The Southern Black

Slave and Free

The Southern Black
Slave and Free

∽

A Bibliography of Anti- and Pro-Slavery Books and
Pamphlets and of Social and Economic Conditions in the
Southern States From the Beginnings to 1950.

∽

Works available in Microform

∽

compiled by
Lawrence S. Thompson

Whitston Publishing Company
Incorporated
Troy, New York
1970

INTRODUCTION

It was difficult to select an appropriate title for
the present work. Specifically, it is a list of books
and pamphlets which have been issued in Microcard editions by the Lost Cause Press, Louisville, Kentucky,
relative to American slavery and the American South,
the home of the vast majority of North American Blacks
before World War II. It consists of Microcard editions
based on T.D. Clark's monumental bibliographies of <u>Tra-
vels in the Old and New South</u> (including E.M. Coulter's
<u>Travels in the Confederate States</u>), substantial portions
of the Oberlin College Library's slavery collection and
works which have been incorporated into this collection
or associated with it (usually relative to the time or
milieu), a few titles from the first two volumes of Sa-
bin which are pertinent to our subject and which have
been included in the Lost Cause Press' Microcard edition
of works included in this great work, a few titles from
Lyle Wright's bibliographies of American fiction before
1900 (also being reproduced in a Microcard edition by the
Lost Cause Press), a few titles from the Lost Cause Press'
"Kentucky Culture Series", and a few titles from its
"Civil War Pamphlets".

The quality of the material in the present volume
could be refined substantially; or, in quantitative terms,
it could be multiplied several times within the broad de-
finitions used here for inclusion. It should be considered simply a library author catalog, a guide to books
and pamphlets which have been available so far to the
Lost Cause Press for reproduction in a Microcard edition.
It is essentially a library collection (as of the present date); and library collections, unlike comprehensive
author or subject bibliographies based on all available
printed and manuscript sources, are never complete. They
strive towards completeness, but the fact of their existence and availability, in any stage of bibliographical

development, enriches scholarship. The student of slavery, the southern historical "buff", and, especially, the student of Black American history will find much treasure here.

On the other hand, he must dig for this treasure. The entries in this guide range from meticulously accurate printed cards with all subject and secondary entries noted down to entries copied directly from the old Hubbard catalog of the Oberlin Slavery Collection and some entries copied from the title-page with minimum effort to establish the proper entry. Yet the important fact is that each entry can be matched with a specific Microcard edition.

If some industrious student of library science or American history will revise the entries, provide fully acceptable subject and secondary entries, and index them all by number, American historical studies will be infinitely richer. A microform publisher would have to charge more for his cards than for his editions if he provided catalog cards which would meet the highest specifications of bibliographical purists.

The compiler would like to be a bibliographical purist; but here he wants to provide a rather impressive corpus of material, readily available to any library, which is indispensable for any student of Black American history. It is not duplicated elsewhere.

Lawrence S. Thompson
Lexington, Kentucky, February, 1969

Aabye, Karen.
    Dejligt at Amerika ikke ligger langt herfra.
Copenhagen, Hasselbach, 1949.
    139 p. map, illus. 16 cm.

[Abbad y Lasierra, Iñigo,] 1745-1813.
    Historia geográfica, civil y política de la isla
de S. Juan Bautista de Puerto Rico. Dala á luz don
Antonio Valladares de Sotomayor. Madrid, Impr. de
A. Espinosa, 1788.
    4 p. 1, 403 p. 21 1/2 cm.
    L. C. card no. 3-2721 rev 2

Abbott, Allen O.
    Prison life in the South: at Richmond, Macon,
Savannah, Charleston, Columbia, Charlotte, Raleigh,
Goldsborough and Andersonville, during the years
1864 and 1865. New York, Harper & brothers, 1865.
    x p., 1 1., [13]-374 p. incl. front., illus.,
plates. 18 1/2 cm.

Abbott, John Stevens Cabot, 1805-1877.
    South and North; or, Impressions received during
a trip to Cuba and the South. By John S. C. Abbott ...
New York, Abbey & Abbot, 1860.
    352 p. 19 cm.
    L. C. card no. 1-21521

Abdy, Edward Strutt, 1791-1846.
    American whites and blacks, in reply to a German
orthodermist. By E. S. Abdy ... London, C. Gilpin,
1842.
    50 p. 21 cm.
    L. C. card no. 11-8346

Abdy, Edward Strutt, 1791-1846.
    Journal of a residence and tour in the United
States of North America, from April, 1833, to October, 1834. By E. S. Abdy ... London, J. Murray,
1835.
    3 v. 19 1/2 cm.

Abolition of apprenticeship. Edinburgh, W. Oliphant
and sons; Glasgow, George Gallie and W. Smeal,
1838.
    20 p. 22 cm.

Abolition society of New York City. Exposition.
Duty of the federal government to abolish slavery.
New York, The Society,[n.d.]
16 p. 16 1/2 cm.

The abrogation of the seventh commandment, by the
American churches. New York, David Ruggles, 1835.
23 p. 17 cm.

Account of a shooting excursion on the mountains near
Dromilly estate, in the parish of Trelawny, and
island of Jamaica, in the month of October, 1824!!!
London, Printed by Harvey and Barton, 1825.
15 p. 20 cm.

Account of Charles Dunsdon, of Semington, Wiltshire,
England. Philadelphia, Published by the Tract
association of Friends, [n.d.]
16 p. 18 cm.

An account of the important debate in the House of Commons, on Monday April 2, on Mr. Wilberforce's motion
for the abolition of the slave trade. In the
Universal magazine, April, 1792.
p. 289-295. 22 cm.

An account of the interviews which took place on the
fourth and eighth of March, between a committee
of the Massachusetts anti-slavery society and the
committee of the legislature, [n.p.] 1836.
26 p. 24 cm.

An account of the late intended insurrection among a
portion of the blacks of this city. Published by
the authority of the corporation of Charlestown.
Second Edition, Charlestown, A. E. Miller, 1822.
48 p. 21 1/2 cm.

An account of the Spanish settlements in America. In
four parts ... To which is annexed, a succinct
account of the climate, produce, trade, manufactures,
& c. of old Spain. Illustrated with a map of America. Edinburgh, Printed by A. Donaldson and J. Reid
for the author [etc.] 1762.
xvi, 512 p. fold. map. 21 cm.

Achenbach, Hermann.
Tagebuch meiner reise nach den Nordamerikanischen
freistaaten, oder: Das neue Kanaan ... Von Hermann
Achenbach ... Düsseldorf, Gedruckt auf kosten des
verfassers, bei J. Wolf, 1835.

2

2 v. front., fold. map. 22 cm.
L. C. card no. 1-26179

Achenwall, Gottfried, 1719-1772.
Einige anmerkungen über Nord-Amerika und über
dasige grosbrittannische colonien. Aus mündlichen
nachrichten des Herrn D. Franklins verfasst von hrn.
d. Gottfried Achenwall. Nebst ... John Wesleys
schrift von den streitigkeiten mit den colonien in
Amerika. Helmstedt, J. H. Kühnlin, 1777.
27 (i.e.72) p. 19 cm.
L. C. card no. 2-6032

Adair, James, trader with Indians.
The history of the American Indians; particularly those nations adjoining to the Mississippi, East
and West Florida, Georgia, South and North Carolina,
and Virginia ... London, Printed for E. and C.
Dilly, 1775.
464 p. 6 p. 1. front. (fold. map) 27 1/2 cm.

Adam, Paul Marie Auguste, 1862-
Vues d'Amérique. 5. éd. Paris, Société
d'éditions littéraires et artistiques, 1906.
568 p. 19 cm.

Adams, Charles Francis, 1807-
The Republican party a necessity. Speech of
Charles Francis Adams, of Massachusetts. Delivered
in the House of Representatives, May 31, 1860.
[Washington?] 1860.
7 p. 22 cm.

Adams, Charles Francis, 1807-1886.
What makes slavery a question of national con-
cern? A lecture, delivered, by invitation, at New
York, January 30, at Syracuse, February 1, 1885.
By Charles Francis Adams. Boston, Little, Brown,
and co., 1855.
46 p. 24 cm.
L. C. card no. 11-7607

Adams, Francis Colburn.
Manuel Pereira, or The Sovereign rule of South
Carolina. With views of Southern laws, life, and
hospitality. Washington, D. C., Buell and Blanchard, 1853.
302 p. 19 cm.

Adams, Francis Colburn.
    A review of the reviewers and repudiators of
Uncle Tom's cabin. London, Clarke, Beeton, and
co., Philadelphia, Willis P. Hazzard [n.d.]
    vii, 151 p.   17 cm.

Adams, Francis Colburn.
    The story of a trooper. With much of interest
concerning the campaign on the Peninsula, not before written. By F. Colburn Adams ... New York,
Dick & Fitzgerald, 1865.
    2 p. 1., [3]-616 p.   19 1/2 cm.

Adams, Francis Colburn.
    Uncle Tom at home. A review of the reviewers
and repudiators of Uncle Tom's cabin by Mrs. Stowe.
By F. C. Adams ... Philadelphia, W. P. Hazard, 1853.
    vi, 7-142 p.   19 cm.
    L. C. card no. 5-28419

Adams, Herbert Baxter, 1850-
    The life and writings of Jared Sparks, com-
prising selections from his journals and correspondence ... Boston and New York, Houghton, Mifflin
and company, 1893.
    2v. 6 port. (incl. fronts.)   24 cm.

Adams, John, 1750?-1814.
    The flowers of modern travels; being elegant,
entertaining and instructive extracts, selected
from the works of the most celebrated travellers...
Intended chiefly for young people of both sexes.
By the Rev. John Adams ... Boston: Printed for
John West, No. 75, Cornhill, 1797.
    2 v.   17 1/2 cm.
    L. C. card no. 5-37218

Adams, John Gregory Bishop, 1841-
    Reminiscences of the Nineteenth Massachusetts
regiment, by Captain John G. B. Adams. Boston,
Wright & Potter printing company, 1899.
    viii, 186 p. incl. front. (port.) ports. 23 cm.

Adams, John Quincy, pres. U. S., 1767-
    Speech of John Quincy Adams of Massachusetts
upon the right of the people, men and women, to
petition; on the freedom of speech and of debate
in the House of Representatives of the United
States; on the resolutions of seven state legis-
latures, and the petition of more than one hundred
thousand petitioners, relating to the annexation

4

of Texas to this union ... Washington, Gales and
Seaton, 1838.
131 p. 22 cm.

Adams, Nehemiah, 1806-
A south-side view of slavery; or, Three months
at the South, in 1854 ... Boston, T. R. Marvin
[etc.] 1854.
viii, 7-214 p. 19 cm.

Adams, William Edwin, 1832-
Our American cousins: being personal impressions
of the people and institutions of the United States.
London and Newcastle-on-Tyne, W. Scott, 1883.
x, 357 p. 19 cm.

Adamson, Augustus Pitt, 1844-
Brief history of the Thirtieth Georgia regiment.
Griffin, Ga., The Mills printing co., 1912.
157 p. front. (ports.) illus. 23 cm.

Address of the committee appointed by a public meeting
at Faneuil Hall, September 24, 1846, for the purpose of considering the recent case of kidnapping
from our soil, and of taking measures to prevent
the recurrence of similar outrages. With an appendix. Boston, White and Potter, 1846.
42 p. 22 cm.

Address of the committee appointed by a public meeting
held at Faneuil Hall, September 21, 1846, for the
purpose of considering the recent case of kidnapping from our soil, and of taking measures to prevent the recurrence of similar outrages. With an
appendix. Boston, White and Potter, printers,
1846.
42 p. 23 cm.

Address of the Free constitutionalists to the people of
the United States. [2d ed.] Boston, Thayer &
Eldridge, 1860.
54 p. 22 cm.
L. C. card no. 21-12500

Address of the New York City Anti-slavery society to
the people of the city of New York. New York,
Printed by West & Trow, 1833.
46 p. 21 cm.

The address of the southern and western liberty convention held at Cincinnati, June 11 & 12, 1845, to the

people of the United States, with notes by a
citizen of Pennsylvania. [n.p., n.d.]
  15 p.   23 cm.

Address of the southern rights association of Yazoo
county. [n.p.] Mississippian press, [1850?]
  7 p.   22 cm.

An address on the state of slavery in the West India
islands, from the committee of the Leicester auxiliary anti-slavery society. London, Sold by T.
Hamilton, Pater Noster Row; and by T. Combs, Leicester, 1824.
  28 p.   21 cm.

An address to the anti-slavery Christians of the United
States. [New York? John A. Gray, printer, 1852?]
  17 p.   22 cm.

Address to Christians of all denominations, on the inconsistency of admitting slave-holders to communion
and church membership ... Philadelphia, S. C.
Atkinson, 1831.
  19 p.   17 cm.

Address to the free colored people of the United States.
Philadelphia, Printed by Merrihew and Gunn, 1838.
  12 p.   17 cm.

An address to the friends of Negro emancipation in
Liverpool. Liverpool, Printed by Rushton and
Melling, 1824.
  16 p.   20 1/2 cm.

An address to the inhabitants of Europe on the iniquity
of the slave trade; issued by the religious Society
of friends, commonly called Quakers, in Great
Britain and Ireland. London, Printed by W. Phillips, 1822.
  15 p.   22 cm.

An address to King Cotton. New York, [n.d.]
  19 p.   22 cm.

Adger, John B.
    Christian missions and African colonization.
Columbia, S. C., Steam power press of E. H.
Britton, 1857.
  53 p.   22 cm.

Adger, John Bailey, 1810-1899.
A review of reports to the legislature of S. C.,
on the revival of the slave trade. By John B. Ad-
ger. From the April number of the Southern Presby-
terian review. Columbia, S.C., Press of R. W.
Gibbes, 1858.
Cover-title, 36 p. 23 cm.
L. C. card no. 11-8380

Advocate of freedom. Brunswick, Maine, v. 1, 1838 (?)-

Aflalo, Frederick George, 1870-
Sunshine and sport in Florida and the West Indies with forty-seven illustrations. Philadelphia,
G. W. Jacobs & co. [1907]
xv, 272 p. front., plates, ports. 23 cm.

The African captives. Trial of the prisoners of the
Amistad on the writ of habeas corpus, before the
circuit court of the United States for the district of Connecticut, at Hartford; Judges Thompson and Judson, September term, 1839. [n.p.,n.d.]
47 p. 22 cm.

African education society. Board of managers. Report
of the proceedings at the formation of the African
education society; instituted at Washington,
December 28, 1829 ... Washington, printed by
James C. Dunn, 1830.
16 p. 21 cm.

African institution. Extracts from the eighteenth and
nineteenth reports of the directors of the African
institution, read at their annual general meetings,
held in London on the 11th day of May, 1824, and
on the 15th day of May, 1825. Philadelphia,
Printed by Joseph R. A. Skerrett, 1826.
40 p. 22 cm.

African institution. Fifteenth report of the directors.
London, Printed by Ellerton and Henderson, sold
by J. Hatchard and son, 1821.
viii, 108 p. fold., diag. 20 cm.

African servitude: when, why, and by whom instituted.
By whom, and how long, shall it be maintained?
Read and consider ... New York, Davies & Kent, 1860.
54 p., 1 1. 22 1/2 cm.
L. C. card no. 1-25923

Agitation-- the doom of slavery. Cincinnati, American
reform tract and book society, n.d.
16 p. 18 cm.

The agitation of slavery. Who commenced! and Who
    can end it! Buchanan and Fillmore compared from
    the record. [n.p., n.d.]
        32 p.   24 cm.

Agnew, John Holmes, 1804-1865.
        Reply to Professor Tayler Lewis' review of
    Rev. Henry J. Van Dyke's sermon on Biblical slavery;
    also, to his other articles on the same subject,
    published in "The World". By J. Holmes Agnew.
    New York, D. Appleton and company, 1861.
        63 p.   22 cm.
        L. C. card no.   11-11590

Agutter, William.
        The abolition of the slave trade considered in
    a religious point of view. A sermon preached be-
    fore the corporation of the city of Oxford, at
    St. Martin's church, on Sunday, February 3, 1788...
    London, Printed for J. F. and C. Rivington and G.
    Philips, 1788.
        29 p.   19 cm.

Aikman, William, 1824-1909.
        The future of the colored race in America:
    being an article in the Presbyterian quarterly re-
    view of July, 1862. By William Aikman ... New
    York, A. D. F. Randolph, 1862.
        35 p.   23 1/2 cm.
        L. C. card no. 12-3259

Aldunate Philips, Arturo, 1902-
        Estados Unidos, gran aventura del hombre. San-
    tiago de Chile, Nascimento, 1943.
        382 p.   illus.   19 cm.

[Alexander, Charles Wesley] 1837-1927.
        Maud of the Mississippi. A companion to Pauline
    of the Potomac. By Wesley Bradshaw [pseud.] ... A
    thrilling narrative of the adventures of Miss
    Pauline d'Estraye, a young and beautiful French
    lady ... during the Vicksburg campaign under Major-
    General U. S. Grant. Philadelphia, C. W. Alexan-
    der & co. [1864]
        1 p. 1., 21-30, 39-52, 61-74, 85-94 p. front.,
    plates.   23 1/2 cm.
        L. C. card no. 44-35021

[Alexander, Charles Wesley] 1837-1927.
        Pauline of the Potomac, or, General McClellan's

spy. An authentic and thrilling narrative of the
beautiful and accomplished Miss Pauline D'Estraye,
who since the opening of the southern rebellion
has performed some of the most startling and noble
deeds that have ever been recorded in history ...
Beautifully illuminated with magnificently colored
engravings ... Philadelphia, Barclay & co. [1862]
    1 p. l., 13-100 (i.e.88) p. incl. plates. front.
25 cm.
    L. C. card no. CA9-4796 Unrev'd

Alexander, George William, 1802-1890.
    Letters on the slave-trade, slavery, and emanci-
pation; with a reply to objections made to the liberation of the slaves in the Spanish colonies; addressed to friends on the continent of Europe,
during a visit to Spain and Portugal. By G. W.
Alexander. London, C. Gilpin [etc.] 1842.
    xvi, 176 p. 16 cm.
    L. C. card no. 17-8659

Alexander, George William, 1802-1890.
    Liberté immédiate et absolue, ou esclavage. Ob-
servations sur le rapport de m. de duc de Broglie,
président de la commission instituée par décision
royale du 26 mai 1840, pour l'examen des questions
relatives à l'esclavage et à la constitutuon politique des colonies françaises; adressées à tous les
français amis de la liberté et de l'humanité par
Geo. W. Alexander et John Scoble ... Paris, Firmin
Didot frères, 1844.
    2 p. l., 55 p. 23 cm.
    L. C. card no. 10-2739

Alexander, J   E
    Transatlantic sketches, comprising visits to the
most interesting scenes in North and South America,
and the West Indies. With notes on negro slavery
and Canadian emigration ... Philadelphia, Key and
Biddle, 1833.
    vii, [9]-378 p. 24 cm.

Alexander, Sir James Edward, 1803-
    Transatlantic sketches, comprising visits to
the most interesting scenes in North and South
America, and the West Indies. With notes on Negro
slavery and Canadian emigration ... London, R.
Bentley, 1833.
    2v. fronts., plates, map. 22 1/2 cm

Alexander, William.
    Dominion of the Prince of peace: with its
application to the slave trade and slavery. York,
1840.
    54 p.   20 cm.

[Algar, W   H]
    Some notes on America. [Plymouth, England, W.
Brendon and son, printers, 1884?]
    101 p.   14 x 11 cm.

Alger, William Rounseville, 1822-1905.
    The genius and posture of America. An oration
delivered before the citizens of Boston, July 4,
1857, by William Rounseville Alger. Boston, J. E.
Farwell and company, printers to the city, 1864.
    53 p.   23 1/2 cm.
    L. C. card no. 20-2090

Alger, William Rounseville, 1822-1905.
    The genius and posture of America. An oration
delivered before the citizens of Boston, July 4,
1857, by William Rounseville Alger. With preface
and appendix. Boston, Office Boston daily bee,
1857.
    60 p.   23 1/2 cm.
    L. C. card no. 2-6439

Alger, William Rounseville, 1822-1905.
    Public morals: or, The true glory of a state.
A discourse delivered before the executive and
legislative departments of the government of
Massachusetts, at the annual election, Wednesday,
January 1, 1862. By Rev. William Rounseville
Alger. Boston, W. White, printer to the state,
1862.
    55 p.   21 1/2 cm.
    L. C. card no. 40-19169

[Allan-Olney, Mary]
    The new Virginians, by the author of 'Junia'
[etc.] Edinburgh and London, William Blackwood and
sons, 1880.
    2 v.   20 cm.

Allardice, Robert Barclay, 1779-
    Agricultural tour in the United States and Upper
Canada, with miscellaneous notices ... Edinburgh
[etc.] W. Blackwood & sons, 1842.
    [v]-xxiii, 181 p.   1 p.l.   20 cm.

[Allemagne, d']
    Nouvelles du Scioto, ou Relation fidèle du
voyage et des infortunes d'un Parisien qui arrive
de ces pays-là, où il étoit allé pour s'établir ...
A Paris: Chez Lenoir et Leboucher, imprimeurs,
1790.
    16 p. 8°

Allen, George
    Mr. Allen's report of a declaration of senti-
ments on slavery, Dec. 5, 1837. Worcester,
Printed by Henry J. Howland, 1838.
    12 p. 21 cm.

Allen, George.
    Mr. Allen's speech on ministers leaving a moral
kingdom to bear testimony against sin; liberty in
danger, from the publications of its principles;
the Constitution a shield for slavery; and the
Union better than freedom and righteousness.
Boston, Published by Isaac Knapp, 1838.
    46 p. 21 cm.

[Allen, George] 1792-1883.
    Resistance to slavery every man's duty. A re-
port on American slavery, read to the Worcester
central association, March 2, 1847. Boston, W.
Crosby & H. P. Nichols, 1847.
    40 p. 24 cm.
    L. C. card no. 11-8379

Allén, Isaac.
    Is slavery sanctioned in the Bible? A premium
tract. Boston, American tract society [1860?]
    26 p. 18 cm.

Allen, James Lane, 1849-1925.
    The blue-grass region of Kentucky, and other
Kentucky articles, by James Lane Allen ... New York
and London, Harper & brothers, 1899.
    5 p.l., 3-301p. [2] p. front., plates.
19 1/2 cm.

Allen, William G.
    The American prejudice against color. An
authentic narrative, showing how easily the nation
got into an uproar. By W. G. Allen, a refugee from
American despotism. London, W. and F. G. Cash;
[etc.,etc.] 1853.
    2 p. l., 107, [1] p. 16 1/2 cm.
    L. C. card no. 1-26231 Revised

11

Allgemeine historie der reisen zu wasser und lande; oder
Sammlung aller reisebeschreibungen, welche bis
itzo in verschiedenen sprachen von allen völkern
herausgegeben worden ... durch eine gesellschaft
gelehrter männer im englischen zusammen getragen.
und aus demselben ins deutsche übersetzet ...
Leipzig, Bey Arkstee und Merkus, 1747-74.
    21 v. front., plates (part fold.) maps (part
fold.) plans (part fold.)   25 cm.
    L. C. card no. 6-3062

Almbert, Alfred d', 1813-1887.
    Flânerie parisienne aux États-Unis. par Alfred
d'Almbert. Paris, Librairie théâtrale, 1856.
    2 p. 1., 278 p., 1 1.   16 1/2 cm.
    L. C. card no. 2-839

Alsop, George, 1638-
    A character of the province of Maryland ...
Also a small treatise on the wilde and naked In-
dians (or Susquehanokes) of Mary-land ... London,
Printed by T. J. for P. Dring, 1666.
    118 p. 10 p.1., port., map. 13 1/2 cm.

Alston, William Jeffreys, 1800-
    The slavery question. Speech ... in the House
of representatives, April 18, 1850, in committee
of the whole on the state of the union, on the
president's message transmitting the constitution
of California. [Washington, Printed at the Congressional globe office, 1850?]
    8 p.   24 cm.

Alvarez, Francisco, Asturian.
    Noticia del establecimiento y poblacion de las
colonias inglesas en la America Septentrional; religion, orden de gobierno, leyes y costumbres de
sus naturales y habitantes; calidades de su clima,
terreno, frutos, plantas y animales; y estado de
su industria, artes, commercio y navegacion:
sacada de varios autores por don Francisco Alvarez
... Madrid, A. Fernandez, 1778.
    196 p.   21 cm.

Alvord, Clarence Walworth, 1868, ed.
    The new régime, 1765-1767, ed. with introduction
and notes by Clarence Walworth Alvord ... and
Clarence Edwin Carter ... Springfield, Ill., Illinois state historical library, 1916.
    iii-xxvii p., 4 p.1., 1 1., 700 p. ports.
(incl. front.) map. facsim. 23 cm.

Ambrose, Daniel Leib.
    History of the Seventh regiment Illinois volun-
teer infantry, from its first muster into the U.S.
service, April 25, 1861, to its final muster out,
July 9, 1865. By D. Leib Ambrose. Springfield,
Ill., Illinois journal co., 1868.
    xii, 391, [1] p.   19 1/2 cm.

America compared with England. The respective social
effects of the American and English systems of
government and legislation; and the mission of
democracy. London, Effingham Wilson, Royal Exchange, 1848.
    xxiv, 289 p.   18 cm.

American abolition society.
    Slavery-limitation abandoned in theory and
practice, by the defenders of the Crittenden-
Lecompton compromise. Annual report of the
American abolition society, September, 1858. New
York, American abolition society, 1858.
    31 p.   23 cm.

American and foreign anti-slavery society.
    The [8th] annual report ... presented at New
York, May 9, 1848, with the resolutions and addresses. New York, Published by the A. & F. anti-
slavery society, 1848.
    48 p.   19 cm.

American and foreign anti-slavery society.
    The [10th] annual report ... presented at New
York, May 7, 1850 ... New York, Published by the
A. & F. anti-slavery society, 1850.
    172 p.   20 cm.

American and foreign anti-slavery society.
    The annual report of the American and foreign
anti-slavery society presented at New York, May 6,
1851; with the addresses and resolutions. New-York
Published by the Am. & for. anti-slavery society,
1851.
    118 p.   23 cm.

American and foreign anti-slavery society.
    Thirteenth annual report. [n.p., John A. Gray,
printer, n.d.]
    216 p.   21 cm.

American and foreign anti-slavery society. Executive
committee. Address to the friends of liberty. [New
York, American and foreign slavery society, 1848?]
12 p. 18 cm.

American and foreign anti-slavery society. Executive
committee. Protest and remonstrance. To the
Christian abolitionists of Great Britain and Ireland who met at Freemasons' hall, London, August
19, 1846, to form an evangelical alliance. [New
York, 1847?]
16 p. 22 cm.

American anti-slavery society.
The declaration of sentiments and constitution
of the American anti-slavery society. New York,
American anti-slavery society, 1835.
16 p. 18 cm.

American anti-slavery society.
Letter to Louis Kossuth, concerning freedom and
slavery in the United States ... Boston, Published
by R. F. Wallcut, 1852.
112 p. 24 cm.

American anti-slavery society.
Platform of the American anti-slavery society
and its auxiliaries. New York, Published by the
American anti-slavery society, 1836.
35 p. 19 cm.

American anti-slavery society.
Platform of the American anti-slavery society
and its auxiliaries. New York, Published by the
American anti-slavery society, 1855.
36 p. 18 cm.

American anti-slavery society. Executive committee.
Address to the Friends of Constitutional liberty,
on the violation by the United States House of
Representatives of the right of petition. New
York, American anti-slavery society, 1840.
12 p. 23 cm.

American board of commissioners for foreign missions.
Committee on anti-slavery memorials... Report...
September, 1845. With a historical statement of
previous proceedings. Boston, Press of T. R.
Marvin, 1845.
32 p. 23 cm.

The American coast pilot; containing, the courses and
    distance from Boston to all the principal harbours,
    capes and headlands included between Passamaquady
    and the capes of Virginia ... Newburyport, Printed
    by Blunt and March, and sold by them and the prin-
    cipal booksellers, 1796.
        [3]-125 p. 5 p.1. 22 1/2 cm.

The American coast pilot; containing directions for the
    principal harbors, capes, and headlands on the
    coast of North and part of South America ... With
    the prevailing winds, setting of the currents, &
    c., and the latitudes and longitudes of the prin-
    cipal harbors and capes; together with tide tables
    and variations. By Edmund M. Blunt. 21st ed.,
    New York, Published by Geo. W. B. Blunt, 1867.
        vi, 78, 841, [1] p. illus., fold. charts.
    25 cm.

The American churches, the bulwarks of American slavery
    ... Second American edition, revised by the author.
    Newburyport, Published by Charles Whipple, 1842.
        44 p. 21 cm.

The American churches the bulwarks of American slavery.
    By an American. London, Printed by Johnston and
    Barrett, 1840.
        40 p. 20 cm.

American colonialization society.
        Address of board of managers ... to the auxili-
    ary societies and the people of United States.
    Washington, printed by Davis and Force, 1820.
        32 p. 23 cm.

American colonization society.
        Address of the board of the American coloniza-
    tion society to its auxiliary societies. Washing-
    ton, D. C., Printed by Gales and Seaton, 1831.
        11 p. 21 cm.

American colonization society.
        Address of the managers of the American coloni-
    zation society to the people of the United States ...
    Washington, Printed by James C. Dunn, 1832.
        16 p. map. 24 cm.

American colonization society.
        First annual report ... and the proceedings of
    the society at their annual meeting in the city of

Washington on the first day of January, 1818.
Washington, Printed by D. Rapine, 1818.
49 p.   21 cm.

American colonization society.
Second annual report .   Washington, printed by
Davis and Force, 1819.
80 p.   23 cm.

American colonization society.
Third annual report .   Washington, Printed by
Davis and Force, 1820.
146 p.   21 cm.

American colonization society.
Fifth annual report.   Washington, Printed by
Davis & Force, 1822.
120 p.   23 cm.

American colonization society.
Sixth annual report.   Washington, Printed by
Davis & Force, 1823.
72 p.   22 cm.

American colonization society.
Seventh annual report.   Washington, Printed by
Davis & Force, 1824.
173 p.   24 cm.

American colonization society.
Eighth annual report.   Washington, James C.
Dunn, printer, 1825.
68 p.   21 cm.

American colonization society.
Ninth annual report.   Washington, Printed by
Way & Gideon, 1826.
67 p.   21 cm.

American colonization society.
Tenth annual report.   Washington, Way & Gideon,
printers, 1827.
101 p.   21 cm.

American colonization society.
Twelfth annual report.   Washington, Printed by
James C. Dunn, 1829.
80 p.   21 cm.

American colonization society.
Thirteenth annual report ... Washington, Printed by James C. Dunn, 1830.
xvi, [61] p.   map.   21 cm.

American colonization society.
Fourteenth annual report ... Washington,
Printed by James C. Dunn, 1831.
42 p.   21 cm.

American colonization society.
Fifteenth annual report ... Washington, Printed
by James C. Dunn, 1832.
xxix, 63 p.   21 cm.

American colonization society.
Sixteenth annual report ... Washington, Printed
by James C. Dunn, 1833.
xxii, 40 p.   21 cm.

American colonization society.
Seventeenth annual report ... Washington,
Printed by James C. Dunn, 1834.
xxxii, 46 p.   21 cm.

American colonization society.
Twenty-first annual report ... Washington,
James C. Dunn, printer, 1838.
48 p.   21 cm.

American colonization society.
Twenty-fourth annual report ... Washington,
Joseph Etter, printer, 1841.
49 p.   21 cm.

American colonization society.
Twenty-fifth annual report ... J. & G. S.
Gideon, printer, 1842.
24 p.   21 cm.

American colonization society.
Twenty-eighth annual report ... Washington,
C. Alexander, 1845.
32 p.   21 cm.

American colonization society.
Twenty-ninth annual report... Washington,
C. Alexander, printer, 1846.
43 p.   21 cm.

American colonization society.
Thirtieth annual report ... Washington, C.
Alexander, printer, 1847.
43 p.   illus.   21 cm.

American colonization society.
Thirty-first annual report ... Washington, C.
Alexander, printer, 1848.
60 p.   21 cm.

American colonization society.
Thirty-second annual report ... Washington,
C. Alexander, printer, 1849.
59 p.   21 cm.

American colonization society.
Thirty-third annual report ... Washington, C.
Alexander, printer, 1850.
46 p.   21 cm.

American colonization society.
Thirty-fourth annual report ... Washington, C.
Alexander, printer, 1851.
84 p.   21 cm.

American colonization society.
Thirty-fifth annual report ... Washington, C.
Alexander, printer, 1852.
52 p.   21 cm.

American colonization society.
Thirty-sixth annual report ... Washington, C.
Alexander, printer, 1853.
36 p.   21 cm.

American colonization society.
Thirty-seventh annual report ... Washington, C.
Alexander, printer, 1854.
43 p.   21 cm.

American colonization society.
Thirty-eighth annual report ... Washington,
C. Alexander, printer, 1855.
56 p.   21 cm.

American colonization society.
Thirty-ninth annual report ... Washington, C.
Alexander, printer, 1856.
40 p.   21 cm.

American colonization society.
Fortieth annual report ... Washington, C.
Alexander, printer, 1857.
45 p.   illus.   21 cm.

American colonization society.
Forty-first annual report ... Washington, C.
Alexander, 1858.
60 p.   21 cm.

American colonization society.
Forty-second annual report ... Washington, C.
Alexander, 1859.
56 p.   21 cm.

American colonization society.
Forty-third annual report ... Washington, C.
Alexander, printer, 1860.
72 p.   21 cm.

American colonization society.
Forty-fourth annual report ... [Washington?
1861?]
56 p.   21 cm.

American colonization society.
Forty-fifth annual report ... Washington, H. S.
Bowen, printer, 1862.
59 p.   21 cm.

American colonization society.
Forty-sixth annual report ... Washington,
William S. Moore, printer, 1863.
52 p.   illus.   21 cm.

American colonization society.
Forty-seventh annual report ... Washington,
1864.
67 p.   21 cm.

American colonization society.
Forty-eighth annual report ... Washington,
1865.
52 p.   21 cm.

American colonization society.
Forty-ninth annual report ... Washington, 1866.
56 p.   21 cm.

American colonization society.
Fiftieth annual report ... Washington, 1867.
65 p.   21 cm.

American colonization society.
Fifty-first annual report ... Washington,
1868.
56 p.   21 cm.

American colonization society.
Fifty-second annual report ... Washington,
1869.
67 p.   21 cm.

American colonization society.
Fifty-third annual report ... Washington, 1870.
40 p.   21 cm.   map.

American colonization society.
Fifty-fourth annual report ... Washington, 1871.
56 p.   21 cm.

American colonization society.
Fifty-fifth annual report ... Washington, 1872.
48 p.   21 cm.

American colonization society.
Fifty-sixth annual report ... Washington, 1873.
80 p.   21 cm.

American colonization society.
Fifty-seventh annual report ... Washington,
1874.
80 p.   21 cm.

American colonization society.
Fifty-eighth annual report ... Washington, 1875.
28 p.   21 cm.

American colonization society.
Fifty-ninth annual report ... Washington, 1876.
28 p.   21 cm.

American colonization society.
Sixtieth annual report ... Washington, 1877.
32 p.   21 cm.

American colonization society.
        Sixty-first annual report ... Washington, 1878.
    22 p.   21 cm.

American colonization society.
        Sixty-second annual report ... Washington,
    1879.
        26 p.   21 cm.

American colonization society.
        Sixty-third annual report ... Washington, 1880.
    27 p.   21 cm.

American colonization society.
        Sixty-fourth annual report ... Washington, 1881.
    28 p.   21 cm.

American colonization society.
        Sixty-fifth annual report ... Washington, 1882.
    24 p.   21 cm.

American colonization society.
        Sixty-sixth annual report ... Washington, 1883.
    26 p.   21 cm.

American colonization society.
        Sixty-seventh annual report ... Washington,
    1884.
        23 p.   21 cm.

American colonization society.
        Sixty-eighth annual report ... Washington, 1885.
    27 p.   21 cm.

American colonization society.
        Sixty-ninth annual report ... Washington, 1886.
    25 p.   21 cm.

American colonization society.
        Seventieth annual report ... Washington, 1887.
    26 p.   21 cm.

American colonization society.
        Seventy-first annual report ... Washington,
    1888.
        20 p.   21 cm.

American colonization society.
        Seventy-second annual report ... Washington,
    1889.
        16 p.   21 cm.

American colonization society.
Seventy-third annual report ... Washington,
1890.
15 p.   21 cm.

American colonization society.
Seventy-fourth annual report ... Washington,
1891.
18 p.   21 cm.

American colonization society.
Seventy-fifth annual report ... Washington,
1892.
20 p.   21 cm.

American colonization society.
Seventy-six annual report ... Washington,
1893.
19 p.   21 cm.

American colonization society.
Seventy-seventh annual report ... Washington,
1894.
22 p.   21 cm.

American colonization society.
Seventy-eighth annual report ... Washington,
1895.
21 p.   21 cm.

American colonization society.
Seventy-ninth annual report ... Washington,
1896.
24 p.   21 cm.

American colonization society.
Eightieth annual report ... Washington,
1897.
26 p.   21 cm.

American convention for promoting the abolition of
slavery. Minutes of the adjourned session ... convened at Baltimore the twenty-fifth of October,
1826. Baltimore, Printed by order of the Convention, 1826.
49 p.   21 cm.

American convention for promoting the abolition of
slavery. Minutes of the twenty-first biennial
convention ... Philadelphia, Printed by order of

the convention, 1829.
    72 p.   22 cm.

The American gazetteer, containing a distinct account
    of all the parts of the New world: their situation,
    climate, soil, produce, former and present con-
    dition; commodities, manufactures, and commerce.
    Together with an accurate account of the cities,
    towns, ports, bays, rivers, lakes, mountains,
    passes, and fortifications ... London, Printed for
    A. Millar [etc.] 1762.
    3 v. fronts., fold. maps.   17 1/2 cm.

American home missionary society and slavery. [n.p.,
    n.d.]
    8 p.   23 cm.

The American in Algiers; or, The patriot of seventy-
    six in captivity. A poem, in two cantos ... New
    York, Printed and sold by J. Buel, 1797.
    36 p.   18 1/2 cm.
    L. C. card no. 12-11546

American jubilee [edited by] William Goodell.   New
    York, William Goodell, 1854 - Mar. 1858 Nos. 1-12.
    35 cm.

American missionary. Published by the American mis-
    sionary association. New York, November, 1852.
    66 p.   28 1/2 cm.

The American question. Secession. Tariff. Slavery.
    Brighton, H. Taylor, 1862.
        iv, [5]-73, [1] p.   18 cm.
    L. C. card no. 19-12109

American slavery. Organic sins: or the iniquity of
    licensed injustice. Edinburgh, William Oliphant
    and sons, 1846.
    31 p.   18 1/2 cm.

American society for colonizing the free people of
    colour of the United States.
        The sixteenth annual report of the American
    society for colonizing the free people of colour
    of the United States. With an appendix. Wash-
    ington, Dunn, 1833.
        xxiii, 40 p.   20 cm.

American society for promoting national unity.
      American society for promoting national unity...
[Programme, constitution and proposed members]
New York, J. F. Trow, 1861.
      10, 6 p.   22 1/2 cm.
      L. C. card no. 11-20401

American union commission.
      The American union commission: its origin,
operations and purposes. Organized to aid in the
restoration of the Union upon the basis of freedom, industry, education, and Christian morality
...October 1865. New York, Sanford, Harroun &
co., printers, 1865.
      cover-title, 24 p.   22 1/2 cm.
      L. C. card no. 11-21126

Americus, pseud.
      Thoughts for the times: addressed to the con-
siderate people of the northern states. By Americus ... London, Printed for the author, 1862.
      125 p.   25 cm.
      L. C. card no. 3-30673

Amerika, in alle zyne byzonderheden beschouwd, ter
verkryging eener naauwkeumaakend waerelddeel.
Amsterdam, P. Meijer, 1780-82.
      4 v.   fold.   maps.   16 1/2 cm.

[Ames, Julius Rubens?]
      "Liberty." The image and subscription of every
coin issued by the United States of America.
[n.p.]   1837.
      231 p.   illus., map.   21 cm.

[Ames, Julius Rubens] 1801-1850.
      "Liberty" ... [New York, American anti-slavery
society] 1837.
      231 p.   illus.   23 cm.
      L. C. card no. 4-35716 rev

Ames, Mary, 1831-
      From a New England woman's diary in Dixie in
1865 ... Springfield [Mass., Plimpton press, Norwood, Mass.] 1906-
      vi, 125 p.   front. (ports.)   18 cm.

Ames, Mary (Clemmer) Hudson, 1839-
      Ten years in Washington. Life and scenes in the
national capital, as a woman sees them ... Hartford,

Conn., A.D. Worthington & co. [etc., etc.] 1873.
xx, 21-587 p. plates, ports. (incl. front.)
21 1/2 cm.

Amory, Charles Bean, 1841-
A brief record of the army life of Charles B.
Amory; written for his children. [Boston?] Priv.
pub., 1902.
2 p.l., [3]-43 p. front. (port.) 22 1/2 cm.

Ampère, Jean Jacques Antoine, 1800-
Promenade en Amérique; États-Unis, Cuba -
Mexique. Paris, Michel Lévy Frères, 1855.
2 v. 22 cm.

Amphlett, William.
The Emigrant's directory to the western states
of North America ... London, Longman, Hurst, Rees,
Orme, and Brown, 1819.
viii, 208 p. 21 1/2 cm.

Analysis of the report of a committee of the House of
Commons on the extinction of slavery, with notes
by the editor. London, Printed for the Society
for the abolition of slavery throughout the British dominions, 1833.
213 p. 21 cm.

[Anburey, Thomas]
Travels through the interior parts of America.
In a series of letters. By an officer ... London,
Printed for W. Lane, 1789.
2v. front. (fold. map) 5 pl. (part fold.),
fold. plan, 8 facsim. on 1 1. 21 cm.

An ancient landmark, or the essential element of civil
and religious liberty: dedicated to the young men
of New-England. By a pastor. Middletown, C. M.
Pelton - print., 1838.
43 p. 17 cm.

Anderson, Ephraim McD.
Memoirs: historical and personal; including
the campaigns of the First Missouri Confederate
brigade. By Ephraim McD. Anderson. Saint Louis,
Times printing co., 1868.
2 p.l., vi p., 1 1., [9]-436, [2] p. front.
(port.) plates. 22 cm.

[Anderson, James S.]
Nineteen months a prisoner of war in the hands
of the Rebels: experiences at Belle Isle, Richmond, Danville, and Andersonville: some items with
reference to Capt. Wirz, with a map of Andersonville prison camp, called Camp Sumter. Milwaukee,
Starr & son, printers, 1865.
67 p. front. (fold. plan) 22 cm.

Anderson, Osborne P.
A voice from Harper's Ferry. A narrative of
events at Harper's Ferry; with incidents prior
and subsequent to its capture by Captain Brown
and his men ... Boston, Printed for the author,
1861.
72 p. 18 1/2 cm.

Anderson, Thomas.
Interesting account of Thomas Anderson, a
slave. Taken from his own lips. [n.p., 1854?]
12 p. 18 cm.

Andreasen, H.
Amerika, seet fra et landbostandpunkt. Udgivet af H. Andreasen. København, I hovedkom-
mission hos C. A. Topp, 1884.
3 p.l., 382 [3] p. illus. (incl. maps: 1
double) double plates. 24 cm.

Andree, Karl [Theodor] 1808-
Geographische wanderungen ... Dresden, Rudolf
Kuntze, 1859.
2 v. 19 1/2 cm.

Andree, Karl Theodor, 1808-
Nord-Amerika in geographischen und geschicht-
lichen umrissen. Mit besonderer berücksichtigung
der eingeborenen und der indianischen alterthümer,
der einwanderung und der ansiedelungen, des acker-
baues, der schiffahrt und des handels ... 2.
aufl... Braunschweig, G. Westermann, 1845.
xiii, 810 p. illus. 25 cm.

Andrew, Abram Piatt, 1843-
Some civil war letters of A. Piatt Andrew, III.
Gloucester, Mass., Priv. Print., 1925.
x p., 2 l., 3-146 p., 1 l. front., plates,
ports., facsims. 21 cm.

Andrew, James Osgood, bp., 1794-1871.
Miscellanies: comprising letters, essays, and
addresses; to which is added a biographical sketch
of Mrs. Ann Amelia Andres ... Louisville, Morton
& Griswold, 1854.
viii, [9]-395 p.   19 1/2 cm.

Andrew, John A.
Speeches of John A. Andrew at Hingham and
Boston, together with his testimony before the
Harper's Ferry Committee of the Senate, in re-
lation to John Brown. Also the Republican plat-
form and other matters. Published by order of the
Republican state committee [n.p., n.d.]
16 p.   24 cm.

Andrews, Charles C.
The history of the New-York African free-schools,
from their establishment in 1787, to the present
time; embracing a period of more than forty years:
also a brief account of the successful labors, of
the New-York manumission society: with an appendix ... By Charles C. Andrews ... New York, Printed
by M. Day, 1830.
2 p.l., [7]-148 p.   front.   18 1/2 cm.
L. C. card no. 7-42229

Andrews, Christopher Columbus, 1829.
Suffrage the armor of liberty. Speech ... at
St. Paul, October 26, 1865, as originally reported
in the St. Paul press. [n.p.] Printed at the
office of the Great republic [n.d.]
8 p.   22 cm.

Andrews, Eliza Frances, 1840-
The war-time journal of a Georgia girl, 1864-
1865, by Eliza Frances Andrews; illustrated from
contemporary photographs. New York, D. Appleton
and company, 1908.
4 p.l., 387 p.   front., plates, ports.
21 1/2 cm.

Andrews, Ethan Allen, 1787-
Slavery and the domestic slave-trade ... In a
series of letters addressed to the Executive committee of the American union for the relief and
improvement of the colored race ... Boston, Light
& Stearns, 1836.
xii, [9]-201p.   17 1/2 cm.

Andrews, Samuel George.
    The Lecompton constitution. Speech of Hon.
S. G. Andrews, of New York. Delivered in the
House of representatives, February 23d, 1858.
Washington, Buell & Blanchard, 1858.
    8 p.   21 cm.

Andrews, Sherlock George, 1796.
    The Lecompton constitution. Speech of Hon.
S. G. Andrews, of New York, Delivered in the
House of representatives, February 23rd, 1858.
Washington, Buell & Blanchard, printers, 1858.
    8 p.   23 cm.

Andrews, Sidney, 1837-
    The south since the war, as shown by fourteen
weeks of travel and observation in Georgia and
the Carolinas. Boston, Ticknor and Fields, 1866.
    viii, 400 p.   18 cm.

Anent the United States and Confederate States of
    North America ... London, J. Ridgway, 1862.
    7 p.   21 1/2 cm.
    L. C. card no. 19-7407

Anglo-Californian, pseud.
    The national crisis. A letter to the Hon.
Milton S. Latham, senator from California ... by
Anglo-Californian ... San Francisco, Towne &
Bacon, printers, 1861.
    cover-title, 21 p.   23 cm.
    L. C. card no. CA30-534 Unrev'd

Anneke, Fritz.
    Der zweite freiheitskampf der Vereinigten
Staaten von Amerika. Von Fritz Anneke ... Erster
band. Mit drei uebersichtskärtchen. Frankfurt am
Main, J. D. Sauerlander, 1861.
    viii, [iii]-vii, 368 p. 3 fold. maps.   17 1/2
cm.
    L. C. card no. 2-7752

Ansted, David Thomas, 1814-1880.
    Scenery, science and art; being extracts from
the note-book of a geologist and mining engineer.
By Professor D. T. Ansted ... London, J. Van Voorst,
1854.
    viii, 323 p. illus., 4 col. pl. (incl. front.)
22 cm.
    L. C. card no. 6-2668

The anti-slavery alphabet ... Philadelphia, Printed
    for the Anti-slavery fair, 1847.
        16 p.   17 cm.

Anti-slavery convention of American women, 1st, New
    York, 1837.
        An address to free colored Americans. Issued
    by an anti-slavery convention of American women,
    held in the city of New-York, by adjournment from
    9th to 12th May, 1837.
        32 p.   18 cm.

Anti-slavery convention of American women, 1st, New
    York, 1837.
        An appeal to the women of the nominally free
    states, issued by an anti-slavery convention of
    American women, held ... by adjournment from 9th
    to 12th of May, 1837. New-York, William S. Dorr,
    1837.
        68 p.   19 cm.

Anti-slavery convention of American women, 1st, New
    York, 1837.
        Proceedings of the anti-slavery convention of
    American women, held in the city of New-York, May
    9th, 10th, 11th, and 12th, 1837. New-York,
    Printed by William S. Dorr, 1837.
        23 p.   21 cm.

Anti-slavery convention of American women, 2d, Phila-
    delphia, 1838.
        Address to anti-slavery societies. Philadel-
    phia, Printed by Merrihew and Gunn, 1838.
        14 p.   18 cm.

Anti-slavery convention of American women.
        Address to the senators and representatives
    of the free states, in the Congress of the United
    States. Philadelphia, Printed by Merrihew and
    Gunn, 1838.
        11 p.   18 cm.

Anti-slavery convention, Philadelphia, December 4-6,
    1833.
        Proceedings of the anti-slavery convention,
    assembled at Philadelphia, December 4, 5, and 6,
    1833. New York, Printed by Dorr & Butterfield,
    1833.
        28 p.   20 cm.

Anti-slavery lecturer [edited by] William Goodell.
Utica, N. Y., William Goodell, Jan., 1839.
Nos. 1-12. 36 cm.

Anti-slavery. More exposures. By the author of the
former specimen. Aberdeen, D. Chalmers & co.,
printers, 1826?
16 p. 20 1/2 cm.

Anti-slavery society of Lane Seminary.
Preamble and constitution of the anti-slavery
society of Lane Seminary. [n.p., n.d.]
Broadside.

[Anville, Jean Baptiste Bourgignon d'] 1697-
Mémoire sur la carte intitulée Canada, Louisiane
& terres angloises. [Paris, 1755]
26 p. 20 cm.

An appeal, not to the government, but to the people of
England, on the subject of West Indian slavery.
London, Baldwin, Cradock, and Joy, 1824.
22 p. 20 1/2 cm.

Appeal of forty thousand citizens, threatened with dis-
franchisement, to the people of Pennsylvania.
Philadelphia, Merrihew and Gunn, 1838.
18 p. 22 cm.

Appeal of the independent democrats in Congress, to the
people of the United States. Shall slavery be
permitted in Nebraska? [n.p., n.d.]
8 p. 24 cm.

An appeal on behalf of the Oberlin Institute, in aid of
the abolition of slavery in the United States of
America. [n.p., n.d.]
3 p. 39 cm.

An appeal to the females of the north, on the subject
of slavery, by a female of Vermont ... Philadelphia,
Printed by John Thompson, 1838.
12 p. 18 cm.

Appeal to the people of Maine. By a citizen ... [n.p.]
August 1, 1855.
11 p. 22 cm.

An appeal to the people of Massachusetts, on the Texas
question. Boston, Charles C. Little and James
Brown, 1844.

20 p.   23 cm.

Appleton, Nathan.
    Correspondence between Nathan Appleton and John
    G. Palfrey intended as a supplement to Mr. Pal-
    frey's pamphlets on the slave power. Boston,
    Eastburn's press, 1846.
        20 p.   23 cm.

Appleton, Nathan.
    Letter to the Hon. Wm. C. Rives, of Virginia,
    on slavery and the union ... Boston, J. H. East-
    burn's press, 1860.
        17 p.   23 cm.

Appleton's general guide to the U. S. & Canada. [n.p.]
    1910-1911.
        2v.   i-xvi, map, 1-32, map.

Appleton's general guide to the United States and
    Canada ... [1879, 1882-1901] New York, D. Apple-
    ton and company, 1879-1901.
        21 v.   illus., plates, maps (part fold.)   fold.
    plans, tables. 17 1/2 cm.

Appleton's hand-book of American travel.
    The southern tour... With maps of the leading
    routes of travel and of the principal cities. By
    Edward H. Hall ... New York, D. Appleton & co.,
    [etc., etc.] 1866.
        xii, 142 p. front., fold maps. fold plans.
    20 cm.

Archdale, John, 1642?
    A new description of that fertile and pleasant
    province of Carolina; with a brief account of its
    discovery and settling, and the government thereof
    to this time ... London, printed in 1707. Charles-
    ton, S. C.: Reprinted and sold by A. E. Miller,
    1822.
        33 p.   22 cm.

Archer, Armstrong.
    A compendium of slavery, as it exists in the
    present day in the United States of America. To
    which is prefixed, a brief view of the author's
    descent from an African king on one side, and from
    the celebrated Indian chief Powhattan on the other;
    in which he refers to the principal transactions
    and negotiations between this noble chief and the
    English colony under the famous Captain Smith, on

the coast of Virginia, in the year 1608, as well
as to his still more illustrious daughter, the
Princess Pocahontas, who excited so much interest
in England. By Armstrong Archer. London, The
author, 1844.
iv, 68 p. front. 17 cm.
L. C. card no. 11-7587

Arfwedson, Carl David, 1806-1881
Förenta Staterna och Canada, åren 1832, 1833
och 1834, af C. D. Arfwedson ... Stockholm, L. J.
Hjerta, 1835.
2v. 15 cm.
L. C. card no. 1-26737

Arfwedson, Carl David, 1806-1881.
The United States and Canada, in 1832, 1833, and
1834. By C. D. Arfwedson ... London, R. Bentley,
1834.
2 v. fronts. 22 cm.

Armistead, Wilson, 1819?-1868.
'A cloud of witnesses' against slavery and
oppression. Containing the acts, opinions, and
sentiments of individuals and societies in all
ages. Selected from various sources and for the
most part chronologically arranged, by Wilson
Armistead ... London, W. Tweedie [etc.] 1853.
154 p. 17 1/2 cm.
L. C. card no. 17-4883

Armistead, Wilson.
A tribute to the negro: being a vindication of
the moral, intellectual and religious capabilities
of the coloured portion of mankind; with particular
reference to the African race. Illustrated by
numerous biographical sketches, facts, anecdotes,
etc. and many superior portraits and engravings ...
Manchester, William Irwin; London, Charles Gilpin; American agent, Wm. Harned, New York, 1848.
564 p. 21 cm. illus.

Armstrong, George Dodd, 1813-1899.
The Christian doctrine of slavery. By Geo. D.
Armstrong, D. D., pastor of the Presbyterian
church of Norfolk, Va. ... New York, C. Scribner,
1857.
vi, 7-147 p. 19 cm.

Armstrong, George Dodd.
A discussion on slaveholding. Three letters to

a conservative ... and three conservative replies,
by C. van Rennsselaer ... together with two re-
joinders, on slaveholding, schemes of emancipation,
colonization, etc. Philadelphia, Joseph M.
Wilson, 1858.
137 p.   23 cm.

Arnold, Isaac Newton, 1815-1884.
The power, duty, and necessity of destroying
slavery in the rebel states. Speech of Hon. Isaac
N. Arnold, of Illinois. Delivered in the House of
representatives, January 6, 1864. [Washington]
Towers, printers [1864]
cover-title, 8 p.   23 1/2 cm.
L. C. card no. 12-11019

Arnold, Matthew, 1822-
Civilization in the United States; first and
last impressions of America ... Boston, Cupples
and Hurd, 1888.
4 p.1., 3-192 p.   18 1/2 cm.

Arnold, William E   comp.
... Florida; or, Summer in the winter time. A
condensed gazateer [!] of Florida, and other points
in the South known as winter resorts. Where located: their hotels and boarding-houses and their
rates. Compiled by W. E. Arnold ... [Eastern ed.]
[New York, 1894]
119 [1] xxxii p., incl. front., illus.
22 1/2 cm.

Arredondo, Antonio de.
Arredondo's historical proof of Spain's title
to Georgia; a contribution to the history of one
of the Spanish borderlands, edited by Herbert E.
Bolton. Berkeley, Calif., University of California press, 1925.
xvii, 382 p.   1 1.   front., pl., maps (part
fold.) plan.   22 1/2 cm.

The arrest, trial, and release of Daniel Webster, a
fugitive slave. Correspondence of the anti-
slavery standard. Philadelphia, Pennsylvania
anti-slavery society, 1859.
31 p.   14 cm.

Arricivita, Juan Domingo.
Crónica seráfica y apostólica del Colegio de
propagande fide de la Santa Cruz de Querétaro en

la Nueva España ... Segunda parte. México, Don
Felipe de Zuñiga y Ontiveros, 1792.
605 p.   10 p.1., 7 l.   28 cm.

Arvine, K
Our duty to the fugitive slave: A discourse
delivered on Sunday, Oct. 6, in West Boylston, Mass.,
and in Worcester, Dec. 15.   By Rev. K. Arvine.
Boston, John P. Jewett & co., 1850.
31 p.   22 cm.

Asbury, Francis, 1745-
The journal of the Rev. Francis Asbury, bishop
of the Methodist Episcopal church, from August 7,
1771, to December 7, 1815.   New York, N. Bangs
and T. Mason, 1821.
3v.   22 cm.

[Ashe, Thomas, supposed author]   fl. 1682.
Carolina; or, A description of the present state
of that country, and the natural excellencies
thereof.   London, printed for W. C., and to be
sold by Mrs. Grover in Pelican court in Little
Britain, 1682.
40 p.   2 p.1.   22 cm.

Ashe, Thomas, 1770-
Travels in America, performed in 1806, for the
purpose of exploring the rivers, Alleghany, Monon-
gahela, Ohio, and Mississippi, and ascertaining
the produce and condition of their banks and
vicinity.   London, printed, Newburyport [Mass.]
Reprinted for W. Sawyer & co., by E. M. Blunt,
1808.
ix [11]-366 p.   17 1/2 cm.

Ashmun, Jehudi, 1794-1828.
History of the American colony in Liberia,
from December 1821 to 1823.   By J. Ashmun.   Comp.
from the authentic records of the colony.   Washington city, Printed by Way & Gideon, 1826.
42 p.   front. (fold. map)   22 1/2 cm.
L. C. card no. 5-15271

Ashworth, Henry, 1794-
A tour in the United States, Cuba, and Canada
... A course of lectures delivered before the
members of the Bolton mechanics' institution.   London, A. W. Bennett [etc., etc., 1861]
198 p.   18 1/2 cm.

Association of friends for advancing the cause of the
    slave, and improving the conditions of the free
    people of color. Extracts from the writings of
    friends, on the subject of slavery ... Philadel-
    phia, Merrihew and Thompson, printers, 1839.
        24 p.   19 cm.

Assollant, Alfred, i. e. Jean Baptiste Alfred, 1827-
        Scènes de la vie des États-Unis ... Acacia -
    Les butterfly. Une fantaisie américaine. Paris,
    Hachette, 1859.
        362 p.   1 1.   18 cm.

[Aston, Anthony]
        The fool's opera; or, The taste of the age.
    Written by Mat. Medley [pseud.] And performed by
    his company in Oxford. To which is prefix'd, A
    sketch of the author's life, written by himself.
    London, T. Payne [etc.] 1731?
        22 p.   3 p.l.   front.   20 cm.

At anchor: a story of our civil war. By an American.
    New York, D. Appleton and company, 1865.
        311 p.   19 cm.
        L. C. card no. 6-4535

Aten, Henry J. 1841-   comp.
        History of the Eighty-fifth regiment, Illinois
    volunteer infantry. Comp. and pub. under the
    auspices of the Regimental association, by Henry
    J. Aten ... Hiawatha, Kan., 1901.
        xi, [1], [13]-506 p. incl. front. ports.
    20 1/2 cm.

Atkins, John, 1685-1757.
        A voyage to Guinea, Brasil, and the West-Indies
    ... London, C. Ward and R. Chandler, 1735.
        xxv, 2, 19-265 p.   20 cm.
        L. C. card no. 5-22535 rev

Atlee, Edwin Pitt, 1799-1836.
        An address, delivered before the Female anti-
    slavery society of Philadelphia, in the session
    room of the Second Presbyterian church ... in the
    first month, (January) 1834. By E. P. Atlee, M.D.
    To which is added an appendix. Philadelphia,
    Printed by T. K. Collins & co., 1834.
        27 p.   21 cm.
        L. C. card no. 20-6157

An attempt to demonstrate the practicability of emancipating the slaves of the United States of North America, and of removing them from the country, without impairing the right of private property, or subjecting the nation to a tax. By a New-England man. New-York, Published by G. & C. Carvill, 1826.
75 p. 22 cm.

Atterbury, John Guest, 1811-1887.
God in civil government, a discourse preached in the First Presbyterian church, New Albany, Nov. 27, 1862, by the Rev. John G. Atterbury... New Albany [Ind.] G. R. Beach, printer, 1862.
16 p. 21 1/2 cm.
L. C. card no. 19-13207

Attmore, William.
Journal of a tour to North Carolina, 1787. Chapel Hill, The University, 1922.
35 p. 23 cm.

Atwater, Caleb, 1778-
Writings of Caleb Atwater. Columbus [O.] The author, printed by Scott and Wright, 1833.
7, [1] p., 1 1., [9]-408 p. incl. illus. 10 pl. 20 cm.

Aubertin, John James, 1818-
A fight with distances; the States, the Hawaiian islands, Canada, British Columbia, Cuba, the Bahamas, by J. J. Aubertin ... With eight illustrations and two maps. London, K. Paul, Trench & co., 1888.
viii p., 1 1., 352 p. front., plates, maps (1 fold.) 20 cm.

Audouard, Olympe.
A travers l'Amérique ... États-Unis, constitution, moeurs, usages, lois, institutions, sectes religieuses. Paris, E. Dentu, éditeur. 1871.
xi, 371 p. 17 1/2 cm.

Audubon, John James, 1785-
Journal of John James Audubon made while obtaining subscriptions to his "Birds of America" 1840-1843. Edited by Howard Corning. Foreword by Francis H. Herrick. Cambridge, The Business historical society, 1929.
x, 173 p. 25 cm.

Audubon, John James, 1785-1851.
    Letters of John James Audubon, 1826-1840,
edited by Howard Corning ... Boston, The Club of
odd volumes, 1930.
    2v.   25 cm.

Audubon, John Woodhouse, 1812-
    Audubon's western journal: 1849-1850; being
the ms. record of a trip from New York to Texas,
and an overland journey through Mexico and Arizona
to the gold fields of California ... Cleveland,
The A. H. Clark company, 1906.
    249 p.   incl. front. (port.) 5 pl. fold. map.
25 cm.

Aughey, John Hill, 1828-
    The iron furnace: or, Slavery and secession.
Philadelphia, J. S. Claxton, 1865.
    296 p.   front. (port.)   2pl.   18 1/2 cm.

Aughey, John Hill, b. 1828.
    The iron furnace: or, Slavery and secession.
By Rev. John H. Aughey, a refugee from Mississippi
... Philadelphia, W. S. & A. Martien, 1863.
    206 p.   front. (port.) 2 pl.   18 cm.

Austin, J. P.
    The blue and the gray: sketches of a portion
of the unwritten history of the great American
civil war, a truthful narrative of adventure, with
thrilling reminiscences of the great struggle on
land and sea, by J. P. Austin ... Atlanta, Ga.,
The Franklin printing and publishing co., 1899.
    xi, [1], 246 p.   col. front.   21 cm.

[Austin, James Trecothick] 1784-1870.
    Remarks on Dr. Channing's Slavery. By a citizen
of Massachusetts. Boston, Russell, Shattuck and
co., and J. H. Eastburn, 1835.
    48 p.   24 1/2 cm.
    L. C. card no. 11-10288

Auszüge aus briefen aus Nord-Amerika geschrieben von
    zweien aus Ulm an der Donau gebürtigen, nun im
    staate Louisiana ansässigen geschwistern ... Ulm,
    E. Nübling, 1833.
    214 p.   4 p.l.   front.   17 cm.

Authentic anecdotes of American slavery. Newburyport,
    Charles Whipple [n.d.]

12 p.   18 cm.

Authentic anecdotes of American slavery. Newburyport,
    Charles Whipple [n.d.]
        4 p.   18 cm.

Avary, Mrs. Myrta (Lockett)
        Dixie after the war; an exposition of social
    conditions existing in the south, during the twelve
    years succeeding the fall of Richmond ... with an
    introduction by General Clement A. Evans ... New
    York, Doubleday, Page and company, 1906.
        5 p.l., [ix -x,] 435 p.   front., plates, ports.
    23 1/2 cm.

Avenel, Georges d', vicomte, 1855-
        ... Aux États-Unis. Les champs. Les affaires.
    Les idées. Paris, A. Colin, 1908.
        2 p.l., 255 p.   19 cm.

Aves, Thomas, defendant.
        Case of the slave-child, Med. Report of the
    arguments of counsel, and of the opinion of the
    court, in the case of Commonwealth vs. Aves; tried
    and determined in the Supreme judicial court of
    Massachusetts. Boston, I. Knapp, 1836.
        40 p.   22 cm.
        L. C. card no.   10-34631

Aydelott, B. P.
        Prejudice against colored people. Cincinnati,
    American reform tract and book society [n.d.]
        12 p.   18 cm.

                                B

Bachelder, John Badger, 1825-
        Popular resorts, and how to reach them. Com-
    bining a brief description of the principal summer
    retreats in the United States, and the routes of
    travel leading to them ... Boston, J. B. Bachelder
    1875.
        364 p.   fold map., illus.   20 1/2 cm.

Bachmann, Ida.
        Amerika! Amerika! København, Forlaget Fremad,

38

1947.
192 p. illus., ports., map. 24 cm.

Bacon, Alvin Q. d. 1863.
Thrilling adventures of a pioneer boy (of the
John M. Palmer, 14th Ill. regiment,) while a
prisoner of war. Alvan [!] Q. Bacon, his capture
at the battle of Shiloh, and escape from Macon,
Ga. ... Written by himself ... [n.p., 18__?]
32 p. 21 1/2 cm.

Bacon, Edward, 1830-1901.
Among the cotton thieves. By Edward Bacon ...
Detroit, The Free press steam book and job printing
house, 1867.
299, [1] p. 22 cm.

Bacon, Ephraim.
Abstract of a journal kept by E. Bacon, United
States assistant agent for the reception of recaptured negroes on the western coast of Africa.
Containing an account of the first negotiations
for the purchase of lands for the American colony.
Fourth edition. Philadelphia, Clark & Raser,
printers, 1824.
48 p. 17 1/2 cm.

Bacon, George Washington, 1830-
Bacon's descriptive handbook of America ... by
George Washington Bacon ... and William George
Larkins ... New York, G. W. Bacon & co. [1886]
viii, 392 p. col. front., illus., pl., maps,
19 1/2 cm.

Bacon, Leonard.
Established in righteousness. A discourse to
the First church and society in New Haven. On a
day of public thanksgiving, November 24th, 1859 ...
New Haven, Peck, White and Peck, 1859.
20 p. 22 1/2 cm.

Bacon, Leonard, 1802-1881.
The jugglers detected. A discourse, delivered
by request, in the Chapel street, church, New Haven
December 30, 1860, by Leonard Bacon, pastor of the
First church. With an appendix. New Haven, T. H.
Pease, 1861.
39 p. 22 1/2 cm.
L. C. card no. 12-2601

Bacon, Leonard.
A plea for Africa; delivered in New-Haven,
July 4th, 1825. By Leonard Bacon, pastor of the
First Church in New-Haven. New-Haven, T. G.
Woodward and co., 1825.
22 p.   25 cm.

Bacon, Leonard, 1802-1881.
Slavery discussed in occasional essays, from
1833 to 1846. By Leonard Bacon ... New York.
Baker and Scribner, 1846.
x p., 1 1., [13]-247 p.   19 1/2 cm.
L. C. card no. 11-6905

Bacon, Mrs. Lydia B. (Stetson) 1786-
Biography of Mrs. Lydia B. Bacon. Written
for the Massachusetts Sabbath school society ...
Boston, Massachusetts Sabbath school society
[c1856]
384 p.   19 1/2 cm.

Bacon, Thomas, 1700 (ca.)-1768.
Four sermons, preached at the parish church of
St. Peter, in Talbot county, in the province of
Maryland, by the Rev. Thomas Bacon ... Viz. Two
sermons to black slaves, and two sermons for the
benefit of a charity working-school, in the above
parish, for the maintenance and education of or-
phans and poor children, and negroes. London,
Printed by J. Oliver, 1753. Reprinted at Bath,
by R. Cruttwell, 1783.
1 p.1., [v]-vi p., 1 1., 192 p.   16 1/2 cm.
L. C. card no. 16-23736 Revised

Bacourt, Adolphe Fourier de, 1801-
...Souvenirs d'un diplomate: lettres intimes
sur l'Amérique. Paris, Calmann-Levy, 1882.
xiii, 401 p.   2 p.1.   18 cm.

Badger, George Edmund
Speech ... in the United States Senate, February 16, 1954, on the Nebraska bill.   Washington,
Sentinel office, 1854.
14 p.   23 cm.

Badger, George Edmund.
Speech of Mr. Badger, of North Carolina, on the
slavery question. In Senate, March 18 and 19, 1850.
Washington, Gideon & Co., 1850.
18 p.   24 cm.

[Badin, Stephen Theodore] 1768-
    Origine et progrès de la mission du Kentucky,
par un témoin oculaire ... Paris, A. Le Clèrc,
1821.
    32 p.   20 cm.   1 p.l.

[Bagg, Lyman Hotchkiss] 1846-1911.
    Ten thousand miles on a bicycle.   By Karl Kron
[pseud.] New York, Karl Kron, 1887.
    [1] 799 [1]p.   front.   20 1/2 cm.

Bailey, Nathaniel.
    Our duty as taught by the aggressive nature of
slavery. A discourse preached in the Baptist
church, Akron, O., on Thanksgiving day, November
22nd, 1855 ... Akron, Teesdale, Elkins & co.,
1855.
    24 p.   19 cm.

Bailey, Silas, 1809-1874.
    The moral significance of war.   A discourse
delivered in the Baptist meeting house, in Franklin, Indiana, on the occasion of the national
fast; September 26, 1861.   By Rev. Silas Bailey...
Indianapolis, Dodd & co., printers, 1861.
    cover-title, 20 p.   23 1/2 cm.
    L. C. card no.   18-12663

Baily, Francis, 1774-
    Journal of a tour in unsettled parts of North
America, in 1796 & 1797 ... With a memoir of the
author.   London, Baily brothers, 1856.
    xii, 439 p.   22 cm.

Baird, Robert, 1798-
    Impressions and experiences of the West Indies
and North America in 1849.   Philadelphia, Lea &
Blanchard, 1850.
    354 p.   20 cm.

Baird, Robert ...
    The progress and prospects of Christianity in
the United States of America, and on the inter-
course between British and American churches.   London, Partridge and Oakey, etc. etc.   n.d.
    78 p.   22 cm.

41

[Baird, Robert] 1798-
    View of the valley of the Mississippi: or,
The emigrant's and traveller's guide to the West
... Philadelphia, H. S. Tanner, 1832.
    xii, 341 p. fold. front., fold. map, plans.
19 cm.

Baker, James Loring.
    Slavery: by J. L. Baker ... Philadelphia,
J. A. Norton, 1860.
    19 p.   23 cm.

Baker, La Fayette Charles, 1826-
    The United States secret service in the late
war. Philadelphia, J. E. Potter and company,
[c1889]
    398 p. incl. 16 pl. front. (port.) 8
chromolith. pl.   24 cm.

Baker, William Mumford, 1825-
    The life and labours of the Rev. Daniel Baker,...
Prepared by his son ... Philadelphia, W. W. & A.
Martien, 1858.
    [7]-573 p. 1 p.l. front. (port.) 20 1/2 cm.

Baldwin, Ebenezer, d. 1837.
    Observations on the physical, intellectual, and
moral qualities of our colored population: with
remarks on the subject of emancipation and colonization. By Ebenezer Baldwin ... New Haven, L. H.
Young, 1834.
    iv, [5]-52 p.   22 cm.
    L. C. card no. 10-33469

Baldwin, Joseph Glover, 1815-1864.
    The flush times of Alabama and Mississippi. A
series of sketches. By Joseph G. Baldwin. 2d ed.
New-York, London, D. Appleton & co., 1854.
    x, 330 p. front., 3 pl.   19 1/2 cm.

Baldwin, Joseph Glover, 1815-1864.
    The flush times of Alabama and Mississippi. A
series of sketches. New-York [etc.] D. Appleton
and company, 1853.
    x, 330 p. front. (port.) 3 pl.   19 cm.

[Baldwin, Oliver P] comp.
    Southern and south-western sketches. Fun,
sentiment and adventure. Edited by a gentleman of
Richmond. Richmond, J. W. Randolph [1852].
    190 p., 1 1.   18 1/2 cm.

Baldwin, Roger Sherman.
    Argument ... before the Supreme court of the
United States, in the case of the United States,
apellants, vs. Cinque, and others, Africans of
the Amistad. New York, S. W. Benedict, 1841.
    32 p.   22 cm.

Ball, Charles.
    Slavery in the United States. A narrative of
the life and adventures of Charles Ball ... who
lived forty years in Maryland, South Carolina and
Georgia, as a slave ... 3d ed. Pittsburgh, J. T.
Shryock, 1854.
    [v]-vi, [9]-446 p.   1 p.1.   19 cm.

Ball, Charles.
    Slavery in the United States. A narrative of
the life and adventures of Charles Ball, a black
man, who lived forty years in Maryland, South
Carolina and Georgia, as a slave ... Pittsburgh,
J. T. Shryock, 1853.
    1 p. 1., [v]-vi, [9]-446 p.   19 cm.
    L. C. card no.   17-2411

Ball, Edward.
    Speech by Hon. Edward Ball, of Ohio, on the
Nebraska and Kansas bill, delivered in the House
of Representatives, May 9, 1954. Washington,
Printed at the Congressional Globe office, 1854.
    15 p.   23 1/2 cm.

[Ballentine, George] 1812?
    Autobiography of an English soldier in the
United States army. Comprising observations and
adventures in the States and Mexico. New York,
Stringer & Townsend, 1853.
    xii, [9]-288 p.   front., pl.   19 1/2 cm.

The ballot box a remedy for national crimes. A sermon,
entitled "The remedy for dueling," by Rev. Lyman
Beecher, D. D., applied to the crime of slaveholding. By one of his former parishioners.
Boston, Published by Isaac Knapp, 1838.
    36 p.   16 cm.

Ballou, Adin, 1803.
    A discourse on the subject of American slavery,
delivered in the First Congregational meeting
house, in Mendon, Mass., July 4, 1837 ... Boston,
Isaac Knapp, 1837.
    88 p.   16 cm.

Ballou, Adin, 1803-1890.
    The voice of duty. An address delivered at the anti-slavery picnic at Westminster, Mass., July 4, 1843. By Adin Ballou ... Hopedale, Milford, Mass., Community press, 1843.
    12 p.   24 cm.
    L. C. card no. 11-6922

Balme, Joshua R.
    Letters on the American republic; or, Common fallacies and monstrous errors refuted and exposed... 2d thousand. Enl. ed. London, Hamilton, Adams & co. [1863]
    2 p.l., [iii]-vii, 290 p.   19 1/2 cm.

Balme, Joshua Rhodes.
    Synopsis of the American war. By J. R. Balme... London, Hamilton, Adams & co.; [etc., etc.] 1865.
    2 p. 1., p. 547-776.   17 1/2 cm.
    L. C. card no. 2-7450

Baltimore association for the moral and educational improvement of the colored people.
    First annual report ... [Baltimore?] November, 1865.
    31 p.   22 cm.

Banvard, John, 1815-
    Description of Banvard's panorama of the Mississippi river, painted on three miles of canvas: exhibiting a view of country 1200 miles in length, extending from the mouth of the Missouri river to the city of New Orleans ... Boston, J. Putnam, printer, 1847.
    48 p.   22 1/2 cm.

Barber, Edward D.
    An oration delivered before the Addison county anti-slavery society, on the fourth of July, 1836 ... Middlebury, Knapp and Jewett, printers, 1836.
    16 p.   20 1/2 cm.

Barber, John Warner, 1798, comp.
    A history of the Amistad captives; being a circumstantial account of the capture of the Spanish schooner Amistad, by the Africans on board; their voyage, and capture near Long Island, New York; with biographical sketches of each of the surviving Africans; also, an account of the trials had on their case, before the district and circuit courts

of the United States for the district of Connecticut. 1   Comp. from authentic sources, by John W.
Barber ... New Barber, John Warner, 1798, comp.
   A history of the Amistad captives... New Haven,
(1840), Ct., E. L. & J. W. Barber, 1840.
   32 p.   fold. front., illus. (incl. map)
22 1/2 cm.

Barber, Lucius W. 1839-1872.
   Army memoirs of Lucius W. Barber, Company
"D", 15th Illinois volunteer infantry. May 24,
1861, to Sept. 30, 1865. Chicago, The J.M.W.
Jones stationery and printing co., 1894.
   v p., 1 1., [9]-233 p. front. (port.)
23 1/2 cm.

Barbour, George M.
   Florida for tourists, invalids, and settlers:
containing practical information regarding climate,
soil, and productions; cities, towns, and people;
the culture of the orange and other tropical fruits;
farming and gardening; scenery and resorts; sport;
routes of travel, etc., etc. ... New York, D. Appleton and company, 1882.
   310 p. front., illus., fold. map.   19 1/2 cm.

Barham, J. H.
   Considerations on the abolition of negro
slavery and the means of practically effecting it.
The third edition. London, Printed for James
Ridway, 1824.
   85 p.   20 cm.

[Barinetti, Carlo]
   A voyage to Mexico and Havanna; including some
general observations on the United States. By an
Italian. New York, Printed for the author by C.
Vinton, 1841.
   x, 139 p.   20 cm.

[Barker, Jacob] 1779-1871.
   The ballot box, the palladium of our liberties.
New Orleans, July, 1863. [New Orleans], Printed for
the compiler, 1863.
   65 p.   24 cm.
   L. C. card no. 7-37076

Barker, Joseph.
Slavery and civil war; or, The Harper's Ferry
insurrection, with a review of discourses on the
subject by Rev. W. H. Furness, J. R. Giddings and
Wendell Phillips. [n.p., 18-?]
24 p. 23 cm.

Barker, Mrs. Louisa J. (Whiting)
Influence of slavery upon the white population.
By a former resident of slave states. [New York,
American anti-slavery society, 1855?]
12 p. 19 cm.

[Barnard, Frederick Augustus Porter] 1809-1889.
Letter to the President of the United States,
by a refugee. Philadelphia, J. B. Lippincott &
Co., 1863.
32 p. 22 1/2 cm.

Barnard, John Gross, 1815-1882.
Report of the engineer and artillery operations
of the Army of the Potomac, from its organization
to the close of the Peninsular campaign. By Brig.
Gen. J. G. Barnard, chief engineer, and Brig. Gen.
W. F. Barry, chief of artillery ... New York D.
Van Nostrand, 1863.
1 p.1., [5]-230 p. 5 pl. (incl. front.) 13 maps
and plans (part fold.)   24 cm.

Barnes, Albert.
The conditions of peace. A thanksgiving dis-
course delivered in the First Presbyterian church,
Philadelphia, November 27, 1862. Philadelphia,
Henry B. Ashmead, book and job printer, 1863.
63 p. 22 cm.

Barnes, Albert, 1798-1870.
The conditions of peace. A thanksgiving dis-
course delivered in the First Presbyterian church,
Philadelphia, November 27, 1862. By Albert Barnes.
Philadelphia, W. B. Evans, 1863.
63 p. 21 1/2 cm.

Barnes, Albert, 1798-1870.
An inquiry into the Scriptural views of slavery
... Philadelphia, Perkins & Purves; Boston, B.
Perkins & co., 1846.
384 p. 20 cm.

Barney, C.
Recollections of field service with the Twentieth Iowa infantry volunteers; or, what I saw in the army, embracing accounts of marches, battles, sieges, and skirmishes, in Missouri, Arkansas, Mississippi, Louisiana, Alabama, Florida, Texas, and along the northern border of Mexico. Davenport, Iowa, "Printed for the author at the Gazette job rooms," 1865.
viii, 9-323 p.   19 1/2 cm.

Barr, James.
A correct and authentic narrative of the Indian war in Florida, with a description of Maj. Dade's massacre, and an account of the extreme suffering, for want of provisions, of the army ... New York, J. Narine, printer, 1836.
32 p.   16 cm.

Barr, Knut August, 1871-1929.
På studentsångarfärd till Amerika; illustrerade resebref af Knut Barr. Stockholm, H. W. Tullberg, 1905.
1 p.l., [5]-194 p. illus. (incl. ports., facsims.)   22 1/2 cm.

Barron, Samuel Benton, 1834-1912.
The Lone Star defenders; a chronicle of the Third Texas cavalry, Ross' brigade, by S. B. Barron ... New York and Washington, The Neale publishing company, 1908.
3 p.l., 3-276 p. front., 10 port.   21 cm.

Barrows, Elijah Porter, 1807-1888.
...A view of the American slavery question. By E. P. Barrows, Jr., pastor of the First Free Presbyterian church, New York. New York, J. S. Taylor, 1836.
iv, [5]-114 p.   14 1/2 cm.

Barrows, William, 1815-1891.
The war and slavery and their relations to each other. A discourse, delivered in the Old South church, Reading, Mass., December 28, 1862. Boston, J. M. Whittemore & co., 1863.
18 p.   23 1/2 cm.

Barry, Thomas.
Narrative of the singular adventures and captivity of Thos. Barry, among the Monsipi Indians,

in the unexplored regions of North America ...
[London] A. Neil, 1802.
   vii, [1], [9]-60 p. incl. col. front.   18 cm.

Bartlett, John Russell, 1805-
   Personal narrative of explorations and incidents
in Texas, New Mexico, California, Sonora, and
Chihuahua, connected with the United States and
Mexico boundary commission, during the years 1850,
'51, '52, and '53 ... New York & London, D. Appleton & company, 1854.
   2v. fold. fronts., illus., plates.   23 cm.

[Bartlett, Napier] 1836-1877.
   A soldier's story of the war; including the
marches and battles of the Washington artillery,
and of other Louisiana troops ... New Orleans,
Clark & Hofeline, 1874.
   1 p.l., 252 (i.e. 262) p. front., port.
22 1/2 cm.

Bartley, Thomas W.
   Speech ... on the subject of the law to organize the territories of Kansas and Nebraska,
delivered before a convention of the people, held
at Mansfield on the 20th of July, 1854. Mansfield, John Y. Glessner, 1854.
   35 p.   22 cm.

Barton, Harry Scott, 1862-
   What I did in "The long." Journals home during
a tour through the United States and Canada, in
the long vacation of 1881 ... [London, E. Stanford
printer, 1881?]
   2 p.l., 91 p. illus.   25 1/2 cm.

Barton, Thomas H.   1828-
   Autobiography of Dr. Thomas H. Barton ... including a history of the Fourth Regt. West Va.
vol. inf'y, with an account of Col. Lightburn's
retreat down the Kanawha Valley, Gen. Grant's
Vicksburg and Chattanooga campaigns, together with
the several battles in which the Fourth regiment
was engaged, and its losses by disease, desertion
and in battle. By Dr. T. H. Barton. Charleston,
West Virginia printing co., 1890.
   viii, 340 p. front. (port.) 21 1/2 cm.

Barton, William Eleazar, 1861-1930.
   Life in the hills of Kentucky, by W. E. Barton.

Oberlin, O., E. J. Goodrich, 1890.
[7] [3]-295 p. incl. illus., plates, front.,
plates. 18 cm.

Barton, William Eleazar, 1861-1930.
Pine Knot; a story of Kentucky life, by William
E. Barton ... illustrated by F. T. Merrill. New
York, D. Appleton and company, 1900.
ix, 300 p. front., plates. 19 1/2 cm.

Bartram, William, 1739-
... Travels through North and South Carolina,
Georgia, East & West Florida, the Cherokee country,
the extensive territories of the Muscogulges, or
Creek confederacy, and the country of the Choctaws;
containing an account of the soil and natural
productions of those regions, together with observations on the manners of the Indians. Embellished
with copperplates. Philadelphia, Printed by James
& Johnson, M.DCC.XCI.
[iii]-xxxiv, 522 p. 2 p.l., front. (port.),
plates (part fold.), fold, map. 20 1/2 cm.

Bascom, Henry Bidleman, bp., 1796-1850.
Methodism and slavery: with other matters in
controversy between the North and the South; being
a review of the manifesto of the majority, in reply to the protest of the minority, of the late
General conference of the Methodist E. church, in
the case of Bishop Andrew. By H. B. Bascom ...
Frankfort, Ky., Hodges, Todd & Pruett, printers,
1845.
165 p. 24 1/2 cm.

Bassett, George W.
Slavery examined in the light of nature. Sermon ... at the Congregational church, Washington,
D.C., Sunday, February 28, 1858. [Washington?
1858?]
8 p. 23 cm.

Bassett, William, 1803.
Letter to a member of the Society of friends,
in reply to objections against joining anti-slavery
societies ... Boston, Published by Isaac Knapp,
1837.
41 p. 18 1/2 cm.

Bates, Edward.
Opinion of Attorney General Bates on citizen-

ship. Washington, Government printing office,
1862.
27 p. 23 1/2 cm.

Bates, Edward, 1793-1869.
Opinion of Attorney General Bates on citizenship. Washington, Govt. print. off., 1863.
22 p. 22 cm.

Bates, Emily Katharine.
A year in the great republic, by E. Katherine
Bates ... London, Ward & Downey, 1887.
2 v. 19 cm.

Batten, John Mullin, 1837-
Around and around, by John Mullin Batten ...
[Downingtown? Pa.] For the author, 1906.
226 p. front. (port.) pl. 20 cm.

Battle-fields of the South, from Bull Run to Fredericks-
burg; with sketches of Confederate commanders,
and gossip of the camps. By an English combatant,
(lieutenant of artillery on the field staff.)...
London, Smith, Elder and co., 1863.
2 v. fronts. (fold. maps) 19 1/2 cm.

[Baudry des Lozières, Louis Narcisse] 1761-
Voyage à la Louisiane, et sur le continent de
l'Amérique septentrionale, fait dans les années
1794 à 1798; contenant un tableau historique de
la Louisiane ... Par B*** D***. Orné d'une belle
carte ... Paris, Dentu, an ix. - 1802.
viii, 382 p. front. (fold. map) 20 cm.

Baumann, Felix, 1868-
Im dunkelsten Amerika; sittenschilderungen
aus den Vereinigten Staaten, von Felix Baumann...
Dresden, E. Beutelspacher & co., 1902.
[3] 104 p. 22 1/2 cm.

Baumbach, Ludwig Carl Wilhelm von, 1799-
Neue briefe aus den Vereinigten Staaten von
Nord-amerika in die heimath, mit besonderer rücksicht auf deutsche auswanderer. Cassel, T. Fischer,
1856.
xiv, 333 [2]p. 18 1/2 cm.

Baumgartner, Andreas.
Erinnerungen aus Amerika, von Andreas Baumgart-
ner. Mit 49 abbildungen. Zürich, Art. institut
O. Füssli [1906].

221 p.   incl. front., illus.   19 1/2 cm.

Baxter, William Edward, 1825-
    America and the Americans ... London, New York,
G. Routledge & co., 1855.
    244 p.   2 p.l.   16 1/2 cm.

Bayard, Ferdinand Marie, 1768-
    Voyage dans l'intérieur des États-Unis, à Bath,
Winchester, dans la vallée de Shenandoha [!]
etc., etc. pendant l'été de 1791. Paris, Chez
Cocheris, 1797.
    [iii]-xvi, 336 p.   2 p.l.   20 cm.

Bayard, James Asheton, 1799-1880.
    Abolition, and the relation of races. Speech
of Hon. James A. Bayard, of Delaware. Delivered
in the Senate of the United States, April 8, 1862.
[Washington L. Towers & co., printers, 1862].
    15 p.   24 1/2 cm.

Bazin, René, 1853-
    ... Nord-sud: Amérique - Angleterre - Corse -
Spitzberg. Paris, Calmann-Levy [c1913].
    2 p.l., 348 p.   18 1/2 cm.

[Beadle, Charles]
    A trip to the United States in 1887. Printed
for private circulation.   [London, Printed by
J. S. Virtue and co., limited, 1887].
    3 p.l., 210 p.   fold. map.   19 cm.

Beadle, John Hanson, 1840-
    The undeveloped west; or, Five years in the
territories ... Philadelphia, Chicago [etc.]
National publishing company [1873].
    1 p.l., 15-823 p.   front., illus., plates,
double map.   22 cm.

Beale, George William, 1842-
    A lieutenant of cavalry in Lee's army, by
G. W. Beale. Boston, The Gorham press, 1918.
    231 p.   19 1/2 cm.

Beale, Joseph H.
    Picturesque sketches of American progress.
Comprising official descriptions of great American
cities ... Illustrated sketches of American scenery, and celebrated resorts. With historical
sketches ... of our country, under the various

51

administrations ... New York, The Empire Coopera-
tive association, c1889.
    445 p. front., illus. (incl. ports., map,
facsim.) plates. 24 cm.

Beale, Richard Lee Tuberville, 1819-1893.
    History of the Ninth Virginia cavalry, in the
war between the states. By the late Brig. General
R.L.T. Beale. Richmond, Va., B. F. Johnson publishing company, 1899.
    192 p. front. (port.) 23 cm.

Beatty, John, 1828-1914.
    The citizen-soldier; or, Memoirs of a volunteer.
By John Beatty. Cincinnati, Wilstach, Baldwin
& co., 1879.
    vii, [9]-401 p. 20 cm.

Beaufoy, Henry.
    The speech of Mr. Beaufoy, Tuesday, the 18th
June, 1788, in a committee of the whole House,
on a bill for regulating the conveyance of negroes
from Africa to the West-Indies, to which are
added observations on the evidence adduced against
the bill. London, Printed for J. Phillips, 1788.
    37 p. 20 cm.

Beaujour, Louis Auguste Félix, baron de, 1763-
    Aperçu des États-Unis, au commencement du XIXe
siècle, depuis 1800 jusqu'en 1810, avec des tables
statistiques. Paris, L. G. Michaud, imprimeur
[etc.] 1814.
    274 p. fold. map, xvii fold. tables. 20 1/2 cm.

Beaumont de La Bonninière, Gustave Auguste de, 1802-
    Marie; ou L'esclavage aux États-Unis, tableau
de moeurs américaines ... Bruxelles, Louis Hau-
man et compie., 1835.
    2 v. 21 cm.

Beauvallet, Leon.
    Rachel and the New world. A trip to the United
States and Cuba. Tr. from the French of Leon
Beauvallet. New York, Dix, Edwards & co., 1856.
    [iii]-xiv, 404 p. 2 p.1. 18 cm.

Beck, Carl, 1856-
    Amerikanische streiflichter ... Berlin, L.
Simion nf., 1905.
    vi, 246 p. 23 cm.

Becker, John H.
Die hundertjährige republik. Soziale und politische zustande in den Vereinigten Staaten Nordamerika's ... mit einleitung von Friedrich von Hellwald. Augsburg, Lampart & comp., 1876-
2 p.l., lv, 384 p. 21 1/2 cm.

Beckman, Ernst, 1850-
Från nya verlden; reseskildringar från Amerikas Förenta Stater ... Stockholm, P. A. Norstedt och söner, 1877.
2 p.l., 386 p. front., illus. 21 1/2 cm.

Beecher, Catherine Esther, 1800-1878.
An essay on slavery and abolitionism, with reference to the duty of American females. By Catherine E. Beecher. Philadelphia, H. Perkins; Boston, Perkins & Marvin, 1837.
152 p. 15 1/2 cm.

Beecher, Charles, 1815-1900.
The duty of disobedience to wicked laws. A sermon on the fugitive slave law. By Charles Beecher ... New York, J. A. Gray, printer, 1851.
22 p. 22 1/2 cm.

Beecher, Charles, 1815-1900.
The God of the Bible against slavery. By Rev. Charles Beecher. [New York, American anti-slavery society, 1855].
11 p. 19 cm.

Beecher, Charles.
A sermon on the Nebraska bill ... Published by the First Congregational Society, Newark, N.J. New York, Oliver & brother, 1854.
16 p. 23 cm.

Beecher, Edward.
Narrative of the riots at Alton: in connection with the death of Rev. Elijah P. Lovejoy ... Alton, Illinois, George Holton, 1838.
159 p. 18 1/2 cm.

Beecher, Eunice White (Bullard)
"Mrs. Henry Ward Beecher," 1813.
Letters from Florida. New York, D. Appleton and company, 1879.
85 p. illus. 17 1/2 cm.

Beecher, Henry Ward, 1813-1887.
American rebellion. Report of the speeches of
the Rev. Henry Ward Beecher, delivered at public
meetings in Manchester, Glasgow, Edinburgh, Liverpool, and London; and at the farewell breakfasts
in London, Manchester, and Liverpool. Manchester,
Union and emancipation society; [etc., etc.] 1864.
2 p.1., 175 p.   21 cm.

Beecher, Henry Ward, 1813-1887.
England and America: speech of Henry Ward
Beecher at the Free-trade hall, Manchester, October 9, 1863 ... Boston, J. Redpath, 1863.
39 p.   18 cm.

Beecher, Henry Ward, 1813-1887.
Freedom and war. Discourses on topics suggested
by the times. By Henry Ward Beecher. Boston,
Ticknor and Fields, 1863.
2 p.1., [iii]-iv p., 1 1., 445 p.   19 cm.

Beers, Mrs. Fannie A.
Memories. A record of personal experience and
adventure during four years of war. By Mrs. Fannie A. Beers. Philadelphia, Press of J. B. Lippincott co., 1888.
336 p.   front.   20 cm.

Beknopte en zakelyke beschryving der voornaamste en-
gelsche volkplantingen, in Noord-Amerika; neffens
aanmerkin en over den oorsprong en voortgang der
tegenwoordige geschillen, en des oorlogs, tusschen
Groot-Brittanie en deszelfs kolonisten. Amsterdam,
Petrus Conradi, 1776.
2 v.   22 1/2 cm.

Bell, John Thomas, 1842-
Tramps and triumphs of the Second Iowa infantry,
briefly sketched, by John T. Bell, lieut. Co."C".
Omaha, Gibson, Miller & Richardson, printers,
1886.
32 p.   22 1/2 cm.

Bellin, Jacques Nicolas, 1703-
Remarques sur la carte de l'Amérique Septentrionale, comprise entre le 28e et le 72e dégré
de latitude, avec une description géographique
de ces parties ... A Paris, De l'impr. de Didot,
M.DCC.LV.
131 p.   24 cm.

Beltrami, Giacomo Constantino, 1772-
A pilgrimage in Europe and America, leading
to the discovery of the sources of the Mississippi
and Bloody river; with a description of the whole
course of the former, and of the Ohio ... London, Hunt and Clarke, 1828.
2 v. fronts. (v. I, port.; v. II, fold. map)
plates, fold. plans. 22 cm.

Benavides, Alonso de, fl. 1630.
Memorial qve fray Ivan de Santander, de la
orden de San Francisco, comissario general de
Indias, presenta a la Magestad catolica del rey
Don Felipe Qvarto neustro senor. Hecho por el
padre fray Alonso de Benauides ... En Madrid, en
la Imprenta real, año 1630.
109 [i.e. 103] p. 1 p.l. 21 cm.

Benezet, Anthony.
A caution to Great Britain and her colonies,
in a short representation of the calamitous state
of the enslaved negroes in the British dominions.
A new edition ... Philadelphia printed; London
reprinted and sold by James Phillips, 1785.
46 p. 21 cm.

[Benezet, Anthony]
"Notes on the slave trade". [n.p., n.d.]
8 p. 17 cm.

[Benezet, Anthony]
Observations on the enslaving, importing and
purchasing of Negroes ... 2d ed. Germantown,
printed by Christopher Sower, 1760.
16 p. 19 cm.

Benezet, Anthony.
Some historical account of Guinea, its situation, produce, and general disposition of its
inhabitants. With an inquiry into the rise and
progress of the slave trade, its nature, and la-
mentable effects. London, J. Phillips, 1788.
xv, 131 p. 22 cm.

Benezet, Anthony.
Some historical account of Guinea ... Philadelphia, printed by Joseph Crukshank, 1771.
iv, 144 p. 16 cm.

Benjamin, Judah Philip.
Kansas bill ... Speech ... delivered in Senate
of United States on Thursday, March 11, 1858.
Slavery protected by the common law of the new
world. Guaranteed [sic] by constitution. Vindication of the Supreme Court of the U. S.
Washington, G. S. Gideon, 1858.
29 p.   23 cm.

Benjamin, Judah Philip.
Speech ... on the Kansas question. Delivered
in the Senate May 2, 1856. [n.p., n.d.]
15 p.   24 cm.

Bennett, Andrew J.   b. 1841 or 2.
The story of the First Massachusetts light
battery, attached to the Sixth army corps. A
glance at events in the armies of the Potomac
and Shenandoah, from the summer of 1861 to the
autumn of 1864. By A. J. Bennett ... Boston,
Press of Deland and Barta, 1886.
200 p. pl., port., maps, facsim. 23 1/2 cm.

Bennett, Henry.
Kansas must be free! The political effects of
slavery. Speech ... on the bill for the admission
of Kansas as a free state, delivered in the House
of representatives, June 30, 1856. [n.p., n.d.]
15 p.   22 1/2 cm.

Bennett, William Wallace, 1821-
A narrative of the great revival which pre-
vailed in the southern armies during the late
civil war between the states of the federal union.
Philadelphia, Claxton, Remsen & Haffelfinger,
1877.
vi, [7] - 427 p. front., plates, ports.
19 1/2 cm.

Benson, Henry Clark, 1815-
Life among the Choctaw Indians, and sketches
of the South-west ... With an introduction by Rev.
T. A. Morris ... Cincinnati, Pub. by L.Swormstedt
& A. Poe, for the Methodist Episcopal church,
1860.
314 p.   19 1/2 cm.

Bentley, William H.
History of the 77th Illinois volunteer infantry, Sept. 2, 1862 - July 10, 1865, by Lieut. W.H.

Bentley, with an introduction by General D. P.
Grier. Peoria, Ill., E. Hine, printer, 1883.
396 p. 20 cm.

Benwell, J.
An Englishman's travels in America: his observations of life and manners in the free and slave
states ... London, Binns and Goodwin; [etc., etc.,
1853]
vii, 231 p. col. front. 17 cm.

Berghaus, Erwin, 1894- ed.
USA-nackt! Bilddokumente aus Gottes eigenem
Land. Berlin, Brunnen-Verlag [c1943]
1 v. (chiefly plates, ports.) 25 cm.

Berghoff, Stephan, 1891-
Joes abenteuer im wilden westen, von Stephan
Berghoff; mit bildern von Johannes Thiel. Freiburg im Breisgau, Herder & co., g.m.b.h., 1934.
4 p.1., 199, [3] p. illus. 18 1/2 cm.

Bernard, Jean Frédéric, comp.
Relations de la Louisiane, et du fleuve Mississippi, où l'on voit l'état de ce grand païs & les
avantages, qu'il peut produire & c. Amsterdam,
J. F. Bernard, 1720.
408 p. 1 p.1., 14 pl., map. 17 cm.

Bernard, John, 1756-
Retrospections of America, 1797-1811 ... edited
from the manuscript by Mrs. Bayle Bernard with an
introduction, notes, and index by Laurence Hut-
ton and Brander Matthews. New York, Harper brothers, 1887.
xiii p., 380 p. 1 1., front., plates, ports.
19 1/2 cm.

Bernhard, Karl, duke of Saxe-Weimar-Eisenach, 1792-
Reise sr. hoheit des herzogs Bernhard zu Sach-
sen-Weimar-Eisenach durch Nord-Amerika in den
jahren 1825 und 1826. Hrsg. von Heinrich Luden...
Weimar, W. Hoffmann, 1828.
2 v. in 1. fold. front., illus., plates, maps
(part fold.) fold. plans. 23 1/2 cm.

Berquin-Duvallon.
Vue de la colonie espagnole du Mississippi, ou
des provinces de Louisiane et Floride Occidentale:
en l'année 1802, par un observateur résident sur

les lieux ... Paris, Imprimerie expéditive, an
xi, 1803.
   xx, 318, 5 [4] p. 2 fold. maps. 21 1/2 cm.

Berry, C. B. 1812-
   The other side, how it struck us ... London,
Griffith and Farran; New York, E. P. Dutton & co.,
1880.
   296 p. 22 cm.

Berry, Harrison, b. 1816.
   Slavery and abolitionism, as viewed by a
Georgia slave. By Harrison Berry, the property
of S. W. Price, Covington, Georgia. Atlanta,
Franklin printing house, Wood, Hanleiter, Rice &
co., 1861.
   viii, [9]-41 p., 1 l. port. 21 cm.

Berry, Henry.
   The speech of Henry Berry, (of Jefferson,)
in the House of delegates of Virginia, on the
abolition of slavery. [Richmond, 1832]
   8 p. 22 1/2 cm.

Berry, Philip.
   A review of the Bishop of Oxford's counsel to
the American clergy, with reference to the institution of slavery. Also supplemental remarks on
the relation of the colored class. By the Rev.
Philip Berry ... Washington, W. M. Morrison; New
York, Stanford & Swords; [etc.,etc.] 1848.
   26 p. 22 cm.

Berry, Thomas Franklin, 1832-
   Four years with Morgan and Forrest, by Col.
Thomas F. Berry ... Oklahoma City, Okla., The
Harlow-Ratliff company, 1914.
   1 p.l., [vii]-xv, 476 p. front., plates, ports.
20 1/2 cm.

Besancon's annual register of the state of Mississippi,
   for the year 1838. Compiled from original documents and actual surveys ... v. 1. Natchez, L. A.
   Besancon, 1838.
      232 p. fold. map. 19 1/2 cm.

Beschryving der colonien van Groot-Britanje in Noord-
   Amerika. (In De naauwkeurige hollandsche almanach.
   1779. P. 127-148).

Beste, John Richard Digby, 1806-
The Wabash: or, Adventures of an English gentleman's family in the interior of America ... London, Hurst and Blackett, 1855.
2v. fronts. 20 cm.

Betts, Alexander Davis, 1832-
Experience of a Confederate chaplain, 1861-1864 [i.e. 1865] by Rev. A. D. Betts ... chaplain 30th N. C. troops. Ed. by W. A. Betts. [Greenville? S. C., 190 ?]
103, [1] p. illus., ports. 18 cm.

Bevens, W. E.
Reminiscences of a private, Company "G", First Arkansas regiment infantry, May, 1861 to 1865. [Newport, Ark.? The author? 1913]
89 p. ports.

Beyer, Edward, 1820?-1865.
Edward Beyer's cyclorama, malerische Reise von Bremen nach New York and durch die Vereinigten Staaten von Nordamerika, zurück nach Hamburg. Nach der Natur gemalt und erläutert. 2d ed. Dresden, C. C. Meinhold & Söhne [186?]
60 p. 2 1. 17 1/2 cm.

Beyer, Moritz, 1807-1854.
Das Auswanderungsbuch; oder, Führer und Rathgeber bei der Auswanderung nach Nordamerika ... und Texas ... Leipzig, Baumgartner, 1846.
xii, 236 p. 1 pl. 12°

Bianchi, Alberto G.
Los Estados Unidos. Descripciones de viaje, por Alberto G. Bianchi ... México, N. Lugo Viña, 1887.
5 p.l., vii-xv, [1] 336 p. front. (7 port.) illus., fold. facsim. 21 1/2 cm.

Bibb, Henry, b. 1815.
Narrative of the life and adventures of ... an American slave, written by himself. With an introduction by Lucius C. Matlack. New York, The Author, 1849.
1 p.l., xii, [13]-204, [3] p. illus. 19 cm.

The Bible gives no sanction to slavery. By a Tennessean. [Cincinnati, American reform tract and book society, n.d.]
32 p. 18 cm.

Bickel, Karl August.
The mangrove coast, the story of the west coast of Florida, by Karl A. Bickel, photographs by Walker Evans. New York, Coward-McCann, inc. [1942]
viii, 312 p. 82 pl. on 16 l. 22 cm.

Bickell, Richard.
Negro slavery. No. XIV. The West Indies as they are: or, A real picture of slavery. [London, n.d.]
133-148 p. 21 cm.

Bickell, Richard.
The West Indies as they are; or, A real picture of slavery: but more particularly as it exists in the island of Jamaica. In three parts. With notes. By the Rev. R. Bickell ... London, Printed for J. Hatchard and son [etc.] 1825.
xvi, 256 p. 21 1/2 cm.

Bickham, William Denison, 1827-1894.
Rosecrans' campaign with the fourteenth army corps, or, the Army of the Cumberland: a narrative of personal observations with ... official reports of the battle of Stone river. By "W.D.B." ... Cincinnati, Moore, Wilstach, Keys & co., 1863.
viii, 9-476 p. front. (map) 19 cm.

Bicknell, Rev. George W.
History of the Fifth regiment Maine volunteers, comprising brief descriptions of its marches, engagements, and general services from the date of its muster in, June 24, 1861, to the time of its muster out, July 27, 1864. By Rev. Geo. W. Bicknell ... Portland, H. L. Davis, 1871.
xii, [13]-404 p. front. (port.) pl. 19 cm.

Biddle, Mrs. Ellen (McGowan) 1841-
Reminiscences of a soldier's wife ... Philadelphia, Press of J. B. Lippincott Company, 1907.
256, [3] p. front., plates, ports. 20 1/2 cm.

Bigelow, John, 1817-1911.
France and the Confederate navy, 1862-1868. An international episode. New York, Harper & brothers, 1888.
x p., 1 l., 247 p. 19 1/2 cm.

Bigelow, John.
Jamaica in 1850: or, The effects of sixteen
years of freedom on a slave colony ... New York
& London, George P. Putnam, 1851.
iv, 214 p. 18 cm.

Bilder aus dem gesellschaftlichen leben der Nord-Ameri-
kaner ... Von einer Deutschen. Reutlingen, M.
MacKen, 1835.
254 p. 21 1/2 cm.

Bill, Ledyard, 1836-
A winter in Florida; or, Observations on the
soil, climate, and products of our semi-tropical
state ... New York, Wood & Holbrook, 1869.
222 p. front., plates, map. 19 cm.

Billings, John Davis, 1842-
The history of the Tenth Massachusetts battery
of light artillery in the war of the rebellion.
Formerly of the Third corps, and afterwards of
Hancock's Second corps, Army of the Potomac. 1862-
1865. By John D. Billings ... Boston, Hall &
Whiting, 1881.
xii p., 2 1., 400 p. incl. front., plates (1
col.) ports., 2 plans. 24 cm.

Bingham, John Armor, 1815-1900.
The assault upon Senator Sumner, a crime
against the people. Speech ... in the House of
Representatives, July 9, 1856. [Washington, Buell
& Blanchard, printers, 1856?]
8 p. 23 cm.

Bingham, John Armor, 1815-1900.
Bill and report of John A. Bingham, and vote
on its passage, repealing the territorial New
Mexican laws establishing slavery and authorizing
employers to whip "white persons" and others in
their employment, and denying them redress in
the courts. [Washington? 1858]
7, [1] p. 24 cm.

Bingham, John Armor, 1815-1900.
The Lecompton conspiracy. Speech ... Delivered
in the House of Representatives, January 25, 1858.
Washington, Buell & Blanchard, 1858.
8 p. 23 cm.

Bingley, William, 1774-
    Travels in North America, from modern writers...
London, Printed for Harvey and Darton, 1821.
    346 p. 5 p.1., 3 pl. (incl. front.) 18 1/2 cm.

Birkbeck, Morris, 1784-
    Notes on a journey in America, from the coast
of Virginia to the territory of Illinois. With
proposals for the establishment of a colony of
English, accompanied by a map, illustrating the
route. Dublin, Re-printed for Thomas Larkin, 1818.
    viii, [9]-158 p. fold. map. 21 1/2 cm.

Birkhead, Lennox.
    A voice from the south, discussing, among other
subjects, slavery, and its remedy ... Baltimore,
John W. Woods, printer, 1861.
    iv, [5]-234 p.   18 1/2 cm.

Birney, James Gillespie, 1792.
    The American churches the bulwarks of American
slavery ... 3d American ed. Rev. by the author.
Concord, N. H., P. Pillsbury, 1885.
    48 p.   19 cm.

Birney, James Gillespie, 1792-1857.
    ... Correspondence, between the Hon. F. H. El-
more, one of the South Carolina delegation in
Congress, and James G. Birney, one of the secre-
taries of the American anti-slavery society. New
York, American anti-slavery society, 1838.
    68 p.   23 cm.

Birney, James Gillespie, 1792-
    Correspondence between James G. Birney, of Ken-
tucky, and several individuals of the Society of
Friends. Haverhill [Mass.] Printed at the Essex
gazette office. 1835.
    8 p.   22 cm.

Birney, James Gillespie, 1792.
    Examination of the decision of the Supreme Court
of the United States, in the case of Strader, Gor-
man and Armstrong vs. Christopher Graham, delivered
at its December term, 1850: concluding with an
address to the free colored people, advising them
to remove to Liberia... Cincinnati, Truman &
Spofford, 1852.
    47 p.   23 cm.

Birney, James Gillespie, 1792.
Letter on colonization, addressed to the Rev.
Thornton J. Mills, corresponding secretary of the
Kentucky colonization society ... New-York, Pub-
lished by the American anti-slavery society, 1838.
46 p.   19 cm.

Birney, James Gillespie, 1792.
Letter to ministers and elders on the sin of
holding slaves, and the duty of immediate emancipation.   [New York, S. W. Benedict & co., 1834.]
18 p.   18 1/2 cm.

Birney, James Gillespie, 1792-1857.
Mr. Birney's second letter.   To the ministers
and elders of the Presbyterian church in Kentucky.
[n.p., 1834]
16 p.   18 cm.

Birney, James Gillespie, 1792-
The sinfulness of slaveholding in all circumstances; tested by reason and Scripture.   Detroit,
Printed by C. Wilcox, 1846.
iv, [5]-60 p.   21 cm.

Biron, Armand Louis de Gontaut duc de Lauzun, 1747-
Memoires de M. le duc de Lauzun.   Paris, Chez
Barrois l'âiné, 1822.
xx, 399 p.   1 p.l.   20 1/2 cm.

[Bishop, Isabella Lucy (Bird)] "Mrs. J. F. Bishop,"
1831-
The Englishwoman in America.   London, J. Murray, 1856.
vii, 464 p.   20 cm.

Bishop, Nathaniel Holmes, 1837-
Four months in a sneak-box.   A boat voyage
of 2600 miles down the Ohio and Mississippi
rivers, and along the Gulf of Mexico.   Boston,
Lee & Shepard; New York, C. T. Dillingham, 1879.
xii, 322 p. front., illus., plates, maps,
21 1/2 cm.

Bishop, Nathaniel Holmes, 1837-
Voyage of the paper canoe: a geographical
journey of 2500 miles, from Quebec to the Gulf of
Mexico, during the years 1874-5 ... Boston, Lee
and Shepard; New York, C. T. Dillingham [etc.,etc.]

xv, 351 p. front., illus., plates, maps.
21 1/2 cm.

Bissell, William Harrison, 1811.
    The slave question. Speech ... in the House
of Representatives, Thursday, February 21, 1850.
[Washington, Buell & Blanchard, 1850?]
    8 p.   23 cm.

Bittinger, Joseph Baugher.
    A plea for humanity. A sermon preached in
the Euclid street Presbyterian church, Cleveland,
Ohio. Cleveland, Medall & Cowles & co., 1854.
    28 p.   23 cm.

Bittinger, Joseph Baugher.
    A sermon preached before the Presbyterian
churches of Cleveland, on the national fast day,
September 26, 1861 ... Cleveland, Printed by F.
Cowles & co., 1861.
    21 p.   22 cm.

Bixby, O. H.
    Incidents in Dixie; being ten months' experi-
ence of a Union soldier in the military prisons
of Richmond, N. Orleans and Salisbury. Published
for the benefit of Maryland state fair for the
Christian and Sanitary commissions. Baltimore,
Printed by J. Young, 1864.
    89 p.   15 cm.

Black republican imposture exposed! Fraud upon the
    people! Fremont no soldier! [n.p., n.d.]
    16 p.   20 cm.

Blackburn, James Knox Polk, 1837-
    Reminiscences of the Terry rangers. [Austin]
Published by the Littlefield fund for southern
history, the University of Texas, 1919.
    vii, 79 p.   27 cm.

Blackford, Mrs. Susan Leigh (Colston) 1835- comp.
    Memoirs of life in and out of the army in Vir-
ginia during the war between the states. Comp.
by Susan Leigh Blackford from original and contemporaneous correspondence and diaries. Annotated
and edited exclusively for the private use of
their family by her husband, Charles Minor Blackford ... Lynchburg, Va., J. P. Bell company,

printers, 1894-96.
2 v.   24 cm.

Blair, Francis Preston, 1821.
    ... Letter ... to the Republican association
of Washington, D. C. ... December 10, 1855.
[Washington, Buell & Blanchard, 1855?]
    8 p.   24 cm.

Blair, Francis Preston, 1821.
    Speech ... at the Cooper institute, New York
City, Wednesday, January 25, 1860. Washington,
Buell & Blanchard, 1860.
    14 p.   21 cm.

Blair, Francis Preston, 1821.
    Speech of Hon. Francis P. Blair, Jr., of
Missouri, on the acquisition of Central America;
delivered in the House of Representatives, January
14, 1858. Washington, Printed at the Congressional globe office, 1858.
    16 p.   23 cm.

Blair, Francis Preston, 1821.
    Speech ... on the acquisition of territory in
Central and South America to be colonized with
free blacks, and held as a dependency by the
United States. Delivered in the House of Representatives on the 11th day of January, 1858. With
an appendix. Washington, D. C., Buell & Blanchard,
printers, 1852.
    31 p.   24 cm.

Blair, Francis Preston, 1821.
    A voice from the grave of Jackson! Letter
from Francis P. Blair, Esq., to a public meeting
in New York, held April 29, 1856. [Washington,
D. C., Buell & Blanchard, 1856?]
    15 p.   23 cm.

Blake, Harrison Gray Otis, 1818.
    Equality of rights in the territories. Speech
... made in the House of Representatives, in committee of the whole, June 12, 1860. [n.p., n.d.]
    8 p.   24 cm.

Blake, Henry Nichols, 1838-
    Three years in the Army of the Potomac. By
Henry N. Blake, late captain in the Eleventh regiment Massachusetts volunteers ... Boston, Lee and

Shepard, 1865.
vi, 7-319 p.   18 1/2 cm.

Blakeslee, Bernard F.
   History of the Sixteenth Connecticut volunteers.
   By B. F. Blakeslee ... Hartford, The Case, Lockwood & Brainard co., printers, 1875.
   116 p.   19 cm.

Blanchard, Claude, 1742-
   The journal of Claude Blanchard, commissary of
   the French auxiliary army sent to the United States
   during the American revolution, 1780-1783. Tr.
   from a French manuscript, by William Duane, and
   ed. by Thomas Balch. Albany, J. Munsell, 1876.
   xvi, 207 p.   22 1/2 cm.

Blanchard, J.
   A debate on slavery: held in the city of Cincinnati, on the first, second, third, and sixth
   days of October, 1845, upon the question: Is
   slave-holding in itself sinful, and the relation
   between master and slave, a sinful relation? Af-
   firmative: Rev. J. Blanchard ... Negative: N.L.
   Rice ... Cincinnati, Wm. H. Moore and co., 1846.
   482 p.   19 1/2 cm.

Blanchard, P.
   San Juan de Ulùa, ou Relation de l'expédition
   francaise au Mexique ... Suivi de notes et documents, et d'un apercu général sur l'état actuel
   du Texas, par m. E. Maissin ... Paris, Gide, 1839.
   xii, 591 p.   illus., pl.   28 cm.

Blanding, Stephen F.
   Recollections of a sailor boy; or, The cruise
   of the gunboat Louisiana. By Stephen F. Blanding
   ... Providence, E. A. Johnson & co., 1886.
   vi, [7]-330 p.   19 1/2 cm.

[Blane, William Newnham] 1800-
   Travels through the United States and Canada...
   London, Baldwin and co., 1828.
   511 p.   2 p.l.   2 fold. maps (incl. front.)
   fold. tab.   22 cm.

Bleby, Henry.
   Speech ... on the results of emancipation in
   the British W. I. colonies, delivered at the celebration of the Massachusetts Anti-slavery society,

held at Island Grove, Abington, July 31st, 1858.
Phonographic report by J. M. W. Yerrinton. Boston,
R. F. Wallcut, 1858.
36 p.   15 cm.

Bledsoe, Albert Taylor, 1809-1877.
An essay on liberty and slavery. By Albert
Taylor Bledsoe, LL. D., professor of mathematics
in the University of Virginia. Philadelphia, J.
B. Lippincott & co., 1856.
4, 9-383 p.   19 cm.

[Blessington, Joseph P.]
The campaigns of Walker's Texas division. By
a private soldier. Containing a complete record
of the campaigns in Texas, Louisiana and Arkansas
... including the federal's report of the battles,
names of the officers of the division   diary of
marches, camp scenery, anecdotes ...   &c., &c. ...
New York, Pub. for the author, 1875.
314 p.   23 cm.

Bliss, Philemon, 1813.
Citizenship: state citizens, general citizens.
Speech ... delivered in the House of Representa-
tives, January 7, 1858. [Washington, D. C., Buell
& Blanchard, 1858.]
8 p.   23 cm.

Bliss, Philemon, 1813-1889.
Complaints of the extensionists--their falsity.
Speech ... in the House of Representatives, May
21, 1856. [n.p., n.d.]
16 p.   23 cm.

Bliss, Philemon, 1813.
Congress must govern its territory--man not
property. Speech in the House of Representatives,
January 15, 1857. Washington, D. C., Buell &
Blanchard [1857?]
8 p.   23 cm.

Bliss, Philemon, 1813.
The Federal judiciary. Speech ... in the United States House of Representatives, February 7,
1859. [n.p., n.d.]
8 p.   23 cm.

Bliss, Philemon, 1813.
    Success of the absolutists: their idealism:
what and whence is it: speech ... in the House
of Representatives, May 24, 1858. Washington,
D. C., Buell & Blanchard, 1858.
    15 p.   23 cm.

Blocher, W. D.
    ... Blocher's Arkansas land-guide, containing
instructions how to proceed and to whom to go,
and what to do to obtain titles to lands of the
state, or lands of rail-roads, or of the United
States, within the state of Arkansas. Little
Rock, W. H. Windsor, 1876.
    50 p.   17 1/2 cm.

Blondel, Georges, 1856-
    Les enseignements de l'Exposition de Saint
Louis. Extrait du Correspondant. Paris, De
Soye et fils, imprimeurs, 1904.
    16 p.   24 cm.

The blook-stained leaf. [Cincinnati, American reform tract and book society, n.d.]
    4 p.   17 cm.

[Blouët, Paul, i.e. Léon Paul] 1848-
    A Frenchman in America (the Anglo-Saxon race
revisited) by Max O'Rell [pseud.] ... With upwards of 130 illustrations by E. W. Kemole.
Bristol, J. W. Arrowsmith; London, Simpkin, Marshall, Hamilton, Kent & co., limited [1891?]
    1 p.l., iv, 336 p.   illus.   19 cm.

[Blowe, Daniel]
    A geographical, historical, commercial, and
agricultural view of the United States of America
... Compiled by several gentlemen from a variety
of original manuscripts, and from the latest and
best authorities. London, Edwards & Knibb;
Liverpool, W. Grapel, 1820.
    7, 3-746, xvi p.   front. (port.) maps (1 fold.)
fold. tab.   22 cm.

Blyden, Edward W.
    Liberia's offering: being addresses, sermons,
etc. ... New York, John A. Gray, 1862.
    vi, 167 p.   22 1/2 cm.

68

Board of aid to land ownership, Boston.
    Second exploration of the table-land or plateau
of east Tennessee. Its topography, climate, health-
fulness, productions, minerals, water-power, etc.,
etc. Ample areas. Northern emigration needed
and desired. First exploration of western North
Carolina. Boston, Mass., Priv. printed for the
Board [1878]
    1 p.1., 62, 56, 12, 15 p. maps, plan.
23 1/2 cm.

Bodenstedt, Friedrich Martin von, 1819-
    Vom Atlantischen zum Stillen Ocean. Von Fried-
rich Bodenstedt. Leipzig, F. A. Brockhaus, 1882.
    xi p, 1 1., 426 p. 23 cm.

Boggs, Samuel S.
    Eighteen months a prisoner under the Rebel flag,
a condensed pen-picture of Belle Isle, Danville,
Andersonville, Charleston, Florence and Libby prisons from actual experience. Lovington, Illa.,
S. S. Boggs, 1887.
    69 p. front. 21 cm.

Boggs, William Robertson, 1829-1911.
    ... Military reminiscences of Gen. Wm. R. Boggs,
C.S.A.; introduction and notes by William K. Boyd.
Durham, N.C., The Seeman printery, 1913.
    xxiii, 115 p. front. (port.) 20 cm.

Boies, Andrew J.
    Record of the Thirty-third Massachusetts volun-
teer infantry, from Aug. 1862 to Aug. 1865. By
Andrew J. Boies, Fitchburg, Sentinel printing
company, 1880.
    168 p. front. (port.) 23 1/2 cm.

Bokum, Hermann, 1807-
    The Tennessee hand-book and immigrant's guide:
Giving a description of the state of Tennessee ...
With special reference to the subject of immigra-
tion ... Philadelphia, J. B. Lippincott & co., 1868.
    164 p. front. (fold. map) 19 1/2 cm.

[Bolivar, Fernando S.]
    Recuerdos y reminiscencias del primer tercio
de la vida de Rivolba [pseud.] Paris, Imprenta
americana de Rouge, Dunon y Fresné, 1873.
    64 p. 18 1/2 cm.

Bolles, John R.
A reply to Bishop Hopkins' view of slavery and a review of the times ... Philadelphia, J. W. Daughaday, 1863.
36 p.   19 cm.

Bolles, John R.
A reply to Bishop Hopkins' View of slavery, and a review of the times ... Philadelphia, J. W. Daughaday: etc., etc.   1865.
Cover-title, 36 p.   22 1/2 cm.

Bolton, Charles Edward, 1841-1901.
Travels in Europe and America, by Charles E. Bolton ... New York, T. Y. Crowell & co.   [1903]
4 p.l., 418 p.   front., plates, ports.
19 1/2 cm.

Bonnefoy, Antoine.
Journal of Antoine Bonnefoy, containing the circumstances of his captivity among the Cherokee Indians, from his departure from New Orleans in August, 1741, in the pirogue of the Sieur Chauvin dit Joyeuse, of whom he was engagé, till his arrival among the Allibamous. Johnson City, Tenn., The Watauga press, 1928.
149-162 p.   24 1/2 cm.

Bonnell, George William.
Topographical description of Texas. To which is added an account of the Indian tribes ... Austin, Clark, Wing, & Brown, 1840.
viii, [7]-150 p.   14 1/2 cm.

Bonrepos, Chevalier de.
Description du Mississippi, le nombre des villes & colonies établies par les francois, les isles, rivières & territoires que le bordent depuis le levant jusqu'au couchant, & du nord au sud, les moeurs & negoces des sauvages qui y habitant, la manière de se faire la guerre & la paix, la fertilité du pays, & la chasse aux diférens animaux qui s'y trouvent ... Imprimé à Rouen: se vend à Paris, chez Berthelemy Gyrin, 1720.
45, [1] p.   17 cm.

Booth, Benjamin F.   1837?-
Dark days of the rebellion, or, Life in southern military prisons, giving a correct and thrilling

history of unparalled [!] suffering ... Written
from a diary kept while in Libby and Salisbury
prisons in 1864-5, and now in possession of the
author. By B. F. Booth ... Indianola, Ia.,
Booth publishing company, 1897.
    375 p. front., illus. (incl. ports.)
19 1/2 cm.

[Booth, George Wilson] 1844-1914.
    Personal reminiscences of a Maryland soldier in
the war between the states, 1861-1865. For private
circulation only. Baltimore [Press of Fleet,
McGinley & co.] 1898.
    177 p.   24 cm.

Booth, Walter, 1791.
    Speech of Hon. Walter Booth, of Connecticut,
in the House of Representatives, June 4, 1850.
[Washington, Buell and Blanchard, 1850.]
    7 p.   22 cm.

Booty, James Horatio.
    Three months in Canada and the United States...
London, Printed by the author at his private residence, 1862.
    94 p. 2 p.l.   21 1/2 cm.

Borcke, Heros von, 1835-1895.
    Memoirs of the Confederate war for independence.
By Heros von Borcke ... Philadelphia, J. B. Lippincott & co., 1867.
    4 p.l., [vii]-x, 438 p. map.   18 cm.

[Borden, William] 1689-
    An address To the Inhabitants of North Carolina;
occasioned By the difficult Circumstances the
Government seems to labour under, for Want of a
Medium, or something to answer in lieu of Money
... Williamsburg [Va.]; Printed by William Parks,
M.DCC.XLVI.
    26 p. 2 p.l.   27 cm.

The Border ruffian code in Kansas. [n.p., n.d.]
    15 p.   22 cm.

Bosbyshell, Oliver Christian, 1839-
    The 48th in the war. Being a narrative of the
campaigns of the 48th regiment, infantry, Pennsylvania veteran volunteers, during the war of the

rebellion. By Oliver Christian Bosbyshell ...
Philadelphia, Avil printing company, 1895.
    4 p.1., 17-205 p. front., pl., port.
23 1/2 cm.

Bosshard, Heinrich.
    Anschauungen und erfahrungen in Nordamerika.
Eine monatsschrift. Herausgegeben von Heinrich
Bosshard ... [1.-3. jahrgang] Zürich, Druck von
Zürcher und Furrer, 1853-5.
    3v. illus., diagr.   17 1/2 cm.

Bossu, Jean Barnard, 1720-
    Nouveau voyage aux Indes occidentales ... Paris,
Le Jay, 1768.
    2v. in 1. fronts., 2 pl.   17 cm.

Boston female anti-slavery society.
    Report ... with a concise statement of events
previous and subsequent to the annual meeting of
1835. Second ed. Boston, Published by the
Society, 1836.
    108 p.   17 cm.

Boston female anti-slavery society.
    Report ... with a concise statement of events
previous and subsequent to the annual meeting of
1835. Boston, Published by the Society, 1836.
    108 p.   18 cm.

Boston female anti-slavery society.
    Annual report ... being a concise history of
the slave child, Med, and of the women demanded
as slaves of the Supreme judicial court of Mass.
with all the other proceedings of the Society.
Boston, Published by the Society, 1836.
    90 p.   18 cm.

Boston female anti-slavery society.
    Seventh annual report ... presented October 14,
1840. Boston, Published by the society, 1840.
    36 p.   17 cm.

Boston female anti-slavery society.
    Ninth annual report ... presented October 12,
1842. Boston, Oliver Johnson, 1842.
    47 p.   20 1/2 cm.

Boston slave riot, and trial of Anthony Burns ...
Boston, Fetridge and company, 1854.
86p.   24 cm.

Botts, John Minor.
Interesting and important correspondence between opposition members of the legislature of
Virginia and Hon. John Minor Botts, January 17,
1860.   Washington, Lem. Towers [n.d.]
16 p.   22 cm.

Botume, Elizabeth Hyde.
First days amongst the contrabands ... Boston,
Lee and Shepard, 1893.
iii, 286 p.   19 cm.

Bourget, Paul Charles Joseph, 1852-
Outre-mer: impressions of America, by Paul
Bourget ... New York, C. Scribner's sons, 1895.
v, 425 p.   20 cm.

Bourne, George.
An address to the Presbyterian church, en-
forcing the duty of excluding all slaveholders
from the "Communion of saints." New York, 1833.
16 p.   21 cm.

Bourne, George.
A condensed anti-slavery Bible argument; by
a citizen of Virginia ... New York, Printed by
S. W. Benedict, 1845.
91 p.   22 1/2 cm.

Bourne, George.
Man-stealing and slavery denounced by the Presbyterian and Methodist churches ... Boston.
Garrison & Knapp, 1834.
19 p.   24 cm.

[Bourne, George?]
Picture of slavery in the United States of
America ... Middletown, Con. [!] 1834.
[228] p.   16 cm.

Bourne, Theodore.
Rev. George Bourne, the pioneer of American
antislavery. In Methodist quarterly review,
January, 1882.
p. 67-91.

Bowditch, H. I.
    Proceedings of the citizens of the borough of
Norfolk, on the Boston outrage, in the case of
the runaway slave George Latimer. Norfolk, T. G.
Broughton & son, 1843.
    20 p.   21 1/2 cm.

Bowditch, H. I.
    To the public. [n.d., n.p.]
    11 p.   16 cm.

Bowditch, William Ingersoll, 1819-1909.
    The rendition of Anthony Burns ... Boston,
Published by Robert F. Wallcut, 1854.
    40 p.   24 cm.

Bowditch, William Ingersoll, 1819-1909.
    Slavery and the constitution. Boston, Robert
F. Wallcut, 1849.
    156 p.   24 cm.

Bowditch, William Ingersoll.
    The United States constitution. [New York,
American anti-slavery society, 1855?]
    12 p.   19 cm.

Bowditch, William Ingersoll.
    White slavery in the United States. [New York,
American anti-slavery society, 1855?]
    8 p.   19 cm.

Bowen, Eli, 1824-
    Rambles in the path of the steam-horse. An
off-hand olla podrida, embracing a general historical and descriptive view ... of the travelled
route from Baltimore to ... Louisville ... Philadelphia, W. Bromwell and W. W. Smith; Baltimore,
S. B. Hickcox, agent, 1855.
    v-viii, 432 p. 3 p.l. incl. illus., plates.
24 cm.

Bowen, Elias.
    Slavery in the Methodist episcopal church...
Auburn, [N.Y.] William J. Moses, printer, 1859.
    viii, [9]-317p.   19 1/2 cm.

Bownas, Samuel, 1676-
    An account of the life, travels, and Christian
experiences in the work of the ministry of Samuel

Bownas.   London, Printed by L. Hinde, 1756.
viii, 198 p.   20 1/2 cm.

Boyle, James.
A letter ... to William Lloyd Garrison, respecting the clerical appeal, sectarianism, true
holiness, etc. Also, lines on Christian rest, by
Mr. Garrison. Boston, I. Knapp, 1838.
xi,   43 p.   14 1/2 cm.

Boynton, Charles Brandon, 1806.
The duty which the colored people owe to them-
selves, a sermon delivered at Metzerott hall,
Washington, D. C., November 17, 1867. [Washington,
Printed at the office of the Great republic, 1867?]
8 p.   22 cm.

Bracht, Viktor, 1819-
Texas im jahre 1848. Nach mehrjährigen beobachtungen dargestellt von Viktor Bracht ... Mit ver-
schiedenartigen zügen, auszügen aus briefen.
Elberfeld, u. Iserlohn, J. Bädeker, 1849.
xii p., 1 1., 322 p.   18 cm.

Brackenridge, Henry Marie, 1786-
Views of Louisiana; together with a Journal of
a voyage up the Missouri river, in 1811. Pittsburgh, Printed and published by Cramer, Spear and
Eichbaum, Franklin head office, 1814.
304 p.   21 1/2 cm.

Bradbury, John, fl. 1809-
Travels in the interior of America, in the
years 1809, 1810, and 1811; including a description
of upper Louisiana, together with the states of
Ohio, Kentucky, Indiana, and Tennessee, with the
Illinois and western territories. Liverpool,
Printed for the author, by Smith and Galway, and
published by Sherwood, Neely, and Jones, London,
1817.
xii, [9]-364 p.   23 cm.

Bradley, Arthur Granville, 1850-
Other days. Recollections of rural England and
old Virginia, 1860-1880. London, Constable and
company, 1913.
xi, 427 [1] p. front. (port.)   22 1/2 cm.

Bradley, Arthur Granville, 1850-
    Sketches from old Virginia ... London, New
York, Macmillan and co., 1897.
    ix p., 1 1., 284 p. incl. front.   20 cm.

Bradley, George S.
    The star corps; or, Notes of an army chaplain,
during Sherman's famous "march to the sea." Rev.
G. S. Bradley ... Milwaukee, Jermain & Brightman,
printers, 1865.
    xi, [13]-304 p. front. ports. 19 1/2 cm.

Brady, William.
    Glimpses of Texas: its divisions, resources,
development and prospects. Houston, Tex. [A. C.
Gray & co., printers] 1871.
    104 p. 1 1. front. (fold. map)   18 cm.

Branagan, Thomas.
    The penitential tyrant; or, Slave trader re-
formed: a patriotic poem in four cantos. Second
ed., enlarged. New York, Samuel Wood, 1807.
    xii, 290 p. front.   15 cm.

Bray, Thomas, 1656-
    Apostolick charity, its nature and excellence
consider'd. In a discourse ... at the ordination
of some Protestant missionaries to be sent into
the plantations. To which is prefixt, A general
view of the English colonies in America with respect to religion ... London, Printed by W.
Downing for W. Hawes, 1698.
    30 p. 6 p.1.   21 cm.

Bray, Thomas, 1656-
    A memorial representing the present state of
religion on the continent of North America. London, Printed by William Downing, 1700 ... reprinted for the Thomas Bray club. [n.p., 1916]
    7-30 p. 2 p.1.   24 1/2 cm.

Breckinridge, Robert Jefferson, 1800.
    An address delivered before the Colonization
society of Kentucky, at Frankfort, on the 6th day
of January, 1831. Frankfort, K., A. G.Hodges,
printer, 1831.
    24 p.   22 cm.

Breckinridge, Robert Jefferson, 1800-
    The great deliverance and the new career. An
oration delivered before the Phi beta kappa society of Union college at Schenectady, N. Y., on
the 25th July, 1865. Pub. by order of the society.
Philadelphia, J. S. Claxton, 1865.
    1 p.l., 32p.   22 1/2 cm.

[Breckinridge, Robert Jefferson] 1800-
    Hints on slavery. Founded on the state of the
constitution, laws and politics of Kentucky, thirteen years ago. [Lexington, Ky.? 1843?]
    26 p.   20 1/2 cm.

Breckinridge, Robert Jefferson, 1800-1871.
    Our country: its peril and its deliverance.
From advance sheets of the Danville quarterly review, for March, 1861 ... Cincinnati, Published
at the office of the Danville review, 1861.
    43 p.   22 1/2 cm.

Breckinridge, Robert Jefferson, 1800.
    The second defence of Robert J. Breckinridge
against the calumnies of Robert Wickliffe; being
a reply to his printed speech of November 9, 1840
... Louisville, Ky., Prentice and Weissinger,
1841.
    39 p.   21 cm.

Breckinridge, Robert Jefferson, 1800-
    Speech of Robert J. Breckinridge, delivered in
the court-house yard at Lexington, Ky., on the
12th day of October, 1840, in reply to the "Speech
of Robert Wickliffe, delivered in the courthouse
in Lexington, on the 10th day of August, 1840,
upon the occasion of resigning his seat as senator
from the county of Fayette" ... More particularly
in regard to the questions of the power of the
legislature on the subject of slavery ... Lexington,
Ky., N. L. & J. W. Finnell, printers, 1840.
    iv, [5]-32 p.   20 1/2 cm.

Bremer, Fredrika, 1801-1865.
    The homes of the New world; impressions of Ameri-
ca ... Tr. by Mary Howitt ... New York, Harper &
brothers, 1853.
    2 v.   19 1/2 cm.

Briant, Charles C.
History of the Sixth regiment Indiana volunteer infantry. Of both the three months' and three years' services ... by ... C. C. Briant ... Indianapolis, W. B. Burford, printer and binder, 1891.
iv p., 1 l., 428 p. front., ports. 19 1/2 cm.

Brickell, John, 1710?
The natural history of North Carolina. With an account of the trade, manners, and customs of the Christian and Indian inhabitants. Dublin, 1737.
iii-xv, [4], 408 p. 1 p.l., illus., 4 p.l., fold. map. 20 1/2 cm.

[Bridge, James Howard] 1858-
Uncle Sam at Home. By Harold Brydges [pseud.] New York, H. Hoit, 1888.
244 p. illus. 19 cm.

Brief account of Samuel Neale, a minister of the gospel in the Society of friends. Philadelphia, Published by the Tract association of Friends [n.d.]
12 p. 18 cm.

A brief chapter in the life of General Franklin Pierce. From the national era of June 17, Mr. Pierce and the anti-slavery movement. Washington, Buell & Blanchard [n.d.]
8 p. 23 cm.

A brief sketch of the trial of William Lloyd Garrison, for an alleged libel on Francis Todd, of Newburyport, Mass. Boston, Garrison and Knapp, 1834.
iv, 24 p. 20 1/2 cm.

[Bright, J. D.]
A review of the troubles in Kansas, and of the Senate's bill for the admission of Kansas as a state into the union. By an Indianian. Washington, Union office, 1856.
16 p. 22 1/2 cm.

Brinton, Daniel Garrison, 1837-
A guide-book of Florida and the south, for tourists, invalids and emigrants ... Philadelphia, G. Maclean; Jacksonville, Fla., C. Drew, 1869.
v, 9-136 p. fold. map. 16 1/2 cm.

Brinton, John Hill, 1832-1907.
      Personal memoirs of John H. Brinton, major
and surgeon U.S.V., 1861-1865 ... New York, The
Neale publishing company, 1914.
      361 p. front. (port.) 21 cm.

Brion de la Tour, Louis.
      Almanach intéressant dans les circonstances
présentes. Description abrégée des États-Unis
de l'Amérique; des possessions angloises; et des
pays qui y sont contigus, dans des Index Orien-
tales ... Paris, Desnos [1780]
      72 p. 1 p.l. pl., fold. maps. 12 cm.

Brisbane, William Henry.
      Slaveholding examined in the light of the
Holy Bible ... New York, American and foreign
anti-slavery society [1847?]
      viii, x, [11]-222 p. 14 cm.

Brisbane, William Henry.
      Speech of the Rev. Wm. H. Brisbane, lately a
slaveholder in South Carolina; containing an
account of the change in his views on the subject of slavery. Delivered before the Ladies
anti-slavery society of Cincinnati, February 12,
1840. Hartford, Published by S. S. Cowles, 1840.
      12 p. 22 cm.

Brissot de Warville, Jacques Pierre, 1754-
      Nouveau voyage dans les États-Unis de l'Améri-
que septentrionale, fait en 1788 ... Paris, Buisson,
1791.
      3 v. fold. tab. 20 cm.

Brissot de Warville, Jean Pierre, 1754-1793.
      New travels in the United States of America,
performed in 1788. Translated from the French.
Boston, Joseph Bumstead, 1797.
      xxvi, 276 p. chart. 18 cm.

British and foreign anti-slavery society.
      Proceedings of the general anti-slavery con-
vention, called by the committee of the British
and foreign anti-slavery society, and held in London, from Friday, June 12th, to Tuesday, June
23rd, 1840. London, British and foreign anti-
slavery society, 1841.
      xi, 597 p. 21 1/2 cm.

British and foreign anti-slavery society.
Proceedings of the general anti-slavery convention, called by the committee of the British and foreign anti-slavery society, and held in London, from Tuesday June 13th, to Tuesday, June 20th, 1843. By J. F. Johnson, short-hand writer. London, John Snow 1843?
viii, 360 p. 22 cm.

British opinions of the American colonization society. Boston, Garrison & Knapp, 1833.
36 p.   20 cm.

Britton, Wiley.
Memoirs of the rebellion on the border, 1863, by Wiley Britton ... Chicago, Cushing, Thomas & co., 1882.
458 p.   19 1/2 cm.

Broadway tabernacle, New York, N. Y.
Proceedings of the session of Broadway tabernacle, against Lewis Tappan with the action of the presbytery and general assembly. New York, 1839.
64 p.   21 cm.

[Brockway, Thomas]
The European traveller in America. Contained in three letters to his friend in London. Hartford, Printed by Hudson & Goodwin, M.DCC.LXXXV.
40 p.   18 1/2 cm.

Brodnax, William H.
The speech of William H. Brodnax, (of Dinwiddie) in the House of delegates of Virginia, on the policy of the state with respect to its colored population. Delivered January 19, 1832. Richmond, Va., Thomas W. White, printer, 1832.
44 p.   23 cm.

Broke, Hezekiah.
On two continents. A long life's experience. Topeka, Kansas, Crance and company, 1896.
240 p.   19 1/2 cm.

Bromme, Traugott, 1802-
Reisen durch die Vereinigten Staaten und Ober-Canada ... Baltimore, Md., C. Scheld & co.; [etc., etc.] 1834-35.

80

3 v. fold. map, tables (part fold.)
18 1/2 cm.

Bronson, Francis S.
    Bronson's travelers' directory, from New York
to New Orleans, embracing all the most important
routes, with a condensed outline of the country
through which they pass ... La Grange, Ga.,
Printed at the American star office, 1845.
    32 p.   25 cm.

Brooke, Samuel.
    The slave-holder's religion. Cincinnati,
Sparhawk and Lyttle, 1845.
    45 p.   19 cm.

Brooke, Samuel.
    Slavery, and the slaveholder's religion; as
opposed to Christianity ... Cincinnati, Published
by the author, 1846.
    72 p.   17 1/2 cm.

Brookes, R[ichard] fl. 1750.
    The general gazetteer; or, Compendious geo-
graphical dictionary ... London, J. Newberry, 1762.
    viii, xxxii [756] p. fold. front., fold.
maps.   21 1/2 cm.

Brooks, A. L.
    An appeal for the right. A sermon ... Chicago,
Daily democrat office, 1856.
    18 p.   22 cm.

[Brooks, Abbie M.]
    Petals plucked from sunny climes. By Sylvia
Sunshine [pseud.] ... 2d ed. Nashville, Southern
Methodist publishing house, 1883.
    495 p.   front., illus., plates., 3 maps and
plan on fold. sheet. 19 cm.

Brooks, John, 1792-
    The life and times of the Rev. John Brooks,
in which are contained a history of the great revival in Tennessee; with many incidents of thrilling interest ... To which are appended two sermons
by the author, and a discourse by the late Rev.
Learner Blackman ... Nashville, Nashville Christian
advocate office, 1848.
    175 p.   18 1/2 cm.

Broomall, John Martin, 1816.
    Speech of Hon. John B. Broomall of Pennsylvania,
on the civil rights bill; delivered in the House
of Representatives, March 8, 1866. Rights of
citizens. [Washington? 1866?]
    7 p.   24 cm.

Broomall, John Martin, 1816.
    Speech ... on the civil rights bill; delivered
in the House of Representatives, March 8, 1866.
Rights of citizens. [n.p. Chronicle print, 1866?]
    7 p.   22 cm.

Broome, Mary Ann (Stewart) Barker, lady, d. 1911.
    Travelling about over new and old ground, by
Lady Barker ... London, New York, George Routledge
& sons, 1872.
    xii, 353 [1] p. front. (port.) plates, maps.
19 1/2 cm.

Brothers, Thomas.
    The United States of North America as they are;
not as they are generally described; being a cure
for radicalism ... London, Longman, Orme, Brown,
Green & Longmans, 1840.
    v, 517 p.   23 cm.

Brougham and Vaux, Henry Peter Brougham, 1st baron.
    Immediate emancipation. The speech of Lord
Brougham in the House of Lords on Tuesday, February 20, 1838, on slavery and the slave-trade.
Prepared from the most full and accurate reports,
and corrected by his lordship. London, Printed
for the Central emancipation committee [1838].
    24 p.   17 cm.

Brougham, John.
    ... Dred: or, The dismal swamp. A play, in
five acts ... New-York, Samuel French [n.d.]
    43 p.   19 cm.

Brown, Aaron Venable, 1795.
    An address on the progress of the United States
and on the slavery question ... Nashville, Tenn.,
Harvey M. Watterson, printer, 1850.
    19 p.   22 cm.

Brown, Albert G.
Address ... before the members of the legislature of the state of Mississippi, November 8,
1859. Washington, Printed by Lemuel Towers, 1859.
15 p.   23 cm.

Brown, Albert Gallatin, 1813.
Speech ... delivered at Elwood Springs, near
Port Gibson, Miss., November 2, 1850. [Washington,
D. C., Printed at the Globe Office, 1850?]
16 p.   23 cm.

Brown, Augustus Cleveland, 1839-
The diary of a line officer, by Captain Augustus
C. Brown ... [New York, 1906?]
1 p.1., 117 p.   front.   (port.)   19 cm.

Brown, C. S.
Memoir of Rev. Abel Brown, by his companion,
C. S. Brown.   Worcester, Mass., Published by the
author, 1849.
xii, [13]-228 p.   front.   19 cm.

[Brown, David] 1786-1875.
The planter: or, Thirteen years in the South.
By a northern man... Philadelphia, H. Hooker, 1853.
275 p.   20 cm.
L. C. card no. 2-6942

Brown, Edmund Randolph, 1845-
The Twenty-seventh Indiana volunteer infantry
in the war of the rebellion, 1861 to 1865.   First
division, 12th and 20th corps.   A history of its
recruiting, organization, camp life, marches and
battles, together with a roster of the men com-
posing it ... By a member of Company C.   [Monti-
cello, Ind., 1899].
640, [2] p.   incl.   front., illus. (incl.
ports.)   23 cm.

Brown, James.
American slavery, in its moral and political
aspects, comprehensively examined, to which is
subjoined an epitome of ecclesiastical history,
showing the mutilated state of modern Christianity ... Oswego, Geo. Henry, 1840.
102 p.   17 cm.

Brown, John, 1800, defendant.
Testimonies of Capt. John Brown, at Harper's Ferry, with his address to the court ... New York, American anti-slavery society, 1860.
16 p.   18 cm.

Brown, Josephine
Biography of an American bondman, William Wells Brown, by his daughter ... Boston, R. F. Wallcut, 1856.
104 p.   19 cm.

Brown, Philip Francis, 1842-
Reminiscences of the war of 1861-1865. By Philip F. Brown ... [Roanoke, Va., Printed by the Union printing co.,   c1912]
cover-title, 54 p.   illus.   (incl. port.)
22 1/2 cm.

Brown, Samuel R. 1775-
The western gazetteer; or, emigrant's directory, containing a geographical description of the western states and territories ... Auburn, N. Y., Printed by H. C. Southwick, 1817.
vi, [7]-360 p.   22 cm.

Brown, Tarleton, 1757-
Memoirs of Tarleton Brown, a captain of the revolutionary army, written by himself, with a preface and notes, by Charles I. Bushnell.   New York, Priv. print., 1862.
iv p., 1 l., [7]-65 p.   front., ports.
25 1/2 cm.

Brown, Thomas.
Brown's three years in the Kentucky prisons, from May 30, 1854, to May 18, 1857.   Indianapolis Courier company print, 1857.
21 p.   22 cm.

Brown, Thomas.
Brown's three years in the Kentucky prisons, from May 30, 1854, to May 18, 1857.   Indianapolis, Indianapolis journal company, 1858.
19 p.   22 cm.

Brown, Thomas C.
Examination of Mr. Thomas C. Brown, a free colored citizen of S. Carolina, as to the actual

state of things in Liberia in the years 1833 and
1834 at the Chatham Street chapel, May 9th and
10th, 1834. New-York, S. W. Benedict & co.,
printers, 1834.
40 p. 23 cm.

Brown, William Wells.
The anti-slavery harp: a collection of songs
for anti-slavery meetings ... Boston, Bela Marsh,
1848.
48 p. 18 cm.

Brown, William Wells.
The black man, his antecedents, his genius,
and his achievements ... New York, Thomas Hamilton; Boston, R. F. Wallcut, 1863.
288 p. 19 cm.

Brown, William Wells.
Clotel; or, The president's daughter: a
narrative of slave life in the United States ...
London, Partridge & Oakey, 1853.
viii, 245 p. front. 18 cm.

Brown, W[illiam] W[ells] b. 1814.
Clotelle: a tale of the southern states. By
W. W. Brown. Boston, J. Redpath; New York, H.
Dexter, Hamilton & co. [1864].
104 p. incl. front., plates. 17 1/2 cm.
L. C. card no. 6-17232

Brown, William Wells, b. 1814-
My southern home: or, The South and its people
... 3d ed. Boston, A. G. Brown & co., 1882.
vii, 253 p. illus. 19 1/2 cm.

Brown, William Wells.
Narrative of William W. Brown, a fugitive
slave. Written by himself ... Second ed., enl.
Boston, Published at the Anti-slavery office,
1848.
144 p. illus. 18 cm.

Brown, William Wells, 1815.
Narrative of William W. Brown, a fugitive
slave. Written by himself. Boston, The Anti-
slavery office, 1847.
xi, [13]-110 p. front. (port.) 17 1/2 cm.

Browne, Junius Henri, 1833-1902.
Four years in Secessia: adventures within and beyond the Union lines: embracing a great variety of facts, incidents, and romance of the war ... By Junius Henri Browne ... Hartford, O. D. Case and company; [etc., etc.] 1865.
vi, 450 p. 8 pl. (incl. front.) 21 1/2 cm.

Brownlow, W. G.
American slavery to be perpetuated? A debate between Rev. W. G. Brownlow and Rev. A. Pryne. Held at Philadelphia, September, 1858. Philadelphia, Published for the authors by J. B. Lippincott & co. [1858?]
iv, [5]-305 p. front. (port.) 19 cm.

Brownlow, William Ganaway, 1805.
The great iron wheel examined; or, Its false spokes extracted, and an exhibition of Elder Graves, its builder, in a series of chapters ... Nashville, Tenn., For the author, 1856.
xvii, 19-331 p. 2 pl. 20 cm.

Brownlow, William Gannaway, 1805-1877.
Sketches of the rise, progress, and decline of secession; with a narrative of personal adventures among the rebels. By W. G. Brownlow ... Philadelphia, G. W. Childs; Cincinnati, Applegate & co., 1862.
458 p. front. (port.) plates, facsim. 17 1/2 cm.

Bruce [Miss] John Jessie.
A trip to Florida, spring of 1883 ... Cumberland, Md., The Daily news, 1883.
1 p.l., xxiii p. 12 cm.

Bruce, Peter Henry, 1692-
Memoirs of Peter Henry Bruce, esq., a military officer, in the services of Prussia, Russia, and Great Britain. Containing an account of his travels in Germany, Russia, Tartary, Turkey, the West Indies, &c., as also very interesting private anecdotes of the Czar, Peter I, of Russia. London, Printed for the author's widow, and sold by T. Payne and son, 1782.
446 p. 6 p.l. 26 1/2 cm.

Bruun, Ellen (Raon) 1892-
Her er Amerika; artikler om amerikanske sam-

fundsforhold, forfattet i de Forenede stater paa opfordring af Svensk radiojänst. [Overs efter Meet America, a radio course. Versene overs. af A. Veng Christensen] København, Danske forlag, 1945.
134 p. illus., ports., map. 26 cm.

Bryant, William Cullen, 1794-1878.
Letters of a traveller; or, Notes of things seen in Europe and America ... 2d. ed. New York, G. P. Putnam; [etc., etc.] 1850.
442 p. 20 1/2 cm.

Bryce, James Bryce, viscount, 1838-
The American commonwealth ... New ed., completely rev. throughout, with additional chapters. New York, The Macmillan company, 1910.
2 v. 21 cm.

Bryner, Byron Cloyd, 1849-
Bugle echoes; the story of Illinois 47th ... By Cloyd Bryner ... [Springfield, Ill., Phillips bros., printers, 1905]
ix p., 1 l., 11-262 p. front., plates, ports. 23 1/2 cm.

Buchanan, James., pres. U. S., 1791-1868.
Independent treasury. Speech by Hon. James Buchanan, of Pennsylvania. In the Senate of the United States, January 22, 1850, on the independent treasury bill; in reply to Mr. Clay, of Kentucky. [n.p., n.d.]
16 p. 20 cm.

Buckingham, G.
The Bible vindicated from the charge of sustaining slavery ... Columbus, Printed at the Temperance advocate office, 1837.
24 p. 22 cm.

Buckingham, J. S.
The slave states of America ... Fisher, son & co. [n.d.]
2 v. 22 1/2 cm.

Buckingham, James Silk, 1786-
The slave states of America. London, Paris, Fisher, son & co. [1842]
2 v. fronts., plates. 22 cm.

[Buechler, Johann Ulrich]
Land-und seereisen eines St. Gallischen kan-
tonsbürgers nach Nordamerika und Westindien ...
in den Jahren 1816, 1817 und 1818 ... St. Gallen,
Gedruckt bey Zollikofer und Zühlin, 1819.
228 p. 16 1/2 cm.

Bullock, William.
Sketch of a journey through the western states
of North America, from New Orleans ... to New
York, in 1827 ... London, J. Miller, 1827.
[v]-xxxi, viii, 135 p. 3 p.l. (fold. plan)
fold. map. 18 1/2 cm.

Bullock, William, fl. 1649.
Virginia impartially examined, and left to
public view, to be considered by all judicious
and honest men ... London, Printed by John Hammond, 1649.
66 p. 6 p.l. 18 cm.

Bülow, Dietrich i. e. Adam Heinrich Dietrich, freiherr
von, 1757-
Der freistaat von Nordamerika in seinem neuesten zustand ... Berlin, J. F. Unger, 1797.
2 v. 17 1/2 cm.

[Burke, Edmund] 1729?
An account of the European settlements in
America ... London, R. and J. Dodsley, 1757.
2 v. fronts. (fold. maps). 20 cm.

Burke, Emily P.
Reminiscences of Georgia. [Oberlin, O.]
J. M. Fitch, 1850.
viii, 252 p. port. 17 cm.

Burke, William.
The mineral springs of western Virginia: with
remarks on their use, and the diseases to which
they are applicable ... New York, Wiley and Putnam, 1842.
291 p. front. (fold. map) 16 1/2 cm.

Burleigh, Charles C.
Slavery and the north. New York, American
anti-slavery society, 1855?
12 p. 19 cm.

[Burlend, Mrs. Rebecca] 1793-
    A true picture of emigration: or Fourteen
years in the interior of North America; being a
full and impartial account of the various difficulties and ultimate success of an English family
who emigrated ... in the year 1831. London, G.
Berger; [etc., etc., 1848]
    [5]-62p. 1 p.l.   18 cm.

Burlingame, Anson, 1820.
    Defence of Massachusetts. Speech... in the
House of Representatives, June 21, 1856. [Wash-
ington, Buell & Blanchard, printers, 1856?]
    7 p.   23 cm.

Burman, Ben Lucien, 1895-
    ... Big river to cross; Mississippi life today;
drawings by Alice Caddy. New York, The John Day
company [c1940]
    294, [1] p. incl. front., illus., plates.
22 cm.

Burnaby, Andrew, 1734?
    Travels through the middle settlements in
North America, in the years 1759 and 1760; with
observations upon the state of the colonies ...
edition the 3d; rev., cor., and greatly enl., by
the author. London, T. Payne, 1798.
    xix, 209 p. incl. fold. tables. front.
(fold. maps) 2 pl.   28 cm.

Burnap, Uzziah Cicero.
    Bible servitude. A sermon, delivered to the
Appleton-St. Church, Lowell on the day of annual
thanksgiving, Nov. 30, 1843 ... Lowell, A. E.
Newton and A. O. Ordway, 1843.
    20 p.   22 cm.

Burns, Barnabas.
    Speech of Mr. Burns of Richland on the several
resolutions on the subject of the "Fugitive
slave law." In Senate--January 17, 1850. Columb-
bus, Ohio Statesman print, 1851.
    8 p.   25 cm.

Burns, Jabez, 1805-1876.
    Notes of a tour in the United States and Canada,
in the summer and autumn of 1847 ... London, Houl-
ston and Stoneman, 1848.

vi, [9]-180 p.   16 cm.

Burnyeat, John, 1631-
    The truth exalted in the writings of that
eminent and faithful servant of Christ, John
Burnyeat ... London, T. Northcott, 1691.
    20, 264 (i.e. 260) p.   4 p.1.   19 1/2 cm.

Burritt, Elihu, 1811.
    A plan of brotherly copartnership of the
north and south for the peaceful extinction of
slavery ... New York, Dayton and Burdick, 1856.
    18 p.   19 cm.

Burritt, Elihu, 1810-
    Washington's words to intending emigrants to
America. With an introduction and appendix by
Elihu Burritt. London, S. Low, son & Marston,
1870.
    127 p.   16 cm.

Burson, William, 1833-
    A race for liberty; or, My capture, imprison-
ment, and escape. By William Burson, of Company
A, 32d reg't. O.V.I. With an introduction by
W. B. Derrick ... Wellsville, O., W. G. Foster,
printer, 1867.
    xii, [5]-135 p.   16 1/2 cm.

Burt, Jairus.
    The law of Christian rebuke, a plea for slave-
holders. A sermon delivered at Middletown,
Conn., before the anti-slavery convention of ministers and other Christians, October 18, 1843 ...
Hartford, N. W. Goodrich & co., 1843.
    20 p.   22 cm.

Burton, Elijah P.
    Diary of E. P. Burton, surgeon, 7th reg. Ill.,
3rd brig., 2nd div. 16 A. C. Prepared by the
Historical records survey, Division of professional
and service projects, Work projects administration. Des Moines, Iowa, The Historical records
survey, 1939.
    8 p.1., 92 numb. 1.   28 cm.

Busch, Moritz, 1821-
    Wanderungen zwischen Hudson und Mississippi,
1851 und 1852 ... Stuttgart und Tübingen, J. G.

Cotta, 1854.
2 v.   21 1/2 cm.

Bush, George, 1796.
New church miscellanies; or, Essays ecclesiastical, doctrinal and ethical ... New-York, Wm.
McGeorge; Boston, O. Clapp [etc.,etc.] 1855.
372 p.   18 1/2 cm.

Bushnell, Horace.
The census and slavery; a Thanksgiving dis-
course, delivered at the chapel at Clifton Springs,
New York, November 29, 1860. Hartford, Lucius
E. Hunt, 1860.
24 p.   19 cm.

Bushnell, Horace.
A discourse on the slavery question, delivered in the North church, Hartford, Thursday, Jan.
10, 1839 ... second edition. Hartford, Printed
by Case, Tiffany & co., 1838.
32 p.   22 cm.

Bushnell, Horace.
Politics under the law of God. A discourse
delivered in the North Congregational church,
Hartford, on the annual fast of 1844 ... Third
edition. Hartford, Edwin Hunt, 1844.
23 p.   23 cm.

[Butel-Dumont, Georges Marie] 1725-
Histoire et commerce des colonies angloises,
dans l'Amérique septentrionale ... A Londres, et
se vend à Paris, chez le Breton [etc.] M.DCC.LV.
xxiv, 336 p.   18 cm.

Butler, Andrew Pickens, 1796-1857.
The Massachusetts resolutions on the Sumner
assault and the slavery issue. Speeches of Senators Butler, Evans, and Hunter, delivered in the
Senate of the United States. [Washington, D.C.,
Published at the office of the Congressional
globe, 1856?]
24 p.   23 cm.

Butler, Andrew Pickens, 1796.
Speech ... upon the bill providing for the
surrender of fugitive slaves. Delivered in the
Senate of the United States, January 24, 1850.

Washington, Printed at the Globe office, 1850.
12 p.   23 cm.

Butler, Andrew Pickens, 1796-
Speeches of senators Butler, Evans and Hunter,
delivered in the Senate of the United States.
Washington, 1856.
24 p.   20 cm.

Butler, Jay Caldwell, 1844-1885.
Letters home [by] Jay Caldwell Butler, captain,
101st. Ohio volunteer infantry, arranged by his
son Watson Hubbard Butler ... [Birmingham, N.Y.]
Priv. print., 1930.
x, 153 p.   21 1/2 cm.

Butterworth, Hezekiah, 1839-
A zigzag journey in the sunny South; or, Won-
der tales of early American history ... Boston,
Estes and Lauriat, 1887.
320 p.   incl. front., illus., plates, ports.
21 1/2 x 16 1/2 cm.

Butterworth, Hezekiah, 1839.
Zigzag journeys on the Mississippi, from
Chicago to the islands of the discovery, by
Hezekiah Butterworth ... Boston, Estes and Lauriat
[1892]
311 p.   incl. front., illus., plates.   21 1/2
x 17 1/2 cm.

Büttner, Johann Carl, 1754-
Narrative of Johann Carl Buettner in the
American revolution. New York, Printed for C. F.
Heartman [1915]
69 p.   3 p.l.   col. front. (port.)   20 cm.

Büttner, Johann Gottfried.
Die Vereinigten Staaten von Nord-Amerika. Mein
aufenthalt und meine reisen in denselben, vom
jahre 1834 bis 1841 ... Hamburg, M. Geber, 1844.
2 v.   fold. tab.   21 cm.

Buzhardt, Beaufort Simpson, 1838-
[Diary] n.p. [1916?]
73 p.   2 ports.   20 cm.

Byers, Samuel Hawkins Marshall, 1838-
What I saw in Dixie; or, Sixteen months in Re-

bel prisons. By Adjutant S.H.M. Byers. Dansville,
N. Y., Robbins & Poore, printers, 1868.
3 p.l., 126 p. 18 cm.

Byrd, William, 1674-
The Westover manuscripts: containing the history of the dividing line betwixt Virginia and
North Carolina; a Journey to the land of Eden,
A. D. 1733; and A progress to the mines. Written
from 1728 to 1736, and now first published.
Petersburg [Va.] Printed by E. and J. C. Ruffin,
1841.
iv, 143 [1] p. 1 illus. 24 1/2 cm.

C

C, O.
O. C's letters from the south, on northern and
southern views respecting slavery and the American
tract society. First published in the Boston
Courier. Boston, Crocker & Brewster; New York,
D. Appleton & co., 1857.
16 p. 22 cm.

Cabot, Susan C.
What have we, as individuals, to do with
slavery? [New York, American anti-slavery society,
1855?]
7 p. 19 cm.

Cadogan, George.
The Spanish hireling detected, being a refutation of the several calumnies and falsehoods in a
late pamphlet, entitl'd An impartial account of
the late expedition against St. Augustine under
General Oglethorpe ... London, Printed for J.
Roberts, 1743.
3-68p. 2 p.l. 20 cm.

Cadwell, Charles K.
The old Sixth regiment, its war record, 1861-5,
by Charles K. Cadwell ... New Haven, Tuttle, More-
house & Taylor, printers, 1875.
227, [1] p. 20 1/2 cm.

Cairnes, J. E.
　　The slave power: its character, career, and probable designs: being an attempt to explain the real issues in the American contest ... New York, Carleton, 1862.
　　xv, [16]-171 p.　23 1/2 cm.

Caldwell, James Fitz James.
　　The history of a brigade of South Carolinians, known first as "Gregg's" and subsequently as "McGowan's brigade". By J. F. J. Caldwell ... Philadelphia, King & Baird, printers, 1866.
　　247 p.　20 cm.

[Caldwell, John Edwards] 1769-
　　A tour through part of Virginia, in the summer of 1808 ... New-York, Printed for the author. H. C. Southwick, printer, no. 2, Wall-street, 1809.
　　31 p.　21 cm.

Calhoun, John Caldwell, 1782.
　　Speech ... on the slavery question. Delivered in the Senate of the United States, March 4, 1850. [Washington, Buell & Blanchard, 1850?]
　　8 p.　24 cm.

...A call for national nominating convention. [n.p., n.d.]
　　8 p.　23 cm.

Callicot, Theophilus Carey.
　　Speech ... against the personal liberty bill. In Assembly, March 14, 1860. Albany, Comstock & Cassidy, 1860.
　　13 p.　22 cm.

Calvert, Henry Murray.
　　Reminiscences of a boy in blue, 1862-1865, by Henry Murray Calvert. New York and London, G. P. Putman's sons, 1920.
　　vii, 347 p.　20 1/2 cm.

Camacho Roldan, Salvador, 1827-
　　... Notas de viaje (Colombia y Estados Unidos de America). Bogotá, Camacho Roldan & Tamayo, 1890.
　　1 p.1., [v]-vi, 900 [2] p.　20 cm.

Campbell, A. W.
　　Cassius Marcellus Clay; a visit to his home
in Kentucky. His peculiar habits and remarkable
career - the peaceful ending of a stormy life.
By Hon. A. W. Campbell. [Philadelphia, J. B.
Lippincott company, 1888?]
　　15 p.　22 cm.

Campbell, Sir George, 1824-
　　White and black; the outcome of a visit to
the United States ... New York, R. Worthington,
1879.
　　xvii, 420 p.　21 cm.

Campbell, John.
　　A letter to Sir Robert Peel, bart., on the
subject of British colonial slavery ... Edinburgh,
Printed by James Colson, and sold by William
Oliphant, Waugh & Innes, and J. Wardlaw, 1830.
　　64 p.　20 cm.

Campbell, John Archibald, 1811-
　　Reminiscences and documents relating to the
civil war during the year 1865. Baltimore, J.
Murphy & co., 1886.
　　68 p.　23 1/2 cm.

Campbell, John Charles, 1867-1919.
　　The southern highlander and his homeland, by
John C. Campbell ... New York, Russell Sage
foundation, 1921.
　　xxi, [1], 405 p.　front., illus. (music)
plates, ports., fold. maps.　23 1/2 cm.

[Campbell, John Francis]
　　A short American tramp in the fall of 1864,
by the editor of "Life in Normandy." Edinburgh,
Edmonston and Douglas, 1865.
　　2 p.l., vii, 427 p.　incl. front., illus.,
map.　21 1/2 cm.

Campbell, Lewis Davis, 1811.
　　Americanism ... delivered at the American mass
meeting, held in Washington City, February 29th,
1856, as reported and published in the "American
organ." Washington, D. C., Buell & Blanchard,
printers, 1856?
　　8 p.　23 cm.

Campbell, Lewis Davis.
  Kansas and Nebraska, Georgia and Ohio. Free
labor and slave labor. Speech ... in the House
of Representatives, December 14, 1854. Washington, Congressional globe office [n.d.]
  16 p.   22 cm.

Campbell, Lewis Davis, 1811.
  Speech ... on southern aggression, the purposes of the union, and the comparative effects
of slavery and freedom. Delivered in the House
of Representatives, February 19, 1850. Washington, Buell & Blanchard, [1850?]
  8 p.   23 cm.

Campbell, Lewis Davis, 1811.
  "Union for the cause of freedom." Letter of
Hon. L.D.Campbell, of Ohio, to the Hon. Daniel
R. Tilden, as to the proper means of securing
freedom to the territories. [Washington? 1850?]
  8 p.   22 cm.

Can abolitionists vote or take office under the United
  States Constitution? New York, American anti-
  slavery society, 1845.
  39 p.   24 cm.

Canada mission.
  Seventh annual report. Rochester, Printed
by Erastus Shepard, 1844.
  25 p.   21 cm.

Canadian anti-slavery association.
  Constitution. [n.p., n.d.]
  14 p.   21 cm.

[Candler, Isaac]
  A summary view of America: comprising a description of the face of the country, and of
several of the principal cities: and remarks on
the social, moral and political character of the
people: being the result of observations and en-
quiries during a journey in the United States.
By an Englishman. London, T. Cadell; [etc.,etc.]
1824.
  viii, 503 p.   22 cm.

Cannon, J. P.
  Inside of rebeldom: the daily life of a private in the Confederate army ... By J. P. Cannon

Washington, D.C., The National tribune, 1900.
xx, 21-288 p. incl. front. (port.) illus.
21 1/2 cm.

Canova, Andrew P.
Life and adventures in south Florida. By
Andrew P. Canova ... Assisted by L. S. Perkins,
with an introduction by Hon. R. W. Davis. Palatka, Fla., Southern sun publishing house, 1885.
136 p. plates. 21 1/2 cm.

Carey, John.
The claims of agriculture. Speech of Hon.
John Carey, of Ohio. Delivered in the U. S. House
of Representatives, April 27, 1860. [n.p., n.d.]
7 p. 21 1/2 cm.

Carey, Mathew, 1760-
Carey's American pocket atlas: containing
nineteen maps ... With a brief description of each
state. 2d ed. greatly impr. and enl. Philadelphia, Printed by H. Sweitzer for M. Carey, 1801.
114 p. 4 p.l. 19 maps (1 fold.) 21 cm.

Carey, Matthew.
Letters on the Colonization society with a
view of its probable results ... addressed to
the Hon. Chas. F. Mercer, M. H. R. U. S. ... Second edition, enlarged and improved ... Philadelphia, Young, printer, April 26, 1832.
32 p. map., diagr. 22 cm.

[Carlé, Erwin] 1876-
Der deutsche lausbub in Amerika; erinnerungen
und eindrücke von Erwin Rosen [pseud.] Stuttgart,
R. Lutz [c1911-13]
3v. 20 cm.

Carlier, Auguste.
De l'esclavage dans l'union américaine ...
Paris, Michel Lévy frères, 1862.
495 p. 21 1/2 cm.

Carlisle, George William Frederick Howard, 7th earl
of, 1802-1864.
Travels in America. The poetry of Pope. Two
lectures delivered to the Leeds mechanics' institution and literary society, December 5th and 6th,
1850. By the Right Honorable the Earl of Car-

97

lisle (Lord Morpeth). New York, G. P. Putnam,
1851.
135 p.   19 cm.

Carneiro Leão, Antonio, 1887-
   Visão panoramica dos Estados Unidos.   Rio de
Janeiro, Civilização Brasileira [1950]
   233 p.   illus., ports.   23 cm.

Carolina described more fully than heretofore.   Being
an impartial collection made from the several relations of that place in print ... Dublin: Printed 1684.
   [24], 17-56p.   20 1/2 cm.

Carpenter, James S.
   Speech ... on the resolutions of Mr. Fisher,
of Hardin. House of Representatives, Ohio, Feb.
24, 1840. [Medina? 1840?]
   16 p.   20 cm.

Carroll, Anna Ella.
   The relation of the national government to
the revolted citizens defined ... [Washington,
D.C., Henry Polkinhorn, printer, 186-?]
   16 p.   22 cm.

Carter, Howell.
   A cavalryman's reminiscences of the civil war.
By Howell Carter. New Orleans, The American
printing co., 1td. [19--]
   2 p.1., [9]-212 p.   incl. ports.   ports.   18
cm.

Cartter, David Kellogg, 1812.
   Speech of Hon. David K. Cartter, of Ohio, on
the finality of the compromise, delivered in the
House of Representatives, May 25, 1852. Washington, Printed at the Congressional globe office,
1852.
   8 p.   22 cm.

Cartwright, Peter, 1785-1872.
   Autobiography of Peter Cartwright, the backwoods preacher. Edited by William Peter Strickland. New York and Cincinnati, The Methodist
book concern [n.d.]
   525 p.   20 cm.

Carver, Jonathan, 1710-1780.
The new universal traveller; containing a full
and distinct account of all the empires, kingdoms,
and states, in the known world... London, Printed
for G. Robinson, in Paternoster-row, 1779.
iii, [1], 668, [6] p. illus., 37 pl.
(part col.) 18 maps. 38 cm.

Case of the slave-child, Med. Report of the arguments
of counsel, and of the opinion of the court, in
the case of Commonwealth vs. Aves; tried and determined in the Supreme judicial court of Massachusetts. Boston, Published by Isaac Knapp, 1836.
40 p. 22 cm.

Casey, Charles.
Two years on the farm of Uncle Sam. With
sketches of his location, nephews, and prospects
... London, R. Bentley, 1852.
[v]-ix, 311 p. 1 p.l. 20 cm.

Casler, John Overton, 1838-
Four years in the Stonewall brigade. By
John O. Casler. Private, Company A, 33d regiment
Virginia infantry, Stonewall brigade, 1st division, 2d corps, Army of Northern Virginia, Gen.
Robert E. Lee, commanding ... Guthrie, Okl., State
capital printing company, 1893.
495 p. incl. illus., plates, ports., facsims.
fold. facsim. 20 1/2 cm.

Cass, Lewis, 1782.
Cass and Taylor on the slavery question ...
Boston, Damrell & Moore, 1848.
23 p. 18 cm.

Cass, Lewis, 1782.
Question de l'esclavage. [n.p., n.d.]
7 p. 23 cm.

Cass, Lewis, 1782-1866.
Speech of Hon. Lewis Cass, of Michigan. Delivered in the Senate of the United States, May
12-13, 1856. [n.p.] 1856.
24 p. 20 cm.

Cass, Lewis, 1782.
Speech of Mr. Cass, of Michigan, delivered
in the Senate of the United States, May 15, 1854,
on the subject of the religious rights of Ameri-

can citizens residing or traveling in foreign
countries. Washington, Printed at the Congressional Globe office, 1854.
21 p.   23 cm.

Cassell, John, 1817-
Amerika i vor tid ... oversat of M. J. Ruse.
København, J. H. Schuboths Boghandel, 1863.
488 p.   17 1/2 cm.

Caste. New York [Published by R. G. Williams for the
American anti-slavery society, 1839?]
24 p.   11 cm.

Castelnau, Francis, 1812-
Vues et souvenirs de l'Amérique du Nord ...
Paris, A. Bertrand, 1842.
viii, 165, [2]p.   35 pl.   (part col.)   31 cm.

Castiglioni, Luigi, conte, 1757-
Viaggio negli Stati Uniti dell'America Settentrionale, fatto negli anni, 1785, 1786, e 1787 ...
Con alcune osservazioni sui vegetabili più utili
di quel paese ... Milano, Stamperia di G.Marelli,
1790.
2v.   xiv fold. pl.   (incl. maps, plans)   III
fold. tab.   21 cm.

Castillo, Benjamin E.   del.
... Dos Américas.   Valencia, F. Sempere y
compañia [1910?]
3 p.l., [9]-250 [8] p. port. 19cm.

Castro, Henry, 1786-
Le Texas ... [Anvers, 1845]
38 p., 1 1.   24 cm.

Caswall, Henry, 1810-
America, and the American church ... London,
Printed for J. G. & F. Rivington, 1839.
xviii, 368 p.   1 1., front., 3 pl., fold.
map.   20 cm.

Caswall, Henry.
The western world revisited ... Oxford and
London, J. H. Parker, 1854.
xvi, 351 p.   16 1/2 cm.

Cate, Wirt Armistead, ed., 1900-
    Two soldiers: the campaign diaries of Thomas
J. Key, C.S.A., December 7, 1863-May 17, 1865,
and Robert J. Campbell, U.S.A., January 1, 1864-
July 21, 1864; edited, with an introduction, notes,
and maps, by Wirt Armistead Cate. Chapel Hill,
The University of North Carolina press, 1938.
    xiii, 277 p. front., illus. (maps) 2 port. on
1 pl., facsims.   22 cm.

... Catechism for free working men. By the son of a
blacksmith. [Cincinnati, American reform tract
and book society, n.d.]
    4 p.   18 cm.

Catesby, Mark, 1679?-1749.
    The natural history of Carolina, Florida and
the Bahama islands: containing the figures of
birds, beasts, fishes, serpents, insects, and
plants ... London, Printed at the expense of the
author, 1731-43.
    2v.   220 col. pl., fold. map.   53 cm.

Catlin, George, 1796.
    Letters and notes on the manners, customs, and
condition of the North American Indians ... Written during eight years' travel amongst the wildest
tribes ... In 1832, 33, 34, 35, 36, 37, 38, and
39 ... London, Pub. by the author; Printed by
Tosswill and Myers, 1841.
    2v.   front. (v. I) plates, ports., 2 maps (1
fold.)   25 1/2 cm.

Caulkins, Nehemiah.
    Narrative of Nehemiah Caulkins, an extract
from "American slavery, as it is." New York,
American and foreign anti-slavery society, 1849.
    iv, [5]-22p.   18 1/2 cm.

Cavling, Henrik, 1859-
    Fra Amerika, af Henrik Cavling. Med 74
helsidebilleder paa saerligt papir, flere hun-
drede afbildninger i teksten, samt et koloreret
kort over Nord-amerika. Kjøbenhavn, Gyldendal,
1897.
    2 v.   illus., pl., port., fold. map, plan,
facsim.   24 cm.

Chaffin, William Ladd, 1837-
    History of the town of Easton, Massachusetts.

Cambridge, J. Wilson and son, 1886.
xviii p. 1 1., 838p. front., plates, ports,
4 maps (1 fold.) 24 cm.

Chalkley, Thomas, 1675-
The journal of Thomas Chalkley. To which is
annexed, a collection of his works. New-York:
Printed and sold by Samuel Wood, no. 362, Pearl-
street. Sold also, by Abraham Shearman, jun.
New-Bedford: and by Kimber and Conrad, Philadelphia ... 1808.
7, 556 p. 22 cm.

Challis, B. C.
The substance of a speech on negro slavery,
delivered at the Rev. Mr. Barker's chapel, High
Street, Deptford, on Tuesday evening, 2nd November, 1830 ... Deptford, Sold by Warcup [etc.]
1830.
28 p. 20 cm.

Chalmers, Lionel, 1715-
An account of the weather and diseases of
South-Carolina ... London, Printed for E. and C.
Dilly, 1776.
2 v. in 1. 2 fold. tab. 21 cm.

Chamberlain, Ebeneezer Mattoon.
Speech ... against the repeal of the Missouri
compromise act; delivered in the House of Representatives, Monday, March 13, 1854. Washington,
A. O. P. Nicholson, 1854.
23 p. 23 cm.

Chamberlaine, William W. 1836?-
Memoirs of the civil war between the northern
and southern sections of the United States of
America, 1861-1865, by Captain William W. Chamberlaine ... Washington, D. C., Press of B. S. Adams,
1912.
138 p. front. (port.) 21 cm.

Chamberlayne, John Hampden, 1838-1882.
Ham Chamberlayne - Virginian: letters and
papers of an artillery officer in the war for
southern independence, 1861-1865; with introduction, notes and index, by his son, C. G. Chamberlayne. Richmond, Va., Press of the Dietz
printing co., 1932.
xxx p., 1 1., 440 p. front., plates, ports,

maps (2 fold) facsims. 23 1/2 cm.

Chambers, William.
American slavery and colour. London, W. & R.
Chambers, 1837.
216 p. 21 cm.

Chambers, William, 1800-
American slavery and colour ... London, W. &
R. Chambers; New York, Dix and Edwards, 1857.
218 p. 2 p.l. front. (map) 21 cm.

Chambers, William, 1800-
Things as they are in America ... London and
Edinburgh. W. and R. Chambers, 1854.
vi, 364 p. 19 cm.

Champigny, Jean, chevalier de, 1717-
La Louisiane ensanglantée, avec toutes les
particularités de cette horrible catastrophe, re-
digées sur le serment de témoins dignes de foi ...
London, Aux dépens de l'éditeur: chez Fleury
Mesplet, 1773.
xii, 123, xxxi, [1], 32 p. 4 p.l. 21 cm.

[Champigny, Jean Chevalier de] 1717-
The present state of the country and inhabitants, Europeans and Indians, of Louisiana, on
the north continent of America. By an officer
at New Orleans to his friend at Paris ... London,
Printed for J. Millan, 1744.
53 p. 19 cm.

Champlin, James, 1821-
Early biography, travels and adventures of
Rev. James Champlin ... with a description of the
different countries through which he has traveled in America, and of the different institutions,
etc., visited by him ... 2d ed. rev. Columbus,
O. [C. Scott's Power Press] 1842.
206 p. 19 cm.

Chandler, Elizabeth Margaret, 1807-
Essays, philanthropic and moral ...principally
relating to the abolition of slavery in America
...Philadelphia, L. Howell, 1836.
120 p. front. 18 1/2 cm.

Chandler, John A.
    The speech of John A. Chandler, (of Norfolk
county,) in the House of delegates of Virginia,
on the policy of the state with respect to her
slave population. Delivered January 17, 1832.
Richmond, Va., Thomas W. White, printer, 1832.
10 p.   21 cm.

Channing, William Ellery, 1780-1842.
    A discourse occasioned by the death of the
Rev. Dr. Follen.   Boston, James Monroe and company, M.DCCC.XI.
29 p.   22 cm.

Channing, William Ellery, 1780-1842.
    The duty of the free states, remarks sug-
gested by the case of the Creole.   Boston,
William Crosby & co., 1842.
93 p.   11 1/2 cm.

Channing, William Ellery, 1780.
    Dr. Channing's last address, delivered at
Lenox, on the first of August, 1842, the anniversary of emancipation in the British West
Indies.   Boston, Oliver Johnson, 1842.
21 p.   18 cm.

Channing, William Ellery, 1780-1842.
    Essay X.   Slavery.   Originally published in
1836, in review of "Slavery.   By William E.
Channing."   [n.p.] 1836.
312 p.   21 cm.

Channing, William Ellery, 1780.
    Letter of William E. Channing to James G.
Birney.   Boston, James Monroe and company, 1837.
36 p.   17 cm.

Channing, William Ellery, 1780.
    A letter to the abolitionists ... with com-
ments.   First published in the Liberator, Dec.
22, 1837.   Boston, Isaac Knapp, 1837.
32 p.   16 1/2 cm.

Channing, William Ellery, 1780-1882.
    A letter to the Hon. Henry Clay, 1777-1852,
on the annexation of Texas to the United States.
Boston, James Munroe and company, 1837.
72 p.   21 1/2 cm.

Channing, William Ellery, 1780.
On the evils of slavery ... Richmond, Ind.,
Republished by the Central book and tract committee of Friends [n.d.]
30 p.   17 cm.

Channing, William Ellery, 1780.
Remarks on the slavery question, in a letter
to Jonathan Phillips, esq. ... Boston, James
Munroe and company, 1839.
91 p.   19 cm.

Channing, William Ellery, 1780.
Slavery ... Fourth ed., rev. Boston, James
Munroe and company, 1836.
187 p.   17 cm.

Channing, William Ellery, 1780.
Tribute of William Ellery Channing to the
American abolitionists, for their vindication of
freedom of speech ... New York, American anti-
slavery society, 1861.
24 p.   19 cm.

Chapman, Maria Weston.
"How can I help to abolish slavery?" Counsels
to the newly converted. [New York, American
anti-slavery society, 1855?]
12 p.   19 cm.

Chapman, Mrs. Maria (Weston) 1806.
Pinda: a true tale. New York, Published by
the American A. S. society, 1849.
23 p.   17 cm.

Chapman, Maria Weston.
Right and wrong in Massachusetts ... Boston,
Dow & Jackson's anti-slavery press, 1839.
177 p.   18 cm.

Chapman, Robert D.   1839-
A Georgia soldier in the civil war, 1861-1865,
by R. D. Chapman. Houston, Tex. 1923.
108 p., 1 1. ports.   19 cm.

Charlevoix, Pierre Francois Xavier de 1682-1761.
Histoire et description générale de la Nouvelle
France, avec le Journal historique d'un voyage
fait par ordre du roi dans l'Amérique septentrionale. Paris, Nyon fils, 1744.

105

3v.   plates,   maps (part fold.)   26 cm.

Charlton, William Henry.
    Four months in North America. Hexham, The
Courant office, by J. Catherall and company, 1873.
    2 p.l.,   55 p.   16 cm.

Chase, Ezra B.
    Teachings of patriots and statesmen; or, The
"founders of the republic" on slavery ... Philadelphia, J. W. Bradley, 1861.
    495 p.   front. (port.)   19 cm.

Chase, Henry.
    The north and the south: being a statistical
view of the conditions of the free and slave
states, by Henry Chase and C. H. Sanborn. Boston,
John P. Jewett, 1857.
    vi, 191 p.   10 1/2 cm.

Chase, Lucien Bonaparte, 1817-1864.
    English serfdom and American slavery: or, Our-
selves--as others see us. By Lucien B. Chase ...
New York, H. Long & brother [c1854]
    viii, [9]-259 p.   19 1/2 cm.
    L. C. card no. 15-21834 Revised

Chase, Philander, bp., 1775-
    Bishop Chase's Reminiscences: an autobiography.
Second edition: comprising a history of the principal events in the author's life to A. D. 1847
... Boston, J. B. Dow: etc., etc. 1848.
    2 v.   fronts. (v. 1: port.) illus., plates.
23 1/2 cm.

Chase, Salmon Portland.
    Anti-slavery addresses of 1844 and 1845, by
Salmon Portland Chase and Charles Dexter Cleveland.
London, Sampson Low, son, and Marston; Philadel-
phia, J. A. Bancroft and co., 1867.
    167 p.   18 1/2 cm.

Chase, Salmon Portland, 1808.
    Maintain plighted faith. Speech ... in the
Senate, February 3, 1854. Against the repeal of
the Missouri prohibition of slavery north 36° 30',
Washington, Printed at the Congressional globe
office, 1854.
    16 p.   23 cm.

Chase, Salmon Portland, 1808.
   Maintain plighted faith. Mr. Chase's speech
in the Senate, February 3, 1854, against the repeal of the Missouri prohibition. Washington,
Printed by John T. and Lem. Towers [1854]
   30 p.   22 cm.

Chase, Salmon Portland, 1808.
   Politics in Ohio. Senator Chase's letter to
Hon. A. P. Edgerton. [Cincinnati, 1854?]
   16 p.   25 cm.

Chase, Salmon Portland, 1808.
   The radical democracy of New York and the independent democracy. Letter from Senator Chase,
of Ohio, to Hon. B. F. Butler, of New York
[Washington? 1852?]
   8 p.   22 cm.

Chase, Salmon Portland, 1808.
   Speech of Senator Chase, delivered at Toledo,
May 30, 1851, before a mass convention of the
democracy of northwestern Ohio. [Cincinnati?
Printed at Ben Franklin book and job office,
1851?]
   8 p.   24 cm.

Chase, Salmon Portland, 1808.
   Union and freedom without compromise. Speech
... on Mr. Clay's compromise resolutions, in
Senate, May 26, 1850. [Washington, Buell & Blanchard, 1850?]
   16 p.   24 cm.

Chastellux, Francois Jean, marquis de, 1734-
   Travels in North-America, in the years 1780,
1781, and 1782 ... Tr. from the French by an
English gentleman, who resided in America at that
period. With notes by the translator ... Dublin,
Printed for Colles, Moncrieffe, White, H. White-
stone, Byrne, Cash, Marchbank, Henry and Moore,
1787.
   2v.   fold. plates, fold. maps.   20 1/2 cm.

Cheap cotton by free labor. By a cotton manufacturer.
   Boston, A. Williams & Co., 1861.
   52 p.   22 1/2 cm.

Cheek, Philip, 1841-
   History of the Sauk County riflemen, known as

Company "A", Sixth Wisconsin veteran volunteer
infantry, 1861-1865; written and comp. by Philip
Cheek, Mair Pointon. [Madison, Wis., Democrat
printing company] 1909.
    220 p., 1 1. front., pl., ports., plan.
21 1/2 cm.

Cheever, George B.
    God against slavery: and the freedom and the
duty of the pulpit to rebuke it, as a sin against
God. New York, Joseph H. Ladd, 1857.
    viii, [9]-272 p.   18 1/2 cm.

Cheever, George Barrell, 1807.
    American missionary supplement. Address ...
before the American missionary association, Boston, May 27, 1858. [n.p., 1858?]
    169-192 p.   23 cm.

Cheever, George Barrell, 1807.
    The fire and hammer of God's word against the
sin of slavery. Speech ... at the anniversary
of the American abolition society, May, 1858.
New-York, American abolition society, 1858.
    16 p.   22 cm.

Cheever, George Barrell, 1807.
    The guilt of slavery and the crime of slave-
holding, demonstrated from the Hebrew and Greek
scriptures ... New York, 1860.
    viii, xx, 21-472,   19 cm.

Cheever, George Barrell, 1807.
    The salvation of the country secured by im-
mediate emancipation. A discourse ... delivered
in the Church of the Puritans, Sabbath evening,
Nov. 10, 1861. New-York, John A. Gray, 1861.
    24 p.   19 cm.

Cheever, Henry T.
    A tract for the times, on the question, Is it
right to withhold fellowship from churches or
from individuals that tolerate or practice slavery?
Read by appointment, before the Congregational
ministers' meeting, of New-London County ... New
York, John A. Gray, 1859.
    23 p.   23 cm.

Chesnut, James, 1815.
Relations of states. Speech ... delivered in
the Senate of the United States, April 9, 1860,
on the resolutions submitted by the Hon. Jefferson Davis, of Miss., on 1st March, 1860. Baltimore, Printed by John Murphy & co., 1860.
24 p.   23 cm.

Chester, Anthony.
Scheeps-togt van Anthony Chester, na Virginia,
gedaan in het jaar 1620 ... Leyden, Pieter Vander
Aa, 1707.
14, [4] p.   1 p.l., 1 fold. pl.   18 cm.

Chester, Greville John, 1830-
Transatlantic sketches in the West Indies,
South America, Canada, and the United States ...
London, Smith, Elder & co., 1869.
xvi, 405, [1] p.   19 1/2 cm.

Chesterman, William Dallas, 1845-
Guide to Richmond, Printed by J. E. Goode,
1881.
68 p. incl. plates, map.   17 1/2 cm.

Chesterman, William Dallas, 1845-
The James River tourist. A brief account of
historical localities on James River. Prepared
by W. D. Chesterman. Pub. by L. D. Tatum, supt.
of the Virginia steamboat co. Richmond, Dis-
patch steam printing house, 1878.
69 p. front., illus., plates (1 fold), maps
(1 fold)   17 1/2 cm.

[Chetwood, William Rufus]
The voyages, dangerous adventures and imminent
escapes of Captain Richard Falconer ... Intermix'd
with the voyages and adventures of Thomas Randal
... London, W. Chetwood [etc.] 1720.
[vii]-viii, 72, 136, 179p. 1 p.l., front.
20 cm.

Chevalier, Michel, 1806-
Lettres sur l'Amérique du Nord ... avec une
carte des États-Unis d'Amérique ... Paris, C.
Gosselin et cie., 1836.
2v. fold. map.   22 cm.

Child, David L.
... The despotism of freedom; or, The tyranny
and cruelty of American republican slave-masters,
shown to be the worst in the world; in a speech,
delivered at the first anniversary of the New England anti-slavery society, 1833 ... Boston, Boston
young men's anti-slavery association, 1833.
iv, [5]-72 p.   19 cm.

Child, David Lee, 1794.
Oration in honor of universal emancipation in
the British empire, delivered at South Reading,
August first, 1834 ... Boston, Published by Garrison & Knapp, 1834.
38 p.   21 cm.

Child, David Lee, 1794.
Rights and duties of the United States relative
to slavery under the laws of war.   No military
power to return any slave.   "Contraband of war"
is applicable between the United States and their
insurgent enemies ... Boston, R. F. Wallcut, 1861.
48 p.   19 cm.

Child, Mrs. Lydia Maria (Francis) 1802.
Anti-slavery catechism ... Newburyport, C.
Whipple, 1836.
36 p.   18 cm.

Child, Mrs. Lydia Maria (Francis) 1802.
An appeal in favor of that class of Americans
called Africans ... Boston, Allen and Ticknor,
1833.
232 p.   front.   18 cm.

Child, Mrs. Lydia Maria (Francis) 1802.
Correspondence between Lydia Maria Child, and
Gov. Wise and Mrs. Mason, of Virginia.   New York,
American anti-slavery society, 1860.
28 p.   18 cm.

Child, Mrs. Lydia Maria (Francis) 1802.
The duty of disobedience to the Fugitive slave
act: an appeal to the legislators of Massachusetts
... Boston, American anti-slavery society, 1860.
36 p.   19 cm.

Child, Mrs. Lydia Maria (Francis) 1802.
The evils of slavery and the cure of slavery ...
Newburyport, Published by Charles Whipple, 1836.

19 p.   17 cm.

Child, Mrs. Lydia Maria (Francis), 1802-1880.
Isaac T. Hopper: a true life. By L. Maria
Child ... Boston, J. P. Jewett & co.; Cleveland
O., Jewett, Proctor & Worthington; [etc.,etc.]
1853.
xvi, 493 p.   2 port. (incl. front.) 19 1/2 cm.

Child, Mrs. Lydia Maria (Francis) 1802-1880, ed.
The oasis. Ed. by Mrs. Child ... Boston, B.
C. Bacon, 1834.
xvi, 276 p. front., illus., plates, ports.,
facsim.   16 cm.

Child, Mrs. Lydia Maria (Francis) 1802.
The patriarchal institution, as described by
members of its own family ... New York, American
anti-slavery society, 1860.
55 p.   18 cm.

Child, Mrs. Lydia Maria (Francis) 1802.
The right way the safe way, proved by emancipation in the British West Indies, and elsewhere
... New York, Published and for sale at 5 Beek-
man street, 1862.
108 p.   19 cm.

Child, Mrs. Lydia Maria (Francis) 1802.
The right way the safe way, proved by emancipation in the British West Indies, and elsewhere
... New York. Published and for sale at 5 Beek-
man street [by the American anti-slavery society]
1860.
96 p.   19 cm.

The child's anti-slavery book; containing a few words
about American slave children, and stories of
slave life ... New York, Carleton & Porter [n.d.]
158 p.   illus.   15 cm.

The child's book on slavery; or, Slavery made plain...
Cincinnati, American reform tract and book society,
1857.
iv, 143 p.   illus.   14 1/2 cm.

Chittenden, Lucius Eugene, 1824-
Recollections of President Lincoln and his administration. New York and London, Harper &

brothers, 1901.
   viii, 470 p.   front. (port.)   22 1/2 cm.

Christian anti-slavery convention, Cincinnati, April
   17-20, 1850.
       The minutes of the Christian anti-slavery con-
   vention assembled April 17th-20th, 1850. [Cin-
   cinnati] Ben Franklin book and job rooms, 1850.
       84 p.   21 cm.

Christian anti-slavery convention, Chicago, July 3,4,
   5, 1851.
       Minutes ... Chicago, Printed at the office of
   the Western citizen, 1851.
       31 p.   22 cm.

Christian investigator [edited by] William Goodell.
   Whitesboro, N. Y., William Goodell, Feb. 1843 -
   Aug. 1848.
       529 p.   31 cm.

A Christian memento, with observations on some of the
   prevalent amusements of the day ... Philadelphia,
   Published by the Tract association of Friends
   [n.d.]
       12 p.   18 cm.

... Christianity and war. [Cincinnati, American reform tract and book society, n.d.]
       16 p.   17 cm.

[Christie, Thomas]
       A description of Georgia, by a gentleman who
   has resided there upwards of seven years and was
   one of the first settlers. London, Printed for
   C. Corbett, 1741.
       8 p.   26 cm.

Christ's doctrine of future punishment--life a season
   of probation. [Cincinnati, American reform tract
   and book society, n.d.]
       16 p.   18 cm.

Christy, David.
       African colonization of the free colored people
   of the United States an indispensable auxiliary
   to African missions ... Cincinnati, Published by
   J. A. and U. P. James, 1854.
       64 p.   22 cm.

112

Christy, David.
Cotton is king: or, the culture of cotton, and
its relation to agriculture, manufactures and commerce; and also to the free colored people of the
United States, and to those who hold that slavery
is in itself sinful ... Second edition, revised
and enlarged. New York, Derby & Jackson, 1856.
xxiii, [24]-298 p. 17 1/2 cm.

Christy, David.
Pulpit politics: ecclesiastical legislation
on slavery, in its disturbing influences on the
American union ... Fifth edition. Cincinnati,
Faran & McLean, 1863.
xvi, [17]-624 p. 21 cm.

Chunn, Ida F.
Descriptive illustrated guide-book to North
Carolina mountains. Their principal resorts ...
New York, E. J. Hale & son, 1881.
87 p. phot. 18 1/2 cm.

The church and slavery. [Philadelphia, Stereotyped
by L. Johnson, 1856?]
196 p. 19 cm.

Church anti-slavery society.
Proceedings of the convention which met at
Worcester, Mass., March 1, 1859. New York, John
F. Trow, 1859.
31 p. 24 cm.

Church, Jeremiah.
Journal of travels, adventures, and remarks,
of Jerry Church. Harrisburg, 1845.
72 p. 15 1/2 cm.

Churchman, John, 1705-1775.
An account of the gospel labours, and Christian
experiences of a faithful minister of Christ,
John Churchman, late of Nottingham in Pennsylvania,
deceased. To which is added a short memorial of
the life and death of a fellow labourer in the
church, our valuable friend Joseph White, late of
Bucks county ... Philadelphia: Printed by Joseph
Cruckshank, on the north side of Market-street,
between Second and Third streets, MDCCLXXIX.
vii, 256 p. 19 1/2 cm.

Civil liberty outraged. [New York, John A. Gray, printer, n.d.]
36 p. 19 cm.

Claiborne, John Francis Hamtramck, 1809–
Life and times of Gen. Sam Dale, the Mississippi partisan ... Illustrated by John M'Lenan. New York, Harper & brothers, 1860.
xi, [15]-233 p., 1 l., incl. front. 12 pl. 19 1/2 cm.

Clapp, Theodore, 1792–
Autobiographical sketches and recollections, during a thirty-five years' residence in New Orleans ... 4th ed. Boston, Phillips, Sampson & company, 1859.
viii, 419 p. 20 cm.

[Clare, Mrs. Josephine]
Narrative of the adventures and experiences of Mrs. Josephine Clare, a resident of the South at the breaking out of the rebellion, her final escape from Natichitoches, La., and safe arrival at home, in Mariette, Pa. Lancaster, Pa., Pearson & Geist, 1865.
36 p. 16 1/4 cm.

Clarinda, a pious coloured woman of South Carolina, who died at the age of 102 years. Philadelphia, Published by the Tract association of Friends [n.d.]
4 p. 18 cm.

Clark, Benjamin C.
A plea for Hayti, with a glance at her relations with France, England and the United States, for the last sixty years ... Third edition. Boston, Eastburn's Press, 1853.
50 p. 24 1/2 cm.

Clark, George, 1841–
A glance backward; or, some events in the past history of my life, by George Clark. [Houston, Press of Rein & sons company, 1914?]
93 p. 22 1/2 cm.

Clark, George W., comp.
The harp of freedom ... New York [etc.,etc.] Miller, Orton & Mulligan [etc., etc.] 1856.
335 p. front. (port.), music. 18 1/2 cm.

Clark, George W., comp.
    The liberty minstrel ... Sixth ed.   New-York,
Published by the author, 1846.
    iv, 219 p.   music.   16 1/2 cm.

Clark, James H. 1842-
    The iron hearted regiment: being an account
of the battles, marches and gallant deeds performed
by the 115th regiment N. Y. vols. ... By James H.
Clark ... Albany, J. Munsell, 1865.
    xii, 337 p.   19 cm.

Clark, James Samuel, 1841-
    Life in the Middle West; reminiscences of J.
S. Clark.   Chicago, The Advance publishing company [1916]
    226 p.   incl.   front., ports.   20 cm.

Clark, John Alonzo, 1801-
    Gleanings by the way.   Philadelphia, W. J. &
J. K. Simon; New York, R. Carter, 1842.
    v, [7]-352 p.   19 1/2 cm.

Clark, Lewis Garrard, 1812.
    Narrative of the sufferings of Lewis Clarke
[!], during a captivity of more than twenty-five
years, among the Algerines of Kentucky, one of
the so called Christian states of America.   Dictated by himself.   Boston, David H. Ela, printer,
1845.
    108 p.   front.   22 cm.

Clark, Lewis Garrard, 1812.
    Narratives of the sufferings of Lewis and
Milton Clarke [!], sons of a soldier of the Revolution, during a captivity of more than twenty
years among the slaveholders of Kentucky, one of
the so called Christian states of North America.
Dictated by themselves.   Boston, Published by
Bela Marsh, 1846.
    144 p.   front. (port.)   18 cm.

Clark, Rufus Wheelwright, 1813.
    The African slave-trade ... Boston, American
tract society [n.d.]
    102 p.   17 cm.

Clark, Rufus Wheelwright, 1813.
    Review of the Rev. Moses Stuart's pamphlet on
slavery, entitled Conscience and the Constitution

Boston, Published by C. C. P. Moody, 1850.
103 p.   21 cm.

Clark, Thomas March, bp., 1812-
Reminiscences ... New York, T. Whitaker [n.d.]
[5], 266 p. front. (port.) 19 1/2 cm.

Clark, Walter Augustus.
Under the stars and bars; or, Memories of four
years service with the Oglethorpes, of Augusta,
Georgia. By Walter A. Clark ... Augusta, Ga.,
Chronicle printing company, 1900.
230 [3] p.   20 1/2 cm.

Clarke, Beverly Leonidas, 1809.
The veto power -- relation of parties.
Speech ... in the House of Representatives, Monday, June 26, 1848. [Washington, D. C.? 1848?]
8 p.   23 cm.

Clarke, George, 1676-
Voyage of George Clarke, esq., to America
[1703] With introduction and notes, by B. B.
O'Callaghan. Albany, J. Munsell, 1867.
lxxxi,   126 p. front. (mounted phot.)
20 1/2 cm.

Clarke, James Freeman.
Secession, concession, or self-possession:
which? Boston, Walker, Wise and company, 1861.
48 p.   23 cm.

Clarkson, Matthew.
Diary west of the Alleghanies, in 1766. (In
Henry Rowe Schoolcraft. Information respecting
the history, condition, and prospects of the Indian tribes of the United States ... 1852-57.
v. 4, p. 265-278).

Clarkson, Thomas, 1760.
Abolition of the African slave-trade, by the
British Parliament. Abridged from Clarkson.
2 v. illus.   15 cm.

Clarkson, Thomas.
The cries of Africa, to the inhabitants of
Europe; or, A survey of that bloody commerce
called the slave-trade ... London, Sold by Harvey
and Barton, and W. Phillips [n.d.]
50 p.   diagrs.   20 cm.

Clarkson, Thomas, 1760.
An essay on the comparative efficiency of regulation or abolition, as applied to the slave trade shewing that the latter only can remove the evils to be found in that commerce ... London, Printed by James Phillips, 1789.
xi, 82 p. 19 cm.

Clarkson, Thomas, 1760.
An essay on the impolicy of the African slave trade. In two parts ... London, Printed and sold by J. Phillips, 1788.
iv, 3-134 p. 22 cm.

Clarkson, Thomas, 1760.
An essay on the slavery and commerce of the human species, particularly the African; translated from a Latin dissertation, which was honoured with the first prize in the University of Cambridge, for the year 1785. The second edition ... London, Printed and sold by J. Phillips, 1788.
xxii, 167 p. 22 cm.

Clarkson, Thomas, 1760.
History of the rise, progress, and accomplishment of the abolition of the African slave-trade by the British parliament ... A new edition. London, John W. Parker, 1839.
viii, 615 p. front. (port.) 22 cm.

Clarkson, Thomas, 1760.
A letter to the clergy of various denominations and to the slave-holding planters, in the southern parts of the United States of America... London, Printed by Johnston and Barrett, 1841.
64 p. 21 cm.

Clarkson, Thomas, 1760.
Negro slavery. No. XI. The argument that the colonial slaves are better off than "the British peasantry," answered, from the Jamaica Royal gazette of June 21, 1823. [London, n.d.]
93-100 p. 21 cm.

Clarkson, Thomas, 1760.
Thoughts on the necessity of improving the conditions of the slaves in the British colonies, with a view to their ultimate emancipation; and on the practicability, the safety, and the advan-

tages of the latter measure ... Second ed. corrected. London, Printed for the Society for the
mitigation and gradual abolition of slavery
throughout the British dominions, and sold by J.
Hatchard and son, 1823.
  iv, 57 p.   22 cm.

Clarkson, Thomas, 1760.
     Thoughts on the necessity of improving the
conditions of slaves in the British colonies, with
a view to their ultimate emancipation; and on
the practicability, the safety, and the advantages of the latter measure ... London, Printed
by Richard Taylor, 1823.
  60 p.   21 cm.

Clay, Cassius Marcellus, 1810-
     Appeal of Cassius M. Clay to Kentucky and the
world. Boston, J. M. Macomber & E. L. Pratt,
1845.
  35 p.   20 1/2 cm.

Clay, Cassius Marcellus, 1810-
     Speech of Cassius M. Clay, at Frankfort, Ky.,
from the Capitol steps, January 10, 1860 ...
[Cincinnati? 1860]
  20 p.   23 cm.

Clay, Cassius Marcellus, 1810-
     Speech of C. M. Clay, at Lexington, Ky. De-
livered August 1, 1851. [n.p., 1851]
  20 p.   25 cm.

Clay, Cassius Marcellus, 1810-
     Speech of C. M. Clay before the Young men's
Republican central union of New York in the
Tabernacle, October 24th, 1856. [New York? 1856?]
  Cover-title, 19 p.   21 1/2 cm.

Clay, Henry, 1777.
     Speech ... on taking up his compromise resolu-
tions on the subject of slavery. Delivered in
Senate, Feb. 5th & 6th, 1850 ... New York, Stringer & Townsend, 1850.
  32 p.   23 cm.

Clay, Thomas S.
     Detail of a plan for the moral improvement of
negroes on plantations. Read before the Georgia

presbytery ... [n.p.]   Printed at the request of
the presbytery, 1833.
23 p.   22 cm.

Clemens, Jeremiah, 1814.
Remarks of Messrs. Clemens, Butler, and Jefferson Davis, on the Vermont resolutions relating
to slavery. Delivered in Senate of the United
States, January 10, 1830. Washington, D. C.,
Printed at the Congressional globe office, 1850.
15 p.   23 cm.

[Clemens, Samuel Langhorne] 1835-
Life on the Mississippi, by Mark Twain [pseud.]
With more than 300 illustrations ...   Sold by
subscription only.   Boston, J. S. Osgood and
company, 1883.
624 p. incl. front., illus., plates.   23 cm.

Cleveland, Chauncey Fitch, 1799.
The homestead bill -- the fugitive slave
bill -- the compromise measures. Speech of Hon.
C. F. Cleveland, of Connecticut, in the House of
Representatives, April 1, 1852, on the homestead
bill [n.p., 1852?]
7 p.   22 cm.

Cleveland, Henry.
Alexander H. Stephens in public and private.
With letters and speeches before, during, and
since the war. Philadelphia, Chicago, Ill.
[etc.] National publishing company [c1866]
1 p.l., [7]-833 p. plates, 2 port. (incl.
front.) facsim.   22 1/2 cm.

[Clinton, Charles A.] supposed author.
A winter from home. New-York, J. F. Trow,
printer, 1852.
60 p.   19 cm.

[Cluny, Alexander]
The American traveller; or, Observations on
the present state, culture and commerce of the
British colonies in America, and the further improvements of which they are capable ... By an
old and experienced trader. London, Printed for
E. and C. Dilly [etc.] 1769.
122 p. 4 p.l., front., fold. map.   28 cm.

Cluskey, Mich. W., comp.
Buchanan and Breckinridge. The democratic
hand-book, compiled by Mich. W. Cluskey, of Washington City, D. C. Recommended by the Democratic
National Committee. Washington, 1856.
310 p. 20 cm.

Coale, Charles B.
The life and adventures of Wilburn Waters, the
famous hunter and trapper of White Top Mountain;
embracing early history of southwestern Virginia,
sufferings of the pioneers, etc., etc. ... Richmond, G. W. Gary & co., printers, 1878.
2 p.l., [vii-xiv], [17]-265 p. 20 1/2 cm.

Coates, Benjamin.
Cotton cultivation in Africa. Suggestions on
the importance of the cultivation of cotton in
Africa, in reference to the abolition of slavery
in the United States, through the organization
of an African Civilization Society ... Philadelphia, C. Sherman & Son, 1858.
52 p. 23 cm.

[Cobb, Charles, comp.]
American railway guide, and pocket companion,
for the United States; containing correct tables,
time of starting from all stations, distances,
fares, etc. on all railway lines in the United
States; together with a complete railway map.
Also many stage lines running in connection with
railroads. Subscription per annum, $1; single
numbers, 12 1-2 cts; wholesale price, $7 per 100.
New York, Dinsmore, 1850.
133 p. (22 p. of advertisements) 15 cm.

Cobb, Howell.
Scriptural examination of the institution of
slavery in the United States; with its objects
and purposes. Georgia [sic], Printed for the
author, 1856.
173 p. 19 cm.

Cobb, Joseph Beckham, 1819-
Leisure labors; or, miscellanies historical,
literary, and political ... New York, D. Appleton
and company, 1858.
408 p. 19 cm.

Cobb, Joseph Beckham, 1819-
Mississippi scenes; or, Sketches of southern
and western life and adventure, humorous, satirical, and descriptive, including The Legend of
Black Creek. Philadelphia, A. Hart, 1851.
vii, [13]-250 p.   20 1/2 cm.

Cobb, Thomas Reade Rootes, 1823.
An inquiry into the law of negro slavery in
the United States of America. To which is prefixed, an historical sketch of slavery ... Vol. 1.
Philadelphia, T. & J. W. Johnson & co.; Savannah,
W. Thorne Williams, 1858.
ccxxviii, 358 p.   22 1/2 cm.

Cochin, Augustin, i.e. Pierre Suzanne Augustin, 1823.
L'abolition de l'esclavage ... Paris, J.
Lecoffre [etc.] 1861.
2v.   tables.   23 1/2 cm.

Cochin, Augustin, i.e. Pierre Suzanne Augustin, 1823.
... Results of emancipation ... Translated by
Mary L. Booth ... Boston, Walker, Wise, and
company, 1864.
xiv, 412 p.   tables.   19 cm.

[Cochran]
Address to anti-slavery Whigs on third party-
ism [n.p., n.d.]
8 p.   22 cm.

Coffin, Charles Carleton, 1823-1896.
Four years of fighting: a volume of personal
observation with the army and navy, from the first
battle of Bull Run to the fall of Richmond.   By
Charles Carleton Coffin ... Boston, Ticknor and
Fields, 1866.
xv, [1].   558 p.   front. (port.)   illus.,
plates, plans.   22 cm.

Coffin, Joshua.
An account of some of the principal slave insurrections, and others, which have occurred, or
been attempted, in the United States and elsewhere, during the last two centuries ... New York,
American anti-slavery society, 1860.
36 p.   20 cm.

Coffin, Levi, 1798-
Reminiscences of Levi Coffin, the reputed
president of the Underground railroad ... Cincinnati, Western tract society [1876]
viii, 3-712 p. 1 p.l., 2 port. (incl. front.)
19 1/2 cm.

Coggeshall, S. W.
An anti-slavery address, delivered in the M.
E. church, Danielsonville, Conn., July 4th 1849
... West Killingly, E. B. Carter, 1849.
58 p. 17 1/2 cm.

Cogley, Thomas Sydenham, 1840-
History of the Seventh Indiana cavalry volunteers, and the expeditions, campaigns, raids,
marches, and battles of the armies with which it
was connected, with biographical sketches of Brevet
Major General John P. C. Shanks, and of Brevet
Brig. Gen. Thomas M. Browne, and other officers
of the regiment; with an account of the burning
of the steamer Sultana on the Mississippi river,
and of the capture, trial, conviction and execution of Dick Davis, the guerrilla. By Thomas S.
Cogley ... Laporte, Ind., Herald company, printers,
1876.
2 p.l., v, [5]-267 p. front., illus. port.
19 cm.

Cohen, Ernest Julius, 1869.
Uit het land van Benjamin Franklin. Zutphen,
W. J. Thieme & cie., 1928.
320 p. illus. 22 cm.

Cohen, Myer M.
Notices of Florida and the campaigns. By M.
M. Cohen, (an officer of the left wing.) Charles-
ton, S. C., Burges & Honour; New-York, B. B.
Hussey, 1836.
240 p. front. (fold. map) pl. 18 1/2 cm.

[Cohen, Myer M.]
Sketch of the Seminole War, and sketches during a campaign. By a lieutenant, of the left
wing. Charleston, Dan J. Dowling, 1836.
iv, 311, [1] p., 1 l. 18 cm.

Coke, Edward Thomas, 1807-
A subaltern's furlough; descriptive of scenes
in various parts of the United States, upper and

lower Canada, New-Brunswick, and Nova Scotia,
during the summer and autumn of 1832 ... New
York, J. & J. Harper, 1833.
2v.   20 1/2 cm.

Coke, Henry John, 1827-
A ride over the Rocky mountains to Oregon
and California. With a glance at some of the
tropical islands, including the West Indies and
the Sandwich isles ... London, R. Bentley, 1852.
x, 388 [2] p.   incl. front. (port.)   22 cm.

Coke, Thomas, 1747-
Extracts of the journals of the late Rev.
Thomas Coke, LL. D.; comprising several visits
to North-America and the West-Indies ... Dublin,
Printed by R. Napper for the Methodist book-room,
1816.
271 p.   17 cm.

Cole, Jacob H[enry] 1847-
Under five commanders; or, A boy's experience
with the Army of the Potomac, by Jacob H. Cole...
Paterson, N. J., News printing company, 1906.
ix p., 1 1., 253 p.   incl. illus., plates,
ports.   ports.   21 cm.

[Coleman, Elihu] 1600.
[Tract on slavery] [n.p.] Reprinted 1934.
22 p.   18 cm.

Coleraine, George Hanger, 4th baron, 1751?-1824.
The life, adventures, and opinions of Col.
George Hanger. Written by himself ... London,
J. Debrett, 1801.
2v.   21 1/2 cm.

Colfax, Richard H.
Evidence against the views of the abolitionists, consisting of physical and moral proofs,
of the natural inferiority of the negroes ... New
York, James T. M. Blakeley, 1833.
33 p.   22 cm.

Colfax, Schuyler.
The "laws" of Kansas. Speech ... in the House
of Representatives, June 21, 1856. [n.p., n.d.]
15 p.   22 cm.

Colfax, Schuyler.
 The "laws" of Kansas. Speech ... in the House
of Representatives, June 21, 1856. Washington,
Buell & Blanchard, 1856.
 16 p.   23 cm.

Collamer, Jacob.
 Report of the Kansas conference committee.
Speech ... Delivered in the Senate of the United
States, April 27, 1858. [n.p., n.d.]
 7 p.   22 1/2 cm.

Collamer, Jacob, 1791.
 ... Views of the minority on the constitution
of Kansas, adopted by the convention which met
at Lecompton on Monday, the 4th of September,
1857.
 7 p.   22 cm.

A collection of valuable documents, being Birney's
vindication of abolitionists -- protest of the
American A. S. society -- To the people of the
United States; or, To such Americans as value
their rights -- Letter from the executive committee of the N. Y. A. S. society, to the exec. com.
of the Ohio state A. S. S. at Cincinnati -- Outrage upon southern rights. Boston, Isaac Knapp,
1836.
 80 p.   19 cm.

[Collier, Price] 1860-
 America and the Americans from a French point
of view. 6th ed. New York, C. Scribner's sons,
1897.
 x, 293 p.   18 1/2 cm.

Collins, Elizabeth.
 Memories of the southern states. By Elizabeth Collins ... Taunton [Eng.] Barnicott, 1865.
 3 p.1., 116 p.   18 cm.

Collins, P. G.
 The Scinde & the Punjaub, the gems of India,
in respect to their value and unparalleled capabilities of supplanting the slave states of
America in the cotton markets of the world: or,
An appeal to the English nation on behalf of the
great cotton interest, threatened with inade-
quate supplies of the raw material ... Manchester,
A. Ireland and co., 1858.

64 p.   20 cm.

Collins, R. M., lieut. 15th Texas infantry.
    Chapters from the unwritten history of the
war between the states; or, The incidents in the
life of a Confederate soldier in camp, on the
march, in the great battles, and in prison. By
Lieut. R. M. Collins ... St. Louis, Nixon-Jones
printing co., 1893.
    335 p. front., illus. (incl. facsim.) port.
19 1/2 cm.

Collins, Robert.
    Essay on the treatment and management of
slaves. Written for the seventh annual fair of
the Southern Central Agricultural Society. By
Robert Collins, of Macon, Ga. Second edition.
Boston, Eastburn's press, 1853.
    18 p.   24 1/2 cm.

Collins, S. H.
    The emigrant's guide to and description of the
United States of America ... 4th ed. Hull, J.
Noble; [etc., etc. 1830]
    180 p. 3 p.l. front. (fold. map) 15 cm.

Collyer, Robert H.
    Lights and shadows of American life. Boston,
Brainard & co. [1838?]
    40 p. port.   25 cm.

Colonization. New York [Published by R. G. Williams
    for the American anti-slavery society, 1839?]
    24 p.   11 cm.

Colonization and abolition contrasted. Philadelphia,
    Herman Hooker [n.d.]
    16 p.   22 cm.

Colonization herald and general register. V. 1, no.
    1-4, Jan.-Apr. 1839. [Philadelphia, Pennsylvania
    colonization society] 1839.
    4 nos. in 1v. (192p.)   23 cm.

Colonization society of the city of New York.
    Proceedings of the colonization society of the
city of New York, at their third annual meeting,
held on the 13th and 14th of May, 1835, including
the annual report of the board of managers, to

the society. New York, Printed by Wm. A. Mercein
and son, 1835.
   62, [1] p.   20 cm.

Colonization society of the city of New York.
   Sixth annual report of the Colonization society of the city of New-York, &c.   New-York,
Mercein and Post's press, 1838.
   46 p.   20 cm.

Colonization society of the city of New York.
   Seventh annual report of the Colonization
society, of the city of New-York, &c.   New-York,
Mercein & Post's press, 1839.
   48 p.   20 cm.

Colonization society of the city of New York.
   Eighth annual report of the Board of managers
of the New-York City colonization society, presented May, 1840. New-York, Alexander S. Gould,
printer, 1840.
   56 p.   20 cm.

Colonization society of the state of Connecticut.
   Third annual report of the managers ... with
an appendix. May, 1830. New-Haven, Printed by
Baldwin and Treadway, 1830.
   28 p.   tables.   24 cm.

Colonization society of the state of Connecticut.
   Sixth annual report of the managers ... May,
1833. Hartford, Printed by Peter B. Bleason
and co., 1833.
   15 p.   21 cm.

The colonizationist and journal of freedom. Boston,
Geo. W. Light, 1834.
   383 p. front. (port.)   22 cm.

Colored citizens of Ohio. State convention, Columbus,
January 10-13, 1849.
   Minutes and address ... Oberlin, From J. M.
Fitch's power press, 1849.
   28 p.   22 cm.

Colored freemen of Pennsylvania.
   Proceedings of the state convention ... held
in Pittsburgh on the 23rd, 24th and 25th of August, 1841, for the purpose of considering their
condition and the means for its improvement.

Pittsburgh, Matthew M. Grant, 1841.
16 p.   23 cm.

[Colton, Calvin]   1789.
Abolition a sedition.   By a northern man.
Philadelphia, George W. Donohue, 1839.
187 p.   14 1/2 cm.

Colton, Joseph Hutchins, 1800-
Colton's traveler and tourist's guidebook
through the United States of America and the
Canadas: containing the routes and distances
on the great lines of travel by railroads, canals,
stageroads, and steamboats; together with a description of the several states ... New York, J.
H. Colton & co., 1856.
v-xiv,   250 p.   1 p.l.   fold map.   15 1/2 cm.

Columbiana (Ohio) county anti-slavery society.
An address of the board of managers of the
Columbiana county anti-slavery society, to the
citizens of Ohio.   [n.p., n.d.]
8 p.   21 cm.

Columbus, Ohio.   State convention of colored men,
1851.
Address to the constitutional convention of
Ohio, from the state convention of colored men,
held in the city of Columbus, January 15th, 16th,
17th and 18th, 1851.   [n.p.]   E. Glover, printer,   [1851?]
8 p.   22 cm.

[Colwell, Stephen]
The five cotton states and New York; or, Remarks upon the social and economical aspects of
the southern political crisis.   [n.p., January,
1861].
64 p.   23 cm.

[Colwell, Stephen]   1800.
The south: a letter from a friend in the
north.   With special reference to the effects of
disunion upon slavery.   Philadelphia, Printed
for the author, by C. Sherman & son, 1856.
46 p.   22 cm.

Combe, George, 1788-
    Notes on the United States of North America
    during a phrenological visit in 1838-9-40 ...
    Philadelphia, Carey & Hart, 1841.
    2v. illus. 20 cm.

Comettant, Jean Pierre Oscar, 1819-
    Trois ans aux États-Unis; étude des moeurs et
    coutumes américaines ... Paris, Pagnerre, 1857.
    364 p. 2 p.1. 18 1/2 cm.

The commemorative wreath: in celebration of the ex-
    tinction of negro slavery in the British domin-
    ions ... London, Published by Edmund Fry, 1835.
    viii, 112 p. front. 18 cm.

A compendious description of the thirteen colonies,
    in British-America. London: Printed for Herman,
    Strong and Co., 1777.
    22 p., 1 1. 20 1/2 cm.

Concessions and compromises. [Philadelphia? 1860?]
    14, iv, p. 22 cm.

A concise historical account of all the British
    colonies in North-America, comprehending their
    rise, progress, and modern state; particularly
    of the Massachusetts-Bay, (the seat of the
    present civil war) together with the other pro-
    vinces of New-England. To which is annexed, an
    accurate descriptive table of several countries
    ...London, Printed for J. Bew, 1775.
    iv, 196p. fold. table. 22 1/2 cm.

A concise statement of the question regarding the
    abolition of trade. Third edition. London,
    Printed for J. Hatchard and T. N. Longman and
    O. Rees, 1804.
    108 p. 20 cm.

Conder, Josiah, 1789-
    ... [United States of America and Canada]...
    London, J. Duncan, 1830.
    2v. fronts. (fold. maps) plates. 16 cm.

Condition of the American colored population, and of
    the colony of Liberia. Boston, Published by
    Pierce & Parker, 1833.
    24 p. 22 cm.

The condition of the Free people of colour in the
   United States of America, Reprint from Anti-
   slavery examiner, no. 13, to which are added,
   resolutions passed at the late meeting of the
   Anti-slavery convention, held in London, in
   June, 1840 ... London, Thomas Ward and co., and
   British and foreign anti-slavery society, 1841.
      22 p.   20 cm.

Congregational church, Franklin, Mass.
      Action of the church in Franklin, Mass., in
   regard to the American tract society and the
   American board. New-York, J. A. Gray, printer,
   1854.
      8 p.   22 1/2 cm.

Connor, Mrs. Jeannette M. (Thurber), ed. and tr.
      Colonial records of Spanish Florida; letters
   and reports of governors and secular persons...
   translated and edited by Jeannette Thurber Connor.
   v. I, 1570-1577. Deland, The Florida state historical society, 1925.
      xxxiv, 367 p.   front., facsim.   25 1/2 cm.

The conquerors of the new world and their bondsmen,
   being a narrative of the principal events which
   led to negro slavery in the West Indies and
   America ... London, William Pickering, 1848.
      2v.   20 cm.

Conser, Solomon L. M., 1812-
      Virginia after the war. An account of three
   years' experience in reorganizing the Methodist
   Episcopal church in Virginia at the close of the
   civil war ... Indianapolis, Baker-Randolph litho.
   & eng. co., 1891.
      82 p.   23 1/2 cm.

Considérant, Victor Prosper, 1808-
      Au Texas ... 2. éd. contenant: 1° Rapport à
   mes amis; 2° Bases et statutes de la Société de
   colonisation européo-Américaine au Texas; 3° ...
   Les bases d'un premier établissement sociétaire
   ... Bruxelles, Société de colonisation; [etc.,etc.]
   1855.
      [3]-334 p.   3 p.1.   fold. map, tables (part
   fold.)   18 1/2 cm.

Considerations on Negro slavery; with a brief view of
the proceedings relative to it, in the British
parliament. Edinburgh, Edinburgh society for
promoting the mitigation and ultimate abolition
of Negro slavery, 1824.
24 p.   20 1/2 cm.

The conspiracy to break up the union. The plot and
its development. Breckinridge and Lane candidates
of a disunion party. Washington, Lemuel Towers
[n.d.]
16 p.   24 cm.

The Constitution against slavery. [n.p., n.d.]
6 p.   24 cm.

The Constitution, a pro-slavery compact; or, Selections
from the Madison papers. Second ed. enlarged.
New York, American anti-slavery society, 1845.
x, 131 p.   23 cm.

The constitutional duty of the federal government to
abolish American slavery; an exposé of the position of the American abolition society. New-
York, Published by the American abolition society,
1856.
[18] p.   17 cm.

Convention of Congregational ministers of Massachusetts.
Committee on slavery. Report ... presented May
30, 1849. Boston, Press of T. R. Marvin, 1849.
92 p.   23 cm.

Convention of delegates from the abolition societies
established in different parts of the United
States, 2d, Philadelphia, 1795. Minutes of the
proceedings. Philadelphia, Printed by Zachariah
Poulson, junior, 1795.
32 p.   18 cm.

Convention of delegates from the abolition societies
established in different parts of the United
States, Philadelphia, 1796. Minutes of the
proceedings. Philadelphia, Printed by Zachariah
Poulson, junior, 1796.
32 p.   22 cm.

Convention of delegates from the abolition societies
established in different parts of the United

States, 4th, Philadelphia, 1797. Minutes of the
proceedings. Philadelphia, Printed by Zachariah
Poulson, junior, 1797.
59 p. 20 cm.

Convention of radical political abolitionists. Syracuse, N. Y., 1855.
Proceedings. New-York, Published by the
Central abolition board, 1856.
68 p. 23 cm.

Converse, John Kendrick.
A discourse on the moral, legal and domestic
condition of our colored population, preached before the Vermont colonization society, at Montpelier, October 17, 1832 ... Burlington, Edward
Smith, 1832.
32 p. 22 cm.

Conway, Moncure D.
The golden hour... Boston, Ticknor and Fields,
1862.
160 p. 20 cm.

Conyngham, David Power, 1840-1883.
Sherman's march through the South. With
sketches and incidents of the campaign. By Capt.
David P. Conyngham. New York, Sheldon and co.,
1965.
431 p. 19 cm.

Cook, Benjamin F. b. 1835 or 6.
History of the Twelfth Massachusetts volunteers (Webster regiment) By Lieutenant-Colonel
Benjamin F. Cook. Boston, Twelfth (Webster) regiment association, 1882.
167 p. pl., 2 port. (incl. front.) map (in
pocket) 23 1/2 cm.

Cook, Ebenezer.
Early Maryland poetry; the works of Ebenezer
Cook, gent.: laureat of Maryland, Ed. by Bernard
Christian Steiner, Baltimore, 1900.
102 p. facsims. 25 cm.

Cook, Joel, 1842-
The siege of Richmond: a narrative of the
military operations of Major-General George B.
McClellan during the months of May and June, 1862.
Philadelphia, G. W. Childs, 1862.

viii, 7-358 p.   18 1/2 cm.

Cooke, John Henry, 1791-
A narrative of events in the south of France,
and of the attack on New Orleans, in 1814   and
1815.   London, T. & W. Boone, 1835.
iv, 318 p.   19 cm.   -

Cooke, Philip St. George, 1809-
Scenes and adventures in the army: or, Romance of military life ... Philadelphia, Lindsay
& Blakiston, 1857.
xii, [13]-432 p.   19 cm.

Cooper, Alonzo.
In and out of rebel prisons, by Lieut. A.
Cooper ... Oswego, N. Y., R. J. Oliphant, printer, 1888.
vii, [8]-335 p. incl.   10 pl. front. (port.)
23 cm.

[Cooper, James Fenimore] 1789-
Notions of the Americans: picked up by a
travelling bachelor ... Philadelphia, Carey,
Lea & Carey, 1828.
2 v.   18 cm.

Cooper, Thomas.
Correspondence between George Hibbert, Esq.,
and the Rev. T. Cooper, relative to the condition
of the Negro slaves in Jamaica, extracted from
the Morning chronicle: also, a libel on the
character of Mr. and Mrs. Cooper, published in
1823, in several of the Jamaica journals; with
notes and remarks ... London, J. Hatchard and
son and Lupton Relfe, 1824.
67 p.   20 1/2 cm.

Cooper, Thomas.
Facts illustrative of the condition of the
Negro slaves in Jamaica; with notes and an appen-
dix ... London, J. Hatchard and son and Lupton
Relfe, 1824.
64 p.   20 1/2 cm.

Cooper, Thomas, 1759-
Some information respecting America ... London, Printed for J. Johnson, 1794.
iv, 240 p.   1 l.   front. (fold. map)
21 1/2 cm.

Copley, Esther.
A history of slavery and its abolition ...
Second edition, with an appendix. London, Houls-
ton & Stoneman, 1839.
xi, 648 p. front. (port.) 16 cm.

Copley, John M.
A sketch of the battle of Franklin, Tenn.;
with reminiscences of camp Douglas. By John M.
Copley ... Austin, Tex., E. Von Boeckmann, printer, 1893.
206 p. plates. 17 1/2 cm.

Copp, Elbridge J. 1844-
Reminiscences of the war of the rebellion,
1861-1865, by Col. Elbridge J. Copp, the youngest
commissioned officer in the Union army who rose
from the ranks. Published by the author. Nashua,
N. H., printed by the Telegraph publishing company, 1911.
536, iv.p. incl. illus., plates. ports.
front. 24 cm.

Corby, William, 1833-1897.
Memoirs of chaplain life, by Very Rev. W. Corby ... Three years chaplain in the famous Irish
brigade, "Army of the Potomac." Notre Dame, Ind.,
"Scholastic" press, 1894.
391 p. front., plates, ports. 20 cm.

Corcoran, Michael, 1827-1863.
The captivity of General Corcoran. The only
authentic and reliable narrative of the trials
and sufferings endured, during his twelve months
imprisonment in Richmond and other southern cities,
by Brig.-General Michael Corcoran ... Philadelphia, Barclay & co., 1862.
1 p.1., [21]-100 (i.e. 54) p. 3 pl. 24 cm.

Cornelius, Elias, 1794-
. Tour in Virginia, Tennessee, & c. (In Sansom,
Joseph. Travels in Lower Canada ... 1820. p.
96-116. [Modern voyages and travels, vol. III,
no. 1. March 15, 1820])

Cornwallis, Kinahan, 1839-
Royalty in the New World; or, The Prince of
Wales in America ... New York, M. Doolady, 1860.
xii, 289p. front. (port.) 19 1/2 cm.

Correspondence on the slave trade with foreign powers, parties to treaties and conventions, under which captured vessels are to be tried by tribunals of the nation to which they belong. From January 1 to December 31, 1846, inclusive. London, T.R. Harrison, 1847.
79 p. 33 cm.

Correspondence with foreign powers relating to slave trade. 1837. London, William Clowes and sons, 1838.
79 p. 33 cm.

Corsan, W. C.
Two months in the Confederate States; including a visit to New Orleans under the domination of General Butler. By an English merchant. London, R. Bentley, 1863.
2 p.1., 209 p. 19 cm.

Cortambert, Louis Richard, 1808?
Voyage au pays des Osages. Un tour en Sicile ... Paris, A Bertrand, 1837.
94 p. 22 cm.

Corwin, Thomas.
Speech ... In the House of Representatives, January 23, and 24, 1860. Washington, Republican Congressional committee [1860?]
16 p. 22 cm.

Corwin, Thomas, 1794.
State of the Union. Speech ... delivered to the House of Representatives, Jan. 21, 1861. Washington, Printed by Henry Polkinhorn, 1861.
16 p. 24 cm.

Cory, Charles Barney, 1857-
Hunting and fishing in Florida, including a key to the water birds known to occur in the state ... 2d ed. Boston, Mass., Estes & Lauriat, 1896.
4 p.1., 3-4, 1 1., 5-8, 7-304 p. illus., 2 pl. (incl. front.) 23 1/2 cm.

[Cory, Charles Barney] 1857-
Southern rambles. Florida. By Owen Nox [pseud.] Boston, A. Williams & co., 1881.
149 p. front., illus. 20 cm.

Cosmopolitan ideas on the union. [n.p., 1861?]
    23 p.   22 cm.

Cotton cultivation in Africa. Suggestions on the
    importance of the cultivation of cotton in Africa
    in reference to the abolition of slavery in the
    United States, with a few observations addressed
    to the friends of emigration among the colored
    population of the northern states. By a coloni-
    zationist. Philadelphia, Printed at the Evening
    register job office, 1854.
    25 p.   22 cm.

Cotton stealing. A novel. Chicago, J. R. Walsh &
    co., 1866.
    iv, [5]-487 p.   18 cm.

A country gentleman's reasons for voting against Mr.
    Wilberforce's motion for a bill to prohibit the
    importation of African negroes into the colonies.
    London, Printed for J. Debrett, 1792.
    78 p.   22 cm.

The cousins' journey; or, Sketches of American scenery.
    Boston, L. C. Bowles, 1833.
    102 p.   16 cm.

Cowan, John F.
    A new invasion of the South. Being a narra-
    tive of the expedition of the Seventy-first in-
    fantry, National guard, through the southern
    states, to New Orleans. February 24 - March 7,
    1881. New York city, Board of officers, Seventy-
    first infantry, 1881.
    3 p.l., [5]-103, 24 [3] p. front. (port.)
    plates.   18 1/2 cm.

Cooper, William.
    The negro's complaint: a poem. To which is
    added, Pity for poor Africans. London, Printed
    for Harvey and Darton, 1826.
    22 p.   illus.   18 cm.

Cox, Samuel Hanson.
    Correspondence between the Rev. Samuel H. Cox,
    D. D., of Brooklyn, L. I., and Frederick Douglass,
    a fugitive slave. New-York, American anti-slavery
    society, 1846.
    16 p.   21 cm.

Coxe, Daniel, 1673-
A description of the English province of
Carolana, by the Spaniards call'd Florida, and
by the French La Louisiane. As also of the great
and famous river Meshacebe or Missisipi   ...
London, Printed for B. Cowse, 1722.
122 p.   27 p.l., front. (fold. map)   20 cm.

[Coyner, David H.]
Cheap, healthy and happy homes in West Virginia for northern and New England emigrants.
Wheeling, John Frew, 1870.
16 p.   23 1/2 cm.

Crafford, John.
A new and most exact account of the fertile
and famous colony of Carolina.   Dublin, Printed
for Nathan Tarrant, 1683.
7 p.   19 cm.

Craft, David, 1832-1908.
History of the One hundred forty-first regiment. Pennsylvania volunteers, 1862-1865. By
David Craft, chaplain ... Published by the author.
Towanda, Pa., Reporter-journal printing company,
1885.
ix, 270, [4] p.   front., pl., port.   23 cm.

[Crafton, William Bell]
A short sketch of the evidence for the abolition of the slave trade, delivered before a committee of the House of Commons ... London, printed, Philadelphia, re-printed by Daniel Lawrence,
1792.
28 p.   17 cm.

Craib, Alexander.
America and the Americans; a narrative of a
tour in the United States and Canada, with chapters on American home life, by Alexander Craib ...
Paisley and London, A. Gardner, 1892.
2 p.l. [3]-325 p.   incl. front., illus.
20 1/2 cm.

Crandall, Reuben, 1805? defendant.
The trial of Reuben Crandall, M. D., charged
with publishing seditious libels, by circulating
the publications of the American anti-slavery
society. Before the Circuit court for the District of Columbia, held at Washington, in April,

1836, occupying the court the period of ten days.
New-York, H. R. Piercy, 1836.
    62 p.   21 cm.

Crawford, J. Marshall.
    Mosby and his men: a record of the adventures
of that renowned partisan ranger, John S. Mosby,
Colonel C.S.A. including the exploits of Smith,
Chapman, Richards, Montjoy, Turner, Russell,
Glasscock, and the men under them. By J. Marshall
Crawford, of Company B. New York, G. W. Carleton
& co., [etc., etc.] 1867.
    375 p. front., port.   18 cm.

Crawford, William, 1788-
    Penitentiaries (United States). Report ...
on the penitentiaries of the United States ...
Ordered by the House of Commons, to be printed,
11 August 1834. [London, 1834]
    56, 229 p. 18 plans (partly fold.) 34 1/2
cm.

Cresswell, Nicholas, 1750-
    The journal of Nicholas Cresswell, 1774-1777.
New York, L. MacVeagh, The Dial press, 1924.
    ix p., 1 1., 287 p. front. (port.) p 1.,
facsim.   24 1/2 cm.

Creuzbaur, Robert.
    Route from the Gulf of Mexico and the lower
Mississippi valley to California and the Pacific
Ocean, illustrated with a general map and section-
al maps; with directions to travellers. New York,
H. Long & brother; Austin, Tex., Robert Creuzbaur,
1849.
    40 p. maps. 11 cm.

Crèvecoeur, Michel Guillaume St. Jean de, called Saint
John de Crèvecoeur, 1735-1813.
    Letters from an American farmer ... Written
for the information of a friend in England, by
J. Hector St. John ... London, Printed for Thomas
Davies [etc.] 1782.
    318 p. 8 p.1., maps. 21 1/2 cm.

The crisis, no. 1. Or, thoughts on slavery, occasioned
by the Missouri question. New-Haven, Printed by
A. H. Maltby & co., 1820.
    14 p.   22 cm.

Criswell, Robert.
"Uncle Tom's Cabin" contrasted with Buckingham
Hall, the planter's home, or, A fair view of both
sides of the slavery question. By Robert Criswell,
esq., author of "Letters from the South and West."
New-York, D. Fanshaw, 1852.
152 p.   18 cm.

Crittenden, John Jordan.
The Kansas conference bill.   Speech ... Delivered in the Senate of the United States, April 27,
1858.   Washington, Buell & Blanchard, 1858.
8 p.   22 1/2 cm.

Crocker, Samuel Leonard, 1804.
Eulogy upon the character and services of
Abraham Lincoln ... delivered by invitation of
the authorities of the city of Taunton, on the
occasion of the national fast, June 1, 1865 ...
Boston, Printed by J. Wilson and son, 1865.
28 p.   23 cm.

Crockett, David, 1786-1836.
Col. Crockett's exploits and adventures in
Texas ... a full account of his journey from
Tennessee ... to San Antonio.... together with
a topographical, historical, and political view
of Texas ... Philadelphia, T. K. and P. G.
Collins, 1836.
viii, 13-216 p.   front. (port.)   18 cm.

[Croghan, John]
Rambles in Mammoth Cave, during the year 1844,
by a visitor.   Louisville, Ky., Morton & Griswold, 1845.
xii [9] -101 p.   6 pl.   18 cm.

Croom, Wendell D.
The war-history of Company "C", (Beauregard
volunteers) Sixth Georgia regiment, (infantry)
with a graphic account of each member.   Written
by Wendell D. Croom ... and pub. by the survivors
of the company.   Fort Valley, Ga., Printed at
the "Advertiser" office, 1879.
2 p.l., 37 p.   22 1/2 cm.

Cropper, James, 1773.
The interests of the country and the prosperity
of the West India planters mutually secured by

138

the immediate abolition of slavery; being a review of the House of Commons on the state of the
West India colonies ... Second edition. London,
J. and A. Arch, 1833.
30 p.   21 1/2 cm.

Cropper, James, 1773.
A letter addressed to the Liverpool society
for promoting the abolition of slavery, on the
injurious effects of high prices of produce, and
the beneficial effects of low prices, on the
conditions of slaves ... Liverpool, Printed by
James Smith, Published by Hatchard & son,
Piccadilly, and J. & J. Arch, Cornhill, London,
1823.
32 p.   21 cm.

Cropper, James, 1773.
Letters addressed to William Wilberforce, M.
P., recommending the encouragement of the culti-
vation of sugar in our dominions in the East
Indies, as the natural and certain means of ef-
fecting the general and total abolition of the
slave-trade ... Liverpool, Printed by James
Smith; published by Longman, Hurst, and co.,
London, 1822.
54 p.   21 cm.

Cropper, James, 1773.
Relief for the West-Indian distress, shewing
the inefficiency of protecting duties on East-
India sugar, and pointing out other modes of certain relief ... London, Printed by Ellerton and
Henderson, Gough Square, and sold by Hatchard
and son, Piccadilly, and J. & J. Arch, Cornhill,
London, 1823.
36 p.   21 cm.

Cropper, James, 1773.
The support of slavery investigated ... Liver-
pool, Printed by George Smith; published by
Hatchard & son, Piccadilly, and J. & J. Arch,
Cornhill, London [etc.] 1824.
27 p.   20 1/2 cm.

Crosly, Oliver Marvin.
Florida facts both bright and blue. A guide
book to intending settlers, tourists, and investors, from a northerner's standpoint. Plain un-
varnished truth, without "taffy", no advertisements

or puffs.   Appendix by resident experts.   New
York, 1887.
iv, 240, ix p.   illus.   19 1/2 cm.

Crossley, William J.
Extracts from my diary, and from my experiences
while boarding with Jefferson Davis, in three of
his notorious hotels, in Richmond, Va., Tusca-
loosa, Ala., and Salisbury, N. C., from July,
1861, to June, 1862.   By William J. Crossley,
late sergeant Company C, Second Rhode Island infantry volunteers.   Providence, The Society, 1903.
49 p.   21 cm.

Crothers, Samuel.
The gospel of the jubilee ... Re-print of the
author's edition of 1839.   With an introduction
by Rev. John Rankin.   Cincinnati, American reform tract and book society, 1856.
iv, [5]-222 p.   18 1/2 cm.

Crothers, Samuel, 1783.
The Gospel of typical servitude: The substance of a sermon preached in Greenfield,
Jan. 1, 1834 ... Published by Abolition society
of Paint Valley, Hamilton, O., Printed at the
office of the Intelligencer, by Gardner & Gibbon, 1835.
22 p.   20 cm.

Crothers, Samuel, 1873.
Strictures on African slavery.   Pub. by the
Abolition society of Paint valley.   Rossville,
Butler co., O., Printed by T. Webster, 1833.
46 p.   21 cm.

Crouin, David Edward, 1839-
The evolution of a life, described in the
memoirs of Major Seth Eyland [pseud.] ... New
York, S. W. Green's son, 1884.
336 p.   19 1/2 cm.

Crowe, Eyre, 1824-
With Thackeray in America ... New York, C.
Scribner's sons, 1893.
xvi p., 179 p.   incl. front., illus.   1 1.
21 1/2 cm.

Crummell, Alex.
The future of Africa: being addresses, ser-
mons, etc., etc., delivered in the republic of
Liberia ... Second edition. New York, Charles
Scribner, 1862.
372 p.   19 cm.

Crummell, Alexander.
The relations and duties of the free colored
men in America to Africa. A letter to Charles
B. Dunbar, M. D., Esq., of New York City ... Hartford, Press of Case, Lockwood and company, 1861.
54 p.   23 cm.

Cudworth, Warren Handel, d. 1883.
History of the First regiment (Massachusetts
infantry), from the 25th of May, 1861, to the 25th
of May, 1864; including brief references to the
operations of the Army of the Potomac. By Warren H. Cudworth, chaplain of the regiment ...
Boston, Walker, Fuller and co., 1866.
528 p.   pl.   20 cm.

Cuffy's description of the progress of cotton. Boston, Lilly, Wait, Colman, and Holden, 1833.
11 p.   17 1/2 cm.

Cullom, William.
Speech ... on the Nebraska and Kansas Bill,
in the House of Representatives, April 11, 1854.
Washington, Congressional globe office, 1854.
13 p.   23 cm.

Cumback, Will, 1829-
Speech ... on the affairs in Kansas. Delivered in the House of Representatives, March
7, 1856. Washington, Congressional globe office,
1856.
7 p.   23 cm.

Cuming, Fortescue, 1762-
Sketches of a tour to the western country,
through the states of Ohio and Kentucky; a voyage
down the Ohio and Mississippi rivers, and a trip
through the Mississippi territory, and part of
West Florida ... Pittsburgh, Printed and pub. by
Cramer, Spear & Eichbaum, 1810.
viii, [9]-504 p.   17 1/2 cm.

Cumings, Samuel.
The western pilot, containing charts of the
Ohio river, and of the Mississippi from the mouth
of the Missouri to the Gulf of Mexico ... Cincinnati, Morgan, Lodge and Fisher, printers, 1825.
143 p.   43 maps (incl. front.)   22 1/2 cm.

Cumming, Kate, 1835-
A journal of hospital life in the Confederate
army of Tennessee, from the battle of Shiloh to
the end of the war: with sketches of life and
character, and brief notices of current events
during that period. By Kate Cumming. Louisville,
J. P. Morgan & co., New Orleans, W. Evelyn
[ᶜ1866]
199, [1] p.   23 1/2 cm.

Cunynghame, Sir Arthur Augustus Thurlow, 1812-
A glimpse at the great western republic ...
London, R. Bentley, 1851.
337, [1] p.   2 p.l.   22 cm.

Curtis, Newton Martin, 1835-1910.
From Bull Run to Chancellorsville; the story
of the Sixteenth New York Infantry together with
personal reminiscences, by Newton Martin Curtis...
New York & London, G. P. Putnam's sons, 1906.
xix, 384 p.   4 port. (incl. front.)   23 1/2
cm.

Curtis, Orson Blair, 1841?-1901.
History of the Twenty-fourth Michigan of the
Iron brigade, known as the Detroit and Wayne
county regiment ... By O. B. Curtis ... Detroit,
Mich., Winn & Hammond, 1891.
483 p.   incl.   illus. (incl. maps, plans)
pl., ports. front., col.   pl.   25 1/2 cm.

Cushing, Caleb.
An oration presented at Boston before the
Colonization society of Massachusetts, on the
anniversary of American independence, July 4,
1833 ... Boston, Lyceum press - G. E. Light &
co., 1833.
24 p.   22 cm.

Cushing, S. W., 1818-
Wild oats sowings; or, The autobiography of
an adventurer ... New York, D. Fanshaw, 1857.

483 p.　20 cm.

[Cutler, Jervis] 1768-
　A topographical description of the state of
Ohio, Indiana territory, and Louisiana ... To
which is added, an interesting journal of Mr.
Chas. Le Raye, while a captive with the Sioux
nation, on the waters of the Missouri river.
By a late officer in the U. S. army.　Boston:
Published by Charles Williams.　J. Belcher,
printer, 1812.
　v, [7]-219 p.　5 pl.　18 1/2 x 11 cm.

Cutler, Theodore L.
　To the seeker after Christ.　Cincinnati,
American reform tract and book society [n.d.]
　4 p.　18 cm.

D

Dabney, Robert Lewis, 1820-
　A defence of Virginia, (and through her, of
the South,) in recent and pending contests against
the sectional party.　New York, E. J. Hale &
son, 1867.
　356 p.　22 cm.

Dabney, Robert Lewis, 1820-
　The new South.　A discourse delivered at the
annual commencement of Hampden-Sydney college,
June 15th, 1882, before the Philanthropic and
Union literary societies.　Raleigh, N. C., Edwards, Broughton & co., printers, 1883.
　cover-title, 16 p.　22 1/2 cm.

Dacus, Joseph A.
　A tour of St. Louis; or, the inside of a
great city.　By J. A. Dacus, Ph.D., and James
W. Buel.　St. Louis, Western publishing company, 1878.
　564 p.　front (port.) illus.　23 1/2 cm.

Dale, Robert William, 1829-
　... Impressions of America ... New York, D.
Appleton and company, 1878.
　163 p.　16 1/2 cm.

Dame, William Meade, 1844 or 5-
    From the Rapidan to Richmond and the Spott-
sylvania campaign; a sketch in personal narration
of the scenes a soldier saw, by William Meade
Dame ... Baltimore, Green-Lucas company, 1920.
    4 p.l., xi-xvi, 218 p. 3 port. (incl. front.)
23 1/2 cm.

Dana, Charles Anderson, 1819-1897.
    Recollections of the civil war; with the
leaders at Washington and in the field in the
sixties, by Charles A. Dana ... New York, D.
Appleton and company, 1898.
    xiii, 296 p. front. (port.) 21 1/2 cm.

Dana, Edmund.
    Geographical sketches on the western country:
designed for emigrants and settlers: being the
result of extensive researches and remarks ...
Cincinnati: Looker, Reynolds & co., printers,
1819.
    iv, [5]-312 p.   18 1/2 cm.

Dana, James.
    A discourse delivered in the city of New
Haven, September 9, 1790, before the Connecticut
society for the promotion of freedom [Foretitle:
Doctor Dana's sermon on the African slave trade
1790] New Haven, printed by Thomas and Samuel
Green, 1791.
    33 p.   20 cm.

Danger and safety. New York [Published by R. G.
Williams for the American anti-slavery society,
1839?]
    24 p.   11 cm.

[Daniel, Frederick S.]
    Richmond howitzers in the war. Four years
campaigning with the Army of northern Virginia.
By a member of the company. Richmond, 1891.
    155 p.   19 1/2 cm.

Darby, George W.
    Incidents and adventures in rebeldom; Libby,
Belle-Isle, Salisbury. By Geo. W. Darby. Pitts-
burg, Pa., Press of Rawsthorne engraving & printing company, 1899.
    1 p.l., [7]-228 p. front. (port.) illus., pl.
23 1/2 cm.

Darby, William, 1775-
    The emigrant's guide to the western and south-
western states and territories comprising a geographical and statistical description of the
states ... Accompanied by a map of the United
States ... New York, Kirk & Mercein, 1818.
    xiii,p. 311 p. 3 p.1. 2 fold. maps (incl.
front) plan. tables. 22 cm.

Darby, William, 1775-
    A geographical description of the state of
Louisiana, the southern part of the state of
Mississippi, and the territory of Alabama ...
Together with a map from actual survey and ob-
servation ... of the state of Louisiana, and
adjacent countries. 2d ed. enl. and improved.
New-York, Published by James Olmstead, sold also
by B. Levy & co., booksellers, New-Orleans.
J. Seymour, printer, 1817.
    xi, [1], [13]-356 p. 3 maps (2 fold. incl.
front.) 22 cm.

Darby, William, 1775-
    A geographical description of the state of
Louisiana ... with an account of the character
and manners of the inhabitants. Being an accompaniment to the map of Louisiana ... Printed
for the author, and published by John Melish,
Philadelphia. J. Bioren, printer ... 1816.
    ix, [11]-270, [14] p., 1 1., [2], xvii, [17]
p. map. 21 cm.

Darby, William, 1775-
    Memoir on the geography, and natural and civil
history of Florida, attended by a map of that
country, connected with the adjacent places: and
an appendix, containing the Treaty of cession,
and other papers relative to the subject ...
Philadelphia, Printed by T. H. Palmer, 1821.
    vii, [1], [5]-92 p. front. (fold. map)
23 1/2 cm.

Darby, William, 1775, comp.
    A new gazetteer of the United States of Ameri-
ca ... including ... geographical, historical,
political, and statistical information, with the
population of 1830. By William Darby and Theodore
Dwight, jr. Hartford, E. Hopkins, 1833.
    iv, 9-630 p. 24 cm.

Darby, William, 1775-
View of the United States, historical, geographical, and statistical ... Philadelphia, H. S. Tanner, 1828.
iv, 5-654 p. 2 p.1. fold. maps. 15 cm.

Darling, Henry.
Slavery and the war: a historical essay ... Philadelphia, J. B. Lippincott & co., 1863.
48 p. 23 cm.

[D'Arusmont, Mme. Frances (Wright)] 1795-
Views of society and manners in America; in a series of letters from that country to a friend in England, during the years 1818, 1819 and 1820. By an Englishwoman. From the 1st London ed. With additions and corrections by the author. New York, E. Bliss and E. White, 1821.
xii, 387 [1] p. 24 cm.

Daubeny, Charles Giles Bridle, 1795-
Journal of a tour through the United States, and in Canada made during the years 1837-38 ... Oxford, Printed by T. Combe, 1843.
vi, 231 p. fold. map. 18 cm.

Davenport, Alfred.
Camp and field life of the Fifth New York volunteer infantry. (Duryee zouaves.) By Alfred Davenport. New York, Dick and Fitzgerald, 1879.
485 p. front. (port.) pl. 19 1/2 cm.

Davenport, Bishop.
A new gazetteer, or geographical dictionary. Of North America and the West Indies ... A new edition with alterations and additions to 1836... Philadelphia, B. Davenport & co., 1836.
518 p. illus., fold. col. map. 23 cm.

Davenport, Montague.
Under the gridiron. A summer in the United States and the far West, including a run through Canada ... London, Tinsley brothers, 1876.
xi [1] 143 p., incl. tables. front., plates. 17 cm.

David, Michael.
Father Ignatius in America. By Father Michael, O. S. B., with a preface by Ernest A. Farnol.

London, J. Hodges, 1893.
xx, xvi, 373 p. front. (ports.) 20 cm.

Davidson, Henry M.   d. 1900.
Fourteen months in southern prisons; being a
narrative of the treatment of federal prisoners
of war in the rebel military prisons of Richmond,
Danville, Andersonville, Savannah and Millen ...
By H. M. Davidson ... Milwaukee, Daily Wisconsin
printing house, 1865.
viii, [9]-393 p. front. (fold. plan)   20 cm.

Davidson, James Wood, 1829-
The Florida of to-day; a guide for tourists
and settlers ... New York, D. Appleton and company, 1889.
254 p. front. (fold. map) illus.   18 1/2 cm.

Davidson, Robert.
The evils of disunion: a discourse delivered
on Thanksgiving day, December 12, 1850 ... New
Brunswick, N. J., Press of J. Terhune and son,
1850.
15 p.   21 1/2 cm.

Davidson, Robert, 1808-
An excursion to the Mammoth Cave and the
barrens of Kentucky. With some notices of the
early settlement of the state ... Lexington, Ky.,
A. T. Skillman & son, 1840.
ix p. [13]-148 p.   1 1.   14 1/2 cm.

Davies, Ebenezer, 1808-
American scenes and Christian slavery; a recent tour of four thousand miles in the United
States ... London, J. Snow, 1849.
xii, 324 p.   18 1/2 cm.

Davis, Charles E.   b. 1842 or 1843-1915.
Three years in the army. The story of the
Thirteenth Massachusetts volunteers from July 16,
1861, to August 1, 1864. By Charles E. Davis,
jr. Boston, Estes and Lauriat, 1894.
xxxv, 476 p.   maps.   23 1/2 cm.

Davis, Jefferson, 1808.
Relations of states. Speech ... delivered in
the Senate of the United States, May 7th, 1860,
on the resolutions submitted by him on 1st of

147

March, 1860. Baltimore, John Murphy & co., 1860.
15 p. 23 cm.

Davis, Jefferson, 1808-1887.
The rise and fall of the Confederate government. New York, D. Appleton and co., 1881.
2v. fronts., plates, ports., maps (part
fold.) 23 1/2 cm.

Davis, John, 1774-
Travels of four years and a half in the United
States of America; during 1798, 1799, 1800, 1801,
and 1802 ... London, sold by T. Ostell [etc.]
and H. Caritat; New-York, for R. Edwards, printer, Bristol, 1803.
454 p. 21 1/2 cm.

Davis, Joseph Jonathan, 1828-1892.
Southern claims. Speech ... in the House of
Representatives, Wednesday, May 29, 1878.
[n.p., n.d.]
8 p. 23 cm.

Davis, Mrs. Mary Evelyn (Moore), 1852-
In war times at La Rose Blanche. Twelve
illustrations by E. W. Kemble. Boston, D. Lothrop company [c1888]
vi, 11-257 p. 1 l. incl. front., plates.
17 1/2 cm.

Davis, Nicholas A.
The campaign from Texas to Maryland. By Rev.
Nicholas A. Davis ... Richmond, Printed at the
office of the Presbyterian committee of publication of the Confederate States, 1863.
165, [1] p. 2 port. (incl. front.) 19 1/2
cm.

Davis, Stephen.
Notes of a tour in America, in 1832 and 1833
... Edinburgh, Waugh & Innes; [etc., etc.] 1833.
[vii]-xii, [13]-150 p. 4 p.l. 15 1/2 cm.

Dawes, Henry Laurens, 1816.
The Lecompton constitution founded neither in
law nor in the will of the people. Speech of
Hon. Henry L. Dawes, of Massachusetts. Delivered
in the U. S. House of Representatives, March 8,
1858. [Washington, Buell & Blanchard, printers,
1858].

8 p. 24 cm.

Dawes, Henry Laurens, 1816.
The new dogma of the south-- "Slavery a blessing." Speech ... delivered in the House of Representatives, April 12, 1860. [n.p., n.d.]
7 p. 22 cm.

Dawes, Rufus R. 1838-1899.
Service with the Sixth Wisconsin volunteers. By Rufus R. Dawes ... Marietta, O., E. R. Alderman & sons, 1890.
2 p.1., v, [5] -830 p. front., illus., port. 22 1/2 cm.

Dawson, Mrs. Sarah (Morgan)
A Confederate girl's diary, by Sarah Morgan Dawson; with an introduction by Warrington Dawson, and with illustrations. Boston and New York, Houghton Mifflin company, 1913.
xviii, 1, 439, [3] p. front., plates, ports., double facsim. 21 cm.

Day, George Edward.
The dangers of our country, and the means of averting them. A discourse delivered in Marlborough, Mass., on the day of the annual state fast, April 7, 1842 ... Boston, Press of T. R. Marvin, 1842.
17 p. 23 cm.

Day, Lewis W. b. 1839 or 40.
Story of the One hundred and first Ohio infantry. A memorial volume. By L. W. Day. Cleveland, W. M. Bayne printing co., 1894.
xiv, [15]-463 p. incl. illus., port. front. 21 cm.

Day, Samuel Phillips.
Down South: or, An Englishman's experience at the seat of the American war. By Samuel Phillips Day, special correspondent of the Morning herald ... London, Hurst and Blackett, 1862.
2 v. front. (port.) 19 1/2 cm.

Day, Samuel Phillips.
Life and society in America ... London, Newman and co., 1880.
2v. 22 cm. (v. 2, 23 cm.)

Day, Timothy Crane, 1819.
The Democratic party as it was as it is! Speech ... in the House of Representatives, April 23, 1856. [n.p., n.d.]
8 p. 22 cm.

Day, W[illiam] W.
Fifteen months in Dixie; or, My personal experience in Rebel prisons ... Owatonna, Minn., The People's press, 1889.
2 p.l., 80 pp. 8 cm.

Daylight before sunrise. [Cincinnati, American reform tract and book society, n.d.]
36 p. 18 cm.

Dayton, William Louis, 1807.
Speech ... on the territorial question. Delivered in the Senate of the United States, March 22, 1850. Washington, Printed by John T. Powers, 1850.
32 p. 22 cm.

[Dean, Henry Clay].
Letter to Governor Wright, of Indiana, upon the connexion of the Methodist Episcopal church with the subject of slavery. [n.p., n.d.]
13 p. 25 cm.

Dearborn, Henry, 1751-
Revolutionary war journals of Henry Dearborn, 1775-1783, edited from the original manuscripts by Lloyd A. Brown and Howard H. Peckham; with a biographical essay by Hermon Dunlap Smith. Chicago, The Caxton club, 1939.
xvi, 264 p., 1 l. front. (port.) 2 fold. maps, facsims (1 fold.)

Debar, J. H. Diss.
The West Virginia hand-book and immigrant's guide. A sketch of the state of West Virginia ... Parkersburg, Gibson bros., printers, 1870.
viii, [9]-19, 3 p. fold. map. 19 1/2 cm.

Debouchel, Victor.
Histoire de la Louisiane, depuis les premières découvertes jusqu'en 1840. Nouvelle-Orléans, J. F. Lelievre, 1841.
3 p.l., ii, [7]-197 p. 17 1/2 cm.

De Bow, James Dunwoody Brownson, 1820.
The industrial resources, etc., of the southern and western states ... New-Orleans, New-
York [etc.] Published at the office of De Bow's
review, 1853.
3v.   tables.   22 1/2 cm.

De Brahm, John Gerar William, 1717-
History of the province of Georgia; with maps
of original surveys ... Wormsloe [Ga.] 1849.
55 p.,   1 1.   2 maps, 4 plans.   38 1/2 cm.

De Cordova, Jacob.
Lecture on Texas delivered by Mr. J. De Cor-
dova ... Also, a paper read by him before the
New York geographical society, April 15th, 1858
... Philadelphia, Printed by E. Crozet, 1858.
32 p.   19 cm.

Deedes, Henry.
Sketches of the south and west; or, Ten months'
residence in the United States ... Edinburgh and
London, Blackwood and sons, 1869.
vi, 170 p.   18 1/2 cm.

A defence of southern slavery against the attacks of
Henry Clay and Alexander Campbell ... by a
southern clergyman.   Hamburg, S. C., Robinson and
Carlisle, 1851.
ii, 46 p.   20 cm.

DeForest, Bartholomew S.
Random sketches and wandering thoughts; or,
What I saw in camp, on the march, the bivouac,
the battle field and hospital, while with the
army in Virginia, North and South Carolina, during the late rebellion.   With a historical sketch
of the second Oswego regiment, Eighty-first New
York state V.L.; a record of all its officers,
and a roster of its enlisted men; also an appendix.   By B. S. DeForest ... Albany, A. Herrick,
1866.
324 p.   pl.   19 1/2 cm.

Deiler, John Hanno, 1849-
Die europäische einwanderung nach den Vereinigten Staaten von 1820 bis 1896 ... Von J.
Hanno Deiler.   New Orleans, La., Im selbstverlage,
1897.
2 p.l.,   32 p.   23 1/2 cm.

Deiler, John Hanno, 1849.
Louisiana, ein heim für deutsche ansiedler ...
herausgegeben von der Deutschen gesellschaft von
New Orleans. New Orleans, Druck der "New Orleans
Zeitung," 1895.
63 p. fold. map. 22 cm.

Deland, Mrs. Margaret Wade (Campbell), 1857-
Florida days, by Margaret Deland ... Illustrated by Louis K. Harlow. Boston, Little,
Brown and company, c1889.
xviii p., 1 l., [21]-200 p. incl. illus.,
plates. col. front., col. plates. 22 cm.

De La Warr, Thomas West, 3d lord, 1577-1618.
The relation of the Right Honourable the Lord
De-La-Warre, lord gouvernour and captaine generall
of the colonie, planted in Virginea. London,
Printed by William Hall for William Welbie, Dwell-
ing in Paul's church-yeard at the signe of the
Swan, 1611.
[17]p. 19 cm.

DeLeon, Thomas Cooper, 1839-1914.
Four years in Rebel capitals: an inside view
of life in the southern confederacy, from birth
to death. From original notes, collated in the
years 1861 to 1865, by T. C. DeLeon ... Mobile,
Ala., The Gossip printing co., 1890.
6, vii, 11-376 p. 22 1/2 cm.

[Delius, Eduard]
Wanderungen eines jungen norddeutschen durch
Portugal, Spanien und Nord-Amerika. In den jahren
1827-1831. Hrsg. von Georg Lotz ... Hamburg,
Harold, 1834.
4v. 14 1/2 cm.

Demetz, Frédéric Auguste, 1796-
Rapports à m. le comte de Montalivet ... sur
les penitenciers des États-Unis, par m. Demetz...
et par m. Abel Blouet. Paris, Imprimerie royale,
1837.
144, 114 p. 2 p.l., 1 l. 45 pl. (part fold.,
incl. plans) 35 cm.

Democratic national executive committee.
To the democracy of the United States. [Wash-
ington, D. C.? 1860?]
16 p. 25 cm.

Democratic party, National committee, 1852-1856.
The issue fairly presented. The senate bill
for the admission of Kansas as a state. Democracy, law, order and the will of the majority of
the whole people of the territory, against black
republicanism, usurpation, revolution, anarchy,
and the will of a meagre minority. Washington,
Union office, 1856.
30 p. 20 cm.

Democratic party. National convention, Cincinnati,
1856.
Official proceedings of the National Democratic Convention, held in Cincinnati, June 2-6,
1856. Cincinnati, Enquirer company steam printing
establishment, 1856.
78 p. 20 cm.

...Democratic text book. Slavery in the territories.
A compilation from the leading authorities of the
democratic party, showing what is meant by the
doctrine of non-intervention ... Aberdeen, Miss.,
Issued from the "Independent" office [n.d.]
16 p. 23 cm.

Dennett, Daniel.
Louisiana as it is: its topography, and material resources ... New Orleans, "Eureka" press,
1876.
xiii, [14]-288 p. fold. map. 22 cm.

Denny, Ebenezer, 1761-
Military journal of Major Ebenezer Denny, an
officer in the revolutionary and Indian wars.
With an introductory memoir [by W. H. Denny]
Philadelphia, Historical society of Pennsylvania,
1859.
288 p. 2 port. (incl. front.) 6 fold.
plans. 24 1/2 cm.

Denny, John F.
An essay on the political grade of the free
coloured population under the constitution of the
United States, and the constitution of Pennsylvania; in three parts ... Chambersburg, Pa.,
Printed by Nickok & Blood, 1836.
60 p. 23 cm.

Derby, William P.
Bearing arms in the Twenty-seventh Massachusetts regiment of volunteers infantry during the civil war, 1861-1865. By W. P. Derby. Boston, Wright & Potter printing co., 1883.
xvi, 607 p. front., port., maps. 24 cm.

Derry, Joseph Tyrone, 1841-
Georgia: a guide to its cities, towns, scenery and resources ... Philadelphia, J. B. Lippincott & co., 1878.
199 p. front., illus., fold. map. 19 1/2 cm.

Descourtilz, Michel Étienne, 1775-
Voyages d'un naturaliste ... Paris, Dufart, père, 1809.
3v. fronts. (part. fold.) fold. tables. 21 cm.

Descrizione geografica di parte dell'America settentrionale ... Amsterdam, Venezia, Bassaglia, MDCCLVIII.
13 p. map. 19 cm.

The design of civil government and the extent of its authority, as set forth in the holy scriptures. [n.p., n.d.]
16 p. 21 cm.

A detail of some particular services performed in America, during the years 1776, 1777, 1778, and 1779. Compiled from journals and original papers, supposed to be chiefly taken from the journal kept on board of the ship Rainbow, commanded by Sir George Collier, while on the American station during that period ... Printed for Ithiel Town, from a manuscript obtained by him, while in London, in the summer of 1830. New York, 1835.
ix, 117 p. 20 cm.

Detraction. Philadelphia, Published by the Tract association of Friends [n.d.]
8 p. 18 cm.

Deux-Ponts, Guillaume, comte de, 1745-
My campaigns in America: a journal kept by Count William de Deux-Ponts, 1780-81. Translated from the French manuscript, with an introduction and notes, by Samuel Abbott Green. Boston, J. W. Wiggin & W. P. Lunt, 1868.

xvi p., 176 p.   1 1.   23 cm.

Devol, George H.   1829-
    Forty years a gambler on the Mississippi.
Cincinnati, Devol & Haines, 1887.
    vii, 9-300p.   front. (port.) 4 pl.   22 cm.

Dewees, Jacob.
    The great future of America and Africa; an
essay showing our whole duty to the black man,
consistent with our own safety and glory ...
Philadelphia, H. Orr, 1854.
    236 p.   23 cm.

Dewees, William B.
    Letters from an early settler of Texas ...
Comp. by Cara Cardelle [pseud.] 2d ed. Louisville, Kentucky [New Albany tribune print.]
1858.
    viii, [9]-312 p.   18 1/2 cm.

Dexter, Henry M.
    Our national condition, and its remedy. A
sermon, preached in the Pine street church, Boston, on Sunday, June 22, 1856 ... Boston, John
P. Jewett & co., 1856.
    44 p.   23 cm.

Dicey, Edward, 1832-1911.
    Six months in the federal states. By Edward
Dicey ... London and Cambridge, Macmillan and
co., 1863.
    2 v.   18 1/2 cm.

Dick, David.
    All modern slavery indefensible; intended for
all places where slavery does exist, and for all
legislative powers by whom it is allowed; with a
desire, in due deference, to be presented to His
Majesty, through the medium of the Right Honourable Lord Viscount Melbourne, whose favour for
the doing of which is hereby requested: For in-
troducing to the consideration of His Majesty and
the Government those places yet in slavery, and
hitherto overlooked, in British India and Sierra
Leone in Africa, which still require interference.
By David Dick, Arbroath. Sold by P. Milne, Mon-
trose; A. Allardice, Dundee; P. Gray, Aberdeen,
and the booksellers in London, Manchester, Dublin,
Newcastle, and Liverpool, 1836.

xx, 323 p.   17 cm.

Dickens, Charles, 1812-1870.
    American notes for general circulation ... London, Chapman and Hall, 1842.
    2v.   20 1/2 cm.

Dickert, D. Augustus.
    History of Kershaw's brigade, with complete roll of companies, biographical sketches, incidents, ancedotes, etc., by D. Augustus Dickert. Introduction by Associate Justice Y. J. Pope. Newberry, S.C., E. H. Aull company, 1899.
    583, 5, 2 p. front., ports.   22 1/2 cm.

Dickinson, James, 1659-1741.
    A journal of the life, travels, and labour of love in the work of the ministry, of that worthy elder, and faithful servant of Jesus Christ, James Dickinson, who departed this life on the 6th of the 3d month 1741, in the 23d year of his age. London, Printed and sold by T. S. Raylton and L. Hinde, 1745.
    xxvii, 172 p.   17 cm.

Dickinson, James Taylor.
    A sermon, delivered in the Second Congregational church, Norwich, on the fourth of July, 1834, at the request of the Anti-slavery society of Norwich and vicinity ... Norwich, Published by the Anti-slavery society, 1834.
    40 p.   23 cm.

Dickinson, Jonathan, 1663-
    God's protecting providence, man's surest help and defence, in times of the greatest difficulty, and most eminent danger. Evidenced in the remarkable deliverance of Robert Barrow, with divers other persons, from the devouring waves of the sea ... and also, from the cruel, devouring jaws of the inhuman cannibals of Florida. Faithfully related by one of the persons concerned therein... Philadelphia, printed: London, Reprinted, and sold by T. Sowle, 1700.
    89 p. 5 p.l.   17 1/2 cm.

Dickson, William.
    Letters on slavery ... London, Printed and sold by J. Phillips [etc.] 1789.
    x, [191]p.   23 cm.

156

Did the world make itself. [Cincinnati, American reform tract and book society, n.d.]
16 p. illus. 18 cm.

Diehl, Louis.
Meine schicksale und erlebnisse in Nord-
amerika, nebst einem anhang: Die licht- und
schattenseit der Neuen welt ... Darmstadt,
Gedruckt bei C. F. Will, 1851.
vi, 96 p. 23 cm.

Dilke, Sir Charles Wentworth, bart., 1843.
Greater Britain. A record of travel in
English-speaking countries during 1866-7 ... With
maps and illustrations. Philadelphia, J. B.
Lippincott & co. [etc., etc.] 1869.
2 v. in 1. front., pl., port., maps. 19 1/2
cm.

Dimock, Anthony Weston, 1842-1918.
Florida enchantments, by A. W. and Julian A.
Dimock, with numerous illustrations from photographs. New York, The Outing publishing company,
1908.
3 p.l., v-x, 318 p. front. 88 pl. 24 1/2
cm.

District of Columbia. Laws, statutes, etc. The
slavery code of the District of Columbia, together with notes and judicial decisions explanatory of the same. By a member of the Washington
bar. Washington, L. Towers & co., 1862.
38 p. 22 cm.

Disturnell, John, 1801-
Disturnell's American and European railway
and steamship guide, giving the arrangements on
all the great lines of travel through the United
States and Canada, across the Atlantic ocean,
and throughout central Europe ... New York, J.
Disturnell, 1853.
208 p. front., illus., fold map. 15 1/2 cm.

Disturnell, John, 1801-
Springs, water-falls, sea-bathing resorts, and
mountain scenery of the United States and Canada
... New York, J. Disturnell, 1855.
xii, [13]-227 p. front., plates, maps (part
fold.) 15 1/2 cm.

157

The disunionist. Can abolitionists vote or take office under the United States constitution? Cincinnati, Sparhawk and Lytle, 1845.
   36 p.   18 cm.

The divided house, or, The irrepressible conflict. The doctrine of Washington, Jefferson, Madison, Martin, Pinkney, Reid, Clay, Faulkner, McDowell, Webster, Birney, Douglas, Shields, Louisville Courier, Parker, Wade, Fitzhugh, Richmond Inquirer, Baker, Valparaiso Observer, Lincoln, Seward, Hickman, Everett, Clark, C. M. Clay, Phillips, Schurz. [n.p., n.d.]
   7 p.   23 cm.

[Dix, John] 1800?
   Transatlantic tracings; or, Sketches of persons and scenes in America. By the author of "Lions: living and dead" ... London, W. Tweedie, 1853.
   xii [13]-337 p.   incl. front. (port.)
   18 1/2 cm.

Dixon, James, 1788-
   Personal narrative of a tour through a part of the United States and Canada: with notices of the history and institutions of Methodism in America ... 2d ed.   New York, Lane & Scott, 1849.
   431, [1]p.   front. (port.)   19 cm.

Dixon, William Hepworth, 1821-
   New America ... London, Hurst and Blackett, 1867.
   2 v.   fronts., plates, ports.   22 1/2 cm.

Dixon, William Hepworth, 1821-
   White conquest ... London, Chatto and Windus, 1876.
   2 v.   22 cm.

Doak, Henry Melvil, 1841-
   The Wagonauts abroad. Two tours in the wild mountains of Tennessee and North Carolina, made by three regs, four Wagonauts, and a canteen. In two parts. By A. T. Ramp [pseud.] Edited by H. M. Doak, from the journal of the Wagonauts... Nashville, Tenn., Southwestern publishing house, 1892.
   300 p.   incl. illus., ports.   19 cm.

Dr. Nelson's lecture on slavery. New York, Published
by R. G. Williams for the American anti-slavery
society, 1839?
16 p. 11 cm.

Dod, Albert B.
Essays, theological and miscellaneous, reprinted from the Princeton review. Second series.
Including the contributions of the late Rev. Albert B. Dod, D. D. New York and London, Wiley
and Putnam, 1847.
342 p. 23 cm.

[Dodge, Mary Abigail] 1833-
Wool-gathering. By Gail Hamilton [pseud.]...
Boston, Ticknor & Fields, 1867.
vii [9]-335 p. 18 cm.

Dodge, William Sumner.
A waif of the war; or, The history of the
Seventy-fifth Illinois infantry, embracing the
entire campaigns of the Army of the Cumberland.
By Wm. Sumner Dodge ... Chicago, Church & Goodman, 1866.
vii, [17]-241, [1] p. 22 cm.

Dodson, John.
A report of the case of the Louis, forest,
master; appealed from the vice-admiralty court
at Sierra Leone, and determined in the high court
of admiralty, on the 15th of December 1817.
With an appendix ... London, Printed for J. Butterworth & son, 1817.
56 p., 13 unnumb. p. 21 cm.

Doggett, Simeon, 1765.
Two discourses on the subject of slavery ...
Boston, Printed by Minot Pratt, 1835.
28 p. 23 cm.

Döhla, Johann Conrad, 1750-
Tagebuch eines Bayreuther soldaten, des Johann
Conrad Döhla aus dem nordamerikanischen freiheits-
kriege von 1777 bis 1783. Mit einem vorwort von
W. frhr. v. Waldenfels ... Bayreuth, Druck von
L. Ellwanger vorm. T.Burger, 1913.
241 p. 1 p.l., plates, fold. map. 23 cm.

Domenech, Emmanuel Henri Dieudonné, 1826-
Journal d'un missionaire au Texas et au Mexi-

que, par l'abbé E. Domenech, 1846-1852. Paris,
Gaume frères, 1857.
[v]-xii, 477 p. 1 p.1., 1 l. fold. map.
21 cm.

Domenech, Emmanuel Henri Dieudonné, 1825 or 6-1886.
Seven years' residence in the great deserts
of North America, by the abbé Em. Domenech ...
Illustrated with fifty-eight woodcuts by A. Joliet,
three plates of ancient Indian music, and a map
showing the actual situation of the Indian tribes
and the country described by the author... London,
Longman, Green, Longman, and Roberts. 1860.
2v. fronts., col. plates, fold. map. 22 cm.

Domestic committee.
Journal of a tour on the "Indian territory,"
performed by order of the Domestic committee...
in the spring of 1844 ... New York, Published for
the Domestic committee of the Board of missions
by Danial Dana, jr., 1844.
74 p. 2 p.1., front., 3 maps (2 fold.)
22 cm.

Doolittle, James Rood, 1815.
The Calhoun revolution: its basis and its
progress. Speech ... delivered in the United
States Senate, December 14, 1859. [Washington,
Buell & Blanchard, 1860].
16 p. 24 cm.

Doolittle, James Rood.
The union Kansas and the Lecompton Constitution. Speech ... in the Senate of the United
States, March 4 and 8, 1858. Washington, Congressional globe office, 1858.
16 p. 23 cm.

Dore, James.
A sermon on the African slave trade, preached
at Maze-Pond, Southwark, Lord's day afternoon,
Nov. 30, 1788 ... Third edition. London, Printed by J. Phillips and sold by J. Buckland [etc.]
1788.
39 p. 19 cm.

[Dörnberg, Karl Ludwig, freiherr von] 1749-
...Tagebuchblätter eines hessischen offiziers
aus der zeit des nord-amerikanischen unabhängig-
keits-krieges, von Gotthold Marseille ... Pyritz,

Backe'sche buchdruckerei, 1899-1900.
2v. in 1. double map. 25 cm.

Dornblaser, Thomas Franklin, 1841-
Sabre strokes of the Pennsylvania dragoons,
in the war of 1861-1865. Interspersed with personal reminiscences. By T. F. Dornblaser ...
Published for the author. Philadelphia, Lutheran
publication society, 1884.
viii, 9-264 p. fold. map. 19 cm.

Doubts on the abolition of the slave trade; by an old
member of Parliament ... London, Printed for John
Stockdale, 1790.
vii, 123 p. 20 1/2 cm.

Dougherty, Michael.
Prison diary, of Michael Dougherty, late Co.
B, 13th, Pa., cavalry. While confined in Pemberton, Barrett's Libby, Andersonville and other
southern prisons. Sole survivor of 127 of his
regiment captured the same time, 122 dying in
Andersonville. Briston, Pa., C. A. Dougherty,
printer, 1908.
2 p.l., 75, [1] p. front. (port.) 19 1/2 cm.

Douglas, Stephen Arnold, 1813.
Execution of United States laws. Speeches ...
delivered in the Senate of the United States,
February 23, 1855, on the bill ... to protect
officers and other persons acting under the authority of the United States. [Washington, Congressional Globe office, 1855].
8 p. 24 cm.

Douglas, Stephen Arnold, 1813-1861.
Kansas-Lecompton convention. Speech ... on
the President's message, delivered in the Senate
of the United States, December 9, 1857. Washington, Lemuel Towers, 1857.
15 p. 22 1/2 cm.

Douglas, Stephen Arnold, 1813-1861.
Letter ... in explanation of the Nebraska
and Kansas Territorial Bill. Washington, Robert
Armstrong, 1854.
7 p. 23 cm.

Douglas, Stephen Arnold, 1813-1861.
The Nebraska question comprising speeches in

161

the United States Senate by Mr. Douglas, Mr.
Chase, Mr. Smith, Mr. Everett, Mr. Wade, Mr.
Badger, Mr. Seward and Mr. Sumner together with
the history of the Missouri Compromise. Daniel
Webster's memorial in regard to it. History of
the annexation of Texas - the organization of
Oregon territory. And the compromises of 1850.
New York, J. S. Redfield, 1854.
    119 p.   23 1/2 cm.

Douglas, Stephen Arnold, 1813.
    Non-interference by Congress with slavery in
the territories. Speech ... in the Senate of the
United States, May 15 & 16, 1860. Washington,
D. C., Printed by Lem. Towers [1860?]
    32 p.   22 cm.

Douglas, Stephen Arnold, 1813.
    Non-intervention, popular sovereignty. Speech
in the Senate of the United States, February 23,
1859, in reply to Hon. A. G. Brown, of Mississippi ... Washington, Lemuel Towers, 1859.
    32 p.   25 cm.

Douglas, Stephen Arnold, 1813.
    Popular sovereignty in the territories. Re-
joinder of Judge Douglas to Judge Black. [Washing-
ton? 1859?]
    15 p.   24 cm.

Douglas, Stephen Arnold, 1813.
    Remarks of Senator Douglas, of Illinois, in
reply to Senator Collamer, on Kansas territorial
affairs. Delivered in the Senate of the United
States April 4, 1856. Washington, Printed at the
Union office, 1856.
    15 p.   22 cm.

Douglas, Stephen Arnold, 1813-1861.
    Speech ... in the Senate, January 30, 1854,
on the Nebraska territory. Washington, Sentinel
office, 1854.
    14 p.   23 cm.

Douglas, Stephen Arnold, 1813.
    Speech ... in the United States Senate, March
3, 1854, on Nebraska and Kansas. Washington,
Printed at the Sentinel office, 1854.
    30 p.   21 cm.

Douglas, Stephen Arnold, 1813.
Speech of Mr. Douglas of Illinois, on the
territorial question. Delivered in Senate of
the United States, March 13 and 14, 1850.
Washington, Printed by John T. Towers, 1850.
31 p. 25 cm.

Douglas, Stephen Arnold, 1813.
Speech ... on the invasion of the states;
and his reply to Mr. Fessenden. Delivered in
the Senate of the United States, January 28, 1860.
[Washington] Printed by Lemuel Towers [1860?]
15 p, 24 cm.

Douglas, Stephen Arnold, 1813-1861.
Speech ... on the Kansas territorial affairs.
Delivered in the Senate United States, March 20,
1856. Washington, Union office, 1856.
29 p. 23 cm.

Douglas, Stephen Arnold, 1813.
Speech ... on the "measures of adjustment."
delivered in the city hall, Chicago, October 27,
1850. Washington, Gideon & co., 1851.
32 p. 23 cm.

Douglas, Stephen Arnold, 1813.
State of the union. Speeches of Hon. Stephen
A. Douglas, of Illinois, in the Senate of the
United States, March 15, 25, and 26, 1861.
[Washington? 1861?]
24 p. 24 cm.

Douglass, Frederick, 1817.
Lectures on American slavery ... delivered at
Corinthian hall, Rochester, N. Y. [n.p., 1850?]
32 p. 22 cm.

Douglass, Frederick, 1817.
My bondage and my freedom. Part I. - Life as
a slave. Part II. - Life as a freeman ... With
an introduction by Dr. James M'Cune Smith ...
New York and Auburn, Miller, Orton & Mulligan,
1855.
xxxi, [32]-464 p. illus. 17 1/2 cm.

Douglass, Frederick, 1817.
Narrative of the life of Frederick Douglass,
an American slave. Written by himself. Boston,
Published by the anti-slavery office, 1846.

xvi, 125 p. front. (port.) 19 cm.

Douglass, Frederick, 1817.
Oration, delivered in Corinthian hall, Rochester ... July 5th, 1852 ... Rochester, Printed by
Lee, Mann & co., 1852.
39 p. 21 1/2 cm.

Douglass, Frederick, 1817.
Sklaverei und Freiheit ... aus dem Englischen
uebertragen von Ottilie Assing. Hamburg, Hoffmann und Campe, 1860.
xiv, 366 p. 18 cm.

Douglass, Frederick, 1817.
Two speeches ... one on West India emancipation, delivered at Canandaigua, Aug. 4th, and
other on the Dred Scott decision, delivered in
New York, on the occasion of the anniversary of
the American abolition society, May, 1857. Rochester, N. Y., C. P. Dewey, printer, American
office [n.d.]
46 p. 21 cm.

[Douglass, William] 1691? - 1752.
A summary, historical and political, of the
first planting, progressive improvements, and
present state of the British settlements in
North-America; with some transient accounts of
the bordering French and Spanish settlements...
Boston: Printed and sold by Rogers and Fowle
in Queen-street, next to the prison, 1747-1752.
2 vols. in 62 (?) Nos. 21 cm.

Dow, Lorenzo, 1777-
History of Cosmopolite: or The writings of
Rev. Lorenzo Dow: containing his experience and
travels, in Europe and America, up to near his
fiftieth year. Also, his polemic writings. To
which is added, the "Journey of Life," by Peggy
Dow. Rev. and cor. with notes ... Philadelphia,
S. B. Smith & co., 1859.
vii, 9-720p. 2 port. (incl. front.) 22 cm.

Dow, Mrs. Peggy, 1780-
Vicissitudes exemplified; or, The journey of
life. New York, Printed by J. C. Totten, 1814.
124 p. front. (port.) 14 cm.

Dowling, Morgan E.
Southern prisons; or, Josie the heroine of
Florence. Four years of battle and imprisonment.
Richmond, Atlanta, Belle Isle, Andersonville and
Florence, a complete history of all southern
prisons ... By Morgan E. Dowling ... Detroit, W.
Graham, 1870.
xii, [13]-506 p. 16 pl., 2 port. (incl.
front.) 22 cm.

Doy, John.
The narrative of John Doy, of Lawrence, Kansas ... New York, Thomas Holman, 1860.
132 p. 18 cm.

Drake, James Madison, 1837-
Fast and loose in Dixie. An unprejudiced
narrative of personal experience as a prisoner
of war at Libby, Macon, Savannah, and Charleston,
with an account of a desperate leap from a moving
train of cars, a weary tramp of forty-five days
through swamps and mountains, places and people
visited, etc., etc. By J. Madison Drake ... New
York, The Author's publishing company, 1880.
x, [11]-310 p. incl. front., plates, ports.
20 cm.

Drake, Samuel Adams, 1833-
Florida: its history, condition, and resources ... Boston, Little, Brown & co., 1878.
15 p. fold. map. 19 cm.

Drake, Samuel Adams, 1833-
Georgia: its history, condition, and resources ... New York, C. Scribner's sons, 1879.
31 p. map. 16 cm.

Drayton, Daniel.
Personal memoir of Daniel Drayton for four
years and four months a prisoner (for charity's
sake) in Washington jail including a narrative
of the voyage and capture of the schooner Pearl
... Boston, Bela Marsh; New York, American and
foreign anti-slavery society, 1855.
122 p. front. (port.) 19 cm.

Drayton, John, 1766-
A view of South-Carolina, as respects her
natural and civil concerns ... Charleston: Printed by W. P. Young, no. 41, Broad street, 1802.

252 p., 2 p.l., 1 1. plates (part fold.)
fold. maps (incl. front.) fold. tables.
22 cm.

Dresser, Amos.
The Bible against war ... Oberlin, Printed
for the author, 1849.
276 p.   15 cm.

[Dresser, Amos]
The narrative of Amos Dresser, with Stone's
letter from Natchez ... and two letters from
Tallahassee, relating to the treatment of slaves.
New York, Published by the American anti-slavery
society, 1836.
42 p.   18 cm.

Dresser, Amos.
Narrative of the arrest, lynch law trial, and
scourging of Amos Dresser, at Nashville, Tennessee, August, 1835. Oberlin, printed for the
author, 1849.
24 p.   15 cm.

Drew, Benjamin.
A north-side view of slavery. The Refugee:
or the narratives of fugitive slaves in Canada.
Related by themselves, with an account of the
history and condition of the colored population
of Upper Canada ... Boston, Published by John
P. Jewett and company, 1856.
xii, 387 p.   19 cm.

Driggs, George W.
Opening of the Mississippi; or, Two years'
campaigning in the South-west. A record of the
campaigns, sieges, actions and marches in which
the 8th Wisconsin volunteers have participated.
Together with correspondence, by a non-com-
missioned officer. Madison, Wis., W. J. Park
& co., printers, 1864.
149, [1] p.   21 cm.

Du Bose, John Witherspoon, 1836-
The life and times of William Lowndes Yancey.
A history of political parties in the United
States from 1834 to 1864; especially as to the
origin of the Confederate States. Birmingham
[Ala.] Roberts & son, 1892.
xiv p., 1 1., 752 p. pl., 8 port. (incl.

front.)   25 cm.

Duden, Gottfried.
   Bericht über eine reise nach den westlichen
staaten Nordamerika's und einem mährjährigen Aufenthalt am Missouri (in den Jahren 1824, 25, 26
und 1827) in bezug auf auswanderung und ueber-
völkerung ... Elberfeld, Gedruckt bei S. Lucas,
1829.
   xvi, 348 p.   21 1/2 cm.

[Dudley, Mary]
   Scripture evidence of the sinfulness of injustice and oppression. Respectfully submitted
to professing Christians, in order to call forth
their sympathy and exertions, on behalf of the
much-injured Africans ... London, Printed for
Harvey and Barton, 1828.
   26 p.   front.   18 cm.

Duffield, George, 1794-
   A sermon on American slavery: its nature and
the duties of Christians in relation to it.   Detroit, J. S. and S. A. Bagg, printer, 1840.
   32 p.   22 1/2 cm.

Duffield, George.
   Travels in the two hemispheres ... by George
Duffield [et al.] ... Second edition ... Detroit,
Doughty, Straw & co., and Raymond and Selleck,
1858.
   vi, 576 p.   front.   21 1/2 cm.

Dufur, Simon Miltimore, 1843-
   Over the dead line; or, Tracked by blood-hounds;
giving the author's personal experience during
eleven months that he was confined in Pemberton,
Libby, Belle Island, Andersonville, Ga., and
Florence, S. C., as a prisoner of war.   Describing
plans of escape and recapture; with numerous and
varied incidents and anecdotes of his prison life.
By S. M. Dufur ... [Burlington, Vt., Printed by
Free press association, 1902].
   viii, 283 p.   front.   (port.)   21 cm.

Dugan, James.   corporal 14th Ill. infantry.
   History of Hurlbut's fighting Fourth division:
and especially the marches, toils, privations,
adventures, skirmishes and battles of the Fourteenth
Illinois infantry; together with camp scenes,

anecdotes, battle-incidents; also a description
of the towns, cities and countries through which
their marches have extended since the commencement of the war; to which is added official reports of the battles in which they were engaged;
with portraits of many distinguished officers;
by James Dugan ... Cincinnati, E. Morgan & co.,
1863.
viii, 9-265 p. front., port. 20 cm.

Duganne, Augustine Joseph Hickey, 1823-1884.
Camps and prisons. Twenty months in the department of the Gulf. By A.J. H. Duganne ...
New York, 1865.
424 p. front., pl. 19 cm.

Dugard, Marie, 1862-
La société américaine; moeurs et caractère -
la famille - role de la femme - écoles et uni-
versités, par M. Dugard. 2. éd. Paris, Hachette
et cie, 1896.
2 p.l., 320 p. 18 1/2 cm.

Duke, John K. 1844-
History of the Fifty-third regiment Ohio volunteers infantry, during the war of the rebellion,
1861 to 1865. Together with more than thirty
personal sketches of officers and men. By John
K. Duke, company F, Fifty-third O.V.V.I. Portsmouth, O., The Blade printing company, 1900.
4 p.l., 303, [1] p. front., plates, ports.
22 cm.

Dumas, Mathieu, comte, 1753-
Memoirs of his own time; including the revolution, the empire, and the restoration ... Philadelphia, Lea & Blanchard, 1839.
2v. 20 1/2 cm.

Dumont de Montigny, Lieutenant.
Mémoires historiques sur la Louisiana, contenant ce qui y est arrivé de plus mémorable depuis l'année 1687, jusqu'à présent ... Composés
sur les mémoires de M. Dumont, par M. L. L. M.
... Paris, C. J. B. Bauche, 1753.
2v. 6 plates, fold. maps, 3 fold. plans.
16 cm.

Duncan, James.
A treatise on slavery ... Vevay, Printed at the Indiana Register office; New York, Reprinted and published by the American anti-slavery society, 1840.
136 p.   19 cm.

[Duncan, Mrs. Mary (Grey) Lundie]
America as I found it. By the mother of Mary Lundie Duncan ... New York, R. Carter & brothers, 1852.
[v]-vii, [11]-440 p.   1 p.1.,   1 l.   17 1/2 cm.

Duncan, Thomas D.
Recollections of Thomas D. Duncan, a Confederate soldier. Nashville, Tenn., McQuiddy printing company, 1922.
213 p.   ports.   20 cm.

Du Pont, Henry Algernon, 1838-1926.
The campaign of 1864 in the valley of Virginia and the expedition to Lynchburg, by H. A. Du Pont ... New York, National Americana society, 1925.
5 p.1., 3-188 p.   front. (port.)   maps.
23 1/2 cm.

[Durand, of Dauphine]
Voyages d'un François, exilé pour la religion, avec une description de la Virginie & Marilan dans l'Amérique. La Haye, Impr. pour l'auteur, 1687.
140 p.   13 1/2 cm.

Dureau, B. 1820-
Les États-Unis en 1850, notes et souvenirs ... Paris, Chez l'auteur, 1891.
iv, 540 p.   2 p.1.   19 cm.

[Durell, Edward Henry] 1810-
New Orleans as I found it. By H. Didimus [pseud.] New York, Harper & Brothers, 1845.
125, [2] p.   25 cm.

Du Roi, August Wilhelm.
Journal of Du Roi the elder, lieutenant and adjutant, in the service of the Duke of Brunswick, 1776-1778. Translated from the original German manuscript in the Library of Congress ... by Charlotte S. J. Epping. Philadelphia, Uni-

versity of Pennsylvania; New York, D. Appleton &
co., agents, 1911.
189 p. 3 p.l., 2 facsim., tables. 25 1/2 cm.

Du Ru, Paul, 1666-
Journal of Paul du Ru [February 1 to May 8,
1700] missionary priest to Louisiana; translated,
with introduction and notes, from a manuscript
in the Newberry library, by Ruth Lapham Butler.
Chicago, Printed for the Caxton club, 1934.
x, 74 p., 1 l. 24 cm.

The duty and safety of immediate emancipation. [n.p.,
n.d.]
12 p. 17 1/2 cm.

The duty of Pennsylvania concerning slavery. [Phila-
delphia, Anti-slavery office, n.d.]
8 p. 23 cm.

Duty of voting for righteous men for office. [Cin-
cinnati, American reform tract and book society,
n.d.]
8 p. 18 cm.

Duvergier de Hauranne, Ernest, i.e. Louis Prosper
Ernest, 1843-
Huit mois en Amérique, lettres et notes de
voyage, 1864-1865 ... Paris, Lacroix, Verboeck-
hoven & cie., 1866.
2 v. 18 1/2 cm.

Dwight, Theodore.
An oration, spoken before "The Connecticut
society, for the promotion of freedom and the relief of persons unlawfully holden in bondage,"
Convened in Hartford, on the 8th day of May, A.D.
1794 ... Hartford, Hudson and Goodwin, 1794.
24 p. 19 1/2 cm.

Dyer, John Will.
Reminiscences; or, Four years in the Confederate army. A history of the experiences of the
private soldier in camp, hospital, prison, on
the march, and on the battlefield. 1861 to 1865.
Evansville, Ind., Keller printing and publishing
co., 1898.
323 p. front., illus. 19 1/2 cm.

Dymond, Jonathan.
    The rights of self-defence. Philadelphia,
Published by the Tract association of Friends
[n.d.]
    8 p.   18 cm.

E

Eastman, Mary H.
    Aunt Phillis's cabin; or, Southern life as
it is ... Philadelphia, Lippincott, Grambo & co.,
1852.
    280 p.   front., title vignette.   20 cm.

[Eastman, Z.]
    Slavery a falling tower. A lecture on slavery,
the cause of the civil war in the United States.
Delivered at Alley Chapel, Bristol, June, 1862 ...
Second edition. Chicago, John R. Walsh [1862?]
    24 p.   19 cm.

Easton, Hosea.
    A treatise on the intellectual character, and
civil and political condition of the colored
people of the U. States; and the prejudice exer-
cised towards them: with a sermon on the duty
of the church to them... Boston, Isaac Knapp, 1837.
    54 p.   23 cm.

Eby, Henry Harrison, 1841-
    Observations of an Illinois boy in battle,
camp and prisons - 1861 to 1865, by Henry H. Eby.
Mendota, Ill., The author, 1910.
    284 p.   incl. front., illus., port., map.
20 cm.

Eddis, William, 1745?
    Letters from America, historical and descrip-
tive; comprising occurrences from 1769, to 1777,
inclusive ... London, Printed for the author, 1792.
    455 p.   24 p.l.   21 cm.

Eddy, Richard, 1828-1906.
    History of the Sixtieth regiment New York state
volunteers, from the commencement of its organization in July, 1861, to its public reception at

Ogdensburgh as a veteran command, January 7th,
1864. By Richard Eddy, chaplain. Philadelphia,
Pub. by the author, 1864.
xii, 360 p. 19 1/2 cm.

Eden, Robert C. d. 1907.
The sword and gun, a history of the 37th Wis.
volunteer infantry. From its first organization
to its final muster out. By Major R. C. Eden.
Madison, Atwood & Rublee, printers, 1865.
120 p. 16 1/2 cm.

Edgerton, Sidney, 1818.
The irrepressible conflict. Speech ... delivered in the House of Representatives, February 29, 1860. [n.p., n.d.]
8 p. 24 cm.

Edinburgh society for promoting the mitigation and
ultimate abolition of Negro slavery. The first
annual report ... with an appendix. Edinburgh,
Printed for the Society, 1824.
29 p. 20 1/2 cm.

Edmonds, S. Emma E.
Nurse and spy in the Union army: comprising
the adventures and experiences of a woman in hospitals, camps, and battle-fields. By S. Emma E.
Edmonds ... Hartford, W. S. Williams & co.; Philadelphia [etc.] Jones bros. & co., 1865.
384 p. front. (port.) pl. 21 1/2 cm.

Edmunds, George Franklin, 1828.
Enforcement of fourteenth amendment. Speech...
in the Senate of the United States, April 14, 1871.
[Washington, D. C., Congressional Globe office,
1871?]
24 p. 25 cm.

Edmundson, William, 1827 -
A journal of the life, travels, sufferings and
labour of love in the work of the ministry, of
that worthy elder and faithful servant of Jesus
Christ, William Edmundson ... The 2d ed. London,
Printed and sold by M. Hinde, 1774.
lxxv, 371, [32] p. 21 cm.

Edward, David B.
    The history of Texas; or, The emigrant's, far-
mer's and politician's guide to the character,
climate, soil and productions of that country ...
Cincinnati, J. A. James & co., 1836.
    xii, 13-336 p.   front. (fold. map) 18 1/2 cm.

Edwards, Bela Bates, 1802.
    Inquiry into the state of slavery in the early
and middle ages of the Christian era ... Edinburgh,
Thomas Clark, 1836.
    45 p.   17 cm.

Edwards, Bela Bates, 1802-
    Memoir of the Rev. Elias Cornelius. Boston,
Perkins & Marvin; Philadelphia, H. Perkins, 1833.
    ix, [13]-360 p.   1 1., front. (port.) 19 cm.

Edwards, Bela Bates, 1802-
    Writings ... with a memoir by Edwards A. Park.
Boston, John P. Jewett and company [etc.] 1853.
    2 v.   20 cm.

Edwards, John L.
    Edwards' guide to east Florida. Historical,
geographical, descriptive, climatic, &c. ...
[Jacksonville, Fla., Ashmead bros., 1881]
    vi, 7-148 p.   24 cm.

Edwards, Jonathan, 1745.
    The injustice and impolicy of the slave trade,
and of the slavery of the Africans: illustrated
in a sermon preached ... September 15, 1791 ...
Third edition. New Haven, Published by the New
Haven Anti-slavery society, 1833.
    32 p.   21 cm.

Edwards, Richard, ed.
    Statistical gazetteer of the state of Virginia,
embracing important topographical and historical
information ... together with the results of the
last census population, in most cases, to 1854.
Edited by Richard Edwards ... Richmond, For the
proprietor, 1855.
    [53]-456 p.   2 p.1., illus.   23 1/2 cm.

Egan, Michael, 1826?-
    The flying, gray-haired Yank; or, The adven-
tures of a volunteer ... A true narrative of the

civil war. [n.p.] Edgewood [c1888]
  414 p. incl. front., plates, ports. plates.
19 1/2 cm.

Eggleston, George Cary, 1839-1911.
  A rebel's recollections. New York, Hurd and
Houghton; Cambridge [Mass.] The Riverside press,
1875.
  vi p., 1 l., 260 p. 18 cm.

Egleston, R. S.
  Human legislation void when it conflicts with
the law of God. A discourse, delivered in the
Congregational church, Madison, O., August 31,
1856 ... Cleveland, Harris, Fairbanks & co.,
1856.
  20 p. 23 cm.

Ehrenberg, Hermann.
  Texas und seine revolution ... Leipzig, O.
Wigand, 1843.
  iv, 258 p. 21 1/2 cm.

The eleventh Massachusetts anti-slavery fair. Boston, 1844. Broadside.
  25 cm.

Ellet, Elizabeth Fries (Lummis) 1818-
  Rambles about the country. New York, Harper,
1847.
  257 p. 16 cm.

Ellet, Mrs. Elizabeth Fries (Lummis) 1818-
  Summer rambles in the West. New-York, J. C.
Riker, 1853.
  viii, 269 p. 19 cm.

Ellicott, Andrew, 1754-
  The journal of Andrew Ellicott, late commissioner on behalf of the United States during part
of the year 1796, the years 1797, 1798, 1799, and
part of the year 1800; for determining the boundary
between the United States and the possessions of
his Catholic Majesty in America ... Philadelphia,
Printed by Budd & Bertram, for Thomas Dobson, 1803.
  vii, 299, 151 p., 1 l. illus., 6 fold. plates,
8 fold. maps. 25 1/2 cm.

Elliott, Charles.
The Bible and slavery ... Cincinnati, L.
Swormstedt and A. Poe, for the Methodist Episcopal church, 1859.
354 p.   19 cm.

Elliott, Charles
Sinfulness of American slavery; proved from
its evil sources; its wrongs; its contrariety to
many scriptural commands, prohibitions and principles, and to the Christian spirit; and from its
evil effects; together with observations on emancipation, and the duties of American citizens in
regard to slavery ... Cincinnati, L. Swormstedt &
J. H. Power, 1851.
2 v.   18 1/2 cm.

Elliott, E. N.
Cotton is king, and pro-slavery arguments:
comprising the writings of Hammond, Harper, Christy, Stringfellow, Hodge, Bledsoe, and Cartwright,
on this important subject ... with an essay on
slavery in the light of international law, by the
editor ... Augusta, Ga., Pritchard, Abbott &
Loomis, 1860.
xv, [16]-908 p.   front., ports.   24 1/2 cm.

Elliott, John A.
All about Texas, a handbook of information for
the home seeker, the capitalist, the prospector,
the tourist, the health hunter, containing a
description of the state, its area, topography ...
Austin, J. H. Traynham, 1888.
3 p.l., [3-47] [23] p.   23 1/2 cm.

Elliott, William, 1788.
The letters of Agricola, Pub. in the Southern
standard, June, 1851. Greenville, S. C., Office
of the Southern patriot, 1852.
15 p.   22 1/2 cm.

Ellis, Daniel, 1827-
Thrilling adventures of Daniel Ellis, the
great Union guide of east Tennessee, for a period
of nearly four years during the great southern
rebellion. Written by himself. Containing a
short biography of the author ... New York, Harper & brothers, 1867.
1 p.l., [5]-430 p.   incl. illus., ports., map.

front.   19 1/2 cm.

Ellis, George E.
"The preservation of the states united:" A
discourse delivered in Harvard Church, Charles-
town, on Thanksgiving day, Nov. 29, 1860 ...
Charlestown, Abram E. Cutler, 1860.
29 p.   23 cm.

Ellis, Thomas T.
Leaves from the diary of an army surgeon; or,
Incidents of field, camp, and hospital life. By
Thomas T. Ellis ... New York, J. Bradburn, 1863.
312 p.   facsim.   19 cm.

Ellison, Thomas.
Slavery and secession in America, historical
and economical ... London, Sampson Low, son & co.
[n.d.]
xvi, 371 p.   fold. map.   19 cm.

Elmore, Franklin Harper, 1799-
Correspondence between the Hon. F. H. Elmore...
and James G. Birney ... New York, American anti-
slavery society, 1838.
68 p.   22 cm.

Ely, Alfred, 1815-1892.
Journal of Alfred Ely, a prisoner of war in
Richmond. Edited by Charles Lanman. New York,
D. Appleton and company, 1862.
359 p.   front. (port.) pl.   20 1/2 cm.

...Emancipation. By a member of the Board. Boston?
1839?
At head of title: Poem dedicated to the board
of the Boston female anti-slavery society, to the
women of Great Britain, in commemoration of their
untiring efforts in the cause of the British West
Indies.
35 p.   15 cm.

...Emancipation. Cincinnati, American reform tract
and book society, [n.d.]
12 p.   17 cm.

Emancipation in the West Indies, in 1838.
[n.p., n.d.]
32 p.   21 cm.

176

Emancipation league.
    Facts concerning the freedmen. Their capacity
and their destiny. Collected and published by
the Emancipation league. Boston, Press of Commercial printing house, 1863.
    12 p.   23 cm.

The emancipator (complete).
    Published by Elihu Embree, Jonesborough, Ten-
nessee, 1820. A reprint ... to which are added a
biographical sketch of Elihu Embree ... and two
hitherto unpublished anti-slavery memorials bearing the signature of Elihu Embree. Nashville,
Tenn., B. H. Murphy, publisher, 1932.
    xi, 112 p.   25 cm.

Emch, Arnold, 1871-
    Reise- und kulturbilder aus den Vereinigten
Staaten von America, insbesondere aus dem "fer-
nen Westen." Eine sammlung von studien von dr.
Arnold Emch and Hermann Emch. Mit 12 vollbildern.
Aarau, H. R. Sauerländer & co., 1908.
    iv, 272 p.   12 pl.   (incl. front.)   23 1/2 cm.

Emerson, Ralph Waldo, 1803.
    An address delivered in the court-house in
Concord, Massachusetts, on 1st August, 1844, on
the anniversary of the emancipation of the Negroes in the British West Indies ... Boston, James
Munroe and company, 1844.
    34 p.   20 1/2 cm.

The Emigrant's guide, or pocket geography of the wes-
    tern states and territories, containing a des-
    cription of the several cities and towns, rivers,
    antiquities, population, manufactories, prices
    of land, soil, productions, and exports. Com-
    piled from the best and latest authorities. Cin-
    cinnati: Published by Phillips & Speer, book-
    sellers, Main-street, near Front. Morgan, Lodge
    & co., printers, 1818.
    iv, [5] - 266 p.   15 cm.

Emmerton, James Arthur.
    A record of the Twenty-third regiment Mass.
vol. infantry in the war of the rebellion 1861-
1865 with alphabetical roster; company rolls ...
etc., by James A. Emmerton ... Boston, W. Ware
& co., 1886.

xx, 352 p. front., pl., port., maps (partly fold.) 23 1/2 cm.

The enemies of the constitution discovered, or, An inquiry into the origin and tendency of popular violence. Containing a complete and circumstantial account of the unlawful proceedings at the city of Utica, October 21st, 1835; the dispersion of the state anti-slavery convention by the agitators ... By Defensor. New York, Leavitt, Lord & co., 1835.
xii, [9] - 183 p. 17 cm.

Engleheart, Sir John Gardner Dillman, 1823-
Journal of the progress of H.R.H. the Prince of Wales through British North America; and his visit to the United States, 10th July to 15th November, 1860 ... [London, Priv. print., 1860?]
110 p. 3 p.l., 1 l. illus. 9 pl. (incl. front.) 2 fold. maps. 24 cm.

English, William Hayden, 1822-
Conquest of the country northwest of the river Ohio, 1778-1783; and life of George Rogers Clark ... Indianapolis, Ind., and Kansas City, Mo., The Bowen-Merrill company, 1869.
xv. fronts., illus., plates, ports., maps, facsims. 25 1/2 cm.

Ennis, John W.
Adventures in rebeldom; or, Ten months experience of prison life ... New York, "Business mirror" print, 1863.
60 p. 12 cm.

An enquiry which of the two parties is best entitled to freedom? The slave or the slaveholder? From an impartial examination of the conduct of each party, at the bar of public justice ... London, Baldwin, Cradock and Joy, 1824.
28 p. 1 20 1/2 cm.

Entick, John, 1703?
The present state of the British empire. Containing a description of the kingdoms, principalities, islands, colonies, conquests, and of the military and commercial establishments, under the British crown, in Europe, Asia, Africa and America. By the late Rev. John Entick, M. A., and

178

other gentlemen. Illustrated with maps... engraved
from the best authorities, by T. Kitchen & co. ...
London, B. Law [etc.] 1774.
4 v. front. (v. 4) fold. maps. 21 cm.

Escalante Fontaneda, Hernando d'.
Memoir of Dᵒ Escalante Fontaneda respecting
Florida. Written in Spain, about the year 1575.
Translated from the Spanish with notes by Buckingham Smith. Washington: 1854. Reprinted, with
revisions. Miami, Fla., 1944.
[3]-77 p., 1 l. incl. front. (map) illus.
(facsim.) 24 cm.

Espy, Josiah Murdoch, 1771-1847.
Memorandums of a tour made by Josiah Espy in
the states of Ohio and Kentucky and Indiana territory in 1805. Cincinnati, R. Clarke & co., 1870.
viii, 28 p. 1 l. 25 cm.

Esquisse intéressant du Tableau fidèle des causes qui
ont occasioné les révolutions actuelles de l'Amérique Septentrionale ... Revu & corrigé à Versailles.
Philadelphia, 1783.
124 p. 20 cm.

Estabrooks, Henry L.
Adrift in Dixie; or, A Yankee officer among
the Rebels. With an introduction by Edmund
Kirke [pseud.] New York, Carleton, 1866.
224 p. 19 cm.

Estournelles de Constant, Paul Henri Benjamin, baron
d', 1852-
...Les États-Unis d'Amérique. Paris, A. Colin,
1913.
ix, 536 p. fold. map. 19 cm.

Estvan, Bela, b. 1827.
War pictures from the South. By E. Estvan ...
New York, D. Appleton and company, 1863.
viii, 332 p. 21 cm.

Etheridge, Emerson, 1819-
Nebraska and Kansas. Speech ... In the House
of Representatives, May 17, 1854. Washington,
Buell & Blanchard, 1854.
14 p. 23 cm.

179

Etheridge, Emerson, 1819.
State of the union. Speech ... delivered in
the House of Representatives, Jan. 23, 1861.
Washington, Printed by Henry Polkinhorn, 1861.
15 p. 25 cm.

Étourneau.
Livret-guide de l'émigrant, du négociant et
du touriste dans les États-Unis d'Amérique et au
Canada, contenant les renseignements les plus ex-
acts, pris sur les lieux memes, sur ces contrées
... Paris, A. Petit-Pierre, 1855.
211, [1]p. 2 p.l. 16 cm.

Evangelical consociation, Rhode Island.
Fellowship with slavery. Report republished
from the minutes of the Evangelical consociation,
Rhode Island. Cincinnati, American reform tract
and book society, [n.d.]
32 p. 18 cm.

Evans, Estwick, 1787-
A pedestrious tour, of four thousand miles,
through the western states and territories, during
the winter and spring of 1818. Interspersed with
brief reflections upon a great variety of topics
...Concord: N. H., printed by Joseph C. Spear,
1819.
256 p. front. (port.) 18 cm.

Evans, Lewis, 1700?
Geographical, historical, political, philosophical and mechanical essays. The first, containing An analysis of a general map of the
middle British colonies in America ... Philadelphia: Printed by B. Franklin and D. Hall, 1755.
iv, 32 p. fold. map. 28 cm.

Everest, Robert.
A journey through the United States and part
of Canada. London, John Chapman, 1855.
xi, 178 p. 23 cm.

Everett, Edward, 1794.
An address delivered at the inauguration of
the Union club, 9 April, 1863 ... Boston, Little,
Brown, and company, 1863.
61 p. 23 cm.

Everett, Edward, 1794.
    Address of Hon. Edward Everett. [n.p., n.d.]
    19 p.   23 cm.

Everett, Edward, 1794.
    Address of the Hon. Edward Everett, at the an-
niversary of the American colonization society,
January 15, 1853. [Boston, Massachusetts colonization society, 1853?]
    11 p.   22 cm.

Everett, Edward, 1794.
    Address of Hon. Edward Everett, delivered in
Faneuil Hall, October 10, 1864. The duty of supporting the government in the present crisis of
affairs. [n.p., n.d.]
    16 p.   21 cm.

Everett, Edward, 1794.
    The questions of the day. An address, de-
livered in the Academy of music, in New York, on
the fourth of July, 1861 ... New York, Geo. P.
Putnam, 1861.
    46 p.   24 cm.

Everett, Edward.
    Speech of Mr. Everett, of Massachusetts, de-
livered in the Senate of the United States, Feb.
8, 1854, on the Nebraska and Kansas Territorial
Bill. Washington, Congressional Globe Office,
1854.
    14 p.   22 cm.

Ewbank, Thomas.
    Inorganic forces ordained to supersede human
slavery ... (Originally read before the American
ethnological society) New York, William Everdell
& sons, 1860.
    32 p.   22 cm.

Ewbank, Thomas, 1792-
    Life in Brazil; or, A journal of a visit to
the land of the cocoa and the palm. With an appendix, containing illustrations of ancient South
American arts ... New York, Harper & brothers,
1856.
    [v]-xvi, [17]-469 p. 1 p.l. illus.   23 cm.

181

Ewell, John D.
  Life of Rev. William Keele, a noted preacher
of the Baptist church for fifty-five years. Written by John D. Ewell, A. M., from data furnished
by William Keele, jr. Noah, Tenn., W. J. Stephenson, 1884.
  244 p.   19 cm.

Excursion guide to the Virginia springs and health resorts of western North Carolina and north Georgia.
Issued by the Passenger department of the Richmond
and Danville Railroad.   New York, Leve and Alden's
publication department, 1883.
  76 p.   map, illus.   24 1/2 cm.

The expedition of Major General Braddock to Virginia;
with the two regiments of Hacket and Dunbar.   Being extracts of letters from an officer in one
of those regiments to his friend in London, describing the march and engagement in the woods...
London: Printed for H. Carpenter, MDCCLV.
  [iii]-iv, 5-29 (i.e. 30) p.   2 p.l.   19 cm.

An exposition of the African slave trade, from the
year 1840, to 1850, inclusive.   Prepared from
official documents, and published by direction of
the religious Society of friends, in Pennsylvania,
New Jersey, and Delaware.   Philadelphia, For
sale at Friends' book store, 1851.
  160 p.   21 cm.

... The extinction of slavery.   A national necessity,
before the present conflict can be ended.   [n.p.,
n.d.]
  8 p.   19 cm.

Extracts from the American slave code.   Philadelphia?
Published by the Philadelphia female anti-slavery
society, [n.d.]
  4 p.   22 cm.

Extracts from remarks on Dr. Channing's Slavery, with
comments, by an abolitionist.   Boston, D. K. Hitchcock, 1836.
  55 p.   20 cm.

Extrait du journal d'un officier de la marine de l'es-
cadre de M. le comte d'Estaing.   [n.p.] 1782.
  126 p.   front. (port.)   20 cm.

Eyma, Louis Xavier, 1816-
Les deux Amériques; histoire, moeurs et voyages par Xavier Eyma. Paris, D. Giraud, 1853.
374 p. 2 p.l. 18 cm.

Eyma, Louis Xavier, 1816-
La vie aux États-Unis, notes de voyage ... Paris E. Plon et cie., 1876.
307 p. 2 p.l. 18 cm.

F

Faber, Kurt.
Rund um die Erde; Irrfahrten und Abenteuer eines Grünhorns. Berlin, Globus [n.d.]
319 p. 20 cm.

Fackler, Samuel A.
Ups and downs of a country editor, mostly downs, Tallahassee, Fla., Collins job print [1908?]
103 p. illus. (fronts.) 21 cm.

Facts and documents for the people. [n.p., n.d.]
24 p. 21 cm.

Facts for the people. No. 1. [n.p., n.d.]
16 p. 24 cm.

Facts for the people. v. 1, no. 4; Sept. 1843. Pittsburgh, 1843.
25-32 p. 22 1/2 cm.

Facts for the people. Nos. v, vi, viii, ix, x. [n.p., n.d.]

Facts for the people. New series. v. 1., nos. 3, 6, 8, 9, 12; Mar., June, Aug., Sept., Dec. 1843. Cincinnati, 1843.
5 nos. 24 cm.

Facts for the people; new series. v. 1.; May 1855-Apr. 1856. Washington, D. C., 1855-56.
192 p. 22 cm.

...Facts for the people of the free states. New York, Published by William Harned for the American and foreign anti-slavery society [n.d.]
[12] p. illus. 19 cm.

Fairbank, Calvin, 1816-
Rev. Calvin Fairbank during slavery times. How he "fought the good fight" to prepare "the way". Ed. from his manuscript. Chicago, Patriotic publishing co., 1890.
xi, 207 p. front. [2 port.] 20 1/2 cm.

Fairfield, Edmund B.
Christian patriotism: A sermon delivered in the Representatives' Hall, Lansing, Michigan, February 22, 1863, by Rev. Edmund B. Fairfield, LL. D., president of Hillsdale College. Lansing, John A. Kerr & co., Book and job printers, 1863.
40 p. 22 cm.

Fairfield, Edmund Burke.
Christian patriotism. A sermon delivered in Representatives' Hall, Lansing, Michigan, February 22, 1863 ... Lansing, John A. Kerr & co., book and job printers, 1863.
40 p. 22 cm.

Faithfull, Emily, 1835-
Three visits to America ... New York, Fowler & Wells co. [c1884]
xvi, 400 p. 19 1/2 cm.

Falconbridge, Alexander.
An account of the slave trade on the coast of Africa ... London, Printed by J. Phillips, 1788.
iv, 55 p. 19 cm.

Falk, Alfred.
Trans-Pacific sketches; a tour through the United States and Canada ... Melbourne [etc.] George Robertson, 1877.
xv, 313 p. 18 1/2 cm.

The family and slavery. By a native of the south-west. [Cincinnati, American reform tract and book society, n.d.]
24 p. 18 cm.

Famous adventures and prison escapes of the civil war.
New York, The Century co., 1893.
x p., 1 1., 338 p. incl. front., illus.
21 cm.

Fanning, David, 1756?
The narrative of Colonel David Fanning, (a
Tory in the revolutionary war with Great Britain;)
giving an account of his adventures in North
Carolina, from 1775 to 1783, as written by himself,
with an introduction [by John H. Wheeler] and
explanatory notes. Richmond, Va., printed for
private distribution only, in the first year of
the independence [!] of the Confederate States
of America, 1861.
xxv, 92 p.   28 1/2 cm.

Farley, Ephraim Wilder.
Nebraska and Kansas.   Speech of Hon. E. W. Far-
ley, of Maine, in the House of Representatives,
May 10, 1854. Washington, Congressional Globe
Office, 1854.
8 p.   22 1/2 cm.

Farley, Joseph Pearson, 1839-
Three rivers, the James, the Potomac, the
Hudson; a retrospect of peace and war, by Joseph
Pearson Farley ... New York and Washington, The
Neale Publishing company, 1910.
277 p.   col. front., 9 col. pl.   21 cm.

Farquhar, Robert Townsend.
Suggestions, arising from the abolition of
the African slave trade, for supplying the de-
mands of the West India colonies with agricultural labourers ... London, Printed for John
Stockdale, 1807.
66 p.   21 cm.

Faux, William.
Memorable days in America ... London, W. Simpkin and R. Marshall, 1823.
xvi, 488 p.   incl. front.   22 cm.

Favill, Josiah Marshall.
The diary of a young officer serving with the
armies of the United States during the war of the
rebellion, by Josiah Marshall Favill, adjutant,
captain, and brevet major 57th New York infantry,

brevet lieutenant-colonel, and colonel U. S. volunteers. Chicago, R. R. Donnelley & sons company,
1909.
298 p. fronts., plates, ports. 21 cm.

Fawcett, Joseph W.
Journal of Jos. W. Fawcett. (Diary of his
trip in 1840 down the Ohio and Mississippi rivers
to Gulf of Mexico and up the Atlantic coast to
Boston ...) Chillicothe, Ohio, D. K. Webb, private
press, 1944.
59 p. 14 cm.

The fearful issue to be decided in November next!
Shall the constitution and the union stand or fall?
Fremont, the sectional candidate of the advocates
of dissolution! Buchanan, the candidate of those
who advocate one country! one union! one constitution! and one destiny! [n.p., n.d.]
24 p. 20 cm.

Fearon, Henry Bradshaw, b. ca. 1770-
Sketches of America ... London, Printed for
Longman, Hurst, Rees, Orme, and Brown, 1818.
vii, [1]-462 p. 22 cm.

Featherstonhaugh, G. W.
Excursion through the slave states, from
Washington on the Potomac to the frontier of
Mexico; with sketches of popular manners and
geological notices ... New-York, Published by
Harper & brothers, 1844.
x, [11]-168 p. 23 cm.

Featherstonhaugh, George William, 1780-
A canoe voyage up the Minnay Sotor; with an
account of the lead and copper deposits in Wisconsin; of the gold region in the Cherokee country; and sketches of popular manners ... London,
R. Bentley, 1847.
2 v. fronts., illus., 2 fold maps. 23 cm.

Featherstonhaugh, George William, 1780-
Excursion through the slave states, from
Washington ... to the frontier of Mexico; with
sketches of popular manners and geological
notices ... London, J. Murray, 1844.
2 v. fronts., illus., fold. map. 23 cm.

186

Fedric, Francis.
Slave life in Virginia and Kentucky; or, Fifty
years of slavery in the southern states of America. By Francis Fedric, an escaped slave. With
preface, by the Rev. Charles Lee. London, Wert-
heim, Macintosh, and Hunt, 1863.
viii, 115 p.   15 1/2 cm.

Fee, John Gregg, 1816-
Autobiography of John G. Fee, Berea, Kentucky.
Chicago, Ill., National Christian association,
1891.
211 p.   front.   [port.]   18 1/2 cm.

Fee, John Gregg, 1816.
Colonization. The present scheme of colonization wrong, delusive, and retards emancipation.
[Cincinnati, American reform tract and book society n.d.]
48 p.   18 cm.

Fee, John Gregg, 1816.
Non-fellowship with slaveholders the duty of
Christians ... New York, John A. Gray, printer,
1851.
68 p.   19 cm.

Fee, John Gregg, 1816.
The sinfulness of slaveholding shown by appeals
to reason and scriptures. New York, Printed by
John A. Gray, 1851.
36 p.   17 cm.

Feemster, Zenas E.   1813-
The traveling refugee; or, The cause and cure
of the rebellion in the United States; embracing
a sketch of the state of society in the South,
before, and at the commencement of the rebellion.
Illustrated by facts and incidents. By Rev. Zenas
E. Feemster, refugee, from Mississippi, in 1862.
Springfield, Ills., Steam press of Baker & Phillips, 1865.
iv p., 2 l., [9]-195, [1] p.   18 cm.

Feltman, William.
The journal of Lieut. William Feltman, of the
First Pennsylvania regiment, 1781-82. Including
the march into Virginia and the siege of Yorktown.
Philadelphia, Published for the Historical Society

of Pennsylvania, by H. C. Baird, 1853.
    48 p.   24 1/2 cm.

Female anti-slavery society.
    Constitution and address. New-York, Printed
by William S. Dorr, 1834.
    16 p.   17 cm.

Fenning, Daniel.
    A new system of geography: or, A general des-
cription of the world. Containing a particular
and circumstantial account of all the countries,
kingdoms, and states of Europe, Asia, Africa, and
America ... By D. Fenning ... J. Collyer ... and
others ... London, Printed for S. Crowder, and
sold by Mr. Jackson [etc.] 1764-1765.
    2 v. front., 29 plates, 28 maps. (6 fold.)
35 1/2 cm.

Fenton, Feuben Eaton, 1819.
    Position of parties and abuse of power. Speech
...delivered in the House of Representatives,
February 16, 1860. [n.p., 1860?]
    8 p.   22 cm.

Ferguson, Fergus, 1824-
    From Glasgow to Missouri and back ... Glasgow,
T. D. Morison [etc.] 1878.
    vii, [1] 370 p.   19 cm.

Ferguson, Joseph.
    Life-struggles in Rebel prisons: a record of
the sufferings, escapes, adventures and starva-
tion of the Union prisoners. By Joseph Ferguson...
Containing an appendix with the names, regiments,
and date of death of Pennsylvania soldiers who
died at Andersonville. With an introduction by
Rev. Joseph T. Cooper, D. D. ... Philadelphia,
J. M. Ferguson, 1865.
    206, xxiv p. incl. front. (port.) pl.
17 1/2 cm.

Ferguson, Robert, 1817-
    America during and after the war ... London,
Longmans, Green, Reader and Dyer, 1866.
    4 p.l., ii p., 1 l. 280 p. 19 1/2 cm.

Ferguson, William.
    America by river and rail; or, Notes by the

way on the New world and its people ... London,
J. Nisbet and co., 1856.
  viii, 511 p.   2 pl. (incl. front.)   23 1/2
cm.

Ferree, Barr, 1862-1924.
  American estates and gardens, by Barr Ferree
... New York, Munn and company, 1904.
  xvi, 306 p. incl. front., illus. 7 pl.
34 1/2 x 28 cm.

Fessenden, William Pitt.
  Speech of W. P. Fessenden, of Maine, against
the repeal of the Missouri prohibition, north of
36 30'. Delivered in the Senate of the United
States, March 3, 1854, on the bill to establish
territorial governments in Nebraska and Kansas.
Washington, Buell & Blanchard, 1854.
  16 p.   22 1/2 cm.

Fessenden, William Pitt.
  Speech of Mr. Fessenden, of Maine, on the
message of the President transmitting the Lecompton Constitution. Delivered in the United States
Senate, February 8, 1858. Washington, Buell &
Blanchard, 1858.
  24 p.   22 1/2 cm.

A few facts respecting the American colonization society and the colony at Liberia ... Washington,
  Printed by Way and Gideon, 1830.
  16 p.   24 cm.

Fieharty, Stephen F.
  Our regiment. A history of the 102d Illinois
infantry volunteers, with sketches of the Atlanta
campaign, the Georgia raid, and the campaign of
the Carolinas. By S. F. Fieharty, Chicago, Brewster & Hanscom, printers, 1865.
  192, xxiv p.   19 1/2 cm.

Field, Charles D.
  Three years in the saddle from 1861 to 1865;
memoirs of Charles D. Field; thrilling stories of
the war in camp and on the field of battle ...
By Charles D. Field ... [Goldfield? Ia.,   c1898]
  74 p. front. (port.)   21 1/2 cm.

Field, Henry Martyn, 1822-
     Bright skies and dark shadows, by Henry M.
Field ... New York, C. Scribner's sons, 1890.
     [6] i-ii, [1] 9-316 p. front., illus. (plans)
map. 21 cm.

Field, Joseph E.
     Three years in Texas. Including a view of the
Texan revolution, and an account of the principal
battles, together with descriptions of the soil,
commercial and agricultural advantages, &c. ...
Greenfield, Mass., J. Jones; Boston, A. Tompkins,
1836.
     iv, [5]-47 p.   20 1/2 cm.

Fifteenth annual report, presented to the Pennsylvania
     Anti-Slavery Society, by its executive committee,
     October 25, 1852. With the proceedings of the
     annual meeting. Philadelphia, Anti-slavery of-
     fice, 1852.
     57 p.   23 cm.

[Figg, Royall W.]
     "Where men only dare to go!" or, The story of
a boy company (C.S.A.) By an ex-boy ... Richmond,
Whittet & Shepperson, 1885.
     viii, [17]-263 p. front., port.   20 1/2 cm.

Fillmore, Millard, pres. U. S., 1800.
     Mr. Fillmore's views on slavery. Answer to
"The crisis." Published by the Democratic state
central committee. [New Orleans? 1848?]
     3 p.   22 cm.

Filson, John, 1747?
     The discovery, settlement and present state
of Kentucke ... Wilmington [Del.] Printed by
James Adams, 1784.
     118 p. map.   21 1/2 cm.

Finch, John, fl. 1835-
     Travels in the United States of America and
Canada, containing some account of their scientific institutions, and a few notices of the geology
and mineralogy of those countries ... London,
Longman, Reese, Orme, Brown, Green, and Longman,
1833.
     [ix]-xv, 455 p. 3 p.l.   21 1/2 cm.

Finch, Marianne.
An Englishwoman's experience in America ...
London, R. Bentley, 1853.
viii, 386 p.   20 1/2 cm.

Finlay, Hugh.
Journal kept by Hugh Finlay, surveyor of the
post roads on the continent of North America ...
begun the 13th Septr., 1773 and ended 26th June
1774. Brooklyn, F. H. Norton, 1867.
xxv p., 94 p. 1 l., 1 illus., 2 maps (1 fold)
27 cm.

First annual report of the New York Young Men's Anti-
slavery Society; with addresses, delivered at the
anniversary. May, 1835, New York, Coolidge &
Lambert, 1835.
20 p.   22 cm.

The first Lincoln and Douglas debate. At Ottawa, Ill.,
Aug. 21, 1858.   [Boston, Directors of the Old
South work, Old South Meeting House, n.d.]
32 p.   19 cm.

First of August. Abolition of apprenticeship. Edinburgh, W. Oliphant and sons; Glasgow, George
Gallie & W. Smeal, 1838.
20 p.   21 cm.

Fish, Hamilton, 1808.
Fremont, the conservative candidate. Correspondence between Hon. Hamilton Fish, U. S. senator from New York, and Hon. James A. Hamilton,
son of Alexander Hamilton. [n.p., 1856?]
20 p.   21 cm.

[Fisher, Charles Edward]
Kansas [!] and the Constitution. By "Cecil"
[pseud.] Boston, Printed by Damrell & Moore, 1856.
16 p.   23 cm.

Fisher, Ellwood.
Lecture on the north and south, delivered before the Young men's mercantile library association, of Cincinnati, Ohio, January 16, 1849 ...
Cincinnati, Daily chronicle job rooms, 1849.
46 p.   22 cm.

Fisher, Ellwood.
The south and the north: being a reply to a
lecture on the north and the south, by Ellwood
Fisher, delivered before the Young Men's Mercantile Library Association of Cincinnati, January
16, 1849 ... Washington, Buell & Blanchard, 1849.
32 p.   25 cm.

Fisher, George Adams, 1835-
The Yankee conscript; or, Eighteen months in
Dixie. By George Adams Fisher. With an intro-
duction by Rev. William Dickson. Philadelphia,
J. W. Daughaday, 1864.
251 p.   front.   (port.)   plates.   18 cm.

Fisher, George E.
The church, the ministry, and slavery. A
discourse delivered at Rutland, Mass., July 14,
1850 ... Worcester, Printed by Henry J. Rowland
[1850].
23 p.   23 cm.

Fisher, Ruth A., comp.
Extracts from the records of the African companies, collected by Ruth A. Fisher. Washington,
D. C., The Association for the study of Negro
life and history, inc. [1930?]
108 p.   24 cm.

Fisk, Willbur.
Substance of an address delivered before the
Middletown colonization society, at their annual
meeting, July 4, 1834. Middletown, Printed by
G. F. Olmsted, 1834.
23 p.   22 cm.

[Fiske, Samuel Wheelock] 1828-1864.
Mr. Dunn Browne's experiences in the army ...
Boston, Nichols and Noyes; New York, O. S. Felt,
1866.
2 p.l., iii-xii, 11-390 p.   front. (port.)
19 cm.

Fitch, Charles.
Slaveholding weighed in the balance of truth,
and its comparative guilt illustrated. Boston,
Isaac Knapp, 1837.
36 p.   18 cm.

Fitch, Graham Newell.
    The slave question. Speech ... In the House
of Representatives, February 14, 1850. In committee of the whole on the state of the union,
on the resolutions referring the President's
message to the various standing committees. Washington, Congressional Globe office [n.d.]
    7 p.   23 cm.

Fithian, Philip Vickers, 1747-
    Philip Vickers Fithian, journal and letters,
1767-1774, student at Princeton college, 1770-72,
tutor at Nomini Hall in Virginia, 1773-74; edited
for the Princeton historical association by John
Rogers Williams. Princeton, N. J., The University
library, 1900-34.
    2 v. front., plates, ports., maps (1 fold.)
24 1/2 cm.

Fitzhugh, George.
    Cannibals all! Or, Slaves without masters ...
Richmond, Va., A. Morris, 1857.
    xxiii, [24]-379 p.   18 cm.

Fitz-Patrick, T.
    A transatlantic holiday; or, Notes of a visit
to the eastern states of America, by T. Fitz-Patrick ... London, S. Low, Marston & company, 1891.
    viii, 2 1., 210 p. front., pl., maps.
19 cm.

Flack, Capt.
    A hunter's experiences in the southern states
of America; being an account of the natural history of the various quadrupeds and birds which
are the objects of chase in those countries ...
London, Longmans, Green and co., 1866.
    359 p. 4 p.1.   19 1/2 cm.

Flack, Capt.
    The Texas rifle-hunter; or, Field sports on
the prairie, by Captain Flack ... ("the Ranger,")
late of the Texas rangers. London, John Maxwell
and company, 1866.
    viii, 333 p.   18 1/2 cm.

[Flagg, Edmund] 1815-1890.
    The far West: or, A tour beyond the mountains.
Embracing outlines of western life and scenery;

193

sketches of the prairies, rivers, ancient mounds,
early settlements of the French, etc. ... New-York,
Harper & brothers, 1838.
2 v.   18 1/2 cm.

[Flanders, Mrs. G. M.]
    The ebony idol ... New York, D. Appleton &
company, 1860.
    283 p.   front.   19 1/2 cm.

Fletcher, John.
    Studies on slavery, in easy lessons. Compiled
into eight studies, and subdivided into short les-
sons for the convenience of readers. Natchez,
Jackson, Warner, 1852 [c1851]
    637 p.   22 1/2 cm.

Fletcher, William Andrew, 1839-
    Rebel private, front and rear; experiences and
observations from the early fifties and through
the civil war, by W. A. Fletcher. Beaumont, Press
of the Greer print, 1908.
    193 p.   incl. port.   24 cm.

Flint, James (Scotchman).
    Letters from America, containing observations
on the climate and agriculture of the western
states, the manners of the people, the prospects
of emigrants, &c.   ... Edinburgh, W. & C. Tait;
[etc., etc.] 1822.
    viii, 330 p.   incl.   illus., tables.   21 cm.

Flint, Timothy, 1780-
    Journal of the Rev. Timothy Flint, from the
Red river, to the Quachitta or Washita, in
Louisiana, in 1835.   [Alexandria? La., 1835?]
    31 p.   16 cm.

Flint, Timothy, 1780-
    Recollections of the last ten years, passed in
occasional residences and journeyings in the valley of the Mississippi, from Pittsburgh and the
Missouri to the Gulf of Mexico, and from Florida
to the Spanish frontier ... Boston, Cummings,
Hilliard, and company, 1826.
    395 p.   1 p.l.   22 1/2 cm.

Florida. Commissioner of lands and immigration.
Florida: its climate, soil and productions,
with a sketch of its history, natural features
and social condition; a manual of reliable information concerning the resources of the state and
the inducements to settlers ... New York, The
Florida improvement company, 1869.
128 p. front. (fold. map), illus., pl.
23 cm.

Florida. Commissioner of lands and immigration.
Florida: its climate, soil and productions,
with a sketch of its history, natural features
and social condition ... Published for the state
by J. S. Adams, commissioner of immigration.
[New York, Printed by Fisher & Field] 1870.
69 p. front. (fold. map) illus., pl.   23 cm.

Florida. Commissioner of lands and immigration.
Florida: its climate, soil and productions,
with a sketch of its history, natural features
and social condition ... Jacksonville, L. F. Dewey
and company, 1868.
64 p. fold. map.   22 1/2 cm.

Florida. Commissioner of lands and immigration.
The Florida settler, or immigrants' guide; a
complete manual of information concerning the
climate, soil, products and resources of the
state. Prepared by D[ennis] Eagan ... Tallahassee, Printed at the office of the Floridian, 1873.
160 p.   23 1/2 cm.

Florida, the Italy of America.   The winter garden of
the North.   The world's sanitarium, Hernando the
richest most attractive and picturesque county in
south Florida, and the famous Annuttaliga Hammock,
the richest and most productive land in Hernando
county.   Palatka, Fla., Southern sun publishing
company, 1885.
63 p.   21 1/2 cm.

Florida, its climate and productions.   Deland, a famous
resort and educational center.   Deland, Agricul-
turist job print, 1887-88.
5 1., 66 p.   19 cm.

Florida railway and navigation company.
The Florida railway and navigation company.
The key line comprising the Gulf coast route from

the sea to the Gulf, New York, The south publishing co., 1884.
75 p. front., illus., map. 23 1/2 cm.

Flournoy, John Jacobus.
An essay on the origin, habits, etc., of the African race: incidental to the propriety of having nothing to do with Negroes: addressed to the good people of the United States ... New York, 1835.
56 p. 21 1/2 cm.

Flower, George, 1780-
... History of the English settlement in Edwards county, Illinois, founded in 1817 and 1818, by Morris Birkbeck and George Flower ... With preface and footnotes, by E. B. Washburne ... Chicago, Fergus printing company, 1882.
viii p. 2 p.l., 1 1., [9]-402 p. front. (port.) pl. 24 1/2 cm.

Flower, Richard, 1761?
Letters from Lexington and the Illinois. London, J. Ridgway, 1819.
iv, [5]-32 p. 22 cm.

Floyd, David Bittle.
History of the Seventy-fifth regiment of Indiana infantry volunteers, its organization, campaigns, and battles (1862-1865). By Rev. David Bittle Floyd ... With an introduction by Major-General J. J. Reynolds ... Published for the author. Philadelphia, Lutheran publication society, 1893.
457 p. front., illus., port., maps. 22 1/2 cm.

Foley, Daniel.
The people and institutions of the United States of America: a summer vacation tour ... Dublin, George Herbert; London, James Nisbet & company, 1858.
79 p. 18 1/2 cm.

Follen, E. L.
The life of Charles Follen. In one volume. Boston, Thomas Webb and company, 1844.
viii, 386 p. 18 cm.

Follen, Mrs. Eliza Lee (Cabot)
   The liberty cap ... Boston, Leonard C. Bowles,
   1846.
      36 p.   16 cm.

Follen, Mrs. Eliza Lee (Cabot)
   To mothers in the free states. [New York,
   American anti-slavery society 1856?]
      4 p.   19 cm.

Fonerden, Clarence A.
   A brief history of the military career of
   Carpenter's battery, from its organization as a
   rifle company under the name of the Alleghany
   Roughs to the ending of the war between the
   states, by C. A. Fonerden. New Market, Va.,
   Henkel & company, printers, 1911.
      78 p.   3 pl.   20 1/2 cm.

Fontaine, Jacques, 1658-
   Memoirs of a Huguenot family; tr. and comp.
   from the original autobiography of Rev. James
   Fontaine, and other family manuscripts; comprising an original journal of travels in Virginia, New-York, etc. in 1715 and 1716 ... By
   Ann Maury. New York, G. P. Putnam & co., 1853.
      512 p.   incl. front., port.   19 1/2 cm.

Foot, Jesse.
   A defence of the planters of the West-Indies;
   comprised in four arguments, on comparative humanity, on comparative slavery, on the African
   slave trade, and on the condition of the negroes
   in the West-Indies ... London, Printed for J.
   Debrett, 1792.
      iv, 101 p.   22 cm.

Foote, C. C.
   American women responsible for the existence
   of American slavery. Conversation between an
   anti-slavery lecturer and a lady ... Rochester,
   E. Shepard, book and job printer, 1816.
      24 p.   22 cm.

Foote, Henry Stuart, 1804-
   War of the rebellion; or, Scylla and Charybdis.
   Consisting of observations upon the causes, course,
   and consequences of the late civil war in the
   United States. New York, Harper & brothers, 1866.

1 p. 1., xii, [13]-440 p. front. (port.)
19 1/2 cm.

Foote, William Henry, 1794-
Sketches of North Carolina, historical and
biographical, illustrative of the principles of
a portion of her early settlers. New York, R.
Carter, 1846.
2 p.1., [ix]-xxxii, [33]-557 p. 23 1/2 cm.

Foote, William Henry, 1794-
Sketches of Virginia, historical and biographical. [1st]-2d series. Philadelphia, W.
S. Martien [etc.] 1850-55.
2 v. front. (v. 2: port.) 23 1/2 cm.

Forbes, Eugene, d. 1865.
Diary of a soldier, and prisoner of war in
the Rebel prisons, Written by Eugene Forbes ...
Trenton, [N.J.] Murphy & Bechtel, printers,
1865.
iv, 68 p. 22 1/2 cm.

Forbes, James Grant.
Sketches, historical and topographical, of
the Floridas; more particularly of East Florida...
New-York, C. S. VanWinkle, 1821.
viii, [9]-226 p. fold. pl. (map and plan)
24 1/2 cm.

The foreign slave trade, a brief account of its state,
of the treaties which have been entered into, and
of the laws enacted for its suppression, from the
date of the English abolition act to the present
time. London, John Hatchard and son [etc.], 1837.
62 p. 21 cm.

Forest, Michael.
Travels through America. A poem ... Philadelphia, Printed by Johnston & Justice, at Franklin's
Head, no. 41, Chestnut street, 1793.
50 p. 18 1/2 cm.

Forman, Samuel S. 1765-
Narrative of a journey down the Ohio and Mississippi in 1789-90 ... with a memoir and illustrative notes by Lyman C. Draper. Cincinnati, R.
Clarke & co., 1888.
67 p. 20 1/2 cm.

Forney, John Wien, 1817-
What I saw in Texas ... Philadelphia, Ringwalt & Brown, prs. [1872]
Cover-title, 92 p. incl. illus., port., map.
24 cm.

Forten, James.
An address delivered before the Ladies' anti-
slavery society of Philadelphia, on the evening
of the 14th of April, 1836 ... Philadelphia,
Printed by Merrihew and Gunn, 1836.
16 p.   23 cm.

Fortier, Alcée, 1858-
Louisiana studies. Literature, customs and
dialects, history and education. New Orleans,
F. F. Hansell & bro. [1894]
vi, 307 p.   19 1/2 cm.

Fosdick, Charles.
Five hundred days in Rebel prisons, by Charles
Fosdick, formerly of Co. K, 5th Iowa vols. ...
Bethany, Mo., Printed at the Clipper book and job
office, 1887.
132 p.   incl. port.   20 cm.

Foss, A. T.
Facts for Baptist churches, collected, arranged
and reviewed by A. T. Foss and E. Matthews.   Utica,
American Baptist free mission society, 1850.
408 p.   front.   18 1/2 cm.

[Foss, James H.]
Florida: its climate, soil, productions, and
agricultural capabilities. Washington, Government
printing office, 1882.
98 p.   23 cm.

Foster, Eden Burroughs, 1813.
A north-side view of slavery. A sermon on
the crime against freedom, in Kansas and Washington. Preached at Henniker, N. H., August 31,
1856 ... Concord, N. H., Jones & Cogswell, 1856.
39 p.   22 1/2 cm.

Foster, Eden Burroughs, 1813.
The rights of the pulpit, and perils of free-
dom. Two discourses preached in Lowell, Sunday,
June 25th, 1854 ... Lowell, Mass., Published by

J. J. Judkins, 1854.
72 p.   23 cm.

Foster, Lillian.
Way-side glimpses, north and south ... New
York, Rudd & Carleton, 1860.
xi, [13]-250 p.   18 1/2 cm.

Foster, Stephen Clark, 1799.
The rights of white men vindicated. Speech
... delivered in the House of Representatives,
March 10, 1858. [Washington, Buell & Blanchard,
1858?]
8 p.   24 cm.

Foster, Stephen Symonds.
Letter to Nathaniel Barney and Peter Masy
[!] of Nantuckut [!] [n.p., 1843?]
68 p.   16 cm.

Foster, Stephen Symonds.
Revolution the only remedy for slavery.   [New
York, American anti-slavery society, 1855?]
20 p.   19 cm.

Fothergill, John, 1787-
An account of the life and travels in the work
of the ministry, of John Fothergill.   To which
are added, divers epistles to friends in Great
Britain and America, on various occasions.   London.
Printed and sold by Mary Hinde, 1773.
v, 338, xxix p.

The fountain, for every day in the year.   New York,
John S. Taylor, 1836.
208 p.   7 cm.

Fountain, Paul.
The great deserts and forests of North Ameri-
ca, by Paul Fountain. With a preface by W. H.
Hudson ... London, New York and Bombay, Longmans,
Green, and co., 1901.
ix, 295 p.   23 cm.

Fournel, Henri Jérome Marie, 1799-1876.
Coup d'oeil historique et statistique sur le
Téxas, par Henri Fournel ... Paris, Delloye, 1841.
57 p.   fold.   map.   25 1/2 cm.

Fowler, Orin, 1791.
Slavery in California and New Mexico. Speech
... in the House of Representatives, March 11,
1850, in committee of the whole on the state of
the union, on the president's message communicating
the constitution of California. [n.p., 1850?]
15 p.   24 cm.

[Fowler, Philemon Halsted] 1814-1879.
Memorials of William Fowler. New York, A.D.F.
Randolph & company, 1875.
172 p.   front.   (port.)   21 cm.

Fowler, Reginald.
Hither and thither; or, Sketches of travels
on both sides of the Atlantic. London, F. R.
Daldy, 1854.
viii, 272 p.   22 cm.

[Fox, Francis William]
A crusade against the slave trade. [n.p.,
1889?]
3 p.   22 cm.

Fox, George, 1624-1691.
A journal or historical account of the life,
travels, sufferings, Christian experiences and
labour of love in the work of the ministry, of
that ancient, eminent and faithful servant of
Jesus Christ, George Fox ... The first volume ...
London, Printed for Thomas Northcot, in Georgeyard, in Lombard-street, MDCXCIV.
xviii, 632 (i.e., 729), [16] p. 25 p. 1.
30 1/2 cm.

Fox, James D.
A true history of the reign of terror in
southern Illinois, a part of the campaign in western Virginia, and fourteen months of prison
life at Richmond ... Macon ... Charleston ... and
Columbia. By James D. Fox ... Aurora, Ill.,
J. D. Fox, 1884.
vi p., 1 1., [7]-60 p.   incl. front., pl.
21 1/2 cm.

Fox, John, 1862-
Blue-grass and rhododendron; out-doors in old
Kentucky, by John Fox, jr. New York, C. Scrib-
ner's sons, 1901.

x, 294 p. front., illus., plates. 21 cm.

Fox, Simeon M. 1842-
The Seventh Kansas cavalry: its service in
the civil war. An address before the State historical society, December 2, 1902. By S. M. Fox
... Also, a brief narration of the first eight
Kansas regiments. Topeka, State printing office,
1908.
59 p. 23 cm.

Fox, W.
A defence of the decree of the National Convention of France, for emancipating the slaves
in the West Indies. London: Sold by M. Gurney,
no. 128, Holborn Hill; and D. I. Eaton, no. 74,
Newgate street [n.d.]
16 p. 20 1/2 cm.

Fox, William.
An address to the people of Great Britain, on
the propriety of abstaining from West India sugar
and rum ... The tenth edition, with additions.
London, printed, Philadelphia, reprinted by Daniel
Lawrence, 1792.
16, [3] p. 17 cm.

France. Laws, statutes, etc.
Précis de l'abolition de l'esclavage dans le
colonies anglaises, imprimé par ordre de M. l'
Amiral Baron Duperre ... Paris, Imprimerie, royale, 1840.
5 v. 21 cm.

Francis, Charles Lewis.
Narrative of a private soldier in the volunteer
army of the United States, during a portion of
the period covered by the great war of the rebellion of 1861. By Charles Lewis Francis ...
Brooklyn, W. Jenkins and co., 1879.
viii, [7]-185 p. 16 1/2 cm.

[Francklyn, G.]
Substance of a speech intended to have been
made on Mr. Wilberforce's motion for the abolition of the slave trade on Tuesday, April 3,
1792 ... Second edition, corrected. London,
Printed for J. Owen, 1792.
56 p., 28 unnumb. p. 22 cm.

Franklin, pseud.
    To the people of Kentucky. Fellow citizens.
At this eventful period, when the fundamental
principles of our government are about to be
established ... [Lexington? 1798]
    20 1/2 x 17 1/2 cm.

Franklin, James.
    The philosophical & political history of the
thirteen United States of America ... London, J.
Hinton & W. Adams, 1784.
    156 p.   3 p.l.   19 cm.

Frederick, Francis, 1809?-
    Autobiography of Rev. Francis Frederick, of
Virginia. Baltimore, J. W. Woods, printer, 1869.
    40 p.   19 1/2 cm.

Frederick, Gilbert, b. 1841 or 1842.
    The story of a regiment: being a record of
the military services of the Fifty-seventh New
York state volunteer infantry in the war of the
rebellion, 1861-1865. By Gilbert Frederick ...
[Chicago] Pub. by the Fifty-seventh Veteran
association, 1895.
    xii, 349 p.   front., illus., pl., port.
21 1/2 cm.

Free convention, Rutland, Vt., June 25-27, 1858.
    Proceedings ... Boston, J. B. Yerrington &
son, 1858.
    185 p.   23 cm.

Free produce association of Friends of Ohio.
    Extracts from the minutes of the annual meet-
ing of the Free Produce Association of Ohio yearly
meeting. Held 3d of ninth month, 1850, with the
report of the board of managers. Mountpleasant,
Ohio, published by the Managers of the Free produce association of Friends at Ohio yearly meeting. E. Harris, printer, 1851.
    12 p.   18 cm.

Free produce association of Friends of Ohio.
    Second annual report ... yearly meeting. Held
9th of month, 1851. Mountpleasant, Ohio, Enoch
Harris, printer, 1851.
    6 p.   19 cm.

Free produce society of Pennsylvania.
Constitution of the Free Produce Society of
Pennsylvania. Philadelphia, Printed on the Ver-
tical Press by D. & S. Neall [1827]
12 p.   18 1/2 cm.

Free remarks on the spirit of the federal constitution,
the practice of the federal government, and the
obligation of the union, respecting the exclusion
of slavery from the territories and new states
... By a Philadelphian. Philadelphia, A. Finley,
1819.
116 p.   22 cm.

Free soil, free speech, free men.
Proceedings of the democratic Republican state
convention, at Syracuse, July 24, 1856. The address and resolutions, with the list of delegates.
Albany, J. D. Parsons, 1856.
16 p.   23 cm.

The free soil minstrel ... New York, Martyn & Ely,
1848.
228 p.   17 1/2 cm.

Freedom's gift; or, Sentiments of the free. Hartford,
Printed by S. W. Cowles, 1840.
108 p.   front.   18 cm.

Freeman, Edward Augustus, 1823-
Some impressions of the United States ... New
York, H. Holt and company, 1883.
x p., 1 1., 304 p.   19 1/2 cm.

Freeman, F.
A plea for Africa ... Third ed.   Philadelphia,
William Stavely, 1838.
359 p.   19 cm.

Freeman, Mrs. Julia Susan (Wheelock) 1833-
The boys in white; the experience of a hospital
agent in and around Washington. By Julia S.
Wheelock ... New York, Printed by Lange & Hill-
man, 1870.
vii, [1] p., 1 1., [9]-274 p.   2 port. (incl.
front.)   19 cm.

[Freeman, Warren Hapgood] 1844?-
    Letters from two brothers serving in the war
for the union to their family at home in West
Cambridge, Mass. Cambridge, Printed for private
circulation [by H. O. Houghton and company] 1871.
    2 p.l., 164 p., 2 l. front. (port.) 17 1/2
cm.

Freemantle, Sir Arthur James Lyon.
    Three months in the southern states: April-
June, 1863. New York, John Bradburn, 1864.
    309 p. front. (port.) 19 cm.

French, Mrs. A. M.
    Slavery in South Carolina and the ex-slaves;
or, The Port Royal mission ... New York, Win-
chell M. French, 1862.
    xii, 13-312 p. 19 cm.

French, Benjamin Franklin, 1799, ed.
    Historical collections of Louisiana. New
York, Wiley and Putnam [etc.] 1846-75.
    7 v. front., port., fold. maps. facsims.
24 1/2 cm.

French, Samuel Gibbs, 1818-1910.
    Two wars: an autobiography of General Samuel
G. French ... Mexican war; war between the states,
a diary; reconstruction period, his experience;
incidents, reminiscences, etc. Nashville, Tenn.,
Confederate veteran, 1901.
    xv, [2], 404 p. incl. illus., port. front.
(port.) 24 cm.

Freytas, Nicolas de.
    The expedition of Don Diego Dionisio de
Peñalosa ... from Santa Fé to the river Mischipi
and Quivira in 1662, as described by Father Nicolas de Freytas, C.S.F., with an account of Peñalosa's projects to aid the French to conquer the
mining country in northern Mexico; and his connection with Cavelier de la Salle. By John Gil-
mary Shea. New York, J. G. Shea, 1882.
    101 [1] p. 24 1/2 cm.

Friends in council: a series of readings, and discourses thereon ... New York, James Miller, 1861.
    279 p. 18 1/2 cm.

Friends of African colonization.
Proceedings of a convention of the friends of
African colonization held in Washington city, May
4, 1842. Washington, Alexander and Barnard,
printers, 1842.
64 p.   25 cm.

Friends, Society of.
Address of the representatives of the religious
society of friends, commonly called Quakers, in
Pennsylvania, New Jersey, Delaware, & etc., to
the citizens of the United States. Philadelphia,
Joseph & William Kite, 1837.
15 p.   23 cm.

Friends, Society of (U. S.)
An address to friends and friendly people;
being an exhortation to faithfulness in the maintenance of our Christian testimony against slavery ... Philadelphia, T. Ellwood Chapman, 1848.
24 p.   18 cm.

Friends, Society of.
The appeal of the religious Society of friends
in Pennsylvania, New Jersey, Delaware, etc., to
their fellow-citizens of the United States on behalf of the coloured races. Philadelphia, Friends'
book-store, 1858.
48 p.   21 1/2 cm.

Friends, Society of.
The case of our fellow-creatures, the oppressed
Africans, respectfully recommended for the serious
consideration of the legislature of Great Britain, by the people called Quakers. London, Printed by James Phillips, 1783.
16 p.   22 cm.

Friends, Society of.
Free Produce association of friends, New-York
yearly meeting. Report of the board of managers
... New-York, Collins, Browne & co., printers,
1854.
9 p.   15 cm.

Friends, society of.
Free Produce association of Friends of Ohio
yearly meeting. Considerations on abstinence
from the use of the products of slave labor;

addressed to the members of the Ohio yearly
meeting ... [Mount Pleasant, Ohio? Enoch Harris,
printer, 1850].
   8 p.   18 cm.

Friends, Society of.
   Proceedings in relation to the presentation
of the address of the yearly meeting of the religious Society of friends, on the slave-trade
and slavery, to sovereigns and those in authority
in the nations of Europe and in other parts of
the world, where the Christian religion is professed.   London, Printed by Edward Newman, 1854.
   62 p.   21 cm.

Friends, Society of.
   Committee in charge of Friends' mission in
Washington, for the relief of the freed people
of color.   Report ... printed for the information
of Friends of New England yearly meeting, New
Bedford, 1865.
   4 p.   22 cm.

Friends, Society of.
   Committee on freedmen, in parts of Tennessee
and the Mississippi valley.   Report ... to
Friends' board of control, third month, 1865.
Cincinnati, R. W. Carroll & co., 1865.
   16 p.   22 cm.

Friends, Society of.   Farmington, N. Y., quarterly
   meeting.
   Address of Farmington quarterly meeting (New
York) to the monthly meetings constituting it,
and to membership of the same generally.   "Are
there not at this moment slaves toiling for us."
[n.p.] Published by the managers of the Free produce association of Friends of Ohio yearly meeting, 1850.
   8 p.   19 cm.

Friends, Society of.   Free Produce association of
   friends.
   An address to our fellow members of the religious society of friends on the subject of
slavery and the slave-trade in the western world ...
Philadelphia, 1849.
   17 p.   22 cm.

Friends, Society of. Indiana yearly meeting.
    Address to the citizens of the state of Ohio,
concerning what are called the black laws. Issued in behalf of the Society of friends of Indiana yearly meeting, by their meeting for sufferings, representing the said yearly meeting in
its recess ... Cincinnati, A. Pugh, 1848.
    15 p.   18 cm.

Friends, Society of. London yearly meeting.
    Address on the slave trade and slavery, to
sovrereigns, and those in authority in the nations
of Europe, and other parts of the world where
the Christian religion is professed. From the
yearly meeting of Friends in London, held in
1847. Richmond, Ind., Published by the Central
book and tract committee of Friends [n.d.]
    8 p.   18 cm.

Friends, Society of. London yearly meeting.
    An appeal in the iniquity of slavery and the
slave-trade: issued by the yearly meeting of the
religious Society of friends, held in London,
1844. Re-published for general circulation, by
Indiana yearly meeting of friends ... 1844. Cincinnati, A. Pugh & co., 1844.
    9 p.   22 cm.

Friends, Society of. New England yearly meeting.
    An appeal to the professors of Christianity,
in the southern states and elsewhere, on the subject of slavery ... Providence, Printed by Knowles
and Vose, 1842.
    24 p.   22 cm.

Friends, Society of. New England yearly meeting.
    Report upon the condition and needs of the
freed people of color in Washington and Virginia.
New Bedford, E. Anthony & sons. 1864.
    8 p.   22 cm.

Friends, Society of. New England yearly meeting.
Executive committee.
    Second report of the proceedings ... in be-
half of the freed people of color. New Bedford,
E. Anthony & sons, 1865.
    8 p.   22 cm.

Friends, Society of. New York yearly meeting.
    Address of the yearly meeting of the religious
society of friends, held in the city of New-
York, in the sixth month, 1852, to the professors
of Christianity in the United States, on the subject of slavery. New-York, James Robert, 1852.
    10 p.   19 cm.

Friends, Society of. New York yearly meeting.
    Address to the citizens of the United States
of America on the subject of slavery, from the
yearly meeting of the religious society of friends
(called Quakers) held in New-York, Published by
the New-York yearly meeting of friends, 1837.
    11 p.   18 cm.

Friends, Society of. New York yearly meeting.
    Second report of a committee of the represen-
tatives of New York yearly meeting of friends
upon the condition and wants of the colored re-
fugees. [New York?] 1863.
    15 p.   22 cm.

Friends, Society of. New York yearly meeting.
    Third report of a committee of the representa-
tives of the New York yearly meeting of friends
upon the condition and wants of the colored refu-
gees. [New York?] 1864.
    23 p.   22 cm.

Friends, Society.of. New York yearly meeting.
    Fifth report of a committee of the representa-
tives of the New York yearly meeting of friends
upon the condition and wants of the freedmen.
[New York?] 1864.
    15 p.   22 cm.

Friends, Society of. Ohio yearly meeting. Free pro-
    duce association.
    ... Considerations on the abstinence from the
use of the products of slave labor addressed to
the members of the Ohio yearly meeting. [Mount
Pleasant, Ohio]. Published by the managers of
the Free produce association of Friends of Ohio
yearly meeting, 1851.
    12 p.   18 1/2 cm.

Friends, Society of.   Ohio yearly meeting.   Free produce association.
Considerations on abstinence from the use of
the products of slave labor ... [n.p.] Published
by the managers of the Free produce association
of Friends of Ohio yearly meeting, 1850.
8 p.   19 cm.

Friends, Society of.   Ohio yearly meeting.   Free produce association.
... The plea of necessity.   [Mount Pleasant,
Ohio] Published by the managers of the Free produce association of Friends of Ohio yearly meeting, 1851.
12 p.   18 1/2 cm.

Friends, Society of.   Philadelphia yearly meeting.
A brief statement of the rise and progress of
the testimony of the religious society of friends,
against slavery and the slave trade.   Published
by direction of the yearly meeting, held in Philadelphia, in the fourth month, 1843.   Philadelphia,
Printed by Joseph and William Kite, 1843.
59 p.   19 cm.

Friends, Society of.   Philadelphia yearly meeting.
Extracts and observation on the foreign slave
trade.   Published by the committee appointed by
the yearly meeting of friends held in Philadelphia in 1839.   On the subject of slavery.
Philadelphia, Printed for the committee, 1839.
12 p.   19 cm.

Friends, Society of.   Philadelphia yearly meeting.
Second report of the executive board of the
Friends' association of Philadelphia and its
vicinity, for the relief of colored freedmen.
Read at the annual meeting of the contributors,
held at Arch Street meeting-house, Philadelphia,
4th month 17th, 1865.   Philadelphia, Ringwalt &
Brown, 1865.
19 p.   23 cm.

Friends, Society of.   Philadelphia yearly meeting.
Third annual report of the executive board
of the Friends' association of Philadelphia and
its vicinity for the relief of colored freedmen,
read at the annual meeting of the contributors,
held at Arch Street meeting-house, Philadelphia,

4th month 16th, 1866. Philadelphia, Ringwalt & Brown, 1866.
17 p.   22 cm.

Friends, Society of. Philadelphia yearly meeting.
Fourth annual report of the executive board of the Friends' association of Philadelphia and its vicinity for the relief of colored freedmen, read at the annual meeting of the contributors, held at Arch Street meeting-house, Philadelphia, 4th month, 15th, 1867. Philadelphia, Sherman & co., 1867.
24 p.   22 cm.

Friends, Society of. Philadelphia yearly meeting.
Slavery and the domestic slave trade, in the United States. By the committee appointed by the late yearly meeting of Friends held in Philadelphia, in 1839. Philadelphia, Printed by Merrihew and Thompson, 1841.
46 p.   19 cm.

Fritsch, William August, 1841-
Aus Amerika, alte und neue heimat, von W. A. Fritsch. Stargard i. Pom., W. Prange [1905].
2 p.1., 82 p.   20 cm.

Fröbel, Julius, 1805-1893.
Aus Amerika. Erfahrungen, reisen und studien... Leipzig, J. J. Weber, 1857-58.
2 v. illus.   17 1/2 cm.

From ocean to ocean, being a diary of three months' expedition from Liverpool to California and back, from the Atlantic to the Pacific by the overland route ... [London] Printed [by W. Clowes and son] for private circulation, 1871.
3 p. 1., 108, [2] p.   23 cm.

Frossard, Benjamin-Sigismond.
La cause des esclaves nègres et des habitans de la Guinée, portée au tribunal de la justice, de la religion et de la politique, ou Historie de la traite et de l'esclavage des nègres, preuves de leur illégitimité, moyens de les abolir ... Lyon, Impr. de A. de La Roche, 1789.
2 v. front.

Frothingham, Frederick.
　　Significance of the struggle between liberty
and slavery in America. A discourse ... at Portland, Maine, on fast day, April 16th, 1857. New
York, American anti-slavery society, 1857.
　　21 p.　17 cm.

Frothingham, Octavius Brooks.
　　Colonization. [New York, American anti-slavery society, 1855?]
　　8 p.　19 cm.

Frothingham, Octavius Brooks.
　　The new commandment; a discourse delivered in
the North church, Salem, on Sunday, June 4, 1854...
Second edition. Salem, Printed at the Observer
office, 1854.
　　21 p.　23 cm.

The Fugitive slave bill: its history and unconstitutionality; with an account of the seizure and en-
slavement of James Hamlet and his subsequent
restoration to liberty. New York, William Harned,
1850.
　　36 p.　18 cm.

A full and impartial account of the Company of Mississippi, otherwise call'd the French East-India company, projected and settled by Mr. Law ... London,
Printed for R. Francklin [etc., etc.] 1720.
　　79 (i.e. 71) p.　2 p.l.　19 1/2 cm.

A full statement of the reasons which were in part
offered to the committee of the legislature of
Massachusetts, on the fourth and eighth of March,
showing why there should be no penal laws enacted, and no condemnation resolutions passed by
the legislature, respecting abolitionists [!]
and anti-slavery societies. Boston, Massachusetts
anti-slavery society, 1836.
　　48 p.　25 cm.

Fuller, Richard, 1808.
　　Domestic slavery considered as a scriptural
institution: in a correspondence between the Rev.
Richard Fuller of Beaufort, S. C., and the Rev.
Francis Wayland, of Providence, R.I. Revised
and corrected by the authors. New York, Published by Lewis Colby; Boston, Gould, Kendall

and Lincoln, 1845.
viii, 254 p.   15 cm.

Fuller, Thomas J. D.
Democracy national and not sectional. Speech
of Hon. Thomas J. D. Fuller, of Maine. Delivered
in the House of Representatives, August 28, 1856.
In vindication of the Democratic Party from the
charge of sectionalism, made by his colleagues,
and defending its action upon the disagreement
of the two Houses of Congress upon the Army Ap-
propriation Bill. [n.p.] 1856.
8 p.   20 cm.

Fünf wochen im osten der Vereinigten Staaten und
Kanadas; reiseerinnerungen von einem, der seinen
bruder besuchte; mit 41 ansichten nach aufnah-
men des verfassers. Bern, A. Francke, 1913.
124 p.   illus.   23 cm.

Furness, William Henry.
A discourse delivered on the occasion of the
national fast, September 26th, 1861, in the First
Congregational Unitarian church in Philadelphia
... Philadelphia, T. B. Pugh, 1861.
20 p.   23 cm.

Furniss, William Henry.
A discourse occasioned by the Boston fugitive
slave case, delivered in the First Congregational
Unitarian church, Philadelphia ... Philadelphia,
Merrihew & Thompson, 1851.
15 p.   23 cm.

The further progress of colonial reform; being an analysis of the communication made to Parliament by
His Majesty, at the close of the last session,
respecting the measures taken for improving the
condition of the slave population in the British
colonies ... London, Society for the mitigation
and gradual abolition of slavery throughout the
British dominions, 1827.
78 p.   21 cm.

G, J. S.
The detector detected: or, State of affairs
on the Gold Coast and conduct of the present
managers consider'd. With a comparison of the
trade in the late company's time, and benefits
since received by the open plan for extending the
same. Wrote on the coast, by J. S. G. last commandant of the Commenda, under the Royal African
company ... London, Printed for the author,
1753.
64 p. 19 cm.

Gaddis, Maxwell Pierson, 1811-
Foot-prints of an itinerant ... Cincinnati,
Printed at the Methodist book concern, for the
author, 1855.
546 p. front. (port.) 19 1/2 cm.

Gadsby, John, 1809-
A visit to Canada and the United States of
America. Also a second visit to Spain. London,
Gadsby, 1873.
104 p. 18 cm.

Gage, Moses D.
From Vicksburg to Raleigh; or, A complete history of the Twelfth regiment Indiana volunteer
infantry, and the campaigns of Grant and Sherman,
with an outline of the great rebellion, by M. D.
Gage, chaplain. Chicago, Clarke & co., 1865.
xiv, [15]-356 p. 19 cm.

Gaillardet, Frédéric, 1808-
L'aristocratie en Amérique, par Frédéric
Gaillardet ... Paris, E. Dentu, 1883.
2 p.l., 375 p. 18 1/2 cm.

Gall, Ludwig, 1791-
Meine auswanderung nach den Vereinigten-Staaten
in Nord-Amerika im frühjahr 1819 und meine rück-
kehr nach der heimath im winter 1820 ... Trier,
F. A. Gall, 1822.
2 v. 10 pl. (part fold., incl. fronts., maps,
plan, diagr.) fold. tab. 20 1/2 cm.

Gallenga, Antonio Carlo Napoleone, 1810-
Episodes of my second life. (American and English experiences.) By Antonio Gallenga. (L. Mariotti.) Philadelphia, J. B. Lippincott & co., 1885.
xii, 466 p. 19 cm.

Galloway, Samuel.
Kansas contested election. Speech ... in the House of Representatives, March 17, 1856, on the resolution reported by the committee of elections in the contested election case from the territory of Kansas. [n.p., n.d.]
7 p. 22 1/2 cm.

The Gallynipper in Yankeeland. By himself. London, Tinsley brothers, 1882.
viii, 102 p. incl. front., illus. 19 cm.

Galveston Bay and Texas land company.
Address to the reader of the documents relating to the Galveston Bay & Texas land company, which are contained in the appendix. New York, Printed by G. F. Hopkins & son, 1831.
37, [1], 69 p. 21 cm.

Gammage, W. L.
The camp, the bivouac, and the battlefield, being the history of the Fourth Arkansas regiment, from its first organization down to the present date: its campaigns and its battles ... Selma, Ala., Cooper & Kimball, Mississippian [sic] book and job office, 1864.
6 p.1., [7]-164 p. 19 1/2 cm.

Gannett, Ezra Stiles.
Relation of the north to slavery. A discourse preached in the Federal street meeting-house, in Boston, on Sunday, June 11, 1864 ... Boston, Crosby, Nichols & company, 1854.
23 p. 24 cm.

Gano, John, 1727-
Biographical memoirs of the late Rev. John Gano, of Frankfort, (Kentucky). Formerly of the city of New York. Printed by Southwick & Hardcastle for John Tiebout, 1806.
vii, [9] - 151 p. 17 cm.

Ganse, Harvey Doddridge.
Bible slaveholding not sinful; a reply to
"Slaveholding not sinful, by Samuel B. Howe, D.
D." ... New York, R. & R. Brinckerhoff, 1856.
85 p. 21 cm.

Garcia Mérou, Martin, 1862-
... Estudios americanos. Buenos Aires, F.
Lajouane, 1900.
492 p. 22 1/2 cm.

Gardiner, O. C.
The great issue: or, The three presidential
candidates; being a brief historical sketch of
the free soil question in the United States, from
the Congress of 1744 and '87 to the present time
... [n.p., 1848?]
176 p. 22 1/2 cm.

Gardini, Carlo.
Gli Stati Uniti, ricordi di Carlo Gardini ...
Bologna, N. Zanichelli, 1887.
2 v. front. (port.) illus., pl. (part fold.)
maps (part fold.) fold. plans, tab., diagr.
18 1/2 cm.

[Garnett, R. H.]
The union, past and future: how it works,
and how to save it. By a gentleman of Virginia
... Fourth edition ... Charleston, S. C., Southern rights association, 1850.
43 p. 23 1/2 cm.

Garrett, Alexander Charles, Bp., 1832-
"Homes for the people." Lecture on Texas, its
climate, soil, resources and how to get and enjoy
them ... Delivered ... October 3, 1882 ... St.
Louis, Times printing house, 1883.
31 p. 22 cm.

Garrettson, Freeborn, 1752-
The experience and travels of Mr. Freeborn Garrettson, minister of the Methodist-Episcopal church
in North-America ... Philadelphia: Printed by
Joseph Crukshank ... and sold by John Dickins ...
1791.
vii, 9-265 p. 13 cm.

Garrison, Wendell Phillips, 1840.
    The preludes of Harper's Ferry. Two papers
... reprinted from the Andover review, December
1890, January, 1891. [Boston? 1891]
    cover-title, 21 p. 23 1/2 cm.

Garrison, William Lloyd, 1805.
    An address delivered at the Broadway Taber-
nacle, N. Y., August 1, 1838. By request of the
people of color of that city, in commemoration
of the complete emancipation of 600,000 slaves
on that day, in the British West Indies ... Boston, Published by Isaac Knapp, 1838.
    46 p. 16 cm.

Garrison, William Lloyd, 1805.
    An address, delivered before the free people
of color, in Philadelphia, New York, and other
cities, during the month of June, 1831 ... Third
edition. Boston, Printed by Stephen Foster, 1831.
    24 p. 23 cm.

Garrison, William Lloyd, 1805.
    An address delivered in Marlboro' Chapel,
Boston, July 4, 1838 ... Boston, Published by
Isaac Knapp, 1838.
    48 p. 16 cm.

Garrison, William Lloyd, 1805.
    A fresh catalogue of southern outrages upon
northern citizens. New York, American anti-
slavery society, 1860.
    72 p. 19 cm.

[Garrison, William Lloyd] 1805
    In memoriam. Testimonials to the life and
character of the late Francis Jackson ... [by
William Lloyd Garrison, Wendell Phillips, and
Samuel May, Jr.] Boston, Published by R. F.
Wallcut, 1861.
    36 p. 18 cm.

Garrison, William Lloyd, 1805.
    The "infidelity" of abolitionism. New York,
American anti-slavery society, 1860.
    12 p. 19 cm.

Garrison, William Lloyd, 1805.
   Lectures of George Thompson, with a full report of the discussion between Mr. Thompson and
Mr. Borthwick, the pro-slavery agent, held at
the Royal amphitheatre, Liverpool ... also, a
brief history of his connection with the anti-
slavery cause in England ... Boston, Published
by Isaac Knapp, 1836.
   xxxvi, 190 p.   19 cm.

[Garrison, William Lloyd] 1805.
   The new "reign of terror" in the slaveholding
states, for 1859-60. New York, American anti-
slavery society, 1860.
   144 p.   19 cm.

Garrison, William Lloyd, 1805.
   No compromise with slavery. An address delivered to the Broadway tabernacle, New York,
February 14, 1854 ... New York, American anti-
slavery society, 1854.
   36 p.   16 cm.

Garrison, William Lloyd, 1805.
   Selections from the writings and speeches of
William Lloyd Garrison ... Boston, R. F. Wallcut,
1852.
   xii, 13-416 p.   19 cm.

[Garrison, William Lloyd] 1805.
   Southern hatred of the American government,
the people of the north, and free institutions.
Boston, Published by R. F. Wallcut, 1862.
   48 p.   18 cm.

[Garrison, William Lloyd] 1805.
   The spirit of the south towards northern freemen and soldiers defending the American flag
against traitors of the deepest dye. Boston,
Published by R. F. Wallcut, 1861.
   24 p.   18 cm.

Garrison, William Lloyd, 1805.
   Thoughts on African colonization: or, An
impartial exhibition of the doctrines, principles
and purposes of the American colonization society.
Together with the resolutions, addresses and re-
monstrances of the free people of color ... Boston, Garrison and Knapp, 1832.

2 v.   22 cm.

Gartrell, Lucius Jeremiah, 1821.
    The dangers of black-republicanism, and the
duty of the south. Speech ... in the House of
Representatives, January 10, 1860. [Washington]
Printed by Lemuel Towers [1860?]
    16 p.   24 cm.

Gartrell, Lucius Jeremiah, 1821.
    Domestic slavery in the south. Speech ...
delivered in the House of Representatives, January 25, 1858. [n.p., n.d.]
    7 p.   24 cm.

Gartrell, Lucius Jeremiah, 1821.
    Speech ... in defense of slavery and the
south. Delivered in the House of Representatives,
January 25, 1858. Washington, Printed by Lemuel
Towers, 1858.
    16 p.   23 cm.

Gauld, George.
    Observations on the Florida kays, reef and
gulf; with directions for sailing along the kays,
from Jamaica by the Grand Cayman and west end of
Cuba: also, a description, with sailing instructions, of the coast of west Florida, between the
bay of Spiritu Santo and Cape Sable ... London,
W. Faden, 1796.
    28 p.   25 1/2 cm.

Gause, Isaac, 1843-
    Four years with five armies: Army of the Fron-
tier, Army of the Potomac, Army of the Missouri,
Army of the Ohio, Army of the Shenandoah. By
Isaac Gause, Late of Co. E. Second Ohio cav.
New York and Washington. The Neale publishing
company, 1908.
    2 p. 1., [3] 384 p. pl., 1 1. port. (incl.
front.)   21 cm.

Gay, Mary Ann Harris, 1827.
    Life in Dixie during the war. 1861-1862-1863-
1864-1865. 3d ed. (enl.) Atlanta, Ga., C. P.
Byrd, 1897.
    410 p.   20 1/2 cm.

Gayarré, Charles Etienne Arthur, 1805-
    Romance of the history of Louisiana. A series
of lectures. New York, D. Appleton & company;
Philadelphia, G. S. Appleton, 1848.
    [5] - 265 p.   18 1/2 cm.

Geer, John James, 1833-
    Beyond the lines: or, A Yankee prisoner loose
in Dixie. By Captain J. J. Geer ... With an introduction by Rev. Alexander Clark ... Philadelphia, J. W. Daughaday, 1863.
    285 p. front. (port.) pl.   18 cm.

Geist, Margarethe.
    ... Mit dem eselwagen durch U.S.A.; herausge-
geben von Adelgunde Gruner, mit farbigen und
schwarzen bildern von Marie Luise Scherer. Stuttgart, K. Thienemann [c1933]
    108 p., illus., 2 col. pl. (incl. front.)
21 cm.

General Grant and the republican party. By a republican. New York, 1880.
    13 p.   21 1/2 cm.

General Taylor and the Wilmot proviso. [n.p., n.d.]
    31 p.   23 cm.

A general view of the African slave-trade, demonstrat-
ing its injustice and impolicy: with hints
towards a bill for its abolition. London, Printed for R. Faulder, 1788.
    39 p.   21 cm.

The genius of universal emancipation, a monthly paper
containing original essays and selections, on the
subject of African slavery. Benjamin Lundy,
editor ... v. II, no. 1 - v. III, no. 14; July
1822 - June 1824. Greeneville, Tenn. Published
by the proprietor, 1822-24.
    2 v. illus.   23 cm.

The genius of universal emancipation, a monthly peri-
odical work, containing original essays, documents,
and facts, relative to the subject of African
slavery ... Benjamin Lundy, ed. 3d ser. v. I,
III; Apr. 1830 - Mar. 1831, Nov. 1832 - Oct.
1833. Washington and Baltimore, Published by
Benjamin Lundy, 1830-33.

2 v.   24 cm.

A geographical view of the United States.   Boston, A.
K. White, 1827.
130, [2] p.   20 cm.

[Georgia (Colony) Trustees for establishing the colony
of Georgia in America]
An account shewing the progress of the colony
of Georgia in America from its first establishment.
London, Printed in the year 1741.
71 p., 1 p.1.   31 cm.

Gerrish, Theodore, 1846-
Army life; a private's reminiscences of the
civil war, by Rev. Theodore Gerrish ... With an
introduction by Hon. Joshiah H. Drummond.   Portland [Me.] Hoyt, Fogg & Donham [1882]
872 p.   19 1/2 cm.

Gerrit Smith and the Vigilante association of the city
of New York.   New York, John A. Gray, printer,
1860.
29 p.   15 cm.

The Gerrit Smith banner.   Temperance and equal rights
edited by William Goodell.   Nos. 1-13, Oct. 16,
1858 - Nov. 1, 1858.   New York.
45 cm.

Gerritsen, Carel Victor, 1850-
Brieven uit en over Amerika, door C. V. Gerritsen en Dr. Aletta H. Jacobs.   Amsterdam, F.
van Rossen, 1906.
179 p.   front. (port.)   21 1/2 cm.

Gerstäcker, Friedrich Wilhelm Christian, 1816-1872.
Wild sports in the far West ... Tr. from the
German.   With tinted illustrations by Harrison
Weir.   London, New York, G. Routledge & co., 1854.
xi, 396 p.   front., plates,   18 1/2 cm.

Gerstner, Clara (von Epplen-Härtenstein) von.
Beschreibung einer reise durch die Vereinigten Staaten von Nord-Amerika in den jahren 1838
bis 1840.   In gesellschaft des ritters Franz Anton
von Gerstner unternommen.   Leipzig, J. C. Hin-
richs, 1842.
xii, 456 p.   17 1/2 cm.

221

Gerstner, Franz Anton, ritter von, 1795-
Die innern communicationen der Vereinigten
Staaten von Nord-amerika. Von Franz Anton ritter
von Gerstner ... Nach dessen tode aufgesetzt,
redigirt und hrsg. von L. Klein ... Wien, L.
Förster's artistische anstalt, 1842-43.
2 v. 35 fold. pl. 28 1/2 cm.

Geschichte und handlung der franzö-sischen pflanzstädte
in Nordamerika, nebst einer zuverlässigen nachricht
von deren bevölkerung, ihren einwohnern ... wie
auch einer kurzen einleitung in die jezige strit-
tigkeiten der Engländer und Franzosen wegen Aka-
dien; und den ansprüchen der erstern auf einen
grossen theil von Canada und Louisiana. Mit einer
landcharte. Stutgart [!] J. B. Mezler, 1756.
376 p. 4 p.1. fold. map. 17 1/2 cm.

Gibbon, John, 1827-1896.
Personal recollections of the civil war, by
John Gibbon, brigadier-general, U.S.A. New York,
London, G. P. Putnam's sons, 1928.
vii, 426 p. front. (port.) maps. 24 cm.

Gibbons, J. A.
The Kanawha Valley, its resources and development. Also, special business directory of Charleston and other cities ... Charleston, W. Va., Gibbons, Atkinson & co., printers, 1872.
64 p. 21 1/2 cm.

Giddings, Joshua Reed, 1795.
Amistad claim. History of the case ... Speech
... in the House of Representatives, Dec. 21,
1853. [n.p., n.d.]
7 p. 24 cm.

Giddings, Joshua Reed, 1795.
Baltimore platforms ... slavery question.
Speech ... in the House of Representatives, June
23, 1852. [n.p., n.d.]
8 p. 24 cm.

Giddings, Joshua Reed, 1795.
The exiles of Florida: or, The crimes com-
mitted by our government against the maroons,
who fled from South Carolina and other slave
states, seeking protection under Spanish laws...
Columbus, Ohio, Published by Follett, Foster

and company, 1858.
viii, 338 p. front. 20 cm.

Giddings, Joshua Reed, 1795.
... Florida war. Speech ... delivered in the
House of Representatives, February 9, 1841. Hal-
lowell, Published by the Bangor female anti-
slavery society, 1841.
24 p. 20 cm.

Giddings, Joshua Reed, 1795.
A letter from Hon. J. R. Giddings, upon the
duty of anti-slavery men in the present crisis.
Ravenna, Ohio, Printed by William Wadsworth,
1844.
16 p. 23 cm.

Giddings, Joshua Reed.
Moral responsibility of statesmen. Speech ...
on the bill organizing territorial governments
in Kansas and Nebraska, in committee of the whole
on the state of the union, May 17, 1954 [!] Washington, Buell & Blanchard, 1854.
8 p. 23 1/2 cm.

Giddings, Joshua Reed.
Organization of the House. Speech ... delivered in the House of Representatives, Dec. 18, 1855.
Washington, Congressional globe office, 1855.
8 p. 23 1/2 cm.

Giddings, Joshua Reed, 1795.
Our domestic policy. Speech of Hon. J. R.
Giddings on the reference of the President's
message, made, December 9, 1850, in Committee
of the whole on the state of the union. [n.p.,
1850?]
8 p. 22 cm.

Giddings, Joshua Reed, 1795.
Payment for slaves. Speech of Mr. J. R. Gid-
dings, of Ohio, on the bill to pay the heirs of
Antonio Pacheco for a slave sent west of the
Mississippi with the Seminole Indians in 1838.
Made in the House of Representatives, Dec. 28,
1848, and Jan. 6, 1849. Washington, Buell and
Blanchard, 1849.
14 p. 22 cm.

[Giddings, Joshua Reed] 1795
The rights of the free states subverted, an
enumeration of some of the most prominent instances in which the federal constitution has been
violated by our national government, for the
benefit of slavery. [n.p., 1844?]
16 p. 21 1/2 cm.

Giddings, Joshua Reed, 1795.
Slavery in the territories. Speech of Hon.
J. R. Giddings, of Ohio, in the House of Represen-
tatives, Monday, March 18, 1850. [Washington,
Buell & Blanchard, 1850?]
8 p. 22 cm.

Giddings, Joshua Reed, 1795.
Speech of the Hon. J. R. Giddings, of Ohio,
on the compromise measures. Delivered in the
House of Representatives, March 6, 1852. [Wash-
ington] Buell & Blanchard [1852?]
8 p. 22 cm.

Giddings, Joshua Reed, 1795.
Speech ... on Cuban annexation. Delivered in
the House of Representatives, December 14, 1852.
[Washington, Buell & Blanchard, 1852?]
7 p. 22 cm.

Giddings, Joshua Reed.
Speech ... upon adopting the rule of the
House excluding petitions in relation to slavery.
House of Representatives, February 13, 1844.
Washington, J. & G. S. Gideon [n.d.]
8 p. 22 1/2 cm.

Gihon, John H.
Geary and Kansas. Governor Geary's administration in Kansas: with a complete history of
the territory until July 1857 ... Philadelphia,
Chas. C. Rhodes, 1857.
xii, [13]-348 p. 19 cm.

Giles, Leonidas Blanton, 1841-
Terry's Texas rangers, by L. B. Giles. [Aus-
tin, Tex., Von Boeckmann-Jones co., printers,
c1911].
165 p. 18 cm.

[Gill, John] 1841-
    Reminiscences of four years as a private sol-
dier in the Confederate army, 1861-1865. Baltimore
Sun printing office, 1904.
    xii, [13]-136 p., 1 l.   front. (port.)   22 cm.

Gillette, Francis, 1807.
    National slavery and national responsibility.
Speech ... in the Senate of the United States,
February 23, 1855 ... Washington, D. C., Buell &
Blanchard, printers, 1855.
    15 p.   25 cm.

Gillette, Francis, 1807.
    A review of the Rev. Horace Bushnell's dis-
course on the slavery question, delivered in the
North church, Hartford, January 10, 1839 ... Hartford, Published by S. S. Cowles, 1839.
    44 p.   21 cm.

Gilman, Mrs. Caroline (Howard) 1794-1888.
    The poetry of travelling in the United States.
By Caroline Gilman. With additional sketches,
by a few friends; and A week among autographs,
by Rev. S. Gilman ... New York, S. Colman, 1838.
    430 p.   5 p.l.   18 cm.

Gilman, Mrs. Caroline (Howard), 1794-
    Recollections of a New England bride and of
a southern matron. New ed. rev. New York, G.
P. Putnam & co., 1852.
    [3], [iii]-iv, [5]- 403 p.   front.   19 cm.

Gilman, Caroline (Howard) 1794-1888.
    Recollections of a southern matron. By Caro-
line Gilman ... New-York, Harper & brothers, 1838.
    1 p. l., [vii]-viii, [9]- 272 p.   19 1/2 cm.

Gilmer, John Adams.
    The Kansas question. Speech ... delivered in
the House of Representatives, on the 30th of
March, 1858.   Washington, C. W. Fenton, 1858.
    7 p.   23 cm.

Gilmer, John Adams, 1805.
    State of the union ... Delivered in the House
of Representatives, January 26, 1861. [Wash-
ington, D. C., H. Polkinhorn, printer, 1861?]
    8 p.   25 cm.

225

Gilmor, Harry, 1838-1883.
    Four years in the saddle. By Colonel Harry
Gilmor ... New York, Harper & brothers, 1866.
    xii, [13] - 291 p. incl. front. 19 1/2 cm.

Gilmore, H. S., comp.
    A collection of miscellaneous songs, from
the liberty minstrel, and Mason's juvenile harp;
for the use of the Cincinnati high school ...
Cincinnati, Sparhawk and Lytle, 1845.
    48 p.   16 1/2 cm.

[Gilmore, James Roberts] 1822-1903.
    Among the pines: or, South in secession-time.
By Edmund Kirke [pseud.]   New York, J. R. Gilmore [etc.] 1862.
    310 p.   18 1/2 cm.

[Gilmore, James Roberts] 1822-1903.
    Down in Tennessee, and back by way of Rich-
mond. By Edmund Kirke [pseud.] ... New York,
Carleton, 1864.
    282 p.   18 1/2 cm.

[Gilmore, James Roberts) 1822-1903.
    Here and there in our own country. Embracing
sketches of travel and descriptions of places,
etc., etc. Philadelphia, J. B. Lippincott company, 1885.
    214 p. illus.   22 cm.

[Gilmore, James Roberts] 1822-
    The workingman's paradise; or, West Virginia
as a home. With hints to new settlers.   By Edmund
Kirke [pseud.]   New York, Fords, Howard & Hurlbert, 1879.
    72 p.   17 cm.

[Gilpin, Thomas] 1776, ed.
    Exiles in Virginia: with observations on the
conduct of the Society of Friends during the revolutionary war, comprising the official papers of
the government relating to that period, 1777-1778.
Philadelphia, Pub. for the subscribers [C. Sherman, printer] 1848.
    [v]-xvi, [17]-302 p.   1 p.l., 3 fold. facsims.
22 1/2 cm.

226

[Girard, Charles Frédéric] 1822-1895.
Les Etats Confédérés d'Amérique visités en
1863. Mémoire adressé a S. M. Napoléon III.
Paris, E. Dentu, 1864.
viii, [9]-160 p. fold. map. 21 1/2 cm.

Girard, Just [pseud. for Just Jean Étienne Roy] 1794-
1870.
The adventures of a French captain, at present
a planter in Texas, formerly a refugee of Camp
Asylum. By Just Girard. Translated from the
French by Lady Blanche Murphy. New York, Ben-
ziger Bros. [1878].
180 p. 18 cm.

Gisborne, Thomas.
Remarks on the late decision of the House of
commons respecting the abolition of the slave
trade ... London, Printed for R. White and sons,
1792.
49 p. 20 cm.

Gislén, Torsten, 1893-
Från Hawaiis strander till New-Yorks sky-
skrapor; minnen från en naturvetenskaplig forsk-
ningsfärd, av Torsten Gislén. Illustrerad med
90 fotografier. Stockholm, Saxon & Lindström
[1935]
196, [1] p. plates. 21 1/2 cm.

Gist, Christopher.
Christopher Gist's journals with historical,
geographical and ethnological notes and bio-
graphies of his contemporaries, by William M.
Darlington. Pittsburgh, J. R. Weldon & co.,
1893.
7-296 p. 1 p.l. maps (part double) 25 cm.

Gladstone, John.
Facts, relating to slavery in the West Indies
and America, contained in a letter addressed to
the Right Hon. Robert Peel, bart. ... Second ed.
London, Baldwin and Craddock [etc., etc.] 1830.
36 p. 22 cm.

Glasgow emancipation society.
Britain and America united in the cause of universal freedom: being the third annual report
of the Glasgow Emancipation society ... 1837.

Glasgow, Printed by Aird & Russell and sold by
G. Gallie [etc., etc.] 1837.
144 p.   22 cm.

Glasgow emancipation society.
Report of the annual meeting of the Glasgow
emancipation society, held August 8, 1840 ...
Glasgow, Printed by John Clark, 1840.
23 p.   18 cm.

Glasgow emancipation society.
Report of the speeches, and reception of the
American delegates, at the great public meeting
of the Glasgow emancipation society, held in
Dr. Wardlaw's chapel, on the evening of Monday,
the 27th July, 1840 ... Glasgow, Printed by John
Clark for George Gallie, 1840.
24 p.   18 cm.

Glasgow emancipation society.
Sixth annual report ... Glasgow, Printed by
Aird & Russell and sold by George Gallie; [etc.,
etc.] 1840.
53 p.   23 cm.

Glasgow ladies' auxiliary emancipation society.
Three years' female anti-slavery effort, in
Britain and America: being a report of the proceedings of the Glasgow ladies' auxiliary emancipation society, since its formation in January,
1834 ... Glasgow, Printed by Aird & Russell and
sold by G. Gallie [etc., etc.] 1837.
72 p.   21 cm.

Glazier, Willard, 1841-1905.
The capture, the prison pen, and the escape;
giving a complete history of prison life in the
South, principally at Richmond, Danville, Macon,
Savannah, Charleston, Columbia, Belle Isle, Millin,
Salisbury, and Andersonville ... embracing, also,
the adventures of the author's escape from Columbia, South Carolina, his recapture, subsequent
escape, recapture, trial as a spy, and final escape, from Sylvania, Georgia ... By Captain Willard W. Glazier ... To which is added an appendix
containing the name, rank, regiment, and post
office address of prisoners ... New York, United
States publishing company, 1868.

xiv, p., 2 l., [19]-422 p. incl. plates.
front. (port.) 18 1/2 cm.

Glazier, Willard, 1841-
Down the great river: embracing an account
of the discovery of the true source of the Mississippi, together with views, descriptive and
pictorial, of the towns, cities, villages and
scenery on the banks of the river ... By Captain
Willard Glazier ... Philadelphia, Hubbard brothers,
1888.
xxvi, [27] - 443, liii p. incl. front. (port.)
plates. maps. fold. map. 19 1/2 cm.

Glazier, Willard, 1841-
Peculiarities of American cities. By Captain
Willard Glazier ... Philadelphia, Hubbard brothers, 1886.
4 p.l., v-xv, 25-570 p. front. (port.) 32
pl. 19 1/2 cm.

Glazier, Willard, 1841-1905.
Three years in the federal cavalry. By Captain Willard Glazier ... New York, R. H. Ferguson & company, 1874.
xvi, [2], [19] - 347 p. incl. front., 8 pl.
port. 19 1/2 cm.

[Gleig, George Robert] 1796-
A narrative of the campaigns of the British
army at Washington and New Orleans, under Generals
Ross, Pakenham, and Lambert, in the years 1814
and 1815; with some account of the countries
visited. By an Officer, who served in the expedition ... London, John Murray, 1821.
377 p. 2 p.l., 1 l. 21 1/2 cm.

Gleitsmann, William, 1840-
Western North Carolina as a health resort ...
Read before the American public health association, November, 1875, at Baltimore, and reprinted
from the Philadelphia medical and surgical reporter, February, 1876. Baltimore, Sherwood &
co., 1876.
1. p. 1., 8 p. 22 cm.

[Glen, James]
A description of South Carolina; containing
many curious and interesting particulars relating
to the civil, natural and commercial history of
that colony ... London, Printed for R. and J.
Dodsley, 1761.
[v]-viii, 110 p. 2 p.l., fold. illus.
21 1/2 cm.

Glover, Thomas.
An account of Virginia, its situation, tem-
perature, productions, inhabitants and their
manner of planting and ordering tobacco &c.
Oxford, Reprinted from the Philosophical transactions of the Royal society, June 20, 1676.
[by H. Hart, printer to the University] and
sold by B. H. Blackwell, 1904.
31 p. 21 cm.

Gobat, Albert, 1843-
... Croquis et impressions d'Amérique.
Berne, G. Grunau [1906?]
3 p.l., 301 p. front., illus. 27 cm.

Goddard, Frederick Bartlett, 1834-
Where to emigrate and why. Homes and for-
tunes in the boundless west and the sunny south
... With a complete history and description of
the Pacific railroad ... Philadelphia, Cincinnati
[etc.] The Peoples publishing company, 1869.
2 p.l., iii-xvi, 9-591 p. front, plates, maps
(part fold.) 23 cm.

Godley, John Robert.
Letters from America ... London, J. Murray,
1844.
2 v. 19 1/2 cm.

Godwin, Benjamin.
Lectures on slavery, by Rev. Benjamin Godwin
... from the London edition, with additions to
the American edition. Boston, J. B. Dow, 1836.
258 p. 17 cm.

Godwin, Benjamin.
The substance of a course of lectures on
British colonial slavery, delivered at Bradford,
York, and Scarborough ... London, J. Hatchard

and son, and J. and A. Arch, 1830.
   171 p.   21 cm.

Godwin, Parke, 1816.
   Political essays ... [From contributions to
Putnam's magazine] New York, Dix, Edwards & co.,
1856.
   345 p.   18 cm.

Gohier, Urbain Degoulet, called, 1862-
   ... Le peuple de xxe siècle aux États-Unis.
[3. mille] Paris, E. Fasquelle, 1903.
   3 p.l., 311 p.   1 l.   19 cm.

Goldberger, Ludwig Max.
   ... Das land der unbegrenzten möglichkeiten;
beobachtungen über das wirtschaftsleben der Vereinigten Staaten von Amerika, von Ludwig Max
Goldberger. Berlin [etc.] F. Fontane & co.;
Chicago, New York [etc.] Brentano's, 1911.
   4 p.l. [7]-299 [1] p.   24 1/2 cm.

Goldsborough, William Worthington, 1831-1901.
   The Maryland line in the Confederate States
army. By W. W. Goldsborough ... Baltimore,
Kelly, Piet & co., 1869.
   357 p.   front., port.   19 1/2 cm.

Goodell, William, 1792.
   Address of the Macedon convention by William
Goodell; and letters of Gerrit Smith. Albany,
S. W. Green, 1847.
   16 p.   25 cm.

Goodell, William, 1792.
   American slavery a formidable obstacle to the
conversion of the world ... New York, American
and foreign anti-slavery society, 1854.
   24 p.   19 cm.

Goodell, William.
   The Kansas struggle, of 1856, in Congress,
and in the presidential campaign; with suggestions
for the future ... [n.p.] 1857.
   80 p.   23 cm.

Goodell, William.
   Our national charters: for the millions. I.
The federal Constitution of 1788-9. II. The

Articles of confederation. III. The Declaration
of independence, 1776. IV. The Articles of
association, 1774. With notes, showing their
bearing on slavery, and the relative powers of
the state and national governments ... New York,
J. W. Alden, 1864.
144 p. 15 1/2 cm.

Goodell, William, 1792.
... The rights and wrongs of Rhode Island:
comprising views of liberty and law, of religion
and rights, as exhibited in the recent and ex-
isting difficulties in that state ... Whitesboro, N. H., 1852.
120 p. 21 cm.

Goodell, William, 1792.
Slavery and anti-slavery; a history of the
great struggle in both hemispheres; with a view
of the slavery question in the United States...
New-York, William Harned, 1852.
x, 603 p. 20 cm.

Goodhart, Briscoe, 1845-1927.
History of the Independent Loudoun Virginia
Rangers. U. S. vol. cav. (scouts) 1862-65. By
Briscoe Goodhart, co. A. Washington, D. C., Press
of McGill & Wallace, 1896.
vi, 234 p. front., illus., plates, ports.,
maps. 22 1/2 cm.

Goodloe, Albert Theodore.
Some Rebel relics from the seat of war. By
Albert Theodore Goodloe ... Nashville, Tenn.,
Printed for the author, 1893.
315 p. front. (port.) 19 cm.

[Goodloe, Daniel Reaves] 1814.
Is it expedient to introduce slavery into
Kansas? A tract for the times. [Cincinnati,
American reform tract and book society, n.d.]
24 p. 17 cm.

[Goodloe, Daniel Reaves] 1814.
The south and the north, being a reply to a
lecture on the north and the south by Ellwood
Fisher, delivered before the Young men's mercantile library association of Cincinnati, January

16, 1849. By a Carolinian. Washington, Buell
& Blanchard, 1849.
32 p.   22 cm.

[Goodloe, Daniel Reaves] 1814.
The southern platform; or, Manual of southern
sentiment on the subject of slavery ... Boston,
John P. Jewett & co., 1858.
79 p.   23 cm.

Goodmane, W. F.
Seven years in America; or, A contrast of
British America, namely, Canada, New Brunswick,
Prince Edward Island, Nova Scotia, Cape Breton,
and Newfoundland, with the United States and
Texas ... London, R. Jones, 1845.
32 p.   22 1/2 cm.

[Goodrich, J. Z.]
[Letter concerning Union emigration society,
dated House of Representatives, Washington, June
29, 1854] [Washington? 1854?]
[2] p.   25 cm.

Goodrich, Samuel Griswold, 1793-
Les États-Unis d'Amérique. Aperçu statistique,
historique, géographique, industriel et social...
accompagné d'une carte des États-Unis ... Paris,
Guillaumin et c^{ie} , 1852.
xvi, 376 p.   fold. map, tables.   22 cm.

Gordon, Armistead Churchill, 1855-
Befo' de war; echoes in Negro dialect, by
A. C. Gordon and Thomas Nelson Page. New York,
C. Scribner's sons, 1888.
3 p.l., [v]-vi, 131 p.   18 1/2 cm.

Gordon, George Henry, 1825?-1886.
A war diary of events in the war of the great
rebellion, 1863-1865. By George H. Gordon ...
Boston, J. R. Osgood and company, 1882.
vi p., 1 1., 437 p.   illus., maps.   21 cm.

Gordon, H. Panmure.
The land of the almighty dollar, by H. Panmure Gordon; the illustrations by Irving Montagu.
London and New York, F. Warne & co. [pref. 1892]
4 p.l., 215 [1] p. incl. illus., plates.
front. (port.)   21 cm.

233

Gordon, Harry.
   Journal of an expedition from Philadelphia to
the Illinois and down the Mississippi to New Orleans. [Springfield, Ill., 1916].
   290-311 p.   22 cm.

Gordon, Joseph, 1819.
   The life and writings of Rev. Joseph Gordon.
Written and compiled by a committee of the Free
Presbyterian synod. Cincinnati, Published for
the Free Presbyterian synod, 1860.
   312p.   front. (port.)   19 cm.

Gordon, Marquis Lafayette, 1843-1900.
   M. L. Gordon's experiences in the civil war
from his narrative, letters and diary; edited
by Donald Gordon ... Boston, Priv. print., 1922.
   7 p.l., [3]-72 p.   front., illus., plates,
ports., facsims. (part fold.)   28 1/2 cm.

Goss, Warren Lee, 1835-
   The soldier's story of his captivity at
Andersonville, Belle Isle, and other Rebel prisons. By Warren Lee Goss ... With an appendix,
containing the names of the Union soldiers who
died at Andersonville ... Boston, Lee and
Shepard, 1869.
   1 p.l., 357 p.   front. (port.)   plates, map,
3 plans (1 fold)   22 cm.

Gosse, Philip Henry, 1810-
   Letters from Alabama, (U. S.) chiefly relating
to natural history. London, Morgan and Chase,
1859.
   xii, 306 p.   illus.   18 cm.

Gottschall, Amos H., 1854-
   Boys, stay at home ... Marietta, Pa., The
author, 1877.
   2 p.l., [9] - 24 p.   21 1/2 cm.

[Gottshall, Amos. H.] 1854-
   Travels from ocean to ocean, and from the
lakes to the gulf; being the narrative of a
twelve years' ramble, and what was seen and experienced ... By the author of "The Chippewa's last
turn" ... 3d ed. Harrisburg, Penn., A. H. Gottschall, 1882.
   viii, 9-287 p.   17 cm.

Götz, Karl, 1903-
... Brüder über dem meer; schicksale und
begegnungen. Stuttgart, J. Engelhorns nachf.
[1938]
254, [2] p. 20 1/2 cm.

Gould, John Mead, 1839-
History of the First - Tenth - Twenty-ninth
Maine regiment. In service of the United States
from May 3, 1861, to June 21, 1866. By Maj. John
M. Gould. With the History of the Tenth Me.
battalion, by Rev. Leonard G. Jordan. Portland,
S. Berry, 1871.
709, [1] p. front., illus., port., maps.
23 cm.

Graham, Samuel, 1756-
Memoir of General Graham, with notices of the
campaigns in which he was engaged from 1779 to
1801. Ed. by his son, Colonel James J. Graham...
Edinburgh, Priv. printed by R. & R. Clark, 1862.
xvii p., 318 p. 1 1. front. (port.) 4
plates, 2 maps. 20 cm.

Graham, Sylvester.
Letter to the Hon. Daniel Webster, on the
compromises of the constitution ... Northampton,
Mass., Hopkins, Bridgman & co., 1850.
19 p. 21 cm.

Grandfort, Marie (Fontenay) de "Mme. Manoël de Grandfort."
... L'autre monde. 2 éd. Paris, Librairie
nouvelle, 1857.
272 p. 2 p.l., 1 1. 18 1/2 cm.

Grandy, Moses.
Narrative of the life of Moses Grandy, late a
slave in the United States of America ... Second
American from the last London edition ... Boston,
Oliver Johnson, 1844.
45 p. 17 cm.

Granger, Arthur.
The Apostle Paul's opinion of slavery and
emancipation. A sermon, preached to the Congregational church and society in Meriden. At the
request of several respectable anti-abolitionists

Middletown, Conn., Printed by Charles Felton, 1837.
27 p.   22 cm.

Grant, Ulysses Simpson, pres. U.S., 1822-1885.
Personal memoirs of U. S. Grant ... New York,
C. L. Webster & co., 1885-86.
2 v. front. (port.) plates, maps, facsims.
23 1/2 cm.

Grantham, Sir Thomas.
An historical account of some memorable actions,
particularly in Virginia; also against the admiral
of Algier, and in the East Indies; performed for
the service of his prince and country, by Sir
Thomas Grantham, knight, with an introduction by
R. A. Brock ... London, Printed for J. Roberts,
1716. Richmond, Va., Reprinted by C. McCarthy &
co., 1882.
viii, 72 p.   24 cm.

Grattan, Thomas Colley, 1792-
Civilized America ... 2d. ed.   London, Bradbury and Evans, 1859.
2 v. 2 maps (1 fold.)   22 cm.

Gravier, Jacques, 1651-
Lettre du père Jacques Gravier, de la Compagnie de Jésus, le 23 février 1708, sur les
affaires de la Louisiane. Nouvelle-York, 1865.
18 p.   21 1/2 cm.

Gravier, Jacques, 1651-
Relation ou Journal du voyage du r.p. Jacques
Gravier, de la Compagnie de Jésus, en 1700,
depuis le pays des Illinois jusqu'à l'embouchure
du Mississippi. Nouvelle-York, Isle de Manate,
De la presse Cramoisy de Jean-Marie Shea,
M.DCCC.LIX.
68 p., 1 l.   20 1/2 cm.

Gray, Edgar Harkness.
Assaults upon freedom! or, Kidnapping an outrage upon humanity and abhorrent to God.   A discourse occasioned by the rendition of Anthony
Burns ... Shelburne Falls [Mass.] D. B. Gunn,
1854.
22 p.   23 cm.

Gray, Iron.
     The gospel of slavery, a primer of freedom ...
[n.p., n.d.]
     [28] p.   illus.   17 cm.

Gray, John W.
     The life of Joseph Bishop, the celebrated old
pioneer in the first settlements of middle Tennessee ... Nashville, Tenn., The Author, 1858.
     236 p.   19 cm.

Gray, William F.
     From Virginia to Texas, 1835. Diary of Col.
William F. Gray giving details of his journey to
Texas and return in 1835-36 and second journey
to Texas in 1837 ... Houston, Tex., Gray, Dillaye
& co., printers, 1909.
     viii, 230 p.   23 1/2 cm.

Grayson, Andrew J. sergeant.
     "The spirit of 1861." History of the Sixth
Indiana regiment in the three months' campaign
in western Virginia ... With the names of every
officer and private in the Sixth regiment. By
A. J. Grayson. [Madison, Ind., Courier print.
1875?]
     52 p.   23 cm.

Grayson, William John, 1788-
     The hireling and the slave, Chicora and other
poems. Charleston, S. C., McCarter and co., 1856.
     xv, [21]-169 p.   2 l.   20 cm.

Great Britain. Parliament. House of commons.
     The debate on a motion for the abolition of
the slave-trade, in the House of commons, on
Monday and Tuesday, April 18 and 19, 1791. London, Printed by and for W. Woodfall, 1791.
     123 p.   21 cm.

Great Britain. Parliament. House of commons.
     The debate on a motion for the abolition of
the slave-trade &c. on Monday, the 2d of April,
1792. [n.p., n.d.]
     178 p.   21 cm.

Great Britain. Parliament. House of commons.
     Report of the debate in the House of commons,
June the 16th, 1825, on Dr. Lushington's motion

237

respecting the deportation of Messrs. L. C. Lec-
esne and J. Escoffery, two persons of colour,
from Jamaica (from Hansard's parliamentary debates,
new series, vol. xiii, p. 1173) London, Printed
for Hatchard and son [1823?]
19 p.   21 cm.

Great Britain. Parliament. House of commons.
        Select committee on the abolition of the slave
trade. An abstract of the evidence delivered before a select committee of the House of commons,
in the years 1790 and 1791; on the part of the
petitioners for the abolition of the slave trade.
The second edition. Bury, Printed by R. Haworth
[n.d.]
        260 p.   19 cm.

Great Britain. Parliament. House of commons.
        Select committee on the abolition of the slave-
trade. An abstract of the evidence delivered before a select committee of the House of commons
in the years 1790 and 1791, on the part of the
petitioners for the abolition of the slave trade.
Cincinnati, American reform tract and book society, 1855.
        xvi, [17]- 117 p.   diag.   18 cm.

Gt. Brit. Parliament. House of commons. Select committee on the slave trade.
        Third report together with the minutes of
evidence and appendix. [Communicated from the
Commons to the Lords] [n.p.]   1848.
        233 p.   33 cm.

Great Britain. Parliament. House of lords. Committee on the condition and treatment of the colonial
slaves.
        Abstract of the report of the Lords committees
on the condition and treatment of the colonial
slaves, and of the evidence taken by them on that
subject, with notes to the editor. London, Society for the abolition of slavery throughout the
British dominions, 1833.
        122 p.   21 cm.

Great southern railway, a trunk line, between the north
and the tropics, to within ninety miles of
Habana, connecting at the nearest possible point
with the West Indies, Central and South America.

New York, W. P. Hickok, printer, 1878.
xiii, 267 p. fold map. 22 1/2 cm.

The great surrender to the rebels in arms. The armi-
stice. [n.p., n.d.]
7 p. 25 cm.

Greeley, Horace, 1811, comp.
A history of the struggle for slavery extension or restriction in the United States, from
the Declaration of independence to the present
day. Mainly compiled and condensed from the
journals of Congress and other official records,
and showing the vote by yeas and nays ... New
York, Edwards & co., 1856.
iv, 164 p. 24 1/2 cm.

Greeley, Horace, 1811-
Mr. Greeley's letters from Texas and the
lower Mississippi; to which are added his address to the farmers of Texas, and his speech on
his return to New York, June 12, 1871. New York,
Tribune office, 1871.
56 p. 23 cm.

Greeley, Horace, comp.
A political text-book for 1860: comprising
a brief view of presidential nominations and
elections: including all the national platforms
ever yet adopted; also, a history of the struggle
respecting slavery in the territories, and of
the action of congress as to the freedom of the
public lands, with the most notable speeches and
letters of Messrs. Lincoln, Douglas, Bell, Cass,
Seward, Everett, Breckinridge, H. V. Johnson,
etc., etc., touching the questions of the day;
and returns of all presidential elections since
1836. Compiled by Horace Greeley and John F.
Cleveland. New York, The Tribune association,
1860.
x, 248 p. 21 cm.

Green, Beriah, 1795.
Belief without confession. A sermon preached
at Whitesboro, N. Y. ... Utica, Published by J.
C. Jackson, 1844.
15 p. 22 cm.

Green, Beriah, 1795-
     The chattel principle, the abhorrence of
Jesus Christ and the Apostles ... New York, American anti-slavery society, 1838.
     67 p.   23 cm.

Green, Beriah, 1795-
     The Chattel principle; the abhorrence of Jesus
Christ and the Apostles ... New York, American
anti-slavery society, 1839.
     71 p.   20 cm.

Green, Beriah, 1795.
     The church carried along, or the opinions of
a doctor of divinity on American slavery ...
New-York, W. S. Dorr, printer, 1836.
     41-61 p.   19 cm.

Green, Beriah, 1795.
     Iniquity and a meeting. In The tract distri-
butor (published by William Goodell, Honcoye,
Ontario county, N. Y.), v. 1, no. 1, March, 1844.
     p. 1-8.   24 cm.

Green, Beriah, 1795.
     The martyr. A discourse, in commemoration of
the martyrdom of the Rev. Elijah P. Lovejoy, delivered in Broadway Tabernacle, New York, and
in the Bleecker street church, Utica ... [New
York] Published by the American anti-slavery society, 1838.
     18 p.   20 cm.

Green, Beriah, 1795.
     Sermons, preached in the chapel of the Western
Reserve college ... Cleveland, Printed at the
office of the Herald, 1833.
     52 p.   20 cm.

Green, Beriah, 1795.
     Things for northern men to do: a discourse
delivered Lord's day evening, July 17, 1836, in
the Presbyterian church, Whitesboro', N. Y. ...
New York, Published by request, 1836.
     22 p.   22 cm.

[Green, John Paterson] 1845-
     Recollections of the inhabitants, localities,
superstitions, and Kuklux outrages of the Carolinas.

By a "Carpet-bagger" who was born and lived there. [Cleveland?]   1880.
    205 p.   22 cm.

Green, Samuel B.
    A pamphlet on equal rights and privileges, to the people of the United States ... St. Joseph Mo., Printed by Pfouts and Cundiff, Gazette office, 1857.
    cover-title, 24 p.   24 cm.

Green, William, 1748-
    The sufferings of William Green, being a sorrowful account of his seven years transportation, wherein is set forth the various hardships he underwent ... Likewise an account of their manner of living; the climate of the country; and in what it principally abounds. London: Printed by J. Long [1774?]
    16 p. illus.   17 1/2 cm.

Greene, John W.
    Camp Ford prison; and how I escaped. An incident of the civil war. Toledo, Ohio, Barkdull printing house, 1893.
    140 p. front., illus.   20 1/2 cm.

Greenleaf, A. B.
    Ten years in Texas ... Selma, Alabama, W. G. Boyd, 1881.
    vii, [9] - 131 p. front., pl.   23 1/2 cm.

Greenwood, Thomas, 1851-
    A tour in the states & Canada. Out and home in six weeks. By Thomas Greenwood ... London, L. U. Gill, 1883.
    vii, 170 p. illus.   20 cm.

Grégoire, [Henri] constitutional bp. of Blois, 1750.
    De la noblesse de la peau; ou, Du préjugé des blancs contre la couleur des Africains et celle de leurs descendans noirs et sang-melés; par M. Grégoire, ancien évêque de Blois, etc. Paris, Baudouin frères, 1826.
    3 p. 1., 75, 1 p.   21 1/2 cm.

Griesinger, Theodor, 1809-
Freiheit und Sclaverei unter dem Sternen-
banner; oder, Land und Leute in Amerika ... Stuttgart, A. Kroner, 1862.
2 pts. in 1v. fold. map. 19 cm.

Griffin, Edward D.
A plea for Africa. A sermon preached October
26, 1817, in the First Presbyterian church in the
city of New-York ... New-York, Gould, printer,
1817.
76 p. 22 cm.

Griffing, Jane R.
Letters from Florida on the scenery, climate,
social and material conditions, and practical
advantages of the "Land of flowers," by Jane R.
Griffing. Lancaster, N. H., Printed at the Republican office, 1883.
2 p.l., 122 p. 15 1/2 cm.

Griffith, Barton.
The diary of Barton Griffith, Covington, Indiana, 1832-1834, now edited and published for
the first time by permission of his great great
nephew, J. Barton Griffith, M. D. Crawfordsville,
Ind., R. E. Banta, 1932.
17 p. 2 p.l., illus. (map) 19 1/2 cm.

Griffith, John, 1713-
A journal of the life, travels, and labours
in the work of the ministry of John Griffith.
London, Printed and sold by James Phillips, in
Georgeyard, Lombard street, 1779.
iv, 427 p. 21 cm.

[Griffith, Mattie]
Autobiography of a female slave. New York,
Redfield, 1857.
viii, [9] - 401 p. 18 cm.

[Griffith, William]
Address of the president of the New-Jersey
society, for promoting the abolition of slavery,
to the general meeting at Trenton, on Wednesday
the 26th of September, 1804 ... Trenton, Printed
by Sherman & Mershon, 1804.
12 p. 22 cm.

[Griffiths, Julia] ed.
 Autographs for freedom. Boston, John P.
Jewett and company [etc.]
 viii, 263 p. front. 18 1/2 cm.

Grigsby, Melvin, 1845-
 The smoked Yank, by Melvin Grigsby. Sioux
Falls, Dakota, Bell publishing co., 1888.
 ix, [10] - 227 p. 24 cm.

Grimes, Absalom Carlisle, 1834-1911.
 Absalom Grimes, Confederate mail runner,
edited from Captain Grimes' own story by M. M.
Quaife ... New Haven, Yale university press;
London, H. Milford, Oxford university press, 1926.
 xii, 216 p. front. (port.) plates, facsim.
23 1/2 cm.

Grimes, Bryan, 1828-1880.
 Extracts of letters of Major-Gen'l Bryan
Grimes to his wife, written while in active service in the Army of northern Virginia. Together
with some personal recollections of the war,
written by him after its close, etc. Compiled
from original manuscripts by Pulaski Cowper ...
of Raleigh, N. C. Raleigh, N. C., Edwards,
Broughton & co., printers, 1883.
 137, [1] p. 22 1/2 cm.

Grimké, Angelina Emily.
 Appeal to the Christian women of the south.
[n.p., 1836?]
 36 p. 21 cm.

Grimké, Angelina Emily, 1805.
 Letters to Catherine Esther Beecher in reply
to an essay on slavery and abolitionism, addressed
to A. E. Grimke. Revised by the author. Boston,
Printed by Isaac Knapp, 1838.
 130 p. 18 cm.

Grimké, Angelina Emily.
 Slavery in America. A reprint of an appeal
to the Christian women of the slave states of
America ... With introduction, notes, and appendix by George Thompson ... Edinburgh, William
Oliphant and son, 1837.
 xxiii, [9] - 56 p. 23 cm.

Grimké, Sarah Moore, 1792.
    An epistle to the clergy of the southern
states. [New York, 1836]
    20 p.   21 cm.

Gripenberg, Alexandra, friherrinna, 1857-
    Ett halfår i Nya verlden. Strödda resebilder
från Förenta Staterna, af Alexandra Gripenberg.
Helsingfors, G. W. Edlung, 1889.
    2 p.1., 290 p.   1 1.   18 1/2 cm.

Gronovius, Joannes Fredericus, 1611-
    Flora virginica, exhibens plantas quas v. c.
Johannes Clayton in Virginia observavit atque
collegit. Easdem methodo sexuali disposuit, ad
genera propria retulit, nominibus specificus in-
signivit, & minus cognitas descripsit Joh. Fred.
Gronovius. Lugduni Batavorum, apud Cornelium
Haak, 1739-1743.
    2 v.   19 1/2 cm.

[Grose, William]   1812-1900.
    The story of the marches, battles and inci-
dents of the 36th regiment Indiana volunteer infantry. By a member of the regiment. New Castle,
Ind., The Courier company press, 1891.
    256 p.   front., ports.   23 1/2 cm.

Groussac, Paul.
    ... Del Plata al Niágara ... Buenos Aires,
Administración de La Biblioteca, 1897.
    xxiii, 486 p.   1 1.   21 1/2 cm.

Grow, Galusha Aaron.
    Nebraska and Kansas. Speech ... in the House
of Representatives, May 10, 1854. [n.p., n.d.]
    8 p.   22 cm.

Grund, Francis Joseph, 1805-
    The Americans in their moral, social and poli-
tical relations ... London, Longman, Rees, Orme,
Brown, Green & Longman, 1837.
    2 v.   22 1/2 cm.

Guest, Lady Theodora (Grosvenor), 1840-
    A round trip in North America, by Lady Theo-
dora Guest. With illustrations from the author's
sketches. London, E. Stanford, 1895.
    4 p.1., 270 p.   xvi pl. (incl. front.)   23 cm.

Guide des émigrans francais dans les états de Kentucky
et d'Indiana, ou Renseignemens fidèles sur les
États-Unis de l'Amérique Septentrionale en générale,
et sur les états de Kentucky et d'Indiana en par-
ticulier ... Paris, A. Bertrand, 1835.
    55 p.   2 p.l.   22 cm.

Guimaraes, Celso Foot, 1907-
    Um sonho! Impressões de uma viagem aos Esta-
dos Unidos. Rio de Janeiro, Editora Civilização
Brasileira, 1947.
    292 p.   illus., ports., map.   21 cm.

Gulliver, John P.
    The lioness and her whelps: a sermon on
slavery, preached in the Broadway congregational
church, Norwich, Conn., December 18, 1859 ...
Second edition ... Norwich, Manning, Perry &
co., 1860.
    35 p.   19 cm.

Gunn, Lewis Carstairs.
    Address to abolitionists ... Philadelphia,
Merrihew and Gunn, printers, 1838.
    16 p.   22 cm.

Gurley, Ralph Randolph, 1797.
    Address at the annual meeting of the Pennsyl-
vania colonization society, November 11, 1839 ...
Philadelphia, Published by Herman Hooker, 1839.
    40 p.   23 cm.

Gurley, Ralph Randolph, 1797.
    Letter of Mr. Gurley. Office of the Coloniza-
tion society, Washington, April 9, 1833. [n.p.,
n.d.]
    [3] - 7 p.   20 cm.

Gurley, Ralph Randolph, 1797.
    Mission to England, in behalf of the American
colonization society. Washington, Wm. W. Morrison, 1841.
    264 p.   19 cm.

Gurney, Alfred, 1845-
    A ramble through the United States; a lecture
delivered (in part) in S. Barnabas' school February 3, 1886, by Alfred Gurney ... [London, Printed by W. Clowes and sons, limited, 1886?]

4 p.1., 63 p.   22 cm.

Gurney, Joseph John, 1788-
    A journey in North America, described in fami-
liar letters to Amelia Opie ... Norwich [Eng.]
Printed for private circulation, by J. Fletcher,
1841.
    414 p. 1 p.1., 1 1.   22 1/2 cm.

Gurney, Joseph John, 1788.
    Speech of J. J. Gurney, Esq., on the abolition
of Negro slavery, delivered at a public meeting,
held in the Guildhall, in the city of Norwich,
on Wednesday, 28th January, 1824. [Liverpool,
Rushton and Melling, printers, n.d.]
    15 p.   21 cm.

Gurney, Joseph John, 1788.
    A winter in the West Indies, described in
familiar letters to Henry Clay, of Kentucky ...
London, John Murray, 1840.
    xvi, 282 p. illus.   23 cm.

Gurowski, Adam, 1805-
    America and Europe ... New York, D. Appleton
and company, 1857.
    viii, 411 p.   20 1/2 cm.

Gurowski, Adam.
    Slavery in history ... New York, A. B. Bur-
dick, 1860.
    xiv, 260 p.   18 1/2 cm.

Guthrie, Thomas.
    "I have fought a good fight." 2 Timothy,
IV: 7. Cincinnati, American reform tract and
book society, n.d.
    4 p.   17 cm.

Guthrie, William, 1708-
    A new geographical, historical, and commercial
grammar; and present state of the several kingdoms of the world ... With a table of the coins
of all nations, and their value in English money ...
Illustrated with a new and correct set of maps,
engraved by Mr. Kitchin. London, J. Knox, 1770.
    xiii, xlvi, 656 p. 19 fold. maps (incl.
front.), fold. table.   21 1/2 cm.

[Habard?, R. T.]
Review of the Massachusetts proposition for
abolishing the slave representation. Republished
from the Southern literary messenger of August,
1845. Washington, D. C., Printed by John T.
Towers, 1847.
30 p. 21 1/2 cm.

Habersham, S. E.
Health and profit: as found in the hilly pine
region of Georgia & South Carolina. Together with
an account of its horticultural, agricultural,
and manufacturing resources, and the topography,
geology, botany and climatology of the region.
Augusta, Ga., Augusta press book and job office,
1869.
vii, [8] - 147 p. 18 1/2 cm.

[Hachard, Marie Madeleine, in religion, Sister Saint
Stanislas]
Relation du voyage des dames religieuses Ursulines de Rouen à la Nouvelle-Orléans, avec une
introduction et des notes par Gabriel Gravier ...
Paris, Maisonneuve et cie, 1872.
lix, 122 p. 1 1. 22 1/2 cm.

Hadley, John Vestal, 1840-
Seven months a prisoner, by J. V. Hadley.
New York, Charles Scribner's sons, 1898.
3 p.l., 258 p. 16 1/2 cm.

[Hager, Heinrich?]
Warhaffte Nachricht, von einer Hochteutschen
Evangelischen Colonie, zu Germantown, in Nord-
Virginien in America, und derselben dringendliches
Ansuchen an ihre Glaubens-Genossen in Europa.
(In Historical notes relating to the Pennsylvania
Reformed church. Edited by Henry S. Dotterer.
v. 1. [May 10, 1899 - April 10, 1900] Philadel-
phia, Perkiomen publishing company, 1900. p. 8-10)

Hague, Mrs. Parthenia Antoinette [(Vardaman)] 1838-
A blockaded family: life in southern Alabama
during the civil war. Boston and New York,
Houghton, Mifflin and co., 1888.
v., 176 p. 18 cm.

Hague, William.
    Christianity and slavery: a review of Doctors
Fuller and Wayland, on domestic slavery ... Boston, Gould, Kendall, & Lincoln, 1847.
    54 p.   16 cm.

Hague, William.
    Christianity and statesmanship; with kindred
topics ... New York, Edward H. Fletcher, 1855.
    429 p.   18 cm.

[Haines, Zenas T.]
    Letters from the Forty-fourth regiment M.V.M.:
a record of the experience of a nine months regiment in the Department of North Carolina in 1862-
3. By "Corporal" [pseud.] Boston, Printed at
the Herald job office, 1863.
    121 p.   24 cm.

Haiti. Laws, statutes, etc.
    Rural code of Haiti. [n.p., n.d.]
    48 p.   20 cm.

Hale, John Parker, 1806.
    Speech ... on the territorial question. De-
livered in the Senate of the United States, Tuesday, March 19, 1850. Washington, Buell & Blanchard, 1850?
    16 p.   24 cm.

Hale, John Parker.
    The wrongs of Kansas. Speech ... In the
United States Senate, February, 1856. Washington,
Buell & Blanchard, 1856.
    16 p.   23 cm.

Hale, Mrs. Sarah Josepha (Buell)
    Liberia; or, Mr. Peyton's experiments ... New
York, Harper and brothers, 1853.
    304 p.   19 cm.

Hall, Abraham Oakley, 1826-
    The Manhattaner in New Orleans; or, Phases of
"Crescent city" life ... New York, J. S. Redfield;
New Orleans, J. C. Morgan, 1851.
    x, 190 p.   18 1/2 cm.

Hall, Basil, 1788-
    Forty etchings, from sketches made with the
camera lucida, in North America, in 1827 and 1828

Edinburgh, Cadell & co.; [etc., etc., 1829]
ii p., 21 1. 1 p.1., front. (fold. map) XL
pl. on 20 1. 33 1/2 cm.

Hall, Basil, 1788-
Travels in North America in the years 1827 and
1828 ... Edinburgh, Printed for Cadell and co.;
London, Simpkin and Marshall, 1829.
3 v. fold. map, fold. tab. 19 1/2 cm.

Hall, Baynard R.
Frank Freeman's barber shop; a tale ... Illustrated by Rush B. Hall. New York, Charles Scribner, 1852.
ix, 343 p. 19 cm.

Hall, Clayton Colman, 1847, ed.
... Narratives of early Maryland, 1633-1684...
New York, Charles Scribner's sons, 1910.
ix p., 3-460 p. 2 1., front. (fold. map) 2
facsim. (1 fold.) 22 1/2 cm.

[Hall, F.]
The importance of the British plantations in
America to this kingdom with the state of their
trade, and methods for improving it; as also a
description of the several colonies there. London, Printed for J. Peele, 1731.
114 p. 3 p.1. 19 cm.

Hall, Francis.
Travels in Canada and in the United States, in
1816 and 1817 ... London, Longman, Hurst, Rees,
Orme & Brown, 1818.
543 p. 2 p.1., front. (fold. map) illus.
?^ i/2 cm.

Hall, Frederick, 1780-
Letters from the East and from the West. Washington city, F. Taylor and W. M. Morrison; Baltimore, F. Lucas, jr., [etc., etc., 1840]
xi, 168 p. 23 cm.

Hall, James, 1744-
A brief history of the Mississippi territory,
to which is prefixed, a summary view of the country between the settlements on Cumberland River
& the territory. Salisbury [N. C.] Printed by
Francis Coupée, 1801.
70 p. 1 p.1. 19 cm.

Hall, James, 1793-
    Statistics of the West, at the close of the
year 1836. Cincinnati, J. A. James & co., 1836.
xviii, [2] - 284 p.   18 1/2 cm.

Hall, Marshall, 1790-
    The two-fold slavery of the United States; with
a project of self-emancipation ... London, A.
Scott, 1854.
    [3], ix-xii, 159 p. 1 1. 2 fold. maps (incl.
front.)   17 1/2 cm.

Hall, Nathaniel.
    The iniquity: a sermon preached in the First
Church, Dorchester, on Sunday, Dec. 11, 1859 ...
Boston, John Wilson & Son, 1859.
    37 p.   23 1/2 cm.

Hall, Nathaniel.
    The moral significance of the contrasts be-
tween slavery and freedom: a discourse preached
in the first church, Rochester, May 19, 1864 ...
Boston, Walker, Wise and company [and] Ebenezer
Clapp, 1864.
    15 p.   23 cm.

Hall, Nathaniel.
    Righteousness and the pulpit: a discourse
preached in the First church, Rochester, on
Sunday, Sept. 30, 1855 ... Boston, Crosby,
Nichols and company, 1855.
    27 p.   21 cm.

Hall, Robert.
    The works of the Rev. Robert Hall, A. M., with
a memoir of his life, by Dr. Gregory; reminiscences,
by John Greene, and his character as a preacher,
by the Rev. John Foster. Published under the
superintendence of Olinthus Gregory, professor
of mathematics in the Royal Military Academy; and
Joseph Belcher, D. D. New-York, Harper & brothers,
1849.
    4 v.   23 cm.

Hall, Winchester, 1819-
    The story of the 26th Louisiana infantry, in
the service of the Confederate States. By Winchester Hall. [n.p., 1890?]
    4 p.l., 228, [2] p. plan.   24 cm.

Hallock, Charles, 1834-
An angler's reminiscences. A record of sport, travel and adventure. With autobiography of the author ... Notes and introductory chapter by Fred E. Pond ("Will Wildwood") Cincinnati, Sportsman's review publishing co., 1913.
vii, 135 p. front., plates, ports.   23 1/2 cm.

Hallock, Charles, 1834-
Camp life in Florida; a handbook for sportsmen and settlers. Comp. by Charles Hallock ... [New York] Forest and stream publishing company, 1876.
vi, [7] - 348 p.   maps.   19 cm.

Hamilton, Andrew Jackson, 1815.
Letter of Gen. A. J. Hamilton, of Texas to the president of the United States. [n.p., n.d.]
18 p.   21 cm.

Hamilton, Andrew Jackson.
... Letter of Gen. A. J. Hamilton, of Texas, to the president of the United States. New York, published by the Loyal publication society, 1865.
18 p.   21 cm.

Hamilton, Andrew Jackson, 1815.
Origin and objects of the slaveholders' conspiracy against democratic principles, as well as against the national union, illustrated in the speeches of Andrew Jackson Hamilton, in the statements of Lorenzo Sherwood, ex-member of the Texas legislature, and in the publications of the Democratic league, etc. [New York? 1862?]
16 p.   22 cm.

Hamilton, Henry.
Account of the expedition of Lieut. Gov. Hamilton. [Lansing, 1908]
489-516 p.   23 cm.

Hamilton, James A.
State sovereignty. Rebellion against the United States by the people of a state in its political suicide ... New York, Baker & Godwin, 1862.
32 p.   22 cm.

[Hamilton, Thomas] 1789-
    Men and manners in America. By the author of
"Cyril Thornton", etc. ... Edinburgh, W. Blackwood;
[etc., etc., pref. 1833]
    2 v. in 1. front. 21 cm.

Hamlin, Hannibal.
    Remarks ... on resigning his position as chair-
man of the Committee on commerce, and the tests
of the Cincinnati convention. In the Senate of
the United States, June 12, 1856. Washington,
Buell & Blanchard, 1856.
    8 p. 22 cm.

[Hammett, Samuel A.] 1816-1865.
    A stray Yankee in Texas. By Philip Paxton
[pseud.] New York, Redfield, 1853.
    xvi, [17] - 416 p. 3 p.l., front. 18 cm.

[Hammett, Samuel Adams] 1816-1865.
    Piney Woods tavern; or, Sam Slick in Texas.
By the author of "A stray Yankee in Texas" ...
Philadelphia, T. B. Peterson and brothers
[c1858]
    x, 11-309 p. front. 18 1/2 cm.

Hammond, James Henry, 1807.
    Remarks of Mr. Hammond, of South Carolina, on
the question of receiving petitions for the abolition of slavery in the District of Columbia.
Delivered in the House of Representatives, February 1, [1836] Washington city, C. Green 1836.
    20 p. 22 1/2 cm.

Hammond, James Henry.
    Speech ... on the admission of Kansas, under
the Lecompton Constitution. Delivered in the
Senate of the United States, March 4, 1858.
Washington, Lemuel Towers, 1858.
    15 p. 23 cm.

Hammond, John.
    Hammond versus Heamans. Or, an answer to an
audacious Pamphlet published by an impudent and
ridiculous Fellow, named Roger Heamans ... where-
in he endeavours by lies and holy expressions,
to colour over his murthers and treacheries com-
mitted in the Province of Maryland ... Printed
at London for the use of the author, and are to

be sold at the Royall Exchange in Cornhill
[1655]
17 numb. 1, 2 p.1.   21 cm.

Hammond, Stephen Hallet.
   Freedom national -- slavery sectional. Speech
... on the governor's message in Senate, February,
1860. Albany, Weed, Parsons & co., 1860.
   14 p.   22 cm.

Hamor, Ralph, the younger.
   A true discourse of the present estate of
Virginia, and the successe of the affaires there
till the 18 of June, 1614 ... London, Printed by
John Beale for W. Welby, 1615.
   69, [1] p.   4 p.1.   18 1/2 cm.

Hampton, John S.
   The North Carolina guide and business office
companion ... Raleigh, News and steam book and
job office and bindery, 1877.
   3 p.1., 4-42 p. fold. map.   17 cm.

Hancock, Richard R.   1841?-1906.
   Hancock's diary: or, A history of the Second
Tennessee Confederate cavalry, with sketches of
First and Seventh battalions; also, portraits and
biographical sketches.   Two volumes in one.
Nashville, Tenn., Brandon printing co., 1887.
   644 p.   front., port.   23 1/2 cm.

Hancock, William Jay.
   A letter to the Hon. Samuel A. Eliot, repre-
sentative in Congress from the city of Boston,
in reply to his apology for voting for the fugitive slave bill ... Boston, Wm. Crosby & H. P.
Nichols, 1851.
   57 p.   21 cm.

Handbook for immigrants to the United States.   New
   York, for the Association, by Hurd and Houghton,
1871.
   vi, 1-117 p.   fold.   map.   19 1/2 cm.

Haney, William Henry, 1882-
   The mountain people of Kentucky.   An account
of present conditions with the attitude of the
people toward improvement.   Cincinnati, O.,
Roessler bros., 1906.

196 p.   front., plates, ports., map.   21 cm.

Hannaford, Ebenezer, 1840-
      The story of a regiment: a history of the
campaigns, and associations in the field, of the
Sixth regiment Ohio volunteer infantry. By E.
Hannaford ... Cincinnati, The author, 1868.
      xvi, 17-622 p.   22 cm.

Hanson, John Wesley, 1823-
      Historical sketch of the old Sixth regiment of
Massachusetts volunteers, during its three campaigns in 1861, 1862, 1863, and 1864. Containing
the history of the several companies previous to
1861, and the name and military record of each
man connected with the regiment during the war.
By John W. Hanson, chaplain ... Boston, Lee and
Shepard, 1866.
      352 p.   front., port.   19 1/2 cm.

Hanstrom, Bertil, 1891-
      ... Skisser från en Kaliforniafard.   Lund,
C. W. K. Gleerup [1922]
      143 p.   illus.   20 1/2 cm.

Hard, Abner.
      History of the Eighth cavalry regiment, Illi-
nois volunteers, during the great rebellion; by
Abner Hard ... Aurora, Ill., 1868.
      4 p.1., [33] - 368 p.   22 1/2 cm.

Hardman, William.
      A trip to America. By William Hardman. With
map. London, T. V. Wood, 1884.
      [5], [v]-vi, 210 p.   front. (map)   19 cm.

Hardy, Iza Duffus.
      Between two oceans: or, Sketches of American
travel. By Iza Duffus Hardy ... London, Hurst
and Blackett, 1884.
      3 p.1., 355 p.   23 cm.

Hardy, Iza Duffus.
      Oranges and alligators: sketches of south
Florida life ... London, Ward and Downey, 1886.
      viii, 240 p.   19 1/2 cm.

Hardy, Mary (McDowell) Duffus, lady, 1825?
Down South, by Lady Duffus Hardy ... London,
Chapman and Hall, limited, 1883.
vii, 276 p.   23 cm.

Hardy, Mary [McDowell] Duffus, lady, 1825?
Through cities and prairie lands. Sketches of
an American tour. By Lady Duffus Hardy. New York,
R. Worthington, 1881.
xii, 338 p.   21 1/2 cm.

[Hare, Joseph Thompson]
The dying confession of Joseph Hare. Second
edition. Baltimore, Printed for the publisher,
1818.
23 p.   20 1/2 cm.

Harlan, James, 1820.
Shall the territories be africanized? Speech
... delivered in the United States Senate, January
4, 1860. [n.p., n.d.]
8 p.   21 cm.

Harlan, Mary B.
Ellen; or, The chained mother; and pictures of
Kentucky slavery. Drawn from real life. Cincinnati, For the author, by Applegate & co., 1853.
vi, [7] - 259 p.   front., plates. 18 cm.

Harley, Timothy.
Southward ho! Notes of a tour to and through
the state of Georgia in the winter of 1885-6.
By the Rev. Timothy Harley ... London, S. Low,
Marston, Searle & Rivington, 1886.
vi p., 1 l., 198 p.   incl. illus., plates.
17 1/2 cm.

Harriott, John, 1745-
Struggles through life, exemplified in the
various travels and adventures in Europe, Asia,
Africa, & America, of Lieut. John Harriott ...
London printed. Philadelphia reprinted by James
Humphreys; and sold by him at his store on Change-
walk ... 1809.
2 v.   18 1/2 cm.

Harris, James Sidney.
Historical sketches. Seventh regiment, North
Carolina troops. Mooresville [N.C.] Mooresville

printing co. [1893?]
70 p. 23 cm.

Harris, Lewis Birdsall, 1816-
Journal of Lewis Birdsall Harris, 1836-1842:
Personal history for my sons. In Southwestern
historical quarterly, XXV (1921-22), 63-71, 131-
146, 185-197.

Harris, Nathaniel Edwin, 1846-
Autobiography; the story of an old man's life,
with reminiscences of seventy-five years, by
Nathaniel E. Harris ... Macon, Ga., The J. W.
Burke company, 1925.
550 p. front., illus. (incl. ports.)
20 cm.

Harris, R.
Scriptural researches on the licitness of the
slave-trade, shewing its conformity with the
principles of natural and revealed religion, delineated in the sacred writings of the word of
God ... London, Printed for John Stockdale, 1788.
77 p. 20 cm.

Harris, Thaddeus Mason, 1768-
The journal of a tour into the territory northwest of the Alleghany mountains; made in the spring
of the year 1803. With a geographical and historical account of the state of Ohio. Boston:
Printed by Manning & Loring, no. 2, Cornhill,
1805.
viii, [11]-271 p., 1 1. fold. pl., 3 fold.
pl., 3 fold. maps, plan. 23 cm.

Harris, William C.
Prison-life in the tobacco warehouse at Richmond. By a Ball's Bluff prisoner, Lieut. Wm. C.
Harris ... Philadelphia, G. W. Childs, 1862.
2 p.1., 9-175 p. incl. front. 18 1/2 cm.

Harris, William Tell.
Remarks made during a tour through the United
States of America, in the years 1817, 1818, and
1819. In a series of letters to friends in
England. London, Sherwood, Neely & Jones, 1821.
196 p. 17 cm.

Harrison, Benjamin, pres. U. S., 1833-
    Through the South and West with the President,
April 14 - May 15, 1891. The only complete and
authorized collection of President Harrison's
great and eloquent speeches made during the tour.
Comp. by John S. Shriver ... New York, The Mail
and express, 1891.
    2 p.l. [vii]-xvi, 152 p. port. fold. map.
23 cm.

[Harrison, Samuel Alexander] 1822-
    Memoir of Lieut. Col. Tench Tilghman, secre-
tary and aid to Washington, together with an appendix, containing revolutionary journals and
letters, hitherto unpublished ... Albany, J. Munsell, 1876.
    176 p. front. (port.)   25 1/2 cm.

Harrison, Z.
    Description of the Cincinnati southern rail-
way from Cincinnati to Chattanooga ... Cincinnati,
Spencer and Craig printing works, 1878.
    viii, 120 p. plates, fold. map.   23 1/2 cm.

Harrold, John.
    Libby, Andersonville, Florence. The capture,
imprisonment, escape and rescue of John Harrold,
a Union soldier in the war of the rebellion ...
Philadelphia, W. B. Selheimer, 1870.
    132 p.   18 1/2 cm.

Hart, Albert Bushnell, 1854-
    The southern South, by Albert Bushnell Hart
... New York and London, D. Appleton and company, 1910.
    3 p.l., 445 p., 1 l. incl. tables. map.
20 cm.

Hart, Ephraim J.
    History of the Fortieth Illinois inf., (volun-
teers). By Sergeant E. J. Hart ... Cincinnati,
H. S. Bosworth, 1864.
    196 p.   19 1/2 cm.

Hartford, Conn. Fourth Congregational church.
    The unanimous remonstrance of the Fourth Con-
gregational church, Hartford, Conn., against the
policy of the American tract society on the subject of slavery. [New York, American anti-

slavery society, 1855?]
  36 p.   19 cm.

The Hartley coal pit. [Cincinnati, American reform
tract and book society, n.d.]
  4 p.   18 cm.

Hartpence, William R.
    History of the Fifty-first Indiana veteran
volunteer infantry. A narrative of its organization, marches, battles and other experiences
in camp and prison; from 1861 to 1866. With revised roster. By Wm. R. Hartpence ... Harrison,
O., Pub. by the author; Cincinnati, The Robert
Clarke company, printers, 1894.
    viii, 405 p. pl., 7 port. (incl. front.)
24 cm.

Hartwell, Henry.
    The present state of Virginia, and the college;
by Messieurs Hartwell, Blair, and Chilton. To
which is added, the charter for erecting the said
college ... London, Printed for J. Wyat, 1727.
    95 p. 2 p.1.   23 cm.

Haskel, Daniel, 1784-
    A complete descriptive and statistical gazet-
teer of the United States ... With an abstract
of the census and statistics for 1840 ... By
Daniel Haskel and J. Calvin Smith. New York,
Sherman & Smith, 1848.
    754 p.   24 cm.

Hasson, Benjamin F.
    Escape from the confederacy; over-powering the
guards - midnight leap from a moving train -
through swamps and forest - blood hounds - thrilling events. [By] B. F. Hasson ... [Bryant? O.,
c1900]
    3 p.1., [9]-59, [1] p.   illus.   20 cm.

[Hasted, Frederick]
    A copy of a letter written to the president
of the United States, on slave emancipation.
[n.p., n.d.]
    4, 8, 5-8, 4, 4, 8, 4, 4, 8, 16 p.   23 cm.

Hastings, George.
    Speech ... on the Nebraska and Kansas Bill,
delivered in the House of Representatives, April
20, 1854. Washington, Congressional globe office,
1854.
    7 p.   23 cm.

[Hastings, John K.]
    Anti-slavery landmarks in Boston ... (From
the Boston Transcript, Sept. 1, 1897) [Boston?
1897?]
    8 p.   23 cm.

Hatch, Reuben.
    Bible servitude re-examined; with special re-
ference to pro-slavery interpretations and infidel
objections ... Cincinnati, Applegate & co., 1862.
    284 p.   19 cm.

Hatton, Joseph, 1841-
    Henry Irving's impressions of America, nar-
rated in a series of sketches, chronicles, and
conversations by Joseph Hatton ... Boston, J. R.
Osgood and company, 1884.
    xii, 475 p.   19 1/2 cm.

Hatton, Joseph.
    To-day in America. Studies for the Old world
and the New ... London, Chapman and Hall (limited)
1881.
    2 v.   20 cm.

Haussonville, Gabriel Paul Othenin de Cléron, comte
    d', 1843-
    A travers les États-Unis; notes et impressions
par le comte d'Haussonville ... Paris, Calmann-
Lévy, 1888.
    2 p.l., 400 p.   19 cm.

Have we any need of the Bible? [Cincinnati, American
reform tract and book society, n.d.]
    24 p.   18 cm.

Have you an anchor? [Cincinnati, American reform
tract and book society, n.d.]
    4 p.   18 cm.

Have you a friend? [Cincinnati, American reform tract
and book society, n.d.]
4 p. 18 cm.

Haven, Gilbert, bp., 1821.
National sermons. Sermons, speeches and letters
on slavery and its war: from the passage of the
Fugitive slave bill to the election of President
Grant ... Boston, Lee & Shepard, 1869.
xxiv, 656 p. 21 1/2 cm.

Haviland, Mrs. Laura (Smith) 1808.
A woman's life-work: labors and experience
of Laura S. Haviland. Cincinnati, Printed by
Walden & Stowe, 1882.
2 p. 1., 520 p. front. (port.) plates.
19 1/2 cm.

Haweis, Hugh Reginald, 1839-
Travel and talk, 1885-93-95. My hundred
thousand miles of travel through America, Australia, Tasmania, Canada, New Zealand, Ceylon,
and the paradises of the Pacific; by the Rev.
H. R. Haweis ... London, Chatto & Windus; New
York, Dodd, Mead, & company, 1896.
2 v. fronts. (ports.) 19 1/2 cm.

Hawes, Jesse, 1843-1901.
Cahaba. A story of captive boys in blue, by
Jesse Hawes ... New York, Burr printing house
[c1888]
xviii, 480 p. incl. fornt. pl., ports.,
plan. 23 1/2 cm.

Hawes, Joel.
North and south: or, Four questions considered: What have we done? What have we to do?
What have we to hope? What have we to fear? A
sermon preached in the First church in Hartford,
on the day of the national fast, Sept. 26th, 1861
... Hartford, Press of Case, Lockwood and company, 1861.
31 p. 23 cm.

Hawks, John Milton, 1826-
The east coast of Florida. A descriptive
narrative by J. M. Hawks ... Lynn, Mass., Lewis
& Winship [c1887]
137 p. fold. front. (map) illus. 17 1/2 x
18 1/2 cm.

Hawks, John Milton, 1826-
    The Florida gazetteer, containing also a guide
through the state; complete official and business directory; state and national statistics ...
New Orleans, Bronze pen stfam [!] book and job
office, 1871.
    214 p.   21 1/2 cm.

Hayden, William, 1785.
    Narrative of William Hayden, containing a
faithful account of his travels for a number of
years, whilst a slave, in the south.   Cincinnati,
[Pub. for the author] 1846.
    156 p.   plates.   port.   18 cm.

Haygood, Atticus Greene, bp., 1839.
    Pleas for progress.   Nashville, Tenn., Printed
for the author, Pub. house of the M. E. church,
South, 1889.
    320 p.   19 cm.

Haynes, Edwin Mortimer, 1836-
    A history of the Tenth regiment, Vermont vol-
unteers, with biographical sketches of the officers who fell in battle.   And a complete roster
of all the officers and men connected with it-
showing all changes by promotion, death or resig-
nation, during the military existence of the
regiment.   By Chaplain E. M. Haynes.   [Lewiston,
Me., printed] Pub. by the Tenth Vermont regimental association, 1870.
    viii, [9] - 249 p.   22 cm.

Haynes, Martin A.   1845-
    History of the Second regiment New Hampshire
volunteers: its camps, marches and battles.   By
Martin A. Haynes ... Manchester, N. H., C. F.
Livingston, printer, 1865.
    viii, [9] - 223, [1] p.   19 1/2 cm.

Hayward, John, 1781-
    A view of the United States: historical,
geographical and statistical.   November, 1832 ...
New York, J. & W. Day, 1832.
    20 l.   incl. tables.   27 cm.

Hearn, Lafcadio, 1850-1904.
    Letters from the Raven; being the correspon-
dence of Lafcadio Hearn with Henry Watkin; with

introduction and critical comment by the editor,
Milton Bronner. New York, Brentano's, 1907.
  5 p.l., [9]-201 p. illus., plates. facsims.
19 1/2 cm.

Heartsill, William Williston, 1839-
  Fourteen hundred and 91 days in the Confederate
  army. A journal kept by W. W. Heartsill, for four
  years, one month, and one day: or, Camp life;
  day--by-day, of the W. P. Lane Rangers, from April
  19th, 1861, to May 20th, 1865. [Marshall, Tex.,
  W. W. Heartsill, 1876]
    4 p.l., 264 p., 1 l. 61 phot. on 19 pl.
  20 1/2 cm.

Hebrew servitude and American slavery. [Cincinnati,
  American reform tract and book society, n.d.]
    8 p.   18 cm.

Hecke, J. Valentin.
  Reise durch die Vereinigten Staaten von Nord-
  Amerika in den jahren 1818 und 1819. Nebst einer
  kurzen uebersicht der neuesten ereignisse auf
  dem kriegs-schauplatz in Süd-Amerika und West-In-
  dien ... Berlin, In commission bei H. P. Petri,
  1820-1821.
    2 v. front.   21 1/2 cm.

[Hedge, Mary Ann]
  [Samboe, or, The African boy. London, Harvey,
  Darton & co., n.d.]
    175 p., [5] l.   14 cm.

Hedley, Fenwick Y.
  Marching through Georgia. Pen-pictures of
  every-day life in General Sherman's army, from
  the beginning of the Atlanta campaign until the
  close of the war, by F. Y. Hedley ... Illustrated
  by F. L. Stoddard. Chicago, Donohue, Henneberry
  & co., 1890.
    490 p. incl. illus., plates, facsims. front.,
  pl.   20 cm.

Heikel, Karl Felix, 1844-
  Från Förenta Staterna. Nitton bref jemte bi-
  hang ... Helsingfors, Tryckt i Hufvudstadsbladets
  tryckeri, 1873.
    4 p.l., 182, [2] p.   19 cm.

Hellwald, Friedrich Anton Heller von, 1842-
        Amerika in wort und bild. Eine schilderung
    der Vereinigten Staaten von Friedrich von Hell-
    wald ... Leipzig, H. Schmidt & C. Günther [1883-
    85].
        2 v. fronts., illus., plates, ports, maps
    (1 fold.)   36 1/2 cm.

Helm, Mary (Sherwood) Wightman, 1807-
        Scraps of early Texas history, by Mrs. Mary
    S. Helm, who, with her first husband, Elias R.
    Wightman, founded the city of Matagorda, in
    1828-9. Austin, the author, 1884.
        iv, 198 p. 1 p.l., 1 1.   21 1/2 cm.

Helper, Hinton Rowan, 1829.
        Compendium of the Impending crisis of the
    south. New York, A. B. Burdick, 1860.
        214 p.   19 cm.

Helps, Arthus.
        The Spanish conquest in America, and its re-
    lation to the history of slavery and to the
    government of colonies ... New York, Harper &
    brothers, 1856.
        4 v. fold. map.   19 1/2 cm.

Hennepin, Louis.
        Description de la Louisiane, nouvellement dé
    couverte au sud'ouest de la Nouvelle France, par
    ordre du roy. Avec la carte du pays: Les moeurs
    & la manière de vivre des sauvages ... A Paris,
    Chez la veuve Sebastien Hure, 1683.
        312, 107 p. 6 p.l. map.   17 cm.

Henshall, James Alexander, 1844-
        Camping and cruising in Florida ... Cincinnati,
    R. Clarke & co., 1884.
        2 p.l., xv-xvi p., 1 1., v-xiii, 248 p. front.,
    illus., plates, map.   20 cm.

Henshall, James Alexander, 1844-
        ... Notes of fishes collected in Florida in
    1892. By James A. Henshall, M. D. Washington,
    Govt. print. off., 1895.
        1 p.l., 209-221 p.   29 1/2 cm.

Henson, Josiah.
        Truth stranger than fiction. Father Henson's

story of his own life. With an introduction by
Mrs. H. B. Stowe. Boston, John P. Jewett and company; Cleveland, Ohio, Henry P. B. Jewett, 1858.
 xii, 212 p. front. (port.) 19 cm.

Hentz, Caroline Lee (Whiting) 1800-1856.
 The planter's northern bride. A novel. By
Caroline Lee Hentz ... Philadelphia, Parry &
M'Millan, 1854.
 2 v. fronts., illus. 20 cm.

Heras, Antonio.
 ... De la vida norteamericana; impresiones
frívolas. Madrid [Sucesores de Hernando] 1924.
 242 p. 19 1/2 cm.

Hermann, Isaac, 1838-
 Memoirs of a veteran who served as a private
in the 60's in the war between the states; personal incidents, experiences and observations,
written by Capt. I. Hermann ... Atlanta, Ga.,
Byrd printing company, 1911.
 285 p. incl. front. (port.) plates. 21 cm.

Herrera Oria, Enrique.
 Norteamérica al día, memorias de un viajero
español. 1. ed. Madrid, Ediciones Studium de
Cultura [1946]
 181 p. 20 cm.

Herter, August.
 Im zweiten vaterland. Briefe aus Amerika für
auswanderer, von August Herter ... Getreue darstellung der reisebedürfnisse, der natürlichen,
gesellschaftlichen und politischen verhältnisse
der Union, der wichtigsten vorsichtsmassregeln
für die ansiedelung, der jetzigen aussichten für
land und industriearbeiter, & c. & c. ... Bern,
K. J. Wyss, 1886.
 iv, 327 [4] p. fold. map. 18 1/2 cm.

Herz, Henri, 1803-
 Mes voyages en Amérique ... Paris, Achille
Faure, 1866.
 328 p. 3 p.l. port. 18 1/2 cm.

Hesse-Wartegg, Ernst von, 1854-
 Curiosa aus der Neuen welt. Von Ernst von
Hesse-Wartegg. Leipzig, C. Reissner, 1893.

vi p., 1 1., 327 p.   19 1/2 cm.

Hesse-Wartegg, Ernst von, 1854-
    Mississippi-fahrten. Reisebilder aus dem
    amerikanischen süden (1879-1880) ... Mit zahl-
    reichen abbildungen ... Leipzig, C.Reissner,
    1881.
        vi, 354 p. illus., map.   23 cm.

[Hewatt, Alexander]
    An historical account of the rise and progress
    of the colonies of South Carolina and Georgia ...
    London, A. Donaldson, 1779.
        2 v.   22 cm.

Hewett, Daniel.
    The American traveller; or, National directory,
    containing an account of all the great post roads,
    and the most important cross roads in the United
    States ... a geographical and statistical view
    of the United States, with information on other
    subjects interesting to travellers ... Washington,
    Printed by Davis & Force, 1825.
        440 (i.e., 464) p.   18 1/2 cm.

[Heyrick, Mrs. Elizabeth (Coltman)]
    Immediate, not gradual abolition; or, An in-
    quiry into the shortest, safest, and most ef-
    fectual means of getting rid of West Indian
    slavery.   London, Hatchard and son [etc.] 1824.
        24 p.   20 1/2 cm.

[Heyrick, Mrs. Elizabeth (Coltman)]
    Immediate, not gradual abolition; or, An in-
    quiry into the shortest, safest, and most effectual
    means of getting rid of West Indian slavery.
    Philadelphia, Anti-slavery society, 1836.
        24 p.   22 cm.

Hintrager, Oscar, 1871-
    Wie lebt und arbeitet man in den Vereinigten
    Staaten? Nordamerikanische reiseskizzen, von Dr.
    Hintrager ... Berlin, F. Fontane & Co.; New York
    [etc.] Brentano's, 1904.
        4 p.1., 291 [1] p.   21 1/2 cm.

Hickman, John.
    Southern sectionalism. Speech ... delivered

in the U. S. House of Representatives, May 1,
1860. [n.p., 1860?]
    8 p.   22 cm.

[Hicks, Elias]
    Observations on the slavery of the Africans
and their descendants, and on the use of the produce of their labour. New York, Samuel Wood,
1814.
    23 p.   17 cm.

Higginson, Thomas Wentworth, 1823-1911.
    Army life in a black regiment. By Thomas
Wentworth Higginson ... Boston, Fields, Osgood &
co., 1870.
    iv, 296 p.   18 1/2 cm.

Higginson, Thomas Wentworth, 1823.
    Does slavery christianize the Negro? [New
York, American anti-slavery society, 1855?]
    8 p.   19 cm.

Higginson, Thomas Wentworth, 1823.
    The new revolution: a speech before the Ameri-
can anti-slavery society, at their annual meeting
in New York, May 12, 1857 ... phonographically
reported. Boston, R. F. Wallcut, 1857.
    16 p.   22 cm.

Higginson, Thomas Wentworth, 1823.
    A ride through Kansas. [New York, American
anti-slavery society, 1856?]
    24 p.   19 cm.

High, Edwin W. 1841-
    History of the Sixty-eighth regiment, Indiana
volunteer infantry, 1862-1865, with a sketch of
E. A. King's brigade, Reynold's division, Thomas'
corps, in the battle of Chickamauga; by Edwin W.
High ... Published by request of the Sixty-eighth
Indiana infantry association, 1902. [Metamora ?
Ind.] 1902.
    xii p., 1 1., 416 p.   front, pl., port.
23 1/2 cm.

Hight, John J. 1834-1886.
    History of the Fifty-eighth regiment of Indiana
volunteer infantry. Its organization, campaigns

and battles from 1861 to 1865. From the manuscript prepared by the late chaplain John J.
Hight, during his service with the regiment in
the field. Comp. by his friend and comrade, Gilbert R. Stormont ... Illustrated with maps of
campaigns and marches, and portraits of a number
of officers and enlisted men of the regiment.
Princeton, Press of the Clarion, 1895.
    577 p. front., illus. (incl. maps) ports.
23 1/2 cm.

Hildreth, Richard.
    The "ruin" of Jamaica. [New York, American
anti-slavery society, 1855?]
    12 p. 19 cm.

[Hildreth, Richard] 1807.
    The slave; or, Memoirs of Archy Moore ...
Boston, John H. Eastburn, printer, 1836.
    2 v. 19 cm.

Hill, Alonzo F.
    Our boys. The personal experiences of a sol-
dier in the Army of the Potomac. By A. F. Hill...
Philadelphia, J. E. Potter, 1864.
    xii, 13-412 p. incl. front. 18 1/2 cm.

Hill, Benjamin Harvey, jr., 1823-1882.
    Senator Benjamin H. Hill of Georgia; his life,
speeches, and writings, written and comp. by his
son, Benjamin H. Hill, jr. Atlanta, T.H.P. Blood-
worth, 1893.
    2 p. 1., iii-ix, 11-823 p. front., plates,
port. 24 cm.

Hill, Isaac J. 1826-
    A sketch of the 29th regiment of Connecticut
colored troops, by J. [!] J. Hill, giving a full
account of its formation; of all the battles
through which it passed, and its final disband-
ment. Baltimore, Printed by Daugherty, Maguire
& co., 1867.
    42 p. 22 1/2 cm.

Hiller, Oliver Prescott, 1814.
    A chapter on slavery: presenting a sketch of
its origin and history, with the reasons for its
permission, and the probable manner of its re-
moval ... London, Hodson & son; New York, Mason

brothers: [etc., etc.] 1860.
    v p., 1 1., 175 p.   17 1/2 cm.

Hilton, William.
    A relation of a discovery lately made on the
coast of Florida, (from lat. 31, to 33 deg. 45
min. north-lat.) by William Hilton ... Anthony
Long, and Peter Fabian ... London, Printed by J.
C. for S. Miller, 1664.
    34 p.   2 p.1.   18 cm.

Hinman, Wilbur F.
    The story of the Sherman brigade. The camp,
the march, the bivouac, the battle; and how "the
boys" lived and died during four years of active
field service ... with 368 illustrations ... by
Wilbur F. Hinman ... Alliance, O., The author,
1897.
    xxxii, 33-1104 p.   illus., ports. (incl. front.)
23 1/2 cm.

History and record of the proceedings of the people
    of Lexington and vicinity, in the suppression of
    the True American, from the commencement of the
    movement on the 14th of August, 1845, to its
    final termination on Monday, the 18th of the
    same month. Lexington [Ky.] Virden, printer,
    1845.
        35 p.   24 cm.

The history of North America. Containing an exact
    account of their first settlements ... With the
    present state of the different colonies; and a
    large introduction ... London, Sold by Millar
    [etc.] 1776.
        284 p.   2 p.1., front. (fold. map)   18 cm.

A history of the trial of Castner Hanway and others,
    for treason, at Philadelphia in November, 1851,
    with an introduction upon the history of the
    slave question. By a member of the Philadelphia
    bar. Philadelphia, Uriah Hunt & sons, 1852.
        86 p.   22 cm.

Hitchcock, Henry, 1829-1902.
    Marching with Sherman; passages from the
letters and campaign diaries of Henry Hitchcock,
major and assistant adjutant general of volunteers,
November 1864 - May 1865, edited, with an intro-

duction, by M. A. DeWolfe Howe. New Haven, Yale
university press; London, H. Milford, Oxford university press, 1927.
6 p.l., 332 p. plates, 2 ports. (incl. front)
fold, map, facsim. 23 1/2 cm.

Hitchcock, Peter.
Speech ... on the "Bill to prevent giving aid
to fugitive slaves" in the House of Representatives,
Feb. 23, 1861. Columbus, Richard Nevins' steam
printing house, 1861.
15 p. 22 cm.

Hjelm-Hansen, Paul, 1810-
Om Nordamerika ... Udgivet af Selskabet for
folkeoplysningens fremme ... Kristiana, P. T.
Mallings bogtrykkeri, 1874.
84 p. 19 1/2 cm.

Hobart-Hampden, Hon. Augustus Charles, 1822-1886.
Sketches from my life. By the late Admiral
Hobart Pasha ... New York, D. Appleton and company, 1887.
viii, 282 p. front. (port.) 18 1/2 cm.

Hodges, Charles E.
Disunion our wisdom and our duty. [New York,
American anti-slavery society, 1855?]
12 p. 19 cm.

Hodgkin, Thomas.
A letter to Richard Gobden, M. P., on free
trade and slave labour [London, W. Watts, 1848]
16 p. 20 1/2 cm.

Hodgson, Adam.
A letter to M. Jean-Baptiste Say, on the comparative expense of free and slave labour ... The
second edition. Liverpool, Printed by James
Smith; published by Hatchard and son, Piccadilly,
and J. and J. Arch, Cornhill, London, 1823.
[60] p. 21 cm.

Hodgson, Adam.
A letter to M. Jean-Baptiste Say, on the comparative expense of free and slave labour ...
Liverpool, printed, 1823; New York, Reprinted for
the Manumission society by Mahlon Day, 1823.

50, 14 p.   21 1/2 cm.

Hodgson, Adam.
    Letters from North America, written during a
tour in the United States and Canada.   London
[etc.] Hurst, Robinson & co., 1824.
    2 v. front., illus. fold. map.   22 1/2 cm.

Hodgson, Adam.
    Remarks during a journey through North America
in the years 1819, 1820, and 1821, in a series of
letters ... Collected, arranged, and published
by Samuel Whiting. New York [J. Seymour, printer]
1823.
    355 p.   24 cm.

Hølaas, Odd.
    ... Nederst ved bordet. Oslo, Gyldendal, 1936.
195, [1] p. front., pl.   22 cm.

[Hoffman, Charles Fenno] 1806-1884.
    A winter in the West. By a New Yorker ... New
York, Harper & brothers, 1835.
    2 v.   19 1/2 cm.

Hoffman, Wickham, 1821-1900.
    Camp, court and siege; a narrative of personal
adventure and observation during two wars: 1861-
1865; 1870-1871. By Wickham Hoffman ... New York,
Harper & brothers, 1877.
    285 p.   19 1/2 cm.

Holbrook, John C.
    Our country's crisis. A discourse delivered
in Dubuque, Iowa, on Sabbath evening, July 6,
1856.... [n.p., 1856?]
    12 p.   23 cm.

Holcombe, Henry, 1762-
    The first fruits, in a series of letters.
Philadelphia, Printed for the author by Ann Cochran, 1812.
    228, xi p. front. (port.)   17 1/2 cm.

Holdombe, James P.
    The election of a black republican president
as an overt act of aggression on the right of property in slaves: The South urged to adopt concerted action for future safety. A speech before

the people of Albemarle on the 2nd day of January, 1860, by James P. Holcombe, professor of law in the University of Virginia. [n.p.] 1860.
16 p.   20 cm.

Holcombe, James Philemon, 1820.
The election of a Black Republican president an overt act of aggression on the right of property in slaves: the South urged to adopt concerted action for future safety. A speech before the people of Albermarle, on the 2d day of January, 1860 ... Richmond, C. H. Wynne, printer, 1860.
cover-title, 16 p.   23 cm.

[Holcombe, William Henry]
The alternative: a separate nationality, or, the Africanization of the south. [Waterproof, Tensas parish, La. n.d.]
15 p.   22 cm.

Holitscher, Arthur, 1869-
Amerika heute und morgen; reiseerlebnisse von Arthur Holitscher. Berlin, S. Fischer, 1912.
429 p.   illus.   21 1/2 cm.

Hollander, Arie Nicolaas Jan den.
De landelijke arme blanken in het Zuiden der Vereenigde Staten; een sociaal-historische en sociografische studie ... Groningen [etc.] J. B. Wolters' uitgeversmattschappi] n.v., 1933.
xiv p., 1 1. 517 p.   25 cm.

Holley, Mary Austin.
Texas. Observations, historical, geographical and descriptive, in a series of letters, written ... in the autumn of 1831 ... Baltimore, Armstrong & Plaskitt, 1833.
167 p.   front. (fold. map)   17 cm.

Holme, Benjamin, 1683-
A collection of the epistles and works of Benjamin Holme. To which is prefix'd an account of his life ... written by himself. London, Luke Hinde, 1753.
vii, 194 p.   20 1/2 cm.

Holmes, Daniel.
Dialogue on slavery, and miscellaneous subjects, based on the word of God. Dayton [O.] Gazette

book and job rooms, 1854.
29 p.   22 cm.

Holmes, Frederick Lionel, 1883-
Abraham Lincoln traveled this way; the log
book of a pilgrim to the Lincoln country, by Fred
L. Holmes; foreword by Glenn Frank ... with map
and thirty-two plates from original photographs.
Boston, L. C. Page & company [1930].
xviii, 350 p. front., plates, ports., fold.
map.   23 cm.

Holmes, Isaac.
An account of the United States of America,
derived from actual observation, during a residence of four years in that republic: including
original communications.   London, Printed at the
Caxton press, by H. Fisher [1823]
476 p.   2 p.l.   illus., fold. map. fold.
tab.   21 1/2 cm.

Holyoake, George Jacob, 1817-
Among the Americans and A stranger in America
... Chicago, Belford, Clarke & co., 1881.
[5] xiv, [17]-246 p.   18 1/2 cm.

Holyoake, George Jacob, 1817-
Travels in search of a settler's guide-book
of America and Canada ... London, Trübner & co.,
1884.
3 p.l., 148 p.   21 1/2 cm.

A home in the south, or Two years at Uncle Warren's.
By a lady. Written for the American reform tract
and book society, and approved by the committee
of publication. Cincinnati, American reform tract
and book society [n.d.]
134 p.   illus.   15 cm.

Hood, John Bell, 1831-1879.
Advance and retreat.   Personal experiences in
the United States and Confederate States armies.
By J. B. Hood ... New Orleans, Pub. for the Hood
orphan memorial fund, 1880.
358 p.   front., port., plans.   22 1/2 cm.

Hooton, Charles, 1813?
St. Louis' isle, or Texiana; with additional
observations made in the United States and in

Canada ... London, Simmonds and Ward, 1847.
[vii]-xiii, 204 p.   2 p.l., 1 l., front. (port)
plates.   22 1/2 cm.

Hopkins, Samuel.
A dialogue concerning the slavery of the Africans. Boston, Doctrinal tract and book society,
1852.
547 — 624 p.   24 cm.

Hopkins, Samuel.
Timely articles on slavery ... Boston, Congregational board of publication, 1854.
vi, [547]- 624 p.   21 cm.

[Hopley, Catherine Cooper]
Life in the South: from the commencement of
the war. By a blockaded British subject. Being
a social history of those who took part in the
battles, from a personal acquaintance with them
in their own homes. From the spring of 1860 to
August 1862 ... London, Chapman and Hall, 1863.
2 v.   fold.   plan.   19 1/2 cm.

Hopp, Ernst Otto, 1841-
Transatlantisches skizzenbuch. Federzeich-
nungen aus dem amerikanischen leben. Berlin, O.
Janke, 1876.
3 p.l., 360 p.   18 cm.

Hopper, Isaac Tatem.
Narrative of the proceedings of the monthly
meeting of New York and their subsequent confir-
mation at the quarterly and yearly meetings, in
the case of Isaac T. Hopper ... New York, Printed
for the author, 1843.
126 p.   18 cm.

Horner, Hattie.
"Not at home." By Hattie Horner ... New York,
J. B. Alden, 1889.
3 p.l., [9] - 307 p.   19 1/2 cm.

Horrall, Spillard F.   1829-
History of the Forty-second Indiana volunteer
infantry. Comp. and written ... by S.F. Horrall,
late captain of Company G, 42d Indiana regiment.
[Chicago, Donohue & Henneberry, printers] 1892.
x, 11-283 p.   front., ports.   20 cm.

Horrs of West Indian slavery. [n.p., C. Whittingham, n.d.]
12 p. 18 1/2 cm.

[Horton, George Moses] 1798?
Poems by a slave. [Philadelphia, 1837].
23 p. 17 cm.

Horton, Joshua H.
A history of the Eleventh regiment, (Ohio volunteer infantry.) containing the military record ... of each officer and enlisted man of the command - a list of deaths - an account of the veterans - incidents of the field and camp - names of the three months' volunteers, etc., etc. Compiled from the official records by Horton & Teverbaugh ... Dayton, W. J. Shuey, 1866.
xv, 17-287 p. 22 cm.

Hoskens, Jane Fenn, 1694-
The life and spiritual sufferings of that faithful servant of Christ, Jane Hoskens, a public preacher among the people called Quakers. Never before printed. Philadelphia, Printed and sold by William Evitt, 1771.
31 p. 16 1/2 cm.

Hoskin, James.
Narrative of a voyage from England to the United States of North America; with travels through part of eight of the states; and remarks on the soil, produce, prices and agriculture in general; in the year 1811. Penzance, Printed for the author, by T. Vigurs, 1813.
[3] - 49 p. 2 p.1. 22 1/2 cm.

Hosmer, James Kendall, 1834-1927.
The color-guard: being a corporal's notes of military service in the Nineteenth army corps. By James K. Hosmer ... Boston, Walker, Wise and co., 1864.
xii, 9-244 p. 18 cm.

Hosmer, William.
The higher law, in the relations to civil government: with particular reference to slavery, and the fugitive slave law ... Auburn, Derby & Miller, 1852.
204 p. front. (port.) 18 cm.

Hossack, John.
    Speech of John Hossack, convicted of a violation
of the Fugitive slave law, before Judge Drummond,
of the United States district court, Chicago, Ill.
New York, American anti-slavery society, 1860.
    12 p.   19 cm.

Houstoun, Matilda Charlotte (Jesse) Fraser, 1815?
    Hesperos: or, Travels in the West ... Lon-
don, J. W. Parker, 1850.
    2 v. in 1.   19 1/2 cm.

Houstoun, Mrs. Matilda Charlotte (Jesse) Fraser, 1815?
    Texas and the Gulf of Mexico; or, Yachting in
the New world ... London, J. Murray, 1844.
    2 v.   fronts., plates, ports.   20 cm.

Hovey, Horace Carter.
    Freedom's banner. A sermon preached to the
Coldwater light artillery and the Coldwater zouave
cadets, April 28th, 1861 ... Coldwater, Michigan,
Republican print, 1861.
    11 p.   21 cm.

Hovey, Horace Carter, 1833-
    Hovey's hand-book of the Mammoth cave of Ken-
tucky; a practical guide to the regulation routes,
with maps and illustrations ... Louisville, Ky.,
J. P. Morton & company, 1909.
    63 [1] p. incl. illus., maps.   19 cm.

Hovey, Horace Carter, 1833-
    Mammoth cave of Kentucky; an illustrated manual
by Horace Carter Hovey ... and Richard Ellsworth
Call ... With historical notes, scenic accounts
and descriptive and scientific matters of interest
to visitors, based upon new and original explorations. Louisville, J. P. Morton and company, 1897.
    v, [1]111[1] p.   13 pl. (Incl. front.) fold.
map.   22 cm.

Hovey, Sylvester.
    Letters from the West Indies: relating es-
pecially to the Danish island St. Croix, and to
the British islands Antigua, Barbadoes and Jamaica ... New York, Gould and Newman, 1838.
    iv, 212 p.   18 cm.

How, Samuel B.
    Slaveholding not sinful. An argument before
the general synod of the Reformed Protestant Dutch
church, October, 1855 ... New York, John A. Gray,
1855.
    32 p.   22 cm.

Howard, Benjamin Chew, 1791.
    Report of the decision of the Supreme Court
of the United States, and the opinions of the
judges thereof, in the case of Dred Scott versus
John F. A. Sandford. December term, 1856 ...
Washington, Cornelius Wendell, 1857.
    239 p.   22 cm.

Howard, George C.
    St. Clare to Little Eva in heaven. Words and
music by Geo. C. Howard ... Boston, Oliver Dit-
son [n.d.]
    [4] p.   music.   33 cm.

Howard, Henry, 1868-
    The yacht "Alice". Planning and building,
by Henry Howard. A cruise from New York to Miami
through the inland water way, by Alice Sturtevant
Howard. A West Indies cruise, by Katharine Howard. Boston, Charles E. Lauriat company [c1926]
    xvii, 268 p.   front., plates, ports., plans,
tab., diagrs.   22 1/2 cm.

Howard, McHenry.
    Recollections of a Maryland Confederate soldier
and staff officer under Johnston, Jackson and Lee.
Baltimore, Williams & Wilkins company, 1914.
    1 p.l., 423 p.   front, illus., pl., ports.,
fold. map.   facsim.   23 cm.

Howard of Glossop, Winifred (De Lisle).
    Journal of a tour in the United States, Canada
and Mexico. London, Sampson, Low, Marston and
company, 1td., 1897.
    vii, 355 p.   19 cm.

Howard, Richard L.
    History of the 124th regiment Illinois infantry
volunteers, otherwise known as the "Hundred and
two dozen", from August, 1862, to August, 1865.
By R. L. Howard ... Springfield, Ill., Printed
and bound by H. W. Rokker, 1880.
    ix, 519 p.   20 1/2 cm.

[Howe, Mark Anthony De Wolfe] bp., 1808-
A reply to the letter of Bishop Hopkins, addressed to Dr. Howe, in the print called "The Age," of December 8th, 1863. Philadelphia, King & Baird, Printers, 1864.
18 p.   21 cm.

[Howe, Thomas H.]
Adventures of an escaped Union prisoner from Andersonville. San Francisco, H. S. Crocker & co., printers, 1886.
48 p.   22 1/2 cm.

Howell, Peter, 1805-
The life and travels of Peter Howell, written by himself; in which will be seen some marvellous instances of the gracious Providence of God. Newbern, N. C., W. H. Mayhew [1849].
320 p.   2 p.l.   front. (port.)   15 cm.

Howitt, William, 1792.
George Fox and his first disciples: or, The Society of friends as it was, and as it is.
[Philadelphia, Merrihew & Gunn, printers, 1834?]
38 p.   17 cm.

Hoyle, William.
The negro question and the I. O. G. T.   A historical and critical disquisition ... Second edition. London, E. Curtice & co.; Manchester, A. Ireland & co. [1876?]
24 p.   21 cm.

[Hubbard, Charles Eustis] 1842-
The campaign of the Forty-fifth regiment, Massachusetts volunteer militia.   "The cadet regiment." Boston, Printed by J. S. Adams, 1882.
xiv p., 1 l., 126 p.   front., plates.
25 1/2 cm.

Hubbard, John Milton.
Notes of a private, by John Milton Hubbard, Company E, 7th Tennessee regiment, Forrest's cavalry corps, C.S.A. ... Memphis, Tenn., E. H. Clarke & brother, 1909.
3 p.l., 189 p.   front. (port.) pl.   20 cm.

Hudson, Charles.
Speech ... on the constitutional power of Congress over the territories, and the right of ex-

cluding slavery therefrom. Delivered in the House
of Representatives of the U. S., June 20, 1848.
Washington, Printed by J. & G. S. Gideon, 1848.
    16 p.   23 cm.

Hughes, Thomas 1822-   ed.
    G. T. T. Gone to Texas; letters from our boys,
ed. by Thomas Hughes. New York, Macmillan and
co., 1884.
    xiii p., 2 1, [3]-228 p.   19 1/2 cm.

Hugo, Victor Marie, comte, 1802.
    Letters on American slavery from Victor Hugo,
de Tocqueville, Emile de Girardin, Garnot, Passy,
Mazzini, Humboldt, O. Lafayette -- & c. Boston,
American anti-slavery society, 1860.
    24 p.   18 cm.

Hull, John Simpson.
    Remarks on the United States of America; drawn
up from his own observations, and from the observations of other travellers by John Simpson Hull
... Dublin, Printed by W. M'Kenzie [1801?]
    72 p.   21 cm.

Hulme, Thomas.
    Mr. Hulme's journal, made during a tour in the
western countries of America, in which tour he
visited Mr. Birkbeck's settlement.
    3 pt. in 1v.   22 cm.

Humphrey, Edward Porter, 1809.
    The color question in the United States. A
paper prepared for the sixtieth annual meeting
of the American colonization society, Washington,
D. C., January 16, 1877 ... Washington city,
Colonization building, 1877.
    10 p.   23 cm.

Humphrey, Heman.
    Parallel between intemperance and the slave
trade. An address delivered at Amherst College,
July 4, 1828 ... Amherst, J. S. and C. Adams, 1828.
    40 p.   22 1/2 cm.

Humphreys, Charles Alfred, 1838-
    Field, camp, hospital and prison in the civil
war, 1863-1865; Charles A. Humphreys, chaplain,
Second Massachusetts cavalry volunteers. Boston,
Press of Geo. H. Ellis co., 1918.

278

xi p., 1 1., 428 p.   front., plates, ports.
20 1/2 cm.

Hundley, Daniel Robinson, 1832-
    Social relations in our southern states.
New-York, H. B. Price, 1860.
    vi, [7]-367 p.   19 1/2 cm.

Hunnicut, James W.   1814-
    The conspiracy unveiled. The south sacrificed;
or, The horrors of secession. Philadelphia, J.
B. Lippincott & co., 1863.
    xiv, 13-454 p.   front. (port.)   18 cm.

Hunt, Richard S.
    Guide to the Republic of Texas; consisting of
a brief outline of the history of its settlement
... New York, J. H. Colton, 1839.
    63, [1] p.   fold.   map.   15 1/2 cm.

Hunter, Alfred G.
    History of the Eighty-second Indiana volunteer
infantry, its organization, campaigns and battles.
Written at the request of the members by Alf. G.
Hunter ... Indianapolis, W. B. Burford, printer,
1893.
    255 p.   incl. front., port.   19 cm.

Huret, Jules, 1864-
    ... En Amérique; de New-York à la Nouvelle-
Orléans.   5. mille.   Paris, E. Fasquelle, 1904.
    3 p.1., 420 p.   18 1/2 cm.

Hurst, Samuel H.
    Journal-history of the Seventy-third Ohio
volunteer infantry; by Samuel H. Hurst ... Chillicothe, O., 1866.
    viii, [9] - 258, [1] p.   20 cm.

Hussey, H.
    The Australian colonies; together with notes
of a voyage from Australia to Panama, in the "Golden Age". Descriptions of Tahiti and other islands in the Pacific and a tour through some of
the states of America, in 1854 ... London, Blackburn & Burt; Adelaide, E. S. Wigg [1855]
    vi, 174 p.   18 cm.

Hutcheseon, R.
    Speech of Hon. R. Hutcheseon of Madison county

delivered in the House of Representatives, March
12, 1860. The tendency of the principles and
teachings of the Republican party -- disunion,
insurrection and negro equality. Columbus,
Statesman steam printing house, 1860.
  12 p.   22 cm.

Hutchins, Frank.
  Houseboating on a colonial waterway, by Frank
and Cortelle Hutchins; illustrated with many
photographs by the authors. Boston, L. C. Page
& company, 1910.
  xii, 299 p.   front., plates, ports.   20 cm.

Hutchins, Thomas, 1730-
  An historical narrative and topographical description of Louisiana and West-Florida, comprehending the river Mississippi with its principal
branches and settlements, and the rivers Pearl,
Pascagoula ... &c. ... with directions for sailing into all the bays, lakes, harbours and rivers
on the north side of the Gulf of Mexico ... Philadelphia, Printed for the author, 1784.
  iv, [5] - 94 p.   1 1.   20 cm.

Hutchins, Thomas, 1730-
  A topographical description of Virginia, Pennsylvania, Maryland and North Carolina, comprehending the rivers Ohio, Kenhawa, Sioto, Cherokee,
Wabash, Illinois, Mississippi, &c.   the climate,
soil and produce, whether animal, vegetable or
mineral ... And an appendix, containing Mr. Patrick Kennedy's Journal up the Illinois river, and
a correct list of the different nations and
tribes of Indians, with the number of fighting
men, &c. London, Printed for the author, and sold
by J. Almon, 1778.
  ii, 67 [1] p.   1 p.l.   2 fold. plans, fold.
table.   20 1/2 cm.

[Huth, Friedrich] 1866-
  Vom Rhein zum Mississippi. Reiseberichte von
Fred Hood [pseud.] Possneck i. Thür., B. Feigen-
span [1904?]
  3 p.l., 279 p.   20 cm.

[Hyde, John] 1848-
  Homeward through America. By a fellow of the
Royal society of literature. Chicago, Poole
bros., printers, 1892.

36 p.   illus., plates.   24 cm.

Hyde, Solon.
A captive of war, by Solon Hyde, hospital
steward Seventeenth regiment Ohio volunteer infantry. New York, McClure, Phillips & co., 1900.
389 p.   19 1/2 cm.

I

I don't believe in religion. [Cincinnati, American
reform tract and book society, n.d.]
12 p. illus.   18 cm.

Ichikawa, Haruko, 1896-
Japanese lady in America, by Haruko Ichikawa
(Mrs. Sanki Ichikawa) Tokyo, Kenkyusha co, [1939]
2 p.1., 7-347 p., 1 l.   20 1/2 cm.

Ide, George B..
The freedmen of the war: a discourse delivered
at the annual meeting of the American Baptist
home mission society, Philadelphia, May 19th,
1864 ... Philadelphia, American Baptist publication society, 1864.
44 p.   15 cm.

Ikin, Arthur.
Texas: its history, topography, agriculture,
commerce, and general statistics. To which is
added a copy of the treaty of commerce entered into by the republic of Texas and Great Britain ...
London, Sherwood, Gilbert, and Piper, 1841.
vii, [1], 100 p. front. (fold. map)   15 cm.

Illinois Central Railroad.
About the South, on lines of the Illinois Central and Yazoo & Mississippi Valley railroads.
Important questions tersely answered for the information of home seekers and investors. Comp.
by J. F. Merry, general immigration agent. Ed.
3. Chicago, Illinois Central railroad company,
1905.
63 p.   map, illus.   23 cm.

Illinois. Republican state central committee.
Political record of Stephen A. Douglas on the

slavery question. [n.p., 1860?]
16 p.   24 cm.

Imlay, Gilbert, fl. 1755-1796.
A topographical description of the western
territory of North America ... London, J. Debrett,
1792.
xv, 247 p. 2 p.l.   21 1/2 cm.

An impartial account of the late expedition against
St. Augustine under General Oglethorpe. Occasioned
by the suppression of the report, made by a committee of the General assembly in South Carolina,
transmitted under the great seal of that province,
to their agent in England, in order to be printed
... London, Printed for J. Huggonson, 1742.
viii, [9]-68 p. front. (port.)   20 cm.

An impartial enquiry into the right of the French king
to the territory west of the great river Mississippi, in North America, not ceded by the prelim-
inaries, including a summary account of that river,
and the country adjacent ... London, W. Nicoll
[1762]
58 p. 1 p.l.   20 cm.

"The impending crisis of the south -- how to meet it."
-- By Hinton Rowan Helper. In National democratic quarterly review, Washington, D. C., 1860.
p. 207-222. A review.

Impolicy of slavery. [n.p., n.d.]
3 p. map.   40 cm.

Inconsistency and hypocrisy of Martin Van Buren on the
subject of slavery. [n.p., n.d.]
16 p.   22 cm.

Indiana anti-slavery society.
Proceedings of the Indiana convention assembled
to organize a state anti-slavery society, held
in Milton, Wayne co., September 12th, 1838. Cincinnati, Samuel A. Alley, printer, 1838.
28 p.   21 cm.

Infidelity among the stars. [Cincinnati, American reform tract and book society, n.d.]
28 p.   18 cm.

Infidelity and abolitionism, an open letter to the
    friends of religion, morality, and the American
    union. [n.p., n.d.]
        Unpaged. 20 cm.

Information for emigrants: in three parts. I. -
    North America. II. - New South Wales, Port
    Phillip, Cooksland, South Australia, and New
    Zealand. III. - The Cape of Good Hope, Algoa
    Bay, and Port Natal; also, a view of Canada ...
    London, Kent and Richards. 1848.
        48, 52, 52 p. 16 1/2 cm.

[Ingersoll, Charles]
        A letter to a friend in a slave state. By a
    citizen of Pennsylvania. Philadelphia, John
    Campbell, 1862.
        60 p. 21 1/2 cm.

Ingle, Edward.
        Southern sidelights; a picture of social and
    economic life in the South a generation before
    the war. New York, Boston, T. Y. Crowell & com-
    pany [1896].
        3 p.1., 373 p. 19 1/2 cm.

[Ingraham, Joseph Holt] 1809-1860.
        The quadroone; or, St. Michael's day. By
    the author of "Lafitte," "Captain Kyd," "Bur-
    ton," &c. ... New York, Harper & brothers,
    1841.
        2 v. 19 1/2 cm.
        L. C. card no. 7-9721 Revised

[Ingraham, Joseph Holt] 1809-1860.
        The South-west. By a Yankee ... New-York,
    Harper & brothers, 1835.
        2 v. 18 x 10 1/2 cm.
        L. C. card no. 1-6606

Ingraham, Joseph Holt, 1809-
        The sunny South; or, The southerner at home,
    embracing five years' experience of a northern
    governess in the land of the sugar and the cot-
    ton. Ed. by Professor J. H. Ingraham ... Phila-
    delphia, G. G. Evans, 1860.
        526 p. 19 1/2 cm.

Ingram, [Mrs.] H[elen] K.
        Tourists' and settlers' guide to Florida ...

1895-6. [Jacksonville, Da Costa, 1895].
135 p. pl. 22 1/2 cm.

The injurious effects of slave labour: an impartial
appeal to the reason, justice, and patriotism
of the people of Illinois on the injurious effects of slave labour. Philadelphia, printed;
London, reprinted for the Society for the mitigation and gradual abolition of slavery throughout the British dominions, 1824.
18 p. 20 1/2 cm.

An inquiry into the causes of the insurrection of the
negroes in the island of St. Domingo ... London,
Printed and sold by J. Johnson, 1792.
39 p. 21 cm.

Intelligent negroes. [n.p., n.d.]
32 p. illus. 17 1/2 cm.

International American conference. 1st, Washington,
D. C., 1889-1890.
... Excursion appendix. Narrative of the
tour of the delegates through the United States;
together with descriptions of places visited,
and reports of addresses delivered. Washington,
Govt. Print. off., 1890.
ii, 3-343 p. 30 x 24 1/2 cm.

International and great northern railroad.
How to go to Texas. A guide to western, central, eastern and southern Texas ... Houston,
Tex., Mercury steam news, book and job print
[1874].
76 p. fold. map. 19 1/2 cm.

Iredale, Andrew.
An autumn tour in the United States and Canada. By Andrew Iredale. Torquay [Eng.] G. H.
Iredale, 1901.
3 p. 1., 164 p. 19 1/2 cm.

Irving, John Beaufain, 1800-
A day on Cooper river ... Charleston [S.C.]
Printed by A. E. Miller, 1842.
83 p. 2 p.1. 19 cm.

[Irving, Washington] 1783-
A tour of the prairies. By the author of the
Sketch book. Philadelphia, Carey, Lea & Blan-

chard, 1835.
    xv, [17]-274 p.   18 1/2 cm.

Is God every body and every body God? [Cincinnati,
    American reform tract and book society, n.d.]
    16 p.   18 cm.

Is the Gospel fact or fable? [Cincinnati, American
    reform tract and book society, n.d.]
    16 p.   18 cm.

Is the system of slavery sanctioned or condemned by
    Scripture? To which is subjoined an appendix,
    containing two essays upon the state of the
    Canaanite and Philistine bondmen, under the
    Jewish theocracy ... London, Printed for John
    and Arthur Arch, 1824.
    92 p.   20 1/2 cm.

Isham, Asa Brainerd, 1844-
    Prisoners of war and military prisons; per-
    sonal narratives of experience in the prisons
    of Richmond, Danville, Macon, Andersonville,
    Savannah, Millen, Charleston, and Columbia ...
    with list of officers who were prisoners of war
    from January 1, 1864. By Asa B. Isham ... Hen-
    ry M. Davidson ... and Henry B. Furness ...
    Cincinnati, Lyman, & Cushing, 1890.
    xii, 571 p.   front., illus., pl., port.,
    diagr.   24 cm.

Ivimey, Joseph, 1773.
    The utter extinction of slavery an object of
    scripture prophecy. A lecture ... delivered at
    the annual meeting of the Chelmsford ladies'
    anti-slavery association in the Friends' meeting
    house, on Tuesday, the 17th of April, 1832 ...
    with elucidatory notes ... London, Sold by G.
    Wightman etc. 1832.
    viii, 74 p.   20 cm.

Izlar, William Valmore.
    A sketch of the war record of the Edisto
    rifles, 1861-1865, by William Valmore Izlar;
    Company "A", 1st regiment S.C.V. infantry ...
    Provisional army of the Confederate States 1861-
    1862; Company "G", 25th regiment S.C.V. infantry
    Confederate States Army 1862-1865. Pub. by
    August Kohn. Columbia, S. C., The State company,

1914.
168 p. 2 pl., 16 port. (incl. front.)
19 1/2 cm.

J

Jackson, Andrew, 1814.
Narrative and writings of Andrew Jackson,
of Kentucky ... Narrated by himself; written by
a friend. Syracuse, Daily and weekly star office
1847.
vi, [7], 120 p. 18 1/2 cm.

Jackson, Henry W. R.
The southern women of the second American revolution. Their trials, &c. Yankee barbarity
illustrated. Our naval victories and exploits of
Confederate war steamers. Capture of Yankee gun-
boats, &c. Atlanta, Ga., Intelligencer steam-
power press, 1863.
120, [2] p. 21 cm.

Jackson, Oscar Lawrence, 1840--1920.
The colonel's diary; journals kept before and
during the civil war by the late Colonel Oscar
L. Jackson ... sometime commander of the 63rd
regiment O.V.I. [Sharon ? Pa., 1922]
3 p. 1., 232 p., 1 1., 233-262 p. front.,
ports. 22 1/2 cm.

Jacques, Daniel Harrison, 1825-
Florida as a permanent home: embracing a
description of the climate, soil and productions
of the state, together with hints to new-comers
and prospective settlers. Jacksonville, Fla.,
Chas. W. Blew, 1877.
32 p. 20 cm.

Jagger, William.
To the people of Suffolk co. Information,
acquired from the best authority, with respect
to the institution of slavery ... New York, R.
Craighead, printer, 1856.
28 p. 22 cm.

James, Bushrod Washington, 1836-
      American resorts; with notes upon their cli-
mate ... With a translation from the German by
Mr. S. Kauffmann of those chapters of "Die kli-
mate der erde" written by Dr. A. Woeikof ... that
relate to North and South America and the islands
and oceans contiguous thereto ... Philadelphia
and London, F. A. Davis, 1889.
      285 p. fold. map. 24 1/2 cm.

James, Henry, 1843-1916.
      The American scene, by Henry James. London,
Chapman and Hall, 1td., 1907.
      vi p., 1 1., 465 [1] p. 22 1/2 cm.

[James, Joshua]
      A journal of a tour in Texas; with observa-
tions, &c., by the agents of the Wilmington
emigrating society. [Wilmington? N. C.] Printed by T. Loromg, 1835.
      16 p. 25 1/2 cm.

[James, Thomas Horton]
      Rambles in the United States and Canada during
the year 1845, with a short account of Oregon.
By Rubio [pseud.] London, J. Ollivier, 1846.
      viii, 259 p. front. 19 1/2 cm.

Jamieson, John, 1789.
      The sorrows of a slave, a poem. Containing
a faithful statement of facts respecting the
African slave trade ... London, Printed for J.
Murray, 1789.
      80 p. 17 cm.

Jannet, Claudio, 1844-
      Les États-Unis contemporains; ou, Les Moeurs,
les institutions et les idées depuis la guerre de
la sécession ... Ouvrage précédé d'une lettre de
M. Le Play. 2. éd. Paris, E. Plon, 1876.
      2 p.1., vii-xxiii, 524 p. 18 cm.

Janson, Charles William.
      The stranger in America: containing observa-
tions made during a long residence in that country, on the genius, manners and customs of the
people of the United States ... London, Printed
for J. Cundee, 1807.
      xiii [1] [15]-22, 499 [1] p. front., plates.
27 1/2 cm.

Jaquith, James, 1781-
    The history of James Jaquith, being his travels
through the United States and Upper and Lower
Canada. Containing great geographical information. 3d ed. [n.p.] Pub. by the author, 1830.
    36 p.   19 1/2 cm.

Jarvis, Edward.
    Insanity among the coloured population of the
free states ... (Extracted from the American journal of the medical sciences for January, 1844).
Philadelphia, T. K. & P. G. Collins, Printers,
1844.
    15 p.   21 1/2 cm.

Jay, Aimé, d. 1881.
    A travers les Etats-Unis d'Amérique ... Ou-
vrage posthume, publié par les soins de G. Cha-
birand, orné du portrait de l'auteur gravé a
l'eau-forte par A. Gilbert.   Niort, L. Clouzot,
1884.
    viii, 320 p.   port.   27 1/2 cm.

Jay, John.
    The progress and results of emancipation in
the English West Indies.   A lecture delivered before the Philomathian society of the city of New-
York ... New-York, Wiley and Putnam, 1842.
    39 p.   21 cm.

Jay, William, 1789.
    An examination of the Mosaic laws of servitude
... New York, Published by M. W. Dodd, 1854.
    56 p.   22 cm.

Jay, William, 1789.
    Inquiry into the character and tendency of the
American colonization and American anti-slavery
societies ... Tenth edition.   New York, American
anti-slavery society, 1840.
    206 p.   19 cm.

Jay, William, 1789.
    Letter to the American tract society. [n.p.,
1853?]
    16 p.   21 cm.

Jay, William.
    A letter to Hon. William Nelson, M. C., on

Mr. Webster's speech, from William Jay. New York, William Harned, 1850.
12 p. 19 1/2 cm.

Jay, William, 1789.
A letter to the Right Rev. L. Silliman Ives, bishop of the Protestant Episcopal church in the state of North Carolina, occasioned by his late address to the convention of his diocese. [n.p., 1848?]
32 p. 18 cm.

Jay, William, 1789.
Miscellaneous writings on slavery ... Boston, J. P. Jewett & company; Cleveland, O., Jewett, Proctor, and Worthington: [etc., etc.] 1853.
x, 11 - 670 p. incl. front. (port.) 20cm.

Jay, William, 1789.
Reply to remarks of Rev. Moses Stuart ... on Hon. John Jay, and an examination of his scriptural exegesis, contained in his recent pamphlet entitled "Conscience and the Constitution" ... New-York, Printed by John A. Gray, 1850.
22 p. 21 cm.

Jefferson, Thomas, pres. U. S., 1743-
Notes on the state of Virginia; written in the year 1781, somewhat corrected and enlarged in the winter of 1782, for the use of a foreigner of distinction, in answer to certain queries proposed by him ... 1782. [Paris, printed 1784-85].
391 p. 1 p.l., 1 illus., tables. 20 cm.

Jefferys, Charles.
George's song of freedom ... The words by Charles Jefferys, the music by Stephen Glover. London, C. Jefferys [n.d.]
6 p. front., music. 35 cm.

Jefferys, Charles.
Sleep my child, let no one hear you. Eliza's song. Sung by Miss Stabbach. Written by Charles Jefferys composed by Stephen Glover. London, Charles Jefferys [n.d.]
4 p. front., music. 34 cm.

Jefferys, Thomas.
The natural and civil history of the French

dominions in North and South America ... London,
Printed for T. Jefferys, 1760.
    2 pt. in 1 vol. fold. maps, fold. plans.
36 cm.

Jeffrey, Mrs. Rosa (Vertner) 1828-1894.
    The crimson hand, and other poems. By Rosa
Vertner Jeffrey. Philadelphia, J. B. Lippincott
& co., 1881.
    200 p. front. (port.) 18 1/2 cm.

Jenkins, Timothy, 1799.
    Slavery in the territories. Speech ... de-
livered in the House of Representatives, February
17, 1849. [Washington, D. C.? 1849?]
    16 p. 22 cm.

Jenks, John Whipple Potter.
    Hunting in Florida in 1874 ... [Providence?
R. I.] c1884.
    cover-title, 70 p. fold. map. 23 1/2 cm.

Jennings, Napoleon Augustus, 1856-
    A Texas ranger ... New York, C. Scribner's
sons. 1899.
    1 p. 1., iii-x p., 1 1., 321 p. 19 cm.

Jensen, Johannes Vilhelm, 1873-
    ... Den Ny verden; til international belysning
of nordisk bondekultur. Med 12 portraeter.
[Kristiania og Kjøbenhavn]. Gyldendalske boghandel, Nordisk forlag, 1907.
    5 p.1., 254 p. illus. (ports.) 19 1/2 cm.

Jewell, Henry.
    Life and writings of Rev. Enoch M. Pingree,
who died in Louisville, Kentucky, January 6,
1849, aged 32 years ... Cincinnati, Longley &
brother, 1850.
    vi, [9] - 385 p. front. (port.) 19 cm.

Jobson, Frederick James, 1821-
    America and American Methodism ... With pre-
fatory letters by the Rev. Thomas B. Sargent ...
and the Rev. John Hannah ... Illustrated from
original sketches by the author. New York, Virtue, Emmins & co., 1857.
    [vii], xvi, 399 p. 5 p.1. front., plates.
20 1/2 cm.

Johns, Henry T. b. 1827 or 8.
   Life with the Forty-ninth Massachusetts vo1-
unteers. By Henry T. Johns ... Pittsfield, For
the author, 1864.
   391 p. front., pl., port.   19 1/2 cm.

[Johnson, Adam Rankin] 1834-
   The Partisan rangers of the Confederate States
army; ed. by William J. Davis. Louisville, Ky.,
G. G. Fetter company, 1904.
   xii, p., 1 1., 476 p. front., plates, ports.
23 cm.

Johnson, Charles Beneulyn, 1843-
   Muskets and medicine: or, Army life in the
sixties, by Charles Beneulyn Johnson ... Philadelphia, F. A. Davis company; [etc., etc.] 1917.
   276 p. front., plates, ports.   21 1/2 cm.

Johnson, Clifton, 1865-
   Highways and byways of the Mississippi valley,
written and illustrated by Clifton Johnson. [New
ed.] New York, The Macmillan company; [etc.,etc.]
1906 [1913].
   xiii, 250, 250a - 250b, 251-287 p. incl.
front., plates.   20 cm.

Johnson, Clifton, 1865-
   Highways and byways of the South, written and
illustrated by Clifton Johnson. New York, The
Macmillan company; London, Macmillan and co.,
limited, 1904.
   xv, 362 p. incl. front., illus.   32 pl.
21 cm.

Johnson, Hannibal Augustus, 1841-
   The sword of honor. From captivity to freedom. By Hannibal A. Johnson, Lieutenant Third
Maine infantry. Providence, The Society, 1903.
   72 p.   21 cm.

Johnson, Oliver, 1809.
   An address delivered in the Congregational
church, in Middlebury, by request of the Vermont
anti-slavery society, on Wednesday evening,
February 18, 1835. Montpelier, Knapp and Jewett,
printers, 1835.
   32 p.   20 1/2 cm.

Johnson, Oliver, 1809.
    Correspondence between Oliver Johnson and
George F. White, a minister of the Society of
friends. With an appendix. New York, Oliver
Johnson, 1841.
    48 p.   18 cm.

Johnson, Richard W.   1827-1897.
    A soldier's reminiscenses in peace and war.
By Brig-Gen. R. W. Johnson ... Philadelphia,
Press of J. B. Lippincott company, 1886.
    428 p.   front. (port.)   pl.   23 cm.

[Johnson, Robert] fl. 1586-1626, supposed author.
    The new life of Virginea: declaring the for-
mer syccesse and present estate of that planta-
tion, being the second part of Noua Britannia.
Published by the authoritie of His Majesties
Counsell of Virginea. London, Imprinted by F.
Kyngston for W. Welby, 1612.
    [54] p.   17 1/2 cm.

[Johnson, Robert] fl. 1586-1626, supposed author.
    Nova Britannia, offering most excellent
fruites by planting in Virginia. Exciting all
such as be well affected to further the same.
London, Printed for S. Macham, and are to be
sold at his shop in Pauls church-yard, at the
sign of the Bul-head, 1609.
    [35] p.   18 cm.

Johnson, Robert Ward.
    Address ... to the citizens of Arkansas.
Washington, Jno. T. Towers, 1850.
    16 p.   22 1/2 cm.

Johnston, Elizabeth Bryant, 1833-
    The days that are no more. New York, London
[etc.] The Abbey press [c1901]
    224 p.   plates, port.   20 1/2 cm.

Johnston, Mrs. Elizabeth (Lichtenstein) 1764-
    Recollections of a Georgia loyalist ... writ-
ten in 1836; ed. by Rev. Arthur Wentworth Eaton.
New York and London, M. F. Mansfield & company,
1901.
    224 p.   front., ports.   18 cm.

Johnston, Gideon, 1671 (ca.)
   Carolina chronicle; the papers of Commisson
Gideon Johnston, 1707-1716. Edited, with an
introduction and notes, by Frank J. Klingberg.
Berkeley and Los Angeles, University of California press, 1946.
   x, 186 p.   24 cm.

Johnston, Sir Harry Hamilton, 1858-1927.
   The Negro in the New world, by Sir Harry H.
Johnston ... With one illustration in colour by
the author and 390 black and white illustrations
by the author and others; maps by Mr. J. W.
Addison ... London, Methuen & co., ltd.   1910.
   xxix, 499 [1] p. incl. illus., plates, maps.
col. front., 2 fold. maps.   26 1/2 cm.

Johnston, Isaac N.
   Four months in Libby, and the campaign against
Atlanta. By Capt. I. N. Johnston, Co. H, Sixth
Kentucky volunteer infantry. Cincinnati, Printed at the Methodist book concern, for the
author, 1893.
   191 p. front. (ports.)   17 cm.

Johnston, James Finlay Weir, 1796-
   Notes on North America, agricultural, economical, and social ... Edinburgh and London, W.
Blackwood and sons, 1851.
   2 v. front. (fold. map)   20 cm.

Johnston, Joseph Eggleston, 1807-1901.
   Narrative of military operations, directed
during the war between the states, by Joseph E.
Johnson, general, C.S.A. New York, D. Appleton
and co., 1874.
   602 p. front., ports., maps (1 fold.)
23 cm.

Johnston, Richard Malcolm, 1822-
   Life of Alexander H. Stephens. By Richard
Malcolm Johnston and William Hand Browne. New
and rev. ed. Philadelphia, J. B. Lippincott &
co., 1883.
   635 p. front., port.   23 cm.

Johnston, Richard Malcolm, 1822-1898.
   Old times in middle Georgia. New York, London, The Macmillan company, 1897.

vi, 249 p.   19 cm.

Johnston, William.
Speech of Wm. Johnston, esq., before the
Franklin circuit court of Kentucky. [n.p.,
1846?]
23 p.   22 cm.

Johnston, William.
The state of Ohio vs. Forbes and Armitage,
arrested upon requisition of the government of
Ohio, on charge of kidnapping Jerry Phinney, and
tried in the Franklin circuit court of Kentucky,
April 10, 1846. [n.p., 1846?]
41 p.   22 cm.

Joinville, Francois Ferdinand Philippe Louis Marie
d'Orleans, prince de, 1818-1900.
The Army of the Potomac: its organization,
its commander, and its campaign. By the Prince
de Joinville. Tr. from the French, with notes,
by William Henry Hurlbert. New York, A. D. F.
Randolph, 1862.
118 p. front. (fold. map)   23 cm.

Jolliffe, John.
In the matter of George Gordon's petition for
pardon ... Cincinnati, Gazette company steam
printing house, 1862.
56 p.   22 cm.

Jollivet.
La commission presidee par m. le duc de
Broglie, et les gouverneurs de nos colonies,
theorie et pratique ... Paris, Imprimerie de
Boule et cie, 1843.
56 p.   20 cm.

Jollivet.
Observations sur le rapport de M. de Tocqueville, relatif a l'abolition de l' esclavage dans
les colonies, et quelques mots sur la loi des
sucres ... Paris, Imprimerie de Cosse et G. -
Laguionie, 1840.
59 p.   20 cm.

Jollivet.
Question des sucres dans la Chambres des com-
munes d'Angleterre. Du travail libre et du tra-

vail force, leur influence sur la production
coloniale ... Mai. - 1841. Paris, Imprimerie
d Ad. Blondeau, 1841.
27 p. 21 cm.

Jonathan, pseud.
Brieven uit en over de Vereenigde Staten van
Noord-Amerika. Uitgegeven met eene inleiding en
bijschrift, door Dr. E. B. Swalue, predikant te
Amsterdam. Met platen en eene kaart. Schoon-
hoven, S. E. Van Nooten, 1853.
xiv, 304 p. front., plates, fold. map.
22 1/2 cm.

[Jones, Benjamin Washington] 1841-
Under the stars and bars; a history of the
Surry light artillery; recollections of a private
soldier in the war between the states ... Richmond, E. Waddey co., 1909.
xiii, 297 p. 20 1/2 cm.

Jones, Calvin.
A description of Wier's cave, in Augusta coun-
ty, Virginia, in a letter from General Calvin
Jones, to Mr. *** in North-Carolina; [communi-
cated to the editor of the Star, Raleigh, North
Carolina] Printed and sold by Henry C. Southwick,
Albany, 1815.
8 p. front. (fold. map) 21 cm.

Jones, Charles Colcock, 1831-1893.
Historical sketch of the Chatham artillery
during the Confederate struggle for independence.
By Charles C. Jones, jr. ... Albany, J. Munsell,
1867.
240 p. maps. 24 cm.

Jones, Charles Colcock, 1831-
Memorial history of Augusta, Georgia; from its
settlement in 1735 to the close of the eighteenth
century, by Charles C. Jones, jr., LL.D. From
the close of the eighteenth century to the present
time, by Salem Dutcher. Syracuse, D. Mason &
co., 1890.
512, 57 p. ports. 26 cm.

Jones, Charles Colcock, 1831-
Negro myths from the Georgia coast told in the
vernacular. Boston and New York, Houghton,

Mifflin and company, 1888.
x, 171 p.   18 cm.

Jones, Charles Colcock, 1804.
The religious instruction of the Negroes in
the United States ... Savannah, Thomas Purse,
1842.
277 p.   18 1/2 cm.

Jones, Evan Rowland, 1840-
The emigrants' friend; containing information
and advice for persons intending to emigrate to
the United States by Major Jones ... London,
Hamilton, Adams & co.; [etc., etc.] 1880.
xiv, 234 p.   front. (fold. map) fold. tab.
18 1/2 cm.

Jones, Hugh, 1669-
The present state of Virginia ... London,
Printed for J. Clarke, 1724.
viii, 151, [1] p.   2 p.l.   20 1/2 cm.

Jones, J. Elizabeth.
The young abolitionists; or, Conversations
on slavery ... Boston, Published at the Anti-
slavery office, 1848.
131 p.   15 cm.

Jones, John Richter.
Slavery sanctioned by the Bible. The first
part of a general treatise on the slavery question ... Philadelphia, J. B. Lippincott, 1861.
34 p.   22 cm.

Jones, John William, 1836-
Christ in the camp; or, Religion in Lee's
army; by Rev. J. Wm. Jones ... With an introduction by Rev. J. C. Granberry ... bishop of the
Methodist Episcopal church, South ... Richmond,
Va., B. F. Johnson & co., 1887.
528 p.   front. (port.) illus., plates.
21 1/2 cm.

Jones, Samuel Calvin, 1838-
Reminiscences of the Twenty-second Iowa volunteer infantry, giving its organization, marches, skirmishes, battles, and sieges, as taken
from the diary of Lieutenant S. C. Jones of Company A.   Iowa City, Ia., 1907.

164, [2] p. 2 double pl., ports. 23 1/2 cm.

[Jörg, Eduard] 1808-
Briefe aus den Vereinigten Staaten von Nord-
Amerika. Leipzig, J. J. Weber, 1853.

Journal of the siege of York-town. Unpublished journal of the siege of Yorktown in 1781 operated by
the General Staff of the French Army, as recorded
in the hand of Gaspard de Gallatin and translated
by the French Department of the College of William
and Mary. Presented by Mr. Fess. Washington,
U. S. Govt. Print. Off., 1931.
iv, 48 p. 24 cm.

Joutel, Henri, 1640?
Journal historique du dernier voyage qui feu
M. de la Sale fit dans le golfe de Mexique, pour
trouver l'embouchure, & le course de la rivière
de Missisipi, nommée à présent la rivière de
Saint Loüis qui traverse la Louisiane. Où l'on
voit l'histoire tragique de sa mort, & plusieurs
choses curieuses du Nouveau monde. Par Monsieur
Joutel, l'un des compagnons de ce voyage. Re-
digè & mis en ordr [e] par Monsieur de Michel.
Paris, Chez E. Robinet, 1713.
xxxiv, 386 p. fold. map. 17 cm.

Judson, A[mos] M.
History of the Eighty-third regiment Pennsylvania volunteers. By A. M. Judson ... Erie, Pa.
B. F. H. Lynn [1865].
2 p.l., xiii-xv, 17-139, [1] p. 24 cm.

Judson, Andrew Thompson, 1784.
... Remarks to the jury, on the trial of the
case, State vs. P. Crandall, Superior court,
Oct. term, 1833. Windham county, Ct. Hartford,
John Russell [1833?]
32 p. 21 cm.

Judson, Edward, 1844-
The life of Adoniram Judson, by his son, Edward Judson. New York, A. D. F. Randolph & company [c1883].
xii, 601 p. front., illus. (facsims.) plates,
ports., 11 maps. 21 cm.

Julian, George Washington, 1817.
  The cause and cure of our national troubles.
Speech ... delivered in the House of Representa-
tives, Tuesday, January 14, 1862. Washington,
Scammell & co., 1862.
  15 p. 24 cm.

Julian, George Washington, 1817.
  Confiscation and liberation. Speech in the
U. S. House of Representatives, Friday, May 23,
1862. Washington, Scammell & co., printers,
1862.
  8 p. 22 cm.

Julian, George Washington, 1817.
  The slavery question. Speech ... delivered
in the House of Representatives, May 14, 1850,
in committee of the whole on the state of the
Union, on the president's message transmitting
the constitution of California. [Washington,
Buell & Blanchard, 1850?]
  16 p. 22 cm.

Julius, Nicolaus Heinrich, 1783-
  Nordamerikas sittliche zustände. Nach eigenen
anschauungen in den jahren 1834, 1835 und 1836 ...
Leipzig, F. A. Brockhaus, 1839.
  2 v. fold. map, fold. plans, fold. tables.
23 cm.

Junkin, George.
  Essay XI. Abolitionism. Originally published
in 1844, in review of the following works: 1.
"The Integrity of our National Union vs. Abolitionism. An argument from the Bible, in proof of
the position; that believing masters ought to be
honoured and obeyed by their servants, and
tolerated in, not excommunicated from the Church
of God, being part of a speech delivered before
the Synod of Cincinnati, on the subject of Slavery,
September 19th and 20th, 1843. By Rev. George
Junkin, D. D., President of Miami University."
[n.p.] 1843.
  342 p. 21 cm.

Junkin, George.
  The integrity of our national union, vs.
abolitionism: an argument from the Bible in
proof of the position that believing masters

ought to be honored and obeyed by their own servants ... a speech delivered before the synod
of Cincinnati, on the subject of slavery, September 19th and 20th, 1843 ... Cincinnati, Printed by R. P. Donogh, 1843.
79 p. 22 cm.

Juvenile poems, for the use of free American children,
of every complexion. Boston, Published by Garrison & Knapp, 1835.
72 p. illus. 15 cm.

K

Kane, John K.
Report of the proceedings on the Writ of Habeas
Corpus in the case of the United States of America ex rel. John H. Wheeler vs. Passmore Williamson, including the several opinions delivered,
and the arguments of counsel, reported by Arthur
Cannon, Esq., phonographer. Philadelphia, Uriah
Hunt & son, 1856.
191 p. 23 cm.

Kapp, Friedrich.
Aus und über Amerika. Thatsachen und erlebnisse ... Berlin, J. Springer, 1876.
2 v., 8°.

Kearney, Bell, 1863-
A slaveholder's daughter ... New York, The
Abbey press [c1900].
4 p.l., 269 p. illus. (facsims.), plates,
port, 20 1/2 cm.

[Keasbey, Anthony Quinton] 1824-
From the Hudson to the St. Johns. Newark,
N. J., Press of the Newark daily advertiser,
1874.
104 p. 20 1/2 cm.

Keim, De Benneville, Randolph, 1841-
A guide to the Potomac River, Chesapeake Bay,
and James River, and an ocean voyage to northern

ports. A series of interesting and instructive
excursions by water from Washington ... Washington,
D. C., by the compiler, c1881.
  80 p. front (fold. map), illus.   17 cm.

Keith, George, 1639?
    A journal of travels from New Hampshire to
Caratuck, on the continent of North America ...
London, Printed by J. Downing for B. Aylmer,
1706.
    92 p.   2 p.l.   21 cm.

Kelland, Philip, 1808-
    Transatlantic sketches.   Edinburgh, Adam and
Charles Black, 1858.
    viii, 77 p.   16 cm.

Kelley, Daniel George.
    What I saw and suffered in Rebel prisons. By
Daniel G. Kelley ... With an introduction by
Major Anson G. Chester ... Buffalo, Printing
house of Matthews & Warren, 1866.
    86 p.   18 cm.

Kelley, Samuel, 1784-
    Samuel Kelly, an eighteenth century seaman,
whose days have been few and evil ... Now edited
with an introduction by Crosbie Garstin.   New
York, Frederick A. Stokes company, 1925.
    320 p.   front., plates, map.   24 1/2 cm.

Kelley, William D.
    Speech of Hon. W. D. Kelley, of Pa., on
freedmen's affairs.   Delivered in the House of
Representatives, Feb. 23, 1864. [Washington,
D. C., 1864?]
    8 p.   22 cm.

Kelley, William Darrah, 1814-
    The old south and the new.   A series of letters
... New York and London, G. P. Putnam's sons,
1888.
    viii, 162 p.   20 cm.

Kellogg, John Azor, 1828-1883.
    ... Capture and escape; a narrative of army
and prison life, by John Azor Kellogg ... [Madi-
son] Wisconsin history commission, 1908.

xvi, 201 p.   front.   (port.)   23 1/2 cm.

Kellogg, John Jackson, 1837-
War experiences and the story of the Vicksburg campaign from "Milliden's Bend" to July 4,
1863; being an accurate and graphic account of
campaign events taken from the diary of Capt.
J. J. Kellogg, of Co. B, 113th Illinois volunteer infantry. [Washington, Ia., Evening journal, ᶜ1913].
64 p.   front.   (port.)   17 1/2 cm.

Kellogg, Louise Phelps, ed.
Early narratives of the Northwest, 1634-1699,
ed. by Louise Phelps Kellogg ... with a facsimile and two maps. New York, C. Scribner's
sons, 1917. (Original narratives of early American history).
xiv, 382 p.   2 fold. maps, facsim.
22 1/2 cm.

Kellogg, Robert H.
Life and death in rebel prisons: giving a
complete history of the inhuman and barbarous
treatment of our brave soldiers by rebel authorities, inflicting terrible suffering and fright-
ful mortality, principally at Andersonville, Ga.,
and Florence, S. C., describing plans of escape,
arrival of prisoners, with numerous and varied
incidents and anecdotes of prison life. By
Robert H. Kellogg ... Prepared from his daily
journal. To which is added as full sketches of
other prisons as can be given without repetition
of the above, by parties who have been confined
therein ... Hartford, Conn., L. Stebbins, 1865.
viii, [11] - 400 p.   incl. front., pl., plan.
19 cm.

Kellogg, William.
The incidents of the Lecompton struggle in
Congress. And the campaign of 1858 in Illinois.
Speech ... delivered in the House of Representa-
tives, March 13, 1860. Washington, Buell &
Blanchard, 1860.
16 p.   22 1/2 cm.

Kemble, Frances Anne.
Journal of a residence on a Georgian plantation in 1838-1839. New York, Harper & brothers,

1863.
337 p.   19 cm.

Kemble, Frances Anne, 1809-
Journal of a residence on a Georgian plantation in 1838-1839 ... London, Longman, Green,
Longman, Roberts, & Green, 1863.
434 p.   4 p.l.   18 1/2 cm.

Kemble, Frances Anne, 1809.
The views of Judge Woodward and Bishop Hopkins on negro slavery at the south, illustrated
from the Journal of a residence on a Georgian
plantation ... [Philadelphia? 1863?]
32 p.   21 cm.

Kendall, George Wilkins, 1809-
Narrative of the Texan Santa Fe expedition.
New-York, Harper and brothers, 1844.
2 v.   fronts., plates, fold. map.   20 1/2 cm.

[Kendrick, John]
National dangers, and means of escape.   [n.p.,
n.d.]
7 p.   22 cm.

Kennaway, Sir John Henry, baronet, 1837-
On Sherman's track; or, The south after the
war ... London, Seeley, Jackson, and Halliday,
1867.
x, 320 p.   incl. front. plates.   18 1/2 cm.

[Kennedy, Philip Pendleton] 1808?
The Blackwater chronicle, a narrative of an
expedition into the land of Canaan in Randolph
county, Virginia ... By "the Clerke of Oxenforde"
... New York, Redfield, 1853.
[3]-223 p.,   2 p.l., incl. illus., pl.   front.
18 cm.

Kennedy, William, 1799-
Texas: the rise, progress, and prospects of
the Republic of Texas ... London, R. Hastings, 1841.
2v.   maps (2 fold.)   22 cm.

Kent, Mrs. E. C.
"Four years in Secessia." A narrative of a
residence at the South previous to and during the

southern rebellion, up to November, 1863, when
the writer escaped from Richmond. By Mrs. E. C.
Kent. Buffalo, Franklin printing house, 1865.
31 p. 23 cm.

Kentucky and Tennessee. A complete guide to their railroads, stations and distances ... connections
north and south. Their rivers, their landings and
distances, with a complete county map of each
state and railway map of the United States. Alphabetical list of post offices in each state,
rate of U. S. postage, a souvenir of Mammoth
Cave together with a list of Adams express offices. Louisville, H. E. Mead, 1867.
144 p. maps. 13 cm.

Kenworthy, Charles James.
Climatology of Florida, by Charles J. Kenworthy ... Savannah, Morning news steam printing
house, 1860.
70 p. 21 1/2 cm.

Ker, Henry.
Travels through the western interior of the
United States from the year 1808 up to the year
1816 ... Elizabethtown, N. J., Printed for the
author, 1816.
viii, [9] - 372 p. 22 1/2 cm.

Kerbey, Joseph Orton, d. 1913.
The boy spy; a substantially true record of
events during the war of the rebellion. The only practical history of war telegraphers in the
field ... thrilling scenes of battles, captures
and escapes, by Major J. O. Kerbey. Chicago,
New York [etc.] Belford, Clarke & co., 1889.
vii, 8-556 p. front., plates. 20 1/2 cm.

[Kerwood, Asbury L.]
Annals of the Fifty-seventh regiment Indiana
volunteers. Marches, battles, and incidents of
army life, by a member of the regiment. Dayton,
O., W. J. Shuey, 1868.
374 p. 19 1/2 cm.

Kettell, Thomas Prentice.
Southern wealth and northern profits, as exhibited in statistical facts and official figures
showing the necessity of union to the future

prosperity and welfare of the republic ... New
York, George W. & John A. Wood, 1860.
173 p.   23 cm.

A key to Sterne's exposure of Jamaica justice, or A
brief account of the author's individual wrongs.
[London, J. Chappell, n.d.]
15 p.   22 cm.

Keyes, Charles M.   ed.
The military history of the 123d regiment of
Ohio volunteer infantry.   Edited by C. M. Keyes ...
Sandusky, Register steam press, 1874.
196 p.   20 cm.

Kidd, James Harvey, 1840-
Personal recollections of a cavalryman with
Custer's Michigan cavalry brigade in the civil
war, by J. H. Kidd, formerly colonel, Sixth
Michigan cavalry ... Ionia, Mich., Sentinel printing company, 1908.
xiv p., 1 l., 476 p.   front., port., 3 maps.
23 cm.

The kidnapped clergyman, or, Experience, the best
teacher.   Boston, Dow and Jackson, 1839.
123 p.   17 1/2 cm.

Kimbell, Charles Bill, 1839-
History of Battery "A", First Illinois light
artillery volunteers [by] Charles B. Kimbell.
Chicago, Cushing printing company, 1899.
viii, [9] - 320 p.   incl. col. front., illus.
(incl. ports.)   plates.   23 1/2 cm.

Kimber, Edward, 1719-
A relation, or, Journal of a late expedition to
the gates of St. Augustine, on Florida; conducted
by the Hon. General James Oglethorpe, with a
detachment of his regiment, etc. from Georgia.
In a letter to the Rev. Mr. Isaac K---r in London.   By a gentleman, volunteer in the said expedition.   London, T. Astley, 1744.
viii, 36 p.   24 cm.

King, Edward, 1848-
The great south; a record of journeys in Louis-
iana, Texas, the Indian Territory, Missouri,
Arkansas, Mississippi, Alabama, Georgia, Florida,

South Carolina, North Carolina, Kentucky, Tennessee, Virginia, West Virginia, and Maryland ... Profusely illustrated from original sketches by J. Wells Champney. Hartford, Conn., American publishing company, 1875.
    1 p. 1., xiv, 17-802, 4 p. front., illus., maps. 26 cm.

King, John T.
    Guide to Baltimore & Ohio railroad ... [Baltimore, 1873?]
        cover-title, 68 p. illus. 18 1/2 cm.

King, Rufus.
    Speeches of Mr. King, in the Senate, and of Messrs. Taylor and Talmadge, in the House of Representatives ... on the bill for authorizing the people of the territory of Missouri to form a constitution and state government ... in the session of 1818-19. With a report of a committee of the Abolition society of Delaware. Philadelphia, printed by Hall and Atkinson, 1819.
        35 p. 22 cm.

Kingdom, William, jr.
    America and the British colonies. An abstract of all the most useful information relative to the United States, the Cape of Good Hope, New South Wales, and Van Diemen's island ... London, Printed for G. and W. B. Whittaker, 1820.
        vii, [1], 359, [1] p. 22 1/2 cm.

[Kingsford, William] 1819-
    Impressions of the West and South during a six weeks holiday. Toronto, A. H. Armour & Co., 1858.
        83 p. 21 1/2 cm.

Kinnear, John R.
    History of the Eighty-sixth regiment, Illinois volunteer infantry, during its term of service. By J. R. Kinnear ... Chicago, Tribune company's book and job printing office, 1866.
        viii, [9] - 139 p. 19 cm.

Kirk, Edward Norris, 1802.
    Annual discourse ... Only one human race. [n.p., n.d.]
        14 p. 22 cm.

Kirsten, A.
    Skizzen aus den Vereinigten Staaten von Nord-
amerika ... Leipzig, F. A. Brockhaus, 1851.
    xx p.   347 p.   1 1.

Kist, Leopold, 1824-
    Amerikanisches ... Mainz, Franz Kirchheim,
New York, F. Pustet, 1871.
    xi, 820 p.   20 cm.

[Kitchen, R.]
    The death of Uncle Tom ... Composed by Alfred
Mullen ... London, B. Williams n.d.
    5 p.   front., music.   34 1/2 cm.

Kleen Emil Andreas Gabriel, 1847-
    Ströftag och irrfärder hos min vän Yankee
Doodle (samt annorstades) af dr. Emil A. G.
Kleen ... Stockholm, Nordin & Josephson [1904,
'03]
    2 v.   20 1/2 cm.

Kleiber, Joseph.
    Amerika wie es ist als: städte, land, verkehr,
eisenbahnen, schiffahrt, maschinerien, handel,
erwerb, verdienst, religiöse zustände, pfarreien
... Erlebnisse von R. P. Jos. Kleiber ... München, Jos. Ant. Finsterlin, 1877.
    viii p., 1 1., 384 p.   18 cm.

Klein, Felix, 1862 -
    ... Au pays de "la yie intense." Paris, Plan-
Nourrit et c^{ie} , 1904.
    3 p.1., 386 p.   19 cm.

Klitgaard, Kaj.
    ... Through the American landscape, by Kaj
Klitgaard. Chapel Hill, the University of North
Carolina press [c1941]
    xi, 323 p.   plates (part col.)   23 1/2 cm.

Knauer, Hermann.
    Deutschland am Mississippi. Neue eindrücke
und erlebnisse von Hermann Knauer. Berlin, L.
Oehmigke's verlag (R. Appelius) 1904.
    vi p., 1 1., 184 p.   illus.   23 1/2 cm.

Knibb, William.
Colonial slavery. Defence of the Baptist missionaries from the charge of inciting the late rebellion in Jamaica; in a discussion between the Rev. William Knibb and Mr. P. Borthwick, at the assembly rooms, Bath, on Saturday, December 15, 1832 ... Second ed. London, Published at the Tourist Office, and sold by Sherwood, Gilbert, & Piper [n.d.]
30 p. 21 cm.

[Knight, Henry Cogswell] 1788-
Letters from the South and West; by Arthur Singleton, esq. [pseud.] Boston, Pub. by Richardson and Lord, J. H. A. Frost, printer, 1824.
159 p. 22 cm.

Knobel, F[ridolin] M[arinus] 1857-
Dwars door het land van Roosevelt, door F. M. Knobel. Amsterdam, H. J. W. Becht, 1906.
5 p.1. [3]-269 p. 21 1/2 cm.

Knortz, Karl, 1841-
Amerikanische lebensbilder. Skizzen und tagebuchblätter von Karl Knortz ... Zürich, Verlags-magazin (J. Schabelitz) 1884.
2 p.1., 208 p. 21 1/2 cm.

Knox, Thomas Wallace, 1835-1896.
Camp-fire and cotton field: southern adventure in time of war. Life with the Union armies, and residence on a Louisiana plantation. By Thomas W. Knox ... New York, Blelock and company, 1865.
524 p. front., plates. 22 cm.

Knox, William.
Three tracts respecting the conversion and instruction of the free Indians and negroe slaves in the colonies ... A new edition. London, Printed for J. Debrett, 1789.
39 p. 21 cm.

Koch, Albrecht Karl.
Reise durch einen theil der Vereinigten Staaten von Nordamerika in den jahren 1844 bis 1846. Dresden und Leipzig, C. Arnold, 1847.
162 p. 2 p.1., front., col. pl. 22 1/2 cm.

Koch, Richert Gerhard Halfred von, 1872-
... Emigranternas land; studier i amerikanskt
samhällslif. Stockholm, Aktiebolaget Ljus, 1910.
2 p.l., 391, vi p. illus. (incl. ports.,
maps, facsims.) 24 cm.

Kollacz, P.
Rewolucya teraznieysza Ameryka polnocney w
dwunastu z konfederowanycho osadach [etc., etc.]
Poznán, w drukarni J. K. Mci y Rzpitey, 1778.

Kotzebue, August Friedrich Ferdinand von, 1761.
The negro slaves, a dramatic-historical piece,
in three acts. Translated from the German ...
London, Printed for T. Cadell, junior, and W.
Davies, and J. Edwards, 1796.
142 p. 20 cm.

[Kriegsau, Adolph, freiherr von]
Skizzen aus Amerika. Von B. Aba [pseud.]
Wien, C. Gerold's sohn, 1885.
1 p.l., 293 [1] p. 20 1/2 cm.

Kroupa, B.
An artist's tour; gleanings and impressions
of travels in North and Central America and the
Sandwich islands. With thirty-four illustrations
by the author. London, Ward and Downey, 1890.
xiv p., 1 1., 339 [1] p. front. plates.
26 cm.

Kuyper, Henriette Sophia Suzanna, 1870-
Een half jaar in Amerika. Door H. S. S.
Kuyper ... Rotterdam, D. A. Daamen [1907].
4 p.l., 450 p. 20 cm.

L

Lade, Robert.
Voyages du Capitaine Robert Lade en differ-
entes parties de l'Afrique, de l'Asie, et de
l'Amerique ... Paris, Didot, 1744.
2 v. fold. maps. 17 cm.

Ladies' New-York city anti-slavery society.
First annual report ... New York, William S.
Dorr, 1836.
19 p. 21 cm.

Lafayette, Marie Joseph Paul Yves Roch Gilbert du
Motier, marquis de, 1757-1834.
The memoirs, correspondence and manuscripts
of Marquis de Lafayette. Published by his family.
London, Saunders and Otley, 1837.
3 v. front. (port., v. 1) 24 cm.

Lafon, Thomas.
The great obstruction to the conversion of
souls at home and abroad ... New York, Union
missionary society, 1843.
23 p. 21 cm.

[La Harpe, Bernard de]
Journal historique de l'établissement des
Français à la Louisiane ... Nouvelle-Orleans,
A. L. Boinare; [etc., etc.] 1831.
412 p. 2 p.l. 20 cm.

Lahontan, Louis Armand de Lom d'Arce, baron de, 1666-
Nouveaux voyages de m^r le baron de Lahontan,
dans l'Amérique Septentrionale, qui contiennent
une relation des differens peuples qui y habitent;
la nature de leur gouvernement; leur commerce,
leurs coutumes, leur religion, et leur manière
de faire la guerre ... Le tout enrichi de cartes
de figures. La Haye, Chez les frères l'Honore,
1703.
2 v. front., plates (part fold.), fold.
maps. 16 1/2 cm.

Lamar, Lucius Quintus Cincinnatus, 1825.
The slavery question. Speech ... in the House
of Representatives, February 21, 1860. [n.p.,
n.d.]
8 p. 24 cm.

Lamb, Roger, 1756-
An original and authentic journal of occurrences during the late American war, from its
commencement to the year 1783 ... Dublin, Printed
by Wilkinson & Courtney, 1809.
iv, xxiv, [5] - 438 p. 22 cm.

Lambert, John.
    Travels through lower Canada, and the United
States of America, in the years 1806, 1807, and
1808. To which are added, biographical notices
and anecdotes of some of the leading characters
in the United States. London, Printed for Richard
Phillips, 1810.
    3 v. fronts. (v. 1) col. plates.   22 cm.

Lambert de Sainte-Croix, Alexandre, 1854-
    De Paris à San Francisco. Notes de voyage,
par Alexandre Lambert de Sainte-Croix. 2 ed.
Paris, C. Levy, 1885.
    3 p.l., iii, 319 p. illus., fold. map.
12 cm.

Lamprecht, Karl Gotthard, 1856-
    Americana. Reiseeindrücke, betrachtungen,
geschichtliche gesamtansicht. Freiburg im Breisgau, H. Heyfelder, 1906.
    5 p.l. [3] - 147 p. illus.   21 cm.

Landolphe, Jean François, 1747-
    Mémoires du capitaine Landolphe, contenant
l'histoire de ses voyages pendant trente-six
ans, aux cotes d'Afrique et aux deux Amériques;
rédigés sur son manuscrit, par J. S. Quesne ...
Paris, A. Bertrand [etc.] 1823.
    2 v. fronts. (ports.) fold. plan.   20 1/2 cm.

Lane Seminary. Cincinnati. Students.
    A statement of the reasons which induced
the students at Lane seminary to dissolve their
connection with that institution. Cincinnati,
1834.
    28 p.   20 cm.

Lane Seminary, Cincinnati. Trustees.
    Fifth annual report ... together with the laws
of the institution, and a catalogue of the officers and students. November, 1834. Cincinnati,
Published by Corey & Fairbank, 1834.
    47 p.   22 cm.

Lang, John D.
    Report of a visit to some of the tribes of
Indians, located west of the Mississippi River.
By John D. Lang and Samuel Taylor, jr. Providence,
Printed by Knowles and Vose, 1843.

47 p.   22 cm.

Lang, John Dunmore, 1799-
    Religion and education in America; with no-
tices of the state and prospects of American
Unitarianism, popery, and African colonization...
London, T. Ward and co., 1840.
    viii, 474 p.   16 1/2 cm.

Langworthy, Daniel Avery, 1832-
    Reminiscences of a prisoner of war and his
escape, by Daniel Avery Langworthy, late captain
85th N. Y. vol. infantry ... Minneapolis, Minn.,
Byron printing company, 1915.
    4 p.1., [13] - 74 p. front., plates, ports.
21 1/2 cm.

Lanier, Sidney, 1842-
    Florida: its scenery, climate, and history.
With an account of Charleston, Savannah, Augusta,
and Aiken ... Philadelphia, J. B. Lippincott and
co., 1875.
    2 p.1., 266 p. incl. front., illus., plates.
19 cm.

Lanman, Charles, 1819-
    Adventures in the wilds of the United States
and British American provinces ... Illustrated
by the author and Oscar Bessau ... with an appendix by Lieut. Campbell Hardy ... Philadelphia,
J. W. Moore, 1856.
    2 v. front., plates.   23 cm.

Lapham, William Berry, 1828-1894.
    My recollections of the war of the rebellion;
by William B. Lapham ... Privately printed.
Augusta, Me., Burleigh & Flynt, printers, 1892.
    240 p.   port.   19 1/2 cm.

Lardner, Dionysius, 1793-
    Railway economy; a treatise on the new art of
transport, its management, prospects and relations
... New York, Harper & brothers, 1850.
    xxiii, [25]-442 p.   20 cm.

Larned, Edwin Channing.
    Arguments of E. C. Larned, esq., counsel for
the defence, on the trial of Joseph Stout, in-
dicted for rescuing a fugitive slave from the

311

United States deputy marshal, at Ottawa, Ill.,
Oct. 20, 1859; delivered in the United States
district court in the northern district of Illinois, Monday and Tuesday, March 12 & 13, 1860.
By R. Hitt, reporter. Chicago, Press & tribune
book and job printing office, 1860.
43 p.   21 cm.

La Rochefoucauld Liancourt, François Alexandre Frédéric,   duc de,   1747-
Voyage dans les Etats-Unis d'Amerique, fait
en 1795, 1796, et 1797. Paris, Du Pont [etc.]
L'an vii de la République [1799].
8 v. 2 fold. maps, 8 fold. tab. 20 1/2 cm.

The last illness and death of George Hardy, a colored
boy. Philadelphia, Published by the Tract association of Friends [n.d.]
4 p.   18 cm.

Latham, Henry, 1794-
Black and white. A journal of a three months'
tour in the United States ... London, Macmillan
and co., 1867.
xii, 304 p.   23 cm.

Latham, Milton Slocum, 1827.
Remarks ... upon slavery in the states and
territories, and the doctrine of an "irrepressible
conflict" between "labor states" and "capital
states." Delivered in the Senate of the United
States, April 10, 1860. Washington, D. C. Printed by Lemuel Towers [1860?]
16 p.   23 cm.

Lathers, Richard, 1820-1903.
Reminiscences of Richard Lathers; sixty years
of a busy life in South Carolina, Massachusetts
and New York; edited by Alvan F. Sanborn. New
York, The Grafton press, 1907.
6 p.1. [3] - 425 p. 4 pl., 9 port. (incl.
front.)   24 1/2 cm.

Lathrop, David.
The history of the Fifty-ninth regiment Illinois volunteers, or A three years' campaign
through Missouri, Arkansas, Mississippi, Tennessee and Kentucky, with a description of the country, towns, skirmishes and battles ... embellished

312

with twenty-four lithographed portraits of the officers of the regiment. By Dr. D. Lathrop. Indianapolis, Hall & Hutchinson, printers, 1865.
    243 p. front., port. 19 1/2 cm.

Latour, Arsène Lacarrière.
    Historical memoir of the war in West Florida and Louisiana in 1814-15. With an atlas ... Written originally in French, and translated for the author, by H. P. Nugent ... Philadelphia, Published by John Conrad and co., J. Maxwell, printer, 1816.
    xx, 264, cxc p. front. (port.) and atlas of 8 maps (part fold.) 21 1/2 cm.

Latrobe, Charles Joseph, 1801-1875.
    The rambler in North America; MDCCCXXXII-MDCCCXXXIII. London, R. B. Seeley and W. Burnside [etc.] 1835.
    2 v. 20 1/2 cm.

Latrobe, John H. B.
    African colonization. An address delivered ... at the anniversary meeting of the American colonization society, held in the hall of the House of Representatives, Washington City, January 21, 1862. Washington, Printed by H. S. Bowen, 1862.
    16 p. 22 cm.

Latrobe, John Hazlehurst Boneval, 1803.
    The Christian civilization of Africa. An address delivered before the American colonization society, January 16, 1877 ... Washington city, Colonization building, 1877.
    10 p. 23 cm.

Laudonnière, René Goulaine de.
    L'histoire notable de la Floride sitvee es Indes Occidentales, contenant les trois voyages faits en icelle par certains capitaines et pilotes françois, descrits par le capitaine Laudonière que y a commande l'espace d'vn an trois moys: à laquelle a este adiouste un quatriesme voyage fait par le capitaine Gourguea. Mise en lumière par M. Basanier ... Paris, G. Auuray, 1586.
    123 numb. l., 1 l. 8 p.l. 17 1/2 cm.

Laval, Antoine Francois, 1664-
    Voyage de la Louisiane, fait par ordre du roy

en l'année mil sept cent vingt: dans lequel
sont traitees diverses matières de physique,
astronomie, géographie et marine ... Paris, J.
Mariette, 1728.
    xxiv, 304, 96, 191 [9] p. maps (part fold.)

Laverrenz, Viktor, 1862-
    Prinz Heinrichs Amerika-fahrt; darstellung der
reise des Hohenzollern-admirals; schilderung
von land und leuten und interessante episoden aus
der geschichte der Vereinigten Staaten; ein
gedenkbuch für jung und alt, von Victor Laverrenz ... Berlin, H. F. Meidinger [1902?]
    257 [2] p. illus. (incl. ports.) 8 pl. (incl.
front.) 24 cm.

The law and testimony concerning slavery. [Cincin-
nati, American reform tract and book society,
n.d.]
    24 p. 18 cm.

[Lawrence, George Alfred] 1827-1876.
    Border and bastille. By the author of "Guy
Livingstone." New York, W. I. Pooley & co.,
[1863].
    xii, 291 p. 19 1/2 cm.

Lawson, John.
    A new voyage to Carolina; containing the exact
description and natural history of that country:
together with the present state thereof. And a
journal of a thousand miles, travel'd thro' several nations of Indians. Giving a particular
account of their customs, manners, &c. London,
Printed in the year 1709.
    258 p. 3 p.l., 1 l. fold. map. 21 cm.

[Lear, Tobias] 1762-
    Observations on the river Potomack, the coun-
try adjacent, and the city of Washington. New-
York, Printed by Loudon and Brower, in Water-
street, 1794.
    29 p. fold. plan. 19 1/2 cm.

Leaven for doughfaces; or, Threescore and ten parables
touching slavery. By a former resident of the
south ... Cincinnati, Bangs and company, Longley
brothers; Cleveland, L.E. Barnard & co., 1856.
    332 p. illus. 19 cm.

Leclerc, Frederic, 1810-1891.
Le Texas et sa revolution. Paris, H. Fournier,
1840.
104 p. map. 22 cm.

Leclercq, Jules Joseph, 1848-
Un été en Amérique, de l'Atlantique aux mon-
tagnes rocheuses. Paris, E. Plon et cie., 1877.
2 p.1., 414 p., 1 1., front., plates.
18 1/2 cm.

Leclerc, Max, 1864-
... Choses d'Amérique; les crises économiques
et religieuses aux Etats-Unis; ouvrage couronné
par l'Académie française. Paris, A. Colin et
cie , 1895.
3 p.1., vii, 282 p. 18 1/2 cm.

Lederer, John.
The discoveries of John Lederer, in three
several marches from Virginia, to the west of
Carolina, and other parts of the continent ...
together with a general map of the whole territory ... Collected and translated out of Latine
... by Sir William Talbot baronet ... London,
Printed by J. C. for S. Heyrick, 1672.
27 p. 4 p.1., double map. 18 cm.

Lee, Henry, 1756-
Memoirs of the war in the southern department
of the United States. Philadelphia: Published
by Bradford and Inskeep; and Inskeep and Bradford; New York, Fry and Kammerer, printers, 1812.
2 v. fronts. (ports.) 20 1/2 cm.

[Lee, Henry] ed.
The tourist's guide of Florida ... New York,
Leve & Alden printing company, 1885.
255 p. illus., maps. (part fold.) 17 1/2 cm.

Leech, Arthur Blennerhassett.
Irish riflemen in America. By Arthur Blennerhassett Leech ... London, E. Stanford; New York,
Van Nostrand, 1875.
vii, 216 p. front., illus., 12 pl. (part
col.) fold. map. 19 1/2 cm.

A legal review of the case of Dred Scott, as decided
by the Supreme Court of the United States. From
the Law Reporter for June, 1857. Boston, Crosby, Nichols, and co., 1857.
62 p.   19 1/2 cm.

The legion of liberty! And force of truth, containing
the thoughts, words, and deeds of some prominent
apostles, champions and martyrs.   2d ed. ... New
York, Sold at the office of the American a. s.
society, 1843.
[308] p. illus. (incl. ports.)   18 1/2 cm.

The legion of liberty! and force of truth, containing
the thoughts, words, and deeds of some prominent
apostles, champions and martyrs.   Second division.   New-York, American anti-slavery society,
1842.
1v. (unpaged) illus.   17 1/2 cm.

The legion of liberty! And force of truth, containing the thoughts, words, and deeds of some prominent apostles, champions and martyrs ... New
York, American anti-slavery society, 1857.
336 p.   illus.   18 1/2 cm.

Leib, Charles.
Nine months in the quartermaster's department;
or, The chances for making a million.   By Charles
Leib ... Cincinnati, Moore, Wilstach, Keys &
co., printers, 1862.
vi, 7-200 p. front., pl., port.   19 cm.

Leigh, Mrs. Frances (Butler), 1838-
Ten years on a Georgia plantation since the
war.   London, R. Bentley & son, 1883.
xi, 347 p.   22 1/2 cm.

Leiste, Christian.
Beschreibung des Brittischen Amerika zur er-
sparung der englischen karten.   Nebst einer spe-
cial-karte der mittlern brittischen colonien ...
[Wolfenbüttel] Gedruckt mit Bindseilschen schrif-
ten, 1778.
29 (i.e. 20), 571 [1] p. fold. map.   18 1/2 cm.

Leng, Sir John, 1828-
America in 1876.   Pencillings during a tour in
the centennial year: with a chapter on the

aspects of American life ... Dundee, Dundee advertiser office, 1877.
  346 p.   18 1/2 cm.

Lenk, Frau Margarete (Klee), 1841–
  Fünfzehn jahre in Amerika. Von Marg. Lenk.
Zwickau i. Sa., J. Herrmann, 1911.
  155 p.   19 cm.

Lente, Frederick Divoux, 1823–
  The constituents of climate with special reference to the climate of Florida ... Louisville,
Ky., Richmond and Louisville medical journal
book and steam job print, 1878.
  58 p.   20 cm.

Leon, L[ouis].
  Diary of a tar heel Confederate soldier.
Charlotte, N. C., Stone publishing company
[c1913]
  2 p.l., 87, [4], 1-14 p.   port.   19 cm.

Leonard, Albert Charles, 1845–
  The boys in blue of 1861-1865; a condensed
history worth preserving ... Lancaster, Pa., A.
C. Leonard [1904].
  79 p.   incl. front. (port.) illus., plates.
23 cm.

Le Page du Pratz, Antoine Simon.
  Histoire de la Louisiane, contenant la découverte de ce vaste pays; sa description géographique; un voyage dans les terres; l'histoire
naturelle, les moeurs, coutumes & religion des
naturels, avec leurs origines; deux voyages dans
le nort du nouveau Mexique, dont un jusqu'à la
mer du Sud; ornee de deux cartes & de 40 planches
en taille douce.   Paris, De Bure, l'aine [etc.]
1758.
  3 v.   plates, fold. maps. fold. plan.
18 1/2 cm.

Leroy Beaulieu, Pierre, 1871–
  ... Les Etats-Unis au xxe siècle.   4. ed.
Paris, A. Colin, 1909.
  2 p.l., xxiii, 469 p.   19 cm.

Lesquereux, Leo, 1806–
    Lettres écrites d'Amérique ... Neuchâtel, De
Henri Wolfrath, 1853.
    300 p.   20 cm.

A letter from Legion to Chas. Gordon Sennox, his Grace
    the Duke of Richmond, 1791–1860, &c., &c., &c.
    Chairman of the slavery committee of the House
    of Lords; containing an exposure of the character
    of the evidence on the colonial side. Produced
    before the committee. London, S. Bagster, 1832.
    196 p.   19 cm.

A letter to John Bull: to which is added the sketch
    of a plan for the safe, speedy, and effectual
    abolition of slavery. By a free-born English-
    man ... London, Printed for J. Hatchard and son,
    1823.
    32 p.   21 cm.

Letters for the people, on the present crisis.
    1.   Slavery in Missouri ... rapidly declining.
    2.   Nebraska territory ... Where is it? and what
    is it?   3.   The American Indians ... How shall
    the government treat them?   4.   The pacific rail-
    road ... where shall it run? and reasons why.
    5.   Compromises ... How kept, and what their ef-
    fects.   6.   The true patriot's duties ... To be
    performed without delay. [n.p., n.d.]
    52 p.   21 cm.

Letters of the members, patrons and friends of the
    branch American tract society in Boston, insti-
    tuted 1841; and those of the national society
    in New York, instituted 1825. By the secretary
    of the Boston society. Boston, Crocker and Brew-
    ster, 1858.
    112 p.   24 cm.

Letters on the condition of Kentucky in 1825; reprin-
    ted from the Richmond enquirer; ed. by Earl Gregg
    Swem ... New York city, Printed for C. F. Heart-
    man, 1916.
    7–76 p.   2 p.l.   24 cm.

Letters on emigration. By a gentleman, lately returned
    from America. London, Printed for C. and G.
    Kearsley, Fleet street, MDCCXCIV.
    76 p.   20 1/2 cm.

Letters respecting a book "Dropped from the catalogue" of the American Sunday school union in compliance with the dictation of the slave power. New York, American and foreign anti-slavery society, 1818.
36 p.   18 cm.

Levasseur, Auguste.
Lafayette en Amerique, en 1824 et 1825, ou, Journal d'un voyage aux Etats-Unis ... Paris, Baudouin, 1829.
2 v. front., plates, ports., fold. map. 21 cm.

Levinge, Richard George Augustus, 1811-
Echoes from the backwoods; or Sketches of transatlantic life ... London, H. Colburn, 1846.
2v. 6 pl. (incl. fronts.)   20 1/2 cm.

Lewis, Sir Charles Edward, 1825-
Two lectures on a short visit to America ... London, Printed by Blades, East, & Blades, 1876.
106 p. 1 l.   21 1/2 cm.

Lewis, George, of Ormiston.
Impressions of America and the American churches: from journal of the Rev. G. Lewis ... Edinburgh, W. P. Kennedy [etc., etc.] 1845.
viii, 432 p.   22 cm.

Lewis, Henry, 1819-
Das illustrirte Mississippithal, dargestellt in 80 nach der natur aufgenommenen ansichten vom wasserfälle zu St. Anthony an bis zum gulf von Mexico ... Nebst einer historischen und geographischen beschreibung der den fluss begränzenden länder, mit besonderer rücksicht auf die verschiedenen den obern Mississippi bewohnenden Indianerstämme. (Deutsch und englisch) Von George R. Douglas ... Düsseldorf, Arnz & comp. [1857].
431 p. front. (eng. title) illus., 78 col. p l. (1 double)   27 1/2 cm.

[Lewis, John Delaware] 1828-
Across the Atlantic. By the author of "Sketches of Cantabs." London, G. Earle, 1851.
x, 274 p. 1 l.   18 cm.

Lewis, John Henry, 1834-
　　　Recollections from 1860 to 1865. With incidents of camp life, descriptions of battles, the
life of the southern soldier, his hardships and
sufferings, and the life of a prisoner of war
in the northern prisons. By John H. Lewis ...
Washington, D. C., Peake & company, 1895.
　　　1 p.1., 92 p.　port.　　15 cm.

Lewis, John W.
　　　The life, labors, and travels of elder Charles
Bowles, of the Free Will Baptist denomination ...
together with an essay on the character and condition of the African race by the same.　Also,
an essay on the fugitive law of the U. S. Congress of 1850, by Rev. Arthur Dearing.　Watertown,
Ingalls & Stowell's steam press, 1852.
　　　285 p.　　19 1/2 cm.

The liberator. Vol. I No. 1.　Boston, Massachusetts-
Saturday, January 1, 1831.　[Boston, Directors
of the Old South work, Old South Meeting House,
n. d.]
　　　24 p.　　19 cm.

Liberty and union, one and inseparable.　Speeches delivered at the Republican union festival.　in
commemoration of the birth of Washington; held
at Irving Hall, Feb. 22., 1862, under the auspices
of the Republican central committees of the city
and county of New York.　New York, G. F. Putnam,
1862.
　　　27 p.　　22 cm.

The liberty bell.　By friends of freedom ... Boston,
American anti-slavery society, 1839.
　　　103 p.　illus.　　16 1/2 cm.

The liberty bell.　Friends of freedom ... Boston,
Massachusetts anti-slavery society, 1841.
　　　144 p.　illus.　　16 cm.

The liberty bell.　By friends of freedom ... Boston,
Massachusetts anti-slavery society, 1842.
　　　204 p.　illus.　　16 cm.

The liberty bell.　By friends of freedom ... Boston,
Massachusetts anti-slavery society, 1843.
　　　208 p.　illus.　　18 1/2 cm.

The liberty bell. By friends of freedom ... Boston,
  Massachusetts anti-slavery society, 1844.
    232 p. illus. 18 1/2 cm.

The liberty bell. By friends of freedom ... Boston,
  Massachusetts anti-slavery society, 1845.
    256 p. illus. 18 cm.

The liberty bell. By friends of freedom ... Boston,
  Massachusetts anti-slavery society, 1846.
    268 p. illus. 18 cm.

The liberty bell. By friends of freedom ... Boston,
  National anti-slavery bazaar, 1847.
    304 p. illus. 18 cm.

The liberty bell. By friends of freedom ... Boston,
  National anti-slavery bazaar, 1848.
    292 p. illus. 18 cm.

The liberty bell. By friends of freedom ... Boston,
  National anti-slavery bazaar, 1849.
    292 p. illus. 17 1/2 cm.

The liberty bell. By friends of freedom ... Boston,
  National anti-slavery bazaar, 1851.
    304 p. illus. 17 cm.

The liberty bell. By friends of freedom ... Boston,
  National anti-slavery bazaar, 1852.
    303 p. illus. 17 cm.

The liberty bell. By friends of freedom ... Boston,
  National anti-slavery bazaar, 1853.
    315 p. illus. 17 cm.

The liberty bell. By friends of freedom ... Boston,
  National anti-slavery bazaar, 1856.
    200 p. illus. 17 cm.

The liberty bell. By friends of freedom ... Boston,
  National anti-slavery bazaar, 1858.
    328 p. illus. 17 cm.

Liebknecht, Wilhelm, 1826-
    Ein blick in die Neue welt, von Wilhelm Lieb-
  knecht. Stuttgart, J. H. W. Dietz, 1887.
    vii, 288 p. 16 1/2 cm.

The life and adventures of Bampfylde-Moore Carew, the noted Devonshire stroller [!] and dog-stealer; as related by himself, during his passage to the plantations in America. Containing, a great variety of remarkable transactions in a vagrant course of life, which he followed for the space of thirty years and upwards. [Vignette] Exon: Printed by Farley's, for Joseph Drew, bookseller, opposite Castle-lane, 1745.
    v, 152 (i. e. 160) p. 1 p.l. front. (port.) 20 1/2 cm.

The life of slavery, or the life of the nation? Mass meeting of the citizens of New York, (without distinction of party,) at the Cooper Institute, New York, March 6, 1862. Hon. James A. Hamilton in the chair. [New York? 1862?]
    11 p. 24 cm.

The life, trial and execution of Captain John Brown, known as "Old Brown of Ossawatomie," with a full account of the attempted insurrection at Harper's Ferry. Compiled from official and authentic sources. Including Cooke's confession, and all the incidents of the execution. New York, Robert M. DeWitt [n.d.]
    108 p. 23 1/2 cm.

[Ligeret de Chazey, Madame Elénore]
    Les Créoles. Reponse à Madame de Grandfort. [New Orleans, imp. de H. Merider, 1855?]
    42 p. 14 1/2 cm.

[Light, Bianca]
    Our American cousins at home. By Vera [pseud.] ... Illustrated with pen-and-ink sketches by the author, and photographs. London, S. Low, Marston, Low and Searle, 1873.
    ix, 268 p. front., illus., port. 18 cm.

Lightcap, William Henry.
    The horrors of southern prisons during the war of the rebellion, from 1861 to 1865, by W. H. Lightcap ... [Platteville, Wis., Journal job rooms, 1902].
    95 p. incl. front. (port.) 22 cm.

Lignereux, Saint-André de.
     ... L'Amérique au xxe siècle ... Préface de
Paul Adam. Paris, J. Tallandier [1908?]
     viii, 291 [3] p. front. (port.)   19 cm.

Lincoln, Abraham, pres. U. S., 1809-1865.
     Political debates between Hon. Abraham Lin-
coln and Hon. Stephen A. Douglas, in the celebrated
campaign of 1858, in Illinois; including the preceding speeches of each, at Chicago, Springfield,
etc.; also, the two great speeches of Mr. Lincoln
in Ohio, in 1859, as carefully prepared by the re-
porters of each party, and published at the times
of their delivery. Columbus, Follett, Foster and
company, 1860.
     268 p.   23 1/2 cm.

Lincoln, Abraham, pres. U. S., 1809.
     U. L. A. The opinions of Abraham Lincoln upon
slavery and its issues; indicated by his apostles,
letters, messages, and proclamations. [n.p.,
n.d.]
     16 p.   22 cm.

Lindau, Paul, 1839-
     Altes und neues aus der Neuen welt. Eine
reise durch die Vereinigten Staaten und Mexico.
Von Paul Lindau ... Berlin, C. Duncker, 1893.
     2 v.   21 1/2 cm.

Lindsly, Philip.
     A sermon, delivered in the chapel of the Col-
lege of New Jersey, August 15, 1824 ... Princeton, N.J., Printed and published by D. A. Borren-
stein, 1824.
     52 p.   24 cm.

Linley, George.
     Uncle Tom's cabin. No. 1. Eva. Ballad.
[n.p., n.d.]
     5 p. front., music.   34 1/2 cm.

Linn, John Joseph, 1798-
     Reminiscences of fifty years in Texas ... New
York, D. & J. Sadlier & co., 1883.
     369 p. plates, 2 port. (incl. front.)   19 cm.

Little sins, a dialogue. To which is added, an abstract of an interesting conversation. Philadelphia, Published by the Tract association of
Friends n.d.
8 p. 18 cm.

Livermore, Mrs. Elizabeth D.
Zoë; or, The quadroon's triumph. A tale for
the times. With illustrations by Henri Lovie and
Charles Bauerle. Cincinnati, Truman and Spofford,
1855.
2 v. illus. 20 cm.

Livermore, Mrs. Mary Ashton (Rice) 1820-1905.
My story of the war: a woman's narrative of
four years personal experience as nurse in the
Union army, and in relief work at home, in hospitals, camps, and at the front during the war
of the rebellion. With anecdotes, pathetic incidents, and thrilling reminiscences portraying
the lights and shadows of hospital life and the
sanitary service of the war. By Mary A. Livermore ... Hartford, A. D. Worthington and company, 1888.
700 p. front., plates (part col.) port.
23 cm.

Livermore, Thomas Leonard, 1844-1918.
Days and events, 1860-1866, by Thomas L.
Livermore ... Boston and New York, Houghton Mif-
lin company, 1920.
x p., 2 l., [3]-485, [1] p. front. (port.)
illus., fold. pl. 24 1/2 cm.

Liverpool East India association.
Report of a committee of the Liverpool East
India association, appointed to take into consideration the restrictions on the East India
trade. Presented to the Association at a general
meeting, 9th May 1822, and ordered to be printed. Liverpool, Printed for the Association by
James Smith, 1822.
58, 40 p. 21 cm.

Liverpool society for the abolition of slavery.
An address from the Liverpool society for the
abolition of slavery on the safest and most effi-
cacious means of promoting the gradual improvement of the Negro slaves in the British West India

islands, preparatory to their becoming free labourers, and on the expected consequences of such
change. Liverpool, Printed by Jonathan & George
Smith, 1824.
    18 p.   21 cm.

Liverpool society for promoting the abolition of
slavery.
    Declaration of the objects of the Liverpool
society for promoting the abolition of slavery,
25th March, 1823. Liverpool, Printed by James
Smith; published by Hatchard & son, Piccadilly,
and J. & J. Arch, Cornhill, London [n.d.]
    14 p.   21 cm.

[Lloyd, William Penn] 1837-1911.
    History of the First reg't. Pennsylvania re-
serve cavalry, from its organization, August, 1861,
to September, 1864, with list of names of all
officers and enlisted men who have ever belonged
to the regiment ... Philadelphia, King & Baird,
printers, 1864.
    216 p.   19 1/2 cm.

Logan, Mrs. Indiana Washington (Peddicord) 1835-
    Kelion Franklin Peddicord of Quirk's scouts,
Morgan's Kentucky cavalry, C.S.A.; biographical
and autobiographical, together with a general
biographical outline of the Peddicord family, by
Mrs. India W. P. Logan. New York and Washington,
The Neale publishing company, 1908.
    170 p.   4 port. (incl. front.)   21 cm.

Logan, James, advocate, of Edinburgh.
    Notes of a journey through Canada, the United
States of America, and the West Indies ... Edinburgh [etc.] Fraser and co., 1838.
    xii, 259 p.   front. (fold. map)   20 1/2 cm.

Löher, Franz von, 1818-
    Aussichten für gebildete Deutsche in Nord-
amerika ... Berlin, Julius Springer, 1853.
    vi, 3-91 p., 1 1.   19 cm.

Löher, Franz von, 1818-
    Geschichte und zustände der Deutschen in Ameri-
ka ... Cincinnati, Eggers und Wulkop; [etc., etc.]
1847.
    xii, 544 p.   2 p.1.   21 1/2 cm.

Löher, Franz von, 1818-
    Land und Leute, in der Alten und Neuen Welt.
Reisekizzen ... Göttingen, George H. Wigand, 1858.
New York, L. W. Schmidt, 1855.
    3 v. in 2.   17 1/2 cm.

Lombardo, Alberto.
    Los Estados-Unidos (notas y episodios de viaje)
Autor Alberto Lombardo. Mexico, Impr. de la Es-
cuela nacional de artes y oficios, 1884.
    3 p.l., 242 p., 1 1., iii p. 22 1/2 cm.

London anti-slavery society.
    Appendix to negro apprenticeship in the British
colonies. London, London anti-slavery society
[etc., etc.] 1838.
    160 p. 20 cm.

[London anti-slavery society]
    Statements and observations on the working of
the laws for the abolition of slavery throughout
the British colonies, and on the present state of
the Negro population. [London, London anti-
slavery society, 1836].
    68 p. 22 cm.

London missionary society.
    ... Report of the proceedings against the
late Rev. J. Smith, of Demerara, minister of the
gospel, who was tried under martial law and condemned to death, on a charge of siding and assist-
ing in a rebellion of negro slaves ... London,
F. Westley, 1824.
    vii, 204 p. 22 cm.

Long, Lessel.
    Twelve months in Andersonville. On the march
- in the battle - in the Rebel prison pens, and
at last in God's country. By Lessel Long ...
Huntington, Ind., T. and M. Butler, 1886.
    199 p., 1 1., i.p. incl. pl. 23 cm.

[Longstreet, Augustus Baldwin] 1790-
    A voice from the South: comprising Letters
from Georgia to Massachusetts, and to the southern
states. With an appendix containing an article
from the Charleston Mercury on the Wilmot proviso
... Baltimore, Western continent press, 1847 [1848].
    72 p. 25 1/2 cm.

Longstreet, James, 1821-
From Manassas to Appomattox; memoirs of the
civil war in America. Philadelphia, J. B. Lippincott company, 1896.
xx, [2], 13-690 p. front., illus., plates, ports.,
maps, facsim. 23 1/2 cm.

[Longworth, Maria Theresa] 1832?
Saint Augustine, Florida. Sketches of its history, objects of interest, and advantages as a resort for health and recreation. By an English
visitor. With notes for northern tourists on St.
John's River, etc. New York, G. P. Putnam & son;
St. Augustine, E. S. Carr [etc., etc.] 1869.
63 p. illus. 17 1/2 cm.

Lopez, Valencia, Federico.
... Del pais gigante; la vida y los negocios
en Norte-america. Madrid, Sucesores de Hernando,
1919.
4 p.l., 7-211 p. 18 1/2 cm.

Lorain, John.
Hints to emigrants, or, A comparative estimate
of the advantages of Pennsylvania, and of the western territory, &c. ... Philadelphia: published
by Littell & Henry. A. Waldie, printer, 1819.
144 p. 1 p.l. 16 cm.

Lord, George A. 1820-1888.
A short narrative and military experience of
Corp. G. A'Lord. formerly a member of Co. G. ...
125th reg't. N. Y. V. ... Containing a four year's
history of the war, the Constitution of the United
States in full, a correct list of stamp duties,
and also patriotic songs of the latest selection.
[n.p., 186-?]
80 p. 15 cm.

Lord, John Chase, 1805.
"The higher law," in its application to the
fugitive slave bill. A sermon on the duties men
owe to God and to governments ... New York, Published by order of the "Union safety committee,"
1851.
16 p. 21 cm.

[Lord, Nathan] 1792.
 A letter of inquiry to ministers of the Gospel
of all denominations of slavery. By a northern
presbyter. Boston, Petridge and company, 1854.
 32 p. 22 1/2 cm.

Loring, Francis William.
 Cotton culture and the south considered with
reference to emigration, by F. W. Loring and C.
F. Atkinson. Boston, A. Williams & co., 1869.
 cover-title, 1 p. l., 188 p. 20 cm.

Lossing, Benson John, 1813-
 Pictorial history of the civil war in the United
States of America ... Illustrated by ... engravings on wood, by Lossing and Barritt, from
sketches by the author and others. Philadelphia,
G. W. Childs, 1866-68.
 3 v. front., illus., port., maps, facsim.
24 cm.

Lost or saved! [Cincinnati, American reform tract and
book society, n.d.]
 4 p. 16 1/2 cm.

Lothrop, Charles Henry, 1831-1890.
 A history of the First regiment Iowa cavalry
veteran volunteers, from its organization in 1861
to its muster out of the United States service in
1866. Also, a complete roster of the regiment.
By Charles H. Lothrop ... Lyons, Ia., Beers &
Eaton, printers, 1890.
 x p., 1 l., [13]-422, v p., 1 l. front., illus., pl., port. 23 cm.

Louisiana. Bureau of immigration.
 Some late words about Louisiana, by T. W.
Poole, commissioner of immigration of the state
of Louisiana. New Orleans, Ernest Marchand,
state printer, 1889.
 163 p. 21 cm.

Louisiana state immigration association.
 Mid-summer convention assembled under the
auspices of the state immigration association of
Louisiana, composed entirely of former citizens
... of northern, western and middle states now
residents of Louisiana ... regarding the health

and climate of Louisiana ... New Orleans, La.,
Aug. 7th and 8th, 1888 ... New Orleans, state
immigration association, 1888.
   81 p.   23 1/2 cm.

Lovejoy, Joseph C.
     Memoir of Rev. Charles T. Torrey, who died in
the penitentiary of Maryland, where he was confined for showing mercy to the poor ... Boston,
John P. Jewett & Co., 1847.
     viii, 364 p.   18 1/2 cm.

Lovejoy, Joseph C.
     Memoir of the Rev. Elijah P. Lovejoy; who was
murdered in defense of the liberty of the press,
at Alton, Illinois, Nov. 7, 1837. By Joseph C.
and Owen Lovejoy. With an introduction by John
Quincy Adams. New York, John S. Taylor, 1838.
     382 p.   17 1/2 cm.

Lovejoy, Owen, 1811.
     The barbarism of slavery. Speech of Hon.
Owen Lovejoy, of Illinois, delivered in the U. S.
House of Representatives, April 5, 1860. [Wash-
ington, Buell & Blanchard, 1860?]
     8 p.   23 cm.

Lovejoy, Owen, 1811.
     Human beings not property. Speech ... de-
livered in the U. S. House of Representatives,
February 17, 1858. [n.p., n.d.]
     8 p.   23 cm.

Lovejoy, Owen, 1811.
     State of the union. Speech ... delivered in
the House of Representatives, January 23, 1861.
[Washington, H. Polkinhorn, 1861?]
     8 p.   24 cm.

Lovewell, Lyman.
     A sermon on American slavery; preached in New
Hudson, Mich., June 18, 1854.
     22 p.   22 cm.

Low, Alfred Maurice, 1860-
     America at home [by] A. Maurice Low ... Lon-
don, G. Newnes, limited [1908].
     xi, 231 [1] p.   12 pl. (incl. front.)   20 cm.

Low, Henry R.
Speech ... on the right of Congress to determine the qualification of its members and to
determine when the public safety will permit the
admission of representatives from the states
lately in rebellion, and the present condition
of national affairs, in the Senate, March 14,
1866. Albany, Weed, Parsons and company, 1866.
19 p.   23 cm.

Löwenstern, Isidor, 1815-1858.
Les Etats-Unis et la Havane; souvenirs d'un
voyageur ... Paris [etc.] A. Bertrand [etc.]
1842.
xii, 372 p.   21 cm.

Löwig, Gustav.
Die Freistaaten von Nord-Amerika.   Beobachtungen und praktische bemerkungen für auswandernde
Deutsche ... Heidelberg und Leipzig, K. Groos,
1833.
x, 264 p.   1 p.l., 1 l.   plan.   18 1/2 cm.

Lowry, James.
A dissertation on the relative duties between the different classes and conditions of
society; also proving slavery consistent with
the spirit of the law and gospel and with the
operations of Providence ... Columbia, [S.C.].
Printed by S. Weir, at the Times and Gazette
office, 1836.
77 p.   21 cm.

The loyalist's ammunition. Philadelphia, Printed for
gratuitous distribution, 1863.
16 p.   22 cm.

Lucas, Daniel R.
History of the 99th Indiana infantry, containing a diary of marches, incidents, biography
of officers and complete rolls. By Chaplain
D. R. Lucas. Lafayette, Ind., Rosser & Spring,
printers, 1865.
iv, [5] - 179, [1] p.   20 1/2 cm.

Lucas, Eliza, see Pinckney, Mrs. Eliza (Lucas), 1723-
Journal and letters of Eliza Lucas, now first
printed. Wormsloe, Ga. 1850.
30 p., 1 l.   33 cm.

Ludecus, Eduard.
Reise durch die mexikanischen provinzen
Tamaulipas, Coahuila und Texas im jahre, 1834...
Leipzig, J. F. Hartknoch, 1837.
xx, 356 p. 21 1/2 cm.

Ludvigh, Samuel Gottlieb, 1801-
Licht- und schattenbilder republikanischer
zustände. Skizzirt von Samuel Ludvigh während
seiner reise in den Vereinigten Staaten von Nord-
Amerika 1846/47. Leipzig, W. Jurany; New York,
Helmich und co., 1848.
viii, 344 p. 19 1/2 cm.

Lundy, Benjamin, 1789-
The life, travels, and opinions of Benjamin
Lundy, including his journeys to Texas and Mexico,
with a sketch of contemporary events, and a notice of the revolution in Hayti ... Philadelphia,
W. D. Parrish, 1847.
[9] - 316 p. 2 p.l. front. (port.) fold.
map. 19 1/2 cm.

Lundy, Benjamin, 1789.
The war in Texas; a review of facts and circumstances, showing that this contest is a long
premeditated crusade against the government, set
on foot by slaveholders, land speculators, &c.
with the view of re-establishing, extending, and
perpetuating the system of slavery and the slave
trade in the republic of Mexico. By a citizen
of the United States. Philadelphia, Printed for
the author, by Merrihew and Gunn, 1836.
56, [1] p. 22 cm.

Lusk, William Thompson, 1838-1897.
War letters of William Thompson Lusk, captain,
assistant adjutant-general, United States volunteers 1861-1863, afterward M. D., LL. D. New
York, Priv. print., 1911.
x p., 1 l., 304 p. front., pl., ports.,
maps. 24 1/2 cm.

Lyell, Sir Charles, bart., 1797-
A second visit to the United States on North
America ... London, J. Murray, 1849.
2 v. illus. 19 1/2 cm.

Lyell, Charles, 1797–
    Travels in North America; with geological ob-
servations on the United States, Canada, and Nova
Scotia ... London, J. Murray, 1845.
    2 v. col. fronts., illus., plates (part fold.)
maps (part fold.) facsims. 19 1/2 cm.

Lyford, William G.
    The western address directory: containing the
cards of merchants, manufacturers, and other business men, in Pittsburgh, (Pa.) Wheeling, (W. Va.)
Zanesville, (O.) Madison, (Ind.) Louisville, (K.)
St. Louis, (Mo.) together with historical, topographical and statistical sketches, (for the year
1837,) of those cities, and towns in the Mississippi valley. Intended as a guide to travellers.
To which is added, alphabetically arranged, a
list of the steamboats on the western waters. By
W. G. Lyford. Baltimore, Printed by J. Robinson, 1837.
    468 p.   18 cm.

Lyman, Theodore, 1833–1897.
    Meade's headquarters, 1863–1865; letters of
Colonel Theodore Lyman from the Wilderness to
Appomattox, selected and ed. by George R. Agassiz.
Boston, The Atlantic monthly press, 1922.
    x p., 3 l., 371 p. front., ports., maps.
25 cm.

Lyon, William Franklin, 1842–
    In and out of Andersonville prison, by W. F.
Lyon ... Detroit, Mich., G. Hariand co., 1905.
    3 p.l., [11]– 121 p. illus., plates, ports.
18 cm.

Lyon, William Penn, 1822–1913.
    Reminiscences of the civil war; comp. from
the war correspondence of Colonel William P.
Lyon and from personal letters and diary by Mrs.
Adelia C. Lyon. Published by William P. Lyon,
jr. [San Jose, Cal., Press of Muirson & Wright]
1907.
    3 p.l., 274 p. front., ports.   24 cm.

M., J.
A sermon intended to enforce the reasonable-
ness and duty, on Christian as well as political,
principles, of the abolition of the African slave-
trade ... London, Sold by J. Johnston, 1788.
35 p.   19 cm.

M., T. J.
Western Kentucky, above ground and below, or,
A trip to the Mammoth Cave.   Containing a full
description of the cave.   Written by T. J. M.,
author of "The unfinished wedding" &c.   ... Albion, Illi., Albion job press company, publishers
[n.d.]
60 p.   20 1/2 cm.

Mabbett, Le.
Stolen goods: or the gains of oppression ...
and Comparison of stolen goods with slave labor
produce.   By Elihu Burritt ...   [n.p.]   Published
by the managers of the Free produce association
of Friends of Ohio yearly meeting, 1850.
4 p.   19 cm.

[Macaulay, Zachary] 1768.
East and west India sugar; or, A refutation
of the claims of the west India colonists to a
protecting duty on east India sugar.   London,
Printed for Lupton Relfe, 13, Cornhill; and
Hatchard and son, Piccadilly, 1823.
128 p.   21 cm.

[Macaulay, Zachary] 1768.
A letter to William W. Whitmore, Esq., M. P.,
pointing out some erroneous statements contained
in a pamphlet by Joseph Marryat, Esq., M. P.,
entitled "A reply to the arguments contained in
various publications recommending an equiliza-
tion of the duties on east and west India sugars."
By the author of a pamphlet entitled "East and
west India sugar."   London, Printed for Lupton
Relfe, 13, Cornhill; and Hatchard and son, Piccadilly, 1823.
38 p.   21 cm.

[Macaulay, Zachary] 1768.
Negro slavery; or, A view of some of the more
prominent features of that state of society, as
it exists in the United States of America and
in the colonies of the West Indies, especially
in Jamaica. Fourth edition. London, Society for
the mitigation and gradual abolition of slavery
throughout the British dominions, 1824.
92 p.   21 1/2 cm.

[Macaulay, Zachary] 1768.
Negro slavery; or, A view of some of the
more prominent features of that state of society,
as it exists in the United States of America and
in the colonies of the West Indies, especially
in Jamaica. London, Printed by Richard Taylor,
1823.
92 p.   21 1/2 cm.

[Macaulay, Zachary] 1768.
Negro slavery; or, A view of some of the more
prominent features of that state of society, as
it exists in the United States of America and
in the colonies of the West Indies, especially
in Jamaica. London, Printed for Hatchard and
son, Piccadilly, and J. and A. Arch, Cornhill,
1823.
118 p.   21 cm.

M'Bride, Robert Ekin, 1846-
In the ranks: from the Wilderness to Appomattox courthouse. The war, as seen and experienced
by a private soldier in the Army of the Potomac.
Cincinnati, Walden & Stowe, 1881.
246 p.   front. (port.)   17 1/2 cm.

McAllister, Ward, 1827-
Society as I have found it. By Ward McAllister. New York, Cassell publishing company
[c1890].
xv, 469 p.   front. (port.)   20 1/2 cm.

McCaine, Alexander.
Slavery defended from scripture, against the
attacks of the abolitionists in a speech delivered before the general conference of the
Methodist Protestant Church, in Baltimore, 1842
... Baltimore, Printed by Wm. Wooddy, 1842.
iv, [5] - 28 p.   22 cm.

McCall, George Archibald, 1802-
    Letters from the frontiers. Written during
a period of thirty years' service in the army of
the United States ... Philadelphia, J. B. Lippincott & co., 1868.
    x, [11], 539 p.   21 cm.

McCalla, William Latta, 1788-
    Adventures in Texas, chiefly in the spring
and summer of 1840 ... accompanied by an appendix containing an humble attempt to aid in establishing and conducting literary and ecclesiastical institutions ... Philadelphia, Printed for
the author, 1841.
    199 p.   15 1/2 cm.

MacCauley, Clay, 1843-
    Through Chancellorsville, into and out of
Libby prison. I. From Chancellorsville into
Libby prison.   II. In Libby prison, and out of
it; home again. By Clay MacCauley, late lieutenant in One hundred and twenty-sixth infantry,
Pennsylvania volunteers.   Providence, The Society, 1904.
    70 p.   front., pl., port.   21 cm.

McClure, Alexander Kelly, 1828-
    The South: its industrial, financial, and
political condition. Philadelphia, J. B. Lippincott company, 1886.
    257 p.   18 1/2 cm.

McCowan, Archibald.
    The prisoners of war; a reminiscence of the
rebellion, by Archibald McCowan ... New York,
London [etc.] The Abbey press [c1901].
    187 p.   front. (port.)   20 cm.

McCoy, Isaac, 1784-
    History of Baptist Indian missions: embracing
remarks on the former and present condition of
the aboriginal tribes; their settlement ... their
future prospects ... Washington, W. M. Morrison;
New York, H. and S. Raynor; [etc., etc.] 1840.
    [3] - 611 p.   5 p.l.   24 cm.

McDanield, H. F.
    The coming empire; or, Two thousand miles in
Texas on horseback. By H. F. McDanield and N. A.

Taylor ... New York, Chicago, New Orleans, A. S.
Barnes & company, c1878.
389 p.   19 cm.

McDonogh, John.
Letter ... on Africa addressed to the editors
of the New Orleans Commercial bulletin. New Orleans, Printed at the Tropic office, 1842.
26 p.   22 cm.

McElroy, John, 1846-1929.
Andersonville: a story of Rebel military
prisons, fifteen months a guest of the so-called
southern confederacy. A private soldier's experience in Richmond, Andersonville, Savannah,
Millen, Blackshear and Florence. By John McElroy
... Toledo, D. R. Locke, 1879.
xxx p., 1 l., [33] - 654 p., 1 l. incl. front.,
illus., plates, maps.   23 cm.

McGee, Benjamin F. 1834-
History of the 72d Indiana volunteer infantry
of the mounted lightning brigade ... Especially
devoted to giving the reader a definite knowledge
of the service of the common soldier. With an
appendix containing a complete roster of officers
and men. Written and comp. by B. F. McGee ...
Ed. by Wm. R. Jewell ... LaFayette, Ind., S.
Vater & co., printers, 1882.
xviii p., 1 l., 698, 21, [1] p. front., port.
24 cm.

McGill, Alexander T.
Patriotism, philanthropy, and religion. An
address before the American colonization society,
January 10, 1877 ... Washington city, Colonization building, 1877.
10 p.   23 cm.

McGuire, Judith White (Brockenbrough) "Mrs. John P.
McGuire."
Diary of a southern refugee, during the war.
By a lady of Virginia, (Mrs. Judith W. McGuire.)
... 3d ed., with corrections and additions. Richmond, Va., J. W. Randolph & English, 1889.
372 p.   10 cm.

Mackay, Alexander, 1808-
    The western world; or, Travels in the United
States in 1846-47; exhibiting them in their latest
development, social, political and industrial;
including a chapter on California ... London, R.
Bentley, 1849.
    3 v. fronts. (v. 1, 3, fold. maps)   20 1/2 cm.

Mackay, Charles, 1814-
    Life and liberty in America; or, Sketches of a
tour in the United States and Canada, in 1857-8
... London, Smith, Elder and co., 1859.
    2 v. front., pl.   20 cm.

Mackay, Robert, 1772-
    Letters to his wife; written from ports in
America and England, 1795-1816; with an intro-
duction and notes by Walter Charlton Hartridge.
Athens, University of Georgia press, 1949.
    xxxi, 325 p. front., plates.   24 cm.

M'Keehan, Hattia.
    Liberty or death; or, Heaven's infraction of
the Fugitive slave law ... Cincinnati, Published
by and for the author, 1858.
    104 p.   21 cm.

McKeen, Silas.
    Scriptural argument in favor of withdrawing
fellowship from churches and ecclesiastical
bodies tolerating slaveholding among them ...
New York, American and foreign anti-slavery
society, 1848.
    37 p.   18 cm.

[Makemie, Francis] 1658-
    A plain and friendly persuasive to the in-
habitants of Virginia and Maryland for promoting
towns and cohabitation. By a well-wisher to
both governments. London, J. Humfreys, 1705.
    iv, 5-16 p.   28 cm.

McKenney, Thomas Lorraine, 1785-
    Memoirs, official and personal; with sketches
of travels among northern and southern Indians
... New York, Paine and Burgess, 1846.
    2 v. in 1. front. (port.) pl., facsim.
23 cm.

337

Mackenzie, Eneas, 1778-
    An historical, topographical, and descriptive
view of the United States of America, and of Upper and Lower Canada ... 2d ed. New Castle-upon-
Tyne. Printed and published by Mackenzie and
Dent, 1819.
        xv, [1], [9] - 712 p. pl., fold. map.   22 cm.

McKim, Randolph Harrison, 1842-1920.
    A soldier's recollections; leaves from the
diary of a young Confederate, with an oration on
the motives and aims of the soldiers of the South,
by Randolph H. McKim ... New York [etc.] Longmans, Green, and co., 1910.
        xvii, 362 p. front., 5 port.   22 cm.

McLanahan, James Xavier, 1809.
    Speech ... on the slave question. Delivered
in the House of Representatives, February 19,
1850. Washington, Printed by Jno. T. Towers,
1850.
        8 p.   24 cm.

M'Lean, D. H. A.
    An address delivered before a Christian anti-
slavery convention, held in Mercer, Pa., August
27 & 28, 1851 ... Mercer, Wm. F. Clark, printer,
1851.
        23 p.   21 cm.

McLeod, Alexander.
    Negro slavery unjustifiable. A discourse ...
1802. Tenth edition. New York, Published by
Alexander McLeod, 1860.
        46 p.   22 cm.

MacMahon, T. W.
    Cause and contrast: an essay on the American
crisis. Richmond, Va., West & Johnston, 1862.
        xv, 192 p.   21 cm.

McMorries, Edward Young.
    History of the first regiment, Alabama volun-
teer infantry, C.S.A., by Edward Young McMorries
... Montgomery, Ala., The Brown co., 1904.
        142 p. front., plates, ports., maps (1 fold.)
plan. facsim.   23 1/2 cm.

Macnamara, Michael II.
    The Irish Ninth in bivouac and battle; or,
Virginia and Maryland campaigns. By M. H. Macnamara ... Boston, Lee and Shepard, 1867.
    1 p.1., 306 p. front., pl. 19 1/2 cm.

McQuade, James.
    The cruise of the Montauk to Bermuda, the West
Indies and Florida, by James McQuade ... New
York, T. R. Knox & co., 1885.
    xv, 441 p. front., illus. (music) plates.
22 cm.

M'Queen, James.
    The West India colonies. The calumnies and
misrepresentations circulated against them by the
Edinburgh review, Mr. Clarkson, Mr. Cropper, &c.
&c. Examined and refuted ... London, Longman,
Hurst, and co. [etc., etc.] 1825.
    xxvi, 427 p. 22 cm.

Macrae, David, 1837-
    America revisited, and men I have met, by Rev.
David Macrae. Glasgow, J. Smith & son, ltd.,
1908.
    325 [1] p. 19 cm.

Macrae, David, 1837-
    The Americans at home: pen-and-ink sketches
of American men, manners and institutions ... Edinburgh, Edmonston and Douglas, 1870.
    2 v. illus., music. 19 1/2 cm.

Madden, Richard Robert, tr.
    Poems, by a slave in the island of Cuba, re-
cently liberated; translated from the Spanish ...
with the history of the early life of the negro
poet, written by himself; to which are prefixed
two pieces descriptive of Cuban slavery and the
slave-traffic, by R. R. M. London, Thomas Ward
and co., 1840.
    188 p. 23 cm.

Maffitt, John Newland.
    A plea for Africa. A sermon delivered at Ben-
nett street church in behalf of the American
colonization society, July 4, 1830 ... Boston,
E. W. Crittenden, 1830.
    14 p. 24 cm.

Maginnis, F.
      Obedience to magistrates. A sermon for the
times; discussing the higher-law theory, as de-
veloped in the recent tragic scenes of Harper's
Ferry ... Cleveland, Fairbanks, Benedict & co.,
printers, Herald office, 1860.
      32 p.   23 cm.

Mahan, John B., defendant.
      Trial of Rev. John B. Mahan, for felony, in
the Mason circuit court of Kentucky. Commen-
cing on Tuesday, the 12th, and terminating on
Monday, the 19th of November, 1838. Reported by
Joseph B. Reid and Henry R. Reeder, Esqs. Cincinnati, Samuel A. Alley, 1838.
      88 p.   21 cm.

Majoribanks, [J.] Captain.
      Slavery: an essay in verse ... Edinburgh,
Printed by J. Robertson, 1792.
      31 p.   20 cm.

Malet, William Wyndham, 1804-1885.
      An errand to the South in the summer of 1862.
By the Rev. William Wyndham Malet ... London, R.
Bentley, 1863.
      viii, 312 p. front.   17 cm.

Malezieux, Emile M. 1822-
      Travaux publics des Etats-Unis d'Amerique en
1870. Rapport de mission ... Publié par ordre de
m. le ministre de travaux publics ... Paris,
Dunod, 1873.
      2 p.l., 572 p. and atlas, 2 p.l., 3 p. 61 fold.
plates (incl. maps, diagr.)   32 cm.

Mallory, Robert, 1815.
      Speech ... on the confiscation of property.
Delivered in the House of Representatives, May
21, 1862. [Washington, Towers, 1862?]
      15 p.   24 cm.

Mandat-Grancey, Edmond, baron de, 1842-
      En visite chez l'Oncle Sam; New-York et
Chicago, par le baron E. de Mandat-Grancey, des-
sins de Crafty et de Martin-Chablis. Paris, E.
Plon, Nourrit et c , 1885.
      vii, 278 p., 2 l. 8 pl. (1 double)   18 1/2 cm.

Manford, Erasmus.
　　　Twenty-five years in the West.　Chicago, E.
Manford, 1867.
　　　[3] - 359 p.　2 p.l.　19 cm.

The 'manifest destiny' of the American union.　Reprinted from the Westminster review.　New York, Published by the American anti-slavery society, 1857.
　　　72 p.　19 cm.

Manigault, G.
　　　The United States unmasked.　A search into the
causes of the rise and progress of these states
and an exposure of their present material and
moral condition.　With additions and corrections
by the author.　By G. Manigault.　London, E. Stanford, 1879.
　　　4 p.l., 168 p.　19 cm.

Mann, Horace, 1796.
　　　The fugitive slave law.　Speech ... in the
House of Representatives ... January 28, 1861 ...
[Washington, D. C., Printed at the Congressional
globe office, 1861?]
　　　24 p.　23 cm.

Mann, Horace, 1796.
　　　Horace Mann's letters on the extension of
slavery into California and New Mexico; and on
the duty of Congress to provide the trial by
jury for alleged fugitive slaves.　[Washington]
Buell & Blanchard [1850].
　　　32 p.　22 cm.

Mann, Horace, 1796.
　　　New dangers to freedom, and new duties for its
defenders:　a letter by the Hon. Horace Mann to
his constituents, May 18, 1850.　Boston, Redding
and company, 1850.
　　　32 p.　23 cm.

Mann, Horace, 1796.
　　　Speech of Horace Mann, of Massachusetts, in
the House of Representatives, Feb. 23, 1849, on
slavery in the United States, and the slave trade
in the District of Columbia ... Boston, Wm. B.
Fowle [1849?]
　　　[14] p.　22 cm.

Mann, Horace, 1796.
      Speech of Hon. Horace Mann of Massachusetts,
on the institution of slavery. Delivered in the
House of Representatives, August 17, 1852.
[n.p., n.d.]
      24 p.   24 cm.

Mann, Horace, 1796.
      Speech ... on the right of Congress to legis-
late for the territories of the United States, and
its duty to exclude slavery therefrom. Delivered
in the House of Representatives in committee of
the whole, June 30, 1848. Revised edition. Boston, William B. Fowle, 1848.
      31 p.   23 cm.

Mann, Horace, 1796.
      Speech ... on the subject of slavery in the
territories, and the consequence of a dissolution
of the Union. Delivered in the United States
House of Representatives, February 15, 1850. Boston, Redding and company, 1850.
      35 p.   22 cm.

Mantegazza, Vico.
      ... Agli Stati Uniti, il pericolo americano ...
Milano, Fratelli Treves.
      4 p.l., [3]-347 [3] p.   plates, ports., map.
20 1/2 cm.

Marjoribanks, Alexander.
      Travels in South and North America ... London,
Simpkin, Marshall, and company; New York, D.
Appleton and co., 1853.
      xiv, 480 p.   col. front., illus.   21 1/2 cm.

Marks, James Junius, 1809-1899.
      The Peninsular campaign in Virginia; or, In-
cidents and scenes on the battlefields and in
Richmond. By Rev. J. J. Marks, D.D. Philadelphia, J. B. Lippincott & co., 1864.
      xx, 21-444 p.   front., pl.   19 1/2 cm.

Marmier, Xavier, 1809-1892.
      Lettres sur l'Amérique, par X. Marmier. Cana-
da - Etats-Unis - Havane, Rio de la Plata. Paris,
A. Bertrand [1851].
      2 v.   18 cm.

342

Marquette, Jacques, 1637-
   Voyage et découverte de quelques pays et nations de l'Amerique Septentrionale, par le père Marquette et sr. Joliet. Paris, E. Michallet, 1681. [Impr. de Maulde et Renou, 1845].
   43 p.   2 p.1.   front. (fold. map).   17 cm.

Marrant, John, 1755-
   A narrative of the Lord's wonderful dealings with John Marrant, a black, (now going to preach the gospel in Nova Scotia) born in New-York, in North-America. Taken down from his relation, arranged, corrected, and published by Rev. Mr. Aldridge. 2d ed. London, Printed by Gilbert and Plummer, 1785.
   v, 7-38 p.   22 cm.

Marriott, Charles.
   An address to the members of the religious Society of friends, on the duty of declining the use of the products of slave labour ... New-York, Isaac T. Hopper, 1835.
   18 p.   22 cm.

Marryat, Frederick, 1792-
   A diary in America, with remarks on its institutions ... London, Longman, Orme, Brown, Green & Longmans, 1839.
   3 v.   20 1/2 cm.

Marryat, Frederick, 1792-1848.
   A diary in America, with remarks on its institutions. Part second ... London, Longman, Orme, Brown, Green & Longmans, 1839.
   3 v.   22 cm.

Mars, James.
   Life of James Mars, a slave born and sold in Connecticut. Written by himself. Hartford, Press of Case, Lockwood & company, 1865.
   36 p.   18 cm.

Marsh, Ephraim.
   "North American" documents. Letters from Geo. Law, Ephraim Marsh, & Chauncey Shaffer. [n.p., n.d.]
   15 p.   23 cm.

Marsh, George Perkins, 1801.
    Remarks ... on slavery in the territories of
New Mexico, California and Oregon; delivered in
the House of Representatives, August 3d, 1848.
[Burlington, Vt., Free press office print, 1848?]
    12 p.   22 1/2 cm.

Marshall, Albert O.
    Army life; from a soldier's journal. By Al-
bert O. Marshall. Incidents, sketches and record
of a Union soldier's army life, in camp and field;
1861-64. Joliet, Ill., Printed for the author,
1883.
    410 p.   20 cm.

Marshall, S. S.
    Letter of Hon. S. S. Marshall, on the parties
and politics of the day, to the freemen of the
Ninth Congressional District of Illinois. Washington, printed at the Union office, 1856.
    27 p.   20 cm.

Marshall, Samuel Scott.
    Kansas - Lecompton constitution proscription
of Democrats - assault upon Illinois; and after
her democracy expelled. Speech ... on the admission of Kansas as a state. Delivered in the
House of Representatives, March 31, 1858. [n.p.,
n.d.]
    16 p.   23 cm.

Marti, Jose, 1853-
    ... En los Estados Unidos ... Habana, G. de
Quesada [etc.] 1902-05.
    2 v.   21 1/2 cm.

Martin, Charles Drake, 1829.
    Speech ... on the Slavery question. Delivered
in the House of Representatives, May 19, 1860.
[Washington, D. C.] Lemuel Towers [1861?]
    16 p.   21 cm.

Martin, Henry William.
    A counter appeal, in answer to "An appeal"
from William Wilberforce, Esq., M. P. designed to
prove that the emancipation of the negroes in
the West Indies, by a legislative enactment, without the consent of the planters, would be a fla-
grant breach of national honour ... London, Prin-

ted for C. & J. Rivington, and sold by Lloyd,
1823.
    52 p.   20 1/2 cm.

Martin, Horace.
    Pictorial guide to the Mammoth Cave, Kentucky
... Illustrated ... by S. Wallen, Jno. Andrew, J.
W. Orr, and N. Orr, New York, Stringer & Town-
send [1851].
    [7] - 116 p.   4 p.l., front., 8 pl.   20 cm.

Martin, Joseph, ed.
    A new and comprehensive gazetteer of Vir-
ginia, and the District of Columbia ... To which
is added a History of Virginia from its first
settlement to the year 1754 ... Charlottesville,
J. Martin, 1835.
    636 p.   23 1/2 cm.

Martineau, Harriet, 1802.
    The martyr age of the United States ... Bos-
ton, Weeks, Jordan & co. Otis, Broaders & co.;
New York - John S. Taylor, 1839.
    84 p.   17 cm.

Martineau, Harriet, 1802-1876.
    Retrospect of western travel ... London,
Saunders and Otley; New York, Sold by Harper &
brothers, 1838.
    2 v.   18 1/2 cm.

Martineau, Harriet, 1802-1876.
    Society in America ... Second edition, London,
Saunders and Otley, 1839.
    3 v.   19 cm.

Martineau, Harriet, 1802.
    Views of slavery & emancipation: from "Society
in America" ... New-York, Piercy & Reed, printers,
1837.
    1 p. l., [iv] - v. 79 p.   20 cm.

Martinez Caro, Ramon.
    Verdadera idea de la primera campaña de Tejas
y sucesos ocurridos despues de la acción de San
Jacinto ... Mexico, Impr. de Santiago Perez a
cargo de A. Sojo, 1837.
    vii, 162 p.   20 cm.

[Martyn, Benjamin] 1699-
    An impartial enquiry into the state and utility
of the province of Georgia. London, Printed for
W. Meadows, MDCCXLI.
    104 p. 2 p.1.   19 cm.

The martyr age of the United States of America, with an
    appeal on behalf of the Oberlin Institute in aid
    of the abolition of slavery. Re-published from
    the London and Westminster Review, by the New-
    castle-upon-Tyne Emancipation and Aborigines Pro-
    tection Society. Newcastle upon Tyne, Finlay and
    Charlton [etc., etc.] 1840.
        xix, 44 p.   20 1/2 cm.

The Maryland scheme, or Expatriation examined. By a
    friend of liberty. Boston, Published by Garri-
    son & Knapp, 1834.
        20 p.   21 cm.

Mason, Frank Holcomb, 1840-1916.
    The Forty-second Ohio infantry: a history of
    the organization and services of that regiment in
    the war of the rebellion; with biographical sket-
    ches of its field officers and a full roster of
    the regiment. Comp. and written for the Veteran's
    association of the Forty-second Ohio, by F. H.
    Mason ... Cleveland, Cobb, Andrews & co., 1876.
        306 p., 1 1. front., port.   22 cm.

Mason, Jonathan, 1756-
    Extracts from a diary kept by the Hon. Jona-
    than Mason of a journey from Boston to Savannah
    in the year 1804. Cambridge [Mass.], John Wilson
    and sons, University press, 1885.
        32 p.   23 1/2 cm.

Massachusetts colonization society.
    ... American colonization society and the
    colony at Liberia ... Boston, Printed by Per-
    kins & Marvin, 1832.
        16 p.   23 cm.

Massachusetts colonization society.
    Proceedings of the annual meeting ... held in
    Park street church, February 7, 1833 ... Bos-
    ton, Pierce and Parker, 1833.
        28 p.   22 cm.

Massachusetts colonization society.
      Third annual report of the Board of managers
... Second edition. Boston, Press of T. R. Marvin, 1844.
      16 p.   23 cm.

Massachusetts colonization society.
      Fourth annual report of the Board of managers
... Boston, Press of T. R. Marvin, 1845.
      24 p.   23 cm.

Massachusetts colonization society.
      Annual meeting [fifth] [Boston? T. R. Marvin?
1846?]
      32 p.   21 cm.

Massachusetts colonization society.
      Sixth annual report of the Board of managers
... Boston, Press of T. R. Marvin, 1847.
      35 p.   23 cm.

Massachusetts colonization society.
      Seventh annual report of the Board of managers
... Boston, Press of T. R. Marvin, 1848.
      36 p.   23 cm.

Massachusetts colonization society.
      Eighth annual report of the Board of managers
... Boston, Press of T. R. Marvin, 1849.
      32 p.   23 cm.

Massachusetts colonization society.
      Ninth annual report of the Board of managers
... Boston, Press of T. R. Marvin, 1850.
      36 p.   23 cm.

Massachusetts colonization society.
      Tenth annual report of the Board of managers
... Boston, Press of T. R. Marvin, 1851.
      40 p.   23 cm.

Massachusetts colonization society.
      Eleventh annual report of the Board of managers
... Boston, Press of T. R. Marvin, 1852.
      24 p.   23 cm.

Massachusetts colonization society.
      Twelfth annual report of the Board of managers
... Boston, Press of T. R. Marvin, 1853.

40 p.   23 cm.

Massachusetts colonization society.
    Fifteenth annual report of the Board of mana-
    gers ... Printed by C. C. P. Moody, 1856.
    32 p. illus.   23 cm.

Massachusetts colonization society.
    Sixteenth annual report of the Board of mana-
    gers ... Boston, Printed by T. R. Marvin, 1857.
    28 p.   23 cm.

Massachusetts colonization society.
    Eighteenth annual report of the Board of mana-
    gers ... Boston, Press of T. R. Marvin and son,
    1859.
    38 p.   24 cm.

Massachusetts colonization society.
    Twenty-first annual report of the Board of
    managers ... Boston, Press of T. R. Marvin and
    son, 1862.
    36 p.   front.   23 cm.

Massachusetts colonization society.
    Twenty-seventh annual report of the Board of
    managers ... Boston, Press of T. R. Marvin & son,
    1868.
    24 p.   23 cm.

Massachusetts colonization society.
    Thirty-second annual report of the Board of
    managers ... Washington City, M'Gill & Witherow,
    1873.
    19 p.   23 cm.

Massachusetts colonization society.
    Thirty-third annual report of the Board of
    managers ... Washington City, M'Gill & Witherow,
    1874.
    8 p.   23 cm.

Massachusetts. General court. House of Representa-
    tives.
    Committee on the admission into Massachusetts
    of free negroes and mulattoes. Free negroes and
    mulattoes ... Report. [Boston, True & Green,
    printers, 1821].
    16 p.   22 cm.

348

Massachusetts. General court. Joint special committee on fugitives from slavery. [Report] [Boston?
1843?]
    37 p.   21 1/2 cm.

Massachusetts. General court. Senate. Joint special
committee on the powers and duties of Congress
upon the subject of slavery and the slave trade.
... Report ...
    36 p.   23 cm.

Massachusetts state anti-Texas committee.
    Report of the Massachusetts committee to pre-
vent the admission of Texas as a slave state.
[n.p., n.d.]
    10 p.   22 1/2 cm.

Massey, Stephen L.
    James's traveler's companion. Being a com-
plete guide through the western states, to the
gulf of Mexico and the Pacific via the Great
Lakes, rivers, canals, etc. ... Cincinnati, J.
A. & U. P. James, 1851.
    vi, 9-224 p.   illus., 2 fold. maps. (incl.
front.)   15 1/2 cm.

Massie, James William, 1799-1869.
    America: the origin of her present conflict;
her prospect for the slave, and her claim for
anti-slavery sympathy; illustrated by incidents
of travel during a tour in the summer of 1863,
throughout the United States, from ... Maine to
the Mississippi. By James William Massie ...
London, J. Snow, 1864.
    viii, 472 p.   fold. map.   18 1/2 cm.

Mather, James.
    Two lectures, delivered at Newcastle-upon-Tyne,
on the constitutions and republican institutions
of the United States ... from data procured on a
visit to that country ... Newcastle-upon-Tyne,
H. Gibb, 1840.
    x, 90, [2] p.   18 cm.

Mathews, Alfred E.
    Interesting narrative; being a journal of the
flight of Alfred E. Mathews ... from the state of
Texas, on the 20th of April, and his arrival at

349

Chicago on the 28th of May, after traveling on
foot and alone a distance of over 800 miles across
the states of Louisiana, Arkansas and Missouri
by the most unfrequented routes. [II. p.] 1861.
1 p.l., [7] - 34 p., 1 l.   22 1/2 cm.

Matlack, Lucius C.
Narrative of the anti-slavery experience of a
minister in the Methodist E. church, who was
twice elected by the Philadelphia annual conference, and finally deprived of license to preach
for being an abolitionist ... Philadelphia, Merrihew and Thompson, 1845.
24 p.   19 cm.

Mauritius. [London, Printed by S. Bagster, jun.,
n.d.]
12 p.   19 cm.

Maury, Dabney Herndon, 1822-1900.
Recollections of a Virginian in the Mexican,
Indian, and Civil wars; by General Dabney Herndon Maury ... New York, C. Scribner's sons, 1894.
xi, 279, [1] p. front. (port.)   20 1/2 cm.

Maury, Matthew Fontaine, 1806-
Physical survey of Virginia. Her geographical
position; its commercial advantages and national
importance. Preliminary report, by M. F. Maury...
2d ed. New York, D. Van Nostrand, 1869.
100 p. 3 fold. maps (incl. front.)   23 cm.

Maury, Matthew Fontaine, 1806-1873.
Resources of West Virginia, by Matthew Fontaine Maury and W. M. Fontaine. Wheeling, W.Va.,
The Register company, 1876.
xii, 430 p.   21 cm.

Maury, Sarah Mytton [(Hughes)] "Mrs. William Maury",
1803-1849.
An Englishwoman in America. London, T. Richardson and son; [etc., etc.] 1848.
[iii]-cxviii p., 251, 204 p., 1 l., 3 p.l.,
1 l.   20 1/2 cm.

Maury, Sarah Mytton (Hughes) "Mrs. William Maury,"1803-
The statesmen of America in 1846 ... London,
Longman, Brown, Green and Longmans, 1847.
vi, 548 p., 1 l.   19 1/2 cm.

Maxwell, Archibald Montgomery.
    A run through the United States, during the
autumn of 1840 ... London, H. Colburn, 1841.
    2 v. front. (port.)   19 1/2 cm.

May, John, 1748-
    Journal and letters of Col. John May, of Bos-
ton, relative to two journeys to the Ohio country
in 1788 and '89. With biographical sketch by Rev.
Richard S. Edes ... and illustrative notes by
William M. Darlington ... Cincinnati, R. Clarke &
co., for the Historical and philosophical society
of Ohio, 1873.
    160 p.   24 1/2 cm.

May, Samuel J.
    A discourse on the life and character of the
Rev. Charles Follen, LL. D., who perished, Jan.
13, 1840, in the conflagration of the Lexington.
Delivered before the Massachusetts anti-slavery
society in the Marlborough chapel, Boston, April
17, 1840. Boston, Henry L. Devereux, 1840.
    30 p.   20 cm.

[May, Samuel, jr.]
    The Fugitive slave law, and its victims.
[New York, American anti-slavery society, 1856?]
    48 p.   19 cm.

May, Samuel J.
    Liberty or slavery, the only question. Ora-
tion: Delivered on the fourth of July, 1856, at
Jamestown, Chautauque co., New York ... Syracuse,
J. G. K. Truair, printer, Daily journal office,
1856.
    30 p.   15 cm.

May, Samuel J.
    The right of colored people to education, vin-
dicated, Letters to Andrew T. Judson, Esq. and
others in Canterbury, remonstrating with them on
their unjust and unjustifiable procedure relative
to Miss Crandall and her school for colored females. Brooklyn, Advertiser Press, 1833.
    24 p.   23 1/2 cm.

Mayer, Brantz, 1809.
    Captain Canot; or, Twenty years of an African

slaver; being an account of his career and adventures on the coast, in the interior, on shipboard, and in the West Indies. Written out and edited from the captain's journals, memoranda and conversations, by Brantz Mayer. New York [etc.] D. Appleton and company, 1854.
xvii, 448 p. front., plates. 18 1/2 cm.

Mayes, Edward, 1846-
Lucius Q. C. Lamar: his life, times and speeches, 1825-1893. Nashville, Tenn., Publishing house of the Methodist Episcopal church, South, 1896.
820 p. front., plates, ports. 26 cm.

Mayo, Amory Dwight.
Herod, John and Jesus: of American slavery and the Christian cure. A sermon preached in Division street church, Albany, N. Y. ... Albany, Weed, Parsons & company, 1800.
29 p. 19 cm.

Mayor des Planches, Edmondo.
... Attraverso gli Stati Uniti. Per L'emigrazione italiana. Torino [etc.] Unione tipografico-editrice torinese, 1913.
viii, 321 p. fold. map. 24 cm.

Mazyck, Arthur, 1850-
Guide to Charleston illustrated. Being a sketch of the history of Charleston, S. C., with some account of its present condition ... Comp. by Arthur Mazyck ... Charleston, S. C., Walter, Evans & Cogswell [1875].
[8], 215 p. front. (fold. map) illus. 19 1/2 cm.

Mazzei, Filippo, 1730-
Memorie della vita e delle peregrinazioni del Fiorentina Filippo Mazzei ... Lugano, Tip. della Svizzera italiana, 1845-46.
2 v. 19 cm.

Meacham, James, 1810.
Defence of the clergy. Speech ... in the House of Representatives, May 17, 1854. [Washington, Buell & Blanchard, 1854?]
16 p. 23 cm.

Mead, Charles.
Mississippian scenery; a poem, descriptive
of the interior of North America. Philadelphia,
Published by S. Potter and co., no. 55, Chestnut
street; W. Fry, printer, 1819.
ix, [11]- 113 p.   20 1/2 cm.

Meadley, G. W.
Memoirs of William Paley, D.D. ... Sunderland,
J. Graham, 1809.
xi, 168 p.   21 cm.

Medley, Julius George, 1829-
An autumn tour in the United States and Canada, by Julius George Medley ... London, H. S.
King & co., 1873.
viii, 180 p.   19 cm.

Mees, Walter.
Stars and stripes en maple leaves; leven en
streven in Amerika en Canada. Amsterdam, Schel-
tens & Giltay [1946].
294 p.   illus., col. fold. map.   25 cm.

Melish, John, 1771-
A description of the roads in the United
States, compiled from the most authentic material.
Philadelphia, 1815.
4, 100 p.   tab.   16 1/2 cm.

Melish, John, 1771-
A geographical description of the United States,
with the contiguous British and Spanish possessions, intended as an accompaniment to Melish's
map of these countries ... Philadelphia, The
author, 1816.
182 p.   5 maps (1 fold.)   20 1/2 cm.

Melish, John, 1771-1822.
Information and advice to emigrants to the
United States: and from the eastern to the wes-
tern states: illustrated by a map of the United
States and a chart of the Atlantic Ocean ...
Philadelphia, Printed for and published by John
Melish, no. 121, Chestnut Street, 1819.
viii, 144 p.   2 fold.   maps (incl. front.)
15 cm.

Melish, John, 1771-
    A statistical account of the United States,
    with topographical tables of the counties, towns,
    population etc. From the census of 1810. In-
    tended as an accompaniment to the portable Map
    of the United States ... Philadelphia, Printed
    by G. Palmer, 1813.
        35 (i.e., 37), [1] p.   15 cm.

Melish, John, 1771-
    The traveller's directory through the United
    States. Consisting of a geographical description
    of the United States, with topographical tables
    of the counties, towns, population &c. and a
    description of the roads, comp. from the most
    authentic materials. Philadelphia, T. & G. Pal-
    mer, 1816.
        iv, [5]- 134 p.   maps.   16 cm.

Melish, John, 1771-
    Travels in the United States of America, in
    the years 1806 & 1807, and 1809, 1810, & 1811
    ... Philadelphia, Printed for the author, and
    for sale by different booksellers in the United
    States, and by Thomas & George Palmer, agents
    for the author, 1812. T. & G. Palmer, printers.
        2 v.   maps (4 fold., incl. front.) 2 fold.
    tables.   22 cm.

Memminger, Christopher Gustavus, 1803.
    Lecture delivered before the Young men's
    library association, of Augusta, April 10th,
    1851. Showing African slavery to be consistent
    with the moral and physical progress of a na-
    tion. Augusta, Ga., W. S. Jones, printer, 1851.
        25 p.   23 1/2 cm.

Memoir of Mrs. Chloe Spear, a native of Africa, who
    was enslaved in childhood, and died in Boston,
    January 3, 1815 ... aged 65 years. By a lady
    of Boston ... Boston, Published by James Loring,
    1832.
        iii, [9]- 108 p.   15 cm.

A memorial to the Congress of the United States, on
    the subject of restraining the increase of slavery
    in new states to be admitted into the Union.
    Boston, Sewell Phelps, printer, 1819.
        22 p.   22 cm.

Mendell, Miss.
　　　Notes of travel and life. By two ladies -
Misses Mendell and Hosmer ... New York, For the
authors, 1854.
　　　288 p.　20 1/2 cm.

Menzel, Gottfried, b. 1798.
　　　Die Vereinigten Staaten von Nordamerika mit
besonderer rücksicht auf deutsche auswanderung
dahin; nach eigener anschauung beschrieben von
Gottfried Menzel. Berlin, G. Reimer, 1853.
　　　viii, 364 p.　22 cm.

Mercier, Alfred, 1816-
　　　L'habitation Saint-Ybars; ou, Maitres et esclaves en Louisiane, récit social. Nouvelle-Orléans, Imprimerie franco-americaine (E. Antoine),
1881.
　　　234 p.　19 1/2 cm.

Meriwether, Lee, 1862-
　　　The tramp at home, by Lee Meriwether ... New
York, Harper & brothers, 1889.
　　　xi p., 1 l., 296 p.　incl. front., illus.,
pl.　19 1/2 cm.

Merlin, Maria de las Mercedes (Jaruco), 1789-
　　　La Havane ... Paris, Librarie d'Amyot, 1844.
　　　3 v.　21 1/2 cm.

Merrell, William Howard, d. 1897.
　　　Five months in rebeldom; or, Notes from the
diary of a Bull Run prisoner, at Richmond. By
Corporal W. H. Merrell ... Rochester, N. Y.,
Adams and Dabney, 1862.
　　　iv, [5]- 64 p.　front.　21 1/2 cm.

Merrill, Samuel, 1831-1924.
　　　The Seventieth Indiana volunteer infantry in
the war of the rebellion, by Samuel Merrill.
Indianapolis, The Bowen-Merrill company [1900].
　　　4 p.l., 372 p.　front., pl., port.　23 1/2 cm.

Merrill, Samuel Hill, 1805-1873.
　　　The campaigns of the First Maine and First
District of Columbia cavalry. By Samuel H. Merrill ... Portland, Bailey & Noyes, 1866.
　　　xv, [17]- 436 p.　port.　20 cm.

Merry, J. F.
    ... The Awakened South. Address by J. F.
Merry, general immigration agent, Illinois central railroad, before the Farmers' demonstration
conference, Louisiana state university, January
18, 1911. Baton Rouge, Ramires-Jones printing
co., 1911.
    23 p.   24 cm.

Meyer, Rudolf Hermann, 1839-
    Ursachen der amerikanischen concurrenz. Er-
gebnisse einer studienreise der herren: grafen
Géza Andrassy, Géza und Imre Széchenyi, Ernst
Hoyos, baron Gabriel Gudenus und dr. Rudolph
Meyer, durch die Vereinigten Staaten. Hrsg. von
dr. R. Meyer. Mit einer verkehrskarte der union.
Berlin, H. Bahr, 1883.
    3 p.l., vi, 825 [1] p. fold. map.   24 cm.

Michaux, André, 1746-
    Journal de André Michaux ... (In Proceedings
of the American Philosophical Society, v. 26,
1889, p. 1-145)

Michaux, François André, 1770-
    Voyage à l'ouest des monts Alleghanys, dans
les etats de l'Ohio, du Kentucky et du Tennessee,
et retour à Charleston par les Hautes-Carolinas ...
Paris, Levrault, Schoell et cie., 1804.
    vi, 312 p. 2 p.l.   21 cm.

Middleton, Charles Theodore.
    A new and complete system of geography. Con-
taining a full, accurate, authentic and interesting
account and description of Europe, Asia, Africa,
and America ... London, Printed for J. Cooke,
1777-78.
    2 v. fronts., plates, maps (part fold.)
36 cm.

Mifflin, Benjamin, 1718-
    Journal of Benjamin Mifflin, the record of a
tour from Philadelphia to Delaware and Maryland,
July 26 to August 14, 1762, ed. by Victor Hugo
Paltsits. The New York Public Library, 1935.
    18 p.   1 l.   25 1/2 cm.

Military order of the loyal legion of the United States.
Indiana commandery.
    War papers, read before the Indiana commandery,
Military order of the loyal legion of the United
States. [v. 1] Indianapolia, Published by the
Commandery, 1898-
    v. front., illus., ports., fold. maps. 25 cm.

Miller, Andrew.
    New states and territories; or, The Ohio, In-
diana, Illinois, Michigan, Northwestern, Missouri,
Louisiana, Mississippi and Alabama in their real
characters, in 1818. Keene, N. H., 1819.
    32 p. 22 1/2 cm.

Miller, C. W.
    Address on re-opening the slave trade, by C.
W. Miller, Esq., of South Carolina, to the citizens of Barnwell at Wylde-Moore August 29, 1857,
Columbia, S. C., Steam power press of the Carolina times, 1857.
    10 p. 23 cm.

Miller, H. L.
    An address delivered before the Tompkins
county colonization society at their third anniversary, held in Ithaca, March 4, 1834 ...
Trumansburg, David Fairchild - printer, 1834.
    16 p. 23 cm.

Miller, James Ira Deese.
    A guide into the South; an open gate to the
laborer, large returns to the investor, an index
for the traveler, a great welcome to the deser-
ving ... Atlanta, Ga., The Index printing company, 1910.
    480 p. plates, ports. 23 1/2 cm.

Miller, James N[ewton].
    The story of Andersonville and Florence. Des
Moines, Ia., Welch, 1900.
    47 p. inc. front. (port.) 8^c.

[Milligen, George].
    A short description of the province of South-
Carolina, with an account of the air, weather,
and diseases, at Charles-town. Written in the
year 1763. London, Printed for J. Hinton, 1770.
    96 p. 21 cm.

Milliroux, J. F.
Aperçus sur les institutions et les moeurs des Américains. Paris, E. Dentu, 1862.
vii, 172 p.   24 cm.

Mills, Samuel John, 1783-
Report of a missionary tour through that part of the United States which lies west of the Allegany mountains; performed under the direction of the Massachusetts missionary society. By Samuel J. Mills and Daniel Smith. Andover: Flagg and Gould, 1815.
64 p.   24 1/2 cm.

Mills, T. B.
A history of the north-western editorial excursion to Arkansas. A short sketch of its inception and the routes traveled over ... By T.B. Mills & co. Little Rock, T.B. Mills & co. 1876.
2 p.l., 384, 20 p. maps (part fold.) (incl. front.)   23 cm.

Minutes of the Christian anti-slavery convention. Held July 3d, 4th, and 5th, 1851, at Chicago, Ill. Chicago, Printed at the office of the Western citizen, 1851.
31 p.   22 cm.

Minutes of the proceedings of a convention of delegates from the abolition societies established in different parts of the United States, assembled at Philadelphia on the first day of January, one thousand seven hundred and ninety-four, and continued, by adjournments, until the seventh day of the same month, inclusive. Philadelphia, Printed by Zachariah Poulson, 1794.
30 p.   22 1/2 cm.

Mississippi. Immigration and Agriculture board.
Hand-book of the state of Mississippi. Pub. by order of the Board of immigration and agriculture, by E. G. Wall, commissioner. Jackson, Miss., 1882.
100 p.   22 cm.

Mitchell, A. jr.
Notes of a tour of America, in August and September, 1865. By A. Mitchell, jun. Glasgow, Printed for private circulation, 1868.

2 p.1., [3] - 152 p.   16 1/2 cm.

Mitchell, David W.
Ten years in the United States: being an Englishman's view of men and things in the North
and South ... London, Smith, Elder and co., 1862.
xii, 332 p.   20 1/2 cm.

Mitchell, Elisha, 1793-
... Diary of a geological tour ... in 1827 and
1828, with introduction and notes by Dr. Kemp P.
Battle ... Chapel Hill [N.C.] The University,
1905.
73 [1] p.   22 cm.

[Mitchell, James].
Letter on the relation of the white and African races in the United States, showing the necessity of the colonization of the latter. Addressed to the president of the U. S. Washington,
Government printing office, 1862.
28 p.   23 cm.

[Mitchell, John].
The present state of Great Britain and North
America, with regard to agriculture, population,
trade, and manufactures, impartially considered ...
London, T. Becket [etc.] 1767.
xvi, 363 [1] p.   4 p.1.   21 cm.

[Mitchell, Samuel Augustus] 1792-
An accompaniment to Mitchell's reference and
distance map of the United States; containing an
index of all the counties, districts, townships,
towns &c. ... With an account of the actual and
prospective internal improvements throughout the
Union ... Philadelphia, Mitchell and Hinman, 1834.
324 p.   22 1/2 cm.

Mitchell, Samuel Augustus, 1792-
A general view of the United States; comprising,
also a description of each individual state and
territory in the Union ... Philadelphia, S. A.
Mitchell, 1846.
128 p.   23 cm.

Mitchell, Samuel Augustus, 1792-
Mitchell's traveller's guide through the United States, containing the principal cities, towns

&c., alphabetically arranged; together with the stage, steamboat, canal, and railroad routes ... Illustrated by an accurate map ... Philadelphia, Thomas, Coperthwait, & co. [1836].
   78 p.   fold. map.   13 1/2 cm.

Mitchell, Samuel Augustus, 1792-
   The principal stage, steamboat, and canal routes in the United States; with the population of each state and other statistical information: being an accompaniment to Mitchell's traveller's guide. Philadelphia, Mitchell & Hinman, 1834.
   96 p.   12 cm.

Mitchell, William M.
   The under-ground railroad from slavery to freedom. London, 1860.
   xv, 172, xi p.   port.   19 cm.

Mixson, Frank M.   1846-
   Reminiscences of a private, by Frank M. Mixson, Company "E" 1st S.C. Vols. (Hagood's) ... Columbia, S.C., The State company, 1910.
   130 p.   3 port.   (incl. front.)   20 cm.

Mob, under pretence of law, or, The arrest and trial of Rev. George Storris at Northfield, N.H. ... Concord, Elbridge G. Chase, printer, 1835.
   24 p.   19 cm.

Moelling, Peter August.
   Reise-skizzen in poesie und prosa. Gesammelt auf einer siebenmonatlichen tour durch die Vereinigten Staaten von Nord-Amerika ... Galveston, Tex., Gedruckt in der office des "Apologeten" [1857?]
   384 p.   front., illus., pl., port.   21 cm.

Molinari, Gustave de, 1819-
   Lettres sur les Etats-Unis et le Canada adressées au Journal des débats par m. G. de Molinari ... Paris, Hachette et cie., 1876.
   3 p.l., 365 p.   19 1/2 cm.

Money, Edward.
   The truth about America, by Edward Money ... London, S. Low, Marston, Searle, & Rivington, 1886.
   iv, 234 p., 1 l.   17 1/2 cm.

Monroe.
        Speech of Mr. Monroe of Lorain, in the House
of Representatives, Jan. 12, 1858, on the bill to
repeal an act to prohibit the confinement of
fugitives from slavery in the jails of Ohio.
Columbus, Ohio, printed by Follett, Foster and
Co., 1858.
        8 p.   22 cm.

Montgomery, Cora, pseud. for Mrs. William Leslie Caz-
    neau.
        The queen of islands, and the king of rivers.
New York; Charles Wood, Washington, D. C., William
Adam, 1850.
        3-50 p.   map.   17 cm.

Montgomery, Franklin Alexander, 1830-
        Reminiscences of a Mississippian in peace and
war, by Frank A. Montgomery ... Cincinnati, The
Robert Clarke company press, 1901.
        xv p., 1 l., 305 p.   front., ports.   23 cm.

Montgomery, James.
        The abolition of the slave trade; written by
James Montgomery, James Grahame, and E. Benger.
Embellished with engravings from pictures painted
by R. Smirke, Esq., R. A.   To His Royal Highness
the Duke of Gloucester, patron, and to the directors and governors of the Society for bettering
the condition of the natives of Africa.   London,
Robert Bowyer [1843].
        141 p.   16 1/2 cm.

Montgomery, James.
        Poems on the abolition of the slave trade, by
James Montgomery, James Grahame, and E. Benger.
Embellished with engravings from pictures painted
by R. Smirke.   London, printed for R. Bowyer by
T. Bensley, 1809.
        ii, 141 p.   front., plates.   30 cm.

The monthly offering.   v.1; July, 1840-Dec. 1841. Bos-
    ton, Anti-slavery office, Dow and Jackson, prin-
    ters, 1840-41.
        184 p.   17 cm.

[Montlezun, baron de].
        Voyage fait dans les années 1816 et 1817, de
New-Yorck à la Nouvelles Orléans, et de L'Orénoque

au Mississippi; par les Petites et les Grandes-
Antilles contenant des détails absolument nouveaux
sur ces contrées; des portraits de personnages
influants dans les Etats-Unis, et des anecdotes
sur les réfugiés qui y sont établis; par l'auteur
des Souvenirs des Antilles. Paris, Gide fils,
1818.
2 v.   20 cm.

Montulé, Edouard de.
Voyage en Amérique, en Italie, en Sicile et en
Egypte, pendant les années, 1816, 1817, 1818 et
1819. Paris, Delaunay [etc.] 1821.
2 v.   20 1/2 cm. and atlas of 59 pl. (incl.
fold. map)   27 cm.

Moore, Edward Alexander, 1842-
The story of a cannoneer under Stonewall Jackson, in which is told the part taken by the Rock-
bridge artillery in the Army of northern Virginia,
by Edward A. Moore ... with introductions by
Capt. Robert E. Lee, jr., and Hon. Henry St.
George Tucker. Fully illustrated by portraits.
New York and Washington, The Neale publishing company, 1907.
375 p. front., pl., ports., facsim.   21 1/2 cm.

Moore, Francis, jr.
Map and description of Texas, containing sketches of its history, geology, geography and statistics ... and some brief remarks upon the character and customs of its inhabitants ... Philadelphia, H. Tanner, junr.; New York, Tanner &
D[i]sturnell, 1840.
143 p. 1 1. 8 pl. (incl. front.) fold. map.
15 cm.

Moore, Francis, fl. 1744.
A voyage to Georgia; begun in the year 1735.
Containing, an account of the settling the town
of Frederica, in the southern part of the province; and a description of the soil, air, birds,
beasts, trees, rivers, islands &c. With the rules
and orders made by the Honorable trustees for
that settlement ... London, Printed for J. Robinson, 1744.
3-108, [2] p. 2 p.l.   20 cm.

362

Moore, George, 1806-
     Journal of a voyage across the Atlantic: with
notes on Canada & the United States; and return
to Great Britain, in 1844 ... London, Printed
for private circulation, 1845.
     96 p.   4 p.1.   18 1/2 cm.

Moore, Theophilus Wilson.
     Treatise and hand-book of orange culture in
Florida. By Rev. T. W. Moore. 2d ed., rev. and
enl. New York, E. R. Pelton & co.; Jacksonville,
Fla., Ashmead brothers [c1881].
     ix, [11]- 184 p.   17 1/2 cm.

Moorhead, Isaac, 1828-
     The occasional writings of Isaac Moorhead;
with a sketch of his life by A. H. C. ... Erie,
Pa., A. H. Caughey, 1882.
     iv, 1 1., 258 p.   19 1/2 cm.

Moorman, John Jennings, 1802-
     The mineral waters of the United States and
Canada, with a map and plates and general direc-
tions for reaching mineral springs. By J. J.
Moorman ... Baltimore, Kelly & Piet, 1867.
     507 p. front. (fold. map) plates.   19 cm.

Moorman, John Jennings, 1802-
     Virginia White Sulphur Springs, with the
analysis of its waters, the diseases to which
they are applicable, and some account of society
and its amusements at the Springs, by J. J. Moorman ... Baltimore, Kelly, Piet & company, 1869.
     27 p. double plan.   19 cm.

Moral condition of slaves. New York [Published by R.
G. Williams for the American anti-slavery society, 1839?]
     24 p.   11 cm.

More, Charles Albert, chevalier de Pont-gibaud, comte
de, 1758.
     Mémoires du comte de More (1758-1837), pub.
pour la Societe d'histoire contemporaine, par M.
Geoffroy de Grandmaison & le cte. de Pontgibaud
... Paris, A. Picard et fils, 1898.
     343 p. 3 p.1., 3 port. (incl. front.)
22 1/2 cm.

Moreau de Saint Méry, Médéric Louis Elie, 1750-
    Voyage aux Etats-Unis de l'Amérique, 1793-
1798. Ed., with an introduction and notes, by
Stewart L. Mims. New Haven, Yale University
press, 1913.
    xxxvi p., 440 p. 1 1., front. (port.)
23 1/2 cm.

Moreau, F Frédéric.
    Aux Etats-Unis; notes de voyage ... Avec un
croquis de l'auteur. Paris, E. Plon, Nourrit et
cie., 1888.
    5 p.1., 263 p. front. 18 cm.

Morford, Henry, 1823-
    Morford's short-trip guide to America. (Uni-
ted States and Dominion of Canada) By Henry
Morford ... New York, C. T. Dillingham; [etc.,
etc.] [1879].
    4 p.1., xiii, [7]- 312, i.e. 374 p. fold.
map. 16 1/2 cm.

[Morford, Henry] 1823-1881.
    Red-tape and pigeon-hole generals: as seen
from the ranks during a campaign in the Army
of the Potomac. By a citizen soldier ... New
York, Carleton, 1864.
    318 p. 19 cm.

Morgan, Edwin Barbour, 1806.
    Tract for Americans. Fillmore's political
history and position. George Law and Chauncey
Shaffer's reasons for repudiating Fillmore and
Donelson and the action of the Know-Nothing state
convention at Syracuse on the resolutions cen-
suring Brook's assault on Senator Sumner, &c.
Speech ... in U. S. House of Representatives,
Aug. 4, 1856. New York, The New York Tribune
[1856?]
    16 p. 22 cm.

[Morgan, Henry James] 1842-
    The tour of H. R. H. the Prince of Wales
through British America and the United States
By a British Canadian. Montreal, Printed by
J. Lovell, 1860.
    ix, [11]- 271, [1] p. 2 p.1., front.
(port.) 21 cm.

Morgan, Julia, "Mrs. Irby Morgan."
How it was; four years among the Rebels. By
Mrs. Irby Morgan ... Nashville, Tenn., Printed
for the author, Publishing house, Methodist Episcopal church, South, 1892.
204 p. front., ports. 19 cm.

Morgan, William Henry, 1836-
Personal reminiscences of the war of 1861-5;
in camp - en bivouac - on the march - on picket -
on the skirmish line - on the battlefield - and
in prison, by W. H. Morgan. Lynchburg, Va.,
J. P. Bell company, inc., 1911.
4 p.l., 7-286 p. front. (port.) 20 1/2 cm.

Morineau, Auguste de.
Essai statistique et politique sur les Etats-
Unis d'Amérique, d'après des documents recueillis
sur les lieux, comprenant 27 tableaux synoptiques
et analytiques de la constitution fédérale et de
celles des états particuliers, avec le portrait
en pied de Washington. Paris, G. Thorel; Blaye,
Chatenet, 1848.
v, 5-39 p. 3 p.l., port., 27 double tables.
31 1/2 cm.

Morris, Eastin.
The Tennessee gazetteer, or topographical
dictionary; containing a description of the several counties, towns, &c. ... To which is prefixed a general description of the state ...
Nashville, W. H. Hunt & co., 1834.
4, cxvi, 178 p. 9 l. 18 cm.

Morris, George W.
History of the Eighty-first regiment of Indiana volunteer infantry in the great war of
the rebellion, 1861 to 1865 ... A regimental
roster. Prison life, adventures, etc., by Corporal Geo. W. Morris. [Louisville, Ky., The
Franklin printing company, 1901].
202 p. 21 1/2 cm.

Morris, Thomas, 1776-
Speech of Hon. Thomas Morris, of Ohio, in
reply to the speech of the Hon. Henry Clay, in
Senate, February 9, 1839. New York, American
anti-slavery society, 1839.
40 p. 22 cm.

Morris, Thomas, 1776.
Speech of the Hon. Thomas Morris, of Ohio, in the Senate of the United States, February 6, 1839, in reply to the Hon. Henry Clay. New-York, Piercy & Reed [1839?]
36 p.   17 cm.

Morris, Thomas Asbury, 1794-
Miscellany: consisting of essays, biographical sketches, and notes of travel ... Cincinnati, L. Swormstedt & J. H. Power, 1852.
390 p.   front. (port.)   19 1/2 cm.

Morris, William.
Ancient slavery disapproved of God. The substance of a lecture by William Morris, M. D. Philadelphia, The Scriptural Knowledge Society, 1862.
20 p.   20 cm.

Morris, William of Swindon, Eng.
Letters sent home. Out and home again by way of Canada and the United States; or, What a summer's trip told me of the people and the country of the great West. By William Morris ... London, F. Warne & co.; New York, Scribner Welford, & Armstrong [1875?]
xv, [1], 477 p.   19 cm.

[Morse, Charles Fessenden] 1839-
Letters written during the civil war, 1861-1865. [Boston, Mass.] Priv. print, 1898.
3 p.l., [5]- 222 p.   front. (port.)   23 1/2 cm.

Morse, Francis W.
Personal experiences in the war of the great rebellion, from December, 1862, to July 1865. Albany, Printed but not published [Munsell, printer] 1866.
iv, [5]- 152 p.   23 cm.

Morse, Isaac Edward, 1809.
Speech ... on the territorial bill. Delivered in the House of Representatives, February 24, 1849. Washington, D. C., John T. Towers, printer, 1849.
8 p.   23 cm.

Morse, Jedidiah, 1761-
The American geography; or, a view of the present situation of the United States of America ... Elizabeth Town, Printed by Shepard Kollock, for the author, 1789.
xii, 534 p., 2 1. 2 fold. maps. 20 1/2 cm.

Morse, Jedidiah, 1761.
A discourse, delivered at the African meetinghouse, in Boston, July 14, 1808, in grateful celebration of the abolition of the African slave-trade, by the governments of the United States, Great Britain and Denmark ... Boston, Printed by Lincoln & Edmunds, 1808.
28 p. 22 1/2 cm.

Morton, John Watson.
The artillery of Nathan Bedford Forrest's cavalry, "the wizard of the saddle," by John Watson Morton ... Nashville, Tenn., Dallas, Tex., Publishing house of the M. E. church, South, Smith & Lamar, agents, 1909.
374 p. front., plates (1 fold.) ports., facsims. 24 cm.

Motley, John Lothrop, 1814-1877.
The causes of the American Civil War ... New York, D. Appleton & company, 1861.
24 p. 23 cm.

Mott, A., comp.
Biographical sketches and interesting anecdotes of persons of color. Of which is added a selection of pieces of poetry ... New York, M. Day, 1839.
vi, [7] - 408 p. 18 1/2 cm.

Mowris, James A.
A history of the One hundred and seventeenth regiment, N. Y. volunteers, (Fourth Oneida) from the date of its organization, August, 1862, till that of its muster out, June, 1865. By J. A. Mowris, M.D., regimental surgeon. Hartford, Case, Lockwood and co., printers, 1866.
xi, [13]- 315 p. 21 1/2 cm.

Mühlenberg, Henry Melchior, 1711-1787.
　　Heinrich Melchior Mühlenberg, patriarch der
Lutherischen kirche Nordamerikas. Selbstbiographie,
1711-1743. Aus dem missions-archive der Franck-
ischen [!] stiftungen zu Halle. Mit zusätzen und
erläuterungen von lic. theol. dr. W. Germann ...
Allentown, Pa., Brobst, Diehl & co.; Halle A. S.,
Waisenhausbuchhandlung, 1881.
　　x p., 256 p. 1 1., incl. front. (port.)
19 cm.

Muirhead, James Fullarton, 1853-
　　The land of contrasts; a Briton's view of his
American kin. By James Fullarton Muirhead ...
Boston, New York [etc.] Lamson, Wolffe & com-
pany, 1898.
　　4 p.1., vii-viii, 282 p.　20 1/2 cm.

Münsterberg, Hugo, 1863-1916.
　　The Americans, by Hugo Münsterberg ... tr. by
Edwin B. Holt ... New York, McClure, Phillips &
co., 1904.
　　2 p.1., [vii]-xiv, 619 p.　24 cm.

Murat, Achille, prince, 1801-
　　Esquisse morale et politique des États-Unis
de l'Amerique du Nord ... Paris, Crochard, 1832.
　　xxvii, 389 p.　2 p.1.　15 1/2 cm.

Murat, Achille.
　　The United States of North America ... With a
note on negro slavery, by Junius Redivivus. Second edition. London, Effingham Wilson [etc.,
etc.] 1833.
　　xxxviii, 402 p. fold. map.　17 cm.

[Murfree, Mary Noailles] 1850-
　　In the Tennessee mountains; by Charles Egbert
Craddock [pseud.] 10th ed. Boston, New York,
Houghton, Mifflin and company, 1885.
　　2 p.1., 322 p.　18 1/2 cm.

Murphey, Claude Charles.
　　Around the United States by bicycle, by Claude
C. Murphey; fully illustrated by Eustace Paul
Ziegler. Detroit, Press of Raynor & Taylor, 1906.
　　362 p. front., plates, map.　16 cm.

Murray, Sir Charles Augustus, 1806-1895.
　　Travels in North America during the years 1834,
1835, & 1836. Including a summer residence with
the Pawnee tribe of Indians, in the remote prairies
of the Missouri, and a visit to Cuba and the Azore
islands. London, R. Bentley, 1839.
　　2 v. front. 22 cm.

Murray, James, 1713-
　　Letters of James Murray, loyalist; edited by
Nina Moore Tiffany, assisted by Susan I. Lesley.
Boston, printed: not published, 1901.
　　ix p. 324 p. 2 l., 1 l., 3 plates, 7 port.
(incl. front.) 3 double facsims. 22 1/2 cm.

Myers, J. C.
　　Sketches on a tour through the northern and
eastern states, the Canadas & Nova Scotia ...
Harrisonburg [Va.] J. H. Wartmann and brothers,
prs., 1849.
　　xvii, [19]-475, [1] p. 16 1/2 cm.

N

Naaukeurige beschryving van Noord-America, vaarin dat
waerelddeel aangeweezen word, de bezittingen der
Spanjaarden, Franschen, Engelschen, Hollandschen,
en andere europeaansche natien ... Door J. C. N.
Amsterdam, C. Gorenwoud, 1783.
　　207 p. front. 17 cm.

[Nairne, Thomas] supposed author.
　　A letter from South Carolina; giving an account
of the soils, air, products, trade, government,
laws, religion, people, military strength, &c. of
that province ... Written by a Swiss gentleman,
to his friend at Berne. London, Printed for A.
Baldwin, 1710.
　　63 p. 21 cm.

A narrative of the adventures and escape of Moses Roper,
from American slavery. London, Harvey and Darton,
1843.
　　122 p. 17 1/2 cm.

Narrative of James Williams, an American slave ... New
York, Published by the American anti-slavery society, 1838.
xxiii, [24]-108 p.   14 cm.

Narrative of the late riotous proceedings against the
liberty of the press, in Cincinnati. With remarks
and historical notices, relating to emancipation.
Addressed to the people of Ohio, by the executive committee of the Ohio Anti-slavery society.
Cincinnati [n.p.] 1836.
48 p.   22 1/2 cm.

Narrative of the life of Thomas Cooper. New York,
Published by Isaac T. Hopper, 1832.
36 p.   front., illus.   15 1/2 cm.

[Nason, Daniel].
A journal of a tour from Boston to Savannah,
thence to Havanna, in the island of Cuba ...
thence to New Orleans and several western cities
... by a citizen of Cambridgeport. Cambridge,
printed for the author, 1849.
114 p.   16 cm.

National anti-slavery bazaar. Gazette. Vol. 1., no.
11. [Boston, n.d.]
4 p.   30 cm.

National convention of union soldiers and sailors,
Cleveland, September 17-18, 1866.
National convention of union soldiers and
sailors held at Cleveland, Ohio ... September 17
and 18, 1866. Official report of the proceedings.
[n.p., 1866?]
32 p.   23 cm.

National Johnson club.
Document no. 1 ... 1.--Address of the National
Johnson club. 2.--Testimony of Alexander H.
Stephens ... [n.p., n.d.]
16 p.   23 cm.

National prosperity the reward of national equity.
Philadelphia, Published by the Tract association
of Friends [n.d.]
24 p.   18 cm.

Naylor, Robert Anderton.
　　Across the Atlantic. Westminster, London,
The Roxburgh press, 1893.
　　xii, 305 p.　22 1/2 cm.

Nebraska: a poem, personal and political. Boston,
John P. Jewett; Cleveland, Jewett, Proctor, and
Worthington, 1854.
　　42 p.　18 cm.

Neck, S. Sanders.
　　The present and future productions of Florida.
Ocala, Fla., Banner steam printing house [c1888].
　　134 p.　illus.　22 1/2 cm.

Needles, Edward.
　　A historical account of the Pennsylvania society: for promoting the abolition of slavery;
the relief of free negroes unlawfully held in bondage, and for improving the condition of the African race, compiled from the minutes of the Society
and other official documents, by Edward Needles...
Philadelphia, Merrihew and Thompson, 1848.
　　116 p.　22 cm.

Needles, Edward.
　　Ten years' progress: or, A comparison of the
state and condition of the colored people in the
city and county of Philadelphia from 1837 to 1847
... Philadelphia, Merrihew and Thompson, 1849.
　　16 p.　19 cm.

Neelmeyer-Vukassowitsch, Heinrich.
　　Die Vereinigten Staaten von Amerika. Nach
eigenen beobachtungen geschildert, von H. Neelmeyer-Vukassowitsch. Leipzig, F. Duncker, 1884.
　　2 p.l., vii, 640 p.　21 cm.

Neese, George Michael, 1839-
　　Three years in the Confederate horse artillery,
by George M. Neese ... New York and Washington,
The Neale publishing company, 1911.
　　4 p.l., 3-362 p.　21 cm.

Negro apprenticeship in the British colonies. London, Published by the office of the anti-slavery
society [etc.,etc.] 1838.
　　32 p.　20 cm.

371

Negro slavery and moral law. In National democratic
quarterly review. Washington, D. C., March, 1860.
p. 264-270.

Negro slavery. No. VI. Predisposing causes to insurrection in Demerara. [London, n.d.]
45-52 p.   21 cm.

Negro slavery. No. VII. Insurrections of slaves in
the West Indies, particularly in Demerara. [Lon-
don, n.d.]
53-64 p.   21 cm.

Negro slavery. No. VIII. Insurrections in the West
Indies. St. Lucia - Trinidad - Dominica-Jamaica -
Demerara. [London, n.d.]
65-76 p.   21 cm.

Negro slavery. No.XVI. State of religious instruction among the slaves of the West Indies. [Lon-
don, n.d.]
165-180 p.   21 cm.

Negro slavery. No. XVII. Attempts to enlist religion on the side of colonial slavery exposed.
[London, n.d.]
181-195 p.   21 cm.

The negro's friend, or, The Sheffield anti-slavery
album ... Sheffield, Printed and sold by J.
Blackwell [etc., etc.].
204 p.   illus.   19 cm.

The negro's memorial, or, Abolitionist's catechism;
by an abolitionist ... London, Printed for the
author, and sold by Hatchard & co., and J. and
A. Arch, 1825.
127 p.   21 1/2 cm.

Neide, Charles A.
The canoe Aurora; a cruise from the Adiron-
dacks to the gulf. By Dr. Chas. A. Neide ...
New York, Forest and stream publishing co., 1885.
215 p.   incl. front. (map)   19 cm.

Neill, Henry.
A letter to the editors of the American Presbyterian and Genesee evangelist ... Philadelphia,

King & Baird, printers, 1858.
    21 p.   22 cm.

Neilson, Peter, 1795-
    Recollections of a six years' residence in
the United States of America, interspersed with
original anecdotes, illustrating the manners of
the inhabitants of the great western republic
... Glasgow, D. Robertson [etc.] 1830.

Nell, William Cooper.
    The colored patriots of the American revolu-
tion, with sketches of several distinguished
colored persons; to which is added a brief survey of the condition and prospects of colored
Americans ... Boston, Robert F. Wallcut, 1855.
    396 p.   illus.   19 cm.

Nell, William Cooper.
    Services of colored Americans, in the wars
of 1776 and 1812 ... Boston, Printed by Prentiss
& Sawyer, 1851.
    24 p.   23 cm.

Nelson, Helge, 1882-
    ... Nordamerika, natur och kulturbygd ...
med 264 bilder och kartor. Stockholm, Bokför-
laget Natur och kultur [1935].
    2 v. illus. (incl. maps, plans) plates,
diagrs.   23 1/2 cm.

Nesterowicz, S.
    Notaki z podrózy po pòłnocnej i strodkowej
Ameryce. Toledo, Ohio, A. A. Pryski, 1909.
    226 p.   illus.   18 cm.

Nevers, Edmond de.
    L'âme américaine ... par Edmond de Nevers ...
Paris, Jouve & Boyer, 1900.
    2 v.   19 cm.

Nevin, Edwin H.
    The religion of Christ at war with American
slavery; or, Reasons for separating from the
Presbyterian church, (O. S.) ... Cleveland,
Steam press of Sanford & Hayward, 1849.
    46 p.   20 cm.

New England anti-slavery convention.
     Address of the New-England anti-slavery con-
vention to the slaves of the United States; with
an address to President Tyler; adopted in Faneuil
hall, May 31, 1843. Boston, Published by Oliver
Johnson, 1843.
     16 p.   18 cm.

The new slave laws of Jamaica and St. Christopher's
examined with an especial reference to the eulo-
gies recently pronounced upon them in Parliament.
London, Society for the mitigation and gradual
abolition of slavery throughout the British dominions, 1828.
     24 p.   21 cm.

A new voyage to Georgia. By a young gentleman. Giving an account of his travels to South Carolina
and part of North Carolina. To which is added,
A curious account of the Indians. By an honorable person. And a poem to James Oglethorpe,
esq. on his arrival from Georgia. 2d ed. London, J. Wilford, 1737.
     62 p.   1 p.l.   19 1/2 cm.

New York anti-slavery convention, Utica, 1835.
     Proceedings of the New York anti-slavery con-
vention held at Utica, October 21, and New York
anti-slavery state society, held at Peterboro',
October 22, 1835. [n.p., n.d.]
     48 p.   23 cm.

New York. Citizens meeting, 1862.
     The life of slavery, or the life of the na-
tion? Mass meeting of the citizens of New York
(without distinction of party,) at the Cooper
Institute, New York, March 6, 1862. Hon. James
A. Hamilton in the chair. [New York? 1862?]
     6 p.   23 cm.

New York city colonization society.
     Proceedings ... at their annual meeting, held
on 13th and 14th of May, including the annual
report of the Board of managers to the society.
New York, Printed by Wm. A. Mercein and son,
1835.
     62 p.   23 cm.

New-York City colonization society.
First report ... read at the annual meeting,
October 29, 1823. New-York, Printed by J. Seymour, 1823.
32 p. 21 cm.

New York City colonization society.
Fifth annual report ... with the constitution
of the society. New-York, Mercein & Post's press,
1837.
48 p. 22 cm.

New York City colonization society.
Seventh annual report ... New-York, Mercein
& Post's press, 1839.
48 p. 22 cm.

New York. Committee of merchants for the relief of
colored people suffering from the late riots in
the city of New York. New York, George A. White-
house, 1863.
48 p. 23 cm.

New York committee of vigilance.
The first annual report ... for the year 1837
... New York, Pierey & Reed, 1837.
84 p. 21 cm.

New York infantry. 2d regt., 1776-1783.
Orderly books of the Fourth New York regiment,
1778-1780, the Second New York regiment, 1780-
1783, by Samuel Tallmadge and others, with diaries
of Samuel Tallmadge, 1780-1782, and John Barr,
1779-1782; Prepared for publication by Almon W.
Lauber. Albany, The University of the state of
New York, 1932.
933 p. front., pl., port., facsims. 26 cm.

New York Quarterly pamphleteer; No. 1, May, 1842.
The slavery of poverty, with a plan for its abolition ... New York, New York Society for the
abolition of all slavery, 1842.
16 p. 21 cm.

New-York state anti-slavery society.
Proceedings of the first annual meeting ...
convened at Utica, October 19, 1836. Utica,
Published for the Society, 1836.
60 p. 21 cm.

New York state colonization society.
     African colonization. Proceedings of the
New-York state colonization society, on its
first anniversary; together with an address to
the public, from the managers thereof. Albany,
Printed by Websters and Skinners, 1830.
     27 p.   22 cm.

New York state colonization society.
     Proceedings of the fortieth annual meeting
... New York, Baker & Godwin, 1872.
     12 p.   23 cm.

New York state colonization society.
     Proceedings ... on its first anniversary...
Albany, N. Y., printed by Websters and Skinners,
1830.
     27 p.   23 cm.

New York state colonization society.
     Eighteenth annual report ... New-York,
Daniel Fanshaw, printer, 1850.
     62 p.   illus., map.   23 cm.

New York state colonization society.
     Twenty-fourth annual report of the Board of
managers ... New-York, John A. Gray, 1856.
     48 p.   illus., map.   23 cm.

New York. Union meeting.
     The proceedings of the union meeting, held
at Castle Garden, October 30, 1850 ... New-York,
Published by order of the "Union safety committee," 1850.
     62 p.   22 cm.

New-York young men's anti-slavery society.
     Preamble and constitution ... New-York,
W. T. Collidge & co., 1834.
     11 p.   17 cm.

[Newcomb, Mary A. "Mrs. H.A.W. Newcomb"] 1817-1893?
     Four years of personal reminiscences of the
war. Chicago, H.S. Mills & co., 1893.
     vii, [9]- 131 p. front. (port.)   19 1/2 cm.

Newcomer, Christopher Armour.
     Cole's cavalry; or, Three years in the saddle
in the Shenandoah Valley, by C. Armour Newcomer...

Baltimore, Cushing and co., booksellers and sta-
tioners, 1895.
x, [9]- 165, [1] p.   front., port.   23 1/2 cm.

Newell, Chester.
History of the revolution in Texas, particularly of the war of 1835 & '36; together with
the latest geographical, topographical, and
statistical accounts of the country ... New York,
Wiley & Putnam, 1838.
[vii]-x, 215 p.   2 p.1.   front. (fold. map)
19 cm.

Newlin, William Henry.
An account of the escape of six federal soldiers from prison at Danville, Va.:   their
travels by night through the enemy's country to
the Union pickets at Gauley Bridge, West Virginia, in the winter of 1863-64.   By W. H. Newlin ... Cincinnati, Western Methodist book concern print, 1888.
136 p.   plates.   23 cm.

Newman, Francis William.
Character of the southern states of America.
Letter to a friend who had joined the southern
independence association ... Manchester, Union
and emancipation society's depot, 1863.
14 p.   21 cm.

[Newsome, Edmund].
Experience in the war of the great rebellion.
By a soldier of the Eighty-first regiment Illinois volunteer infantry.   From August 1862, to
August 1865.   Including nearly nine months of
life in southern prisons, at Macon, Savannah,
Charleston, Columbia and other places.   Carbon-
dale, Ill., E. Newsome, 1879.
1 p.1., 137, [4] p.   14 1/2 cm.

Newton, John.
Thoughts upon the African slave trade ... London, Printed for J. Buckland and J. Johnson,
1788.
41 p.   19 cm.

[Newton, John].
Thoughts upon the African slave trade.   New
York, Samuel Whiting and co., 1811.

[517]-546 p.   22 cm.

Newton, Joseph, of London, Eng.
Emigration to Virginia, [east) "or the Old
Dominion state." (3d ed.) Report from Joseph
Newton ... London, The Virginian land agency
[1871].
cover-title, [3]-52 p.   22 cm.

Nicely, Wilson.
The great Southwest, or, Plain guide for emigrants and capitalists, embracing a description
of the states of Missouri and Kansas ... By
William Nicely. St. Louis, R. P. Studley & co.,
printers, 1867.
115 p.   fold. map.   19 cm.

Nichols, G. W. of Jesup, Ga.
A soldier's story of his regiment (61st Georgia) and incidentally of the Lawton-Gordon-Evans
brigade, Army northern Virginia, by Private G.
W. Nichols ... [Jesup? Ga., 1898].
xi, [1], [13]-291, [2] p. incl. ports.
19 cm.

Nichols, George Ward, 1837-1885.
The story of the great march. From the
diary of a staff officer. By Brevet Major George
Ward Nichols ... 26th ed. New York, Harper &
brothers, 1866.
xii p., 1 1., [15]- 408 p.   incl. front.,
illus., plates.   fold. map.   19 1/2 cm.

Nichols, James Moses, 1835-1886.
Perry's saints; or, The fighting parson's
regiment in the war of the rebellion; by James
M. Nichols. Boston, D. Lothrop and company [1886].
299 p.   incl. illus., plates, maps, plans.
fold. map, plan.   19 cm.

Nichols, Thomas Low, 1815-
Forty years of American life. 2d. ed. ...Lon-
don, Longmans, Green & co., 1874.
xvi, 509 p.   18 1/2 cm.

[Nicklin, Philip Holbrook] 1786-
Letters descriptive of the Virginia springs;
the roads leading thereto, and the doings thereat.

378

Collected, corrected, annotated and edited, by
Peregrine Prolix [pseud.] ... Philadelphia, H.
S. Tanner, 1835.
   xii [9]- 99 p. front. (fold. map). 15 1/2 cm.

Nielsen, Roger, 1888-
   Amerika in bildern und text, von Roger Nielsen ... mit einem vorwort von graf J. H. v. Bern-
storff ... Leipzig, K. F. Koehlers antiquarium
[1925].
   316 p. illus., double maps. 29 1/2 cm.

Nisbet, James Cooper.
   Four years on the firing line, by Col. James
Cooper Nisbet. Chattanooga, The Imperial
press [ᶜ1914].
   2 p.l., 445 p. front. (port.) 20 1/2 cm.

Noble, Frederic Alphonso.
   Blood the price of redemption. A Thanksgiving discourse, delivered in the House of hope,
November 27, 1862 ... Saint Paul, Minnesota ...
Saint Paul, Office of the Press printing company, 1862.
   21 p. 22 cm.

Noel, Theo.
   A campaign from Santa Fe to the Mississippi;
being a history of the old Sibley brigade from
its first organization to the present time; its
campaigns in New Mexico, Arizona, Texas, Louisiana, and Arkansas, in the years of 1861-2-3-4,
by Theo. Noel, 4th Texas cavalry. Shreveport,
La., Shreveport news printing establishment -
John Dickinson, proprietor, 1865.
   152 p. front. (fold. tab.) 22 cm.

Nolte, Vincent Otto, 1779-
   Fifty years in both hemispheres; or, Reminiscences of the life of a former merchant ... Translated from the German ... New York, Redfield,
1854.
   xxii, [11]-484 p. 18 cm.

The non-resistance principle. [n.p., n.d.]
   24 p. 19 cm.

The non-slaveholder ... ed. and publ. by Abm. L. Pen-
nock, Samuel Rhoads, and Geo. W. Taylor. v. II-V,

1847-48; v. II, new ser., 1854. Philadelphia,
Merrihew and Thompson, printers, 1847-48, 1854.
    5 v.   25 cm.

Nordhoff, Charles, 1830-
        The cotton states in the spring and summer of
    1875. By Charles Nordhoff ... New York, D. Ap-
    pleton & company, 1876.
        3 p.1., [9]-112 p.   24 1/2 cm.

Norris, Robert.
        A short account of the African slave-trade ...
    A new edition corrected. London, Printed for W.
    Lowndes, 1789.
        41 p.   20 1/2 cm.

The North-American and West-Indian gazetteer. Con-
    taining an authentic description of the colonies
    and islands in that part of the globe ... Lon-
    don, G. Robinson, 1776.
        xxiv, [220]p.   3 p.1., 2 fold. maps. (incl.
    front.)   18 cm.

The North American tourist. New York, A. T. Goodrich
    [1839].
        ix, 506 p.   plates, fold.   maps.   15 cm.

The north and south. Reprinted from the New York
    Tribune. New York, Published at the office of
    the Tribune, 1854.
        48 p.   23 cm.

The north and south misrepresented and misjudged:
    or, A candid view of our present difficulties
    and danger, and their cause and remedy. Phila-
    delphia, Printed for the author, 1861.
        48 p.   22 cm.

The north and south, slavery and its contrasts. A
    tale of real life. By the author of Way-marks
    in the life of a wanderer ... Philadelphia, Crissy
    and Markley, 1852.
        350 p.   20 cm.

North Carolina. A guide-book of northwest North Caro-
    lina containing historical sketches of the Mora-
    vians in North Carolina, a description of the
    country and its industrial pursuits. Salem, N.C.,
    L. V. and E. T. Blum, 1873.

109 p., [13] p.   21 cm.

North, Thomas.
    Five years in Texas; or, What you did not hear
during the war from January 1861 to January 1866.
A narrative of his travels, experiences, and observations, in Texas and Mexico.   By Thomas North.
Cincinnati, Elm street printing co., 1871.
    viii, [9]-231 p.   18 cm.

Northern dealers in slaves.   [New York Published by
    R. G. Williams for the American anti-slavery
    society, 1839?]
        16 p.   11 cm.

Northrop, John Worrell.
    Chronicles from the diary of a war prisoner
in Andersonville and other military prisons of
the South in 1864 ... An appendix containing
statement of a Confederate physician and officer
relative to prison condition and management.
By John Worrell Northrop ... Wichita, Kan., The
author, 1904.
    228 p.   17 1/2 cm.

Northup, Solomon, 1808-
    ... Twelve years a slave.   Narrative of ...
a citizen of New-York, Kidnapped in Washington
City in 1841, and rescued in 1853, from a cotton plantation near the Red river, in Louisiana.
Auburn, Derby and Miller; Buffalo, Derby, Orton
and Mulligan; [etc.,etc.] 1853.
    xvi, [17]-336 p.   front., pl.   19 cm.

Norton, Charles L[edyard] ed.
    American summer resorts.   American seaside
resorts; a hand-book for health and pleasure
seekers.   New York, Taintor brothers, 1871.
    190 p.   front.   16 cm.

Norton, Charles Ledyard, 1837-1909.
    A handbook of Florida, by Charles Ledyard
Norton.   With forty-nine maps and plans.   New
York, Longmans, Green & co., 1891.
    xxxii, 380 p.   maps (part fold.)   17 cm.

Norton, Jesse O.
    Kansas and the compromises.   Speech ... In
the House of Representatives.   August 9, 1856.

Washington, Buell & Blanchard [n.d.].
8 p.   22 1/2 cm.

Norton, Oliver Willcox.
Army letters, 1861-1865. Being extracts from
private letters to relatives and friends from a
soldier in the field during the late civil war,
with an appendix containing copies of some official documents, papers and addresses of later
date. By Oliver Willcox Norton, private Eighty-
third regiment Pennsylvania volunteers, first
lieutenant Eighth United States colored troops ...
[Chicago, Printed by O. L. Deming, 1903].
355 p.   incl. front., plates (1 col.) ports.
23 1/2 cm.

Norwood, Henry, fl. 1649-
A voyage to Virginia. By Col. Norwood. [Lon-
don, 1732].
145-170 p.   33 cm.

Notes on Florida prepared with special reference to
the Howgate grant on Lake George. New York,
Benj. H. Tyrel, 1881.
23 p.   20 1/2 cm.

Notes on the two reports from the committee of the
honorable House of Assembly of Jamaica, appointed
to examine ... the allegations and charges contained in the several petitions which have been
presented to the British House of Commons, on
the subject of the slave trade, and on treatment
of the negroes ... By a Jamaica planter. London, Printed and sold by James Phillips, 1789.
62 p.   21 cm.

Nott, Charles Cooper, 1827-1916.
Sketches in prison camps: a continuation of
Sketches of the war. By Charles C. Nott, late
colonel of the 176th New York vols. ... 3d ed.
New York, A. D. F. Randolph, 1865.
204 p.   19 1/2 cm.

Nott, Charles Cooper, 1827-1916.
Sketches of the war: a series of letters to
the North Moore street school of New York. By
Charles C. Nott, captain in the Fifth Iowa cavalry and trustee of public schools in the city
of New York. 2d ed. New York, A. D. F. Ran-

dolph, 1865.
viii, [9]- 174 p.   19 1/2 cm.

Nott, Samuel.
Slavery and the remedy; or, Principles and
suggestions for a remedial code ... Sixth edition with a reply and appeal to European advisers.
Boston, Crocker & Brewster, 1859.
137 p.   21 cm.

Nourse, James.
Views of colonization ... Second edition.
New York, American anti-slavery society, 1839.
60 p.   17 cm.

Nourse, James, 1805.
Views of colonization ... Philadelphia, Merrihew and Gunn, printers, 1837.
52 p.   17 cm.

Nouvelle relation de la Caroline, par un gentil-homme
françois arrive, depuis deux mois, de ce nouveau
pais ... A la Haye, Chez Meyndert Uytweff [!]
marchand libraire de Meurant dans le Gorstraet
[1686?]
36 p.   13 1/2 cm.

Noyes, George Freeman, 1824-1868.
The bivouac and the battlefield; or, Campaign sketches in Virginia and Maryland.   By
George F. Noyes ... New York, Harper & brothers,
1863.
xi, [13]- 339 p.   20 cm.

Nuñez Cabeza de Vaca, Alvar, 16th century.
The journey of Alvar Nunez Cabeza de Vaca and
his companions from Florida to the Pacific, 1528-
1536; tr. from his own narrative by Fanny Bandelier, together with the report of Father Marcos
of Nizza and a letter from the viceroy Mendoza;
ed., with an introduction, by Ad. F. Bandelier.
New York, A. S. Barnes & company, 1905.
xxii, 231 p. front. (fold. map) facsims.
18 cm.

Nuttall, Thomas, 1786-
A journal of travels into the Arkansas territory, during the year 1819.   With occasional observations on the manners of the aborigines ...

Philadelphia, T. H. Palmer, 1821.
xii, [9]- 296 p. front. (fold. map) plates,
tables. 22 1/2 cm.

O

Ober, Frederick Albion, 1849-1913.
The Knockabout club in the Everglades; the
adventures of the club in exploring Lake Okecho-
bee ... Boston, Estes and Lauriat [c1887].
213 p. incl. front., illus., plates. 21 x
17 1/2 cm.

Oberländer, Karl.
Ein ausflug nach Amerika. Tagebuchblätter
von Karl Oberländer. Hamburg, Hof-buchdrucherei
F. W. Rademacher, 1893.
212 p. 19 cm.

Oberlin college. Library.
... A classified catalogue of the collection
of anti-slavery propaganda in the Oberlin college
library, compiled by Geraldine Hopkins Hubbard,
edited by Julian S. Fowler. (Oberlin) 1932.
x, 84 p. 25 cm.

Observations on the Rev. Dr. [Ezra Stiles] Gannett's
sermon, entitled "Relation of the north to slavery." Republished from the editorial columns
of the Boston courier, of June 28th and 29th,
and July 6th, 1854. Second thousand. Boston,
Redding and Company, 1854.
29 p. 24 cm.

O'Connell, Daniel.
Daniel O'Connell upon American slavery: with
other Irish testimonies. New York, American
anti-slavery society, 1860.
48 p. 19 cm.

O'Connell, Daniel.
... Speeches of Daniel O'Connell and Thomas
Steele on the subject of American slavery, delivered before the Loyal national repeal association of Ireland, in reply to certain letters

384

received from repeal associations in the U. States. Philadelphia, Anti-slavery office, 1843.
8 p. 24 cm.

[O'Connor, John].
Wanderings of a vagabond. An autobiography. Edited by John Morris [pseud.] ... New York, The author [1873].
492 p. 19 cm.

Odds and ends of travel; or, Adventures, rambles, and recollections, of a trip from Sydney; via South America, Panama, the West Indies, the United States, and Niagara. London, Dean and son, 1851.
viii, 340 p. front. (plates) 20 cm.

Oehler, Andrew, 1781-
The life, adventures, and unparalled sufferings of Andrew Oehler, containing an account of his travels through France, Italy, the East and West Indies, and part of the United States ... Trenton [N. J.], Published by P. Fenton, nearly opposite the bank, L. Deare, printer, N. Brunswick, 1811.
226 p. 17 1/2 cm.

Oeri, Albert, 1875-
Europäische briefe über Amerika von dr. Albert Oeri ... Basel, Buchdruckerei zum Basler Berichthaus a. g., 1930.
131 p. 21 1/2 cm.

O'Ferrall, Simon Ansley.
A ramble of six thousand miles through the United States of America ... London, E. Wilson, 1832.
xii, 360 p. incl. front. (facsim.) 22 cm.

Ogden, George W.
Letters from the West; comprising a tour through the western country and a residence of two summers in the states of Ohio and Kentucky: originally written in a letter to a brother ... New-Bedford [Mass.] Melcher & Rogers, 1823.
iv, [5]-126 p. 18 1/2 cm.

Ohio anti-slavery society.
Memorial ... to the General assembly of the state of Ohio. Cincinnati, Pugh & Dodd, printers, 1838.

34 p.   20 cm.

Ohio anti-slavery society.
    Narrative of the late riotous proceedings
against the liberty of the press, in Cincinnati.
With remarks and historical notices, relating to
emancipation. Addressed to the people of Ohio,
by the executive committee of the Ohio anti-
slavery society. Cincinnati, 1836.
    48 p.   21 cm.

Ohio anti-slavery society.
    Proceedings of the Ohio anti-slavery conven-
tion. Held at Putnam, on the twenty-second,
twenty-third and twenty-fourth of April, 1835.
[n.p., Beaumont and Wallace, printers, n.d.]
    54 p.   21 cm.

Ohio anti-slavery society.
    Report of the first anniversary, 1836. Cin-
cinnati, Published by the Ohio anti-slavery
society, 1836.
    53 p.   23 cm.

Ohio anti-slavery society.
    Report of the second anniversary, 1837. Cin-
cinnati, Published by the Ohio anti-slavery society, 1837.
    67 p.   22 cm.

Ohio anti-slavery society.
    Report of the third anniversary, 1838. Cin-
cinnati, Published by the Ohio anti-slavery society, 1838.
    32 p.   23 cm.

Ohio anti-slavery society.
    Report of the fourth anniversary, 1839. Cin-
cinnati, Published by the Ohio anti-slavery society, 1839.
    23 p.   22 cm.

Ohio anti-slavery society.
    Report of the fifth anniversary, 1840. [Cin-
cinnati? 1840?]
    20 p.   24 cm.

Ohio. Auditor.
    Special report of the auditor of state. [Colum-

bus? 1863?] Shows number of colored persons
immigrated from other states since 1 March 1861.
[4] p. tables.   22 cm.

Ohio state Christian convention, Columbus, 1859.
Proceedings. [n.p., 1859?]
28 p.   21 cm.

Ojetti, Ugo, 1871-
... L'America vittoriosa ... Milano, Fratelli
Treves, 1899.
5 p.1., 343 p.   19 cm.

O'Kelly, Patrick.
Advice and guide to emigrants, going to the
United States of America ... Dublin, Printed by
W. Folds, 1834.
iv, [2], [5]-96, [2] p.   18 1/2 cm.

Olcott, Charles.
Two lectures on the subjects of slavery and
abolition. Compiled for the special use of anti-
slavery lectures and debaters ... Masillon, Ohio,
Printed for the author, 1838.
128 p.   23 cm.

Old Mose; or, The praying negro. [Cincinnati, American reform tract and book society, n.d.]
8 p.   18 1/2 cm.

[Oldmixon, John] 1673-
Das britische reich in America sammt dem ero-
berten Canada mit denen wichtigen inseln Guada-
loupe, Martinique und anderen See-Plätzen, order:
Kurzgefasste beschreibung der englandischen
Pflanzstadte ... in Nord America ... Dritter über
die halfte vermehrter druck. Sorau, Bey Gottlob
Hebold, 1761-62.
2 v. in 1. front., 3 fold. maps.   22 cm.

Oldmixon, John W.
Transatlantic wanderings; or, A last look at
the United States ... London, New York, G. Routledge & co., 1855.
iv, 189 p.   17 1/2 cm.

Olin, Stephen, 1797-
The life and letters of Stephen Olin ... late
president of the Wesleyan University ... New York,

Harper & brothers, 1854.
2 v. front. (port.)   20 cm.

Oliphant, Laurence, 1829.
On the present state of political parties in
America, by Laurence Oliphant ... Edinburgh
and London, W. Blackwood and sons, 1866.
30 p., 1 l.   22 cm.

Oliver, William.
Eight months in Illinois; with information
to emigrants ... Newcastle-upon-Tyne, Printed
by W. A. Mitchell, and sold by E. & T. Bruce
[etc.] 1843.
iv, 141, [1] p. 3 p.l.   20 cm.

Olliffe, Charles.
Scènes américaines; dix-huit mois dans le
Nouveau monde ... 2. ed. Paris, Amyot, 1853.
xvi, 344 p. front. (port.) illus.   19 cm.

Olmstead, Charles H.
Reminiscences of service with the First volunteer regiment of Georgia, Charleston harbor, in
1863. An address delivered before the Georgia
historical society, March 3, 1879, by Colonel
Charles H. Olmstead. Savannah, Ga., Printed
and presented by J. H. Estill, 1879.
15 p.   23 1/2 cm.

Olmsted, Frederick Law, 1822-1903.
A journey in the back country ... New York,
Mason brothers, 1860.
xvi, [11]-492 p.   19 cm.

Olmsted, Frederick Law, 1822-1903.
A journey in the seaboard slaves states, with
remarks on their economy ... New York, Dix &
Edwards; [etc.,etc.] 1856.
[ix]-xv, [1], 723, [1] p. 3 p.l., illus.
19 cm.

[Olney, George Washington] 1835-
A guide to Florida, "The land of flowers,"
containing an historical sketch, geographical,
agricultural and climatic statistics, routes of
travel by land and sea, and general information
invaluable to the invalid, tourist or emigrant...
New York, Cushing, Bardus & co., printers, 1872.

78, iii p. incl. illus., pl. front. (fold. map) 18 cm.

[Olshausen, Theodor] 1802-1869.
Die Vereinigten Staaten von Nordamerika im Jahre 1852. Eine statistische uebersicht mit besonderer rücksicht auf deutsche auswanderer zusammengestellt. Kiel, Akademische Buchhandlung, 1853.
iv, 76 p. 19 1/2 cm.

On protection to West-India sugar ... Second edition, corrected and enlarged, containing an answer to a pamphlet, written by Joseph Marryat, Esq., M. P., entitled "A reply," &c. &c. London, Printed for J. M. Richardson and J. Hatchard, 1823.
159 p. 21 cm.

On the relations of slavery to the war, and on the treatment of it necessary to permanent peace. A few suggestions for thoughtful and patriotic men. [n.p., n.d.]
8 p. 22 cm.

On slavery. [Cincinnati, American reform tract and book society, n.d.]
23 p. 18 cm.

O'Neall, John Belton.
The Negro Law of South Carolina collected and digested by John Belton O'Neall ... Columbia, printed by John G. Bowman, 1848.
56 p. 23 cm.

The operations of the French fleet under the Count de Grasse in 1781-2, as described in two contemporaneous journals. [Edited by John D. G. Shea] New York, 1864.
x, [11]-216 p., incl. plan. front. (port.), plates. 27 cm.

Opie, John Newton.
A rebel cavalryman with Lee, Stuart, and Jackson, by John N. Opie. Chicago, W. B. Conkey company, 1899.
326 p. front., illus., plates, ports., facsim. 20 cm.

O'Rielly, Henry.
    The great questions of the times, exemplified
in the antagonistic principles involved in the
slaveholders' rebellion against democratic institutions ... as set forth in the speech of the Hon.
Lorenzo Sherwood ... delivered at Champlain in
northern N. Y., Oct. 1862 ... New York, C. S.
Westcott & co., printers, 1862.
    31 p.   22 cm.

The origin and object of civil government, according
    to the views of the Society of Friends. Phila-
    delphia, Published by the Tract association of
    Friends [n.d.].
        12 p.   18 cm.

An original memoir, on the Floridas, with a general
    description, from the best authorities. By a
    gentleman of the south. Baltimore, Printed for
    Edward J. Coale, by Richard J. Matchett, March,
    1821.
        43 p.   22 1/2 cm.

Orr, Jehu Amaziah.
    A trip from Houston to Jackson, Miss., in
    1845. In Mississippi historical society publi-
    cations, v. 9, 1906, p. 173-178.

[Orr, Mrs. Lucinda (Lee)].
    Journal of a young lady of Virginia. 1782.
    Baltimore, J. Murphy and company, 1871.
        56 p.   22 1/2 cm.

Osborn, Charles, 1775-
    Journal of that faithful servant of Christ,
    Charles Osborn, containing an account of many of
    his travels and labors in the work of the minis-
    try, and his trials and exercises in the service
    of the Lord, and in defense of the truth, as it
    is in Jesus. Cincinnati, Printed by A. Pugh,
    1854.
        xv, 472 p.   21 cm.

Osborn, Hartwell.
    Trials and triumphs; the record of the Fifty-
    fifth Ohio volunteer infantry, by Captain Hart-
    well Osborn and others; with eighty portraits,
    four views, and ten maps. Chicago, A. C. McClurg
    & co., 1904.
        364 p. front., plates, ports., maps.   23 cm.

Osborne, William H.
The history of the Twenty-ninth regiment of
Massachusetts volunteer infantry, in the late
war of the rebellion. By William H. Osborne ...
Boston, A. J. Wright, printer, 1877.
393 p.   23 1/2 cm.

Ott, Adolf.
Der führer nach Amerika. Ein reisebegleiter
und geographisches handbuch, enthaltend schilderungen über die Verein. Staaten von Amerika
und Canada unter steter berücksichtigung der
wirthschaftlichen verhältnisse sowie der koloni-
sation. Erneute auflage des Handbuches für auswanderer. Mit originalberichten aus 30 ansiedelungen, 78 in der text eingefügten abbildungen
... [etc.] von Adolf Ott ... Basel, Im selbstverlag des verfassers [c1882].
1 p.l., xix [3] 530 p.   illus. (incl. maps)
6 fold. pl., port.   19 cm.

Otto, John.
History of the 11th Indiana battery, connected
with an outline history of the Army of the Cumberland during the war of the rebellion. 1861-
1865. By John Otto ... [Fort Wayne, Ind., W. D.
Page, 1894].
109, [2] p.   22 1/2 cm.

Owen, Robert Dale, 1801.
The wrong of slavery, the right of emancipation, and the future of the African race in the
United States. Philadelphia, J. B. Lippincott
& co., 1864.
246 p.   18 cm.

Owen, William, 1802-
... Diary of William Owen from November 10,
1824, to April 20, 1825, ed. by Joel W. Hiatt.
Indianapolis, The Bobbs-Merrill company, 1906.
vi, [7]-134 p.   24 1/2 cm.

Owen, William Miller, 1832-
In camp and battle with the Washington artillery of New Orleans. A narrative of events during
the late civil war from Bull Run to Appomattox
and Spanish Fort ... By William Miller Owen ...
Boston, Ticknor & co., 1885.
1 p.l., xv p., 1 l., 467 p. front., pl., maps.
22 1/2 cm.

Owens, John Algernon.
Sword and pen; or, Ventures and adventures
of Willard Glazier ... in war and literature ...
By John Algernon Owens ... Philadelphia, P. W.
Ziegler & company, 1881.
xvi p., 1 1., 21-436 p. front. (port.) plates.
19 1/2 cm.

Ozanne, T. D.
The South as it is, or Twenty-one years' experience in the southern states of America. By
the Rev. T. D. Ozanne, M. A. London, Saunders,
Otley, and co., 1863.
v, [1], 306 p. 20 cm.

P

Paasche, Hermann, 1851-
Kultur- und reiseskizzen aus Nord- und Mittel-
Amerika; entworfen auf einer zum studium der
zuckerindustrie unternommenen reise von dr. H.
Paasche ... Magdeburg, A. Rathke, 1894.
vi, 533 p. 22 1/2 cm.

Pacificus: the rights and privileges of the several
states in regard to slavery: being a series of
essays, published in the Western Reserve chronicle, (Ohio,) after the election of 1842. By
a Whig of Ohio. [n.p., n.d.]
16 p. 23 cm.

[Page, Frederic Benjamin].
Prairiedom; rambles and scrambles in Texas
or New Estremadura. By a suthron ... New York,
Paine & Burgess, 1845.
[iii]-vi, [11]-166 p. 2 p.l., 1 1., front.
(fold. map) 18 cm.

Page, James Madison, 1839-
The true story of Andersonville prison: a
defense of Major Henry Wirz, by James Madison
Page, late 2d lieut. Company A, Sixth Michigan
cavalry, in collaboration with M. J. Haley.
With portraits. New York and Washington, The
Neale publishing company, 1908.

248 p. front., ports.   21 1/2 cm.

Page, Karl G[ottfried].
    Darstellung der bürgerlichen verhältnisse in
den freistaaten von Nordamerika; nebst einer
merkwürdigen reise dahin ... Bautzen, Gedruckt
bei J. G. Lehmann (183-?]
    110, [2] p.   19 1/2 cm.

Pagès, Pierre Marie Francois, vicomte de, 1748-
    Voyages autour du monde, et vers les deux
poles, par terre et par mer, pendant les annees
1767, 1768, 1770, 1771, 1773, 1774, & 1776 ...
Paris, Moutard, 1782.
    2 v. 10 fold. plates (incl. 7 maps)   20 cm.

Paine, Albert.
    Clouds in the nation's sky. A discourse, de-
livered before the churches of North Adams, at
a union service held in the Baptist church, on
the day of the annual state thanksgiving, Nov.
25, 1858 ... North Adams, Clark & Phillips,
printers, 1858.
    12 p.   22 cm.

Paine, Robert, 1799-
    Life and times of William M'Kendree, Nash-
ville, Tenn., Publishing house of the Methodist
Episcopal church, south, 1870.
    2 v. front. (port.)   19 1/2 cm.

Pairpoint, Alfred J.
    Rambles in America, past and present ... With
illustrations by Miss N. M. Pairpoint ... Boston, A. Mudge & son, printers, 1891.
    viii [9]-251 p. front. (port.) illus.
19 1/2 cm.

Pairpoint, Alfred J.
    Uncle Sam and his country; or, Sketches of
America, in 1854-55-56 ... London, Simpkin, Marshall & co. [etc.] 1857.
    vii, 9-346 p. 2 p.l.   19 1/2 cm.

Palairet, Jean, 1697-
    A concise description of the English and French
possessions in North-America, for the better ex-
plaining of the map published with that title.
London, Printed by J. Haberkorn, and sold by

Nourse: [etc., etc.] 1775.
71, [1] p.   fold. map.   19 cm.

Palfrey, Francis Winthrop, 1831-1889.
Memoir of William Francis Bartlett. By Francis Winthrop Palfrey. Boston, Houghton, Osgood
and company, 1878.
1 p.l., 309 p. front. (port.) facsim.
18 1/2 cm.

Palfrey, John Gorham, 1796.
The inter-state slave trade. [New York,
American anti-slavery society, 1855?]
8 p.   19 cm.

Palfrey, John Gorham.
A letter to a friend ... Cambridge, Metcalf
and company, 1850.
28 p.   22 cm.

Palfrey, John Gorham, 1796.
Papers on the slave power, first published
in the "Boston Whig", in July, August, and September, 1846 ... Second edition. Boston, Merrill, Cobb & co. [1846?]
92 p.   22 cm.

Palfrey, John Gorham, 1796.
Papers on the slave power, first published
in the "Boston Whig" ... Boston, Merrill, Cobb
& co. [n.d.].
91 p.   23 cm.

Palfrey, John Gorham, 1796.
Speech of Mr. Palfrey, of Massachusetts, on
the political aspect of the slave question. Delivered in the House of Representatives, January
26th, 1848. Washington, J. & G. S. Gideon, 1848.
16 p.   22 cm.

Palisot de Beauvois, Ambroise Marie Francois Joseph,
1752-
Insectes recueillis en Afrique et en Amérique
... Paris, Impr. de Fain et compagnie [etc.]
1805.
xvi, 276 p. 2 p.l., col. plates.   39 cm.

Palliser, John, 1807-1887.
Solitary rambles and adventures of a hunter

in the prairies. London, J. Murray, 1853.
[v]-xiv, 326 p. 3 p.1., 1 1. plates.   19 cm.

Palmer, Abraham John, 1847-1922.
The history of the Forty-eighth regiment New
York state volunteers, in the war for the union.
1861-1865. By Abraham J. Palmer ... Brooklyn,
Pub. by the Veteran association of the regiment,
1885.
xvi, 314, 2 p. front., illus., pl., port.,
maps.   21 1/2 cm.

Palmer, Benjamin Morgan, 1818-1902.
The life and letters of James Henley Thornwell ... ex-president of the South Carolina
college, late professor of theology in the Theological seminary at Columbia, South Carolina.
By B. M. Palmer ... Richmond, Whittet & Shepperson, 1875.
xi p., 1 1., 614 p. front. (port.)   23 cm.

Palmer, Benjamin Morgan.
The south: her peril, and her duty, A discourse, delivered in the First Presbyterian
church, New Orleans, on Thursday, November 29,
1860. New York, Printed at the office of the
True witness and sentinel, 1860.
16 p.   22 cm.

Palmer, Donald McN.
Four weeks in the Rebel army. By Don Mc.N.
Palmer. New London [Conn.] D. S. Ruddock,
1865.
40 p.   22 cm.

Palmer, John, of Lynn, Eng.
Journal of travels in the United States of
North America, and in Lower Canada, performed in
the year 1817; containing particulars relating
to the prices of land and provisions, remarks on
the country and people, interesting anecdotes...
London, Sherwood, Neely, and Jones, 1818.
viii, 456 p. fold. map.   22 cm.

Palmer, Mrs. Sarah A.
The story of Aunt Becky's army life. By S.
A. Palmer. New York, J. F. Trow & co., 1867.
xix, 215 p. front. (port.) plates.   19 1/2 cm.

A pamphlet on equal rights and privileges. [n.p.,
n.d.].
24 p. 22 cm.

Pangborn, J[oseph] G[ladding].
The Glades of the Alleghenies. Deer Park,
Oakland. Baltimore, Baltimore & Ohio railroad
co., 1882.
32 p. incl. illus., plans. 12 cm.

Pangborn, Joseph Gladding, 1844-1914.
Picturesque B. and O. Historical and descriptive. By J. G. Pangborn. Chicago, Knight
and Leonard, 1882.
2 p.l. [7]-152 p. illus. 25 cm.

Parker, Amos Andrew, 1792-
Trip to the West and Texas. Comprising a
journey of eight thousand miles through New
York, Michigan, Illinois, Missouri, Louisiana
and Texas, in the autumn and winter of 1834-5
... Concord, N. H., White & Fischer, 1835.
276 p. 2 pl. (incl. front.) 18 1/2 cm.

Parker, Francis Jewett, 1825-1909.
The story of the Thirty-second regiment,
Massachusetts infantry. Whence it came; where
it went; what it saw, and what it did. By
Francis J. Parker, colonel. Boston, C. W. Cal-
kins & co., 1880.
xi, 200 p. 20 cm.

Parker, Joel.
The true issue, and the duty of the Whigs.
An address before the citizens of Cambridge,
October 1, 1856 ... Cambridge, James Munroe and
company, 1856.
92 p. 23 cm.

Parker, Nathan Howe.
Missouri as it is in 1867; an illustrated
historical gazetteer of Missouri, embracing the
geography, history, resources and prospects ...
The new constitution, the emancipation ordinance,
and important facts concerning "free Missouri."
An original article on geology, mineralogy, soils,
etc. by Prof. G.C. Swallow. Also special articles on climate, grape culture, hemp, and tobacco.
Illustrated with numerous original engravings.

By Nathan H. Parker ... Philadelphia, J. B. Lippincott & co., 1867.
4, [v]-xvi, 17-458 p. pl. 24 cm.

Parker, Nathan H[owe].
Parker's illustrated hand book of the great West. A record of statistics and facts, with practical suggestions for immigrants.... New York, American news co.; Boston, New England news co. [etc.] 1869.
162 p. pl., fold. maps. 8°.

Parker, Theodore, 1810.
An address delivered ... before the New York City Anti-slavery society, at its first anniversary, held at the Broadway Tabernacle, May 12, 1854. New York, American anti-slavery society, 1854.
46 p. 16 cm.

Parker, Theodore, 1810-1860.
The collected works of Theodore Parker ... containing his theological, polemical, and critical writings, sermons, speeches and addresses, and literary miscellanies. London, Trübner & co., 1863-71.
14 v. 20 cm.

Parker, Theodore, 1810-1860.
The dangers of slavery. Boston, Directors of the Old South work, Old South meeting house [1854?]
20 p. 19 cm.

Parker, Theodore, 1810.
The effect of slavery on the American people. A sermon preached at the Music Hall, Boston, on Sunday, July 4, 1858 ... Revised by the author. Boston, William L. Kent & company, 1858.
14 p. 22 cm.

Parker, Theodore, 1810.
The great battle between slavery and freedom, considered in two speeches delivered before the American anti-slavery society at New York, May 7, 1856 ... Boston, Benjamin H. Greene, 1856.
93 p. 22 cm.

Parker, Theodore, 1810-1860.
   John Brown's expedition reviewed in a letter...
to Francis Jackson, Boston, Published by the fraternity, 1860.
   19 p.   18 1/2 cm.

Parker, Theodore, 1810.
   Letter to the people of the United States
touching the matter of slavery. Boston, James
Munroe and company, 1848.
   120 p.   19 cm.

Parker, Theodore, 1810-1860.
   The Nebraska question. Some thoughts on the
new assault upon freedom in America, and the
general state of the country in relation there-
unto, set forth in a discourse preached at the
Music Hall, in Boston, on Monday, Feb. 12, 1854...
Boston, Benjamin B. Mussey & Co., 1854.
   72 p.   24 cm.

Parker, Theodore, 1810.
   The present aspect of slavery in America and
the immediate duty of the north. A speech delivered in the hall of the State House, before
the Massachusetts Anti-slavery convention, on
Friday night, January 29, 1858... Boston, Bela
Marsh, 1858.
   44 p.   22 cm.

Parker, Theodore, 1810-1860.
   The relation of slavery to a republican form
of government. A speech delivered at the New
England anti-slavery convention, Wednesday morning, May 26, 1858 ... Boston, William L. Kent
& Company, 1858.
   21 p.   23 1/2 cm.

Parker, Theodore, 1810.
   A sermon of slavery, delivered Jan. 21, re-
peated June 4, 1843, and now published by request
... Boston, Printed by Thurston and Torry, 1843.
   24 p.   17 cm.

Parker, Theodore, 1810.
   The three chief safeguards of society, con-
sidered in a sermon at the Melodeon, on Sunday,
July 4, 1851 ... Boston, Wm. Crosby and H. P.
Nichols, 1851.
   40 p.   23 cm..

Parker, Thomas H. capt. 51st Pa. infantry.
History of the 51st regiment of P. V. and V. V.,
from its organization, at Camp Curtin, Harrisburg, Pa., in 1861, to its being mustered out of
the United States service at Alexandria, Va.,
July 27th, 1865. By Thomas H. Parker ... Philadelphia, King & Baird, printers, 1869.
xx, [9]-703 p. front., ports. 21 1/2 cm.

Parker, Wooster.
The rule of duty. A sermon delivered in Dover,
on fast day, April 10, 1851. Bangor, Samuel S.
Smith, printer, 1851.
21 p. 18 cm.

Parkinson, Richard, 1748-
The experienced farmer's tour in America: exhibiting, in a copious and familiar view, the
American system of agriculture and breeding of
cattle, with its recent improvements ... London: Printed for the author, by T. Davison,
Whitefriars; and sold by G. and J. Robinson,
Paternoster-Row, 1805.
2 v. 21 1/2 cm.

Parrish, John.
Remarks on the slavery of the black people...
Philadelphia, printed by Kimber, Conrad, and Co.,
1806.
66 p. 21 cm.

Parsons, Charles Grandison, 1807-
Inside view of slavery: or, A tour among the
planters ... with an introductory note by Mrs.
H. B. Stowe. Boston, J. P. Jewett and company;
Cleveland, C. Jewett, Proctor and Worthington,
1855.
xii, [13]-318 p. 20 1/2 cm.

Parsons, Theophilus.
Slavery. Its origin, influence and destiny.
Boston, William Carter and brother, 1863.
36 p. 19 cm.

The past and present -- freedom national, slavery sectional. A document for the people. Contents.
1.-Declaration of independence, and the names of
the signers. 2.-Constitution of the United States,
and the amendments. 3.-The fugitive slave law

of 1850. 4.-Democratic platform, adopted at
Baltimore, June, 1852. 5.-Whig platform, adopted
at Baltimore, June, 1852. 6.-Independent democratic platform, adopted at Pittsburgh, Aug.,
1852. and 7.-Speech of Honorable Charles Sumner,
on his motion to repeal the fugitive slave bill.
Washington, Buell & Blanchard, 1853.
    16 p. 24 cm.

Patten, Edmund.
    A glimpse at the United States and the northern
states of America, with the Canadas, comprising
their rivers, lakes and falls during the autumn
of 1852; including some account of an emigrant
ship. By Edmund Patten, esq. With illustrations,
sketched and zincographed by the author. London, E. Wilson, 1853.
    iv, [5]-109 p. front., plates. 23 cm.

Pattie, James Ohio, 1804?
    The personal narrative of James O. Pattie,
of Kentucky, during an expedition from St. Louis,
through the vast regions between that place and
the Pacific Ocean, and thence back through the
city of Mexico to Vera Cruz, during journeyings
of six years ... Ed. by Timothy Flint. Cincinnati, E. H. Flint, 1833.
    xi, [13]-300 p. 5 pl. 19 1/2 cm.

Patton, Jacob Harris, 1812-1903.
    Natural resources of the United States ...
New York [etc.] D. Appleton and company, 1888.
    xv [1]-523 p. illus., diagrs. 21 cm.

Patton, William.
    The American crisis: or, The true issue,
slavery or liberty? ... London, Sampson Low,
Son, & Co., 1861.
    40 p. 18 cm.

Patton, William Weston, 1821.
    The American board and slaveholding ... Hart-
ford, W. H. Burleigh, printer, 1846.
    47 p. 17 1/2 cm.

Patton, William Weston, 1821.
    Conscience and the law; or, A discussion of
our comparative responsibility to human and
divine government: with an application to the

fugitive slave law ... New York, Mark H. Newman
& co. [etc., etc.] 1850.
    64 p.   16 cm.

Patton, William Weston, 1821.
    Freedom's martyr. A discourse on the death
of the Rev. Charles T. Torrey ... Hartford,
William H. Burleigh, 1846.
    19 p.   16 cm.

Patton, William Weston, 1821.
    Slavery and infidelity: or, Slavery in the
church ensures infidelity in the world ... Cincinnati, Am. reform book and tract society,
[1856].
    70 p.   15 cm.

Patton, William Weston, 1821.
    Slavery -- the Bible -- infidelity. An at-
tempt to prove that pro-slavery interpretations
of the Bible are productive of infidelity ...
Hartford, William H. Burleigh, printer, 1846.
    20 p.   18 cm.

Patton, William Weston, 1821.
    Thoughts for Christians, suggested by the
case of Passmore Williamson: A discourse preached
in the Fourth Cong. Church, Hartford, Conn. ...
October 7, 1855. Hartford, Conn., Press of Montague & co., 1855.
    23 p.   16 cm.

Patton, William Weston, 1821.
    What it is to preach the gospel. [Cincinnati,
American reform tract and book society, n.d.].
    24 p.   16 cm.

[Paulding, James Kirke] 1778-
    Letters from the South, written during an ex-
cursion in the summer of 1816. By the author of
John Bull and Brother Jonathan. New-York: Published by James Eastburn & co., at the Literary
rooms, Broadway, corner of Pine-street. Abraham
Paul, printer, 1817.
    2 v.   18 1/2 cm.

[Paulding, James Kirke] 1778-1860.
    Westward Ho! A tale. By the author of "The
Dutchman's fireside" ... New-York, J. & J. Harper,

1832.
    2 v.   17 1/2 cm.
    L. C. card no. 7-33782

Pavie, Theodore Marie, 1811-
    Souvenirs atlantiques. Voyage aux Etats-Unis
et au Canada ... Angers, Impr. de L. Pavie, 1832.
viii, 550, [2] p.   21 cm.

Paxton, John D. 1784.
    Letters on slavery; addressed to the Cumber-
land congregation, Virginia. By J. D. Paxton,
their former pastor. Lexington, Ky., A. T.
Skillman, 1833.
    2 p. 1., [vii]-viii, 207 p.   18 cm.

Payne, Edwin Waters, 1837-
    History of the Thirty-fourth regiment of Illi-
nois volunteer infantry. September 7, 1861,
July 12, 1865. [By] Edwin W. Payne ... [Clinton,
Ia., Allen printing company, printers, 1903].
viii, 370 p. front., illus., ports., maps.
23 1/2 cm.

Peabody, Andrew Preston.
    Position and duties of the north with regard
to slavery ... Newburyport, Charles Whipple,
1847.
    22 p.   18 cm.

Peabody, Andrew Preston.
    "The word of God is not bound." A sermon,
preached on Sunday afternoon, June 4, 1854 ...
Portsmouth, N. H., James F. Shores, Jr., Joseph
H. Foster, 1854.
    15 p.   23 cm.

Peabody, William Broun Oliver.
    An address delivered at Springfield, before
the Hampden colonization society, July 4th, 1828
... Springfield, Printed by S. Bowles, 1828.
    16 p.   22 cm.

Peak, Howard Wallace, 1856-
    A ranger of commerce; or, 52 years on the road,
by Howard W. Peak. San Antonio, Naylor printing
company [c1929].
    5 p.1., 262 p. front., pl., ports. 22 1/2 cm.

Pearce, James Alfred, 1804.
 Letter ... on the politics of the day. Letter from the Hon. Thomas G. Pratt, United States
senator from Maryland, to the Whigs of that state.
Speech of the Hon. Isaac D. Jones, delivered in
response to the call of a Democratic procession
at Princess Anne, Somerset county, Md., on the
evening of Tuesday, July 15, 1856, responding to
the call of a Democratic procession. Washington,
[Printed at the office of the Standard] 1856.
 16 p.   23 cm.

Pearce, James Alfred.
 Old line Whigs for Buchanan & Breckinridge.
Letters from Hon. James Alfred Pearce, and Hon.
Thomas G. Pratt, to the Whigs of Maryland.
Speeches of Hon. J. W. Crisfield, of Maryland,
and Hon. James B. Clay, of Kentucky. [n.p.,n.d.].
 16 p.   20 cm.

Pearse, James, 1786-
 A narrative of the life of James Pearse, in
two parts ... Rutland [Vt.] Printed by W. Fay,
for the author, 1825.
 vi, [7]-144 p.   18 1/2 cm.

Pease, Giles.
 "Who Is on the Lord's side?" Or, Does the
Bible sanction slavery ... Boston, Published by
Henry Hoyt, 1864.
 64 p.   18 cm.

Peck, John Mason, 1789-
 Forty years of pioneer life. Memoir of John
Mason Peck ... ed. from his journals and correspondence. By Rufus Babcock. Philadelphia, American Baptist publication society [1864].
 360 p.   front. (port.) pl.   20 cm.

Peck, John Mason, 1789-
 A guide for emigrants, containing sketches of
Illinois, Missouri, and the adjacent parts ...
Boston, Lincoln and Edmands, 1831.
 336 p. front. (fold. map).   15 cm.

Peckard, Peter, 1718?
 ... A sermon preached before the University
of Cambridge ... Cambridge, Printed by J. Arch-
deacon, printer to the University, for J. & J.

Merrill [etc.] 1788.
    xi, [13]-48 p.   19 cm.

Peckham, Rufus Wheeler.
    Speech ... on the Kansas and Nebraska question.
    Delivered in the House of Representatives, May 18,
    1854. Washington, John T. & Lem. Towers, 1854.
    15 p.   22 1/2 cm.

Peele, John R.
    From North Carolina to southern California
    without a ticket, and how I did it, giving my
    exciting experiences as a "hobo," by John Peele.
    [Tarboro? N. C.] Edwards & Broughton printing
    company, 1907.
    134 p.   front., illus., port.   18 1/2 cm.

Peet, Frederick Tomlinson.
    Civil war letters and documents.   Newport,
    R. I., Privately printed, 1917.
    285 p.   28 cm.

Pena y Reyes, Juan Antonio de la.
    Derrotero de la expedición en la provincia
    de los Texas, nuevo reyno de Phillipinas, que
    passa a executar el muy illustre senor D. Joseph
    de Azlor.   Mexico, Juan Francisco de Ortego
    Bonilla, 1722.
    20 1.   plans.   29 cm.

Pencil, Mark, pseud.
    White Sulphur papers; or, Life at the springs
    of western Virginia.   By Mark Pencil, esq.   New-
    York, S. Colman, 1839.
    xi, [13]-166 p.   19 1/2 cm.

Pendleton, Louis Beauregard, 1861-
    The sons of Ham.   A tale of the new South.
    Boston, Roberts brothers, 1895.
    3 p.1., 328 p.   19 cm.

Penn, William, 1644.
    ... William Penn's exhortation.   Philadelphia,
    Published by the Tract association of Friends
    [n.d.].
    4 p.   18 cm.

Pennington, James W. C.
    The fugitive blacksmith;   or, Events in the

history of James W. C. Pennington, pastor of a
Presbyterian church, New York ... Third edition.
London, Charles Gilpin, 1850.
    84 p.   16 cm.

Pennington, James W. C.
    The reasonableness of the abolition of slavery
at the south, a legitimate inference from the
success of British emancipation: An address delivered at Hartford, Connecticut, on the first
of August, 1856 ... Hartford, Press of Case,
Tiffany and company, 1856.
    20 p.   23 cm.

Pennington, James W. C.
    A text book of the origin and history, &c.,
&c. of the colored people ... Hartford, L. Skinner, 1841.
    96 p.   13 cm.

Pennsylvania anti-slavery society. Eastern executive
committee.
    Address of the eastern executive committee
of the state anti-slavery society, to the citizens of Pennsylvania. Philadelphia, Printed
by Merrihew and Gunn, 1838.
    16 p.   22 cm.

Pennsylvania colonization society.
    Report of the board of managers ... Philadel-
phia, Printed for the society by Thomas Kite,
1830.
    48 p.   21 cm.

Pennsylvania freedmen's relief association.
    [Report] [n.p., n.d.].
    6 p.   23 cm.

Pennsylvania. House of Representatives. Committee on
the judiciary.
    Report of the Committee on the judiciary re-
lative to the abolition of slavery in the District of Columbia and in relation to the colored
population of this country, Mr. Smith, of Franklin, chairman ... Harrisburg, Boas & Coplan --
printer, 1839,
    14 p.   22 cm.

Pennsylvania society for promoting the abolition of
slaves.
An address from the Pennsylvania society for
promoting the abolition of slavery for the relief of free Negroes unlawfully held in bondage
and for improving the condition of the African
race ... Philadelphia, printed by Hall and Atkinson, 1819.
6 p.   22 cm.

Pepper, George Whitfield, 1833-1899.
Personal recollections of Sherman's campaigns,
in Georgia and the Carolinas. By Capt. George
W. Pepper. Zanesville, O., H. Dunne, 1866.
522 p.   21 cm.

Percival, Charles G.
The trail of the "Bull-dog," a 50,000 mile
journey by motor car through the United States,
Canada, Mexico, B. C., Alaska, and the Klondike
... [n.p., 1911?]
cover-title, 96 p. illus. (incl. facsims.)
28 cm.

Perigny, Maurice de, 1877-
... En courant, le monde, Canada-Etats-Unis-
Corée-Japon-Mexique. Paris, Perrin et c^{ie}, 1906.
3 p.l., 238 p. [3] p.   19 cm.

Perkins, G. W.
Prof. Stuart and slave catching. Remarks on
Mr. Stuart's book "Conscience and the Constitution," at a meeting in Guilford, August 1, 1850,
commemorative of emancipation in the West Indies
... West Meriden, Ct., 1850.
28 p.   22 cm.

Perkins, Justin, 1803.
Our country's sin, a sermon preached to the
members and families of the Nestorian mission,
at Oroomiah, Persia, July 3, 1853 ... New-York,
H. B. Knight, 1854.
24 p.   22 cm.

Perley, Maie Clements.
Without my gloves, by Maie Clements Perley ...
Philadelphia, Dorrance and company [c1940].
279 p.   20 cm.

Perrin du Lac, Francois Marie, 1766-
    Voyage dans les deux Louisianes, et chez les
nations sauvages de Missouri, par les Etats-Unis,
l'Ohio et les provinces que le bordent, en 1801,
1802, et 1803; avec un aperçu des moeurs, des
usages, du caractère et des coûtumes religieuses
et civiles des peuples de ces diverses contrees.
Paris, Capelle et Renand; [etc., etc.] 1805.
    x, 479 p. 3 p.l., fold. pl., fold. map.
20 1/2 cm.

Perry, John Gardner, 1840-1926.
    Letters from a surgeon of the civil war; comp.
by Martha Derby Perry; illustrated from photographs. Boston, Little, Brown, and company, 1906.
    xii, p., 1 1., 225 p. 6 pl., 2 port. (incl.
front.)   21 cm.

Perry, John Jasiel, 1811.
    Freedom national-slavery sectional. Speech...
on the comparative nationality and sectionalism
of the Republican and Democratic parties, in the
House of Representatives, May 1, 1856, in committee of the whole on the state of the union.
[Washington, D. C., Buell & Blanchard, printers,
1856].
    15 p.   25 cm.

Persat, Maurice, 1788-
    Mémoires du commandant Persat, 1806 à 1844;
publiés avec une introduction et des notes par
Gustave Schlumberger ... Paris, Plon-Nouritt &
Cie., 1910.
    [v]-xxx, 367 p. 3 p.l., facsim.   23 cm.

Peters, Richard.
    Report of the case of Edward Prigg against the
Commonwealth of Pennsylvania. Argued and adjudged
in the Supreme Court of the United States, at
January term, 1842. In which it was decided
that all the laws of the several states relating
to fugitive slaves are unconstitutional and void;
and that Congress have the exclusive power of
legislation on the subject of fugitive slaves
escaping into other states ... Philadelphia, L.
Johnson, 1842.
    140 p.   25 cm.

Peters, Theodore Curtis.
A report upon the condition of the South, with regard to its needs for a cotton crop and its financial wants in connection therewith as well as the safety of temporary loans. Baltimore, Printed by H. A. Robinson, 1867.
23 p.   23 1/2 cm.

Peto, Sir Samuel Morton, bart., 1809-
The resources and prospects of America, ascertained during a visit to the States in the autumn of 1865. By Sir S. Morton Peto, bart. ... London and New York, A. Strahan, 1866.
xv, 428 p.   2 col. pl. (incl. front.)
22 1/2 cm.

Pettit, William V.
Addresses delivered in the hall of the House of Representatives, Harrisburg, Pa., on Tuesday evening, April 6, 1852, by William V. Pettit, Esq., and Rev. John P. Durbin, D. D.   Published by order of the Pennsylvania colonization society.   Philadelphia, Printed by W. F. Geddes, 1852.
47 p.   23 cm.

Peyton, John Lewis, 1824-1896.
The American crisis; or, Pages from the notebook of a state agent during the civil war. By John Lewis Peyton ... London, Saunders, Otley and co., 1867.
2 v. front. (port.)   21 cm.

Peyton, John Lewis, 1824-
Over the Alleghanies and across the prairies. Personal recollections of the far West, one and twenty years ago ... 2d ed. ... London, Simkin, Marshall and co., 1870.
xvi, 377 p.   19 1/2 cm.

Pfister, Albert von, 1839-
Nach Amerika im dienste Friedrich Schillers; der völkerfreundschaft gewidmet von Albert Pfister.   Stuttgart und Berlin, J. G. Cotta, 1906.
iv [3]-170 p.   22 1/2 cm.

Pfleiderer, J[oh.] G[ottlob].
Amerikanische reisebilder mit besonderer berücksichtigung der dermaligen religiösen und
kirchlichen zustände der Vereinigten Staaten, von
prof. dr. J. G. Pfleiderer ... Bonn, J. Scher-
gens, 1882.
xi, 212 p. illus. 19 cm.

Phelps, Amos Augustus.
Lectures on slavery and its remedy ... Boston,
Published by the New-England anti-slavery society, 1834.
xi, 284 p. 15 cm.

Phelps, Amos Augustus.
Letters to Professor Stowe and Dr. Bacon, on
God's real method with great social wrongs in
which the Bible is vindicated from grossly erroneous interpretations ... New York, Wm. Harned,
1848.
168 p. 19 cm.

Phelps, Matthew, c. 1748.
Memoirs of and adventures of Captain Matthew
Phelps ... Compiled from the original journal
and minutes kept by Mr. Phelps, during his voyages
and adventures, and revised and corrected according to his present recollection. By Anthony Haswell. From the press of Anthony Haswell, of
Bennington, in Vermont, 1802.
iv, [5]-210, 63 [3] xii p. 16 cm.

Phelps's travellers' guide through the United States;
containing upwards of seven hundred rail-road,
canal, and stage and steam-boat routes ... New
York, Ensigns & Thayer, 1848.
[7]-70 p. 4 p.l. fold. map. 14 1/2 cm.

Philadelphia female anti-slavery society.
Fifth annual report, January 10, 1839. Philadelphia, Merrihew and Thompson, printers, 1839.
15 p. 18 cm.

Philadelphia female anti-slavery society.
Eleventh annual report. January 9, 1845.
Philadelphia, Merrihew and Thompson, printers,
1845.
16 p. 19 cm.

Philadelphia female anti-slavery society.
Nineteenth annual report. [1852]. Philadelphia, Merrihew and Thompson, printers, 1853.
20 p. 18 cm.

Philadelphia female anti-slavery society.
Twenty-first annual report. Philadelphia,
Merrihew and Thompson's steam power printing
office, 1855.
20 p. 19 cm.

Philadelphia female anti-slavery society.
Twenty-second annual report. Philadelphia,
Merrihew and Thompson, printers, 1856.
24 p. 19 cm.

Philadelphia female anti-slavery society.
Twenty-sixth annual report. Philadelphia,
Merrihew and Thompson printers, 1860.
28 p. 19 cm.

Philadelphia female anti-slavery society.
Twenty-seventh annual report. Philadelphia,
Merrihew and Thompson, printers, 1861.
23 p. 19 cm.

Philadelphia female anti-slavery society.
Twenty-eighth annual report. Philadelphia,
Merrihew and Thompson, printers, 1862.
23 p. 19 cm.

Philadelphia female anti-slavery society.
Twenty-ninth annual report. Philadelphia,
Merrihew and Thompson, printers, 1863.
28 p. 19 cm.

Philadelphia female anti-slavery society.
Thirty-first annual report. February, 1865.
Philadelphia, Merrihew and son, printers, 1865.
30 p. 18 cm.

Philadelphia female anti-slavery society.
Thirty-second annual report. February, 1866.
Philadelphia, Merrihew and son, printers, 1866.
27 p. 19 cm.

Philadelphia female anti-slavery society.
Thirty-third annual report. February, 1867.

Philadelphia, Merrihew and son, printers, 1867.
32 p.   19 cm.

Philadelphia female anti-slavery society.
Thirty-fourth annual report. February, 1868.
Philadelphia, Merrihew and son, printers, 1867.
32 p.   19 cm.

Philadelphia female anti-slavery society.
Thirty-fifth annual report. February, 1869.
Philadelphia, Merrihew and son, printers, 1869.
27 p.   19 cm.

Philadelphia female anti-slavery society.
Thirty-sixth and final annual report, April,
1870. Philadelphia, Merrihew and son, printers,
1870.
48 p.   19 cm.

Philanthropist. The guardian genius of the federal
union ... New York, Published for the author,
1839.
288 p.   18 1/2 cm.

Philip, Charles.
The Sabbath the working-man's charter. [Cin-
cinnati, American reform tract and book society, n.d.].
8 p.   illus.   18 cm.

Phillippo, James Mursell, 1798-
The United States and Cuba ... London, Pew-
tress & co.; New York, Sheldon, Blakeman, & co.,
1857.
xi, 476 p.   20 cm.

Phillips, Stephen Clarendon, 1801.
An address on the annexation of Texas, and
the aspect of slavery in the United States, in
connection therewith. Delivered in Boston November 14 and 18, 1845, Boston, Wm. Crosby and
H. P. Nichols, 1845.
56 p.   20 cm.

Phillips, Wendell, 1811.
Argument of Wendell Phillips, Esq., against
the repeal of the personal liberty law, before
the committee of the legislature, Tuesday,

411

January 29, 1861. Phonographic report by J. M. W. Yerrinton. Boston, Published by R. F. Wallcut, 1861.
24 p. 18 cm.

Phillips, Wendell, ed.
The Constitution a pro-slavery compact: or, extracts from the Madison papers, etc. ... Third edition, enlarged. New York, American anti-slavery society, 1856.
208 p. 20 cm.

Phillips, Wendell, 1811.
No slave-hunting in the Old Bay state: an appeal to the people and legislature of Massachusetts. New York, American anti-slavery society, 1860.
23 p. 19 cm.

Phillips, Wendell, 1811.
The philosophy of the abolition movement. New York, American anti-slavery society, 1860.
47 p. 19 cm.

Phillips, Wendell.
Review of Lysander Spooner's essay on the unconstitutionality of slavery. Reprinted from the "Anti-slavery Standard," with additions ... Boston, Andrews & Prentiss, 1847.
95 p. 22 1/2 cm.

Phillips, Wendell, 1811.
Review of Webster's speech on slavery ... Boston, American A. S. society, 1850.
44 p. 21 cm.

Phillips, Wendell.
Speech of Wendell Phillips, Esq. at the Worcester disunion convention, January 15, 1857. Boston, American anti-slavery society, 1857.
16 p. 23 cm.

Phillips, Wendell.
William Lloyd Garrison. Eulogy by Wendell Phillips at the funeral of Garrison, May 28, 1879 [Boston, Directors of the Old South Work, Old South Meeting House, n.d.].
16 p. 19 cm.

Phillips, William.
The conquest of Kansas, by Missouri and her
allies. A history of the troubles in Kansas,
from the passage of the Organic Act until the
close of July 1856 ... Boston, Phillips, Sampson and company, 1856.
x, [11]- 414 p. 19 1/2 cm.

Pickard, Kate E. R.
The kidnapped and the ransomed, being the personal recollections of Peter Still and his wife
"Vina," after forty years of slavery ... with an
introduction by Rev. Samuel J. May; and an appendix by William H. Furness ... Syracuse, William T. Hamilton; New York and Auburn, Miller,
Orton and Mulligan, 1856.
xxiii, [24]-409 p. illus. 20 cm.

Pickering, Joseph.
Emigration, or no emigration; being the narrative of the author, (an English farmer) from the
year 1824 to 1830; during which time he traversed
the United States of America, and the British
province of Canada, with a view to settle as an
emigrant: containing observations on the manners
and customs ... the soil and climate ... London,
Longmans, Reese, Orme, Brown, and Greene, 1830.
x, 132 p. 1 p.l. 18 cm.

A picture of a picturesque country; the Land of the
Sky [resorts along the Southern railway in western North Carolina]. [New York, Frank Presbrey
Co., 1888?]
32 p. map, illus. 25 1/2 cm.

Pierce, Edward Lillie.
The negroes at Port Royal. Report of E. L.
Pierce, government agent to the Hon. Salmon P.
Chase, secretary of the treasury. Boston, Pub-
lished by R. F. Wallcut, 1862.
36 p. 18 cm.

Pierce, Franklin, pres. U. S., 1804-1869.
The Kansas question. An act organizing the
territorial government of Kansas, extracts from
President Pierce's message in regard to the Constitutional relations of slavery; special message
of the President in regard to Kansas affairs;

special message of the President in compliance
with a resolution of the Senate ... Washington,
Union office, 1856.
   31 p.   20 1/2 cm.

Pierce, George Foster, 1811-
   Incidents of western travel; in a series of
letters. Ed. by Thomas O. Summers. Nashville,
Tenn., Southern Methodist Publishing House, 1859.
   259 p.   illus., port.   19 cm.

Pierpont, John, 1785.
   The anti-slavery poems ... Boston, Oliver
Johnson, 1843.
   64 p.   16 1/2 cm.

Pierpont, John, 1785.
   A discourse on the covenant with Judas,
preached in Hollis-Street church, Nov. 6, 1842 ...
Boston, Charles C. Little and James Brown, 1842.
   39 p.   20 1/2 cm.

Pierson, Emily Catharine.
   Jamie Parker, the fugitive ... Hartford,
Conn., Brockett, Fuller, and co., 1851.
   192 p.   17 cm.

Pierson, Hamilton Wilcox, 1817-ed.
   American missionary memorial. Including biographical and historical sketches. Edited by
H. W. Pierson ... New York, Harper & brothers,
1853.
   xv, 504 p.   incl. illus. (incl. facsims.)
plates.   front.   22 1/2 cm.

Pierson, Hamilton Wilcox, 1817-1888.
   In the brush; or, Old-Time social, political,
and religious life in the Southwest.   By Rev.
Hamilton W. Pierson ... with illustrations by
W. L. Sheppard.   New York, D. Appleton & co.,
1881.
   iv, 321 p.   front., plates.   18 1/2 cm.

Pierson, Hamilton Wilcox, 1817-
   A letter to Hon. Charles Sumner, with "statements" of outrages upon freedmen in Georgia, and
an account of my expulsion from Andersonville,
Ga., by the Ku-Klux Klan.   By Rev. H. W. Pierson

414

... Washington, Chronicle print, 1870.
28 p. 20 1/2 cm.

[Pike, Albert] 1809.
Letters to the people of the northern states.
[n.p., n.d.].
35 p. 22 1/2 cm.

Pike, Albert, 1809-
Prose sketches and poems, written in the western country. Boston, Light & Horton, 1834.
viii, [9]-200 p. 18 1/2 cm.

Pike, Albert, 1809-
State or province? Bond or free? ... Addressed particularly to the people of Arkansas. [n.p., 1861].
40 p. 23 cm.

Pike, James, corporal, 4th regt., Ohio cavalry.
The scout and ranger: being the personal adventures of Corporal Pike, of the Fourth Ohio Cavalry. As a Texan ranger, in the Indian wars, delineating western adventure; afterward a scout and spy, in Tennessee, Alabama, Georgia, and the Carolinas, under Generals Mitchell, Rosecrans, Stanley, Sheridan, Lytle, Thomas, Crook, and Sherman. Fully illustrating the secret service. Twenty-five full-page engravings. Cincinnati & New York, J. R. Hawley & co., 1865.
xi, 19-394 p. incl. 24 pl. front. (port.)
22 cm.

Pitt, William.
The speech ... on a motion for the abolition of the slave trade, in the House of Commons, on Monday, the second of April, 1792. London, Printed by James Phillips, 1792.
32 p. 18 cm.

Pittenger, William, 1840-1904.
Capturing a locomotive: a history of secret service in the late war. By Rev. William Pittenger ... Washington, The National tribune, 1885.
354 p. front., plates, ports. 19 cm.

The planter: or, Thirteen years in the south. By a
northern man ... Philadelphia, H. Hooker, 1853.
275 p.   19 1/2 cm.

Platt, S. H.
The martyrs and the fugitive; or, A narrative
of the captivity, sufferings, and death of an
African family, and the slavery and escape of
their son. New York, Daniel Fanshaw, 1859.
95 p.   20 cm.

[Playfair, Hugo] R.N., pseud.?
The Playfair papers, or; Brother Jonathan,
the smartest nation in all creation ... London,
Saunders and Otley, 1841.
3 v. fronts., 5 pl. (part col.)   21 cm.

Playfair, Robert.
Recollections of a visit to the United States
and British provinces of North America, in the
years 1847, 1848, and 1849. Edinburgh [etc.]
T. Constable and co., 1856.
viii, 266 p.   19 cm.

Plum, William Rattle.
The military telegraph during the Civil War
in the United States, with an exposition of ancient and modern means of communication, and
of the federal and Confederate cipher systems;
also a running account of the war between the
states. Chicago, Jansen, McClurg & co., 1882.
2 v. front., illus., port., maps, facsims.
23 1/2 cm.

[Plumer, William].
Freedom's defence: or a candid examination
of Mr. Calhoun's report on the freedom of the
press, made to the Senate of the United States,
Feb. 4, 1836. By Cincinnatus [pseud.] Worcester,
Dorr, Howland & co., 1836.
24 p.   21 cm.

The poet Cowper and his brother. Philadelphia, Published by the Tract association of Friends [n.d.]
12 p.   18 cm.

Polenz, Wilhelm von, 1861-
 ... Das land der zukunft. 2. aufl. Berlin,
F. Fontane & co., 1903.
 3 p.l., 418 [2] p. 23 cm.

The policy of the south: from the Austin (Texas)
 state gazette. [n.p., n.d.]
 15 p. 22 cm.

The political duties of Christians. Report, adopted
 at the Spring meeting of the South Middlesex
 conference of churches, April 18, 1848. Boston,
 Andrews & Prentiss, 1848.
 40 p. 20 cm.

Pollard, Edward Albert, 1828-1872.
 Observations in the North: eight months in
 prison and on parole. By Edward A. Pollard.
 Richmond, E. W. Ayres, 1865.
 vii, [9]- 142 p. 20 1/2 cm.

Pollard, Edward Albert, 1828-
 Southern history of the war. New York, C.B.
 Richardson, 1866.
 2 v. fronts., ports. 23 1/2 cm.

Pollard, Edward Albert, 1828-
 The Virginia tourist. Sketches of the springs
 and mountains of Virginia; containing an exposition of fields for the tourist in Virginia;
 natural beauties and wonders of the state; also
 accounts of its mineral springs; and a medical
 guide to the use of the waters, etc., etc. By
 Edward A. Pollard ... Illustrated by engravings
 from actual sketches. Philadelphia, J. B. Lippincott & co., 1870.
 277 p. front. (fold. map) plates. 19 cm.

Pollard, Edward Alfred, 1831-
 Black diamonds gathered in the darkey homes
 of the South ... New York, Pudney & Russell,
 1859.
 xiv, [17]- 122 p. 19 cm.

Pollard, Edward Alfred, 1831-
 The lost cause regained. New York, G. W.
 Carleton & co., 1868.
 2 p.l., [7]-214 p. 19 cm.

[Pollard, Edward Alfred] 1831.
    The southern spy: or, Curiosities of negro
slavery in the south. Letters from a southerner
to a northern friend. Washington, H. Polkinhorn,
printer, 1859.
    72 p.   18 1/2 cm.

Polley, Joseph Benjamin, 1840-
    Hood's Texas brigade, its marches, its battles,
its achievements, by J. B. Polley ... New York
and Washington, The Neale publishing company,
1910.
    347 p.   front., pl., ports.   22 1/2 cm.

Pond, Enoch.
    Slavery and the Bible ... Boston, American
tract society [n.d.].
    16 p.   18 cm.

Poole, William Frederick, 1821-1894.
    Anti-slavery opinions before the year 1800 ...
To which is appended a facsimile reprint of Dr.
George Buchanan's oration on the moral and political evil of slavery, delivered at a public
meeting of the Maryland Society for promoting
the abolition of slavery, Baltimore, July 4, 1791.
Cincinnati, Robert Clarke & Co., 1873.
    102 p.   24 cm.

Pope, John.
    A tour through the southern and western terri-
tories of the United States of North-America;
the Spanish dominions on the river Mississippi,
and the Floridas; the countries of the Creek nations; and many uninhabited parts. Richmond,
Printed by J. Dixon, for the author, 1792. [New
York, C. L. Woodward, 1888].
    104, iv p.   23 cm.

Pope, William F. 1814-
    Early days in Arkansas; being for the most
part the personal recollections of an old settler
... Arranged and ed. by his son Dunbar H. Pope.
With an introduction by Hon. Sam W. Williams ...
Little Rock, Ark., F. W. Allsopp, 1895.
    330 p.   front., plates, ports.   20 cm.

Popp, Stephan, 1755-
    Popp's journal, 1777-1783, [ed.] by Joseph
G. Rosengarten. [Philadelphia, The Historical
society of Pennsylvania, 1902].
    25-41, 245-254 p. 3 maps.   24 1/2 cm.

Popular sovereignty in the territories. The Demo-
    cratic Record. The purpose of this publication
    is simply to exhibit the Democratic record, as
    it was made by the representative men of the
    party, on the doctrine of popular sovereignty in
    the territories. Baltimore, Murphy & Co. [n.d.].
    24 p.   21 cm.

"Popular sovreignty." The reviewer reviewed. By
    a southern inquirer. [Washington? 1859?]
    45 p.   22 cm.

Porcher, Francis Peyre, 1825-
    Resources of the southern fields and forests,
    medical, economical, and agricultural; being also
    a medical botany of the southern states; with
    practical information on the useful properties
    of trees, plants and shrubs. New ed., rev. and
    largely augm. Charleston, Walker, Evans & Cogs-
    well, printers, 1869.
    xv, 733 p.   23 1/2 cm.

Portalis, Albert Edouard, 1845-
    Les Etats-Unis, le self-government et le
    césarisme, par A. Edouard Portalis ... Paris, A.
    Le Chevalier, 1869.
    2 p.l., 280 p.   18 1/2 cm.

Porter, David Dixon, 1813-1891.
    Incidents and anecdotes of the civil war. By
    Admiral Porter ... New York, D. Appleton and
    co., 1885.
    357 p. front. (port.)   22 1/2 cm.

[Potter, Eliza].
    A hairdresser's experience in high life.
    Cincinnati, The author, 1859.
    iv, 11-294 p.   20 cm.

[Potter, Woodburne].
    The war in Florida: being an exposition of
    its causes, and an accurate history of the cam-

paigns of Generals Clinch, Gaines, and Scott ...
Baltimore, Lewis and Coleman, 1836.
viii, 184 p. front. (fold. map) fold. plans.
19 1/2 cm.

Powdermaker, Hortense.
After freedom; a cultural study in the deep
South, by Hortense Powdermaker. New York, The
Viking press, 1939.
xx, 408 p. incl. tables. 22 cm.

[Powell, Samuel].
Notes on "southern wealth and northern profits." Philadelphia, C. Sherman & son, 1861.
31 p. 23 cm.

Power, Tyrone, 1797-
Impressions of America; during the years
1833, 1834, and 1835 ... Second American edition. Philadelphia, Carey, Lea & Blanchard,
1836.
2 v. 19 cm.

Powers, Elvira J.
Hospital pencillings; being a diary while in
Jefferson general hospital, Jeffersonville, Ind.,
and others at Nashville, Tennessee, as matron
and visitor. By Elvira J. Powers ... Boston,
E. L. Mitchell, 1866.
viii, 211 p. front. 19 1/2 cm.

Powers, George Whitefield, b. 1833 or 4.
The story of the Thirty-eighth regiment of
Massachusetts volunteers. By George W. Powers.
Cambridge, Dakin and Metcalf, 1866.
x p., 1 l., 308 p. 19 1/2 cm.

Powers, Stephen.
Afoot and alone; a walk from sea to sea by
the southern route. Adventures and observations
in southern California, New Mexico, Arizona,
Texas, etc. By Stephen Powers ... Hartford, Conn.,
Columbian book company, 1872.
3 p.l., [xi]-xvi, [17]-327 p. front., illus.,
plates, 20 1/2 cm

Pownall, Thomas, 1722-
    A topographical description of such parts of
North America as are contained in the (annexed)
map of the middle British colonies, &c. in North
America ... London, J. Almon, 1776.
    vi, 46, 16 p. front. (fold. map) 42 1/2 cm.

Prejudice against color. New York [Published by R.
G. Williams for the American anti-slavery society, 1839?]
    16 p.   11 cm.

Prentice, Archibald, 1792-
    A tour in the United States ... London, C.
Gilpin, 1848.
    156 p.   19 cm.

Prentis, Noble Lovely, 1839-
    Southern letters. By Noble L. Prentis ...
Topeka, Kan., G. W. Martin, 1881.
    176 p.   20 1/2 cm.

Presbyterian church, Connecticut.
    Minority report, of a committee of the General
association of Connecticut, on the sin of slavery.
Presented, June 1849, at the meeting of the Association, at Salusbury; Conn. [Meriden, Conn.?
1849?]
    20 p.   25 cm.

Presbyterian church in the U.S.A. Synod of Kentucky.
    Address on slavery. [Newburyport? 1836?]
    24 p.   18 1/2 cm.

Presbyterian church in the U.S.A. Synod of Kentucky.
    An address to the Presbyterians of Kentucky,
proposing a plan for the instruction and emancipation of their slaves, by a committee of the
Synod of Kentucky. Cincinnati, Taylor & Tracy,
1835.
    64 p.   23 cm.

Presbyterian synod of South Carolina and Georgia.
    Report of the committee to whom was referred
the subject of the religious instruction of the
colored population of the synod, at its late
session in Columbia, (South-Carolina,) December

421

5th-9th, 1833 ... Charleston, Observer office
press, 1834.
   35 p.   17 cm.

The present state of the British empire in Europe,
   America, Africa and Asia. Containing a concise
   account of our possessions in every part of the
   globe ... London, Printed for W. Griffin [etc.]
   1768.
      vi, 486 p., 1 l. front., fold. maps. 21 cm.

Price, Isaiah, 1822-
      History of the Ninety-seventh regiment, Penn-
   sylvania volunteer infantry, during the war of
   the rebellion, 1861-65, with biographical sketches...
   Prepared at the request of the regiment, by
   Isaiah Price ... Philadelphia, By the author for
   the subscribers, 1875.
      viii, [3]-608 p., 1 l., front. illus., port.
28 cm.

Price, Morgan Philips, 1885-
      America after sixty years; the travel diaries
   of two generations of Englishmen, by M. Philips
   Price ... London, G. Allen & Unwin, ltd. [1936].
      235 p. incl. front. (ports.) pl.   22 1/2 cm.

Price, Thomas.
      Slavery in America: with notices of the
   present state of slavery and the slave trade
   throughout the world ... London, Published by
   G. Wightman, 1837.
      320 p.   23 cm.

Price, William Newton, 1831-1905.
      One year in the civil war; a diary of the
   events from April 1st, 1864, to April 1st, 1865,
   by William N. Price, a private soldier in company D, 6th Tennessee, United States volunteer
   ₄nfantry. n.p., 190-?
      59 p. 23 1/2 cm.

Priest, William.
      Travels in the United States of America; com-
   mencing in the year 1793, and ending in 1797.
   With the author's journals of his two voyages
   across the Atlantic ... London, Printed for J.

Johnson, 1802.
  ix, [1], 214 p. front. 22 cm.

Priestley, Herbert Ingram, 1875, ed. and tr.
  The Luna papers: documents relating to the
  expedition of don Tristan de Luna y Arellano for
  the conquest of La Florida in 1559-1561 ... translated and edited with an historical introduction
  by Herbert Ingram Priestley ... Deland, The Florida state historical society, 1928.
  2 v. front. (port.) facsims. 25 1/2 cm.

Priestley, Joseph.
  A sermon on the subject of the slave trade;
  delivered to a society of Protestant dissenters,
  at the New Meeting, in Birmingham; and published
  at their request ... Birmingham, Printed for the
  author, by Pearson and Rollason, 1788.
  40 p. 21 cm.

Principles and measures. Declaration of the convention
  of "Radical political abolitionists," at Syracuse,
  June 26th, 27th and 28th, 1855. [n.p.,n.d.]
  2 p. 24 cm.

Proceedings of the constitutional meeting at Faneuil
  hall, November 26th, 1850. Boston, Printed by
  Beals & Greene, 1850.
  46 p. 24 cm.

Proceedings of a convention of delegates, chosen by
  the people of Massachusetts, without distinction
  of party, and assembled at Faneuil Hall, in the
  city of Boston on Wednesday, the 29th day of January, A.D. 1845, to take into consideration the
  proposed annexation of Texas to the United States.
  Published by order of the convention. Boston,
  Eastburn's Press, 1845.
  18 p. 23 cm.

Proceedings of a meeting of the friends of African
  colonization, held in the city of Baltimore, on
  the seventeenth of October, 1827. Baltimore,
  Printed by B. Edes, 1828.
  27 p. 21 cm.

Proceedings of the National Liberty Convention, held
at Buffalo, N. Y., June 14th & 15th, 1848; including the resolutions and addresses adopted by
that body, and speeches of Beriah Green and Gerrit Smith on that occasion. [n.p.] 1848.
52 p. 22 1/2 cm.

Proceedings of the New England Anti-slavery Convention:
held in Boston, May 24, 25, 26, 1836. [n.p.,n.d.]
76 p. 23 cm.

Proceedings of the session of Broadway Tabernacle,
N. Y. City, against Lewis Tappan, with the action
of the presbytery and general assembly. [n.p.]
1839.
64 p. 22 1/2 cm.

The proceedings of the union meeting, held at Brewster's
Hall, October 24, 1850. Published by order of
the "Union Safety Committee". New Haven, William
H. Stanley, 1851.
48 p. 22 1/2 cm.

Proceedings of a union meeting, held in New York.
An appeal to the south. New-York, John H.
Duyckinck, 1860.
36 p. 23 cm.

The progress of colonial reform; being a brief view
of the real advance made since May 15th, 1823,
in carrying into effect the recommendations of
His Majesty, the unanimous resolutions of Parliament, and the universal prayer of the nation
with respect to negro slavery ... London, Anti-
slavery society, 1826.
49 p. 21 cm.

Prophecy. [Cincinnati, American reform tract and
book society, n.d.].
32 p. 18 cm.

The pro-slavery argument; as maintained by the most
distinguished writers of the southern states,
containing the several essays, on the subject,
of Chancellor Harper, Governor Hammond, Dr.
Simms, and Professor Dew. Charleston, S.C.,
Walker, Richards & co., 1852.
490 p. 21 cm.

Pro-slavery Bible. New York [Published by R. G. Williams for the American anti-slavery society, 1839?]
    8 p.   11 cm.

Protectionist ... Arnold Buffum, ed. v. 1, nos. 12-14; June 16 - Dec. 16, 1841. New Garden, Ind., Published by the executive committee of the state anti-slavery society, 1841.
    12 nos.   24 cm.

Protestant Episcopal church in the U.S.A. Board of missions. Domestic committee.
    Journal of a tour on the "Indian territory," performed by order of the Domestic committee... in the spring of 1844 ... New-York, Published for the Domestic committee of the Board of missions by Daniel Dana, jr., 1844.
    2 p.l., 74 p. front., 3 maps. (2 fold.) 22 cm.

Prutsman, Christian Miller.
    A soldier's experience in southern prisons, by C. M. Prutsman ... a graphic description of the author's experiences in various southern prisons. New York, A. H. Kellogg, 1901.
    80 p. front. (port.) 18 1/2 cm.

Pryor, Roger Atkinson, 1828.
    Speech ... on the principles and policy of the Black Republican party; delivered in the House of Representatives, December 29, 1859. Washington, Printed at the Congressional Globe office, 1859.
    14 p.   24 cm.

Pugh, James Lawrence, 1820.
    Speech ... on the election of speaker. Delivered in the House of Representatives, January 11, 1860. [Washington] Printed by Lemuel Towers [1860?]
    7 p.   22 cm.

Pulszky, Ferencz Aurelius, 1814-
    White, red, black. Sketches of society in the United States during the visit of their guest [Louis Kossuth] ... London, Trübner and co., 1853.

3 v.   18 1/2 cm.

Purviance, Levi.
     The biography of elder David Purviance, with
his memoirs ... written by himself: with an
appendix ... Together with a historical sketch
of the great Kentucky revival. Dayton, Pub.
for the author by B. F. & G. W. Ells, 1848.
     viii, [9]-304 p.   incl. front. (port.)
18 1/2 cm.

Purvis, Robert.
     A tribute to the memory of Thomas Shipley,
the philanthropist ... Delivered at St. Thomas'
church, November 23d, 1836 ... Philadelphia,
Merrihew and Gunn, 1836.
     18 p.   22 cm.

Putnam, George.
     God and our country. A discourse delivered
in the First Congregational church in Roxbury,
on fast day, April 8, 1847 ... Second edition.
Boston, Wm. Crosby and H. P. Nichols, 1847.
     29 p.   23 cm.

Putnam, George Haven, 1844-1930.
     A prisoner of war in Virginia 1864-5, by
George Haven Putnam, adjt, and bvt.-major
176th N.Y.S. vols. Reprinted, with additions,
from the report of an address presented to the
N. Y. commandery of the U. S. loyal legion,
December 7, 1910 ... New York and London, G.P.
Putnam's sons, 1912.
     v. 104 p.   incl. plates. front. (port.)
plates.   21 1/2 cm.

[Putnam, George W.]
     Four months with Charles Dickens. During
his first visit to America (in 1842). By his
secretary. In Atlantic Monthly, vol. XXVI
(1870), pp. 476-82.   591-99.

[Putnam, Sallie A. (Brock) "Mrs. Richard Putnam"]
     Richmond during the war; four years of per-
sonal observation. By a Richmond lady. New
York, G. W. Carleton & co.; [etc.,etc.] 1867.
     2 p.l., [ix]-xiv, [15]-389 p.   19 cm.

Putnam, Samuel Henry.
The story of Company A, Twenty-fifth regiment, Mass. vols. in the war of the rebellion.
By Samuel H. Putnam. Worcester, Putnam, Davis
and co.m 1886.
1 p.l., 324 p. front. (port.) maps.
24 1/2 cm.

Q

Quarterly anti-slavery magazine, ed. by Elizur
Wright, jr. v. 1-2; Oct. 1835 - July 1837.
New York, Published by the American anti-
slavery society, 1835-37.
2 v.   21 cm.

Quentin, Karl.
Reisebilder und studien aus dem norden der
Vereinigten Staaten von Amerika ... Arnsberg,
H. F. Grote, 1851.
2 pts. in 1 v.   22 1/2 cm.

[Quesada, Vicente Gregorio] 1830.
... Los Estados Unidos y la América del Sur;
los yankees pintados por si mismos. Buenos
Aires [etc.] J. Peuser, 1893.
xviii, 374 p.   18 cm.

Question of questions. [Cincinnati, American reform tract and book society, n.d.].
2 p.   16 1/2 cm.

Quincy, Josiah.
Address illustrative of the nature and power
of the slave states, and the duties of the free
states: delivered at the request of the inhabitants of the town of Quincy, Mass., on Thursday,
June 5, 1856 ... Boston, Ticknor and Fields,
1856.
32 p.   23 1/2 cm.

Quincy, Josiah, 1772-
Memoir of the life of Josiah Quincy, jun.,
of Massachusetts: by his son, Josiah Quincy...

Boston, Cummings, Hilliard, & company, 1825.
viii, 498 p. 2 facsim. 22 1/2 cm.

Quincy, Samuel Miller, 1833-1887.
History of the Second Massachusetts regiment of infantry. A prisoner's diary. A paper
read at the officers' reunion in Boston, May 11,
1877, by Samuel M. Quincy ... Boston, G. H.
Ellis, printer, 1882.
24 p. 24 cm.

Quint, Alonzo Hall, 1828-1896.
The Potomac and the Rapidan. Army notes
from the failure at Winchester to the reenforce-
ment of Rosecrans. 1861-3. By Alonzo H. Quint...
Boston, Crosby and Nichols; New York, O.S. Felt,
1864.
407 p. front. (fold. map). 20 cm.

Quint, Alonzo Hall, 1828-1896.
The record of the Second Massachusetts infantry, 1861-65. By Alonzo H. Quint, its
chaplain. Boston, J. P. Walker, 1867.
viii p., 1 1., 528 p. front., port. 20 1/2 cm.

Quintard, Charles Todd, bp., 1824-1898.
Doctor Quintard, chaplain C.S.A. and second
bishop of Tennessee; being his story of the war
(1861-1865) ed. and extended by the Rev. Arthur
Howard Noll ... Sewanee, Tenn., The University
press, 1905.
5 p.1., 183 p., 1 1., vi p. front. (port.)
20 1/2 cm.

R

R., J.
The portfolio; or, A view of the manners and
customs of various countries; interspersed with
anecdotes of former times, in letters to a
friend. By J. R., late captain in the Royal Lan-
cashire militia and formerly of the Royal fuzi-
leers. London, Printed by Dean and Schulze, for

T. Egerton, Whitehall, 1812.
2 v. 23 cm.

Rafinesque, Constantine Samuel, 1783-1840.
Ichthyologia ohiensis, or Natural history
of the fishes inhabiting the river Ohio and its
tributary streams, preceded by a physical description of the Ohio and its branches ... Lexington, Ky., Printed for the author by W. G.
Hunt, 1820.
5-90 p., 1 p.1. 23 cm.

Rafinesque, Constantine Samuel, 1783-1820.
A life of travels and researches in North
America and south Europe; or, Outlines of the
life, travels and researches of C. S.Rafinesque
... Philadelphia, Printed for the author by F.
Turner, 1836.
148 p. 20 1/2 cm.

Rainier, Peter William.
American hazard [by] P. W. Rainier. London,
J. Murray [1942].
viii, 262 p. 21 cm.

Rains, George Washington, 1817-
History of the Confederate power works ...
An address delivered by invitation before the
Confederate survivors' association, at its
fourth annual meeting, on Memorial day, April
26th, 1882. Augusta, Ga., Chronicle & consti-
tutionalist print, 1882.
30 p. 22 cm.

Ralph, Julian, 1853-
Dixie; or, Southern scenes and sketches, by
Julian Ralph ... New York, Harper & brothers,
1896.
xii, 1 1., 412 [2] p. front., illus., plates.
23 cm.

[Ramberg, Carl August] 1873-
På ströftag. Resebref till Handelstidningen
från skilda luftstreck. Göteborg, Göteborgs
handelstidnings aktiebolags tryckeri, 1905.
cover-title, 85, 209, 105, 157 p. 19 cm.

The Rambler, or, A tour through Virginia, Tennessee,
    Alabama, Mississippi, and Louisiana; describing
    the climate, the manners, customs and religion
    of the inhabitants. Interspersed with geographi-
    cal and political sketches. By a citizen of
    Maryland. Annapolis, Printed by J. Green, 1828.
    iv, [5]-41, [1] p.   19 cm.

"Rambler," pseud.
    Guide to Florida. By "Rambler." New York,
    The American news company, 1875.
    3 p.l., 7-146 p.   front., plates, fold. map.
    18 1/2 cm.

Ramsay, David, 1749-
    A sketch of the soil, climate, weather, and
    diseases of South-Carolina, read before the medi-
    cal society of that state ... Charleston: Prin-
    ted by W. P. Young, Franklin's head, no. 43,
    Broad-Street, 1796.
    30 p. 2 p.l., 3 fold. tables.   22 1/2 cm.

Ramsay, James.
    An essay on the treatment and conversion of
    African slaves in the British sugar colonies ...
    London, Printed and sold by James Phillips, 1784.
    xx, 298 p.   21 cm.

Ramsay, James.
    Examination of the Rev. Mr. Harris's scriptural
    researches on the licitness of the slave trade ...
    London, Printed by James Phillips, 1788.
    29 p.   20 cm.

Ramsay, James.
    Objections to the abolition of the slave trade,
    with answers ... London, Printed and sold by
    James Phillips, 1778.
    60 p.   22 cm.

Rand, Asa.
    The slave-catcher caught in the meshes of eter-
    nal law ... Cleveland, Steam-press of Smead and
    Cowles, 1852.
    43 p.   19 cm.

Rankin, John.
    An address to the churches in relation to

slavery. Delivered at the first anniversary of
the Ohio state anti-slavery society ... with a
few introductory remarks by a gentleman of the
bar ... Medina, Ohio, Printed at the anti-slavery
office, 1836.
8 p.   24 cm.

Rankin, John.
Letters on American slavery addressed to Mr.
Thomas Rankin, merchant at Middlebrook, Augusta
co., Va. ... Boston, Garrison & Knapp, 1833.
vi, [7]-118 p.   17 cm.

Rankin, John.
A review of the statement of the faculty of
Lane seminary, in relation to the recent diffi-
culties in that institution ... Ripley [Ohio].
Published by the author, 1835.
8 p.   22 cm.

Ransom, John L.
Andersonville diary, escape, and list of the
dead, with name, co., regiment, date of death and
no. of grave in cemetery. John L. Ransom ...
author and publisher. Auburn, N. Y., 1881.
304 p.   incl. illus., ports.   19 cm.

Rantoul, Robert.
Memoirs, speeches and writings of Robert Rantoul, Jr. Edited by Luther Hamilton. Boston,
John P. Jewett and company, 1854.
xii, 864 p.   18 1/2 cm.

Rasmussen, Vilhelm, 1869-
U. S. A., Amerikas forenede stater, af Vilhelm Rasmussen; med 72 illustrationer. København,
I kommission hos G. E. C. Gad, 1932.
243, [3] p. illus.   20 1/2 cm.

Raumer, Friedrich Ludwig George von, 1781-
America and the American people ... Tr. from
the German by William W. Turner. New York, J.&
H. G. Langley, 1846.
512 p.   fold. tab.   22 1/2 cm.

Rauscher, Frank.
Music on the march, 1862-'65, with the Army of
the Potomac. 114th regt. P. V., Collis' Zouaves.

By Frank Rauscher. Philadelphia, Press of W. F.
Fell & co., 1892.
vii, 9-270 p. illus. (music) pl., ports.
(incl. front.)   19 1/2 cm.

Raymond, Daniel.
The Missouri question.   Baltimore, Schaeffer
& Maund, printers, 1819.
39 p.   22 1/2 cm.

Raymond, Henry Jarvis, 1820.
Restoration and the president's policy. Speech
... on changing the basis of representation, and
in reply to Hon. S. Shellabarger, of Ohio; in the
House of Representatives, January 29, 1866. Washington, Printed at the Congressional globe office,
1866.
24 p.   23 cm.

[Raynal, Guillaume Thomas Francois] 1713-
Histoire philosophique et politique, des établ-
issemens & du commerce - - Supplements ... A la
Haye, 1781.
4 v.   fold.   tables.   20 cm.

Reach, Angus B.
The slave chase. From the entertainment of
negro life in freedom & in slavery. Words by
Angus B. Reach. The music composed and dedicated as a mark of esteem to George Bond, Esqr.
by Henry Russell. London, Chappell [n.d.]
7 p.   music.   34 1/2 cm.

Read, Hollis.
The negro problem solved; or, Africa as she
was, as she is, and as she shall be. Her curse
and her cure ... New York, A. A. Constantine,
1864.
418 p.   illus., front.   18 cm.

Read, John M.
Speech ... on the power of Congress over the
territories, and in favor of free Kansas, free
white labor, and of Fremont and Dayton. Delivered on Tuesday evening, September 30, 1856,
at Philadelphia. Philadelphia, Printed by C.
Sherman & son, 1856.
46 p.   23 cm.

Read, Opie Percival, 1852-1939.
    An Arkansas planter ... Cover and illustrations
by W. W. Denslow and Ike Morgan. Chicago and New
York, Rand McNally & company [c1896].
    315 p.   front., illus.   20 cm.

Read, Opie Percival, 1852-1939.
    On the Suwanee River; a romance.   [Golden rod
ed.]   Chicago, Laird & Lee [c1895].
    254 p.   incl. front., illus.   18 1/2 cm.

Reception of George Thompson in Great Britain. Compiled from various British publications. Boston,
Isaac Knapp, 1836.
    xvi, [13]-238 p.   14 cm.

Reck, Philipp Georg Friedrich von, 1710-
    An extract of the journals of Mr. Commissary
Von Reck, who conducted the first transport of
Saltzburgers to Georgia; and of the Reverend
Mr. Bolzius, one of their ministers ... London,
Printed by M. Downing, M.DCC.XXXIV [?]
    72 p.   2 p.l.   17 cm.

Redondo y Godino, Juan, 1859-
    Recuerdos de un viaje a America, por d. Juan
Redondo ... Madrid, Impr. de la "Revista general
de marina," 1905.
    235 p., 1 l.   incl. illus., port.   20 1/2 cm.

Redpath, James.
    Echoes of Harper's Ferry ... Boston, Thayer
and Eldridge, 1860.
    513 p.   19 cm.

Redpath, James.
    The public life of Capt. John Brown, ... with
an auto-biography of his childhood and youth.
Boston, Thayer and Eldridge, 1860.
    408 p.   19 cm.

Redpath, James, 1833-1891.
    The roving editor: or, Talks with slaves in
the southern states. New York, A. B. Burdick,
1859.
    xvi, 349 p.   front., pl.   18 1/2 cm.

Reed, Andrew, 1787-1862.
    A Narrative of the visit to the American
churches, by the deputation from the Congrega-

tional Union of England and Wales. By Andrew
Reed, D. D. and James Matheson, D. D. ... London,
Jackson and Walford, 1835.
  2 v. 8°.

Reed, Henry.
    Southern slavery and its relations to northern
industry: A lecture delivered at the Catholic
Institute, in Cincinnati, January 24, 1862, by
Henry Reed. Cincinnati, Enquirer steam presses,
1862.
    36 p. 23 1/2 cm.

Reed, Isaac.
    The Christian traveller. In five parts. In-
cluding nine years, and eighteen thousand miles.
New York, Printed by J. & J. Harper, 1828.
    242 p. 17 cm.

Reed, William Howell, 1837-
    Hospital life in the Army of the Potomac. By
William Howell Reed. Boston, W. V. Spencer,
1866.
    199 p. 18 1/2 cm.

Reese, David M.
    A brief review of the first annual report of
the American anti-slavery society, with the
speeches delivered at the anniversary meeting,
May 6th, 1834. New York, Published by Howe &
Bates, 1834.
    45 p. 22 cm.

Reese, David Meredith, 1800.
    Letters to the Hon. William Jay, being a re-
ply to his "Inquiry into the American colonization
and American anti-slavery societies" ... New
York, London, Leavitt, Lord & co.; Boston, Crocker & Brewster, 1835.
    xii, 120 p. 18 cm.

Regan, John.
    The emigrant's guide to the western states of
America; or, Backwoods and prairies ... 2d ed.,
rev. and enl. Edinburgh, Oliver & Boyd; [etc.,
etc., 1852].
    vii, [6], [9] - 408 p. front., 1 illus.
18 cm.

Register of traders of the colored people in the city
of Philadelphia and districts. Philadelphia,
Merrihew and Gunn, printers, 1838.
    8 p.   24 cm.

Reid, Hugo, 1809-
    Sketches in North America; with some account
of Congress and of the slavery question ... London, Longman, Green, Longman & Roberts, 1861.
    vi, [9]-320 p.   1 l.   16 1/2 cm.

Reid, Jesse Walton, b. 1824.
    History of the Fourth regiment of S. C. volun-
teers, from the commencement of the war until
Lee's surrender. Giving a full account of all
its movements, fights and hardships of all kinds.
Also a very correct account of the travels and
fights of the Army of northern Virginia ... This
book is a copy of letters written in Virginia at
the time by the author and sent home to his family ... With a short sketch of the life of the
author.   By J. W. Reid ... Greenville, S. C.,
Shannon & co., printers, 1892.
    143 p. incl. front. (port.)   22 1/2 cm.

Reid, John Coleman, 1824-
    Reid's tramp, or, A journal of the incidents
of ten months' travel through Texas, New Mexico,
Arizona, Sonora and California. Including topography, climate, soil ... Selma, Ala., Printed
at the Book and job office of John Hardy & co.,
1858.
    237 p.   21 cm.

Reid, Samuel Chester, 1818-
    The scouting expeditions of McCulloch's Texas
rangers; or, The summer and fall campaign of the
army of the United States in Mexico - 1846 ...
Philadelphia, G. B. Zieber and co., 1847.
    251 p. front., 8 pl., 3 port., plan.
19 cm.

Reid, Whitelaw, 1837-
    After the war; a southern tour. May 1,
1865, to May 1, 1866, by Whitelaw Reid. Cincinnati, New York, Moore, Wilstach & Baldwin; [etc.,
etc.] 1866.
    viii, [9]-589 p. plates, 2 port. (incl.
front.)   20 cm.

Reise von Hamburg nach Philadelphia. Hannover, Rits-
cher sche Buchhandlung, 1800.
208 p. 15 cm.

Rejected stone; or, Insurrection vs. resurrection in
America. By a native of Virginia. Second edition. Boston, Walker, Wise, and company, 1862.
131 p. 18 cm.

A relation of Maryland; together with a map of the
country, the conditions of plantation, His Majesties charter to the Lord Baltimore, translated
into English. These bookes are to bee had, at
Master William Peasley, esq. ... or at Master
John Morgan's house in High Holbourne ... September the 8th Anno Dom. 1634.
56, 25 (i.e. 23) p. 1 p.l., fold. map.
17 x 13 cm.

A relation of the successfull beginnings of the Lord
Baltemore's plantation in Mary- land; being an
extract of certaine letters written from thence,
by some of the adventurers to their friends in
England ... Anno Domini 1634. [Albany, N. Y.,
Reprinted by J. Munsell, 1865].
[5]-23, [1] p. 3 p.l. 22 cm.

Religious anti-slavery convention.
The declaration and pledge against slavery,
adopted by the religious anti-slavery convention,
held at the Marlboro' chapel, Boston, February
26, 1846. Boston, Devereux & Seaman, 1846.
8 p. 22 cm.

Religious duties, consisting chiefly of extracts from
the Holy Scriptures. Philadelphia, Published by
the Tract association of Friends [n.d.].
24 p. 18 cm.

Remarks of Mr. Duncan, of Ohio, on the right of petition: delivered in the House of Representatives,
January 6, 1844. Washington, Globe office, 1844.
8 p. 22 1/2 cm.

Remarks on African colonization and the abolition of
slavery. In two parts. By a citizen of New
England. Windsor, Vt., Richards & Tracy, 1833.
47 p. 22 cm.

Remarks on the constitution, by a friend of humanity,
on the subject of slavery. Philadelphia, Printed
at the office of the "Evening star," 1836.
12 p.   22 cm.

Remarks on Dr. Channing's slavery. By a citizen of
Massachusetts. Third edition. Boston, Russell,
Shattuck and co., and John H. Eastburn, 1835.
48 p.   22 cm.

Remarks on the new sugar bill and on the national com-
pacts respecting the sugar trade and slave trade
... London, J. Johnson, and J. Debrett, 1792.
82 p.   21 cm.

The rendition of fugitive slaves. The acts of 1793
and 1850, and the decisions of the supreme court
sustaining them. The Dred Scott cases--what the
court decided. [n.p.] Published by the National
Democratic campaign committee, 1860.
15 p.   23 cm.

Renz, Hugo.
Eine reise nach den Vereinigten Staaten bei
anlass der weltausstellung. Basel, Krebs, 1905.
77 p.   26 cm.

A report and treatise on slavery and the slavery agitation. Printed by order of the House of Representatives of Texas. December, 1857. Austin,
John Marshall & Co., 1857.
81 p.   21 cm.

Report of the annual meeting of the Glasgow emancipation society, held August 8, 1840:   containing,
with other matter, I. Speech of William Dawes,
giving information respecting Oberlin Institute,
a most interesting seminary in Ohio, U. S. in
aid of the abolition of slavery;   II. Speech of
the Rev. J. Keep;   III. Speech of L. Remond;
and   IV. Speech of the Rev. Alex Harvey, pre-
scribing the duty of British christian churches
towards their christian brethren in the United
States. Reprinted from the Glasgow Argus. Glasgow, John Clark, 1840.
23 ..   18 cm.

Report of the proceedings of the great anti-slavery
meeting, held at the Town hall, Birmingham, on

Wednesday, October 14th, 1835; with an appendix, containing notices of the condition of the apprenticed labourers in the West Indies under the act for the abolition of slavery in the British colonies ... Birmingham, Printed by B. Hudson, 1835.
26 p.   21 cm.

Report of the proceedings of a meeting held at Concert hall, Philadelphia, on Tuesday evening November 3, 1863, to take into consideration the condition of the freed people of the south.   Philadelphia, Merrihew and Thompson, printers, 1863.
24 p.   23 cm.

Report of the select committee on the subject of laws making distinction on account of color.   In House Jan. 2, 1847.   [n.p.] 1847.
7 p.   23 cm.

A report of the trial of Arthur Hodge, Esquire ... at the island of Tortola, on the 25th April, 1811, and adjourned to the 29th of the same month; for the murder of his Negro man slave named Prosper. Stenographically taken by A. M. Belisario, Esquire.   Middletown, [Connecticut] printed by Tertius Dunning, 1812.
18 p.   19 cm.

Report on the deliverance of citizens, liable to be sold as slaves.   Commonwealth of Massachusetts, House of Representatives, March 6, 1839.   No. 38. Thomas Kinnicutt, Chairman.   [Boston, 1839].
36 p.   26 cm.

Republican documents.   Proceedings of the meeting held at the Tabernacle, in the city of New York, on the 29th of April, 1856 ... [n.p., n.d.].
40 p.   23 cm.

The rescuer ... Cuyahoga county jail, July 4, 1859.
v. 1., no. 1 [Cleveland, 1859].   44 cm.

The responsibility of the north in relation to slavery.   Cambridge, Printed by Allen and Farnham, 1856.
15 p.   23 cm.

Revel, [Gabriel] Joachim du Perron, comte de, 1756-
    Journal particulier d'une campagne aux Indes
    occidentales (1781-1782) ... Paris, H. Charles-
    Lavauzelle [1898?]
        287 p. incl. maps. 22 cm.

Revel, James.
    The poor unhappy transported felon's sorrow-
    ful account of his fourteen years transportation
    in Virginia, in America. In six parts. Being a
    remarkable and succinct history of the life of
    James Revel, the unhappy sufferer ... With an
    account of the transports' work, and the punish-
    ment they receive for committing any fault. Lon-
    don, Printed by J. Marshall [n.d.].
        8 p. 21 cm.

Review of Dr. H. Duncan's letters on the West India
    question. [Extracted from the Christian instruc-
    tor for January and September 1831.] Edinburgh,
    Printed for William Whyte & co., 1831.
        49 p. 20 cm.

A review of Mr. Mitchell's sermon, by one of his
    parishioners. Northhampton, Gazette office,
    1837.
        32 p. 21 1/2 cm.

A review of the official apologies of the American
    tract society, for its silence on the subject of
    slavery. From the New-York Daily tribune. New-
    York, Published by the American abolition soci-
    ety, 1856.
        16 p. 23 cm.

Review of pamphlets on slavery and colonization. First
    published in the Quarterly Christian spectator
    for March 1833. Second separate edition. New-
    Haven, Published and sold by A. H. Maltby, 1833.
        24 p. 22 1/2 cm.

Review of the slave question, extracted from the Ameri-
    can quarterly review, Dec. 1832: based on the
    speech of the Marshall, of Fauquier, showing that
    slavery is the essential hindrance to the pros-
    perity of the slave-holding states; with particu-
    lar reference to Virginia, though applicable to
    other states where slavery exists. By a Virginian.
    Richmond, Printed by T. W. White, 1833.
        48 p. 24 cm.

A review of some of the arguments which are commonly
    advanced against parliamentary interference in
    behalf of the Negro slaves, with a statement of
    opinions which have been expressed on that sub-
    ject by many of our most distinguished statesmen
    ... London, Printed by Ellerton and Henderson,
    Gough Square, Fleet Street, sold by J. Hatchard
    and son, Piccadilly, and J. & A. Arch, Cornhill,
    1823.
        32 p.   21 cm.

Revoil, Benedict Henry, 1816-1888.
        The hunter and trapper in North America; or,
    Romantic adventures in field and forest. From
    the French of Benedict Revoil. By W. H. Daven-
    port Adams ... London, New York [etc.] T. Nelson
    and sons, 1874.
        vi p.   [9]-393 p.   1 1., incl. front., illus.
    18 1/2 cm.

Revoil, Bénédict Henry, 1816-1882.
        Pêches dans l'Amerique du Nord.   Paris, L.
    Hachette et cie., 1863.
        320 p.   2 p.l.   18 1/2 cm.

Rewolucya teraznieysza Ameryki połnocney w dwunastu
    zkonfederowanych osadach ... Poznan, w drukarni
    J. K. Mci. y Rzpitey [1778?]
        [101], 208 p.

Rey, William.
        L'Amérique protestante; notes et observations
    d'un voyageur ... Paris [etc.] J. Cherbuliez,
    1857.
        2 v.   18 cm.

[Reynal, Rafael].
        Viage por los Estados Unidos del Norte, dedi-
    cado a los jovenes mexicanos de ambos secsos ...
    Cincinnati, Impreso por E. Deming, 1834.
        164 p.   3 p.l.   plates.   14 1/2 cm.

Reynolds, Charles Bingham, 1856-
        Old Saint Augustine. A story of three cen-
    turies. By Charles B. Reynolds. St. Augustine,
    Fla., E. H. Reynolds, 1888.
        x [11]-144 p.   front., plates, port., maps,
    plans.   19 1/2 cm.

Reynolds, E. W.
The true story of the barons of the south; or
the rationale of the American conflict ... Boston,
Walker, Wise, and company, 1862.
xii, [9]-240 p.   18 cm.

Reynolds, John, 1788-
My own times, embracing also the history of my
life ... [Belleville] Ill. [Printed by B. H.
Perrymen and H. L. Davison] 1855.
xxiii, 600, [1] p.   front. (port.)   18 1/2 cm.

Rhode Island anti-slavery convention.
Proceedings of the Rhode-Island anti-slavery
convention, held in Providence on the 2d, 3d and
4th of February, 1836.   Providence, H. Brown,
printer, 1836.
88 p.   21 cm.

Rhodes, Harrison Garfield, 1871-
A guide to Florida for tourists, sportsmen,
and settlers, by Harrison Rhodes and Mary Wolfe
Dumont; with a chapter on The inland waterways
from New York to Key West.   Three maps and numerous illustrations.   New York, Dodd, Mead and company, 1912.
8 p.l., 456 p.   front., plates, port.   17 cm.

Ricaud, J. A.
... Etude commerciale-industrielle-économique-
constitutionnelle, etc. de la grande république
américaine, 17 années chez les Yankees.   [2. ed.]
Paris, A. M. Beaudelot, 1889.
2 p.l., viii, 311 p.   18 1/2 cm.

Rice, David, 1733.
A Kentucky protest against slavery.   Slavery
inconsistent with justice and good policy, proved
by a speech, delivered in the convention, held
at Danville, Kentucky.   New-York: printed by
Samuel Wood ... 1812.   [New-York] Pub. at the
office of the Rebellion record [1864?]
13 p.   23 1/2 cm.

Rice, N. L.
Ten letters on the subject of slavery: addressed to the delegates from the congregational
associations to the last general assembly of the
Presbyterian Church ... Saint Louis, Keith Woods

& Co., 1855.
47 p.   23 1/2 cm.

Rice, Nathan Lewis, 1807.
Lectures on slavery; delivered in the North
Presbyterian church, Chicago ... Chicago, Church,
Goodman & Cushing, 1860.
100 p.   22 cm.

Rice, Nathan Lewis, 1807.
Ten letters on the subject of slavery ...
Saint Louis, Keith, Woods & co., printers, 1855.
47 p.   23 cm.

Rich, Obadiah, 1783?
A general view of the United States of America.
With an appendix containing the Constitution.
The tariff of duties. The laws of patents and
copyrights, &c. ... London, O. Rich, 1833.
vi, 278 p.   front. (fold. map).   16 1/2 cm.

Rich, R.
Nevves from Virginia. The lost flocke trium-
phant. With the happy arrival of that famous and
worthy knight Sr. Thomas Gates: and the well reputed & valiant capitaine Mr. Christopher Newporte,
and others into England ... London, Printed by
Edw. Allde, and are to be solde by John Wright at
Christ-Church dore, 1610.
14 1. incl. pl.   22 1/2 cm.

Richards, Thomas Addison, 1820-
Rallulah and Jocassee; or, Romances of southern
landscape, and other tales ... Charleston [S.C.]
Walker, Richards & co., 1852.
255 p.   2 p.l.   19 1/2 cm.

Richards, William Carey, 1818, ed.
Georgia illustrated in a series of views embracing natural scenery and public edifices engraved on steel ... Accompanied by historical
and topographical sketches ... Stereotype ed.
Penfield, Ga., W. & W. C. Richards, 1842.
44 p.   15 plates.   28 cm.

Richardson, Albert Deane, 1833-1869.
The secret service, the field, the dungeon,
and the escape ... By Albert D. Richardson ...
Hartford, Conn., American publishing company;

Philadelphia, Jones bros. & co.; [etc., etc.]
1865.
512 p. incl. facsim. front., plates, ports.
22 cm.

Richardson, Frank Herbert, 1867-
Richardson's southern guide; a complete hand-
book to the beauty spots, historical places, noted
battlefields, famous resorts, principal industries and chief points of interest of the South
... Chicago, Monarch book company [c1905].
1 p.1., 7-479 p. 16 cm.

Richardson, John, 1667-
An account of the life of that ancient servant of Jesus Christ, John Richardson, giving a
relation of many of his trials and exercises in
his youth, and his services in the work of the
ministry, in England, Ireland, America, &c. ...
London, Printed: Philadelphia, Reprinted, and
sold by William Dunlap, at the Newest printing-
office, in Market-street, 1759.
vi, 220 p. 19 cm.

Richardson, William Alexander, 1811.
Speech ... delivered in the House of Representatives, May 19, 1862. Washington, L. Towers
& co., 1862].
8 p. 23 cm.

Richmond and Danville Railroad.
The summer of 1882 among the health resorts of
northeast Georgia, upper South Carolina, western
North Carolina, and Virginia. [3d. ed.] [New
York, "The Aldine Press," 1882].
[7] 56 p. front., illus. 27 cm.

Rickman, Thomas M.
Notes of a short visit to Canada and the States,
in August and September, 1885. By Thos. M. Rickman ... [London] Printed for a private circulation [by T. Bosworth] 1886.
v, [7]-54 p. 18 cm.

Riedesel, Friederike Charlotte Luise (von Massow)
freifrau von, 1746-
Auszüge aus den briefen und papieren des
generals freyherrn von Riedesel und seiner gema-
linn, gebornen von Massow. Ihre beyderseitige

443

reise nach America und ihren dortigen aufenthalt
betreffend. Zusammengetragen und geordnet von
ihrem schwiegersohne Heinrich dem XLIV, grafen
Reuss. [Berlin]. Gedruckt als manuscript für
die familie [1800].
386 p. 1 p.l. 20 1/2 cm.

Ries, Julius.
Schilderungen des treibens im leben und handel
in den Vereinigten Staaten und Havana, gesammelt
auf reisen in den jahren 1838 und 1839 ... Berlin,
Selbstverlag des verfassers, 1840.
x, 236, [2] p. 20 1/2 cm.

Rigby, T. C.
Dr. Rigby's papers on Florida, giving a
general view of every portion of the state, its
climate, resources, statistics, society, crops,
trade, &c. By T. C. Rigby, M. D. Cincinnati,
E. Mendenhall, 1876.
63 p. 25 1/2 cm.

Right and wrong in the anti-slavery societies ... Boston, Published at the A. S. office, 1840.
37 p. 18 1/2 cm.

Riland, John.
On the Codrington estates. A letter to the
most reverend William, Lord Archbishop of Canterbury ... London, J. Hatchard and son, 1830.
12 p. 21 cm.

Riland, John.
Two letters, severally addressed to the editor
of the Christian observer and the editor of the
Christian remembrancer, relative to the slave-
cultured estates of the Society for the propaga-
tion of the Gospel ... London, John Hatchard and
son, 1828.
15 p. 21 cm.

Ripley, Mrs. Eliza Moore (Chinn) McHatton, 1832-1912.
From flag to flag; a woman's adventures and
experiences in the South during the war, in Mexico, and in Cuba, by Eliza McHatton-Ripley ...
New York, D. Appleton and company, 1889.
296 p. 18 1/2 cm.

Ritchie, Anna Cora (Ogden) Mowatt, 1819-
    Autobiography of an actress; or, Eight years
on the stage ... Boston, Ticknor, Reed, and
Fields, 1854.
    448 p. front. (port.)   19 cm.

[Ritson, Mrs. Anne].
    A poetical picture of America, being of obser-
vations made, during a residence of several years,
at Alexandria, and Norfolk, in Virginia ... By a
lady. London, Printed for the author [by W.Wil-
son] 1809.
    [3]-177, 1 p. 8 p.l.   17 cm.

Rivera y Villalon, Pedro de, fl. 1740-
    Diario y derrotero de lo caminado, visto y
observado en el discurso de la visita general de
precidios, situados en las provincias ynternas
de Nueva Espana ... Guathemala, S. de Arebale,
1736.
    [76] p. 1 p.l.   28 cm.

[Rivington, Alex.]
    Reminiscences of America in 1869.   By two
Englishmen.   2d ed., rev.   London, S. Low, son,
and Marston, 1870.
    xx, 332 p.   18 cm.

Roach, Alva C.
    The prisoner of war, and how treated. Con-
taining a history of Colonel Steight's expedition
to the rear of Bragg's army, in the spring of
1863, and a correct account of the treatment and
condition of the Union prisoners of war ... and
history of Andersonville prison pen ... Indianapolis, Railroad city pub. house, 1865.
    244 p.   20 cm.

Roah, Sidney.
    Exotic leaves, gathered by a wanderer.   Lon-
don, William Freeman, 1865.
    78 p.   19 cm.

Roberts, Joseph J.
    African colonization.   An address delivered
at the fifty-second annual meeting of the American colonization society, held in Washington,
D. C., January 19, 1869 ... New York, American
colonization society [n.d.].

Roberts, Morley, 1857-
     The western Avernus: or, Toil and travel in
further North America, by Morley Roberts.   New
ed.   Illustrated by A. D. McCormick and from
photographs.   Westminster, A Constable and co.,
1896.
     ix, [2] 277 [1] p.   front., port., plates,
fold. map.   21 1/2 cm.

Roberts, Oran Milo, 1815.
     A description of Texas, its advantages and
resources, with some account of their development, past, present and future ... By O. M. Roberts ... St. Louis, Gilbert book co., 1881.
     2 p.l. [iii]-x, 17-133 p. front. (port.)
col. plates, 5 double maps.   23 1/2 cm.

Roberts, Samuel.
     Slavery, its evils and remedy.   Sheffield,
Printed by J. Blackwell, Iris office, 1829.
     12 p.   16 cm.

Roberts, William, fl. 1763.
     An account of the first discovery, and
natural history of Florida ... Collected from
the best authorities by William Roberts.   London,
Printed for T. Jefferys, 1763.
     viii, [2], 102 p.   fold. plates, 6 fold. maps.
23 1/2 cm.

Robertson, James, of Manchester, Eng.
     A few months in America: containing remarks
on some of its industrial and commercial interests
... London, Longman & co.; [etc., etc., 1855].
     vii, 230, [8] p.   19 cm.

[Robertson, John Blount].
     Reminiscences of a campaign in Mexico; by a
member of the "Bloody-First."   Preceded by a
short sketch of the history and condition of Mexico from her revolution down to the war with the
United States.   Nashville, J. York & co., 1849.
     288 p.   front. (fold. plan).   18 cm.

Robertson, William Parish.
     A visit to Mexico, by the West India islands,
Yucatan and United States, with observations and
adventures on the way.   London, Simpkin, Marshall
& co., 1853.

2 v. fold., fronts. (v.2, map)   19 1/2 cm.

Robin, Claude C. 1750-
Nouveau voyage dans l'Amérique Septentrionale,
en l'année 1781; et campagne de l'armée de M. le
comte de Rochambeau ... A Philadelphie, et se
trouve à Paris, chez Moutard, Imprimeur-Librairie
de la Reine, de madame, & de madame comtesse
d'Artois, rue des Mathurins, Hôtel de Cluni, 1782.
ix, 222 p.   20 cm.

Robinson, John.
The testimony and practice of the Presbyterian
church in reference to American slavery ... Cincinnati, John D. Thorpe, 1852.
256 p.   18 1/2 cm.

Robinson, John Bell.
Pictures of slavery and anti-slavery. Advantages of negro slavery and the benefits of negro
freedom. Morally, socially, and politically considered. Philadelphia, 1863.
viii, [13] 388 p.   20 cm.

[Robinson, Robert].
Miscellaneous works of Robert Robinson ... In
four volumes: to which are prefixed brief memoirs
of his life and writings. Vol. IV. Harlow, printed by B. Flower, 1807.
60-103 p.   25 cm.

Robinson, Sara T. L.
Kansas, its interior and exterior life. Including a full view of its settlement, political
history, social life, climate, soil, productions,
scenery, etc. ... Boston, Crosby, Nichols and
company [etc., etc.] 1856.
ix, 366 p.   19 cm.

Rochambeau, Jean Baptiste Donatien de Vimeur, comte
de 1725-
Mémoires militaires, historiques et politiques
de Rochambeau, ancien maréchal de France, et
grand officier de la Légion d'honneur ... Paris,
Fain [etc.] 1809.
2 v.   21 1/2 cm.

[Rochefort, Charles] 1605-
Histoire naturelle et morale des îles Antilles

de l'Amérique, enrichie d'un grand nombre de bel-
les figures en taille douce ... Avec un vocabulaire
caraibe. Dernière ed. Rev. & augm. par l'auteur
d'un Recit de l'estat present des celèbres colonies
de la Virginie, de Marieland, de la Caroline, du
nouveau duché d'York, de Pennsylvania, & de la
Nouvelle Angleterre ... Rotterdam, R. Leers, 1681.
585, [13], 43 p. 18 p.l. illus. 3 fold. pl.
23 1/2 cm.

Rock, James L.
Southern and western Texas guide for 1878.
James L. Rock and W. I. Smith, authors. St. Louis,
Mo., A. H. Granger, 1878.
282 p. front. (port.) illus., fold. map.
22 1/2 cm.

Rod and gun on the west coast of Florida. Published
by the passenger department of the Plant system.
[Savannah, Ga., 1895].
48 p. map, illus. 18 1/2 cm.

Roe, Alfred Seelye, 1844-1917.
The Ninth New York heavy artillery. A history
of its organization, services in the defenses of
Washington, marches, camps, battles, and muster-
out ... and a complete roster of the regiment.
By Alfred Seelye Roe ... Worcester, Mass., The
author, 1899.
615 p. front., illus. (incl. plans) plates,
ports. 24 cm.

Roe, Mrs. Frances Marie Antoinette (Mack).
Army letters from an officer's wife, 1871-
1888, by Frances M. A. Roe; illustrated by I. W.
Taber from contemporary photographs. New York
and London, D. Appleton and company, 1909.
x, 387 p. incl. illus., plates, front. (port.)
20 1/2 cm.

Roemer, Jacob, 1818-1896.
Reminiscences of the war of the rebellion 1861-
1865, by Bvt.-Maj. Jacob Roemer ... Ed. by L. A.
Furney ... Flushing, N. Y., Pub. by the estate of
J. Roemer, 1897.
316 p., 1 l. front. (port.) 21 cm.

[Rogers, Carlton H.]
Incidents of travel in the southern states and

448

Cuba. With a description of the Mammoth Cave.
New York, R. Craighead, printer, 1862.
[iii]-viii, [9]-320 p.   2 p.l.   19 1/2 cm.

Rogers, Edward Coit.
Letters on slavery, addressed to the pro-slavery men of America; showing its illegality in
all ages and nations: its destructive war upon
society and government, morals and religion. By
O. S. Freeman, pseud. ... Boston, Bela Marsh,
1855.
108 p.   18 cm.

Rogers, Edward H.
Reminiscences of military service in the Forty-third regiment, Massachusetts infantry, during
the great Civil war, 1862-63. By Edward H. Rogers,
Company H, Chelsea, Mass. Boston, Franklin press,
Rand, Avery & co., 1883.
210 p.   front., illus., plates.   23 1/2 cm.

[Rogers, George] fl. 1838-
Memoranda of the experience, labors, and travels of a Universalist preacher ... Cincinnati,
J. A. Gurley, 1845.
400 p.   20 cm.

Rogers, Nathaniel Peabody, 1794.
A collection from the newspaper writings of
Nathaniel Peabody Rogers. Concord, Published
by John R. French, 1847.
380 p.   front. (port.)   18 cm.

Rogers, Robert, 1731-
A concise account of North America; containing
a description of the several British colonies on
that continent, including the islands of Newfoundland, Cape Breton &c. ... London, Printed for
the author, and sold by J. Millan, 1765.
vii, [1], 264 p.   21 cm.

Rogers, Robert, 1731-1795.
Journals of Major Robert Rogers ... London,
Printed for the author, and sold by J. Millan,
1765.
viii, 236 p.   1 l.   20 1/2 cm.

Romans, Bernard, c. 1720-
A concise natural history of East and West

449

Florida ... Vol. I. New-York, Printed for the author, 1775.
    4, viii, 342 (i.e., 340), [2], lxxxix [3] p.
7 plates (incl. front.), 3 maps. fold. table.
18 1/2 cm.

Root, David, 1790.
    The abolition cause eventually triumphant. A sermon, delivered before the Anti-slavery society of Haverhill, Mass. Aug. 1836 ... Andover, Printed by Gould and Newman, 1836.
    24 p.   21 cm.

Root, David.
    A fast sermon on slavery. Delivered April 2, 1835, to the Congregational church and society in Dover, N. H. ... Dover, The Enquirer office, 1835.
    22 p.   22 cm.

Root, David, 1791.
    A tract for the times and for the churches: being the substance of a discourse delivered at South Boston, June, 1845.   Boston, A. J. Wright, printer [1845?]
    16 p.   17 cm.

Root, Joseph Mosley, 1807.
    California and New Mexico.   Speech of Hon. Joseph M. Root, of Ohio, in the House of Representatives, February 15, 1850.   [Washington, Printed at the Congressional globe office, 1850?]
    7 p.   22 cm.

Rose, George, 1817-
    The great country; or, Impressions of America. By George Rose, M. A., "Arthur Sketchley" ... London, Tinsley brothers, 1868.
    xvi, 416 p.   23 cm.

Rose, Victor M.   d. 1893.
    Ross' Texas brigade.   Being a narrative of events connected with its service in the late war between the states.   By Victor M. Rose ... Louisville, Courier-Journal, 1881.
    185 p.   front., port.   20 1/2 cm.

Rosén, Maud, grevinna von, 1902-
    Vi titta pa Amerika; med 76 illustrationer.

450

Stockholm, L. Hokerberg [1933].
3 p.l., [11]-301, [2] p. front., illus. (incl. ports.) 25 cm.

Rosenberg, Charles G.
Jenny Lind in America ... New York, Stringer & Townsend, 1851.
226 p. incl. front. (port.) 19 1/2 cm.

Ross, Fitzgerald.
A visit to the cities and camps of the Confederate states, by Fitzgerald Ross ... Edinburgh and London, W. Blackwood and sons, 1865.
x, 300 p. front. (fold. map) 19 cm.

Ross, Fred A.
Slavery ordained of God ... Philadelphia, J. B. Lippincott & Co., 1857.
186 p. 19 cm.

Ross, Frederick Augustus, 1796-
Dr. Ross and Bishop Colenso: or, the truth restored in regard to polygamy and slavery: by the Rev. Frederick Augustus Ross, D.D., of Huntsville, Alabama, and the right Rev. John William Colenso, D. D., Lord Bishop of Natal. Philadelphia, Henry B. Ashmead, 1857.
82 p. 19 cm.

Ross, Frederick Augustus.
Position of the southern church in relation to slavery. Letter of Dr. F. A. Ross to Rev. Albert Barnes. With an introduction by a constitutional Presbyterian. New-York, John A. Gray, 1857.
23 p. 18 cm.

Ross, George M. von.
Des auswanderers handbuch. Getreue schilderung der Vereinigten Staaten von Nordamerika und zuverlässiger rathgeber für dahin auswandernde jeden standes. Elberfeld u. Iserlohn, J. Bädeker, 1851.
xii, 509, [3] p. 19 cm.

Ross, George M. von.
Der nordamerikanische freistaat Texas, nach eigener anschauung und nach den neuesten und bes-

ten quellen für deutsche auswanderer, geschildert
... Rudolstadt, G. Froebel, 1851.
   85 p. 1 p., 1 . fold. map. 21 cm.

Ross, Ralph Colin, 1923.
   Von Chicago mach Chungking; einem jungen
Deutschen erschliesst sich die Welt, mit einem
Vorwort von Colin Ross. Berlin, Die Heimbücherei,
John Jahr, 1941.
   251 p. illus. 21 1/2 cm.

Rothery, Agnes Edwards, 1888-
   Virginia, the new dominion, by Agnes Rothery,
Illustrated by E. H. Suydam. New York, London,
D. Appleton-Century company, incorporated, 1940.
   xiii, 368 p. col. front., illus., plates.
23 cm.

Rousiers, Paul de, 1857-
   American life, translated from the French by
A. J. Herbertson. Paris, New York, Firmin-Didot
& co., 1892.
   437 p. 25 cm.

Routledge's American handbook and tourist's guide
   through the United States ... London, New York,
G. Routledge & co., 1854.
   vi p., 216 p. 1 1. map. 17 cm.

Roy, J. E.
   Kansas, her struggle and her defense. A discourse preached in the Plymouth Congregational
church of Chicago, Sabbath afternoon, June 1,
1856, by the pastor ... [n.p.] 1856.
   34 p. 21 1/2 cm.

Roy, Joseph Edwin, 1827-
   Pilgrim's letters. Bits of current history
picked up in the West and the South, during the
last thirty years, for the Independent, the Con-
gregationalist, and the Advance, by Joseph E.
Roy. Boston and Chicago, Congregational Sunday-
school and publishing society [c1888].
   310 p. 20 1/2 cm.

The royal African: or, Memoirs of the young prince
of Annamboe ... London, Printed for W. Reeve
[etc.] [n.d.].
   viii, 53 p. 19 cm.

Royall, Anne (Newport) 1769-
    The black book: or, A continuation of travels
in the United States ... Washington City, D. C.,
Printed for the author, 1828-29.
    3 v.   19 1/2 cm.

Royall, Mrs. Anne (Newport) 1769-
    Letters from Alabama on various subjects: to
which is added, an appendix, containing remarks
on sundry members of the 20th & 21st Congress,
and other high characters, &c., &c. at the seat
of government ... Washington, 1830.
    232, 6 p.   23 1/2 cm.

Royall, Anne (Newport) 1769-
    Mrs. Royall's southern tour, or, Second series
of the Black book ... Washington, 1830-31.
    3v.   22 1/2 cm.

[Royall, Mrs. Anne (Newport)] 1769-
    Sketches of history, life, and manners, in the
United States. By a traveller. New Haven, Printed for the author, 1826.
    [13]-392 p.   2 p.l.   front.   19 cm.

Ruffin, Edmund, 1794.
    African colonization unveiled. Washington,
Printed by L. Towers [1859?]
    32 p.   24 1/2 cm.

Ruffin, Edmund, 1794-
    Agricultural, geological and descriptive
sketches of lower North Carolina, and the similar adjacent lands ... Raleigh, Printed at the
Institution for the deaf & dumb, & the blind,
1861.
    xi, [13] - 296 p.   23 cm.

Ruffin, Edmund, 1794.
    The political economy of slavery; or, The
institution considered in regard to its influence
on public wealth and general welfare. [Wash-
ington, Printed by L. Towers, 1857?]
    31 p.   23 1/2 cm.

Ruffner, Henry.
    Address to the people of West Virginia; shew-
ing that slavery is injurious to the public wel-

fare, and that it may be gradually abolished,
without detriment to the rights and interests of
slaveholders. By a slaveholder of West Virginia.
Lexington [Virginia] Printed by R. C. Noel, 1847.
    40 p.   21 cm.

Ruggles, David.
    An antidote for a poisonous combination re-
cently prepared by a "citizen of New-York," alias
Dr. Reese, entitled, "An appeal to the reason and
religion of American Christians", &c. Also David
Meredith Reese's "Humbugs" dissected ... New-York,
W. Stuart, 1838.
    cover-title, 32 p.   20 cm.

Ruggles, David.
    The "extinguisher" extinguished! or, David M.
Reese, M. D. "used up" ... New-York, D. Ruggles,
1834.
    48 p.   18 cm.

Runyan, Morris C.
    Eight days with the Confederates and capture
of their archives, flags, &c. by Company "G"
Ninth New Jersey vol. Written by Captain Morris
C. Runyan, Princeton, N. J., W. C. C. Zapf, printer, 1896.
    44 p. front. (port.)   22 1/2 cm.

[Rush, Benjamin?] 1745.
    An address to the inhabitants of the British
settlements in America upon slave-keeping. New-
York, Printed by Hodge and Shober, 1773.
    3⌐ p.   18 cm.

Rusling, James Fowler, 1834-
    Across America: or, The great West and the
Pacific coast. By James F. Rusling ... New York,
Sheldon & company, 1874.
    xx, [21]-503 p. front., plates, port., fold.
map.   20 cm.

Russell, Charles Russell, baron, 1832-
    Diary of a visit to the United States of Ameri-
ca in the year 1883, by Charles Lord Russell, of
Killowen ... with an introduction by the Rev.
Matthew Russell, S. J. and an appendix by Thomas
Francis Meehan, A. M., ed. by Charles George Her-
bermann, Ph. D. New York, The United States

Catholic historical society, 1910.
235 p. front., plates. ports. 22 1/2 cm.

Russell, David E.
Seven months in prison; or, Life in rebeldom
... Details of real prison life in Richmond and
Danville, with a list of Wisconsin men who died
in the Andersonville prison, in perfect order,
by regiments. Milwaukee, Godfrey & Crandall,
1866.
104 p. 19 cm.

Russell, George G.
Reminiscences of Andersonville prison, a paper
read by Comrade Geo. G. Russell, before Post 34,
G. A. R., Tuesday evening, June 22. Salem, Mass.,
Observer steam book and job print, 1886.
8 p. 23 cm.

Russell, Henry.
The slave ship, a descriptive song, written,
composed and sung by Henry Russell. London,
Brewer & co. [n.d.]
9 p. music. 34 cm.

Russell, Robert.
North America, its agriculture and climate;
containing observations on the agriculture and
climate of Canada, the United States, and the
island of Cuba ... Edinburgh, A. and C. Black,
1857.
390 p. 4 p.l., front. (fold. col. map) 8 pl.
(charts, part fold.) diagrs. 23 cm.

Russell, Sir William Howard, 1820-
Hesperothen; notes from the West; a record of
a ramble in the United States and Canada in the
spring and summer of 1881 ... London, S. Low,
Marston, Searle & Rivington, 1882.
2 v. 19 1/2 cm.

Russell, Sir William Howard, 1820-1907.
My diary North and South. By William Howard
Russell. Boston, T.O.H.P. Burnham; New York,
O. S. Felt, 1863.
xxii, 602 p. 20 cm.

Sabre, Gilbert E.
　　Nineteen months a prisoner of war. Narrative
of Lieutenant G. E. Sabre, Second Rhode Island
cavalry, of his experiences in the war prisons
and stockades of Morton, Mobile, Atlanta, Libby,
Belle Island, Andersonville, Macon, Charleston,
and Columbia, and his escape ... list of officers
confined at Columbia, during the winter of 1864
and 1865. New York, The American news company,
1865.
　　207 p. front., pl. 19 cm.

Sachot, Octave [Louis Marie].
　　Récits de voyages. Les grandes cités de
l'ouest américain. Tableaux de moeurs américaines. Paris, Ducrocq, 1874.
　　334 p. 1 1., front., pl. 18 cm.

St. Domingo. New York. [Published by R. G. Williams
for the American anti-slavery society, 1839?]
　　24 p. 11 cm.

St. Louis, Iron Mountain & southern railway company.
　　A home and where to find one. An accurate
description of the state of Missouri, more particularly southeast Missouri ... to which are
added a few remarks about the state of Arkansas.
Issued by the Land department of the St. Louis,
Iron Mountain and southern railway. [St. Louis?
1880?]
　　32 p. incl. maps. 23 1/2 cm.

Sainte-Croix, M. le marquis de.
　　Emancipation des esclaves aux colonies françaises, memoire présenté au gouvernement par M.
le marquis de Sainte-Croix. Paris, Rosier, 1835.
　　viii, 31 p. 23 cm.

Sala, George Augustus Henry, 1828-
　　America revisited: from the bay of New York
to the gulf of Mexico, and from Lake Michigan to
the Pacific ... London, Vizetelly & co., 1882.
　　2 v. front., illus., pl. 23 cm.

Salmon [Thomas] 1679-
A new geographical and historical grammar ...
and the present state of the several kingdoms of
the world ... Illustrated with a new set of maps
... and other copper-plates. A new ed., with
large additions ... Edinburgh, Murray and Cochran, 1780.
[v]-xii, [2] 7-629 [5] p. 1 p.1., xxxiii pl.
(incl. front., fold. maps) 21 1/2 cm.

Salmon, Thomas, 1679-
The universal traveller; or, A compleat description of the several nations of the world ...
Brought down to the present time. And illustrated with a great variety of maps and cuts ...
London, Printed for R. Baldwin, 1752-53.
2 v. fronts., plates, maps (part fold.),
plans. 38 cm.

Salzbacher, Joseph, 1790-
Meine reise nach Nord-amerika im jahre 1842.
Mit statistischen bemerkungen über die zustände
der katholischen kirche bis auf die neueste zeit
... Wein, In commission bei Wimmer, Schmidt &
Leo, 1845.
viii p., 2 1., 479, [1] p. 1 1., xii p.
fold. map. 22 1/2 cm.

Sanborn, Franklin Benjamin.
Emancipation in the West Indies. Concord,
Mass., March, 1862.
15 p. 24 cm.

Sanchez, Somoano, Jose.
Costumbres yankees; viajes por la America del
Norte. Mexico, Tip. de "El Correo español,"
1894.
208 p. 14 cm.

Sarfatti, Margherita Grassini.
L'America, ricerca della felicità. Milano,
A. Mondadori [1937].
5 p.1., 292, [1] p., 1 1. 19 cm.

Sargent, Angelina M.
Notes of travel and mementos of friendship.
Rochester, N. Y., E. R. Andrews, printer [1894].
130 p. illus. 21 cm.

Sargent, Winthrop, 1825-1870, ed.
The history of an expedition against Fort Du
Quesne, in 1755; under Major-General Edward Braddock ... Edited from the original manuscripts,
by Winthrop Sargent. Philadelphia, for the Historical Society of Pennsylvania, 1855.
vii-xiv, 15-423 p. 4 p.1., front., 1 illus.,
2 fold. maps, 7 plans. (6 fold.) 24 cm.

Sarmiento, Domingo Faustino, pres. Argentine republic,
1811-1888.
Viajes en Europa, Africa i America ... [1.-]2.
entrega. Santiago, Impr. de J. Belin, 1849-51.
2 v. 21 1/2 cm.

Saugrain de Vigni, Antoine Francois, 1763-
L'odyssée américaine d'une famille française
par le docteur Antoine Saugrain; étude suivie des
manuscrits inédits et de la correspondance de
Sophie Michau Robinson, par H. Foure Selter.
Baltimore, the Johns Hopkins press, 1936.
ix, 123 p. front., pl., ports., double maps,
facsims. (1 double) 22 1/2 cm.

Saunders, Prince.
An address delivered at Bethel church, Philadelphia; on the 30th of September, 1818. Before
the Pennsylvania Augustine society, for the education of people of colour ... To which is annexed
the constitution of the society. Philadelphia,
Printed by Joseph Rakestraw, 1818.
12 p. 23 cm.

Saunders, Prince.
A memoir presented to the American convention
for promoting the abolition of slavery, and improving the condition of the African race, December 11th, 1818 ... Philadelphia, Printed by Dennis
Heartt, 1818.
19 p. 22 cm.

Saunders, William, 1823-
Through the light continent; or, The United
States in 1877-8 ... London, New York [etc.] Cassell, Petter and Galpin, 1879.
xi, 409 p., 2 1. [2] p. 23 cm.

Savardan, Augustin.
Un naufrage au Texas; observations et impres-
sions recueillies pendant deux ans et demi au
Texas et à travers les Etats-Unis d'Amerique ...
Paris, Garnier frères, 1858.
344 p.   3 p.l.   18 cm.

Savery, William, 1750-
A journal of the life, travels, and religious
labors of William Savery, a minister ... of the
Society of Friends ... Comp. from his original
memoranda, by Jonathan Evans.   Stereotype ed.
Philadelphia, For sale at Friends' Bookstore,
1873.
485 p.   19 cm.

Sawyer, Leicester Ambrose.
A dissertation on servitude: embracing an
examination of the Scripture doctrines on the
subject, and an inquiry into the character and
relations of slavery ... New Haven, Published
by Durrie & Peck, 1837.
108 p.   18 cm.

Sayer, Robert, 1725-
The American military pocket atlas; being an
approved collection of correct maps, both general and particular, of the British colonies;
especially those which now are, or probably may
be the theatre of war ... London, Printed for
R. Sayer and J. Bennet [1776].
viii, [1] p. 6 fold. maps.   22 cm.

Schade, Louis.
A book for the "impending crisis!" Appeal to
the common sense and patriotism of the people of
the United States.   "Helperism" annihilated!
The "irrepressible conflict" and its consequences!
... Washington, Little, Morris, & co., 1860.
80 p.   23 cm.

Schade, Louis.
The immigration into the United States of America, from a statistical and national-economical
point of view. By Louis Schade, of Washington,
D. C. Washington [n.d.].
15 p.   20 cm.

Scharf, John Thomas, 1843.
    History of the Confederate States navy from
its organization to the surrender of its last
vessel. New York, Rogers & Sherwood; San Francisco, A. L. Bancroft & co.; [etc., etc.] 1887.
    x, [11]-824 p. front., illus. (incl. plans,
diagrs.) plates, ports.   24 cm.

[Schaw, Janet].
    Journal of a lady of quality; being the narra-
tive of a journey from Scotland to the West Indies, North Carolina, and Portugal, in the years
1774 to 1776. Edited by Evangeline Walker Andrews,
in collaboration with Charles McLean Andrews. New
Haven, Yale University press, 1922.
    341 p.   4 p.1. maps, plans, facsim.   23 1/2 cm.

Scheibert, Justus, 1831-1904.
    Sieben monate in den rebellen-staaten während
des nordamerikanischen krieges 1863, von Scheibert. Hierzu viele gefechts- und situationspläne.
Stettin, T. von der Nahmer, 1868.
    v, 126 p., 1 1.   4 fold. plans.   22 cm.

Scherff, Julius.
    Nord-Amerika. Reisebilder, sozial-politische
und wirtschaftliche studien aus den Vereinigten
Staaten. Leipzig, O. Wigand, 1898.
    vi p., 1 1., 269 [4] p.   22 1/2 cm.

Schermerhorn, John Freeman, 1786.
    A correct view of that part of the United
States which lies west of the Alleghany mountains,
with regard to religion and morals. By John F.
Schermerhorn, and Samuel J. Mills. Hartford, P.
B. Gleason and co., printers, 1814.

Schive, Jens, 1900-
    Med kronprinsparet - for Norge! 70 dagers ferd
gjennem Stjernebannerets land. Med innledning av
sendemann Wilhelm Morgenstierne. Oslo, H. Asche-
houg, & co. (W. Nygaard) 1939.
    3 p.1., 9-327 p. plates, ports., fold. map.
25 1/2 cm.

Schlatter, Michael, 1716-
    Getrouw verhaal van den waren toestant der
meest herderloze gemeentens in Pensylvanien en

aangrensende provintien ... Amsterdam, Jacobus
Loveringh, 1751.
    xxii, 56 p.   18 1/2 cm.

Schmidt, Friedrich (Stuttgart).
    Versuch über den politischen zustand der Ver-
einigten Staaten von Nord-Amerika ... Stuttgart
und Tübingen, J. G. Cotta, 1822.
    2 v. xx (i.e. 21) pl. (part fold., incl. maps,
plans) fold. tables. 19 cm.

Schmölder, B.
    Neuer praktischer wegweiser für auswanderer
nach Nord-Amerika, in drei abteilungen ... 1.
abtheilung ... Mainz, Le Roux, 1849 [1851].
    120, [84]-153 p. 4 p.l., 1 l. front. (port.)
3 pl., fold. map. 23 cm.

Schönauer, Georg.
    Tramp und farmer in USA; fünf jahre kreuz und
quer durch die staaten. Berlin, Im Deutschen verlag, 1938.
    269 p. 19 1/2 cm.

Schoolcraft, Henry Rowe, 1793-1864.
    The Indian in his wigwam, or, Characteristics
of the red race of America. From original notes
and manuscripts ... New York, W. H. Graham, 1848.
    5-416 p. 1 p.l., illus. 23 cm.

Schoolcraft, Henry Rowe, 1793-1864.
    Journal of a tour into the interior of Missouri
and Arkansas, from Potosi, or Mine a Burton, in
Missouri Territory, in a south-west direction,
toward the Rocky Mountains; performed in the years
1818 and 1819. London, Printed for Sir R. Phillips and co., 1821.
    102 p. fold. map. 23 cm.

Schoolcraft, Henry Rowe, 1793-1884.
    Travels in the central portions of the Missis-
sippi valley: comprising observations on its
mineral geography, internal resources, and aboriginal population ... New York, Collins and Hannay,
1825.
    iv, 459 p. front., plates. fold. maps.
21 1/2 cm.

Schoolcraft, Henry Rowe, 1793-1884.
A view of the lead mines of Missouri including
some observations on the mineralogy, geology, geography, antiquities, soil, climate, population,
and productions of Missouri and Arkansas and other
sections of the western country ... New York,
Charles Wiley & co., 1819.
299 (i.e. 297) p. front., 2 pl. 21 1/2 cm.

Schöpf, Johann David, 1752-
Reise durch einige der mittlern und südlichen
Vereinigten nord-amerikanischen staaten nach Ost-
Florida und den Bahama-Inseln unternommen in den
jahren 1783 and 1784 ... Erlangen, J. J. Palm,
1788.
2 v. fold, map. 21 cm.

Schrieke, Bertram Johannes Otto, 1890-
Alien Americans; a study of race relations,
by M. Schrieke. New York, The Viking press, 1936.
xi, 208 p. 21 cm.

Schultz, Christian.
Travels on an inland voyage through the states
of New-York, Pennsylvania, Virginia, Ohio, Kentucky and Tennessee, and through the territories
of Indiana, Louisiana, Mississippi and New-Orleans;
performed in the years 1807 and 1808; including
a tour of nearly six thousand miles ... New-York-
Printed by Isaac Riley, 1810.
2 v. in 1. fronts. (v. 1, port.) plates,
fold. maps, fold. plan. 22 cm.

Schurz, Carl, 1829-1906.
Douglas and popular sovereignty. Speech of
Carl Schurz, of Wisconsin. In Hampden hall,
Springfield, Mass., January 4, 1860. Washington,
Buell & Blanchard [n.d.].
8 p. 22 1/2 cm.

Schurz, Carl, 1829.
Speech ... delivered in Brooklyn, New York,
October 7th, 1864. Philadelphia, King & Baird
[1864?]
31 p. 23 cm.

Schurz, Carl, 1829.
Speech of Carl Schurz at Cooper Institute,

N. Y., March 6, 1862. [New York? 1862].
3-11 p. 23 cm.

Schütze, Albert, ed.
Schütze's jahrbuch für Texas und emigranten-
führer für 1883. Austin, Tex., Albert Schütze,
1883.
200 p. 20 cm.

Schwartz, Stephan.
Twenty-two months a prisoner of war. A narrative of twenty-two months' imprisonment by the
Confederates, in Texas, through General Twigg's
treachery, dating from April, 1861, to February,
1863. By Stephan Schwartz ... St. Louis, Mo.,
A. F. Nelson publishing co., 1892.
5 p.1., 17-221 p. front. (port.) plates.
20 cm.

Scott, Job, 1751-
Journal of the life, travels and gospel labours of that faithful servant and minister of
Christ, Job Scott. 4th ed. New-York, Printed
and sold by Isaac Collins, no. 189, Pearl street,
1798.
iii-xii, 360 p. 2 p.1. 18 cm.

Scott, John, 1820-1907.
Partisan life with Col. John S. Mosby. By
Major John Scott ... With portraits and engravings
on wood ... New York, Harper & brothers, 1867.
1 p.1., vii-xvi p., 1 1., 19 - 492 p. front.,
illus., ports., fold. map. facsim. 24 cm.

Scott, Joseph.
The United States gazetteer ... Philadelphia,
F. and R. Bailey, 1795.
vi, [292] p. 1 1., 19 fold. maps. 18 cm.

Scott, Orange.
An appeal to the Methodist Episcopal church
... Boston, David H. Ela, 1838.
156 p. 24 cm.

Scott, Orange.
The grounds of secession from the M. E. church,
or, Book for the times: being an examination of
her connection with slavery, and also of her form

of government ... Revised and corrected, to which
is added Wesley upon slavery. New York, L. C.
Matlack, 1851.
231 p.   15 cm.

Scott, W. A.
    Emigration of free and emancipated negroes to
Africa.   An address delivered at the annual meeting of the Louisiana state colonization society...
New Orleans, Printed at the office of the Picayune,
1853.
    16 p.   20 cm.

Scribner, Benjamin Franklin, 1825-
    How soldiers were made; or, The war as I saw
it under Buell, Rosecrans, Thomas, Grant and Sherman.   [Chicago, Donohue & Henneberry] 1887.
    2 p.1., iii-iv, 5-316 p.   20 cm.

Scull, Gideon Delaplaine, 1824, ed.
    The Montresor journals; ed. and annotated by
G. D. Scull ... [New-York, Printed for the Society, 1882].
    xiv, 578 p.   2 port. (incl. front.) maps (1
fold.) plans.   25 cm.

Seabury, Samuel.
    American slavery distinguished from the slavery
of English theorists, and justified by the law of
nature ... New York, Mason brothers, 1861.
    x, [11]-319 p.   19 cm.

[Sealsfield, Charles] 1793-
    The Americans as they are; described in a tour
through the valley of the Mississippi ... London,
Hurst, Chance, and co., 1828.
    vi, [4]-218, [3] p.   2 p.1.   19 1/2 cm.

Sears, Robert, 1810-
    A pictorial description of the United States;
embracing the history, geographical position,
agricultural and mineral resources ... &c.,&c.,
of each state and territory in the Union ... New
ed. rev. and enl. New York, R. Sears, 1857.
    [v]-viii, 648 p.   3 p.1., incl. front. illus.
(incl. ports., plan)   24 1/2 cm.

Se Chevere11, John Hampton.
    Journal history of the Twenty-ninth Ohio veteran

464

volunteers, 1861-1865. Cleveland, Ohio, By a Committee of the regiment, 1883.
2 p.l., [9]-284 p. front. (port.)　19 cm.

A second address to the right reverend the prelates of England and Wales, on the subject of the slave trade ... London, Printed and sold by J. Johnson, 1795.
22 p.　20 cm.

Sedgwick, Theodore.
Thoughts on the proposed annexation of Texas to the United States. First published in the New York evening post, under the signature of Veto ... together with the address of Albert Gallatin ... Second edition. New York, S. W. Benedict & co., 1844.
56 p.　21 cm.

Segar, Joseph.
Speech ... on the Wilmot proviso. Delivered in the House of delegates, January 19, 1849. Richmond, Va., Printed by Shepherd and Colin, 1849.
22 p.　22 cm.

[Selden, Richard Ely].
Criticism on the Declaration of Independence as a literary document by Mon Droit [pseud.] New York, For sale at the news office, 1846.
44 p.　23 cm.

A selection of anti-slavery hymns, for the use of the friends of emancipation. Boston, Published by Garrison & Knapp, 1834.
36 p.　15 cm.

Self emancipation. A successful experiment on a large estate in Louisiana by Mr. John McDonogh, completed in 1849. [n.p., n.d.].
24 p.　22 cm.

Semmes, Raphael, 1809-
Memoirs of service afloat, during the war between the states. Baltimore, Kelly, Piet & co. [etc., etc.] 1869.
1 p.l., vi, xi-xvi, 17-333 p. front., 6 col. pl., port., diagrs.　24 1/2 cm.

Severance, Frank H.
    Mr. Fillmore's views relating to slavery; the
suppressed portion of the third annual message to
Congress, December 6, 1852. Buffalo, New York,
Buffalo historical society, 1907.
    311-324 p. front. 24 cm.

Seward, William.
    Journal of a voyage from Savannah to Philadel-
phia, and from Philadelphia to England, MCDCCXL.
By William Seward, gent. companion in travel with
the Reverend Mr. George Whitefield ... London,
J. Oswald [etc., etc.] 1740.
    87 p. 3 p.l. 20 cm.

Seward, William Henry, 1801.
    California, union and freedom. Speech of Wil-
liam H. Seward, on the admission of California.
Delivered in the Senate of the United States,
March 11, 1850. [Washington] Buell & Blanchard,
[1850?]
    14 p. 22 cm.

Seward, William Henry, 1801.
    Dangers of extending slavery, and the contest
and the crisis. [Washington, D. C., Published by
the Republican association. Fifth English edition. Buell and Blanchard, printers, 1856].
    16 p. 23 cm.

Seward, William Henry, 1801-1872.
    Freedom and public faith ... Speech ... on the
abrogation of the Missouri compromise, in the
Kansas and Nebraska Bills. Senate of the United
States, February 17, 1854. Washington, Buell &
Blanchard, 1854.
    16 p. 23 1/2 cm.

Seward, William Henry, 1801.
    Freedom and the union. Speech ... in the Se-
nate of the United States in vindication of freedom and the union, Wednesday, February 29, 1860...
Albany, Weed, Parsons & co., 1860.
    12 p. 22 cm.

Seward, William Henry, 1801.
    Freedom in Kansas. Speech of William H. Seward,
in the Senate of the United States, March 3, 1858.

Washington, Buell & Blanchard, printers, 1858.
15 p.   23 cm.

Seward, William Henry, 1801-1872.
Freedom in Kansas. Speech ... in the Senate
of the United States, April 30, 1858, Washington,
Buell & Blanchard, 1858.
15 p.   22 1/2 cm.

Seward, William Henry, 1801-1872.
Great speech of Hon. William H. Seward, against
the Lecompton Constitution, in Senate, March 3d,
1858. [n.p., n.d.]
48 p.   22 cm.

Seward, William Henry, 1801-1872.
The irrepressible conflict. A speech by William H. Seward delivered at Rochester, Monday, Oct.
25, 1858. Albany, Albany Evening Journal, 1858.
15 p.   23 cm.

Seward, William Henry, 1801-1872.
Speech ... for the immediate admission of Kansas into the union. Senate of the United States,
April 9, 1856. [n.p., n.d.]
14 p.   24 cm.

Seward, William Henry, 1801.
The state of the country. Speech ... in the
United States Senate, February 29, 1860. [n.p.,
n.d.]
8 p.   24 cm.

Sewell, William Grant.
The ordeal of free labor in the British West
Indies. New York, Harper & brothers, 1861.
vi, 325 p.   19 cm.

Seymour, William.
A journal of the southern expedition, 1780-
1783 ... Wilmington, The Historical society of
Delaware, 1896.
42 p.   25 1/2 cm.

Shaler, Nathaniel Southgate, 1841-
American highways; a popular account of their
conditions, and of the means by which they may be
bettered ... New York, The Century co., 1896.

467

xv, 2y3 p. incl. illus., plates. front.
19 cm.

Shall we give the Bible to three million of American
slaves? [New York? American and for foreign anti-
slavery society, n.d.].
8 p. 18 cm.

Sharan, James, 1762-
The adventures of James Sharan: compiled from
the journal written during his voyages and travels
in the four quarters of the globe ... Baltimore:
Printed by G. Dobbin & Murphy, 10 Baltimore Street
for James Sharan, 1808.
vi, [7]-225, [1] p., 1 1., [12] p. 17 cm.

Sharp, Granville.
Extract from a representation of injustice and
dangerous tendency of tolerating slavery ... London, printed 1769. Philadelphia, re-printed by
Joseph Crukshank, 1771.
53 p. 16 cm.

Sharp, Granville.
The law of retribution; or, A serious warning
to Great Britain and her colonies, founded on un-
questionable examples of God's temporal vengeance
against tyrants, slaveholders, and oppressors...
London, Printed by W. R. Richardson, for B. White
and E. and C. Dilly, 1876.
357 p. 19 cm.

Sharp, Granville.
A tract on the law of nature and principles
of action in man ... London, Printed for B. White
and E. and C. Dilly, 1777.
447 p. 20 1/2 cm.

Shaver, Lewellyn Adelphus, 1842-
A history of the Sixtieth Alabama regiment,
Gracie's Alabama brigade; by Lewellyn A. Shaver.
Montgomery, Barrett & Brown, 1867.
111 p. 21 cm.

Shaw, Benjamin.
Illegality of slavery. [n.p., n.d.]
12 p. 18 cm.

Shaw, Benjamin.
    Political sin and political righteousness.
[n.p., n.d.]
    12 p.   18 cm.

Shaw, James.
    Twelve years in America; being observations on
the country, the people, institutions and religion;
with notices of slavery and the late war; and
facts and incidents illustrative of ministerial
life and labor in Illinois, with notes of travel
through the United States and Canada. By the Rev.
James Shaw ... 2d thousand. London, Hamilton,
Adams, and co.; Chicago, Poe and Hitchcock; [etc.,
etc.] 1867.
    xvi, 440 p.   front., fold. map.   19 cm.

Shaw, John, M.D.
    A ramble through the United States, Canada,
and the West Indies ... London, J. F. Hope, 1856.
    370 p.   2 p.l.   22 1/2 cm.

Shaw, Joshua.
    United States directory for the use of travel-
lers and merchants, giving an account of the
principal establishments, of business and pleasure,
throughout the Union ... Philadelphia, Printed
by J. Maxwell [1822].
    ix, 156 p.   2 p.l., fold. map. fold. tab.
18 cm.

Shaw, William H. 1833-
    A diary as kept by Wm. H. Shaw, during the
great civil war, from April, 1861 to July, 1865.
[n.p., n.d.]
    76 p.   front. (port.)   22 cm.

Shedd, William G. T.
    Africa and colonization. An address delivered
before the Massachusetts colonization society,
May 27, 1857 ... Andover, Printed by Warren F.
Draper, 1857.
    24 p.   23 cm.

Sheldon, Winthrop Dudley, 1839-1931.
    The "Twenty-seventh." A regimental history.
By Winthrop D. Sheldon ... New-Haven, Morris &
Benham, 1866.

144 p.   front., port.   19 cm.

[Sheridan, Louis].
    Important intelligence from Liberia.   [n.p.,
n.d.]
    [3] p.   30 cm.

Sheridan, Philip Henry, 1831-1888.
    Personal memoirs of P. H. Sheridan, general,
United States army.   New York, C. L. Webster &
company, 1888.
    2 v.   fronts.   (ports.)   illus., fold. maps.
23 cm.

Sherman, Ernest Anderson, 1868-
    Dedicating in Dixie; a series of articles des-
criptive of the tour of Governor Albert B. Cummins
and staff, the members of the Vicksburg, Andersonville, Chattanooga and Shiloh monument commissions and invited guests, through the South
for the purpose of dedicating Iowa memorials on
southern battlefields and cemeteries, November
12th to November 25th, 1906 ... Cedar Rapids, Ia.,
Press of the Record printing company, 1907.
    132 p.   plates.   25 cm.

Sherman, Henry.
    Slavery in the United States of America; its
national recognition and relations, from the establishment of the confederacy, to the present time.
A word to the north and the south ... Second edition.   Hartford, Hurlburt & Pond, 1860.
    xvi, [9]-187 p.   18 cm.

Sherman, John.
    Lecompton Constitution.   Speech ... in the
House of Representatives, Jan. 23, 1858.   On the
admission of Kansas as a state under the Lecompton Constitution.   Washington, Congressional globe
office, 1858.
    8 p.   23 1/2 cm.

Sherman, John, 1823.
    Letter ... in reply to an invitation from "The
working members of the People's party," to attend
a public dinner, at Samson Street hall, in the
city of Philadelphia, Friday evening, December 28,
1860.   [Washington, D. C.? 1860?]

7 p.   24 cm.

Sherman, John, 1823.
Shall the United States be coerced by a state?
Speech ... delivered in the House of Representatives, January 18, 1861. [n.p., n.d.]
8 p.   24 cm.

Sherwood, Adiel, 1791-
A gazetteer of the state of Georgia ... Second
edition. Philadelphia, Printed by J. W. Martin
and W. K. Boden ... 1829.
[1], [v]-vi [2], [9]-300 p., 1 l. front. (fold.
map) 1 illus., plan.   15 cm.

Sherwood, Lorenzo.
Slavocracy against democracy--the great cause
of the rebellion ... [n.p., n.d.]
8 p.   22 cm.

Shillitoe, Thomas.
Extracts from an address to the Society of
Friends. Philadelphia, Published by the Tract
association of Friends [n.d.].
12 p.   18 cm.

Shillitoe, Thomas, 1754-
Journal of the life, labours, and travels of
Thomas Shillitoe, in the service of the Gospel of
Jesus Christ ... London, Harvey and Darton, 1839.
2 v.   23 cm.

Shoemaker, W. B.
Florida as it is. It tells all about the industries of the state, its climate and resources
... By Dr. W. B. Shoemaker. Newville, Pa., Times
steam print, 1887.
199 [1] p.   18 cm.

A short account of that part of Africa, inhabited by
the negroes. With respect of the fertility of the
country; the good disposition of many of the natives, and the manner by which the slave trade is
carried on. Extracted from divers authors ...
The second edition, with large additions and amendments ... Philadelphia, W. Dunlap, 1762.
80 p.   19 cm.

Short answers to reckless fabrications, against the
democratic candidate for president, James Buchanan. Philadelphia, William Rice, book and job
printer, 1856.
32 p.   20 cm.

Short biographical notices of Samuel Emlen, James Pemberton, Daniel Bowly, Junr., Thomas Rutter, and
Job Thomas. Philadelphia, Published by the Tract
association of Friends [n.d.].
16 p.   18 cm.

A short review of the slave trade and slavery, with
considerations on the benefit which would arise
from cultivating tropical productions by free labour. Birmingham, Beilby, Knott, and Beilby,
1827.
129 p.   21 cm.

Short, Rich.
Travels in the United States of America, through
the states of New York, Pennsylvania, Ohio, Michigan territory, Kentucky, Virginia, Maryland, Columbia, North Carolina, Rhode Island and Massachusetts ... 2d ed.   London, R. Lambert [183-?]
24 p.   17 1/2 cm.

Shotwell, Randolph Abbott, 1844-1885.
The papers of Randolph Abbott Shotwell, edited
by J. G. de Roulhac Hamilton, with the collaboration of Rebecca Cameron.   Raleigh, The North Carolina historical commission, 1929-
v, front. (port.)   23 1/2 cm.

Sierra, Justo, 1848-
En tierra yankee (notas a todo vapor) 1895.
Mexico, Tip. de la Oficina impresora del timbre,
1898.
216 p., 1 1.   26 1/2 cm.

Silliman, Augustus Ely, 1807-
A gallop among American scenery; or, Sketches
of American scenes and military adventure ... New
York, D. Appleton & co.; Philadelphia, G. S. Appleton, 1843.
267 p. 4 p.l. illus.   18 1/2 cm.

Simcoe, John Graves, 1752-
    A journal of the operations of the Queen's ran-
gers from the end of the year 1777, to the conclu-
sion of the late American war ... Exeter [Eng.]
Printed for the author [1787].
    184, [48] p. 4 p.l. 10 fold. plans. 30 cm.

Simmons, Louis A.
    The history of the 84th reg't Ill. vols. By
L. A. Simmons. Macomb, Ill., Hampton brothers,
1866.
    345 p., 1 l. 19 1/2 cm.

Simms, William Emmett, 1822.
    Speech ... on the organization of the House,
and the aggressions of the anti-slavery party of
the north; delivered in the House of Representatives, December 16, 1859. Washington, D. C.
Printed at the Congressional globe office, 1859.
    7 p. 22 cm.

Simms, William Gilmore, 1806-1870.
    The geography of South Carolina: being a com-
panion to the history of that state. Charleston,
Babcock & co., 1843.
    viii, [9]-192 p. incl. tables. 17 1/2 cm.

Sims, James Marion, 1813-
    The story of my life ... Ed. by his son, H.
Marion-Sims, M. D. New York, D. Appleton and
company, 1885.
    471 p. 19 1/2 cm.

Singleton, Otho Robards, 1814.
    Speech ... In resistance to black republican
domination; delivered in the House of Representatives, December 19, 1859. Washington, Printed
at the Congressional globe office, 1859.
    16 p. 24 cm.

Sipes, William B. d. 1905.
    The Seventh Pennsylvania veteran volunteer
cavalry; its record, reminiscences and roster;
with an appendix; by William B. Sipes. [Potts-
ville, Pa., Miners' journal print, 1905?]
    1 p.l., iv, 6, 169, [1], 60, 143 p., 3 l.
pl., ports. 24 cm.

Skal, Georg von.
Das amerikanische volk, von Georg von Skal.
Berlin, E. Fleischel & co., 1908.
3 p.l. [ix]-xii, 336 p. 22 1/2 cm.

Skelton, Charles, 1806.
Speech ... in the House of Representatives,
Feb. 14, 1854, against the repeal of the Missouri
compromise. [Washington, Printed at the Congressional globe office, 1854?]
7 p. 23 cm.

Sketch of Daniel O'Connell. [n.p., n.d.].
8 p. 22 cm.

Sketch of western Virginia; for the use of British
settlers in that country. London, Edward Bull,
1837.
vi, 117, 6 p. fold. map. 18 cm.

Skinner, J[ohn] E[dwin] Hilary.
After the storm; or, Jonathan and his neigh-
bours in 1865-6. By J. E. Hilary Skinner ... London, R. Bentley, 1866.
2 v. 19 cm.

Slade, William.
Speech of Mr. Slade, of Vermont, on the right
of petition; the power of Congress to abolish
slavery and the slave trade in the District of
Columbia; the implied faith of the north and the
south to each other in forming the Constitution;
and the principles, purposes, and prospects of
abolition. Delivered in the House of Representatives, on the 18th and 20th January, 1840.
Washington, Printed by Galls and Seaton, 1840.
45 p. 23 cm.

The slave colonies of Great Britain; or, A picture
of negro slavery drawn by the colonists themselves; being an abstract of the various papers
recently laid before Parliament on that subject
... Second edition, corrected. London, Society
for the mitigation and gradual abolition of
slavery throughout the British dominions, 1826.
121 p. 21 cm.

The slave mother. [n.p., n.d.]. Broadside.
   17 cm.

Slavery abolished. [n.p., n.d.].
   20 p.   23 cm.

Slavery and the Bible. [Cincinnati, American reform
   tract and book society, n.d.].
   12 p.   18 cm.

Slavery and missions. New York [Published by R. G.
   Williams for the American anti-slavery society,
   1839?]
   24 p.   11 cm.

Slavery and the slave trade at the nation's capital
   ... New York, Published by William Harned for the
   American anti-slavery society [n.d.].
   [12] p.   illus.   18 cm.

Slavery and the slave trade in British India; with
   notices of the existence of these evils in Ceylon,
   Mallaca, and Penang, drawn from official documents ... London, Thomas Ward and co., 1841.
   viii, 72 p.   20 cm.

Slavery. From the "Hull Rockinham" of January 31,
   1824. Liverpool, Rushton and Melling, printers,
   n.d.
   8 p.   21 cm.

Slavery illustrated in its effects upon woman and
   domestic society ... Boston, Isaac Knapp, 1837.
   127 p.   18 cm.

Slavery in rebellion--an outlaw. How to deal with it.
   [Cincinnati, American reform tract and book
   society, n.d.].
   12 p.   17 cm.

Slavery in the United States: its evils, allevia-
   tions, and remedies. Reprinted from the North
   American review, Oct. 1851. Boston, Charles C.
   Little and James Brown, 1851.
   36 p.   22 cm.

Slavery indispensable to the civilization of Africa.
   Baltimore, Printed by John D. Toy, 1855.

51 p.   22 cm.

Slavery rhymes, addressed to the friends of liberty
    throughout the United States. By a looker on.
    New-York, Johnson & Taylor, 1837.
        84 p.   15 cm.

Slavery--a sin against God. [n.p., n.d.].
        25-45 p.   18 cm.

Slavery vs. abolition. In National democratic quar-
    terly review, Washington, D. C., March, 1860.
        191-207 p.

The slaves' champion, or, the life, deeds, and his-
    torical days of William Wilberforce. Written in
    commemoration of the centenary of his birthday.
    By the author of "The Popular Harmony of the
    Bible," &c., &c. To which is added an account of
    the keeping of the twenty-fifth birthday of free-
    dom ... London, Seeleys, 1859.
        168 p.   16 cm.

The slave's friend ... New York, R. G. Williams, 1836.
        viii, 16 p.   10 1/2 cm.

Slicer, Henry.
        Speech ... delivered in the general conference
    at Indianapolis, 28th May, 1856, on the subject
    of the proposed change in the Methodist discipline,
    making non-slaveholding a test or condition of
    membership in said church. Washington, H. Polkin-
    horn, [n.d.].
        8 p.   22 cm.

Sloan, Jas. A.
        The great question answered according to the
    teaching of the scriptures ... Memphis, Hutton,
    Gallaway & co., 1857.
        288 p.   18 cm.

Smart, Charles Edward.
        Speech ... on the Lecompton Constitution, and
    the report of the committee of conference. De-
    livered in the senate of the United States, April
    28, 1858. Washington, Lemuel Towers, 1858.
        16 p.   22 1/2 cm.

Smectymnuus, pseud.
        Slavery and the church. Two letters addressed

476

to Rev. N. L. Rice ... also a letter to Rev. Nehemiah Adams ... Boston, Crocker and Brewster, 1856.
    44 p.   14 1/2 cm.

Smedley, Charles, 1836-1864.
    Life in southern prisons; from the diary of Corporal Charles Smedley, of Company G, 90th regiment Penn' a volunteers, commencing a few days before the "battle of the Wilderness", in which he was taken prisoner, in the evening of the fifth month fifth, 1864: also, a short description of the march to and battle of Gettysburg, together with a biographical sketch of the author ... [Lancaster? Pa.] Ladies' and gentlemen's Fulton aid society, 1865.
    60 p.   front. (port.)   19 cm.

Smet, Pierre Jean de, 1801-
    Life, letters and travels of Father Pierre-Jean de Smet ... edited from the original unpublished manuscript journals ... New York, F. P. Harper, 1905.
    4 v.   fronts., plates, ports., fold. map in pocket, facsims.   24 1/2 cm.

Smith, Abram P. 1st lieut. 76th N. Y. infantry.
    History of the Seventy-sixth regiment New York volunteers; what it endured and accomplished; containing descriptions of its twenty-five battles; its marches; its camp and bivouac scenes; with biographical sketches of fifty-three officers, and a complete record of the enlisted men. By A. P. Smith ... Cortland, N.Y. [Truair, Smith and Miles, printers, Syracuse] 1867.
    429 p. incl. port. front., pl.   22 cm.

Smith, Adelaide W. 1831-
    Reminiscences of an army nurse during the civil war [by] Adelaide W. Smith, independent volunteer. New York, Greaves publishing company, 1911.
    1 p.l., [7]-263 p.   illus., 2 port. (incl. front.)   19 1/2 cm.

Smith, Daniel, 1748-
    The journal of Daniel Smith, with introduction and notes by St. George L. Sioussat [Nashville, 1915].
    [4]-66 p.   fold. map.   23 1/2 cm.

Smith, Delazon, 1816-
A history of Oberlin, or, New lights of the West. Embracing the conduct and character of the officers and students of the institution; together with the colonists, from the founding of the institution ... Cleveland, S. Underhill & son, printers, 1837.
82 p. 17 1/2 cm.

Smith, E.
An inquiry into scriptural and ancient servitude, in which it is shown that neither was chattel slavery; with the remedy for American slavery. Mansfield, Ohio, published by the author at the Western branch book concern of the Wesleyan Methodist connection of America, 1852.
244 p. 19 cm.

Smith, E.
An inquiry into scriptural and ancient servitude, in which it is shown that neither was chattel slavery; with the remedy for American slavery ... Second thousand. Mansfield, Ohio, Published by the author at the western branch book concern of the Wesleyan Methodist connection of America, 1852.
251 p. 18 cm.

Smith, E. Quincy.
Travels at home and abroad ... New York and Washington, The Neale publishing company, 1911.
3 v. fronts. 21 cm.

Smith, Edward, 1818?
Account of a journey through northeastern Texas, undertaken in 1849, for the purposes of emigration ... London, Hamilton, Adams & co., [etc., etc.] 1849.
vi, [5]-188 p. fold. maps. 18 cm.

Smith, Frederick, 1747.
Memoir of Frederick Smith, written by himself. Philadelphia, Published by the Tract association of Friends [n.d.].
24 p. 18 cm.

Smith, George G[ilbert] 1825-
Leaves from a soldier's diary; the personal record of Lieutenant George G. Smith, Co. C., 1st

Louisiana regiment infantry volunteers white
during the war of the rebellion; also a partial
history of the operations of the army and navy
in the Department of the Gulf from the capture
of New Orleans to the close of the war. Putnam,
Conn., G. G. Smith, 1906.
5, 151 p. front. (port.) 18 cm.

Smith, Gerrit, 1797.
The crime of the abolitionists ... speech of
Gerrit Smith at the meeting of the New York anti-
slavery society, held in Peterboro, October,
22d, 1835. [n.p., 1835?]
[2] p. 23 cm.

Smith, Gerrit, 1797-1874.
Letter of Gerrit Smith to Hon. Henry Clay.
New York, American Anti-slavery society, 1839.
54 p. 21 cm.

Smith, Gerrit, 1797-1874.
Letter of Gerrit Smith to Rev. James Smylie,
of the state of Mississippi, New York, published
by R. G. Williams for the American anti-slavery
society, 1837.
66 p. 22 cm.

Smith, Gerrit, 1797.
Substance of the speech ... in the capital
of the state of New York, March 11th and 12th,
1850. [n.p., n.d.].
30 p. 21 cm.

Smith, Harry, 1815.
Fifty years of slavery in the United States
of America. Grand Rapids, Mich., West Michigan
printing co., 1891.
183 p. incl. illus., port. 21 cm.

Smith, Ichabod Smith.
Fugitive slave law. The religious duty of
obedience to law: a sermon, preached in the Second Presbyterian church in Brooklyn, November
24, 1850 ... New York, Published by M. W. Dodd,
1850.
31 p. 22 cm.

Smith, J. Gray.
A brief historical, statistical, and descrip-

tive review of East Tennessee ...: developing
its immense agricultural, mining, and manufacturing advantages ... London, J. Leath, 1842.
    xii, 71 p. front. (fold. map) fold. pl.
22 1/2 cm.

Smith, J. S., captain.
    A letter from Capt. J. S. Smith to the Revd.
Mr. Hill on the state of the negroe slave ...
London, Printed and sold by J. Phillips, 1786.
    ix, [10]-51 p.   21 cm.

Smith, James, 1737-
    An account of the remarkable occurrences in
the life and travels of Colonel James Smith ...
during his captivity with the Indians in the years
1755, '56, '58, & '59 ... Written by himself.
Philadelphia, J. Grigg, 1831.
    xi, [13]-162 p.   15 cm.

Smith, James.
    The kind assurance. Cincinnati, American re-
form tract and book society, n.d.
    4 p.   11 1/2 cm.

Smith, James.
    Something of advantage to you. [Cincinnati,
American reform tract and book society, n.d.].
    4 p.   17 1/2 cm.

Smith, James E. b. 1831 or 1832.
    A famous battery and its campaigns, 1861-'64.
The career of Corporal James Tanner in war and in
peace. Early days in the Black Hills with some
account of Capt. Jack Crawford, the poet scout;
by Captain James E. Smith, 4th N. Y. independent
battery. Washington, W. H. Lowdermilk & co., 1892.
    vii, 237 p. front., illus., port., pinn.
19 cm.

Smith, Sir James Edward, 1759-
    The natural history of the rarer lepidopterous
insects of Georgia ... Collected from the observation of Mr. John Abbot, many years resident in
that country, by James Edward Smith ... London,
Printed by T. Bensley, for J. Edwards [etc.] 1797.
    2 v. civ. col. pl.   41 1/2 cm.

[Smith, John].
    Across the Atlantic. By the author of "Sketches of Cantabs." London, George Earle, 1851.
    x p., 247 p. 1 1. 18 cm.

Smith, John, 1580-
    A map of Virginia. With a description of the country, the commodities, people, government and religion ... At Oxford, Printed by Joseph Barnes, 1612.
    30 p. 4 p.1., 1 1. [2], 110 p. fold. map. 18 1/2 cm.

Smith, John, 1580-
    A true relation of Virginia ... with an introduction and notes by Charles Deane. Boston, Wiggin and Lunt, 1866.
    xlviii, v, 88 p. front. (fold. map) 22 1/2 cm.

Smith, John Calvin.
    The illustrated hand-book, a new guide for travelers through the United States of America ... New York, Sherman & Smith, 1847.
    233 p. illus., map. 14 1/2 cm.

Smith, Joseph Warren, 1831-
    Visits to Brunswick, Georgia, and travels south [by] Joseph W. Smith, Boston, A. C. Getchell & son, printers, 1907.
    105 p. 3 port. 22 cm.

Smith, L.
    The higher law, or, Christ and his law supreme ... Ravenna, Ohio Star print, 1852.
    24 p. 19 cm.

Smith, R. F., pub.
    Smith's guide to the southwest along the line of the Missouri, Kansas and Texas railway, containing sketches of all the towns and cities on the line ... Sedalia, Mo., 1871.
    216 p. fold. map. 22 cm.

Smith, Samuel, 1759-
    Memoirs of the life of Samuel Smith: being an extract from a journal written by himself, from 1776 to 1786. Middleborough, Mass., 1853.
    24 p. 18 cm.

Smith, Sidney.
The settler's new home: or, The emigrant's
location, being a guide to emigrants in the selection of a settlement, and the preliminary details
of the voyage ... London, J. Kendrick, 1849.
106 p. 1 p.1. 16 1/2 cm.

Smith, Solomon Franklin, 1801-
The theatrical journey - work and anecdotical
recollections of Sol. Smith. Comprising a sketch
of the second seven years of his professional
life ... Philadelphia, T. B. Peterson [1854].
7-254 p. 1 p.1., port. 20 cm.

Smith, Solomon Franklin, 1801-
Theatrical management in the West and South
for thirty years. Interspersed with anecdotical
sketches autobiographically given by Sol. Smith
... New York, Harper & brothers, 1868.
viii, [9]-275, [1] p. incl. illus., port.
24 cm.

Smith, Mrs. Susan E. D. 1817-
The soldier's friend; being a thrilling narrative of Grandma Smith's four years' experience
and observation, as matron, in the hospitals of
the south ... by Mrs. S. E. D. Smith, revised by
the Rev. John Little, and dedicated to the rebel
soldiers. Memphis, Tenn., The Bulletin publishing co., 1867.
300 p. front. (port.) 19 1/2 cm.

Smith, Truman.
Speech ... on the Nebraska question. Delivered
in the Senate of the United States, February 10
and 11, 1854. Washington, John T. and Lem. Towers,
1854.
23 p. 22 1/2 cm.

Smith, W. L. G.
Life at the south: or, "Uncle Tom's Cabin" as
it is. Being narratives, scenes, and incidents
in the real "life of the lowly". ... Buffalo, Geo.
H. Derby and Co., 1852.
vi, [13]-519 p. 19 cm.

Smith, W. R.
Letter of an adopted Catholic, addressed to the
president of the Kentucky Democratic Association

of Washington City, on temporal allegiance to the
Pope, and the relations of the Catholic Church
and Catholics, both native and adopted, to the
system of domestic slavery and its agitation in
the United States. The speech of Hon. W. R. Smith,
of Alabama, delivered in the House of Representatives January 15, 1855, "on the American party and
its mission," reviewed. [n.p.] 1855.
    8 p.   20 cm.

Smith, William, banker.
    Notes of a short American tour, by Wm. Smith,
banker, Moniaive. Dumfries, Printed at the Courier
office by M'Diarmid and Mitchell, 1873.
    3 p.1., [3]-82 p.   17 1/2 cm.

Smith, William Andrew.
    Lectures on the philosophy and practice of
slavery, as exhibited in the institution of domestic slavery in the United States; with the
duties of masters to slaves ... Edited by Thomas
O[smond] Summers. Nashville, Tenn., Stevenson
and Evans, 1856.
    x, [11]-328 p.   19 1/2 cm.

Smith, William B.
    On wheels and how I came there; a real story
for real boys and girls, giving the personal experiences and observations of a fifteen-year-old
Yankee boy as soldier and prisoner in the American civil war, by Private W. B. Smith, of company
K, 14th Illinois infantry. Ed. by Rev. Joseph
Gatch Bonnell ... New York, Hunt & Eaton; Cincinnati, Cranston & Curts, 1893.
    2 p.1., [7]-338 p.   front. (port.) pl., plan.
19 cm.

Smith, William Loughton, 1758-
    Journal of William Loughton Smith, 1790-1791,
ed. by Albert Matthews. Cambridge, the University
press, 1917.
    21-88 p.   2 p.1., front. (port.) pl.   24 cm.

Smith, William Russell.
    Kansas contested election. Speech ... in the
House of Representatives, March 10, 1856, on the
resolution reported by the committee of elections
in the contested election case from the territory
of Kansas: Resolved, that the committee of elec-

tions, in the contested election case from the territory of Kansas be, and are hereby, empowered to send for persons and papers, and to examine witnesses upon oath or affirmation. [n.p., n.d.]
7 p.   22 cm.

Smithwick, Noah, 1808-
The evolution of a state; or, Recollections of old Texas days ... Compiled by his daughter Nanna Smithwick Donaldson. Austin, Tex., Gammel book co. [c1900].
9-354 p.   5 p.l., front., illus. (incl. music) ports.   20 cm.

Smylie, James.
A review of a letter, from the presbytery of Chilicothe, to the presbytery of Mississippi, on the subject of slavery. By Rev. James Smylie, A. M., a member of the Amite presbytery. Quem Deus vult perdere, prius demestat. Woodville, Mi., Printed by Wm. A. Norris and co., 1836.
79 p.   22 1/2 cm.

Smyth, John Ferdinand Dalziel.
A tour of the United States of America ... Dublin, Price, Moncrieffe [etc.] 1784.
2 v.   17 cm.

Snethen, Worthington G., comp.
The black code of the district of Columbia, in force September 1st, 1848 ... New York, Published for the A. & F. anti-slavery society, by William Harned, 1848.
vi, [7]-61 p.   22 cm.

Snyder, W. H.
American slavery contrasted with Bible servitude ... Lexington, Ill., 1857.
16 p.   22 cm.

Society for the amelioration and gradual abolition of slavery. [Liverpool, James Smith, printer, n.d.]
[3] p.   30 cm.

Society for the diffusion of political knowledge.
Bible view of slavery. New-York [n.d.]
16 p.   22 cm.

Society for the mitigation and gradual abolition of
   slavery throughout the British dominions.
      Report of the committee ... read at the general
   meeting of the Society, held on the 25th day of
   June 1824, together with an account of the proceedings which took place at that meeting. London, The Society, 1824.
      112 p.   21 cm.

Society for the mitigation and gradual abolition
   throughout the British dominions.
      Second report of the committee ... read at
   the general meeting of the Society held on the
   30th day of April, 1825. London, Printed for
   the Society, 1825.
      47 p.   21 cm.

Society for the mitigation and gradual abolition of
   slavery throughout the British dominions.
      Third report of the committee ... read at a
   special meeting of the members and friends of
   the Society, held on the 21st day of December
   1825, for the purpose of petitioning Parliament
   on the subject of slavery. With notes and an
   appendix. London, Printed for the Society, 1826.
      24 p.   21 cm.

The soldier, the battle, and the victory. Being a
   brief account of the work of Rev. John Rankin
   in the anti-slavery cause. By the author of
   Life and writings of Samuel Crothers, etc. Cincinnati, Western tract and book society, 1852.
      120 p. front. (port.), illus.   16 1/2 cm.

Solis de Meras, Gonzalo.
      Pedro Menendez de Aviles, adelantado, governor
   and captain-general of Florida, memorial by Gonzalo Solis de Meras; first published in La Florida, su conquista y colonizacion por Pedro Menen-
   dez de Aviles, by Eugenio Ruidiaz y Caravia;
   translated from the Spanish, with notes, by
   Jeannette Thurber Connor. Deland, The Florida
   state historical society, 1923.
      286 p. 1 1. front. (port.) pl., map. 2
   facsim. 26 x 30 cm.

Some considerations on the consequences of the French
   settling colonies on the Mississippi, with respect

to the trade and safety of the English plantations in America and the West-Indies. From a
gentleman of America, to his friend in London...
London, printed for F. Roberts, 1720.
   60 p.   2 p.l., fold. map.   26 cm.

Somers, Robert, 1822-
   The southern states since the war.   1870-1.
By Robert Somers ... London & New York, Macmillan
and co., 1871.
   xii, 286 p. fold. map.   22 1/2 cm.

Songs of the free, and hymns of Christian freedom ...
   Boston, Isaac Knapp, 1836.
   viii, [9]-227 p.   16 1/2 cm.

Soulsby, Lucy Helen Muriel.
   The America I saw in 1916-1918, by L. H. M.
Soulsby ... London, New York [etc.]. Longmans,
Green, and co., 1920.
   xii, 205 p.   19 1/2 cm.

The South Bend fugitive slave case, involving the
   right to a writ of habeas corpus. New York,
For sale at the anti-slavery office, 1851.
   24 p.   18 1/2 cm.

South Carolina. Immigration Commissioner.
   South Carolina, a home for the industrious
immigrant. Charleston, 1867.
   48 p. fold. map.   23 cm.

South Carolina in 1884: a view of the industrial
   life of the state; manufactures, agriculture,
mining ... a brilliant showing 1880-84. Charleston, S. C., News and Courier, 1884.
   [61] p.   22 cm.

The south vindicated from the treason and fanaticism
   of the northern abolitionists. Philadelphia, H.
Manly, 1836.
   314 p.   20 cm.

The Southern bivouac: a monthly literary and historical magazine. v. 1-5; September 1882-May 1887.
Louisville, Ky., E. H. & W. N. McDonald [etc.]
1882-87.
   5 v. illus., plates, ports., maps.   23 1/2 cm.

Southern excursionists' guide-book to cheap and pleasant summer homes in the mountains of Virginia, on
the line of the Atlantic, Mississippi & Ohio railroad. Presented gratuitiously. Lynchburg, John
B. Ege, 1879.
    48 p. illus. 14 1/2 cm.

Southern homeseekers' guide and winter resorts on the
southern division of the Illinois central railroad. Cedar Rapids, Iowa, Daily Republican printing and binding house, 1889.
    92 p. front., illus. 22 1/2 cm.

Southern homeseekers' guide, describing the cities,
towns and country on and adjacent to the Illinois
Central and Yazoo & Mississippi Valley railroads,
in the States of Kentucky, Tennessee, Mississippi,
Louisiana. Louisville, Courier Journal job
printing co., 1898.
    264 p. front., illus. 22 cm.

Southern notes for national circulation ... Boston,
Thayer & Eldridge, 1860.
    32 p. 19 1/2 cm.

Southern rights documents. Cooperation meeting held
in Charleston, S. C., July 29th, 1851. [n.p.,
n.d.].
    23 p. 21 cm.

Southern slavery considered on general principles; or,
A grapple with abstractionists. By a North
Carolinian. New York, Rudd & Carleton, pub-
lishers, 1861.
    24 p. 23 cm.

Sozialistische briefe aus Amerika ... München, C.
Merhoff, 1883.
    iv, 132 p. 19 1/2 cm.

Spalding, Martin, John, abp., 1810.
    Sketches of the life, times, and character
of the Rt. Rev. Benedict Joseph Flaget, first
bishop of Louisville. Louisville, Ky., Webb &
Levering, 1852.
    xvi, [17]-405, [1] p. front. (port.) 20 cm.

Spangler, Edward Webster, 1846-
My little war experience. With historical
sketches and memorabilia, by Edward W. Spangler
... [York, Pa., Printed by the York daily publishing company, 1904].
xv, 202, [3] p. front., plates, ports., facsims. 23 1/2 cm.

Spear, Samuel Thayer.
The duty of the hour ... New-York, Anson D.
F. Randolph, 1863.
16 p. 23 cm.

Spear, Samuel Thayer.
The law-abiding conscience, and the higher
law conscience; with remarks on the fugitive
slave question. A sermon preached in the South
Presbyterian church in Brooklyn, Nov. 24, 1850 ...
New York, Lambert & Lane, 1850.
36 p. 22 cm.

Spear, Samuel Thayer.
The nation's blessing in trial: a sermon
preached in the South Presbyterian church in
Brooklyn ... November 27th, 1862. Brooklyn,
Wm. W. Rose, 1862.
39 p. 23 cm.

Speeches delivered at the anti-colonization meeting,
in Exeter hall, London, July 13, 1833 ... Boston,
Garrison & Knapp, 1833.
39 p. 23 cm.

Spencer, Mrs. Cornelia (Phillips) 1825-
The last ninety days of the war in North Carolina. 2d thousand. New York, Watchman publishing company, 1866.
287 p. 18 cm.

Spencer, Ichabod Smith.
Comparative claims of home and foreign missions:
a sermon, preached in the Second Presbyterian
church in Brooklyn, on the day of the annual contribution for home missions, April 2d, 1843 ...
Brooklyn, A. M. Wilder, 1843.
30 p. 22 cm.

Spencer, Ichabod Smith.
National account ability: a sermon preached

May 14, 1841, the day of the national fast, observed on account of the death of the president of the United States ... New-York, Published by John S. Taylor & co., 1841.
    31 p.   22 cm.

Spencer, Ichabod Smith.
    The national warning: a sermon preached on the sabbath after the death of General Wm. H. Harrison, late president of the United States ... New-York, Published by John S. Taylor & co., 1841.
    32 p.   22 cm.

Spirit of the Chicago convention. Extracts from all the notable speeches delivered in and out of national "Democratic" convention. [n.p., n.d.]
    16 p.   22 cm.

[Spofford, Ainsworth Rand] 1825.
    The higher law tried by reason and authority ... New York, S. W. Benedict, 1851.
    54 p.   21 cm.

Spooner, Lysander.
    A defense for fugitive slaves, against the acts of Congress of February 12, 1793, and September 18, 1850 ... Boston, Bela Marsh, 1850.
    72 p.   23 cm.

Spooner, Lysander.
    The unconstitutionality of slavery. Boston, Published by Bela Marsh, 1847.
    132 p.   19 cm.

Spooner, Lysander.
    The unconstitutionality of slavery ... [n.p., Dow & Jackson's anti-slavery press, n.d.].
    156 p.   23 cm.

Sprague, Homer Baxter, 1829-1918.
    Lights and shadows in Confederate prisons; a personal experience, 1864-5, by Homer B. Sprague ... with portraits, New York and London, G. P. Putnam's sons, 1915.
    viii p., 1 1., 163 p. front. (7 port.) 19 cm.

Spring, Gardiner, 1785-
Memoirs of the Rev. Samuel J. Mills, late mis-
sionary to the south western section of the United
States, and agent of the American colonization
society, deputed to explore the coast of Africa ...
New-York, New-York evangelical missionary society,
J. Seymour, printer, 1820.
[9]-247 p.   2 p.1.   21 cm.

Stadling, Jonas Jonsson, 1847-
Genom den stora vestern. Reseskildringar af
J. Stadling ... Stockholm, Författarens förlag
[1883].
vi, 328 p.   illus., pl.   21 cm.

Stafford, David W.
In defense of the flag. A true war story.
(Illustrated.) A pen picture of scenes and incidents during the great rebellion. - Thrilling
experiences during escape from southern prisons,
etc.   By David W. Stafford ... of Company D,
Eighty-third Pennsylvania volunteers. Kalamazoo,
Mich., Ihling bros. & Everard, printers, 1904.
88 p.   incl. front., 4 pl., port.   22 1/2 cm.

Stanly, Edward, 1810.
Speech of Edward Stanly, of N. Carolina, ex-
posing the causes of the slavery agitation. Delivered in the House of Representatives, March
6, 1850. [Washington, Gideon & co., n.d.]
16 p.   22 cm.

Stanton, Daniel.
A journal of the life, travels, and gospel
labours, of a faithful minister of Jesus Christ,
Daniel Stanton ... Philadelphia printed: London
reprinted and sold by James Phillips & son, 1799.
[4]-120, 119-132 p.   22 cm.

Stanton, Henry Brewster, 1805.
Remarks of Henry B. Stanton, in the representatives' hall on the 23rd and 24th of February,
before the Committee of the House of Representatives, of Massachusetts, to whom was referred
sundry memorials on the subject of slavery. Fifth
edition. Boston, Published by Isaac Knapp, 1837.
90 p.   17 cm.

Star of emancipation ... Boston, Massachusetts female
emancipation society, 1841.
viii, [9] -108 p.   19 1/2 cm.

Starksborough and Lincoln anti-slavery society.
Address of the Starksborough and Lincoln anti-
slavery society to the public.   Presented the 11th
month, 6th, 1834.   Middlebury, Knapp and Jewett,
1835.
36 p.   24 cm.

A statement of facts, illustrating the administration
of the abolition law, and the sufferings of the
negro apprentices in the island of Jamaica.   London, Printed by John Haddon, sold by William Ball,
1837.
36 p.   17 cm.

A statement of the reasons which induced the students
of Lane seminary to dissolve their connection with
that institution.   Cincinnati, 1834.
28 p.   22 cm.

A statement proving Millard Fillmore, the candidate of
the Whig party for the office of vice president,
to be an abolitionist ... [n.p., n.d.]
8 p.   21 1/2 cm.

Stearns, A. M.
Notes on Uncle Tom's Cabin: being a logical
answer to its allegations and inferences against
slavery as an institution   ... Philadelphia, Lippincott, Grambo & co., 1853.
vi, [7] - 314 P.   19 1/2 cm.

Stearns, Amos, Edward, 1833-
Narrative of Amos E. Stearns, member Co. A,
25th regt., Mass. vols., a prisoner at Andersonville. With an introduction by Samuel H. Putnam.
Worcester, Mass., F. P. Rice,   1887.
57 p.   front. (port.)   23 1/2 cm.

Stearns, Charles.
Facts in the life of General Taylor; the Cuba
blood-hound importer, the extensive slaveholder,
and the hero of the Mexican war ... Boston, Published by the author, 1848.
36p.   18 cm.

Stearns, William A.
  Slavery, in its present aspects and relations.
A sermon preached on Fast Day, April 6, 1854, at
Cambridge, Mass. ... Boston and Cambridge, James
Munroe and Company, 1854.
  47 p.   23 cm.

Stearns, William Augustus, 1805.
  Necessities of the war and the conditions of
success in it. A sermon preached in the village
church, before the college and the united congregation of the town of Amherst, Mass., on the
national fast day, Thursday, September 26, 1861
... Second edition -- for the college. Amherst,
Mass., H. A. March, 1861.
  23 p.   22 1/2 cm.

Stebbins, Giles Badger.
  Facts and opinions touching the real origin,
character, and influence of the American coloniz-
zation society: with views of Wilberforce, Clarkson, and others, and opinions of the free people
of color of the United States ... Preface by Hon.
William Jay. Boston, John P. Jewett and company;
Cleveland, Ohio, Jewett, Proctor, and Worthington,
1853.
  224 p.   19 cm.

Steele, Daniel.
  Thanksgiving by faith for our country's future:
a national thanksgiving sermon, delivered at the
Methodist church, Lima, August 6th, 1863, before
the United congregation ... Rochester, Heughes'
book and job power presses, 1863.
  16 p.   22 cm.

Steele, Mrs. Eliza R.
  A summer journey in the west. New York, J. S.
Taylor and co., 1841.
  [13]-278 p.   3 p.l.   18 cm.

Steevens, George Warrington, 1869-
  The land of the dollar, by G. W.Steevens ...
2d ed. Edinburgh and London, W. Blackwood and
sons, 1897.
  viii, 316 p.   19 1/2 cm.

Steiner, Heinrich.
Künstlerfahrten vom Atlantischen bis zum Stillen ocean. Gesammelte reiseskizzen, von H. Steiner. Mit einer vorrede von Marie Geistinger. New York, The International news co., c1883.
119 p. 20 cm.

Stephen, George.
Anti-slavery recollections: in a series of letters addressed to Mrs. Beecher Stowe ... London, Thomas Hatchard, 1854.
xii, 258 p. 16 1/2 cm.

Stephen, James.
New reasons for abolishing the slave trade; being the last section of a larger work, now first published, entitled "The dangers of the country," by the author of "War in disguise." London, Printed for J. Butterworth, 1807.
67 p. 21 cm.

Stephen, James.
West-Indian pretensions refuted; being an extract from the preface of a work, entitled The slavery of the British West-India colonies delineated, as it exists in law and practice, and compared with the slavery of other countries, ancient and modern ... London, Society for the mitigation and gradual abolition of slavery throughout the British dominions, 1824. Impolicy of slavery. [n.p., n.d.]
3 p. map. 40 cm.

Stephens, Alexander H.
Speech of Hon. Alexander H. Stephens, of Georgia, on the bill to admit Kansas as a state under the Topeka constitution. Delivered in the House of Representatives, June 28, 1856. Washington, Printed at the Congressional Globe office, 1856.
16 p. 20 cm.

Stephens, Alexander Hamilton, 1812-1883.
A constitutional view of the late War between the states; its causes, character, conduct and results presented in a series of colloquies at Liberty hall. Philadelphia, Pa., Chicago, Ill. [etc.] The National publishing co. [c1868-70].
2v. in 1. fronts., ports. 23 cm.

Stephens, Alexander Hamilton, 1812-1883.
The reviewers reviewed; a supplement to the
"War between the states," etc., with an appendix
in review of "Reconstruction," so called. New
York, D. Appleton and company, 1872.
273 p.   24 cm.

[Stephens, Thomas].
A brief account of the causes that have re-
tarded the progress of the colony of Georgia, in
America; attested upon oath. Being a proper
contrast to A state of the province of Georgia.
Attested upon oath; and some other misrepresentations on the same subject. London, printed in
the year 1743.
24, 101 p.   2 p.l.   20 cm.

[Stephens, William] 1671-
A state of the province of Georgia, attested
upon oath in the court of Savannah, November 10,
1740. London, Printed for W. Meadows, 1742.
32 p.   2 p.l.   22 cm.

Sterne, Henry.
A statement of facts ... Preparatory to an appeal to be made by the author, to the Commons of
Great Britain, seeking redress for grievances of
a most serious tendency ... under the administration of His Excellency, the late governor, and
Sir Joshua Rowe ... with an exposure of the present system of Jamaica apprenticeship ... London,
Printed by J. C. Chappell, 1837.
xii, 268, xii p. fold. diags.   22 cm.

Stevens, Charles Augustus, b. 1835.
Berdan's United States sharpshooters in the
Army of the Potomac, 1861-1865. By Capt. C. A.
Stevens ... St. Paul, Minn. [Printed by the
Price-McGill company] 1892.
xxiii, 555 p. front., illus., pl., port.
24 cm.

Stevens, Charles Emery.
Anthony Burns, a history. Boston, John P.
Jewett, 1856.
xiv, 295 p. front., illus.   19 cm.

Stevens, George Thomas, 1832-1921.
Three years in the Sixth corps. A concise
narrative of events in the Army of the Potomac
from 1861 to the close of the rebellion, April,
1865. By George T. Stevens ... 2d ed., rev. and
cor., with seven steel portraits and numerous
wood engravings. New York, D. Van Nostrand, 1870.
4 p.l., [v]-xvi, 449 p. front., illus., plates,
ports, plan. 20 1/2 cm.

Stevens, Thaddeus, 1792.
Speech ... in the House of Representatives,
March 19, 1867, on the bill (H.R. no. 20) relative to damages to loyal men, and for other purposes. [n.p., n.d.].
8 p. 24 cm.

Stevens, Thaddeus, 1792.
Speech of Mr. Thaddeus Stevens of Pennsylvania,
in the House of Representatives, on the reference
of the President's annual message. Made in committee of the whole, February 20, 1850. [Wash-
ington, Buell & Blanchard, 1850?]
8 p. 22 cm.

Stevens, Walter Barlow, 1848-
Through Texas. A series of interesting letters
by Walter B. Stevens, special correspondent of the
St. Louis Globe-democrat ... [St. Louis, General
passenger department of the Missouri Pacific railway co.] 1892.
108 p. illus. 21 1/2 cm.

Stevenson, Benjamin Franklin.
Letters from the army, by B. F. Stevenson, surgeon to the Twenty-second Kentucky infantry. Cincinnati, W. E. Dibble & co., 1884.
vi, [7]-311 p. 20 cm.

Stevenson, Thomas M. b. 1825 or 26.
History of the 78th regiment O.V.V.I., from
its "muster-in" to its "muster-out;" comprising
its organization, marches, campaigns, battles
and skirmishes. By Rev. Thomas M. Stevenson,
chaplain ... Zanesville, O., H. Dunne, 1865.
vii, [9]-349, [2] p. 22 1/2 cm.

Stevenson, William G.
    Thirteen months in the Rebel army: being a
narrative of personal adventures in the infantry,
ordnance, cavalry, courier, and hospital services
... By an impressed New Yorker. New York, A. S.
Barnes & Burr, 1862.
    232 p. front.   17 cm.

Steward, Austin.
    Twenty-two years a slave and forty years a
freeman ... Rochester, N. Y., Published by William Allen, 1857.
    xii, [13]-360 p. front. (port.)   17 cm.

Stewart, Alexander Morrison, 1814-1875.
    Camp, march and battle-field; or, Three years
and a half with the Army of the Potomac. By Rev.
A. M. Stewart ... Philadelphia, J. B. Rodgers,
1865.
    x, 413 p. front. (port.)   19 1/2 cm.

Stewart, Alvan.
    Writings and speeches ... on slavery. Ed. by
Luther Rawson Marsh. New York, A. B. Burdick,
1860.
    426 p. front. (port.)   19 cm.

Stewart, Catherine.
    New homes in the West ... Nashville, Cameron
and Fall, 1843.
    iv, [5]-198 p.   17 1/2 cm.

Stewart, Charles.
    Immediate emancipation safe and profitable for
masters -- happy for slaves -- right in government
-- advantageous to the nation -- would interfere
with no feelings but such as are disgraceful and
destructive -- cannot be postponed without contin-
ually increasing danger. An outline for it, and
remarks on compensation ... Reprinted from the
(Eng.) Quarterly magazine, and review for April,
1832. Second American edition. Newburyport, Published by Charles Whipple, 1838.
    35 p.   22 cm.

Stewart, Charles.
    The West India question. Immediate emancipa-
tion would be safe for masters; -- profitable for

the masters; -- happy for the slaves ... an outline for immediate emancipation and remarks on
compensation ... Second American edition. Newburyport, Charles Whipple, 1835.
35 p.   20 cm.

Stewart, James A.
Speech of Hon. James A. Stewart, of Maryland,
on African slavery, its status - natural, moral,
social, legal, and constitutional; and the origin,
progress, present condition, and future destiny
of the United States, considered in connection
with African slavery as a part of its social system; with the bearings of that institution upon
the interests of all sections of the union, and
upon the African race. Delivered in the House of
Representatives, July 23, 1856. Washington, 1856.
24 p.   20 cm.

Stewart, Robert A. M.
The United States of America: their climate,
soil, productions, population, manufactures, religion, arts, government, &c. ... London, W.
Tweedie, 1853.
399 p.   4 p.l., front. (fold. map) 17 1/2 cm.

Stiff, Edward.
The Texan emigrant: being a narrative of the
adventures of the author in Texas, and a description of the soil, climate, productions, minerals
... together with the principal incidents of fifteen years revolution in Mexico ... Cincinnati,
G. Conclin, 1840.
v, [7]-367 p.   front. (fold. map) 1 illus.
19 cm.

Stiles, Joseph Clay, 1795.
Modern reform examined; or, the union of north
and south on the subject of slavery ... Philadelphia, J. B. Lippincott & co., 1857.
310 p.   20 cm.

Stiles, Joseph Clay, 1795.
Modern reform examined; or, The union of North
and South on the subject of slavery. Philadelphia, J. B. Lippincott & co., 1858.
viii, [9]-310 p.   19 1/2 cm.

Stiles, Joseph Clay, 1795.
    The national controversy; or, The voice of the
fathers upon the state of the country ... New York,
R. Brinkerhoff, 1861.
    108 p.   19 cm.

Stiles, Joseph Clay, 1795.
    Speech on the slavery resolutions delivered in
the General assembly which met in Detroit in May
last ... New-York, Mark H. Newman & co., 1850.
    63 p.   23 cm.

Stillwell, Leander, 1843-
    The story of a common soldier of army life in
the civil war, 1861-1865.   2d ed.   By Leander
Stillwell ... [Erie? Kan.]   Franklin Hudson publishing co., 1920.
    278 p.   front., ports.   20 cm.

Stirling, James, 1805-
    Letters from the slave states ... London, J.
W. Parker and son, 1857.
    viii, 374 p.   front. (map)   20 cm.

Stockton, Robert Field.
    Interesting correspondence. Letter of Commo-
dore Stockton on the slavery question. New York,
S. W. Benedict, 1850.
    23 p.   19 cm.

Stockton, Thomas Hewlings.
    Address ... delivered in the hall of the House
of Representatives, on the day of national humi-
liation, fasting, and prayer, Friday, January 4,
1861. Washington, Printed by Lemuel Towers, 1861.
    16 p.   25 cm.

Stockton, Thomas Hewlings.
    American sovreignity; a short sermon, delivered
in the national hall of representatives, Sabbath
morning, July 28, 1861 ... Washington, Printed by
Henry Polkinhorn, 1861.
    8 p.   24 cm.

Stoddard, Amos, 1762-
    Sketches, historical and descriptive, of Louis-
iana ... Philadelphia; Published by Mathew Carey.
A. Small, printer ... 1812.
    viii, 488 p.   21 1/2 cm.

Stone, A. L., 1815-
    Emancipation. A discourse delivered in Park
Street Church, on Fast Day Morning, April 3, 1862
... Boston, Henry Hoyt, 1862.
    28 p.   19 cm.

Stone, Barton Warren, 1772.
    The biography of Eld. Barton Warren Stone,
written by himself: with additions and reflections.
By Elder John Rogers ... Cincinnati, Published for
the author by J. A. & U. P. James, 1847.
    ix, 404, 4 p. front. (port.)   20 cm.

Stone, James W.
    Trial of Thomas Sims, on an issue of personal
liberty, on the claim of James Potter, of Georgia
against him, as an alleged fugitive from service.
Arguments of Robert Rantoul, Jr. and Charles G.
Loring, with the decision of George Ticknor Curtis. Boston, April 7-11, 1851 ... Boston, Wm. S.
Damrell & Co., 1851.
    47 p.   23 1/2 cm.

Stone, Ross Conway.
    The gold mines, scenery and climate of Georgia
and the Carolinas. Compiled by R. C. Stone for
the General passenger department of the Atlanta
& Charlotte air line railway company. New York,
National bank note company, 1878.
    40 p.   illus., 2 fold. maps (incl. front.)
18 cm.

Stone, Thomas T.
    An address before the Salem Female Anti-slavery
Society, at its annual meeting, December 7, 1851
... Salem, William Ives and Co., 1852.
    27 p.   23 cm.

[Stone, Thomas Treadwell] 1801.
    [Discourse on Elijah P. Lovejoy] [n.p., n.d.]
    [3]-31 p.   17 cm.

Stone, Thomas Treadwell.
    The martyr of freedom. A discourse delivered
at East Machias, November 30, and at Machias,
December 7, 1837 ... Boston, Published by Isaac
Knapp, 1838.
    31 p.   18 cm.

499

Stone, William Leete, 1835-
     Letters of Brunswick and Hessian officers dur-
ing the American revolution. Tr. by William L.
Stone ... (Assisted by August Hund.) Albany,
N. Y., J. Munsell's sons, 1891.
     x, 9-258, x [1] p. front. (port.) pl.   22 cm.

[Stork, William].
     An account of East-Florida, with a journal,
kept by John Bartram of Philadelphia, a botanist
to His Majesty for the Floridas; upon a journey
from St. Augustine up the river St. John's.   London: Sold by W. Nicoll, at no. 51 St. Paul's
church-yard and G. Woodfall, Charing-cross.   [Price
four shillings.]   [1766].
     xxii, [4], 23-90, viii, 70 p.   1 p.l.   21 cm.

Storrs, Richard S.
     The obligation of man to obey the civil law:
its ground, and its extent.   A discourse delivered December 12, 1850, on occasion of the
public thanksgiving; in the church of the Pilgrims,
Brooklyn, N. Y. ... New York, Mark H. Newman &
co., 1850.
     44 p.   22 cm.

Story, Thomas, 1662-
     A journal of the life of Thomas Story: con-
taining, an account of his remarkable convince-
ment of, and embracing the principle of truth,
as held by the people called Quakers; and also,
of his travels and labours in the service of the
Gospel: with many other occurrences and observations.   Newcastle-upon-Tyne: Printed by Isaac
Thompson and company, at the New printing-office
on the Side.   MDCCXLVII.
     iv, 768, 8 p.   2 p.l.   25 1/2 x 21 1/2 cm.

Stowe, Harriet Beecher, 1811-1896.
     The story of "Uncle Tom's cabin."   [Boston,
Directors of the Old South meeting house, n.d.]
     28 p.   19 cm.

Stowe, Mrs. Harriet Elizabeth (Beecher), 1811.
     Dred; a tale of the great Dismal swamp ...
Boston, Phillips, Sampson and company; Chicago,
D. B. Cooke & company, 1856.
     2 v.   18 cm.

Stowe, Harriet Elizabeth Beecher, 1811.
The Edmondson family, and the capture of the schooner Pearl ... Cincinnati, American reform tract and book society, 1856.
64 p.   15 cm.

Stowe, Mrs. Harriet Elizabeth (Beecher), 1811-
Palmetto leaves, by Harriet Beecher Stowe ... Boston and New York, Houghton, Mifflin and company [1901].
2 p.l., 321 p.   front., illus., map.   18 cm.

Stowe, Harriet Elizabeth (Beecher) 1811.
The two altars; or, Two pictures in one.   Boston, J. P. Jewett and co., 1852.
12 p.   19 cm.

Stowe, Mrs. Harriet Elizabeth (Beecher), 1811-1896.
Uncle Tom's Cabin; or, life among the lowly ... Boston, John P. Jewett & Company.   Cleveland, Jewett, Proctor & Worthington, 1852.
2 v.   18 1/2 cm.

Strachey, William.
The historie of travaile into Virginia Britannia; expressing the cosmographie and comodies of the country, together with the manners and customes of the people.   Gathered and observed as well by those who went first thither as collected by William Strachey ... London, Printed for the Hakluyt society, 1849.
viii, xxxvi p., 1 l., [2], 203 p.   illus., 5 pl., fold. map, facsim.   22 cm.

Strahan, Edward [pseud.].
Some highways and byways of American travel.
By Edward Strahan [pseud.] Sidney Lanier, Edward A. Pollard, and others ... Philadelphia, J. B. Lippincott & co., 1878.
163 p.   illus.   23 1/2 cm.

Strange news from Virginia; being a full and true account of the life and death of Nathanael Bacon, Esq., who was the only cause and original of all the late troubles in that country.   London, Printed for William Harris, 1677.
8 p.   24 1/2 cm.

Stranger, traveller, and merchant's guide through the
United States. Illustrated with a map. Philadelphia, 1825.
iii, [vii]-ix, 156 p. 1 p.l., front. (fold.
tab.) map. 18 1/2 cm.

[Stratton, Samuel] defendant.
Report on the Holden case, tried at the January term of the court of common pleas, for the
county of Worcester, A. D., 1839. Published by
the board of directors of the Holden anti-slavery
society. Worcester, Printed by Colton & Howland,
1839.
32 p. 21 cm.

Strauss, Louis, 1844-
Les Etats-Unis. Renseignements historiques,
renseignements géographiques, industrie agricole,
par Louis Strauss ... Paris, Librairie interna-
tionale [etc., etc.] 1867.
3 p.l., [5]-436 p. 22 cm.

Streeter, S. W.
American slavery, essentially sinful: a sermon ... Oberlin, Ohio, J. M. Fitch, printer,
1845.
23 p. 22 cm.

Strickland, S., ed.
Negro slavery described by a negro: being the
narrative of Ashton Warner, a native of St. Vincent's ... London, Samuel Maunder, 1831.
144 p. 15 cm.

Stringfellow, Thornton.
Scriptural and statistical views in favor of
slavery ... Richmond, Va., J. W. Randolph, 1856.
149 p. 19 cm.

Stringfellow, Thornton.
Slavery: its origin, nature, and history ...
New York, John F. Trow, 1861.
56 p. 23 cm.

Stroehlin, Ernest, 1844-
Aux Etats-Unis; impressions de nature et souvenirs historiques; conférence faite le 26 février
1903 à l'Athénée pour la séance annuelle de la

Societe des arts, par Ernest Stroehlin. Genéve,
H. Kündig, 1903.
47 p.   23 cm.

Strong, Anna Louise, 1885-
My native land. New York, The Viking press
[c1940].
3 p.l., 5-299 p.   22 cm.

Strong, Leonard, fl. 1655.
Babylon's fall in Maryland; a fair warning to
Lord Baltimore ... [London] Printed for the author,
1655.
[2], 11, [2] p.   22 cm.

Stroud, George McDowell, 1795.
A sketch of the laws relating to slavery in
the several states of the United States of America. With some considerable additions ... Philadelphia, 1856.
ix, 125 p.   19 cm.

Stuart, Charles.
A memoir of Granville Sharp, to which is added
Sharp's "Law of passive obedience" and an extract
from his "Law of Retribution." ... New York, American Anti-slavery Society, 1836.
156 p.   19 cm.

Stuart, James, 1775-
Three years in North America ... Edinburgh,
Printed for R. Cadell; [etc., etc.] 1833.
2 v. front. (fold. map)   21 cm.

Stuart, Martinus Cohen.
Zes maanden in Amerika. Haarlem, Kruseman en
Tjeenk Willink, 1875.
2 v. illus.   23 1/2 cm.

Stuart, Moses.
Conscience and the constitution with remarks
on the recent speech of the Hon. Daniel Webster
in the Senate of the United States on the subject
of slavery ... Boston, Published by Crocker &
Brewster, 1850.
119 p.   23 cm.

Stuart, Villiers, 1827-
    Adventures amidst the equatorial forests and
rivers of South America; also in the West Indies
and the wilds of Florida. To which is added
"Jamaica revisited." By Villiers Stuart, of
Dromana ... London, J. Murray, 1891.
    xxi p., 1 l., 268 p. 21 pl., 2 fold maps
(incl. front.)   25 1/2 cm.

Stuart-Wortley, Emmeline Charlotte Elizabeth (Manners),
    1806-
    Travels in the United States, etc., during 1849
and 1850 ... New York, Harper & brothers, 1851.
    xii, [13]-463 p.   19 1/2 cm.

Stuber, Johann, 1838?-1895?
    Mein tagebuch über die erlebnisse im revolu-
tions-kriege von 1861 bis 1865. Von Johann Stuber.
In ehrender und liebevoller erinnerung herausgegeben von seiner wittwe, frau Roas Stuber. Cincinnati, O., Druck von S. Rosenthal & co., 1896.
    206 p. illus.   24 cm.

Sturge, Joseph, 1793-
    A visit to the United States in 1841 ... Bos-
ton, D. S. King, 1842.
    cxxii, 192 p.   18 1/2 cm.

Subduing freedom in Kansas. Report of the congressional
    committee, presented in the House of Representa-
    tives, Tuesday, July 1, 1856. [n.p., n.d.]
    31 p.   22 cm.

Substance of the debate in the House of Commons, on the
    13th May, 1823, on a motion for the mitigation and
    gradual abolition of slavery throughout the Bri-
    tish dominions. With a preface and appendixes,
    containing the facts and reasonings illustrative of
    colonial bondage. London, Printed by Ellerton
    and Henderson, Gough Square; for the Society for
    the mitigation and gradual abolition of slavery
    throughout the British dominions; and sold by J.
    Hatchard and son, Piccadilly; and J. and A. Arch,
    Cornhill, 1823.
    xxxix, 248 p.   21 cm.

Sullivan, Sir Edward Robert, Bart., 1826-1899.
    Rambles and scrambles in North and South America.

By Edward Sullivan, esq. London, R. Bentley, 1852.
[iii]-viii, [9]-424 p.   2 p.l.   20 cm.

A summary of the evidence produced before the committee
of the Privy council, and before a committee of
the House of Commons; relating to the slave trade.
London, Printed for J. Bell, 1792.
16 p.   22 cm.

A summary view of the progress of reform in the slave
colonies of Great Britain, since the fifteenth of
May, 1823. [n.p., n.d.].
8 p.   21 cm.

A summary view of the slave trade; with an address to
the people of Great Britain, on the utility of
refraining from the use of West India sugar and
rum. The sixth ed., corrected. Birmingham, Printed, and sold, by R. Martin [n.d.].
16 p.   18 1/2 cm.

The Summer-land: a southern story. By a child of the
sun ... New York, D. Appleton and company, 1855.
264 p.   19 1/2 cm.

Sumner, Charles.
    Argument of Charles Sumner, Esq. against the
constitutionality of separate colored schools, in
the case of Sarah C. Roberts vs. the city of Boston. Before the Supreme Court of Mass., Dec. 4,
1849. Boston, B. F. Roberts, 1849.
32 p.   23 cm.

Sumner, Charles.
    The crime against Kansas. [Boston, Directors
of the Old South work, Old South Meeting House,
n.d.].
24 p.   19 cm.

Sumner, Charles, 1811.
    The crime against Kansas. The apologies for
the crime. The true remedy. Speech ... in the
Senate of the United States, 19th and 20th May,
1856. Washington, Buell & Blanchard, printer,
1856.
32 p.   23 cm.

Sumner, Charles, 1811.
    Freedom national; slavery sectional. Speech
... on his motion to repeal the fugitive slave
bill in the senate of the United States, August
26, 1852. Washington, Buell & Blanchard, 1853.
    31 p.   24 cm.

Sumner, Charles.
    The landmark of freedom. Speech ... against
the repeal of the Missouri prohibition of slavery
north of 36 30'. In the Senate, February 21,
1854. Washington, Buell & Blanchard [n.d.].
    23 p.   24 cm.

Sumner, Charles, 1811.
    A lecture on the anti-slavery enterprise. Its
necessity, practicability, with glimpses of the
special duties of the north ... New York, H. Dayton, 1855.
    24 p.   19 cm.

Sumner, Charles, 1811.
    Protection of freedmen: actual condition of
the rebel states. Speech ... on the bill to maintain the freedom of the inhabitants in the states
declared in insurrection and rebellion in the pro-
clamation of the president, December 29, 1865,
delivered in the Senate of the United States,
December 29, 1865. Washington, Printed at the
Congressional globe office, 1865.
    15 p.   25 cm.

Sumner, Charles, 1811.
    The slave oligarchy and its usurpations. Out-
rages in Kansas. The different political parties. Position of the Republican party. Speech
... November 2, 1855, in Faneuil hall, Boston.
[Washington, D. C., Buell & Blanchard, printers,
1855?]
    16 p.   22 cm.

Sumner, Charles, 1811.
    White slavery in the Barbary states, a lecture
before the Boston Mercantile library association,
Feb. 17, 1817 ... Boston, William D. Ticknor and
company, 1847.
    60 p.   24 cm.

Sunderland, Byron.
    God's judgment for national sins. [Cincinnati,
American reform tract and book society, n.d.].
    12 p.   17 cm.

Sunlight upon the landscape, and other poems. By a
    daughter of Kentucky. Cincinnati, Moore, Ander-
son, Wilstach & Keys, 1853.
    48 p.   19 cm.

Surby, Richard W. 1832-
    Grierson raids, and Hatch's sixty-four days
march, with biographical sketches, also the life
and adventures of Chickasaw, the scout. By R. W.
Surby. Chicago, Rounds and James, printers,
1865.
    396 p.   plates, ports.   19 1/2 cm.

Surtees, William Edward.
    Recollections of North America, in 1849-50-51
... [London? Chapman and Hall? 1852?]
    2 pts. in 1v.   21 1/2 cm.

Sutcliff, Robert.
    Travels in some parts of North America, in the
years 1804, 1805, & 1806. York [Eng.] Printed by
C. Peacock for W. Alexander; [etc., etc.] 1811.
    xi, 293 p.   front., plates.   18 cm.

Sutherland, Patrick.
    An account of the late invasion of Georgia,
drawn out by Lieutenant Patrick Sutherland, of
General Oglethorpe's regiment, who lately arrived
in England, and was sent express on that occasion,
but being taken by the Spaniards off the Lizard,
was obliged to throw the said express and his
other papers over-board. [London, 1743].
    4 p.   33 1/2 cm.

Sutter, Archibald.
    American notes, 1881, by Archibald Sutter ...
Edinburgh & London, W. Blackwood & sons, 1882.
    xiv, 118 p.   front. (fold. map) illus., plans.
19 1/2 cm.

Swansea, Henry Hussey Vivian, 1st baron, 1821-
    Notes of a tour in America. From August 7th
to November 17, 1877, by H. Hussey Vivian ...

London, E. Stanford, 1878.
2 p.l., iii, [1] 260 p. front. (fold. map)
22 1/2 cm.

Sweat, Lorenzo de Medici, 1818.
Confiscated property. Speech ... delivered
in the House of Representatives, first session,
thirty-eighth congress, January, 1864. [n.p.,
n.d.].
16 p. 24 cm.

Sweet, Alexander Edwin, 1841-
On a Mexican mustang through Texas, from the
Gulf to the Rio Grande, by Alex. E. Sweet and J.
Armoy Knox ... With two hundred and sixty-five
illustrations. London, Chatto & Windus, 1884.
672 p. front., illus., plates. 21 cm.

Sweet, O. P.
Sweet's amusement directory and travelers'
guide from the Atlantic to the Pacific ... Rochester, N. Y., 1870-71.
480 p. 21 1/2 cm.

Swiggett, Samuel A. 1834-
The bright side of prison life. Experiences,
in prison and out, of an involuntary sojourner
in rebeldom. Baltimore, Press of Fleet, McGinley
& co. [c1897].
254 p. 10 ports. (incl. front.) 19 1/2 cm.

Swisshelm, Mrs. Jane Grey [Cannon] 1815-
Half a century ... Chicago, J. G. Swisshelm,
1880.
363 p. 20 cm.

T

The tables turned. A letter to the Congregational
association of New York, reviewing the report of
their committee on "The relation of the American
tract society to the subject of slavery." By a
Congregational director. Boston, Crocker & Brewster [n.d.]
44 p. 23 cm.

Taddei, Mario.
Strade d'America. Milano, Casa editrice Ces-
china, 1935.
2 p.l., [7]-376, [2] p.   xxiii pl. (incl.
map)   21 cm.

Tafel, Gustav, ed.
"Die neuner."   Eine schilderung der Kriegs-
jahre des 9ten regiments Ohio vol. infanterie
vom 17, April, 1861 bis 7, Juni, 1864. Mit einer
einleitung von Oberst Gustav Tafel. Cincinnati,
S. Rosenthal & co., 1897.
v-ix, 11-290 p., 1 l.   front., illus., ports.
19 1/2 cm.

Tailfer, Patrick.
A true and historical narrative of the colony
of Georgia, in America from the first settlement
thereof until this present period ... By Pat.
Tailfer, M. D., Hugh Anderson, M. A., Da. Douglas,
and others, land-holders in Georgia, at present
in Charles-Town in South Carolina ... Charles-
Town, South-Carolina: Printed by P. Timothy, for
the authors, M.DCC.XLI.
xviii, 118 (i.e. 110) p.   17 1/2 cm.

Tallack, William, 1831-
Friendly sketches in America ... London, A.W.
Bennett, 1861.
xi, 276 p.   19 cm.

Tanner, Henry Schenck, 1786-1858.
The American traveller; or, Guide through the
United States. Containing brief notices of the
several states, cities, principal towns, canals
and railroads, &c.   With tables of distances, by
stage, canal and steamboat routes. The whole
alphabetically arranged, with direct reference to
the accompanying map of the roads, canals, and
railways of the United States. 2d ed. By H. S.
Tanner. Philadelphia, The author, 1836.
144 p. 4 pl. (incl. front.) fold. map, 4
plans.   15 cm.

Tanner, Henry Schenck, 1786-
A description of the canals and railroads of
the United States, comprehending notices of all
the works of internal improvement throughout the

several states ... New York, T. R. Tanner & J. Disturnell, 1840.
vii, [9]-272 p.   2 fold. pl., 3 fold. maps. 23 cm.

Tanner, Henry Schenck, 1786-
A geographical, historical, and statistical view of the central or middle United States; containing accounts of their early settlement; natural features; progress of improvement ... Philadelphia, H. Tanner, jr.; New York, T.R. Tanner, 1841.
v, [3]-524 p.   4 fold. maps.   15 1/2 cm.

Tanner, Henry Schenck, 1786-
Memoir on the recent surveys, observations, and internal improvements, in the United States, with brief notices of the new counties, towns, villages ... Philadelphia, The author, 1829.
108 p.   1 p.l.   18 1/2 cm.

Tansill, Robert.
A free and impartial exposition of the causes which led to the failure of the Confederate states to establish their independence. Washington, 1865.
24 p.   21 1/2 cm.

[Tappan, Lewis].
Address to the non-slaveholders of the south, on the political and social evils of slavery. New York, Published by the Am. & for. anti-slavery society [n.d.].
58 p.   20 cm.

Tarleton, Sir Banastre, bart., 1754-
A history of the campaigns of 1780 and 1781, in the southern provinces of North America ... London, Printed for T. Cadell, 1787.
vii, [1], 518 p.   maps (part fold.)   29 cm.

Tarrant, Eastham.
The wild riders of the First Kentucky cavalry. A history of the regiment in the great war of the rebellion, 1861-1865, telling of its origin and organization; a description of the material of which it was composed; its rapid and severe marches, hard service, and fierce conflicts ... A

regimental roster. Prison life, adventures and
escapes. By Sergeant E. Tarrant ... Pub. by a
committee of the regiment. [Louisville, Press of
R. H. Carothers, ᶜ1894].
x, 503 p. front., port.   22 cm.

Tasistro, Louis Fitzgerald.
Random shots and southern breezes, containing
critical remarks on the southern states and southern
institutions, with semi-serious observations on
men and manners ... New York, Harper & brothers,
1842.
2 v.   18 1/2 cm.

Tatham, William, 1752-
An historical and practical essay on the culture and commerce of tobacco ... London, Printed
for Vernor & Hood, 1800.
xv, 330 p.   4 plates (2 col.)   21 1/2 cm.

Taunton union. Board of managers.
Report of the proceedings and views of the
Taunton Union, for the relief and improvement of
the colored race; together with the Constitution
of the society, and a list of officers, chosen,
May, 1835. Taunton, Printed by Bradford & Amsbury,
1835.
15 p.   22 1/2 cm.

Taylor, Bayard, 1825-1878.
Eldorado, or, Adventures in the path of empire:
comprising a voyage to California, via Panama;
life in San Francisco and Monterey; pictures of the
gold region, and experiences of Mexican travel ....
New York, George P. Putnam; London, Richard Bentley, 1850.
2 v. col. front., col. plates.   20 cm.

Taylor, Benjamin Franklin, 1819-1887.
Mission ridge and Lookout mountain, with pictures of life in camp and field. By Benj. F. Taylor. New York, D. Appleton & company; Chicago,
S. C. Griggs & co., 1872.
vi, [7]-272 p.   21 cm.

Taylor, F[rank] H[amilton].
From the St.Johns to the Apalachicola; or,
Through the uplands of Florida. Illustrated and

prepared by F. H. Taylor and Chas. A. Choate.
[New York] Passenger department, Florida central
& western railroad [1882].
      41 p.   illus.   17 1/2 cm.

Taylor, John.
      Negro emancipation and West Indian indepen-
dence. The true interest of Great Britain ...
Third edition ... Liverpool, R. Rockliff, 1824.
      16 p.   20 1/2 cm.

Taylor, Mrs. Susie King, 1848-
      Reminiscences of my life in camp with the 33d
United States colored troops, late 1st S. C. volunteers, by Susie King Taylor ... Boston, The
author, 1902.
      xii, p., 1 l., 82 p.   front., pl., ports.
19 1/2 cm.

The teaching of the spirit, exemplified in the history
      of two slaves. Philadelphia, Published by the
      Tract association of Friends [n.d.].
      4 p.   18 cm.

Telescopic views of Scripture. [Cincinnati, American
      reform tract and book society, n.d.].
      32 p.   18 cm.

The ten commandments. New York [Published by R. G.
      Williams for the American anti-slavery society,
      1839?]
      16 p.   11 cm.

[Tennant, Charles] 1796-1873.
      The American question and how to settle it ...
London, S. Low, son, and co., 1863.
      2 p.l., 313 p.   19 1/2 cm.
      L. C. card no. 11-32588 Revised

Tennessee. Bureau of agriculture, statistics and
      mines.
      Tennessee; its agricultural & mineral wealth,
with an appendix, showing the extent, value and
accessibility of its ores, with analyses of the
same. By J. B. Killebrew ... com'r of agriculture,
statistics and mines. Nashville, Tavel, Eastman
& Howell, printers, 1876.
      196 p.   illus., fold. map.   22 1/2 cm.

Texan emigration and land company.
Emigration to Texas. Texas: - being a prospectus of the advantages offered to emigrants by the Texan emigration and land company. London, Richardson [1843].
24 p. front. (fold. map)   22 cm.

Texas and Pacific railway company.
Notes on Texas and the Texas and Pacific railway. Compiled from official and other authentic data. Philadelphia, 1873.
48 p. fold. map.

Texas. Bureau of immigration.
Texas: the home for the emigrant from everywhere. Published by authority of the Legislature, and under the auspices of the Bureau of immigration of the state of Texas. Austin, J. Cardwell, state printer, 1873.
29 p.   22 1/2 cm.

Texas Catholic historical society.
Preliminary studies of the Texas Catholic historical society ... distributed under the auspices of the Texas Knights of Columbus historical commission ... [Austin, Tex., 1928-1936].
3 v.   23 cm.

Texas in 1840, or, The emigrant's guide to the new republic; being the result of observations, enquiry and travel ... With an introduction by the Rev. A. B. Lawrence ... New York, W. W. Allen, 1840.
vii-xxii, [23]-275 p.   2 p.1.   19 cm.

Thacher, George.
No fellowship with slavery. A sermon delivered June 29, 1856, in the First Congregational church, Meriden, Conn. ... Meriden, Published by L. R. Webb, 1856.
20 p.   23 cm.

Thacher, James, 1754-
A military journal during the American revolutionary war, from 1775 to 1783 ... To which is added an appendix, containing biographical sketches of several general officers ... Boston, Richardson & Lord, 1823.
viii, [9]-603 p.   22 cm.

Tharin, Robert Seymour Symmes, 1830–
Arbitrary arrests in the South; or, Scenes
from the experience of an Alabama Unionist. By
R. S. Tharin ... New York, J. Bradburn, 1863.
245 p. 16 1/2 cm.

Thatcher, Benjamin Bussey.
Memoir of Phillis Wheatley, a native African
and slave ... Second edition. Boston, Geo. W.
Light; New York, Moore and Payne [etc.] 1834.
36 p. front. (port.) 15 cm.

Thatcher, Marshall P.
A hundred battles in the West, St. Louis to
Atlanta, 1861-65. The Second Michigan cavalry,
with the armies of the Mississippi, Ohio, Kentucky and Cumberland ... with mention of a few
of the famous regiments and brigades of the
West. By Captain Marshall P. Thatcher ... Detroit, The author, 1884.
xiv, [15]-416, 15, [63] p. incl. front.,
illus., port., maps. pl., port. 23 cm.

Thayer, Eli, 1819.
The Central American question. Speech of
Hon. Eli Thayer, of Massachusetts. Delivered in
the House of Representatives, January 7, 1858.
[Washington, Buell & Blanchard, printers, 1858].
8 p. 23 cm.

Thayer, Eli, 1819.
The territorial policy. Speech ... in reply
to Hon. Mr. Curtis and Hon. Mr. Gooch. Delivered
in the U. S. House of Representatives, May 11,
1860. [n.p., n.d.].
8 p. 24 cm.

Thayer, Martin Russell, 1819.
A reply to Mr. Charles Ingersoll's "Letter to
a friend in a slave state" ... Philadelphia, C.
Sherman & son, printers, 1862.
26 p. 23 1/2 cm.

Therou de Sancerre, Louis-Charles-Victor-Auguste.
Le Christianisme et l'esclavage ... suivi d'
un traité historique de Moehler sur la meme sujet,
traduit par M. l'abbe Symon de Latreiche. Paris,

Langlois et Leclercq, 1841.
336 p.   22 cm.

Thomas, Benjamin F.
A few suggestions upon the personal liberty
law and "secession" [so called] in a letter to a
friend. Boston, John Wilson and son, 1861.
22 p.   23 1/2 cm.

Thomas, David, 1776-
Travels through the western country in the
summer of 1816. Including notices of the natural
history, antiquities, topography, agriculture,
commerce and manufactures: with a map of the
Wabash country, now settling. Auburn [N. Y.]
Printed by David Ramsey ... 1819.
320 p.   2 p.l.   front. (fold. map) 17 1/2 cm.

Thomas, Joseph, 1791-
The life of the pilgrim Joseph Thomas, containing an accurate account of his trials, travels
and gospel labours, up to the present date. Winchester, Va., J. Foster, printer ... 1817.
372 p.   18 cm.

Thomas, Joseph, 1791-
Poems, religious, moral and satirical, by
Joseph Thomas, the Pilgrim: to which is prefixed a compend of the life, travels and Gospel
labours of the author. Lebanon, Ohio, Office of
the Western Star, 1892.
264 p.   12 cm.

[Thomas, Thomas E.].
A review of the Rev. Dr. Junkin's synodical
speech in defense of American slavery, delivered
September 19th and 20th, and published December
1843: with an outline of the Bible argument
against slavery ... Cincinnati, Printed at the
Daily atlas office, 1844.
136 p.   22 cm.

Thomassy, Raymond, 1810-
Géologie pratique de la Louisiane. Nouvelle-
Orléans, Chez l'auteur; Paris, Lacroix et Baudry,
1860.
lxviii, 263 p. VI fold. plates (incl. 5 maps)
27 x 21 1/2 cm.

Thome, James A.
Address to the females of Ohio, delivered at the state anti-slavery anniversary, April, 1836. Cincinnati, Ohio anti-slavery society, 1836.
16 p.   22 cm.

Thome, James A.
Emancipation in the West Indies. A six months' tour in Antigua, Barbadoes, and Jamaica, in the year 1837 by Jas. A. Thome, and J. Horace Kimball. Second edition. New York, Published by the American anti-slavery society, 1839.
xx, 412 p.   fold.   map.   19 cm.

Thome, James A.
Emancipation in the West Indies. A six months' tour in Antigua, Barbadoes, and Jamaica, in the year 1837. By Jas. A. Thome, and J. Horace Kimball. New York, Published by the American anti-slavery society, 1838.
xi, 480 p.   18 1/2 cm.

Thome, James Armstrong.
Emancipation in the West Indies. A six months' tour in Antigua, Barbadoes, and Jamaica in the year 1837, by Jas. A. Thome and J. Horace Kimball. New York, American anti-slavery society, 1838.
vi, 128 p.   map.   23 cm.

Thompson, George, 1804.
Discussion on American slavery, between George Thompson, esq. ... and Rev. Robert J. Breckinridge ... holden in the Rev. Dr. Wardlaw's chapel, Glasgow, Scotland; on the evening of the 13th, 14th, 15th, 16th, 17th of June, 1836, with an appendix. Boston, I. Knapp, 1836.
2 p. 1., [3]-187 p.   22 cm.

Thompson, George.
Lectures on British India, delivered in the Friends' meeting house in Manchester, England, in October, 1839 ... with a preface by Wm. Lloyd Garrison. Pawtucket, R. I., Published by William and Robert Adams, 1840.
xii, [13]-206 p.   17 1/2 cm.

Thompson, George.
Pleas for slavery answered. [Cincinnati,
American reform tract and book society, n.d.]
24 p.   18 cm.

Thompson, George.
Prison life and reflexions or, A narrative
of the arrest, trial, conviction, imprisonment,
treatment, observations, reflections; and deliverance of Work, Burr and Thompson.   3 parts in 1
volume.   Oberlin, Ohio, James M. Fitch, 1847.
xvi, 417 p.   18 cm.

Thompson, George.
Prison life and reflections; or, A narrative
of the arrest, trial, conviction, imprisonment,
treatment, observations, reflections, and deliverance of Work, Burr, and Thompson ... Fifteenth thousand.   Dayton, Published by the author,
1860.
xii, [13]-377 p.   17 1/2 cm.

Thompson, George.
Speech of George Thompson, member of the Bri-
tish House of Parliament, at Toronto, May 1851.
Cincinnati, Printed by Wright, Perrin & co. --
Gazette office, 1851.
14 p.   23 cm.

Thompson, George.
A voice to the United States of America; from
the metropolis of Scotland; being an account of
various meetings held in Edinburgh on the subject
of American slavery, upon the return of Mr. George
Thompson, from his mission to that country Edinburgh, William Oliphant and son, 1836.
51 p.   21 cm.

Thompson, George.
Substance of an address to the ladies of Glasgow and its vicinity upon the present aspect of
the great question of Negro emancipation, delivered ... March 5th, 1833 ... Also, some account
of the formation of the Glasgow ladies' anti-
slavery association ... Glasgow, David Robertson,
1833.
42 p.   21 cm.

Thompson, John, 1812.
    The life of John Thompson, a fugitive slave;
containing his history of 25 years in bondage,
and his providential escape. Written by himself.
Worcester, Published by John Thompson, 1856.
    vi, [12]-143 p.   18 cm.

Thompson, Joseph P.
    Memoir of David Hale, late editor of the Jour-
nal of commerce. With selections from his miscellaneous writings ... Second edition. Hartford,
E. Hunt, 1850.
    520 p.   23 cm.

Thompson, Joseph Parrish.
    Teachings of the New Testament on slavery ...
New-York, Published by Joseph H. Ladd, 1856.
    52 p.   18 cm.

Thompson, Maurice, i.e. James Maurice, 1844-
    The witchery of archery; a complete manual
of archery. With many chapters of adventures by
field and flood, and appendix containing practical directions for the manufacture and use of
archery implements. By Maurice Thompson ... New
ed. with a chapter on English archery practice.
New York, C. Scribner's sons, 1879.
    x, [2] 269 p.   front., illus., plates.
17 1/2 cm.

Thompson, Ralph Seymour.
    The sucker's visit to the Mammoth cave: in-
cluding a history of the experience and adventures of a party who undertook to see the cave ...
a full and accurate description of the cave ...
with an account of its living inhabitants. Springfield, O., 1879.
    128 p.   19 cm.

Thompson, Samuel Hunter, 1876-
    The Highlanders of the South, by Samuel H.
Thompson. New York, Eaton & Mains; Cincinnati,
Jennings & Graham [c1910].
    86 p.   front., 3 pl.   19 cm.

Thomson, Andrew, 1779.
    Sermons on various subjects ... Second edition.
Edinburgh, Printed for William Whyte and co. and

Longman and co., London, 1830.
554 p.   22 cm.

Thomson, Andrew.
Substance of the speech delivered at the meeting of the Edinburgh society for the abolition
of slavery, on October 19, 1830 ... Edinburgh,
William Whyte and co., 1830.
42 p.   21 cm.

Thomson, J. R.
Speech of Hon. J. R. Thomson, of New Jersey,
on the conquest of California; delivered in the
United States Senate, August 9, 1856. Washington,
Union office, 1856.
16 p.   20 cm.

Thomson, William.
A tradesman's travels, in the United States
and Canada, in the years 1840, 41 & 42 ... Edinburgh, Oliver & Boyd, 1842.
viii, 228 p.   20 cm.

Thornbury, George Walter, 1828-
Criss-cross journeys ... London, Hurst and
Blackett, 1873.
2 v.   18 1/2 cm.

Thornwell, James Henley, 1812.
The rights and duties of masters. A sermon
preached at the dedication of a church, erected
in Charleston, S. C., for the benefit and instruction of the coloured population ... Charleston,
S. C., Steam power press of Walker & James, 1850.
51 p.   20 cm.

Thorpe, Robert.
A letter to William Wilberforce, containing
remarks on the reports of the Sierra Leone company, and African institution: with hints respecting the means by which an universal abolition of the slave trade might be carried into
effect ... London, Printed for F. C. and J.
Rivington, 1815.
84 p.   21 cm.

Thorpe, Robert.
A reply "point by point" to the special re-

port of the directors of the African institution ... London, Printed for F. C. and J. Rivington, 1815.
113 p.   21 cm.

Thoughts on the abolition of slavery; humbly submitted
in a letter to the king ... London, Baldwin,
Cradock, and Joy, 1824.
22 p.   21 cm.

Three years on the Kansas border. By a clergyman of
the Episcopal church. New York and Auburn, Miller, Orton & Mulligan, 1856.
viii, 240 p.   18 cm.

Thrumbull, Lyman, 1813.
Remarks ... on the seizure of arsenals at
Harper's Ferry, Va. and Liberty, Mo., and in
vindication of the Republican party and its creed,
in response to Senators Chesnut, Yulee, Sauls-
bury, Clay, and Pugh. Delivered in the United
States Senate, December 6, 7, and 8, 1850.
[Washington, D. C., Buell & Blanchard, printers,
1859].
16 p.   23 cm.

Thyfault, I. M.
Fondation d'une colonie française, sous la
direction des Pères du St. Esprit, sol, climat,
ressources de cette magnifique contree et avantages immenses offerts aux immigrants par la
compagnie Little Rock & Fort Smith R. R.   Lettres
du Dr. I. M. Thyfault sur l'ouest de la vallee
de l'Arkansas ... Kankakee, Ill., Impr. du Cour-
rier de l'Illinois, 1878.
39 [2] p.   23 cm.

Tilden, Daniel Rose, 1804.
Daniel R. Tilden's letter to Mr. Giddings,
giving his reasons for supporting General Scott.
[n.p., n.d.].
15 p.   21 cm.

Tilney, Robert.
My life in the army, three years and a half
with the Fifth army corps, Army of the Potomac,
1862-1865, by Robert Tilney ... Philadelphia,

Ferris & Leach, 1912.
247 p. front. (port.)   21 1/2 cm.

Tilton, Theodore, 1835.
The American board and American slavery.
Speech of Theodore Tilton, in Plymouth church,
Brooklyn, January 28, 1860, reported by Wm. Henry
Burr. [n.p., 1860?]
44 p.   15 cm.

Timberlake, Henry, 1730-
The memoirs of Lieut. Henry Timberlake ...
London, Printed for the author, 1765.
viii, 160 p.   front. (fold. map), fold. pl.
21 cm.

Tissandier, Albert, 1839-
Six mois aux Etats-Unis; voyage d'un touriste
dans l'Amerique du Nord, suivi d'une excursion
à Panama; texte et dessins par Albert Tissandier;
avec 82 gravures, 8 planches hors texte et 2
cartes.   Paris, G. Masson [1886].
[5] 298 p., 1 1. incl. illus., plates, 8 pl.,
2 maps (incl. front.)   25 cm.

'To one of the people.' [n.p., Printed by A. E. Miller, No. 5 Broad street, n.d.].
8 p.   24 cm.

To the people of Connecticut.   "The extension of
slavery."   The official acts of both parties in
relation to this question.   [n.p., n.d.].
8 p.   22 cm.

Tobler, Johannes.
Alter und verbesserter schreib-kalender, auf
das G. G. Gnadenreiche Christ-Jahr MDCCLV ...
Neben andern nuz-ergözlichen erforderlichkeiten
mit einer merckwürdigen beschreibung von Süd-
Carolina versehen.   St. Gallen, Hans Jacob Hoch-
reutiner [1754?]
20 unnumb. 1.   20 cm.

Toca Velasco, Jose Ignacio de.
Triaca producida de un veneno.   Naufragio de
española flota.   Poema ... Madrid, Impr. de J.
Sanchez, 1734.
60 p.   10 p.1.   20 1/2 cm.

Tocqueville, Alexis Charles Henri Clerel de, 1805-1859.
De la démocratie en Amérique. Paris, Charles
Gosselin, 1835-40.
4 v. 23 cm.

Todd, William, b. 1839 or 1840.
The Seventy-ninth Highlanders, New York volunteers in the war of rebellion, 1861-1865; by William Todd ... Albany, Press of Brandow, Barton &
co., 1886.
xv, 513 p. incl. front., illus. pl., maps.
25 cm.

Tolmer, J.
Scènes de l'Amérique du Nord en 1849. Leipzig, Avenarius & Mendelssohn, 1850.
vi. 134 p. 18 cm.

Tompkins, Cydnor Bailey, 1810.
Slavery: what it was, what it has done, what
it intends to do. Speech ... delivered in the
House of Representatives, April 24, 1860. [Wash-
ington, D. C., Printed by the Republican congressional committee, 1860?]
8 p. 24 cm.

Toner, Joseph Meredith, 1825-
Notes of a summer trip. Nos. 1-7. [Washing-
ton, 1875]. Mounted newspaper clippings.

Tonti, Henri de.
Relation of Henri de Tonti concerning the explorations of La Salle from 1678 to 1683, tr. by
Melville B. Anderson. Chicago, The Caxton club,
1898.
121 p. 5 p.l., 1 l. 24 cm.

Toombs, Robert, 1810.
A lecture delivered in the Tremont temple,
Boston, Massachusetts, on the 24th January, 1856
... Slavery -- its constitutional status -- its
influence on the African race and society. [n.p.,
n.d.].
16 p. 22 cm.

Toombs, Samuel, 1844-1889.
Reminiscences of the war, comprising a detailed

account of the experiences of the Thirteenth regiment New Jersey volunteers in camp, on the march, and in battle. By Samuel Toombs. With the personal recollections of the author. Orange, Printed at the Journal office, 1878.
4 p.l., 232, 47 p. 17 1/2 cm.

Torrey, Bradford, 1843-
A Florida sketch-book, by Bradford Torrey. Boston and New York, Houghton, Mifflin and company, 1894.
2 p.l., 242 p. 18 cm.

Torrey, Bradford, 1843-
Spring notes from Tennessee, by Bradford Torrey ... Boston and New York, Houghton, Mifflin and company, 1896.
2 p.l., 223 p. 18 cm.

Torrey, Bradford, 1843-
A world of green hills; observations of nature and human nature in the Blue ridge, by Bradford Torrey ... Boston and New York, Houghton, Mifflin and company, 1898.
3 p.l. [3]-285 [1] p. 18 cm.

Torrey, Jesse.
A portraiture of domestic slavery, in the United States ... Philadelphia, published by the author. John Bioren, printer, 1817.
vii, 94 p. front. 23 cm.

Torrey, Rodney Webster, b. 1836.
War diary of Rodney W. Torrey, 1862-1863. [n.p., 19].
96 p. incl. port. front. 20 cm.

Tourgee, Albion Winegar, 1838-1905.
The story of a thousand. Being a history of the services of the 105th Ohio volunteer infantry in the war for the union from August 21, 1862 to June 6, 1865. By Albion W. Tourgee, LL.N. Buffalo, S. McGerald & son, 1896.
8 p.l., 409 p., 1 l., xiv p. incl. illus., port. maps. 23 cm.

Tourists' guide for pleasure trips to the summer resorts, sea bathing and watering places convenient
to Baltimore and its vicinity. Baltimore, Haga-
dorn brothers, 1878.
    59 p. front., illus. 24 cm.

Toutain, Paul, 1848-
    Un Français en Amérique. Yankees, Indiens,
Mormons, par Paul Toutain. Paris, E. Plon et
c^{ie}, 1876.
    2 p.l., iv, 233 p. 18 cm.

Tower, Philo.
    Slavery unmasked: being a truthful narrative
of a three years' residence and journeying in
eleven southern states: to which is added the
invasion of Kansas, including the last chapter of
her wrongs. Rochester, E. Darrow & brother, 1856.
    xv, [17]-432 p. 18 cm.

Towle, George Makepeace, 1841-
    American society ... London, Chapman and Hall,
1870.
    2 v. 19 1/2 cm.

[Townsend, George Alfred].
    The swamp outlaws: or, The North Carolina
bandits. Being a complete history of the modern
Rob Roys and Robin Hoods. New York, M. DeWitt,
1872.
    [vi]-ix, 10-84 p. illus. 23 1/2 cm.

Townshend, Frederick Trench, 1838-
    Ten thousand miles of travel, sport, and ad-
venture ... London, Hurst & Blackett, 1869.
    xiv, 275 p. incl. front. 22 1/2 cm.

Townshend, Frederick Trench, 1838-
    Wild life in Florida, with a visit to Cuba.
By F. Trench Townshend ... London, Hurst and
Blackett, 1875.
    xiv, 319 p. front., map. 23 cm.

Townshend, Norton Strange, 1815.
    The union of the democracy -- resolutions of
'98. Speech ... delivered in the House of Representatives, March 17, 1852. [Washington, D. C.,

Printed at the Congressional Globe office, 1852?]
7 p.   23 cm.

Townshend, Samuel Nugent, 1844-
Our Indian summer in the far West. An autumn
tour of fifteen thousand miles in Kansas, Texas,
New Mexico, Colorado, and the Indian Territory ...
Illustrated by J. G. Hyde. London, Printed by
C. Whittingham, 1880.
2 p.l., 123 p. front., plates.   28 1/2 cm.

A tract for the free states. Let every one read and
consider before he condemns. -- A safe and gener-
ous proposition for abolishing slavery. [Cin-
cinnati, American reform tract and book society,
n.d.].
12 p.   18 cm.

A tract for Sabbath schools [on slavery] [Cincinnati,
American reform tract and book society, n.d.].
4 p. illus.   18 cm.

Tracy, Ebenezer Carter, 1796-
Memoir of the life of Jeremiah Evarts ... Boston, Crocker and Brewster, 1845.
448 p. front. (port.)   23 1/2 cm.

Tracy, Joseph.
Natural equality. A sermon before the Vermont
colonization society, at Montpelier, October 17,
1833 ... Windsor, Vt., 1833.
24 p.   20 1/2 cm.

Trafton, Mark, 1810.
The disturbing element in the body politic.
Speech ... in the House of Representatives, August 6, 1856. [Washington, Buell & Blanchard,
1856].
8 p.   23 cm.

Trafton, Mark, 1810.
Kansas contested election. Speech ... in the
House of Representatives, March 12, 1856, on the
resolution reported from the Committee of elections, in the contested election case from the
territory of Kansas. Washington? 1856?
7 p.   23 cm.

Tranchepain de St.Augustin, Marie.
Relation du voyage des premières Ursulines
à la Nouvelle Orléans et de leur établissement
en cette ville. Par la rev. mère St. Augustin
de Tranchepain, superieure. Avec les lettres
circulaires de quelques unes de ses soeurs, et
de la dite mère. Nouvelle York, isle de Manate,
De la Presse Cramoisy de Jean-Marie Shea.
M.DCCC.LIX.
iv, [5]-62 p., 1 l.   19 1/2 cm.

Transatlantic rambles; or, A record of twelve months
travel in the United States, Cuba, & the Brazils.
By a Rugbaean.   London [etc.] G. Bell [etc.] 1851.
vii, [1] 168 p.   12°.

Travels in North America.   Dublin, Printed by C. Bent-
ham, 1822.
[9]-184 p.   1 p.l., illus.   13 1/2 cm.

Tremain, Lyman, 1819.
Speech ... on the right of Congress to determine the qualification of its members and to determine when the public safety will permit the
admission of representatives from the states
lately in rebellion, and the present state of
national affairs. In assembly, March 1, 1866.
Albany, Weed, Parsons and company, 1866.
16 p.   24 cm.

Tremble, William.
The Liberian crusade ... Louth, Printed by J.
and J. Jackson, 1823.
8 p.   21 cm.

Tremenheere, Hugh Seymour, 1804-
Notes on public subjects, made during a tour
in the United States and in Canada ... London,
J. Murray, 1852.
vi p., 320 p.   1 l., fold. map.   19 1/2 cm.

The trial of Reuben Crandall, M. D., charged with publishing and circulating seditious and incendiary
papers, &c. in the District of Columbia. With
the intent of exciting servile insurrection ...
By a member of the bar. [n.p., 1836].
48 p.   21 1/2 cm.

Tribute to Theodore Parker, comprising the exercises
at the music hall, on Sunday, June 17, 1860, with
the proceedings of the New England anti-slavery
convention, at the Melodeon, May 31, and the resolutions of the fraternity and the twenty-eighth
congregational society. Boston, Published by the
fraternity, 1860.
60 p.   18 1/2 cm.

Trobriand, Philippe Regis Denis de Keredern, comis de,
1816-1897.
Four years with the Army of the Potomac. By
Regis de Trobriand ... Translated by George K.
Dauchy ... Boston, Ticknor and company, 1889.
1 p.l., xix p., 1 1., 757 p. front. (port.)
maps (part fold.)   22 cm.

Trollope, Anthony, 1815-1882.
North America. By Anthony Trollope ... London, Chapman & Hall, 1862.
2 v. fold. map.   22 cm.

Trollope, Frances (Milton) 1780-
Domestic manners of the Americans ... London,
Printed for Whittaker, Treacher & co., 1832.
ix, [1], [iii]-viii, [25]-325 p. 8 pl. (incl.
front.)   23 1/2 cm.

[Trotter, Isabella (Strange)] 1816-
First impressions of the New world on two
travellers from the Old, in the autumn of 1858.
London, Longman, Brown, Green, Longmans, & Roberts, 1859.
xi, 308 p. front. (fold. map) 19 1/2 cm.

Trowbridge, John Townsend, 1827.
Neighbor Jackwood, a domestic drama, in five
acts ... New York, Samuel French & son; London,
Samuel French [n.d.].
72 p.   18 1/2 cm.

Trowbridge, John Townsend, 1827-
The South: a tour of its battlefields and
ruined cities, a journey through the desolated
states, and talks with the people: being a description of the present state of the country -
its agriculture - railroads - business and finan-
ces ... Hartford, Conn., L. Stebbins, 1866.

527

xiii, [14]-590 p.   front., illus. (maps)
plates.   22 cm.

True relation of the hardships suffered by Governor
    Fernando de Soto & certain Portuguese gentlemen
    during the discovery of the province of Florida.
    Now newly set forth by a gentleman of Elvas.
    Translated and edited by James Alexander Robert-
    son ... Deland, The Florida state historical soci-
    ety, 1932-33.
        2 v. facsim.   24 cm.

The true state of the question, addressed to the peti-
    tioners for the abolition of the slave trade.   By
    a plain man, who signed the petition at Derby.
    London, Printed for J. Bell, 1792.
        14 p.   20 cm.

Trumbull, Henry Clay, 1830-
        The knightly soldier; a biography of Major
    Henry Ward Camp, Tenth Conn. vols. Boston, Noyes,
    Holmes & co., 1871.
        xii, 13-335 p. front. (port.) plates.
    18 1/2 cm.

Trumbull, Lyman.
        Great speech of Senator Trumbull, on the
    issues of the day. Delivered in Chicago, Satur-
    day, August 7, 1858. Springfield, Daily Journal
    office, 1858.
        24 p.   21 1/2 cm.

Trumbull, Lynn, 1813-
        Affairs in Kansas territory. Speech ... de-
    livered in the Senate of the United States, March
    4, 1856, on the motion to print thirty-one thou-
    sand extra copies of the reports of the majority
    and minority of the Committee on territories, in
    reference to affairs in Kansas. Washington,
    Buell & Blanchard, 1856.
        16 p.   24 cm.

Truth, Sojourner.
        Narrative of Sojourner Truth, A northern
    slave, emancipated from bodily servitude by the
    state of New York, in 1828 ... Boston, Printed
    for the author, 1850.
        xi, [12]-144 p. front. (port.)   18 1/2 cm.

[Tucker, George] 1775, supposed author.
     Letters from Virginia, translated from the
French ... Baltimore: Published by Fielding Lucas, jr., J. Robinson, printer, 1816.
     viii, [9]-220 p.   12 cm.

Tuckey, Mary B.
     The wrongs of Africa: a tribute to the anti-
slavery cause ... Second edition.   Glasgow, Published for the Glasgow ladies' emancipation society, by George Gallie, 1838.
     48 p.   13 cm.

Tufts, J. B.
     A sermon on American slavery; delivered at
the town house, in Bradford, on Friday evening,
August 22d, 1856 ... Bangor, Wheeler & Lynde,
printers, 1856.
     18 p.   23 cm.

Tunnard, William H.
     A southern record. The history of the Third
regiment Louisiana infantry. By W. H. Tunnard ...
Baton Rouge, La., Printed for the author, 1866.
     [xx], [21]-393, [1] p.   2 port. (incl. front.)
19 1/2 cm.

Turchin, John Basil, 1822-
     Chickamauga. Chicago, Fergus printing com-
pany, 1888.
     4 p.l., 295 p. front (port.) 8 fold. maps.
25 cm.

Turenne d'Aynac, Gabriel Louis, comte de, 1843-
     Quatorze mois dans l'Amérique du Nord. (1875-
1876). Par le c^{te} Louis de Turenne; avec une
carte d'une partie du Nord-^{O}uest ... Paris, A.
Quantin, 1879.
     2 v. fold. map.   18 cm.

Turnbull, Jane M. E.
     American photographs. By Jane M. E. Turnbull
and Marion Turnbull. London, T. C. Newby, 1859.
     2 v. in 1.   19 1/2 cm.

Turner, James William, 1848-
     Wonders of the great Mammoth Cave of Kentucky,
containing thorough and accurate historical and

descriptive sketches of this marvelous under-
ground world, with a chapter on the geology of
cave formation. Carrier Mills, Ill., Turner
publishing company, 1912.
    3 p.l. [3]- 116 p. plates, 3 port. (incl.
front.) 16 cm.

Tutein Nolthenius, R. P. J.
    Nieuwe wereld [door] R. P. J. Tutein Nol-
thenius, indrukken en aanteekeningen tijdens
eene reis door de Vereenigde Staten van Noord-
Amerika. Haarlem, H. D. Tjeenk Willink & zoon,
1900.
    vi p., 1 l., 470 p. illus., fold. map.
23 cm.

[Tuttle, Sarah].
    Claims of the Africans: or, The history of
the American colonization society ... Boston,
Massachusetts, Sabbath school union, 1832.
    252 p. map. 15 cm.

Twining, Thomas, 1776-1861.
    Travels in India a hundred years ago, with
a visit to the United States; being notes and
reminiscences by Thomas Twining ... Preserved
by his son, Thomas Twining of Twickenham, and
ed. by the Rev. William H. G. Twining ... London, J. L. Osgood, McIlwaine & co., 1893.
    xii, 537 p. front. (port.) fold. map.
23 1/2 cm.

The two tract societies; and the three Hartford judges.
    [American tract society, Boston, American tract
    society, New York]. Hartford, Elihu Geer, sta-
    tioner and steam printer, 1859.
        24 p. 22 cm.

Tyler, Daniel F.
    Where to go in Florida, by Daniel F. Tyler
... New-York, W. M.Clarke [1881].
    47 p. illus., map. 17 1/2 cm.

Tyler, Edward Royall.
    Slaveholding a malum in se, or invariably
sinful ... Second edition. Hartford, Printed
by Case, Tiffany & co., 1839.

48 p.   23 cm.

Tyler, Mason Whiting, 1840-1907.
Recollections of the civil war; with many
original diary entries and letters written from
the seat of war, and with annotated references,
by Mason Whiting Tyler, late lieut.-colonel and
brevet-colonel, 37th reg't Mass. vols.   Ed. by
William S. Tyler.   With maps and illustrations.
New York and London, G. P. Putnam's sons, 1912.
xvii, 379 p.   front., ports., fold. maps.
22 1/2 cm.

Tyson, Job Roberts.
A discourse before the Young men's colonization society of Pennsylvania, delivered Oct. 24,
1834, in St. Paul's church, Philadelphia ... with
a notice of the proceedings of the society, and
of their first expedition of coloured emigrants
to found a colony at Bassa Cove.   Philadelphia,
Printed for the society, 1834.
63 p.   22 cm.

U

Uhlendorf, Bernhard Alexander, 1893, ed. and tr.
The siege of Charleston, with an account of
the province of South Carolina: diaries and
letters of Hessian officers from the von Jung-
kenn papers in the William L. Clements library,
translated and edited by Bernhard A. Uhlendorf.
Ann Arbor, University of Michigan press, 1938.
xi, 445 p.   vi pl. (front., facsims., 1 fold.)
2 fold. maps.   23 1/2 cm.

Union Pacific railroad company.
The resources and attractions of the Texas
Panhandle for the home seeker, capitalist and
tourist ... 4th ed.   St. Louis, Woodward and
Tiernen, 1893.
127 p.   map.   20 cm.

Union state central committee.
    Immediate emancipation in Maryland. Proceed-
ings of the Union state central committee, at a
meeting held in Temperance temple, Baltimore,
Wednesday, December 16, 1863. Baltimore, Printed
for Bull & Tuttle, 1863.
    20 p.   23 cm.

U. S. Congress.
    Memorial of the senators and representatives
and the constitution of Kansas; also, the majority
and minority reports of the Committee on territories on the said constitution. Washington,
Cornelius Wendell, printer, 1856.
    59 p.   22 cm.

U. S. Congress. House of Representatives. Committee
appointed to inquire whether any additional provisions are necessary to prevent the importation
of slaves into the territories of the United
States.
    Report ... February 17, 1806, read, and com-
mitted to a committee of the whole House tomorrow
... Washington, A. & G. Way, 1806.
    4 p.   21 cm.

U. S. Congress. House. Committee on naval affairs.
    Report of the Naval committee to the House
of Representatives, August, 1850, in favor of
the establishment of a line of mail steamships
to the western coast of Africa, and thence via
the Mediterranean to London ... with an appendix
added by the American colonization society,
Washington, Gideon and co., 1850.
    79 p.   20 1/2 cm.

U. S. House of Representatives. Committee on the
slave trade.
    Report of the committee to whom was referred,
at the commencement of the present session of
Congress, so much of the president's message as
related to the slave trade, accompanied with a
bill to incorporate the American society for
colonizing the free people of color of the United States. May 8, 1820 ... [n.p., n.d.].
    4p.   23 cm.

U. S. Congress. House. Committee to investigate the
troubles in Kansas. Minority report. [n.p.]

July 11, 1856.
109 p.   20 cm.

U. S. Congress. House of Representatives. Kansas
investigating committee.
Kansas affairs ... [Washington, 1856].
109 p.   23 cm.

U. S. Congress. House of Representatives.
Proceedings and debate in House of Representatives on the election of speaker, January 11,
1856. [Washington, D. C., Printed at the Congressional Globe office, 1856?]
15 p.   24 cm.

U. S. House of Representatives.
Resolutions authorizing the president of the
United States to negotiate with foreign governments on the means of effecting an entire abolition of the African slave trade, and for other
purposes. May 8, 1820 ... [n.p., n.d.].
1 p.   23 cm.

U. S. Congress. House of Representatives. Select
committee on the Amistad case.
Alteration of doc. H. R. no. 185 -- Amistad
case. January 4, 1841. [Washington? 1841?]
9 p.   25 cm.

U. S. Congress. Senate. Committee on territories.
A bill to organize the territories of Nebraska and Kansas, and the report of the Committee
on territories. In the Senate of the United
States, January 4, 1854. Mr. Douglas made the
following report.   (To accompany Bill S. 22.)
[n.p., n.d.].
8 p.   21 cm.

U. S. Congress. Senate.
Proceedings in the U. S. Senate, on the fugitive slave bill. -- The abolition of the slave
trade in the District of Columbia, -- and the
imprisonment of free colored seamen in the southern ports, with the speeches of Messrs. Davis,
Winthrop, and others. [n.p., n.d.].
68 p.   23 cm.

U. S. Congress. Senate.
The spurious Kansas memorial. Debate in the

Senate of the United States, on the memorial of
James H. Lane, praying that the senate receive
and grant the prayer of the memorial presented
by General Cass, and afterwards withdrawn; embracing the speeches of senators Douglas, Pugh,
Butler, Toucet, Rust, etc. Washington, 1856.
    32 p.   20 cm.

U. S. Constitution.
    The Constitution of the United States, with
the acts of Congress, relating to slavery, embracing, the Constitution, the fugitive slave
act of 1793, the Missouri compromise of 1820,
the fugitive slave law of 1850, and the Nebraska and Kansas bill, carefully compiled. Rochester, Published by D. M. Dewey, [n.d.].
    45 p.   22 cm.

U. S. Department of state.
    Report of the secretary of state, communica-
ting the report of the Rev. R. R. Gurley, who
was recently sent out by the government to obtain information in respect to Liberia ...
    116 p.   map., plates.   23 cm.

U. S. Navy dept.
    Recaptured Africans. Letter from the secre-
tary of the Navy ... in relation to the present
condition and probable annual expense of the
United States agency for recaptured Africans
on the Coast of Africa ... Washington, Printed
by Gales & Seaton, 1828.
    15 p.   22 cm.

U. S. President, 1817-1825 (Munroe).
    The message of the president of the United
States, stating the interpretation which has
been given to the act entitled "An act in addi-
tion to the acts prohibiting the slave trade."
December 20, 1819 ... Washington, Printed by
Gales & Seaton, 1819.
    4 p.   23 cm.

U. S. President, 1817-1825 (Munroe).
    Message from the president of the United
States, transmitting a report of the secretary
of State relating to negotiations for the suppression of the slave trade. January 15, 1821
... Washington, Printed by Gales & Seaton, 1821.

534

13 p.   23 cm.

U. S. President, 1829-1837 (Jackson).
   Message from the president of the United
States, in compliance with a resolution of the
Senate, with copies of correspondence, in rela-
tion to the seizure of slaves on board the brigs
"Encomium" and "Enterprise." February 14, 1837
... [Washington? 1837?]
   58 p.   23 cm.

U. S. President, 1837-1841 (Van Buren).
   Africans taken in the Amistad. Congressional
document, containing the correspondence, &c., in
relation to the captured Africans. New York, For
sale at the Anti-slavery depository, 1840.
   48 p.   22 cm.

U. S. Treasury dept.
   Letter from the secretary of the Treasury,
transmitting the information called for, by the
resolution of the House of Representatives, of
the 4th instance, in relation to ships engaged
in the slave trade, which have been seized and
condemned, and the disposition which has been
made of the negroes, by the several state governments, under whose jurisdiction they have fallen.
January 21, 1818 ... Washington, Printed by E.
de Krafft, 1819.
   9 p.   23 cm.

U. S. War department.
   Exploration of the Red river of Louisiana, in
the year 1852: by Randolph B. Marcy ... With
reports on the natural history of the country ...
Washington, R. Armstrong, public printer, 1853.
   xv, 320 p. plates., fold. maps.   23 cm.

Unruh, Conrad Max von, 1842-
   Amerika noch nicht am ziele! Transgermanische
reise-studien von C^d M. von Unruh. Frankfurt a/M.,
Neuer Frankfurter verlag, 1904.
   210 p.   22 cm.

Upham, Charles Wentworth, 1802-
   Nebraska and Kansas. Speech ... in the House
of Representatives, May 10, 1854. [n.p., n.d.]
   7 p.   23 1/2 cm.

Upham, Charles Wentworth, 1802.
Speech ... in the House of Representatives of
Massachusetts, on the compromises of the constitution: with an appendix, containing the ordinance of 1787. Salem, Printed at the Tri-weekly
gazette office, 1849.
40 p. 23 cm.

Upham, Samuel Curtis, 1819-
Notes from Sunland, on the Manatee River,
Gulf coast of south Florida. Its climate, soil,
and productions ... Braidentown, Fla. [etc.]
The author, 1881.
83 p. incl. pl. front. (port.) 18 1/2 cm.

Upson, Theodore Frelinghuysen, 1845-
With Sherman to the sea; the civil war letters,
diaries & reminiscences of Theodore F. Upson,
edited with an introduction by Oscar Osburn Win-
ther. University Station, Baton Rouge, La.,
Louisiana state university press, 1943.
xxii, 181 p. front., plates, port. 21 cm.

Urban, John W.
Battle field and prison pen; or, Through the
war, and thrice a prisoner in rebel dungeons.
A graphic recital of personal experiences. Philadelphia, Hubbard brothers [1882].
xii, 13-422 p. front., plates, ports.
19 1/2 cm.

Uring, Nathaniel.
A history of the voyages and travels of Capt.
Nathaniel Uring. With new draughts of the bay
of Honduras and the Caribbee islands; and particularly of St. Lucia, and the harbour of Petite
Carenage ... London, J. Peele, 1726.
ix, [7], 384, 135, [1] p. fold. maps., fold.
tab. 20 1/2 cm.

[Urquhart, Thomas].
A letter to Wm. Wilberforce, Esq., M. P., on
the subject of empressment; calling on him and
the philanthropists of this country to prove
their feelings of sensibility they expressed in
the cause of humanity on negro slavery, by
acting with the same ardour and zeal in the cause
of the British seamen ... London, Printed by J.
Gillet, Published by R. S. Kirby, 1816.
22 p. 21 cm.

[Urquhart, Thomas].
    Substance of a letter to Lord Viscount Mel-
ville, written in May, 1813, with the outlines
of a plan to raise British seamen, and to form
their minds to volunteer the naval service when
required; to do away with the evils of impres-
sionment, and to man our ships effectually with
mercantile seamen ... London, Printed and sold
by W. Phillips, sold also by J. Richardson.
    16 p.   21 cm.

V

Vail, Stephen Montford.
    The Bible against slavery, with replies to
the "Bible view of slavery" by John H. Hopkins,
Bishop of the Diocese of Vermont, and to "A
northern presbyter's second letter to ministers
of the gospel," by Nathan Lord, D. D., late president of Dartmouth college; and to "X" of the New
Hampshire Patriot ... Concord, Fogg, Hadley & co.,
printers, 1864.
    63 p.   22 cm.

[Vallette Laudun, de].
    Journal d'un voyage à la Louisiane, fait en
1720. Par M***, capitaine de vaisseau du roi.
A la Haye, et se trouve à Paris, Chez Musier,
fils, & Fournier, 1768.
    8, 316, [3] p.   16 cm.

Van Buren, A. De Puy.
    Jottings of a year's sojourn in the South;
or, First impressions of the country and its
people; with a glimpse at school-teaching in
that southern land, and reminiscences of distinguished men. Battle Creek, Mich., 1859.
    x, 11-320 p.   8°.

Van Buren, Martin, pres. U. S., 1782-1862.
    Letter of ex-president Van Buren. [n.p.].
June 28, 1856.
    8 p.   20 cm.

Van Buren, Martin.
The votes and speeches of Martin Van Buren, on the subjects of the right of suffrage, the qualifications of coloured persons to vote, and the appointment or election of Justices of the Peace. In the convention of the state of New York, (assembled to amend the Constitution in 1821). Albany, Thurlow Weed, 1840.
24 p. 23 cm.

Van Dyke, Henry Jackson, 1822.
The character and influence of abolitionism: a sermon preached in the First Presbyterian church of Brooklyn, N. Y., on Sunday morning, December 9, 1860 ... New York, D. Appleton & co., 1860.
38 p. 22 cm.

Van Dyke, Henry Jackson, 1822.
The character and influence of abolitionism. A sermon preached in the First Presbyterian church, Brooklyn, on Sabbath evening, Dec. 9th, 1860 ... New-York, George F. Nesbitt & co., 1860.
31 p. 24 cm.

Van Horn, Burt, 1823.
Democracy and slavery. Speech ... in Assembly. February 18th, 1858. [n.p., n.d.].
11 p. 23 cm.

Van Horn, Burt, 1823.
Liberty and the union, speech ... in Assembly -- January 12, 1860. [n.p., n.d.].
8 p. 23 cm.

Van Vorst, Bessie (McGinnis) "Mrs. John Van Vorst," 1873-
The cry of the children; a study of child-labor ... with an introduction by Hon. Albert J. Beveridge. New York, Moffat, Yard and company, 1908.
xxiii, 9-246 p. 19 1/2 cm.

Van Vorst, Bessie (McGinnis) "Mrs. John Van Vorst," 1873-
The woman who toils; being the experiences of two ladies as factory girls, by Mrs. John Van Vorst and Marie Van Vorst ... New York, Double-

day, Page & company, 1903.
  ix p., 3 l., 303 p. front., plates, ports.
20 1/2 cm.

Vandenhoff, George, 1820-
  Leaves from an actor's note-book; with reminiscences and chit-chat of the green room and the stage, in England and America ... New York [etc.]
D. Appleton and company, 1860.
  vi, 347 p.   20 cm.

Varlo, Charles, 1725?
  Nature display'd, a new work ... A twelve-month's tour of observations through America ...
London, Printed for the editor, 1793.
  xii, [1], 14-320 p.   18 cm.

Vassa, Gustavus.
  The life of Olaudah Equiano, or Gustavus Vassa, the African. Written by himself. Two volumes in one. Boston, Published by Isaac Knapp, 1837.
  vi, [7]-294 p.   front. (port.)   17 cm.

Vaux, Roberts.
  Memoirs of the life of Anthony Benezet ...
York, C. Peacock, 1817.
  156 p.   19 cm.

Vaux, Roberts.
  Memoirs of the lives of Benjamin Lay and Ralph Sandford; two of the earliest public advocates for the emancipation of the enslaved Africans.
Philadelphia, Solomon W. Conrad, 1815.
  ix, 73 p.   17 1/2 cm.

Vay, Peter, gróf, 1864-
  Nach Amerika in einem auswandererschiffe. Das innere leben der Vereinigten Staaten. Von mgr. graf Vay von Vaya und zu Luskod ... Berlin, Gebrüder Paetel, 1908.
  318 p.   24 cm.

Verbrugghe, Louis.
  Promenades et chasses dans l'Amérique du Nord, par Louis & Georges Verbrugghe. Paris, C. Levy, 1879.
  3 p.l., 351 p.   18 cm.

Vermont colonization society.
Twenty-sixth annual report ... presented, October 16, 1845. Burlington, Chauncey Goodrich, 1845.
24 p. 24 cm.

Vermont colonization society.
Forty-eighth annual report ... together with the address of Gen. J. W. Phelps, at the annual meeting in Montpelier, October 17th, 1867. Burlington, Free press steam print, 1867.
42 p. 24 cm.

Verrill, Alpheus Hyatt, 1871-
Isles of spice and palm, by A. Hyatt Verrill ... New York and London, D. Appleton and company, 1915.
xii, [2], 304 p. front., illus. (map) plates. 19 cm.

Vianzone, Therèse.
Impressions d'une Française en Amérique (Etats-Unis et Canada) 3. ed. Paris, Plon-Nourrit et c^{ie}, 1906.
4 p.1., 376 p., 2 1. plates, ports. 19 cm.

View of the law and practice in the Spanish colonies respecting the manumission of slaves. [London, Bagehot and Thomas, printers, n.d.].
6 p. 20 1/2 cm.

A view of the present state of the African slave trade. Published by direction of a meeting representing the religious Society of friends in Pennsylvania, New Jersey, &c. Philadelphia, William Brown, printer, 1824.
69 p. 22 cm.

Vigne, Godfrey Thomas, 1801-
Six months in America. London, Whittaker, Treacher & co., 1832.
2 v. front., pl. 19 cm.

Vinde, Victor.
Amerika slår till ... Stockhom, P. A. Norstedt & söner [1943].
323, [1] p. front., plates, ports., fold map. 22 1/2 cm.

Virginia artillery. Richmond howitzers, 1859-
    Contributions to a history of the Richmond
howitzer battalion. Pamphlet no. 1-4. Richmond,
Va., C. McCarthy & co., 1883-86.
    4 v.   25 cm.
    L. C. card no. 13-11886 Revised

Virginia, Tennessee and Georgia air line.
    The scenic attractions and summer resorts
along the railways of the Virginia, Tennessee,
and Georgia air line, the Shenandoah valley RR.,
the Norfolk and western RR., and the East Tennessee, Virginia, and Georgia RR. New York, Aldine
press, 1883.
    111 p.   front., illus., maps.   4°.

Visconti-Venosta, Enrico, marchese, 1883-
    Impressions of America, by Enrico Visconti-
Venosta. Chicago, A. Kroch, 1933.
    61 p.

The visit of the merchants and manufacturers of Philadelphia to "The World's exposition" at New Orleans. February 11th to 25th, 1885. [Philadel-
phia, Press of McCalla & Stavely, 1885?]
    92 p.   19 x 18 cm.

A visit to the States. A reprint of letters from the
special correspondent of the Times.   1st-[2d]
ser. ... London, G. E. Wright, 1887-88.
    2 v.   15 cm.

A visit to Texas: being the journal of a traveller
through those parts most interesting to American
settlers. With descriptions of scenery, habits,
&c., &c. New York, Goodrich & Wiley, 1834.
    iv, [9]-264, [4] p. front. (fold. map) plates,
19 1/2 cm.

Vivian, Sir Arthur Pendarves, 1834-
    Wanderings in the western land. By A. Pen-
darves Vivian ... With illustrations from original sketches by Mr. Albert Bierstadt and the
author. London, S. Low, Marston, Searle & Rivington, 1879.
    xvi, 426 p. front., illus., 7 pl., 3 maps
(2 fold.]   23 cm.

A voice from Rebel prisons; giving an account of some

of the horrors of the stockades at Andersonville,
Milan and other prisons. By a returned prisoner
of war. Boston, Press of G. C. Rand & Avery,
1865.
16 p.   23 1/2 cm.

Volney, Constantin François Chasseboeuf, comte de,
1757-
Tableau du climat et du sol des Etats-Unis
d'Amérique. Suivi d'éclaircissemens sur la
Floride, sur la colonie française au Scioto, sur
quelques colonies canadiennes, et sur les Sauvages ... Paris, Courcier [etc.] 1803.
2 v.   2 fold. pl., 2 fold. maps.   20 cm.

Vorhees, Daniel Wosley, 1827.
Speech ... delivered in the House of Representatives, January 9, 1866 ... Washington,
Printed at the "Constitutional union" office,
1866.
14 p.   23 cm.

Vries, Hugo de, 1848-
Naar Californië. Reisherinneringen door
dr. Hugo de Vries ... Haarlem, H. D. Tjeenk
Willink & zoon, 1905-07.
2 v. fronts., illus., plates, double map.
22 1/2 cm.

Vries, Hugo de, 1848-
Van Texas naar Florida; reisherinneringen
door Hugo de Vries ... Haarlem, H. D. Tjeenk
Willink & zoon, 1913.
viii, 397 p. incl. illus., plates, maps.
plan.   23 cm.

W

Wachtmeister, Hans, greve, 1828-
Turistskizzer fran andra sidan Atlanten, af
H. Wachtmeister. Stockholm, P. A. Norstedt &
söner [1901].
2 p.l., 250 p. plates, ports. (incl. front.)
25 cm.

Waddington, John.
The American crisis in relation to slavery
... Third Thousand ... London, Elliot Stock,
Warren Hall and co., 1862.
32 p.   20 cm.

Waddle, Angus L. 1826?-
Three years with the armies of the Ohio, and
the Cumberland. By Angus L. Waddle ... Chillicothe [O.]   Scioto gazette book and job office,
1889.
iv p., 1 l., [7]-81 p.   21 1/2 cm.

Wade, Benjamin Franklin, 1800.
Plain truths for the people. Speech of Senator Wade of Ohio. Delivered in the Senate of the
United States, March 13 and 15, 1858. Washington, Buell & Blanchard, printers [1858].
16 p.   24 1/2 cm.

Wade, Benjamin Franklin, 1800-
They "stoop to conquer;" or, the English
swindle. Speech of Senator Wade, of Ohio. Delivered in the United States Senate,April 27,
1858. Washington, Buell & Blanchard, 1858.
7 p.   23 cm.

Wadstrom, Carl Bernhard, 1746.
Observations on the slave trade, and a description of some parts of the coast of Guinea,
during a voyage made in 1787, and 1788, in company with Dr. A. Sparrman and Captain Arrehenius
... London, Printed and sold by James Phillips,
1789.
[xii], 67 p.   19 cm.

Wagner, Charles, 1852-
Vers le coeur de l'Amérique. 2. ed.
Paris, Librairie Fischbacher, 1906.
viii, 401 [1] p.   19 cm.

Wagner, Moritz, 1813-
Reisen in Nordamerika in den jahren 1852 and
1853, von dr. Moritz Wagner und dr. Carl Scherzer
... Leipzig, Arnold, 1854.
3 v.   17 1/2 cm.

Wainwright, J. M.
A discourse on the occasion of forming the

African mission school society, delivered in
Christ church, in Hartford, Connecticut, on Sunday evening, Aug. 10, 1828 ... Hartford, H. & F.
J. Huntington, 1828.
24 p.   21 1/2 cm.

Walcot, James.
The new Pilgrim's progress; or, The pious Indian convert ... London, Printed for M. Cooper
[etc., etc.] 1748.
316 p.   1 p.l.   17 cm.

Walcott, Charles Folsom.
History of the Twenty-first regiment, Massachusetts volunteers, in the war for the preservation of the union, 1861-1865. With statistics
of the war and of Rebel prisons. By Charles F.
Walcott ... Boston, Houghton, Mifflin and co.,
1882.
xiii p., 1 l., 502 p. front., port., maps.
22 1/2 cm.

Waldo, Samuel Putnam, 1780-
Memoirs of Andrew Jackson, major-general in
the army of the United States; and commander in
chief of the division of the south. Hartford,
Published by Silas Andrus, 1819.
317 p.   17 cm.

Walker, Aldace F.
The Vermont brigade in the Shenandoah Valley.
1864. By Aldace F. Walker. Burlington, Free
press association, 1869.
191 p.   front. (map) plans.   20 cm.

Walker, Isaac Pigson, 1815.
The compromise resolutions. Speech ... in
Senate of the United States March 6, 1850, on
the congressional resolution submitted by Mr.
Clay, on the 25th of January. [Washington,
Printed at the Congressional Globe office, 1850?]
16 p.   24 cm.

Walker, Jonathan, 1799.
A brief view of American chattelized humanity,
and its supports ... Second edition. Boston,
Published by the author, 1847.
36 p.   17 cm.

Walker, Jonathan, 1799.
Trial and imprisonment of Jonathan Walker, at Pensacola, Florida, for aiding slaves to escape from bondage. With an appendix containing a sketch of his life ... Boston, Published at the anti-slavery office, 1850.
vi, [7]-126 p. incl. 3 pl., front, (port.) 17 1/2 cm.

Walker, Robert James, 1801.
An appeal for the union. Letter ... New York, Tuesday, Sept. 30, 1856. [New York, John F. Trow, steam book and printer, 1856?]
15 p. 20 1/2 cm.

Walker, Robert James, 1801.
Letter of Mr. Walker of Mississippi, relative to the reannexation of Texas: in reply to the call of the people of Carroll county, Kentucky, to communicate his views on that subject. Philadelphia, Printed by Mifflin and Parry, 1844.
32 p. 23 cm.

Walker, Thomas, 1715-
Journal of an exploration in the spring of the year 1750 ... With a preface by William Cabell Rives ... Boston, Little, Brown, and company, 1888.
69 p. front. 20 cm.

Wallon, H.
De l'esclavage dans les colonies pour servir d'introduction à l'histoire de l'esclavage dans l'antiquité... Paris, Dezobry, E. Magdeleine et c^{ie}. , 1847.
clxxvi p. 19 1/2 cm.

Walsh, Robert, Jr.
An appeal from the judgment of Great Britain respecting the United States of America. Part first, containing an historical outline of their merits and wrongs as colonies ... 2d ed. Philadelphia, Mitchell, Ames, and White, 1819.
lvi, 512 p. 21 cm.

[Walter, John] 1818.
First impressions of America. London, Printed for private circulation, 1867.
2 p.l., 131 p. 18 1/2 cm.

The war and slavery; or, Victory only through emancipation. Boston, Published by R. F. Wallcut,
1861.
   8 p.   18 cm.

Ward, Joseph Ripley Chandler, 1845-
   History of the One hundred and sixth regiment
Pennsylvania volunteers, 2d brigade, 2d division,
2d corps. 1861-1865. By Joseph R. C. Ward ...
Philadelphia, Grant, Faires & Rogers, 1883.
   viii, 351 p.   front., ports.   23 cm.

Ward, Samuel Ringo.
   Autobiography of a fugitive negro: his anti-
slavery labours in the United States, Canada, &
England ... London, John Snow, 1855.
   xii, 412 p.   18 1/2 cm.

Warden, David Baillie, 1772-
   A statistical, political, and historical account of the United States of North America;
from the period of their first colonization to
the present day ... Edinburgh, Printed for A.
Constable and co.; Philadelphia, T. Wardle; [etc.,
etc.] 1819.
   3 v. fold. fronts. (v. 1, 3; map, plan) 1
illus.   23 cm.

Ware, Eugene Fitch, 1841-1911.
   The Lyon campaign in Missouri. Being a history of the First Iowa infantry and of the causes
which led up to its organization, and how it
earned the thanks of Congress, which it got. Together with a birdseye view of the conditions in
Iowa preceding the great civil war of 1861. By
E. F. Ware ... Topeka, Kan., Printed by Crane &
company, 1907.
   xi, 377 p.   front. (facsim.) maps, ports.
20 cm.

Warner, Charles Dudley, 1829-
   On horseback. A tour in Virginia, North Carolina and Tennessee. With notes of travel in
Mexico and California. By Charles Dudley Warner.
Boston and New York, Houghton, Mifflin and company, 1888.
   3 p.1. [3]-331 p.   18 1/2 cm.

Warner, Charles Dudley, 1829-
Studies in the South and West, with comments
on Canada by Charles Dudley Warner ... New York,
Harper & brothers, 1889.
4 p.1. [3]-484 p. 18 1/2 cm.

[Warner, Helen Garnie] 1846.
Home life in Florida. By Helen Harcourt
[pseud.] Lousiville, Ky., J. P. Morton & company, 1889.
433 p. front. 20 cm.

Warren, Edwin R.
The free missionary principle, or Bible missions: A plea for separate missionary action
from slaveholders! ... Second edition. Boston,
J. Howe, 1847.
48 p. 16 cm.

Warville, J. P. Brissot de.
Mémoire sur les noirs de l'Amérique septentrionale, lu à l'Assemblée de la Société des Amis
des Noirs, le 9 février 1789. Paris, Bailly,
1789.
56 p. 19 cm.

Warville, J. P. Brissot de.
New travels in the United States of America.
Performed in 1788, by J. P. Brissot de Warville.
Translated from the French. Boston, Joseph Bum-
stead, 1797.
xxvi, 276 p. 17 cm.

Wash, W. A.
Camp, field and prison life; sketches of ser-
vice in the south ... With an introduction by Gen.
L. M. Lewis, and a medical history of Johnson's
Island by Col. I.G.W. Steedman, M. D. Saint
Louis, southwestern book and publishing company,
1870.
xvi, 382 p. 18 1/2 cm.

Washburn, Israel.
Kansas contested election. Speech ... in the
House of Representatives, March 14, 1856, on the
resolution reported by the committee of elections,
in the contested election case from the territory
of Kansas. Washington, Buell & Blanchard, 1856.
8 p. 22 1/2 cm.

Washburn, Israel, 1813.
Policies of the country. Speech ... in the
House of Representatives, June 21, 1856. [Wash-
ington, Buell & Blanchard, 1856].
14 p. 24 cm.

Washburn, Israel.
Speech ... on the bill to organize territorial
governments in Nebraska and Kansas, and against
the abrogation of the Missouri Compromise. House
of Representatives, April 7, 1854. Washington,
Congressional globe office, 1854.
16 p. 22 cm.

Washington, George, pres. U. S., 1732-1799.
The diaries of George Washington, 1748-1799,
edited by John C. Fitzpatrick. Published for
the Mount Vernon ladies association of the Union.
Boston and New York, Houghton Mifflin company,
1925.
4 v. fronts. (v. 1, port; v. 2-3, facsims.)
map. 23 cm.

Washington, George, Pres. U. S., 1732-
Journal of my journey over the mountains ...
while surveying for Lord Thomas Fairfax ... in
the northern neck of Virginia, beyond the Blue
Ridge, in 1747-8. Copied from the original with
literal exactness and edited with notes by J. M.
Toner, M. D., Albany, N. Y., Munsell's sons,
1892.
144 p. 9 maps. 22 cm.

Washington, George, Pres. U. S., 1732-1799.
Journal sent by the Hon. Robert Dinwiddie,
esq.; His Majesty's Lieutenant-Governor, and
Commander in Chief of Virginia, to the Commandant
of the French forces on Ohio. To which are added
the Governor's letter: and a translation of
the French officer's answer. With a new map of
the country as far as the Mississippi. Williamsburg printed, London: Reprinted for T. Jefferys,
1754.
32 p. front. (fold. map) 22 cm.

[Waterhouse, Edward] fl. 1622.
A declaration of the state of the colony and
state of affairs in Virginia ... London, Imprinted

by G. Eld, for R. Mylbourne, 1622.
    54 p. 3 p.l.   18 cm.

Waterhouse, Sylvester, 1830-
    The resources of Missouri ... St. Louis, Mo.,
Printed by A. Wiebusch & son, 1867.
    96 p.   22 1/2 cm.

Watkins, N. J., ed.
    The pine and the palm greeting; or, The trip
of the northern editors to the South in 1871,
and the return visit of the southern editors in
1872, under the leadership of Maj. N. H. Hotch-
kiss ... Ed. and comp. by N. J. Watkins. Baltimore, J. D. Ehlers & co.'s engraving and printing house, 1873.
    1 p.l., 144 p.   front. (port.) fold. maps.
23 cm.

Watkins, Samuel R.
    1861 vs. 1882. "Co. Aytch", Maury grays,
First Tennessee regiment; or, A side show of
the big show. By Sam. R. Watkins ... Nashville,
Tenn., Cumberland Presbyterian pub. house, 1882.
    236 p.   22 1/2 cm.

Watson, Elkahah, 1758-
    Men and times of the revolution; or, Memoirs
of Elkanah Watson, including journals of travels
in Europe and America, from 1777 to 1842, with
his correspondence with public men and reminiscences and incidents of the revolution, ed. by
his son, Winslow C. Watson. New-York, Dana and
company, 1856.
    xvi, [17]-460 p.   22 1/2 cm.

Watson, John, of Glasgow.
    Souvenir of a tour in the United States of
America and Canada. In the autumn of 1872 ...
Glasgow, Printed for private circulation, 1872.
    91 p. front. (port.)   25 cm.

Watson, William, of Skelmorlie, Scotland.
    Life in the Confederate army, being the ob-
servations and experiences of an alien in the
South during the American civil war. By William
Watson. London, Chapman and Hall, limited [Aird
and Coghill, printers, Glasgow] 1887.
    xvi, [17]-456 p.   19 1/2 cm.

Waylen, Edward.
    Ecclesiastical reminiscences of the United
States. New York, Wiley and Putnam, 1846.
    xv, 501 p.   22 cm.

Wayman, James.
    Impressions of Kentucky.   By an English edi-
tor.   Frankfort, Ky., 1883.
    19 p.   23 cm.

Webb, J. Watson.
    A letter from his excellency J. Watson Webb,
United States envoy extraordinary and minister
plenipotentiary in Brazil, to J. Bramley-Moore,
Esq., M. P.   In reply to a statement in the
"Times" newspaper by his excellency W. D. Chris-
tie.   [Printed for private circulation, n.d.]
    64 p.   21 1/2 cm.

Webb, J. Watson.
    Slavery and its tendencies.   A letter from
J. Watson Webb to the New York Courier and Enquirer.   [Washington, D. C., Buell & Blanchard,
printers, 1856].
    6 p.   22 cm.

Webb, Samuel.
    Speech ... in the national anti-slavery con-
vention held at Albany, N. Y., on the first day
of August, 1839.   Philadelphia, Merrihew and
Thompson, 1840.
    20 p.   20 cm.

Webber, Charles Henry.
    The Eden of the South, descriptive of the
orange groves, vegetable farms, strawberry fields,
peach orchards, soil, climate, natural peculiarities, and the people of Alachua county, Florida,
together with other valuable information for
tourists, invalids, or those seeking a home in
... Florida.   By "Carl" Webber ... New York [Leve
& Alden] 1883.
    [10] [5]-132 p. incl. illus., map.   19 1/2 cm.

Webster, Daniel, 1782.
    Daniel Webster on slavery.   Extracts from
some of the speeches of Mr. Webster, on the subject of slavery: together with his great com-

promise speech of March 7, 1850, entire, and the
Boston memorial, on the subject of slavery, drawn
up by Mr. Webster, to which is added the constitution of the United States. Boston, William
Carter & brother, 1861.
  60 p.   23 cm.

Webster, Daniel, 1782.
    Speech of Hon. Daniel Webster, on Mr. Clay's
resolutions, in the Senate of the United States,
March 7, 1850 ... Washington, Printed by Gideon
and co., 1850.
    64 p.   23 cm.

Webster, Daniel, 1782.
    The voice of Daniel Webster. Remarks in the
Senate of the United States ... on the 12th of
August, 1848. [n.p., n.d.].
    8 p.   24 cm.

[Webster, J. C.].
    Circular [declaration of principles and con-
stitution of the Church anti-slavery society of
the United States]. [Worcester, Mass.? 1858?]
    4 p.   23 cm.

Webster, Noah.
    Effects of slavery on morals and industry ...
Hartford, Conn., Printed by Hudson and Goodwin,
1793.
    56 p.   20 cm.

Weeden, Miss Howard, 1847-
    Bandanna ballads, including "Shadows on the
wall"; verses and pictures ... Introduction by
Joel Chandler Harris. New York, Doubleday &
McClure company, 1899.
    xvi, 90 p.   1 l. incl. front., plates.
19 1/2 cm.

Weichardt, Karl, ed.
    Die Vereinigten Staaten von NordAmerika und
deren territorien, nebst einem blick auf Kanada
... Leipzig, A. Weichardt, 1848.
    x, 447, [1] p. front., fold. map.   21 1/2 cm.

Weichmann, Herbert.
    Alltag in USA.   [Hamburg] E. Hauswedell [1949].
    156 p.   21 cm.

Weiser, George.
Nine months in Rebel prisons ... Philadelphia,
J. N. Reeve & co., 1890.
53, [1] p. incl. front. port. 20 1/2 cm.

Weishampel, John F., comp.
The stranger in Baltimore. A new hand book,
containing sketches of the early history and present condition of Baltimore, with a description
of its notable localities, and other information
... Baltimore, J. F. Weishampel, jr. [1866].
175 p. incl. front., illus., pl. plates.
16 cm.

Weld, Charles Richard, 1813-
A vacation tour in the United States and
Canada ... London, Longman, Brown, Green, and
Longmans, 1855.
xi, 394 p. 20 1/2 cm.

Weld, Isaac, 1794-
Travels through the states of North America,
and the provinces of Upper and lower Canada,
during the years 1795, 1796, and 1797. London,
J. Stockdale, 1799.
xxiv, 464 p. 11 p. (incl. front.) 3 maps
(1 fold.) 2 plans. 27 1/2 cm.

Weld, Theodore Dwight, 1803-1895.
The Bible against slavery. An inquiry into
the patriarchal and mosaic systems on the subject of human rights. Fourth ed. enlarged. New
York American anti-slavery society, 1838.
98 p. 23 cm.

Weld, Theodore Dwight, 1803-1895.
The Bible against slavery. An inquiry into
the patriarchal and mosaic systems on the subject
of human rights. Third ed. revised. New York,
American anti-slavery society, 1838.
74 p. 21 cm.

Weld, Theodore Dwight, 1803-1895.
The Bible against slavery. An inquiry into
the patriarchal and mosaic systems on the subject
of human rights. [n.p., n.d.].
74 p. 22 cm.

Weld, Theodore Dwight, 1803-1895.
    The Bible against slavery. An inquiry into
the patriarchal and mosaic systems on the subject of human rights. New York, published by
R. G. Williams, for the American anti-slavery
society, 1837.
    74 p.   22 cm.

Weld, Theodore Dwight, 1803-1895.
    The power of Congress over the District of
Columbia. With additions by the author. Fourth
ed. New York, American anti-slavery society,
1838.
    56 p.   22 cm.

Weld, Theodore Dwight, 1803-1895.
    The power of Congress over the District of
Columbia. With additions by the author. New
York, American anti-slavery society, 1838.
    55 p.   23 cm.

Weller, John B.
    Speech ... in the Senate, February 13, 1854,
on the Nebraska and Kansas Bill. Washington,
Congressional globe office [n.d.].
    7 p.   23 cm.

Wesley, John, 1703-
    An extract of the Rev. Mr. John Wesley's jour-
nal from his embarking for Georgia to his return
to London ... Bristol, Printed by S. and F. Farley [1739].
    xxiii, 75 p., 2 p.1.   17 cm.

Wesley, John, 1703.
    Wesley's thoughts upon slavery. [Published
in the year 1764]. [New York, American tract
society, n.d.].
    24 p.   17 cm.

West, John C. 1834-
    A Texan in search of a fight. Being the diary
and letters of a private soldier in Hood's Texas
brigade. By John C. West ... Waco, Tex., Press
of J. S. Hill & co., 1901.
    189, 8 p., 1 1.   incl.   port.   19 1/2 cm.

Weston, George Melville.
    The poor whites of the south ... [n.p., 1856?]

7 p.   24 cm.

Weston, George Melville.
    Southern slavery reduces northern wages ...
An address, delivered in Washington, D. C., March
25, 1856. [Washington, D. C.? 1856?]
    8 p.   22 cm.

Wette, Ludwig de.
    Reise in den Vereinigten Staaten und Canada
im jahr 1837 ... Leipzig, Weidmann, 1838.
    xiv, 364 p.   20 cm.

Weygant, Charles H. 1839-1909.
    History of the One hundred and twenty-fourth
regiment, N.Y.S.V. By Charles H. Weygant. New-
burgh, N. Y., Journal printing house, 1877.
    2 p.l., vi, [7]-460 p. front. (port.) fold.
tab.   24 1/2 cm.

What is abolition? New York [Published by R. G. Williams for the American anti-slavery society,
1839?]
    16 p.   11 cm.

Wheaton, Henry.
    Enquiry into the validity of the British
claim to a right visitation and search of American vessels suspected to be engaged in the African slave-trade ... Philadelphia, Lea & Blanchard,
1842.
    151 p.   22 cm.

Wheedon, D. D.
    An address delivered before the Middletown
colonization society, at their annual meeting,
July 4, 1834 ... Middletown, Printed by Joseph
Longking, 1834.
    16 p.   22 cm.

Wheeler, Jacob D.
    A practical treatise on the law of slavery.
Being a compilation of all the decisions made on
that subject, in the several courts of the United
States, and state courts. With copious notes
and references to the statutes and other authorities, systematically arranged ... New York, A.
Pollock, jr.; New Orleans, B. Levy, 1837.
    xviii, 476 p.   24 cm.

Wheeler, John Hill, 1806-
    Historical sketches of North Carolina, from
1584 to 1851. Philadelphia, Lippincott, Grambo
and co., 1851.
    2 v. in 1. fronts. 23 1/2 cm.

Wheeler, John Hill, 1806-
    Reminiscences and memoirs of North Carolina
and eminent North Carolinians. Columbus, O.,
Columbus printing works, 1884.
    15, lxxiv, 478 p. front. (port.) 30 x 23 cm.

Wheeler, William, 1836-1864.
    Letters of William Wheeler of the class of
1855, Y.C. ... [Cambridge, Mass., Printed by H.O.
Houghton and company] printed for private distribution, 1875.
    2 p.l., [iii]-v, 468 p. 22 1/2 cm.

Whipper, William.
    Eulogy on William Wilberforce, esq., deliver-
ed at the request of the people of color of the
city of Philadelphia, in the Second African
Presbyterian church, on the sixth day of December,
1833 ... Philadelphia, Printed by William P.
Gibbons, [1833?]
    35 p. 22 cm.

Whipple, Charles King.
    The family relation, as affected by slavery.
[Cincinnati, American reform tract and book
society, n.d.]
    24 p. 18 cm.

Whipple, Charles King.
    Relation of the American board of commission-
ers for foreign missions on slavery ... Boston,
R. F. Wallcut, 1861.
    247 p. 18 cm.

Whipple, Charles King.
    Relations of anti-slavery to religion. [New
York, American anti-slavery society, 1856?]
    20 p. 19 cm.

[Whipple, Charles King].
    Slavery and the American board of commission-
ers for foreign missions. New York, American

anti-slavery society, 1859.
24 p.   15 cm.

Whitaker, Alexander, 1585-
Good news from Virginia ... At London, Imprinted by Felix Kyngston for William Welby, and
are to be sold at his shop in Paul's church-yard
at the signe of the Swanne, 1613.
44 p.   14 p.l.   17 cm.

Whitcomb, William C.
A discourse on the recapture of fugitive
slaves, delivered at Stoneham, Mass., Nov. 3,
1850 ... Boston, Printed by Charles C. P. Moody,
1850.
37 p.   23 cm.

White, Jonah H.
Guide to and through Florida, "the land of
flowers," containing a historical sketch, geographical, agricultural and climatic statistics,
routes of travel by land and sea, and general
information invaluable to the invalid, tourist
or emigrant. New York, Jonah H. White, 1896.
120 p.   fold. map. illus.   17 cm.

White, Joseph W.
White's guide to Florida and her famous resorts, containing a brief history of Florida;
her climate, health, soil, agricultural products,
fruits, phosphates ... Also a sketch of Jacksonville and other points of interest ... By J.
W. White ... Jacksonville, Fla., Dacosta printing and publishing house, 1890.
112 p.   illus.   22 1/2 cm.

White, Stephen van Culen, 1831.
Address ... upon the race question in the
south, delivered at Salisbury, N. C., before the
literary societies of Livingstone College, May
27th, 1890. [n.p., n.d.].
16 p.   19 cm.

White, T.
An address to the soldiers at Camp Denison
and the union army in general ... [n.p., n.d.]
32 p.   22 cm.

556

Whitefield, George, 1714-
    The works of the Reverend George Whitefield
... To which is prefixed, an account of his life,
comp. from his original papers and letters [by
J. Gillies] London, E. and C. Dilly [etc., etc.]
1771-72.
    6 v. front. (port.)   21 1/2 cm.

[Whitmarsh, Joseph A.]
    To the members of the "First Free church"
Boston. [Boston? 1838?]
    54 p.   16 cm.

Whitney, J. H. E.
    The Hawkins zouaves: (Ninth N.Y.V.) their
battles and marches. By J.H.E. Whitney ... New
York, The author, 1866.
    x p., 1 l., [13]-216 p.   19 cm.

Whitney, John Prescott.
    Whitney's Florida pathfinder. A guide to
Florida. Information for the tourist, traveler
and invalid ... Season 1880-81. New York, J.
P. Whitney, c1881.
    cover-title, 95 [1] p.   15 1/2 cm.

Whitney, William Dwight, 1899-
    Who are the Americans? London, Eyre and Spot-
tiswoode, 1941.
    x p., 1 l., [13]-191 p.   22 cm.

Whittier, John Greenleaf, 1807-1892.
    The anti-slavery convention of 1833. [Boston,
Directors of the Old South work, Old South Meeting House, n.d.].
    16 p.   19 cm.

Whittier, John Greenleaf, 1807-1892.
    The branded hand. Published in The Anti-
slavery Bugle, Salem, Ohio [n.d.].
    36 p.   23 1/2 cm.

Whittier, John Greenleaf, 1807-1892.
    Poems written during the progress of the aboli-
tion question in the United States, between the
years 1830 and 1838. Boston, Isaac Knapp, 1837.
    x, 103 p.   17 cm.

Who wrote the New Testament? [Cincinnati, American
reform tract and book society, n.d.].
16 p. illus. 18 cm.

Why I would not swear. [Cincinnati, American reform
tract and book society, n.d.].
8 p. 18 cm.

Wick, William Watson, 1796.
Apologetic -- explanatory -- denunciatory.
Speech ... in committee of the whole on the
state of the union. Delivered in the House of
Representatives of the United States, August 7,
1848. [Washington, D. C.? 1848?]
7 p. 24 cm.

Wick, William Watson, 1796.
Question of privilege. Speech ... in the
House of Representatives, April 25, 1848. [n.p.,
n.d.].
8 p. 23 cm.

Wickliffe, Robert, 1775.
Reply of Robert Wickliffe, to Robert J.
Breckinridge. Lexington, Ky., Printed at the
Observer & Reporter office, 1841.
64 p. 23 cm.

Wickliffe, Robert, 1775-
Speech of Robert Wickliffe, in reply to the
Rev. R. J. Breckenridge, delivered in the court
house, in Lexington, on Monday, the 9th of November, 1840. Lexington, Ky., Observer and reporter
print, 1840.
55 p. 22 cm.

Wied-Neuwied, Maximilian Alexander Philipp, prinz
von, 1782-
Travels in the interior of North America ...
With numerous engravings on wood and a large
map. Translated from the German, by H. Evans
Lloyd ... London, Ackermann and co. ... 1843.
[v]-x, [2] 520 p. 1 p.l. illus., fold. map.
32 cm.

Wigham, Eliza.
The anti-slavery cause in America and its
martyrs. London, A. W. Bennett, 1863.
vii, 168 p. 18 1/2 cm.

Wilberforce, Samuel.
    A reproof of the American church, by the bishop
of Oxford, extracted from a "History of the Protestant episcopal church in America," by Samuel
Wilberforce, A. M., with an introduction by an
American churchman. New York, William Harned,
1846.
    59 p.   22 cm.

Wilberforce, William, 1759.
    An appeal to the religion, justice, and hu-
manity of the inhabitants of the British empire,
in behalf of the Negro slaves in the West Indies
... A new edition. London, J. Hatchard and son,
1823.
    56 p.   21 cm.

Wilberforce, William, 1759.
    The enormity of the slave-trade; and the duty
of seeking the moral and spiritual elevation of
the colored race. Speeches of Wilberforce and
other documents and records ... New York, American tract society [n.d.].
    144 p.   15 cm.

Wilberforce, William, 1759.
    A letter on the abolition of the slave trade;
addressed to the freeholders and other inhabitants of Yorkshire ... London, Printed by Luke
Hansard & sons, for T. Cadell and W. Davies,
1807.
    396 p.   20 cm.

Wilberforce, William.
    A letter to his excellency the Prince of Tal-
leyrand Perigord &c. &c. &c. on the subject of
the slave trade. [n.p.] 1814.
    354-397 p.   21 cm.

Wild, Ebenezer, 1758-
    The journal of Ebenezer Wild (1776-1781) ...
Cambridge, Mass. [Massachusetts Historical
Society] 1891.
    85 p.   24 1/2 cm.

[Wild, Theodore Dwight] 1803.
    The Bible against slavery: or, An inquiry
into the genius of the Mosaic system, and the

teaching of the Old Testament on the subject of
human rights. Pittsburgh, United Presbyterian
board of publication, 1864.
154 p. 17 1/2 cm.

Wilda, Johannes, 1852–
Amerika-wanderungen eines Deutschen, von
Johannes Wilda ... 2. aufl. Berlin, Allgemeiner
verein für deutsche literatur, 1906-07.
3 v. fronts., plates, ports., 3 fold. maps.
22 1/2 cm.

Wilde, Oscar, 1854–
Impressions of America. Ed., with an introduction, by Stuart Mason [pseud.] Sunderland,
Keystone press, 1906.
40 p. 19 cm.

[Wilhelm, Honor Lupfer] 1870–
Will B. More letters; scenes in the sunny
South. Author's ed. Seattle, The Mail publishing company, 1900.
304 p. 20 cm.

Wilhelm, Paul, Duke of Württemberg, 1797–
Erste reise nach dem nördlichen Amerika in
den Jahren 1822 bis 1824. Stuttgart and Tübingen, J. G. Cotta, 1835.
vi, 394, [2] p. fold. map. 23 cm.

Wilkerson, James.
Wilkerson's history of his travels & labors,
in the United States, as a missionary, in particular, that of the Union Seminary, located in
Franklin co., Ohio, since he purchased his liberty in New Orleans, La. &c. Columbus, Ohio, 1861.
43 p. 22 cm.

Wilkeson, Frank, 1845–
Recollections of a private soldier in the
Army of the Potomac. New York & London, G. P.
Putnam's sons, 1887.
ix, 246 p. 17 1/2 cm.

Wilkeson, Samuel.
A concise history of the commencement, progress and present condition of the American
colonies in Liberia ... Washington, Madisonian
office, 1839.

88 p.   22 cm.

Wilkie, Franc Bangs, 1832-1892.
    Pen and powder, by Franc B. Wilkie (Poliuto)
... Boston, Ticknor and company, 1888.
    383 p.   19 1/2 cm.

Wilkinson, R. A.
    The Gulf coast. Letters written for the New
Orleans "Times-Democrat," by Mr. R. A. Wilkinson.
Published by the Passenger department Louisville
& Nashville R. R.   [Louisville, Press of the
Courier-Journal job printing co.] 1886.
    63 p.   front. (fold. map)   18 1/2 cm.

Wilkinson, Thomas Read.
    Holiday rambles ... Manchester [etc.] J. F.
Wilkinson, 1881.
    3 p.l., 127 p.   front. (port.) pl.   22 cm.

Wilks, Samuel Charles.
    The duty of prompt and complete abolition of
colonial slavery: a sermon ... September 20,
1830 ... London, J. Hatchard and son.   1830.
    53 p.   21 cm.

[Willard, Emma].
    The African in America. To find his true
position, and place him in it, the via media on
which the north and south might meet in a permanent and happy settlement. [Baltimore? 1862?]
    11 p.   22 cm.

[Willer, T. J.]
    La question de l'esclavage aux Etats-Unis,
par un ancien fonctionnaire des Indes neerlandai-
ses ... La Haye, Martinus Nijhoff, Sept. 1862.
    61 p.   21 cm.

William, father, pseud.
    Recollections of rambles in the South ... New
York, Carlton & Porter, 1856.
    196 p.   incl. front., 4 pl.   15 cm.

Williams, Cynric R.
    A tour through the island of Jamaica, from
the western to the eastern end, in the year 1823
... London, Hunt and Clarke, 1826.
    xviii, 352 p.   23 cm.

Williams, Edward, fl. 1650.
Virgo triumphans: or, Virginia richly and
truly valued; more especially The south part
thereof: viz, the fertile Carolina ... London,
Printed by T. Harper, for J. Stephenson, 1650.
47, [8] p. 7 p.l. 18 1/2 cm.

Williams, Edward Peet.
Extracts from letters to A.B.T. from Edward
P. Williams, during his service in the civil war,
1862-1864. New York, for private distribution,
1903.
122 p. 21 cm.

Williams, George Forrester, 1837-
Bullet and shell. War as the soldier saw it;
camp, march, and picket; battlefield and bivouac;
prison and hospital. By Geo. F. Williams ...
Illustrated, from sketches among the actual
scenes, by Edwin Forbes ... New York, Fords,
Howard, & Hulbert, 1883.
454 p. incl. illus., plates. front.
22 1/2 cm.

Williams, George Henry, 1823.
Reconstruction. Speech ... delivered in the
Senate of the United States, February 4, 1868.
Washington, F. & J. Rives and Geo. A. Bailey,
1868.
15 p. 24 cm.

Williams, George W.
Sketches of travel in the Old and New world.
By G. W. W. Charleston, S. C., Walker, Evans &
Cogswell, 1871.
4 p.l., 400 p. front. (port.) plates.
23 1/2 cm.

Williams, James.
Narrative of events, since the first of August
1834 ... London, Printed by John Haddon, sold
by William Ball [n.d.].
23 p. 20 cm.

Williams, James.
A narrative of events, since the first of
August, 1834, by James Williams, an apprenticed
labourer in Jamaica. London, William Ball [1837?]
23 p. 25 cm.

Williams, James.
Narrative of James Williams, an American slave. New York [n.d.].
30 cm.

Williams, James, 1805-
Narrative of James Williams. An American slave; who was for several years a driver on a cotton plantation in Alabama ... New York, The American anti-slavery society; Boston, Isaac Knapp, 1838.
xxiii, [25]-108 p. front. (port.) 15 cm.

Williams, John Lee.
The territory of Florida: or, Sketches of the topography, civil and natural history, of the country, the climate, and the Indian tribes, from the first discovery to the present time... New York, A. T. Goodrich, 1837.
vi, [7]-304 p. front. (port.) plates, fold. map. 21 1/2 cm.

Williams, S.
Rev. William Knibb, missionary to the island of Jamaica. [Cincinnati, American reform tract and book society, n.d.].
8 p. 18 cm.

Williams, Thomas.
Considerations on slavery in the United States ... [Providence, R. I.? 1856?]
24 p. 19 cm.

Williams, W. R.
"No discharge in this war." [Cincinnati, American reform tract and book society, n.d.].
4 p. 18 cm.

Williams, Wellington.
Appleton's railroad and steamboat companion. Being a traveller's guide through New England and the middle states with routes in the southern and western states, and also in Canada... Illustrated with numerous maps and engravings ... New-York, D. Appleton & co.: Philadelphia, G. S. Appleton, 1847.
235, [1] p. front. (fold. plan) illus., fold. maps. 15 1/2 cm.

Williams, Wellington.
Appleton's southern and western travellers'
guide: with new and authentic maps, illustrating
those divisions of the country; and containing
sectional maps of the Mississippi and Ohio rivers;
with plans of cities, views, etc. ... New York,
D. Appleton & co., 1854.
[5]-140 p. 1 p.1., illus., fold. maps, fold.
plans. 16 1/2 cm.

Williams, Wellington.
The traveller's and tourist's guide through
the United States of America, Canada, etc., containing the routes of travel by railroad, steamboat, stage and canal ... Accompanied by an entirely new and authentic map of the United States
... and a map of the island of Cuba ... Philadelphia, Lippincott, Grambo & co., 1851.
iv, 5-216 p. fold. map. 15 cm.

Williams, William, 1763-
Journal of the life, travels, and gospel
labours, of W. Williams, a minister of the Society of Friends, late of White-Water, Indiana.
Cincinnati, Lodge, L'Hommedieu, and Hammond,
1828.
272 p. 18 cm.

Williamson, James Joseph, 1834-1915.
Prison life in the Old capitol and reminiscences of the Civil war, by James J. Williamson
... illustrations by B. F. Williamson. West
Orange, N. J., 1911.
x, 11-162 p. front., illus. 19 1/2 cm.

Williamson, Passmore, defendant.
Narrative of facts in the case of Passmore
Williamson. Philadelphia, Pennsylvania Anti-
slavery Society, 1855.
24 p. 19 cm.

Willis, Nathaniel Parker, 1806-1867.
American scenery; or, Land, lake, and river
illustrations of transatlantic nature. From
drawings by W. H. Bartlett engraved in the first
style of the art ... London, George Virtue,
1840.
2 v. port., plates, map. 28 x 21 cm.

Willis, Nathaniel Parker, 1806-1867.
   Health trip to the tropics. By N. Parker
Willis. New York, C. Scribner, 1853.
   xiii [11]-421, xxiii p.   18 cm.

Willoughby, Hugh Laussat, 1856-
   Across the Everglades; a canoe journey of
exploration, by Hugh L. Willoughby ... Illustrated from photographs taken by the author. Philadelphia, J. B. Lippincott company, 1898.
   xii, 9-192 p.   incl. front. plates (incl.
ports.) maps (1 fold)   19 1/2 cm.

Wills, Charles Wright, 1840-
   Army life of an Illinois soldier, including
a day by day record of Sherman's march to the
sea; letters and diary of the late Charles W.
Wills. Compiled and published by his sister
[Mary E. Kellogg] Washington, D. C., Globe
printing company, 1906.
   383 p.   incl. front. (port.)   23 1/2 cm.

Wilmer, Richard Hooker, bp., 1816-
   The recent past from a southern standpoint.
Reminiscences of a grandfather. New York, T.
Whittaker, 1887.
   281 p.   4 port. (incl. front.)   22 cm.

Wilmot, Franklin A.
   Disclosures and confessions of Franklin A.
Wilmot, the slave thief and negro runner. With
an account of the under-ground railroad. Philadelphia, Barclay & co. [1860].
   1 p., 13-38 p.   front., pl.   25 1/2 cm.

Wilson, Alexander, 1766-1812.
   American ornithology; or, The natural history
of the birds of the United States; illustrated
with plates, engraved and colored from original
drawings taken from nature.... Philadelphia,
Bradford and Inskeep, 1808-14.
   9 v.   illus., 76 col. pl.   36 cm.

Wilson, Daniel.
   The guilt of forbearing to deliver our British colonial slaves. A sermon ... London,
George Wilson, 1830.
   22 p.   21 cm.

Wilson, Henry, 1812.
        Personalities and aggressions of Mr. Butler.
Speech ... in the senate of the United States,
June 13, 1856. Washington, Buell & Blanchard,
printers, 1856?
        8 p.   23 cm.

Wilson, Henry, 1821.
        The state of affairs in Kansas. Speech ...
in the Senate, February 18, 1856. Washington,
Published by the Republican association of the
District of Columbia, Buell & Blanchard, printers, 1856.
        15 p.   23 cm.

Wilson, James, 1797.
        Speech ... on the political influence of
slavery, and the expediency of permitting slavery in the territories recently acquired from
Mexico; delivered in the House of Representatives
of the United States, February 16, 1849. Washington, Printed by J. and G. S. Gideon, 1849.
        16 p.   24 cm.

Wilson, James Falconer, 1828.
        A free constitution. Speech ... delivered
in the House of Representatives March 19, 1864.
[Washington? W. H. Moore, 1864?]
        16 p.   22 cm.

Wilson, John Alfred, 1832-
        Adventures of Alf. Wilson. A thrilling epi-
sode of the dark days of the rebellion. Toledo,
Blade printing & paper company, 1880.
        xiv, 15-237 p.   front. (port.)   plates.
20 cm.

[Wilson, Samuel] fl. 1678-1682.
        An account of the Province of Carolina in
America ... London: Printed by G. Larkin for
F. Smith, 1682.
        27 p.   fold. map.   18 1/2 cm.

Wilson, Thomas, 1655?
        A brief journal of the life, travels and la-
bours of love in the work of the ministry, of
that eminent and faithful servant of Jesus Christ,
Thomas Wilson ... Dublin, Printed by and for S.

Fuller, 1728.
      xlviii, 98 p.   16 cm.

Wilson, William.
      The great American question, democracy vs.
duolocracy: or, Free soil, free labor, free men,
& free speech, against the extension and domination of the slaveholding interest ... Cincinnati,
E. Shepard's steam press, 1848.
      40 p.   21 cm.

Winn, Mary Day.
      The macadam trail; ten thousand miles by motor
coach, by Mary Day Winn; illustrated by E. H.
Suydam. New York, A. A. Knopf, 1931.
      xiv, 319, xii p., 1 l. col. front., illus.,
plates.   23 1/2 cm.

Winn, T. S.
      Emancipation; or, Practical advice to British
slave-holders; with suggestions for the general
improvement of West India affairs ... London,
Sold by W. Phillips [etc.] 1824.
      111 p.   20 1/2 cm.

Winslow, Hubbard, 1799.
      The means of the perpetuity and prosperity
of our republic. An oration, delivered by request of the municipal authorities, of the city
of Boston, July 4, 1838, in the Old South church,
in celebration of American independence ... Boston, John H. Eastburn, city printer, 1838.
      50 p.   21 cm.

A winter in the West Indies and Florida; containing
      general observations ... with a particular de-
      scription of St. Croix, Trinidad de Cuba, Havana,
      Key West, and St. Augustine ... By an invalid.
      New York, Wiley and Putnam, 1839.
      xi, [13]-199 p.   18 cm.

Wisconsin. Legislature.
      Resolution of the Wisconsin legislature, on
the   subject of slavery; with the speech of
Samuel D. Hastings, in the Assembly, Madison,
January 27, 1849. New York, W. Harned, 1849.
      31 p.   18 cm.

Wisconsin. State historical society.
Catalogue of books on the War of the rebellion, and slavery, in the library of the State
historical society of Wisconsin ... Madison,
Democrat printing company, printers, 1887.
61 p.   22 cm.

Wise, Barton Haxall, 1865-
The life and times of Henry A. Wise of Virginia, 1806-1876.   New York, The Macmillan company; London, Macmillan & co., ltd., 1899.
xiii, 434 p.   front. (port.)   23 1/2 cm.

[Wise, George].
History of the Seventeenth Virginia infantry,
C.S.A.   Baltimore, Kelly, Piet & company, 1870.
312 p.   19 1/2 cm.

Wislizenus, Adolphus, 1810-
Ein ausflug nach den Felsen-gebirgen im
jahre 1839.   St. Louis, Mo., W. Weber, 1840.
122, [4] p.   fold. map.   19 1/2 cm.

Wisner, William Carpenter.
A review of Rev. Doctor Lord's sermon on
the higher law, in its application to the fugitive slave bill ... Buffalo, T. and M. Butler,
1851.
32 p.   21 cm.

Withington, Leonard.
A bundle of myth.   Thanksgiving sermon:
preached Nov. 28, 1850, at Newbury, first parish ... Second edition.   Newburyport, Charles
Whipple; Boston, Perkins & Whipple, 1851.
24 p.   19 cm.

Witlenborger, J.
Der rathgeber und wegweiser für auswanderer
nach den Vereinigten Staaten von Nordamerika und
Texas ... Heilbronn, C. Dreschler, 1848.
141 p., 3 1.   fold. map.   14 cm.

Wolcott, Samuel.
Separation from slavery.   Being a consideration of the inquiry, "How shall Christians and
Christian churches best absolve themselves from
all responsible connection with slavery?"   A

premium essay ... Boston, American tract society
[n.d.].
46 p.   15 cm.

Wolfe, Samuel M.
Helper's Impending crisis dissected ... New
York, J. T. Lloyd, 1860.
223 p.   21 cm.

Wood, George L.   1837 or 8-
The Seventh regiment: a record.   New York,
James Miller, 1865.
304 p.   19 1/2 cm.

[Wood, Robert Crooke].
Confederate hand-book; a compilation of important data and other interesting and valuable
matter relating to the War between the states,
1861-1865.   [New Orleans, Graham press, c1900].
126 p., 1 l.   1 illus., 2 col. pl.   22 1/2 cm.

Wood, S.
Letters from the United States ... [London,
Printed by G. Smallfield, 1837].
11 p.   22 cm.

Woodbury, Augustus, 1825-
A narrative of the campaign of the First
Rhode Island regiment, in the spring and summer
of 1861.   Providence, Sidney S. Rider, 1862.
4 p.l., 260 p.   front. (port.)   map.   19 1/2 cm.

[Woodbury, John H. ?]
How I found it, North and South, together
with Mary's statement.. Boston, Lee and Shepard,
1880.
295 p.   17 1/2 cm.

Woodman, David, Jr.
Guide to Texas emigrants ... Boston, printed
by M. Hawes, 1835.
vi, [13]-192 p.   front. (fold. map) pl.
19 cm.

Woodruff, William Edward, 1831-
With the light guns in '61-'65.   Reminiscences of eleven Arkansas, Missouri and Texas
light batteries, in the Civil War.   Little Rock,

Ark., Central printing company, 1903.
8 p., 1 1., 9-115 p. front. (port.) plans.
20 1/2 cm.

Woods, John.
Two years' residence in the settlement on the
English prairie, in the Illinois country, United
States ... London, Longman, Hurst, Rees, Orme,
and Brown, 1822.
310 p. 2 p.1., 3 maps (2 fold., incl. front.)
22 cm.

Woodward, Evan Morrison.
Our campaigns: or, The marches, bivouacs,
battles, incidents of camp life and history of
our regiment during its three years term of service. Together with a sketch of the Army of the
Potomac ... Philadelphia, J. E. Potter, 1865.
vii, 9-362 p. 18 cm.

Woolley, E.
The land of the free, or, A brief view of
emancipation in the West Indies ... Part I ...
Cincinnati, Published by Caleb Clark, 1847.
32 p. front. 22 cm.

Woolman, John, 1720.
Considerations on the keeping of negroes; recommended to the professors of Christianity of
every denomination ... First published in the
year 1754. Philadelphia, Published by the Tract
association of Friends [n.d.].
12 p. 18 cm.

Woolman, John, 1720-1772.
A journal of the life, gospel labors and
Christian experiences, of that faithful minister
of Jesus Christ, John Woolman, to which are
added, his last epistle, and other writings ...
Philadelphia, Association of friends for the
diffusion of religious and useful knowledge, 1860.
viii, [9]-417 p. 16 cm.

Woolman, John, 1720.
Memoir of John Woolman, chiefly extracted
from a journal of his life and travels. Philadelphia, Published by the Tract association of
Friends [n.d.].
23 p. 18 cm.

Woolman, John, 1720-
    The works of John Woolman.   In two parts.
Philadelphia: Printed by Joseph Cruckshank, in
Market-Street, between Second and Third streets.
M.DCC.LXXIV.
    xiv, p., 1 1., 436 p.   21 cm.

Worcester central association.
    Resistance to slavery every man's duty.   A
report on American slavery read to the Worcester
central sssociation, March 2, 1847.   Boston, Wm.
Crosby & H. P. Nichols, 1847.
    40 p.   24 cm.

Worcester county (Mass.).   Ministers.
    Proceedings of the convention of ministers of
Worcester county, on the subject of slavery; held
at Worcester, December 5 & 6, 1837, and January
16, 1838.   Worcester, Massachusetts spy office,
1838.
    22 p.   22 cm.

Words of John Brown.   From his account of his child-
    hood, [Boston, Directors of the Old South work,
    Old South Meeting House, n.d.].
    28 p.   19 cm.

Worsham, John H.
    One of Jackson's foot cavalry; his experiences
and what he saw during the war 1861-1865, including a history of "F" company, Richmond, Va.,
21st regiment Virginia infantry, Second brigade,
Jackson's division.   Second corps, A.N.Va.   New
York, The Neale Publishing company, 1912.
    353 p.   front., plates, ports.   21 cm.

Wrede, Friedrich W. von.
    Lebensbilder aus den Vereinigten Staaten von
Nordamerika und Texas ... In der fortsetzung nach
tagebüchern und mündlichen mittheilungen bear-
beitet von E. D. Cassel, Selbstverlag, 1844.
    iv, 160, [2], iii-v, 161-324 p.   21 1/2 cm.

Wright, Elizur, jr.
    The sin of slavery, and its remedy; containing
some reflections on the moral influence of African colonization.   New York, Printed for the author,
1833.
    52 p.   21 cm.

[Wright, H. C.].
    Duty of abolitionists to pro-slavery ministers
and churches. [Concord, N. H., John H. French,
1811?]
    8 p.   15 cm.

Wright, Henry C.
    No rights, no duties: or, Slaveholders, as
such, have no rights; slaves, as such, owe no
duties. An answer to a letter from Hon. Henry
Wilson, touching resistance to slave holders being the right and duty of the slaves, and of the
people and states of the north ... Boston, Printed for the author, 1860.
    36 p.   19 1/2 cm.

Wright, Henry H.   1840-
    A history of the Sixth Iowa infantry.   Iowa
City, Ia., The State historical society of Iowa,
1923.
    xii, 539 p.   23 cm.

Wright, Henry O.
    The Narick resolution; or, resistance to
slaveholders. The right and duty of southern
slaves and northern freeman ... Boston, Printed
for the author, 1859.
    36 p.   19 1/2 cm.

Wright, Thomas J. captain 8th Kentucky infantry.
    History of the Eighth regiment Kentucky vol.
inf., during its three years campaigns ... St.
Joseph, Mo., St. Joseph steam printing co., 1880.
    286 p., 1 1.   17 1/2 cm.

The wrongs of Africa, a poem. Part the first ... London, Printed for R. Faulder, 1787.
    viii, 33 p.   22 cm.

The wrongs of Africa, a poem. Part the second ... London, Printed for R. Faulder, 1788.
    43 p.   22 cm.

Wynne, John Huddlestone, 1743-
    A general history of the British empire in
North America ... London, W. Richardson and L.Ur-
quhart, 1770.
    2 v. front., port., fold. map. plans.   21 1/2 cm.

Wyse, Francis.
America, its realities and resources: comprising ... present social, political, agricultural,
commercial and financial state of the country, its
laws and customs, together with a review of the
policy ... that led to the War of 1812 ... London,
T. C. Newby, 1846.
3 v.   23 cm.

Y

The Yankee slave drive; or, the black and white rivals.
With illustrations ... New York, H. Dayton: Indianapolis, Asher & co., 1860.
xi, 365 p.   19 cm.

Yates, Richard.
Speech ... on the bill to organize territorial
government in Nebraska and Kansas, and opposing
the repeal of the Missouri Compromise. House of
Representatives, March 28, 1854. Washington,
Congressional globe office, 1854.
16 p.   22 1/2 cm.

Yeatman, James E.
Report to the Western sanitary commission,
in regard to leasing plantations, with rules and
regulations governing the same ... St. Louis,
Western sanitary commission rooms, 1864.
16 p.   22 cm.

Yeatman, James E.
Suggestions of a plan of organization for
freed labor, and the leasing of plantations along
the Mississippi river, under a bureau or commission to be appointed by the government. Accompanying a report presented to the Western sanitary
commission ... Dec. 17, 1863. St. Louis, Rooms
Western sanitary commission, 1864.
8 p.   23 cm.

Yerrinton, J. M. W.
Proeeedings of the State disunion convention,
held at Worcester, Massachusetts, January 15, 1857

   ... Boston, Printed for the Committee, 1857.
    79 p.   23 cm.

[Yonge, Francis].
    A narrative of the proceedings of the people
of South-Carolina, in the year 1719: and of the
true causes and motives that induced them to re-
nounce their obedience to the Lord's proprietors
and to put themselves under the immediate government of the crown. London, Printed in the year
1726.
    40 p.   23 1/2 cm.

[Yonge, Francis].
    A view of the trade of South-Carolina, with
proposals humbly offer'd for improving the same.
[London, 1722?]
    16 p.   22 cm.

[Young, Arthur] 1741-1820.
    Observations on the present state of the waste
lands of Great Britain. Published on the occasion
of the establishment of a new colony on the Ohio.
By the author of the Tours through England. London, Printed for W. Nicoll, 1773.
    83 p.   21 cm.

Young, Jacob, 1776-
    Autobiography of a pioneer; or, The nativity,
experience, travels, and ministerial labors of
Rev. Jacob Young, with incidents, observations,
and reflections ... Cincinnati, L. Swormstedt &
A. Poe, 1857.
    528 p. front. (port.)   19 1/2 cm.

Young, John Clarke, 1803.
    Scriptural duties of masters. A sermon
preached in Danville, Kentucky, in 1846 ... Revised by the author. Boston, American Tract
Society [n.d.].
    43 p.   16 cm.

Young, Thomas M.
    The American cotton industry; a study of work
and workers, contributed to the Manchester guardian by T. M. Young; with an introduction by
Elijah Helm ... London, Methuen & co., New York,
C. Scribner's sons, 1902.
    xvi, 146 p.   19 cm.

[Young, W. A.]
The history of North and South America, containing an account of the first discoveries of
the New World, the customs, genius and persons
of the original inhabitants, and a particular description of the air, soil, natural productions,
manufactures and commerce of each settlement ...
London, Printed for J. Whitaker, 1776.
2 v.   14 1/2 cm.

[Young, William Henry].
Journal of an excursion, from Troy, N. Y.,
to Gen. Carr's head quarters, at Wilson's landing,
(Fort Pocahontas) on the James River, Va. during
the month of May, 1865. By one of the party.
Troy, N. Y., Priv. print., 1871.
59 p.   26 cm.

Z

Zabel, Eugen, 1851-
Bunte briefe aus Amerika.   2. aufl. Berlin,
G. Stilke, 1905.
287 [2] p.   20 cm.

Zannini, Alessandro, conte.
De l'Atlantique au Mississippi, souvenirs
d'un diplomate, par le comte Alexandre Zannini
... Paris, J. Renoult [1884].
271 p.   18 cm.

Zeigler, Wilbur Gleason.
The heart of the Alleghanies: or, Western
North Carolina; comprising its topography, history, resources, people, narratives, incidents,
and pictures of travel, adventures in hunting and
fishing and legends of its wilderness. By Wilbur
G. Zeigler and Ben S. Grosscup ... Raleigh, N.C.,
A. Williams & co.; Cleveland, O., W. W. Williams
[1883].
386 p.   incl. illus., plates.   front., fold,
map.   21 cm.

Zelotes, pseud.
"Astonished at America:" being cursory de-
ductions elucidated from genuine hearsay, intelligent judges, keen land-owners, many nondescripts,
official people, queer republicans, sundry travellers, undoubtedly veritable, without exagera-
tion, yet zealously admiring America. London,
Trübner and co., 1880.
vii, 8 1., 107 p. maps. 18 cm.

Zettler, Berrien McPherson, 1842-
War stories and school-day incidents for the
children. New York, The Neale publishing company,
1912.
168 p. 19 cm.

Zimmermann, Karl.
Onkel Sam; amerikanische reise- und kulturbilder,
von Karl Zimmermann ... 2. unveränderte aufl.
Stuttgart, Strecker & Schröeder, 1904.
4 p.l., 251 p. 22 cm.

Zincke, Foster Barham, 1817-1893.
Last winter in the United States; being table
talk collected during a tour through the late
southern confederation, the far West, the Rocky
mountains, &c. ... London, J. Murray, 1868.
xvi, 314 p. 21 cm.